LIBRARY OF SECOND TEMPLE STUDIES
54

formerly the Journal for the Study of the Pseudepigrapha Supplement Series

Editors
Lester L. Grabbe
James H. Charlesworth

Editorial Board
Randall D. Chesnutt, Philip R. Davies, Jan Willem van Henten,
Judith M. Lieu, Steven Mason, James R. Mueller,
Loren T. Stuckenbruck, James C. VanderKam

Normative and Sectarian Judaism in the Second Temple Period

Moshe Weinfeld

T & T CLARK INTERNATIONAL
A Continuum imprint
LONDON • NEW YORK

Published by T&T Clark International, *a Continuum imprint*
The Tower Building, 11 York Road, London SE1 7NX
15 East 26th Street, Suite 1703, New York, NY 10010

www.tandtclark.com

British Library Cataloguing-in-Publication Data
A catalogue record for this book is available from the British Library

Typeset by Sheffield Typesetting, www.sheffieldtypesetting.com
Printed on acid-free paper in Great Britain by MPG Books Ltd. Bodmin Cornwall

ISBN 0-567-04441-6

CONTENTS

Acknowledgments ix
Abbreviations x

Part I
PRAYER AND WORSHIP

Chapter 1
THE LOYALTY OATH IN THE ANCIENT NEAR EAST 2

Chapter 2
THE HEAVENLY PRAISE IN UNISON 45

Chapter 3
PRAYER AND LITURGICAL PRACTICE IN THE QUMRAN SECT 53

Chapter 4
THE DAY OF THE LORD: ASPIRATIONS FOR THE KINGDOM OF GOD IN THE BIBLE AND THE JEWISH LITURGY 68

Chapter 5
THE ANGELIC SONG OVER THE LUMINARIES IN THE QUMRAN TEXTS 90

Chapter 6
GRACE AFTER MEALS IN QUMRAN 112

Chapter 7
מנחה (*MINḤAH*) 122

Chapter 8
THE MORNING PRAYERS (*BIRKHOTH HASHACHAR*) IN QUMRAN AND IN THE CONVENTIONAL JEWISH LITURGY 126

Chapter 9
THE BIBLICAL ORIGINS OF THE *AMIDAH* PRAYER FOR SABBATH AND HOLY DAYS 137

Part II
THE QUMRAN SCROLLS

Chapter 10
THE TEMPLE SCROLL OR 'THE LAW OF THE KING' 158

Chapter 11
THE ROYAL GUARD ACCORDING TO THE TEMPLE SCROLL 186

Chapter 12
GOD VERSUS MOSES IN THE TEMPLE SCROLL: 'I DO NOT SPEAK ON MY OWN BUT ON GOD'S AUTHORITY' (*SIFRE DEUTERONOMY*, SEC. 5; JOHN 12.48f.) 189

Chapter 13
SARAH AND ABIMELECH (GENESIS 20) AGAINST THE BACKGROUND OF AN ASSYRIAN LAW AND THE GENESIS APOCRYPHON 194

Part III
THEOLOGY AND IDEOLOGY

Chapter 14
THE COVENANTAL ASPECT OF THE PROMISE OF THE LAND TO ISRAEL 200

Chapter 15
THE DAY OF ATONEMENT AND FREEDOM (*DEROR*): THE REDEMPTION OF THE SOUL 227

Chapter 16
THE CRYSTALLIZATION OF THE 'CONGREGATION OF THE EXILE' (קהל הגולה) AND THE SECTARIAN NATURE OF POST-EXILIC JUDAISM 232

Chapter 17
'YOU WILL FIND FAVOUR...IN THE SIGHT OF GOD AND MAN' (PROVERBS 3.4): THE HISTORY OF AN IDEA 239

Chapter 18
UNIVERSALISTIC AND PARTICULARISTIC TRENDS DURING THE EXILE AND RESTORATION 251

Part IV
NEW TESTAMENT

Chapter 19
PENTECOST AS FESTIVAL OF THE GIVING OF THE LAW 268

Chapter 20
THE CHARGE OF HYPOCRISY IN MATTHEW 23 AND IN JEWISH SOURCES 279

Chapter 21
HILLEL AND THE MISUNDERSTANDING OF JUDAISM
IN MODERN SCHOLARSHIP 286

Chapter 22
EXPECTATIONS OF THE DIVINE KINGDOM IN BIBLICAL
AND POSTBIBLICAL LITERATURE 294

Index of References 305
Index of Authors 324

ACKNOWLEDGMENTS

Daren Cohen, Danielle Saranga, Tanya Shapiro, Yonat Stadd and Bar Zecharia have typed the whole material anew.

ABBREVIATIONS

AASOR	Annual of the American Schools of Oriental Research
AB	Anchor Bible
ADD	C.H.W. Jones, *Assyrian Deeds and Documents Recording the Transfer of Property* (Cambridge, 1901)
AfO	*Archiv für Orientforschung*
Arch. D.Hist.d.Droit Orient	*Archives d'histoire de droit orientale*
AHw	Wolfram von Soden, *Akkadisches Handwörterbuch* (Wiesbaden: Harrassowitz, 1959–81)
ANET	James B. Pritchard (ed.), *Ancient Near Eastern Texts Relating to the Old Testament* (Princeton: Princeton University Press, 1950)
AOAT	Alter Orient und Altes Testament
AP	*Aramaic Papyri of the Fifth century B.C.* (edited with translation and notes by A. Cowley; Oxford, 1923)
ARM	Archives royales de Mari
ARN	*'Abot de Rabbi Nathan*
ARW	*Archiv für Religionswissenschaft*
AT	D.J. Wiseman, *The Alalah Tablets* (London, 1954)
ATD	Das Alte Testament Deutsch
BAR	*Biblical Archaeology Review*
BASOR	*Bulletin of the American Schools of Oriental Research*
BBSt	L.W. King, *Babylonian Boundary Stones* (London, 1912)
BKAT	Biblischer Kommentar: Altes Testament
BO	*Bibliotheca orientalis*
BWL	W.G. Lambert, *Babylonian Wisdom Literature* (Oxford, 1960)
BZAW	Beihefte zur *ZAW*
CAD	Ignace I. Gelb *et al.* (eds.), *The Assyrian Dictionary of the Oriental Institute of the University of Chicago* (Chicago: Oriental Institute, 1964–)
CBQ	*Catholic Biblical Quarterly*
CH	*Codex Hammurabi*
CIL	*Corpus inscriptionum latinarum*
CT	*Cuneiform Texts from Babylonian Tablets in the British Museum*
CTA	A. Herdner (ed.), *Corpus des tablettes en cunéiformes alphabétiques découvertes à Ras Shamra–Ugarit de 1929 à 1939* (Paris: Imprimerie nationale Geuthner, 1963)
DDS	M. Weinfeld, *Deuteronomy and the Deuteronomic School* (Oxford, 1972)
DJD	*Discoveries in the Judaean Desert*
EA	*El Amarna Letters:* J.A. Knudtzon, *Die El-Amarna Tafeln* (Leipzig, 1915)
EI	*Eretz Israel*

EJ	*Encyclopaedia Judaica*
FRLANT	Forschungen zur Religion und Literatur des Alten und Neuen Testaments
HAT	Handbuch zum Alten Testament
HKAT	Handkommentar zum Alten Testament
HSS	*Harvard Semitic Studies*
HTR	*Harvard Theological Review*
HUCA	*Hebrew Union College Annual*
IEJ	*Israel Exploration Journal*
IOS	*Israel Oriental Studies*
JANES	*Journal of the Ancient Near Eastern Society of Columbia University*
JAOS	*Journal of the American Oriental Society*
JBL	*Journal of Biblical Literature*
JCS	*Journal of Cuneiform Studies*
JEN	E. Chiera and E.R. Lacherman, *Joint Expedition with the Iraq Museum at Nuzi* (Paris, 1927–39)
JESHO	*Journal of the Economic and Social History of the Orient*
JJS	*Journal of Jewish Studies*
JNES	*Journal of Near Eastern Studies*
JPS	*The Jewish Publication Society of America*
JQR	*Jewish Quarterly Review*
JSOT	*Journal for the Study of the Old Testament*
JSS	*Journal of Semitic Studies*
JTS	*Journal of Theological Studies*
KAI	H. Donner and W. Röllig, *Kanaanäische und aramäische Inschriften* (3 vols.; Wiesbaden: Harrassowitz, 1962–64)
KBo	*Keilschrifttexte aus Boghazköi* (Leipzig, 1916)
KHC	*Kurzer Hand-Kommentar zum Alten Testament*
KUB	*Keilschrifurkunden den aus Boghazköi*
LSS	*Leipziger Semitiische Studien*
MDOG	*Mitteilungen der deutschen Orient-Gesellschaft*
MDP	*Mémoires de la délegation en Perse*
MGWJ	*Monatsschrift für Geschichte und Wissenschaft des Judentums*
MSL	*Materialen zum sumerischen Lexicon* (Materials for the Sumerian Lexicon)
MVAeG	*Mitteilungen der vorderasiatisch-ägyptischen Gesellschaft*
OGI	W. Dittenberger (ed.), *Orientis Graeci Inscriptiones Selectae* (Leipzig 1903–1905)
OLZ	*Orientalistische Literaturzeitung*
Oudt St.	*Oudtestamentische Studiën*
PAAJR	*Proceedings of the American Academy of Jewish Research*
Phil.-hist. Abt. N.F.	*Philosophisch-Historiche Klasse Abhandlungen, Neue Folge*
PRU	*Le palais royal d'Ugarit*
RA	*Revue d'assyriologie et d'archéologie orientale*
Rev. Arch	*Revue archéologique*
RB	*Revue biblique*
RCAE	L. Waterman, *Royal Correspondence of the Assyrian Empire* (Ann Arbor, 1930–36)
RE	A.F. Pauly and G. Wissowa, *Realencyklopädie für protestantische Theologie und Kirche* (Stuttgart 1894–1980)

REJ	*Revue des études juives*
RevQ	*Revue de Qumran*
RGG	K. Galling (ed.), *Religion in Geschichte und Gegenwart* (Tübingen 1957–65)
RHA	*Revue hittite et asianique*
RHPhR	*Revue d'histoire et de philosophie religieuses*
RHR	*Revue de l'histoire des religions*
RS	*Ras Shamra*
SAOC	*Studies in Ancient Oriental Civilisations*
SBL	Society of Biblical Literature
SEL	*Studi Epigrafici e Linguistici*
SPB	S. Singer, *Standard Prayer Book* (New York, 1943)
SVT	Supplements to *VT*
TCL	*Musée du Louvre, Textes cunéiformes*
TDOT	G.J. Botterweck and H. Ringgren (eds.), *Theological Dictionary of the Old Testament* (Grand Rapids, 1977–)
ThLZ	*Theologische Literaturzeitung*
ThWNT	Gerhard Kittel and Gerhard Friedrich (eds.), *Theologisches Wörterbuch zum Neuen Testament* (11 vols.; Stuttgart, Kohlhammer, 1932–79)
TWAT	G.J. Botterweck and H. Ringgren (eds.), *Theologisches Wörterbuch zum Alten Testament* (Stuttgart: W. Kohlhammer, 1973–95)
UF	*Ugarit-Forschungen*
VAB	*Vorderasiatische Bibliothek*
VCaro	*Verbum caro*
Vogt	J. Vogt, *Sklaverei und Humanität: Studien zur antiken Sklaverei und ihrer Erforschung* (Wiesbaden, 1965)
VT	*Vetus Testamentum*
VTE	D.J. Wiseman, 'The Vassal Treaties of Esarhaddon', *Iraq* (1958), pp. 1–99
WMANT	*Wissenschaftliche Monographien zum Alten und Neuen Testament*
YOS	*Yale Oriental Series (Babylonian Texts)*
ZA	*Zeitschrift für Assyriologie*
ZAW	*Zeitschrift für die alttestamentliche Wissenschaft*
ZTK	*Zeitschrift für Theologie und Kirche*

Part I

PRAYER AND WORSHIP

Chapter 1

THE LOYALTY OATH IN THE ANCIENT NEAR EAST*

The political treaties from the ancient Near East which have come to light since the 1920s have contributed much to understanding the nature of formal relationships between peoples, sovereigns and vassals, etc. The relationship between Israel and its God embodied in the so-called 'Covenant' has also been reevaluated following the discovery of the ancient Near Eastern treaties.[1]

In this article we intend to discuss the political documents which though considered as treaties actually constitute fealty oaths. The structure and typology of these documents will be compared with the structure and typology of similar documents in the ancient world, thus revealing a common pattern of fealty oaths prevailing in the Near East for almost 1500 years. Just as the treaties of the ancient Near East have their corresponding parallel in the Biblical Covenant so have the fealty oaths their parallels – as will be shown below – in the Israelite confession of faith and especially as has been crystallized in later Jewish Liturgy.

I

The point of departure for our discussion will be the so-called vassal treaty of Esarhaddon, King of Assyria. This document which was discovered in 1955 and published in 1958[2] is the longest of the political 'treaties' to be unearthed in the ancient Near East. This treaty is actually a loyalty oath on the part of the Median vassals obligating them to remain faithful to Assyria and her king on the occasion of change in the political leadership. On the sixteenth of Iyar (*Ajjāru*) 672, during the *limmu* (eponymy) of Nabû-bēl-uṣur – a date appearing in the treaty's colophon – Esarhaddon, King of Assyria, adjured the vassals to observe allegiance to his son Ashurbanipal who was designated to reign over Assyria, and to his son Shamashsumukin, the crown prince designate of Babylonia. We learn from other documents that not only the vassals were adjured, but that four days earlier (on the

* This is an expanded version of my Hebrew article in *Shnaton, An Annual for Biblical and Ancient Near Eastern Studies* (1975), I, pp. 51–88.

1. See my article 'Brith': *TDOT* II (1975), pp. 253–279.

2. D.J. Wiseman, 'The Vassal Treaties of Esarhaddon', *Iraq* 20 (1958), pp. 1–99. For recent English translations see E. Reiner, *ANET*[3], 534ff., S. Parpola and K. Watanabe, *Neo-Assyrian Treaties and Loyalty Oaths* (1988), pp. 28ff., for a more recent Hebrew annotated translation cf. M. Weinfeld, *Shnaton, An Annual for Biblical and Ancient Near Eastern Studies*, Vol. 1 (1975), pp. 89ff.

twelfth of Iyar) all of the people of Assyria, young and old alike, were required to swear allegiance to the new King Ashurbanipal.[3]

The adjuration, which was carried out in the presence of the gods opens with a declaration that the treaty binds as well the generations to come (ll. 1–12, cf. ll. 380–396). This is followed by a list of deities who are witnesses to the obligations (ll. 13–40), and subsequently by the conditions of obligation which may be summarized as follows:

1. to accept Ashurbanipal's kingship (ll. 41–48).
2. to be obedient to Ashurbanipal and to be prepared to fight and die for him (ll. 49–50, 229–231).
3. to love Ashurbanipal and be wholeheartedly faithful to him (ll. 51–61, 92–100, 231–236, 266–268).
4. to care for the continuation of the dynasty (ll. 83–91, 246–253).
5. to act favourably toward the king's brothers and their households (ll. 269–282).
6. to inculcate loyalty in the coming generations (ll. 283–301, 380–396).
7. not to rebel or install another king (ll. 62–72, 123–129, 147–161, 180–187, 188–211, 212–228).
8. to denounce inciters of rebellion (ll. 73–82, 108–122).
9. not to attack the king (ll. 101–107, 259–265).
10. to capture rebels and eradicate them or bring them to the king (ll. 130–146, 162–172, 302–317).
11. not to cooperate with an enemy or a rebel (ll. 173–179, 237–245).
12. to avenge Ashurbanipal should he be assassinated by conspirators (254–258).
13. not to comply with dissenters and to turn such over to Ashurbanipal (ll. 318–335, 336–352, 353–359, 360–372).
14. not to breach the treaty or damage the treaty document (ll. 373–380, 397–413).

After this come the curses associated with various deities (ll. 414–493), these are followed by the vassals' obligations expressed in the first person plural (ll. 494–512) and last of all comes a series of dramatized curses (ll. 513–665) of the kind found in the Sefire treaties[4] as well as in the Hittite Soldiers oath.[5]

Should we attempt to summarize and find a common denominator to all of the conditions listed above, we will find that they revolve principally about three main topics: (a) loyalty to the king and his dynasty (nos. 1–6); (b) obligation to act against rebels (nos. 7–14); (c) curses for treaty breakers. Similarly, in the vassal oaths themselves, which actually ratify the agreement, we find these three motifs though they start off dealing with rebellion:

3. Cf. M. Streck, *Assurbanipal*, II, p. 4f.; 18–23.

4. See J.A. Fitzmyer, 'The Aramaic Inscriptions of Sefire', *Biblica et Orientalia* 19 (1967), IA: pp. 35–42.

5. *ANET*^{3}, The Soldiers' Oath p. 353. N. Oettinger, *Die Militärischen Eide der Hittiter* (Wiesbaden, 1976). For a transliteration of the Hittite text see J. Friedrich, *ZA* NF 1 (1924), pp. 161–92.

Against rebellion clause: 'May the gods look on if we rebel or revolt... if we hear (men) speaking secretly...unseemly acts... and conceal it and do not report it.'

Loyalty clause: 'If, as long as we, our sons and our grandsons live, the crown prince designate Ashurbanipal will not be our king and lord,... if we place another king...over ourselves, our sons, our grandsons...'

Curses: 'may all the gods mentioned (here) call us, our offspring, and our descendants, to account...' (ll. 494–512).

Similar demands are found in other loyalty oaths from the ancient Near East. From the same period another loyalty oath to Ashurbanipal is known to us,[6] and it too contains clauses reminiscent of those in the vassals' oaths to Esarhaddon:

Loyalty. (1) to be obedient to the king and fight for him (ll. 11, 23–25).
(2) to love the king all the days of their lives (ll. 32–33).
(3) not to install another king over them (ll. 34–35).

Report Rebels: (1) to report to the king any sign of rebellion or instigation (ll. 4–9).
(2) to arrest conspirators and instigators and bring them before the king (ll. 13–16).

Curses. (1) The curses appear at the end of the document (Rev. 1–25).

It should be pointed out that in contrast to the Vassal Treaties of Esarhaddon (henceforth VTE) which are usually phrased as an adjuration by the king and only in one place is an oath of the vassals cited (ll. 494–512, see above), the document which we have brought here is phrased in its entirety as an oath taken by the vassal. This ambivalence (oath vs. adjuration) is already found in the Hittite documents from the 13th–14th centuries known as 'instructions'. There, we encounter on the one hand an adjuration of officials (LÚ. MEŠ. SAG)[7], and military personnel,[8] and on the other hand oaths by military commanders.[9] Furthermore, just as in VTE, where alongside the king's adjuration we found the vassals' oath,

6. L. Waterman, *Royal Correspondence of the Assyrian Empire* (= *RCAE*) (930–36), No. 1105. See also adjuration of Esarhaddon's mother in letter No. 1239, *ibid.*

7. E. von Schuler, *Hethitische Dienstanweisung für höhere Hof- und Staatsbeamte, Archiv für Orientforschung* Beiheft 10 (1957), pp. 1–35. LÚ. SAG is equivalent to *ša rēši* (= Hebrew סריס) and connotes an officer or a minister and not necessarily a castrated courtier (*ša rēši* means 'pertaining to the head', namely one who stands before the head), and see most recently, A.L. Oppenheim, 'A note on *ša rēši*', *Festschrift Th. Gaster*, JANES 5 (1973), 325ff.; M. Heltzer, *Israel Oriental Studies* 4 (1974), pp. 4–11.

8. S. Alp, 'Military Instructions of the Hittite King Tuthaliya IV', *Belleten* 11 (1947), pp. 403ff. And cf. the series of instructions to border guard commanders (*bēl madgalti*) in Schuler, *Dienstanweisung*, pp. 41ff.

9. E. von Schuler, 'Die Würdentragereide des Arnuwanda', *Orientalia* 25 (1956) (=LÚ. MEŠ. DUGUD).

so in the adjuration of the Hittite officers we find the formula of the officials' oaths integrated into the preamble of the document. Therefore it is read:

> Thus says Tudhaliyaš, the great King…you the officers will swear to the Sun (= king) saying: We shall obey the Sun…the sons and grandsons related to his kingdom (Section a, 1).

Only afterward is there an adjuration which makes demands identical to those which we mentioned above:

1. to guard the king and his sons after him (LÚ. MEŠ. SAG A, 6–12).
2. not to install over them another king (LÚ. MEŠ. SAG A, 13–16).
3. to uncover instigators and rebels (*ibid.*, passim).

Also in the 'instructions' to the military personnel[10] and in the oaths of the Hittite army commanders (LÚ. MEŠ. DUGUD)[11] we find clauses which deal mainly with loyalty and uncovering rebellion:

Loyalty (1) to love the king (= to remain loyal), his family and his progeny (see below Section A).
(2) to fight for him constantly (or stubbornly) (see below Section B).
(3) to cherish the life of the king more than their own lives (see belowSection B).
(4) to teach the loyalty oaths to the sons (below Section I).
Against rebellion: (5) to capture rebels and turn them over to the king (below Section F).
(6) to avenge the king (below Section G).

Although these oaths and adjurations contain no curses, this seems to be merely a coincidence since there is a Hittite document which deals with soldiers taking an oath accompanied by dramatic ceremonies meant to illustrate the curses which will come upon those who will not remain loyal to the king, and breach the covenant.[12] This indicates that the curse was a most important feature of Hittite oaths and adjurations of officers, soldiers, etc.

A loyalty oath founded upon the three principles established above – (1) loyalty, (2) uncovering rebels, (3) curses – appears in a Hellenistic document. For example, in a treaty between Smyrna and Magnesia (near Sipylus) from 242 BCE,[13] we find the oaths of the two parties which mainly express loyalty to Seleucus II and may be summed up as follows:

1. to remain loyal (εὐνοήσειν = to have love/affection) to the king and his dependants.

10. In Alp's article (n. 8).
11. In Schuler's article (n. 9).
12. See n. 5.
13. W. Dittenberger, *Orientis Graeci Inscriptiones Selectae* (= *OGI*) No. 229, = H. Bengtson – H.M. Schmitt, *Staatsverträge des* Altertums III, *Die Verträge des griechisch-römischen Welt von 338 bis 200 v. Chr.* (1969), No. 492 (henceforth: Bengtson).

2. to uncover any attempt of conspiracy and agitation.
3. a blessing to the keepers of the pact and curses to its breachers.[14]

Such elements are not confined exclusively to loyalty oaths but also appear in political vassal treaties where, even though the principal concern is the relation between the vassal and the overlord, the three elements mentioned are still prominent:

Loyalty:	(1)	to revere the king and his family just as the vassal reveres his own self and family.[15]
	(2)	to fight wholeheartedly on behalf of the king.[16]
Uncovering rebels:		to uncover rebels and agitators.[17]
Blessing and Curse.[18]		

Here, however, there is the addition of 'to be an enemy to the king's enemies and a friend to his friends' which is very frequent in Greek treaties and has even found its way into loyalty oaths from the Roman period, as we shall see (Section H).

Furthermore, just as in the loyalty oaths cited so far, so also in the vassal treaties the king's adjuration stands alongside the vassal's oath. Thus, in a treaty between Šuppiluliuma and Mattiwaza, after the Hittite King Šuppiluliuma has listed his conditions and the curses that will afflict Mattiwaza should he not keep the pact, Mattiwaza himself says:

> If I Mattiwaza, the prince, and the sons of the Ḫurri (country) do not fulfill the words of this treaty and oath, I...and we the sons of the Ḫurri...we will have no seed...and if (on the other hand) we fulfill the treaty and the oaths of the King Šuppiluliuma, the great king... may the gods, whose name we have invoked, exalt us, guard us, and be king to us...[19]

This combination of imposing an obligation on the one hand, and obligating oneself on the other, appears as well in the treaty between Smyrna and Magnesia which we cited above. Within the treaty in which we found the conditions applying to each party, we also find the oath formula for the two parties which contains the self-obligations which we quoted.

The material so far discussed apparently contains documents of various types:

1. A treaty between an overlord king and his subject vassal kings (the Hittite treaties).
2. Adjurations of the *vassals* to remain loyal to the new crown prince (VTE).
3. Adjuration of *the people and its leaders* to remain loyal to the new crown prince (the oath of Zakutu, Esarhaddon's mother).[20]

14. Lines 60–69 (the settlers of Magnesia), ll. 70–78 (the people of Smyrna). For details of the clauses, see below.
15. Cf. e.g., document No. 17.355 in PRU IV, pp. 85ff. (the treaty between Muršuliš II and Niqmepa King of Ugarit).
16. *Ibid.*, ll. 20–21, p. 89, and see my article in *Leshonenu* 36 (1972), pp. 88–89.
17. See in my book, *Deuteronomy*, etc. pp. 92ff. for references.
18. *Ibid.*
19. E. Weidner, *Politische Dokumente aus Kleinasien* (1923), p. 54.44ff.
20. *RCAE* No. 1239.

4. Adjuration of officials by the king (Schuler, LÚ. MEŠ. SAG).
5. Adjuration of soldiers by the king (Alp, Military Instr.).
6. Adjuration of border guard commanders (Schuler, Bēl Madgalti).[21]
7. Loyalty oaths from army commanders (Schuler, LÚ. DUGUD).
8. Loyalty oaths from soldiers (*RCAE* 1105).

Actually, all of these documents demonstrate one major and central concern, and that is loyalty to the king and his regime. The basic components of these documents are formulated identically and recur in this same formulation over very long periods of time: from the days of the Hittite Empire of the 14th century BCE,[22] through the Assyrian Empire, and into the Roman Empire. Let us examine these basic elements in the Hittite and Assyrian treaties and compare them to documents from the Greek, Hellenistic and Roman periods.

A. *Loyalty*

This concept is expressed in the aforementioned documents by use of terms such as love/kindness[23]: *aššiya* in Hittite and *râmu* in Akkadian.[24] Therefore, in the oath of Hittite army commanders: 'If we will not love (always)[25] our lords, their wives, their children, and their grandchildren'.[26]

And in adjuration of Hittite military personnel.[27] 'Just as you love[28] your wives, your children, and your houses, so shall you love the king's business...'[29]

In VTE: 'If you do not love... Ashurbanipal...your lord...as you do your own lives' (ll. 266–268).

And in a soldier's oath to Ashurbanipal: 'The King of Assyria our lord...we shall love all the days of our lives'.[30]

In the treaties and loyalty oaths of the Greek, Hellenistic and Roman periods, terms of affection φιλεῖν/εὐνοεῖν (to be well inclined or favourable), εὔνοια serve to express political loyalty. Thus, for example, the parties to the treaty between Smyrna and Magnesia (at Sipylus) obligated themselves to be well

21. See n. 8.

22. And especially in the Al-Amarna period. In this period the formula structure of the interna tional treaties crystallized. See my article *JAOS* 93 (1973), pp. 190ff.

23. Concerning חסד and its covenantal connotation see my article in *JAOS* 93 (1973), pp. 190ff.

24. Love (אהב) in the Bible also indicates loyalty. See W.L. Moran, 'The Ancient Near Eastern Background of the love of God in Deuteronomy', *CBQ* 25 (1963), pp. 77–87.

25. *aššiyanušgaweni* (*KUB* 31, 42 II: 23) which is the iterative form.

26. Schuler, *Orientalia* 25 (1956), II: 20–21, p. 227.

27. Alp. (n. 8), p. 392: 30–31.

28. *Genzu harteni* is translated by Alp 'have affection', however *genzu* is equivalent to Akkadian *rêmu* and if so the translation *have love* (=loyalty) is justifiable.

29. LUGAL-*uwaš šakliya*. A concept which in my opinion corresponds to Akkadian *parṣī ša šarrani* – the king's customs/laws. See for example El-Amarna letter 117 line 82: *kīma parṣi ša abūtika* = according to the customs of your fathers, and cf. *kīma paraṣ Ḫalab* (*AT* 17.5). משפט המלך in 1 Sam. 8.11 is in my opinion equivalent to *parṣu ša šarri*, while משפט המלוכה (1 Sam. 10.25) is equivalent to *parṣu ša šarrūti*. In the Hellenistic and Roman loyalty oaths, remaining loyal to the king's affairs is expressed by εὐνοήσειν τὰ πράγματα and in Latin *in acta (iurare)*, and see n. 37.

30. *RCAE* 1105.32ff.

inclined to that which is loyal (εὐνοήσειν) to Seleucus II,[31] and as in the oaths of the Hittite army officers (Schuler, DUGUD) and the oaths of Ashurbanipal's soldiers (*RCAE* 1105), we find that the soldiers pledge to Eumenes I (263 BCE) to be well inclined i.e. to be loyal toward him – καὶ εὐνοήσω αὐτῶι.[32] Similarly, we find that the Roman Sulla[33] bound his opponent Lucius Cinna under oaths and imprecations[34] to be loyal to his interests εὐνοήσειν ἑαυτοῦ πράγμασιν[35] and Josephus tells us that Herod compelled the people to make a sworn declaration that they would maintain loyalty to his rule εὔνοιαν διαφυλάξειν[36] and in another place he has the people swear to be loyal to Caesar and the king's affairs.[37] He also tells us about an oath of loyalty to Gaius Caligula and uses εὔνοια[38]. εὐνοήσειν with connotations of loyalty appears in oaths of loyalty to the Roman Emperors (beginning with Augustus) and especially in those preserved in inscriptions.[39]

B. *Devotion*

The loyalty oaths as well as the vassal treaties contain demands of self-sacrifice for the king.[40] For instance, we find in a Hittite treaty found at Ugarit and written in Akkadian[41]:

> If you Niqmepa do not guard with your army and your chariots and with all your heart (*ina kul libbika*) and if you do not fight with all your heart.

And in a treaty written in Hittite:

31. *OGI 229* = Bengtson III 492, 72, cf. also ll. 2, 8. For discussion of εὔνοια cf. P. Herrmann, *Der römische Kaisereid*, 23f. (see n. 30 below). The verbs στέργω/φιλέω (to love) also appear in contexts of loyalty. Nicholas of Damascus uses this terminology when speaking about decisions concerning loyalty to Caesar (στέργεσθαι) and there we also find εὔνοια (Jacoby, *Fragm. Griech. Hist.* 90, 130 Sec. 180). The verb φιλέω in the sense of loyalty is found in the oath of the Colophons (c. 450 BC), see Bengtson II, 145, 47. For 'love' in the covenantal sense in the Greek-Roman political documents see my article in *JAOS* 93 (1973), pp. 190ff.

32. *OGI* 266 = Bengtson III 481, 26.

33. Plutarch, *Sulla* 10, 6.

34. ἀραῖς καὶ ὅρκοις καταλαβών. The concrete description follows: Cinna swears by taking a stone that if he is not loyal he will be thrown out of the city just as he throws the stone out of his hand. On the dramatization of curses, see below. (Similar dramatization appears in Jer. 51.63).

35. The loyalty to the πράγματα of the ruler corresponds to loyalty to the Latin *acta*, the implication being to his laws and decrees, and cf. n. 29 above concerning loyalty to the king's affairs in the Hittite adjurations. Also, cf. in the oath of loyalty to Eumenes I (above n. 32) in line 29: ὑπὲρ αὐτοῦ καὶ τῶν πραγμάτων τῶν ἐκείνου.

36. Antiq. 15.368.

37. εὐνοήσειν Καίασαρι καὶ τοῖς βασιλέως πράγμασιν (XVII, 42). Compare the letter of Lysias to the Jews: ἐὰν οὖν συντηρήσητε τὴν εἰς τὰ πράγματα εὔνοιαν 'if you keep loyalty to the state-affairs'. (2 Macc. 11.19) and see also 3 Macc. 7.11.

38. XVIII, 124, and cf. the oath to Gaius from Assos, G. Dittenberger, *Sylloge* 3 No. 797, 20: εὐνοήσειν Γαίωι.

39. For those documents and their analysis see P. Hermann, *Der römische Kaisereid*, Hypomnemata 20 (1968). I am grateful to Professor M. Stern who drew my attention to this book.

40. See my article in *Leshonenu* 36 (1972), pp. 88ff.

41. PRU IV 17.353: 20–21 (p. 89) and comp. E. Weidner, *Politische Dokumente* No. 3, Vs. 11.17ff.; No. 4 Vs. 10ff.

> And if you...Šaušgamuwa do not come to aid with your full heart (*šakuuaššarit ZI-it* = Akk. *ina kul libbi*) ...[42] with your army and your chariots and will not be prepared to die (Ú-UL ak-ti) with your wives and your sons (for the King).[43]

In a loyalty oath of the Hittite army officers:[44]

> 'If we will not fight against him stubbornly...[45] if the life of our lord will not be more precious to us than our own lives'.[46]

In an adjuration of Hittite army officers:[47]

> 'They will fight stubbornly'.

In VTE:

> 'If you do not fight and die for him' (ll. 50–51).

This clause also appears in the adjuration of Matʾilu by Ashurnirari V of Assyria:[48]

> 'If our death is not your death, if our life is not your life, if you do not seek the life of Ashurnirari, his sons...as your own life, and as the life of your sons'.

Identical demands are encountered in Greek and Roman loyalty oaths: In these as well, one ally is required to come to the aid of the other 'with all his might and ability' παντὶ σθένει, ὅυι ἄν δύνωμαι, κατὰ τὸ δυνατόι/δύναμιν[49] and here as well each ally is required to remain faithful with all his goodwill μετὰ πάσης προθυμίας[50] This expression of maximal devotion is likewise found in the old amphictyonic oaths: καὶ πάσηι δυνὰμει (Aischines II, 115).

Just as in the oriental documents, the documents from the Greco-Roman world bind the parties to fight until death. In the Greek oath at Plataea before the war with the Barbarians (cf. P. Siewert, *Der Eid von Plataiai*, 1972, p. 6.23) we read: μαχοῦμαι ἕως ἄν ζῶ 'I shall fight as long as I live'. The loyalty oath of the

42. On this phrase cf. H. Freydank, *Mitteilungen der Deutschen Orient-Gesellschaft* (= *MDOG*) 7 (1960), p. 374.

43. C. Kühne and H. Otten, *Der Šaušgamuwa – Verträg*, Studien zu den Boğazkoy-Texten Heft 16 (1971) Vs. 11: 32ff. See also in the treaties and adjurations of Šuppiluliuma II: 'die for the King' or: 'only death will be your border', cf. H. Otten, *MDOG* 94 (1963), p. 5 and R. Stefanini, *Accademia Nazionale dei Lincei*, Rendiconti, Classe di Scienze moralistoriche e filogiche (Ser. VIII) Vol. XX (1965), pp. 50f.

44. Schuler, *Orientalia* 25 (1956), p. 227 II: 14–16.

45. *karši zaḫḫiya* and cf. J. Friedrich, *Staatsverträge* I *MVAeG* 31, I (1926), p. 14: 1–5 and see the commentary *ibid.*, p. 17.

46. *namma-kan anzel* TI-*anni* UL ŠA BELU. NI TI-*tar nakki* (Akkadian *kabtu*). For this sentence see J. Friedrich, *Hethitisches Elementarbuch* I^2 (1960), p. 127, Sec. 222.

47. Alp, *Belleten* 11 (1947), pp. 388.7, 392: 19.

48. See E. Weidner, *Archiv f. Orientforschung* 8 (1932–34), p. 17f., V: 1f., and see E. Reiner's comments to these ll. in *ANET*^{3} p. 533. Cf. also *RCAE* 521.16: 'I am ready to give the blood from my throat in the service of the King, my lord'.

49. Cf. H. Bengtson, *Verträge* II, 263: 16–17, 293.26f. 155.14, 186.22, III s.v. δύναμις and cf. Appian in connection to defending Julius Caesar παντὶ σθένει (BC II. 601), cf. below, No. 63.

50. In the soldiers' oath to Eumenes (*OGI* 266.31) and in the treaty between Smyrna and Magnesia (*OGI* 229.66). In Hannibal's treaty (Polybius VII, 9, 8) which contains many Semitic elements (Bickerman, *Trans. Amer. Philog. Assoc.* 75 (1944), p. 87ff. We find μετὰ πάσης προθυμίας καὶ εὐνοίας.

soldiers to Eumenes I mentioned above tells us that they are obligated to fight... for life or death...: ἀλλὰ μαχοῦμαι ἕως ζωῆς καὶ θανάτου[51] and in the fealty oath to Augustus from Paphlagonia 'not to spare body or soul, life or sons, and to stand up to any danger whatsoever'.[52]

Most surprising is the similarity between the clauses of a loyalty oath from the Roman period in which the vassals pledge to revere the Caesar more than themselves and their sons, and the similar clauses in the Hittite documents. Thus we find in an oath to Gaius Caligula from Aritium,[53] 'and I will not revere myself or my sons more than his well being' (neque me neque liberos meos eius salute cariores habebo),[54] reminding us of the oath of the Hittite army officers quoted above: 'If the life of our lord will not be more precious to us than our own lives'. We can add to this paragraph in the Hittite treaties with the vassals, 'Just as you Niqmepa, you yourself, your head, your wives, your army and your land are dear to you, so may the king himself, the king's head, the king's sons and the land of Hittite be dear to you forever'.[55]

Such clauses are actually contained in the Assyrian treaties in conditions such as 'If you do not love the king as you do your own lives' (VTE 266–268).

In the loyalty oath to Julius Caesar as it is described and cited by various authors[56], similar formulae are reflected.

C. *Guarding the King*

This matter is expressed in all of the documents under study by the expression watch/guard (Hittite: *paḫš*, Akkadian: *naṣāru*). In the oaths of the Hittite officers: 'we shall guard (*paḫšuenni)* the Sun (the King of Heth)[57] and further on in the administration of the oath to the officers: 'guard the Sun and the Sun's progeny'.[58]

In the Hittite treaties with the vassals (written in Akkadian): 'And you Niqmepa shall guard (*tanaṣṣar*) the King of Heth your lord'.[59]

In Esarhaddon's adjuration of his vassals: 'If you do not guard him in city and in open country',[60] and in the soldiers' oaths of loyalty to Ashurbanipal King of Assyria: 'we shall guard the King of Assyria our lord'.[61]

In a treaty between Phillip V and Hannibal[62] we find that Phillip and his dependants are to be aided and guarded σωζόμενοι καὶ φυλαττόμενοι by the

51. Lines 28–29.

52. *OGI* 532.15ff.

53. H. Dessau, *Inscript. Latinae* Vol. 1, No. 190

54. Cf. ...καὶ ὅτι καὶ σφῶν αὐτῶν καὶ τῶν τέκνων καὶ ἐκείνου καὶ τὰς ἀδελφὰς αὐτοῦ προτιμήσουσιν (προτιμᾶν = cariores habere), Dio Cassius 59, 9.2 and see Suetonius, Calig. 15, 3.

55. Treaty of Muršiliš and Niqmepa *PRU* IV 17.353 p. 88, and cf. document No. 17.338 *ibid.*, p. 85ff.

56. Cf. A. von Premerstein, *Von Werden und Wesen des Prizipats* (1937), pp. 32ff. and P. Herman, *Kaisereid*, pp. 66ff.

57. Schuler, *Heth. Dienstanweis* p. 8, I.3.

58. *Ibid.*, p. 9 line 26.

59. *PRU* IV 17.353.5, p. 88.

60. VTE, 49, 50.

61. *RCAE* 1105.11.

62. Polybius Vii. 9, 7.

Carthagines. Admittedly, this expression may be a translation from Semitic, as Bickerman claims,[63] but on the other hand we have found a similar clause in Appian's description of the loyalty oaths to Julius Caesar – 'to guard Caesar and the body of Caesar with all their strength'.[64]

D. *Loyalty to the King's Progeny and Dynasty*

In the preceding section we presented the adjuration of Hittite officers according to which the officers are obliged to guard the king's progeny as well. In addition, a Hittite document has been preserved in which a Hittite officer swears that he inquired as to whether the previous king had progeny who could reign after him but found none. He also inquired as to whether there remained any women pregnant by the king.[65]

In Esarhaddon's adjuration of his vassals we hear explicitly that the vassals were required to wait for the deceased king's wife so as to guarantee the perpetuation of the royal line.[66]

Clauses stipulating loyalty to the king's seed have been found in Greek and Hellenistic pacts. The Athenians pledge to assist Dionysus I of Syracus (367 BCE) and his progeny[67] and the Miletians pledge to be ever loyal to Ptolemy II and his descendants.[68] Similarly, the soldiers pledge to be loyal to Eumenes I and his men.[69]

Such clauses appear in the loyalty oath to Augustus from Paphlagonia,[70] in an oath to Tiberius from Palaipapos in Cyprus[71] and in an oath of loyalty to Caligula of Assos.[72] The two latter examples mention loyalty to 'all the house' of the Emperor, a detail which shows up as well in Esarhaddon's vassal oaths: 'if you… lift your hands against their households' (of the crown prince and his brothers).[73]

E. *Not to Recognize Another King or Lord*

In the adjuration of the Hittite officers we read: 'as to lordship do not recognize (*šak-*) any other man'.[74]

63. *Amer. Journ. of Philology* 73 (1952), p. 9.

64. Appian, *Bella civ.* II, 604: ἦ μὴν φυλάξειν καίσαρα καὶ τὸ καίσαρος σῶμα παντὶ σθένει This description, as other descriptions of the oaths given to Caesar reflects oath formulae as they were actually said, and this may be seen by comparing with oaths of loyalty to the Roman emperors as they have become known from the inscriptions.

65. E. Laroche, *RA* 47 (1953), p. 70, II.3f.; H. Otten, *MDOG* 94 (1963), pp. 3–4.

66. Lines 237–263, and for the obligations of the עם הארץ in Judah to guard the dynasty see Weinfeld, *Deut*. p. 90ff.

67. Bengtson, II, No. 280.18ff.

68. διαφυλάξειν τὴν φιλίαν…πρὸς τόν βασιλέα Πτ. καὶ τοὺς ἐκγόνους αὐτοῦ τὸν ἀεὶ χρόνον. Milet I 3, 139, 4). Cf. Hermann, *Kaisereid*, p. 44.

69. εὐνοήσω αὐτῶι καὶ τοῖς ἐκείνου (Bengtson III, 481: 26–27).

70. Dittenberger, *OGI* 532, 10–11: καὶ τοῖς τέκνοις ἐγγόνοις τε αὐτοῦ.

71. σὺν τῶι ἅπαντι αὐτοῦ οἴκωι (T.B. Mitford, *Journ. of Roman St.* 50 [1960], p. 75, 1.15).

72. Dittenberger, *Sylloge*^{3} 797, 21: καὶ τῶι σύμπαντι οἴκωι αὐτοῦ.

73. VTE 11.271f.

74. Schuler, *Heth. Dienstanw*. p. 9, 11ff., cf. also p. 28.18f. and for Hittite šek-/šak- 'recognize' see A. Goetze *JCS* 22 (1968), pp. 7–8.

In the Hittite treaties with the vassals: 'as to lordship recognize the Sun alone'.[75]

In the soldiers' oath to Ashurbanipal: 'Another king and another lord we shall not seek',[76] and in Esarhaddon's adjuration of his vassals: 'if you install another king, another lord over yourselves' (ll. 71–72).[77]

F. *Not to Hide Rebels or Instigators*

All of the above mentioned documents require extradition of rebels and instigators and warn against hiding them. For example, in the Hittite treaties with the vassals: 'when you hear some evil thing (*idaluš*)[78] spoken against the king and shall conceal it (*šannatti)* and not reveal it (*tekkuššanuši*) or even cover it up (*munnāši)*',[79] and in the Aramaic treaty from Sefire:

> [And should a man come to you] or to your son…or to one of the kings of Arpad…and utter evil words (מלן לחית)[80]…you must turn them over into my hands (תהסכרהם הסכר).[81]

In the adjuration of the Hittite officers: 'And should you hear an evil word against the Sun (= the king)… you shall inform the Sun, and if you have heard and do not tell the Sun (*mematteni*)…'.[82]

In the pledge of Esarhaddon's vassals: 'If we hear rumour mongers, a bad word (*amāt* SAL. ḪUL)[83] not good and not proper…and conceal it (*nupazarruni*)…and do not tell the king Ashurbanipal'.[84]

In the oath of the people of Chalcis to the Athenians[85] they pledged not to listen to rebels, and not only this, but if someone would rebel they were to inform about him (= turn him over) to the Athenians: καὶ ἐὰν ἀφιστε͂ι τις κατερο͂ Ἀθεναίοισι (ll. 24–25). The verb κατερέω (from κατεῖπον) means to turn over by way of informing (denounce)[86]. This is similar to the Oriental sources which use verbs whose literal meaning is *say, tell,* but whose contextual connotations are to turn over or uncover: In Akkadian *qabû*, in Hittite *mema* and in Hebrew הגד.[87]

75. See Friedrich, *MVAeG* 34,1 (1930), 106.14, cf. Goetze, *ibid.*, p. 8.
76. Waterman, *RCAE* 1105.35.
77. All of these should be compared to לא יהיה לך אלהים אחרים in the Decalogue and the formula in Hos. 13.4 ואלהים זולתי לא תדע which appears after אנכי ה׳ אלהיך מארץ מצרים.
78. Concerning 'evil thing' דבר רע meaning instigation to rebellion and breaking a covenant see Weinfeld, *DDS*, p. 93, No. 6, and for דבר טוב in the sense of pact and agreement see my article in *Leshonenu* 36 (1972), pp. 8ff.
79. See Friedrich, *MVAeG* 34 (1930), 108.28f. and cf. my book *Deuteronomy*, p. 97 in connection with the parallels from Deut. 13.
80. See n. 78.
81. Fitzmyer, *Sefire* III, 1–2.
82. Schuler, *Heth. Dienstanw.* p. 14.47–52.
83. See above, n. 78.
84. Lines 499–507, and cf. ll. 73–82, 108–122.
85. *Inscript. Gr.* I^2 39, 20ff. (= Bengtson II 155).
86. Cf. Herodotus III 71 (end): κατερέω πρὸς τὸν μάγον 'I will denounce you to the Magus'.
87. See the discussion in Weinfeld, *DDS*, pp. 94ff.

In a like manner, we find the soldiers' oath to Eumenes I[88] that if someone should hear of a person plotting to rebel (ἐπιβουλεύοντα)...he will inform (ἐξαγγελῶ)[89] as fast as possible, and similarly in the treaty between Smyrna and Magnesia quoted above we find that should someone discern somebody plotting he will inform as soon as possible.[90]

The demand of immediate informing (*ibid.*)[91] already appears in Hittite treaties. In the treaty between Šuppiluliuma[92] and Šunaššura from Kizuwatna it is said:[93]

> If someone, man or city, shall rebel against the Sun, upon hearing this (*kî išamme)* he shall inform (*imaššar*) the Sun.[94]

We find such a clause in the Paphlagonians' oath of loyalty to Augustus,[95] where they swear to turn over/uncover (ἐγμηνύσειν) should they see (detect) or hear (αἴσθωμαι ἢ ἀκούσω)[96] a word, a plot to rebel, or an act against the king and his descendants. Now, the expression 'report all that is seen or heard' is very familiar to us from Neo-Assyrian and Neo-Babylonian documents, once again in conjunction with treaty and loyalty oaths. Certain men write in a letter to Ashurbanipal[97] that they took an oath and are now fulfilling what they swore to the king, to report anything that they may have seen or heard (*mimma mala tammaru u tašemma*). In other places we hear about men who report to the king all that they see and hear: *ša amaruni ašmûni ana šarri...qabû*.[98] In documents from Cyrus' period we hear of artisans in the temple service who pledge not to hide 'what they see or hear' concerning work outside of the temple.[99]

Pursuing the instigators is to take place under all circumstances. Thus in VTE: 'if someone in the palace starts a revolt, *whether by day or night*...you must not let him go, he must not leave, you will keep him under severe guard...' (ll. 198ff.).

Similar clauses are attested in Greek political documents:

88. *OGI* 266, pp. 32ff.

89. In Deut. 13.10 in connection with incitement, the LXX reads: ἀναγγέλων ἀναγγελεῖς based on Hebrew הגד תגדנו. For this matter see in my book *op. cit.* pp. 94ff., see however most recently Z.W. Falk, *Zeitschrift der Savigny-Stiftung* 90 (1973), p. 41.

90. See *OGI* 229, 76: καὶ ἐάν τινα αἰσθάνωμαι ἐπιβούλευοντα...μηνύσω ὡς ἄν τάχιστα δύνωμαι. Cf. also *Sylloge*[3] 360–64ff. and see below pp. 14–15.

91. Cf. in the soldiers' oath to Eumenes: καὶ εξαγγελῶ πα[ραχρῆ]μα (l. 35).

92. He is the partner in the pact and not as Weidner supposed. For this matter see A. Goetze, *Kizzuwatna*, p. 36, No. 141.

93. Weidner, *Polit. Dok.* 96.16ff.

94. Cf. Weinfeld, *DDS*, p. 95.

95. *OGI* 532, p. 18f.

96. αἴσθεσθαι means to see and discern.

97. *RCAE* No. 472.

98. *RCAE* 317.9, 211.11; 831 rev. 3 *et al.* Cf. A.L. Oppenheim, *JAOS* 88 (1968), pp. 174ff., on officials in Assyria and in Persia whose duty was to inform the authorities on plots etc. It seems that Mordechai fulfilled a similar function (Esth. 2.21–23) and like the Assyrian and Persian officials was rewarded for this information (*ibid.* 6.1ff.).

99. D.B. Weisberg, *Guild Structure and Political Allegiance in Early Achaemenid Mesop.* (1967), pp. 35ff.; cf. the oath of an Egyptian worker in Appendix A.

1. In the loyalty oath of the young recruits (ἔφηβοι) from Dreros: (c. 220 BCE): 'I will not be disposed (καλῶς φρονήσειν) to the Lyttians... *whether by day or by night* and I will hasten (as fast) as I can to do wrong to the cities of the Lyttians'. (*Syll.*^{3} 527, 36ff.).
2. In the oath of the Chersonites (Taurica) we read:

> I will not betray...but I will guard for the people of Cherson, I will not dissolve the democracy and will not give up to those who betray or dissolve neither will I join in concealing the matter but will denounce (ἐξαγγελῶ) to the magistrates of the city. I will be an enemy to those who plot and betray... I will guard for the people and will not reveal any of the secrets... (*Syll.*^{3} 360).

G. *Seize Instigators and Punish Them*

In the adjuration of Hittite military personnel we read:[100] 'Should a prince bring an evil thing (*idaluš*) seize him and bring him before the king'.

In the loyalty oaths of the Hittite army officers:[101] 'Should someone send us an evil thing...if we do not capture him (*epp-* = Akkadian *ṣabātu*) and do not bring him before the king'.

In the soldiers' oath to Ashurbanipal: '[Should someone be found] spreading an evil thing (*amāt la ṭābti)* and we should hear...we shall place him in chains and to Ashurbanipal [we shall bring him]' (*RCAE* 1105.13–16).

In Esarhaddon's adjuration of the vassals: 'upon hearing such a thing [about a revolt] from anybody, if you do not seize the instigators of the revolt, do not bring them before the crown prince designate Ashurbanipal [and] if you, being able to seize and kill them, do not eradicate their name and descendants from the country ...' (ll. 130ff.).

Similar provisions against traitors are found in various decrees of the Athenian league and in the old amphyctionic oaths. These occur especially in the attic psephisma against the enemies of democracy.[102] Thus we find in the psephisma of Demophantos (410 BCE) as cited by Andocides:

> If anyone shall dissolve the democracy of Athens...he shall become an enemy of the Athenians and be slain with impunity (νηποινεὶ τεθνάτω)[103] his gods shall be confiscated...and all the Athenians shall take oath...over a sacrifice without blemish to slay such one and this shall be the oath: 'I will slay by word and by deed, by my vote and by my hand, as it is in my power, whosoever shall dissolve the democracy at Athens...' (*On the Mysteries* 96f.).

100. Alp (n. 8), p. 392: 26–27.

101. Schuler, *Orient.* 25 (1956), pp. 226.9–12.

102. For the whole problem see M. Ostwald, 'The Athenian Legislation against Tyranny and Subversion', *Transactions of Amer. Philological Assoc.* 86 (1955), pp. 103ff.

103. For the clarification of this term, which also occurs in the Erythrae Decree and in other writings, cf. L.I. Highby, *The Erythrae Decree, Klio*, Beiheft 36 (1936), p. 28f. The meaning of this term is that anyone could kill the traitor and be free of guilt. If one accept the Hebrew reading in Deut. 13.10 (see however n. 89) he may find the same notion there.

A similar injunction is found in the Erythrae Decree (c. 465 BCE) where we read: 'if anyone is detected who wishes to betray the city to tyrants, he will be put to death with impunity' (see n. 103).

In the amphictyonic oath as cited by Aischines we read:

> if anyone should violate the shrine of the god or be accessory to such violation, or make any plot against the holy places they would punish him with hand and foot and voice and all their mighty power (καὶ χειρὶ καὶ ποδὶ καὶ φωνῆι καὶ πάσηι δυνάμει) (Aischines 2.115).

The latter remind us of the provisions against treason in the religious domain as reflected for example in Deuteronomy 13.[104] Especially instructive in this respect is the injunction there: 'Let your hand be the first against him to put him to death', (ידך תהיה בו בראשונה להמיתו) (v. 10), which is analogous to ἐμαυτοῦ χειρί/ καὶ χειρί in the cited Greek sources.

Similar to the clauses against traitors in Deut. 13, we find in the regulations of a private shrine at Philadelphia[105] of the beginning of the first century BCE that the visitors of the shrine shall not yield to trespassers of the regulations but shall inform on them and take revenge (II 23ff.).

H. *To Avenge the King*

In the oath of the Hittite army officers we read: 'If we do not fight against him (the rebel) stubbornly, and do not retaliate'.[106] (Schuler, *Orient.* 227, II.20–21). Identical clauses are found in other treaties. For instance, we find in the Sefire Treaty: 'If it happens that one of my brothers or one of the house of my father or one of my sons or one of my officers...seeks...to kill me...you must come and avenge my blood from the hand of my enemies... Your son must come to avenge the blood of my son from his enemies ...' (III.9–12).

A similar warning appears in Esarhaddon's treaty: 'If you do not seize and kill the instigators of the revolt, do not eradicate their name and descendants from the country, do not shed blood for blood, and do not avenge (retaliate)[107] the crown prince designate Ashurbanipal, son of the King' (ll. 254–259).

Such a clause is also found in the Paphlagonians' loyalty oath to Augustus:[108] 'and to pursue anyone considered an enemy and to wreak vengeance upon them[109] with arms and sword whether on land or sea'.

104. Cf. Weinfeld, *DDS*, pp. 94ff.

105. For the text with an extensive commentary cf. O. Weinrich, Stiftung und Kultsatzungen eines Privatheiligtums in Philadelphia in Lydien, Sitz.Ber. Heidelberger Akad. Wiss., Phil.-Hist.Kl (1919), p. 16. Abh.

106. UL *kattawatar* (*kattawatar* = Akk. *gimillu*), cf. line 5 there.

107. Akkadian *gimla la tutarraninni*. The Hittite expression for vengeance corresponds to Akkadian *gimillu turru* which appears here, and see n. 106.

108. οὓς τε ἂν ἐχθροὺς αὐτοὶ κρίνωσιν τούτους κατὰ γῆν καὶ θάλασσαν ὅπλοις τε καὶ σιδήρωι διώξειν καὶ ἀμυνεῖσθαι. *OGI* 532, 23–25.

109. ἀμυνεῖσθαι means retribution and revenge, cf. the text quoted in n. 105 line 25: καὶ ἀμυνεῖσθαι and therefore we are confronted with a verb identical to that in VTE and the Hittite oath.

Similarly we find in the loyalty oath to Gaius Caligula from Aritium: 'And should anyone endanger him or his well-being with arms or internal war I will not cease to pursue him on land and at sea until I mete out his punishment'.[110]

I. *To be a Friend to Friends and Foe to Foes*

This clause is particularly characteristic of the Hittite treaties but it is of earlier origin, appearing in a treaty between Naram-Sin and Elam in the third millennium BCE, as well as in private family documents from the Old Babylonian Period.[111] It seems that this element passed by way of the Hittites to the Greek treaties[112] where it is very prevalent. It is true, this clause is absent in oriental treaties of the first millennium BCE, however, because of the small number of treaties from this period in the East, one is not allowed to speak about its disappearance in the first millennium BCE.

From Biblical usage we can learn that this formula was prevalent in the first millennium as well. We read in 2 Sam.19.6: 'You love those that hate you and hate those that love you', – love and hate expressing loyalty and disloyalty to the king.[113] Such is the case of Exod. 23.22, 'then I will be an enemy to your enemies, and I will harass those who harass you', which speaks about recompense for observing the covenant.

This formula is reflected in 2 Chron. 19.2 in connection with the pact between Jehosaphat and the King of Israel: 'Do you take delight in helping the wicked and befriending the enemies of the Lord?' (Comp. Ps. 13.21–22) and also in the covenant ceremony in the Manual of Discipline: 'and to love all that he has chosen and to hate all that he has rejected' (1.4 cf. 10–11), and in the Damascus Covenant: 'to choose him in whom He delights and to reject him whom He hates' (2.15).[114] It is also found in Josephus' account of the Essene vows: 'that he will forever hate the unjust and fight the battle of the just' (*War* 2.139).[115]

This formula is very widespread in Greece and Rome in treaties and oaths of loyalty beginning in the fifth century BCE. It is found not only in treaties between different states but also in agreements between a king and subjects, and between individuals.[116] It is therefore not surprising that this formula is found in the loyalty

110. Dessau, *Inscript. Lat.* No. 190: et si quis periculum ei salutique eius infert inferetque armis bello internecivo terra marique persequi non desinam quiad poenas ei persolverit. And cf. the inscription of Sestinum CIL XI 5998a. For a comparison of the two inscriptions on this point see Herrmann, *Kaisereid*, p. 52f.

111. Concerning this see my article *JAOS* 90 (1970), p. 104. In Greece this clause appears too on the level of interpersonal relationships, see, e.g., Plutarch, *Eum.* 12: τὸν αὐτὸν εχθρὸν ἕξειν καὶ φίλον.

112. This opinion has been accepted by scholars of Greek culture, see for example J. Schwann, *RE* IV A 1, 1109.

113. See W.L. Moran, *CBQ* 25 (1963), p. 81.

114. Cf. additional references in J. Licht, *The Rule Scroll* (Jerusalem, 1965), p. 59 V (Hebrew).

115. Cf. Mt. 5.43 and see M. Smith, *HTR* 45 (1952), p. 71f.

116. See references in P. Hermann, *Kaisereid*, pp. 21–22. Hermann claims that the formula is characteristic only of international relations while the formulae found in contexts of interpersonal relationships and relationships of a king to his subjects (*ibid.*, p. 22) are a late imitation. However, as we have

oaths to the Roman Emperors[117] such as that of the Paphlagonians to Augustus: 'To consider as friends those whom they consider friends and as foes those whom they consider foes'.[118] Such is the case of the loyalty oaths of Aritium, Assos and Palaipapos.[119]

J. *Validity of Covenant upon Succeeding Generations*

The parties to the Assyrian and Aramaic treaties obligate not only themselves but also the generations to come. We read, for example, in the Esarhaddon treaty: '[this is] the treaty of Esarhaddon King of Assyria with Ramataya, his sons, grandsons, and with all the people of Urakazabanu, young and old...with you, your sons, your grandsons, all those who will live in the future after this treaty' (line 1ff.).

And in the Aramaic treaty from Sefire: 'A treaty of Bargaʾyah, King of *Ktk* with Mattiʿel, the son of Attarsamak, King of Arpad; a treaty of the sons [and the offspring] of Bargaʾyah with the offspring of Mattiʿel...and with his (Mattiʿel's) sons who will come up after him'.[120]

Something similar is found in the loyalty oath to Tiberius from Palaipapos[121] where the parties pledge to listen and obey (ὑπακούσεσθαι πειθαρχήσειν) the Emperor and fear him (σεβάσεσθαι), they and their seed (αὐτοι τε καὶ οἱ ἔκγονοι).

The concern for assuring the loyalty of subsequent generations finds special expression in the clauses of the documents which speak of the obligations to teach the stipulations of the covenant to the sons. Such clauses can be found in Hittite and Assyrian loyalty oaths and in the Bible and in the אמת ויציב liturgy which, as we shall see further on, is nothing but a declaration of loyalty.

In the oath of the Hittite army officers we read: 'if we do not bring these matters before our sons'[122], and in the vassals' adjuration of Esarhaddon: 'if you do not tell and do not give orders to your sons, grandsons...saying: keep this treaty... lest you lose your lives'. (ll. 283–295), and in another passage: 'if you do not swear with your entire heart, do not transmit it to your sons who will live after this treaty' (ll. 387–388), and in the book of Deuteronomy, 'But take utmost care and watch yourselves scrupulously, so that you do not forget the things that you saw with your own eyes...And make them known to your children and to your children's children' (4.9 and cf. 31.13), 'Impress upon your children' (6.7), and 'teach them to your children' (11.19).

demonstrated in *JAOS 90*, p. 194 (n. 108), these formulae were already prevalent on the private and familial levels in very early periods and, on the contrary, it seems as if they moved from there to the international realm, and see on this matter in connection to ברית חסד N. Glueck, *Hesed in the Bible*, p. 46.

117. Cf. the clauses compared in the table in Appendix II of Herrmann's *Kaisereid.*

118. For the formula in Greek see below p. 36.

119. In the oath of Aritium we only find the clause of being an enemy to Gaius' enemies but not being a friend to his friends.

120. Cf. Weinfeld, *DDS*, p. 105, and cf. Fitzmyer, *Sefire*, I A 1–5.

121. See n. 71 above.

122. *nammakan ke uddār* ANA DUMU. MEŠ. NI *piran* UL *uwatewani* (Schuler, *Orient.* 25, p. 227: 18–19).

In the אמת ויציב liturgy: 'on our sons and our generations and all generations of the seed of Israel and your servants'.

Formal Aspects of the Covenant Ceremony

K. *The Mass Gathering*

In the Assyrian as well as biblical covenants, we hear of the gathering together of all segments of the population to participate in the covenantal oath.[123] Esarhaddon tells of his enthronement by his father: '[My father] gathered the people of the Land of Assyria, young and old...and adjured them with a solemn oath in the presence of Ashur, Sin, Shamash...the gods of Assyria who dwell in heaven and earth',[124] and in a similar way Ashurbanipal tells of his enthronement by his father Esarhaddon: 'He gathered the people of Assyria young and old...and adjured them by the life of the gods and validated the covenant' (*udannina riksāte*),[125] and in the opening of Esarhaddon's vassal treaty: 'with all the people of Urukazabanu, young and old (*ṣiḫir rabi* [TUR GAL]) (ll. 4–5). All of these should be compared to the Josianic covenant with its gathering of 'the whole population, young and old' (2 Kgs 23.2), and to the covenant of Asa in 2 Chron. 15.13: 'Young and old, men and women alike'.

In Deut. 29.9ff. we are informed that at the covenant ceremony 'all the men of Israel' were standing by including children, wives, and even strangers 'from woodchopper to waterdrawer'. The covenants of Sinai and Gerizim were also ratified in the presence of the entire populace (Exod. 24; Josh. 24).

The Hittite treaty ceremonies were also made in the presence of the entire people who took the pledge. We read for example at the end of the tablet of the adjuration of the Hittite officers that the oath was taken in Usha,[126] but one of the clauses within the document[127] stipulates that the pact is binding on those absent from the gathering.[128] This clause clarifies the passage in Deut. 29.14 according to which the covenant binds 'both those who are standing here with us today before the Lord' and 'those who are not with us here this day'.

The public oath is also known to us from the Greek world. Thus we hear Xenophon saying 'that everywhere in Greece there is a law that the citizens shall promise under oath to agree and everywhere they take this oath' (*Memorabilia* IV 4, 16).

Similarly we find in the pact between the people of Thera and the people of Cyrene[129] which is concerned with the founding of the settlement in Cyrene, that

123. Weinfeld, *DDS*, etc. p. 101.

124. Cf. R. Borger, *Die Inschriften Asarhaddons Königs von Assyrien*, 1956, p. 40.15ff.

125. M. Streck, *Assurbanipal II*, p. 4.18–23, and see also M. Weinfeld, *DDS*, etc. p. 87.

126. Schuler, *Heth. Dienstanw.* p. 17.54–56 and see there in his note to this paragraph, p. 21, and in the commentary to IV 55.

127. *Op. Cit.* p. 14. para. 25 ll. 53–54.

128. Schuler, *op. cit.* p. 21 in his commentary to IV. 55, and for the gathering see also A. Goetze, *Kleinasien*^{2} (1957), p. 104.

129. R. Meiggs and D. Lewis, *A Selection of Greek Historical Inscriptions* 1969, No. 5 and see a

all of those who were gathered, *men, women and children*, recited the covenant oaths. An adjuration of the entire population is also mentioned in other Greek treaties.[130] Furthermore, in the treaty between Smyrna and Magnesia[131] the two parties obligate themselves to appoint people who will administer the oath to the people and will assure that no one will leave the city a day before the adjuration,[132] and in the treaty between Praisos and Stalai[133] we are told that the citizens absent from the city at the time of the oath taking will be required to take the oath upon their return. Special administration of the oath was held for young recruits or minors who became of age and were accepted as full members in the community,[134] reminiscent of the oath of the new initiates who joined the Qumran order, an oath made 'in the sight of all the initiates'.[135]

From the concluding sentences of the oath of the Paphlagonians we also learn that oaths of loyalty to the Roman Emperors were also carried out in the presence of the entire people. We are told that all the people of the province took the oath in their temple alongside the altars of Augustus while the inhabitants of Phacimon all swore in unison (σύμπαντες) alongside the altar of Augustus in the temple of Augustus. In the beginning of the oath we hear that not only inhabitants of Paphlagonia swore loyalty to Augustus but also the Romans who traded with them.[136] Augustus himself writes in his memoirs that all of Italy (tota Italia) swore loyalty to him.[137] We learn from Suetonius (*Augustus* 17.2) that Bononia (= Bolonia) was exempted from this oath since it was considered Antonius' client. This is to say that exemption from taking the oath could be given only to those who were committed to another master and thus freed from pledge to Augustus. Those who did not get the exemption were obliged to take the oath. It seems that the Pharisees and Essenes were also exempted from taking the oath to Herod (*Ant.* 15.368ff). In the Manual of Discipline we find indeed that everyone who refuses to enter the covenant of God 'has separated himself from the group and is not counted in the order (Yaḥad) (Manual of Discipline 2.26–3.2).

comprehensive analysis of this document in V.P. Yailenko, *Viestnik Drevniej Istorii* 1973, Fasc. 2, pp. 43ff. In the opinion of most scholars the date of the inscription in its present form is the fourth century BCE, however its nucleus dates back to the seventh century BCE.

130. In the treaty between Athens and Chalcis from 446/45 (Bengtson II No. 155, 32) and between Athens and Selymbreia (Bengtson II No. 297.24–27). Compare also the oath enacted by Demophantus quoted above.

131. *OGI* 229.

132. Line 80ff. and cf. Polybius III 61 which relates a similar notice in connection with an adjuration of soldiers.

133. Bengtson III No. 553, B. 3ff.

134. See references in P. Hermann, *Kaisereid*, p. 33.

135. Manual of Discipline 5.8 (J. Licht, *Mgylt Hsrkym*, 1965).

136. [καὶ τῶν πραγ]ματευομ[ένων πα]ῤ αὐτοῖς ῥ[ωμαίων] Cf. the oath from Assos (*Syll.*[3] 797, 10)

137. Iuravit in mea verba tota Italia sponte sua (Res Gestae 25). *Tota Italia* is a generalization just like כל ישראל in the Deuteronomic literature in connection with the covenant. For *tota Italia* see R. Syme, *The Roman Revolution*, 1939. Compare also the oath of *tota Syria* to Vespasian (Tacit. Hist. 2, 81).

L. *Annual Covenant Renewal*

Documents from the ancient Near East hint at annual covenant renewal ceremonies,[138] and according to Mowinckel they occurred on the new year's day.[139] Explicit testimony to regularly recurring covenant renewal ceremonies is found in the Manual of Discipline. According to the rules of the sect, the members of the sect are required to undergo the covenant ceremony every year (2.19 cf. 5.24) and it seems that this ceremony had a fixed date. In a yet unpublished version of the Damascus Covenant, the time fixed is the third month[140] and it therefore seems that the covenant ceremony was performed on the holiday of Pentecost which at the time of the second Temple commemorated the Sinai Covenant.

The Greek-Hellenistic and Roman world provides explicit evidence on this matter. In a treaty between Sparta and Athens we find that the treaty will be renewed each year, τὸν δὲ ὅρκον ἀνανεοῦσθαι κατ᾽ ἐνιαυτόν,[141] a phenomenon known to us also from the Hellenistic period which speaks of annual covenant ceremonies.[142] An annual renewal of a loyalty oath to the Caesar is mentioned by Tacitus who tells about a suggestion made in the Senate after the death of Augustus to annually renew the oath of loyalty to Tiberius.[143] We also know that in later periods (Caligula, Nero) it was customary to renew oaths of loyalty at the time of the new year.[144]

M. *Recital of the Covenant*

The gatherings and assembly ceremonies discussed in the preceding paragraphs served the purpose of public proclamation of the covenantal stipulations. Reading of the stipulations of the treaty before the undertaking party is already known in the Hittite Vassal Treaties: 'At regular intervals (*immuti immutima*) shall they read it [the stipulations of the covenant] in the presence of the king of Mittani land and in the presence of the sons of the Hurri land'.[145] Or: 'They shall read this tablet before you three times every year'.[146] The adjuration of the Hittite officers was also read before them at a gathering. The copies of the Assyrian treaties were meant to be read as we may learn from the demonstrative pronouns within the documents such as: 'the oath which is in this tablet' (*māmīt*

138. See my article in *VT* 23 (1973), p. 72.

139. See S. Mowinckel, *The Psalms in Israel's Worship* (1963), Vol. 1, pp. 155ff.

140. See J.T. Milik, *Ten Years of Discovery etc.* SBL No. 26, 1959, pp. 114, 117.

141. Thuc. 5.18.9.

142. ἀναγινωσκόντων δὲ τὰν στάλαν κατ᾽ ἐνιαυτόν, *Inscr. Cret.* I. XIX 231, 1.20 (Bengtson III 511.20). For covenant renewal in religious communes of the Persian and Hellenistic periods see my article *VT* 23 (1973), p. 72 n. 1.

143. (Ann. 1,8) renovandum per annos sacramentum in nomen Tiberii.

144. Cf. the discussions of Premerstein, *Vom Werden* etc., pp. 60ff., and P. Hermann, *Kaisereid*, pp. 107ff.

145. E. Weidner, *Politische Dokumente aus Kleinasien*, p. 28.36–37.

146. J. Friedrich, *MVAeG* 34/1, 1930, p. 76.73–74. This calls to mind the obligation to appear before the Lord three times every year (23.17 and parallel passages) and perhaps also in the Hittite texts the holidays are intended.

tuppi anni), in VTE (line 397), and in the recurring formulae: ‘the oaths which are in this tablet’ (עדיא זי בספרה זנה)[147] in the Aramaic treaty from Sefire.

In the biblical covenants we find explicit evidence that the text of the written covenant was read before the people: ‘Then he took the book of the covenant (ספר הברית) and read it aloud to the people’ (Exod. 24.7), ‘There he read out to them all the book of the covenant discovered in the house of the Lord’(2 Kgs 23.2).

Also in the Hellenistic covenants we hear of the obligation to read the text of the stelae and there is special mention made of an annual reading of the stelae: ἀναγινωσκόντων δὲ τὰν στάλαν κατ’ ἐνιαυτόν (cf. n. 142.)

N. *Witnesses to the Covenant*

In the covenants the gods are called upon to serve as witnesses to the undertaking of obligation and the oath[148] and in the case of a vassal treaty the gods of the administrator and taker of the oath alike are invited.[149] In addition to the gods, the natural forces are involved: mountains, rivers, wells, the abyss,[150] the heavens and earth, wind and clouds.[151] Also mentioned are a thousand gods who serve as punishing[152] witnesses and it is pointed out that all the *gods and goddesses* including the gods of the underworld appear as witnesses. In the treaty between Šuppiluliuma and Mattiwaza it is written:

> let them stand by...listen and serve as witnesses....the Sun-god, the lord of heaven, the Storm-god (^{d}IM)[153], the lord of the Hatti land...(various gods), the gods and goddesses (*ilāni amēlūti ilāni sinnišāti*)...the gods of the underworld[154]...the mountains, the rivers, the Tigris and the Euphrates, heaven and earth, the winds and the clouds.[155]

In the treaty between Šuppiluliuma and Tete:

> [The Sun of heaven...] (all kinds of storm gods) Ereshkigal (= goddess of the netherworld)...(list of the gods)...all of the gods and goddesses...mountains, rivers, wells, the great abyss, heaven and earth, winds and clouds will be witnesses to this covenant and oath.[156]

In the Sefire treaty:

147. Cf. אלות הברית הכתובה בספר הזה (Deut. 29.19, cf. v. 20).

148. Cf. e.g. Il. 22.253f: ‘for they (the gods) shall be the best witnesses and guardians of our covenant’.

149. On this matter see M. Tsevat, *JBL* 78 (1959), pp. 199–204.

150. *Nārāt* (ÍD. MEŠ), *būrātu* (PÚ. MEŠ), *tâmtu rabītu* (A. AB. BA GAL), *KBO* 1 4, IV 153 36, cf. *KUB* 3 7 r. 9. and cf. the various vows in the names of rivers and wells, *CAD* B p. 337d.

151. Weidner, *Polit. Dok.*, pp. 31.53, 68.44–45, 74.9–10.

152. Cf. Weidner, *ibid*, 34.68; PRU UV 43.49; 51.17. For the עֵד as warner cf. I.L. Seeligmann, *SVT* 16 (1967), pp. 251–278.

153. He equals Mesopotamian Adad, Aramaic Hadad, Canaanite Baal, Hurrian Tesub, and Greek Zeus.

154. *Ilani erṣeti* and in a parallel text *Ereškigal*, Queen of the netherworld.

155. Weidner, *Polit. Dokumente*, p. 30.5ff.

156. Weidner, *ibid*, *op. cit.* pp. 66.9ff.

> This treaty concluded by Barga'yah is set up before...Marduk and Zerpanit...before Nergal and Las (the gods of the netherworld), before Shamas and Nur...before Heaven and Earth, before depth and springs, and before Day and Night. Witness all you gods of Ktk and Arpad, open your eyes to behold the treaty...[157]

In Esarhaddon's adjuration of the vassals:

> ...Ashur, the father of the gods...Shamash, Adad...Marduk, Nabu, Nusku, Urash and Nergal (= gods of the netherworld)...all the gods of Sumer and Akkad...all the gods of every land...the gods of heaven and earth. (ll. 25–40)

And in the oath of the vassals themselves:

> 'May these gods see', etc. (line 494)

In the biblical covenant we should obviously not expect any but the one God who is party to the covenant,[158] however, natural forces are invoked as witnesses: heaven and earth (Deut. 4.26; 30.19; 31.28),[159] and in prophecy, mountains and hills (Mic. 6.1–2).[160]

In the treaty between the Achaeans and Trojans in Homer,[161] Agamemnon's address to the divine witnesses is identical to the clauses mentioned above:

> Father Zeus, that rulest from Ida, most glorious, most great, and thou Sun, that beholdest all things and hearest all things, and ye rivers and thou earth, and ye that in the world below take vengeance on men that are done with life, whosoever hath sworn a false oath; be ye witnesses, and watch over the valid oaths (ὅρκια πιστά).[162]

In an oath of the Epheboi of Dreros we read:

> by earth and heaven, the heroes (local deities)...by springs and rivers, all the gods and goddesses. (*Syll.*^{3} 527.30f.)

The divine witnesses listed in the oaths of the treaties occur also in general adjurations. Thus we find in an Assyrian incantation ritual: 'I adjure you by Šamaš... by well, valley, mountains and rivers' (*utammēka kuppu, naḫli, šadê, nārāti*) (Ebeling, *Tod und Leben* 78.6–8, comp. Šurpu VIII 40).

In the Greek sources we find a formulaic oath containing similar elements. Demosthenes is said to proclaim a metric oath:

> 'by earth, by springs, by rivers, and by streams' (μὰ γῆν, μὰ κρήνας, μὰ ποταμούς, μὰ νάματα) (Plut. Demosth. 9).

The common elements to all of the sources brought above are:

157. I A: 10ff., and cf. a similar list in the treaty of Ashurnirari V, *AfO* 8, 17f VI.6.

158. In cases of confrontation between two human parties, such as the case of Samuel and Israel (1 Sam. 12) the god is invited as a witness (*ibid.*, v. 5)

159. In Ps. 89.38 it seems as if the moon (and perhaps the sun which appears in an earlier verse) serves as a witness to God's covenant with David.

160. And see my book *Deuteronomy* p. 62.

161. Iliad III 276ff. (trans. Murray, Loeb Class. L.)

162. For ὅρκια πιστά and its semitic equivalents cf. Weinfeld, *Leshonenu* 36 (1972), p. 11.

1. The appearance of divine witnesses,[163] the most prominent ones being the head of the pantheon, who is usually *the storm god* (IŠKUR = Adad, identical with Canaanite Baal/Hadad, Babylonian Marduk, Assyrian Ashur[164], and Greek Zeus) and *the sun* (god).[165]
2. The gods of the underworld occur among the witnesses, who, as it seems on the basis of Homer,[166] are capable of punishing breakers of the covenant, even after death.
3. Natural phenomena as witnesses to the treaty: heaven and earth,[167] mountains and hills, rivers, wells, lakes, the deep, etc.
4. Address to the divine witnesses to *arise* (*uzuzzu*), *hear*, and *see* or open their eyes to the covenant.

   Such an invocation is found in the Bible in conjunction with the covenant between Jacob and Laban, 'May the Lord watch (יצף) between you and me' (Gen. 31.49 cp. Exod. 5.21), and in the continuation, 'May the God of Abraham and the God of Nahor…judge between us' (Gen. 31.53), a passage which brings to expression the divine witnesses from both sides as we find in the above-mentioned covenants.
5. Emphasis on *all* the gods, be they *male or female*. In the Sefire treaty and in the treaty of Ashurnirari V,[168] this is emphasized by explicit mentioning of the divine spouses along with each of the gods.

The Greek and the Hellenistic treaties and the oaths of loyalty to the Roman Emperor start off by listing as witnesses: Zeus, the Sun and the Earth[169] (Δία,

163. In the Hittite treaties the witnesses usually appear at the end, however we do find them in the beginning as well, such as in the treaty with the Kaskaeans (see E. von Schuler, *Die Kaskäer*, [1965], p. 124f.) and the treaty with Ḫuqannaš (Friedrich *MVAeG*, 1934, p. 111.41) and cf. as well the opening to the adjuration of the army, Alp. (n. 8), 403. The Greek oaths open with the divine witnesses and this is also the case with Esarhaddon's adjuration of the vassals as well as the oath of the vassals themselves which opens: 'may the gods look on' etc., ll. 494ff. The Sefire treaty also commences with the divine witnesses.

164. For Marduk and Ashur in the capacity of storm gods see my article in *Th. Gaster Festschrift. JANES* (1973), pp. 422ff.

165. Cf. the oath between the eagle and the snake in the Neo-Assyrian version of the Mesopotamian Etana myth (*ANET*^{2}, p. 116). The oath is made before Shamash and is contingent on Shamash's curses. Shamash's curse, whose main feature is trapping in a net (*šušgal)* occupies an important position in the treaty of Eannatum (the Vulture Stela) from the third millenium BCE. (Cf. my book *DDS*, p. 73 n. 6) The Sun God in Hurrian-Hittite documents is called *bēl māmīti* 'the Lord of the oath'. See Laroche, *Ugaritica V*, 522.

166. Il. III 276f. (cited above), cf. also Il. XIX 258f.: 'and the Erinyes, that under earth take vengeance on men'.

167. Concerning these witnesses in the biblical covenant see Weinfeld, *DDS*, p. 62 and cf. with the witnesses in the prophetic lawsuit, M.P. Huffmon, *JBL* 78 (1959), pp. 286–95. The oath of 'heaven and earth' occurs already in the Sumerian sources (the oath of Zianna – zikia, cf. Draffkorn-Kilmer, *UF* 3 [1971], pp. 304–305) and cf. also the formula in the Zi-pa incantations: 'adjured by heaven, adjured by earth' (cf. R. Borger, *AOAT* 1, *Festschrift von Soden* [1969], pp. 1–22). Compare also in the Phoenician incantation from the Arslan Tash (7th century BCE): בעלת שמם וארץ 'by oath of heaven and earth' (*KAI* 27.13).

168. Sefire 1 A.8 and Aššurnirari V, Rev. VI.6–27. (*AfO* 8 [1932–33], pp. 17–34).

169. Cf. e.g. Bengtson II, No. 260.2; Bengtson III, No. 429.24; 476.87; 481.23–24; 492.61, 70 and

῞Ηλιον, Γῆν) continue with local gods and goddesses, and conclude with the formula known from the Hittite treaties: 'all the gods and goddesses' (θεοὺς πάντας καὶ πάσας).

In the treaty between Phillip V and Hannibal[170] we find formulae even closer to the oriental type, this is only natural since one of the parties is a Semite.[171] Here we find also rivers, lakes and water,[172] this being similar to the Hittite and Aramaic treaties which we have cited, and just as in the oriental treaties, this treaty goes on to mention the gods of both parties.

Most interesting is the clause concluding the list of witnesses in this treaty: ἐφεστήκασιν ἐπι τοῦδε τοῦ ὅρκου 'who stand by at this oath' (line 3).

The same expression appears in the Hittite treaties in connection with the divine witnesses: 'may (the gods) *stand* together, hear and be witnesses'.[173]

O. *The Blessing and Curse*

This clause is much expanded in the oriental treaties and occupies an important position in the Assyrian and Aramaic treaties. It must be pointed out that, as opposed to the Hittite treaties which list both blessings and curses, the Assyrian treaties mention no blessing at all.[174] We cannot discuss this problem in the utmost detail so we will pay special attention to the blessing and curse formulae common to the treaties and the oath in the Hittite, Aramaic, Greek, and Roman documents. The formulae contained in these documents specially emphasize cutting off *the man, his seed, his house, and all he has*[175] should he break the covenant, and the opposite for his fulfilling all the stipulations. So we read in the Hittite treaties:

> If PN (the vassal) does not fulfill the words of this treaty and oath…may (the gods) blot him out…together with his wives, his sons, his sons' sons, his house, his city and

in the opening of the oath of the Paphlagonians. In some documents we find instead of Sun and Earth, Apollo and Demeter, see Bengtson II.134.16 (The Erythrae Decree), 145.52. In later times there was an inclination to multiply divine witnesses, see P. Siewert, *Der Eid von Plataiai*, p. 33. Philo (Spec. Leg. II, 1, 5) recommends swearing by the earth, sun, stars, heavens (ἀλλὰ γῆν, ἥλιον, ἀστέρας, οὐρανον), see, however, Mt. 23.16–22. It is interesting to point out that Esarhaddon's adjuration of the vassals starts off with Jupiter, Venus, Saturn etc. Invocations by heaven and earth were prevalent within the Jewish masses until late times. See S. Lieberman, *Hellenism in Jewish Palestine* (1950).

170. Polybius VII, 9.

171. For Semitic features in the text of this covenant see E. Bickerman, *Amer. Jour. of Philology* 73 (1952), pp 1–23.

172. ἐναντίον ποταμῶν καὶ λιμένων καὶ ὑδάτων. On the basis of the parallels cited it seems that we should read λιμνῶν (Reiske) from λίμνη meaning lake (cf. F.W. Walbank, *Comm. Polybius* II 1967). It is noteworthy that אגמי מים (Ps. 107.35, 114.8) is translated by the LXX λίμνας ὑδάτων.

173. (*ana aḫāmeš*) *lizzizū lištēmū u lū šībūtu* (Weidner, *Pol. Dok*. 48.11, 50.25, cf. 28.39; 32.58–59).

174. For a possible explanation see Weinfeld, *DDS*, p. 68.

175. And cf. Zech. 5.4 concerning the oath which comes to the house of one who swears falsely: ולנה בתוך ביתו וכלתו ואת עציו ואת אבניו 'it shall dwell inside that house and destroy it, timbers and stone and all'.

> his country and all that he has. If (on the other hand) he fulfills all the words of this treaty and oath which are written in this document, may (the gods) protect him together with his wives, his sons, his sons' sons, his cattle, his house, his city and his country and all he has.[176]

In the Aramaic Sefire Treaty:

> May [he who observes the words of this stela] be guarded by the gods... But whoever does not observe the words of the inscription...may...he and his house be turned upside down...and his seed shall not acquire a name.[177]

Similar formulae appear in Greek and Hellenistic treaties. For example, in the oath (ὅρκια)[178] between the people of Thera and Cyrene in connection with the founding of the Cyrene colony[179] we read that those assembled declared a curse:

> He who does not heed the words of this treaty, and even transgresses them, may he perish and may he melt like wax, he and *his offspring and his property*, and those who do heed the words of the covenant...may it go (very) well for them *and their progeny*.[180]

Similarly, we find in an agreement between two groups of settlers from the fourth century BCE: 'If I swear truthfully, may all be well for me but if I swear falsely may destruction visit *me and my seed*'.[181]

In the treaty between Smyrna and Magnesia:[182] 'If I swear truthfully, may all be well for me but if I swear falsely may destruction visit *myself and my seed*'. A shorter formula appears in other documents: 'If I swear truthfully may all be very well for me (πολλὰ κἀγάθ') but if I swear falsely may the opposite occur (τἀνατία).[183]

The curse in the Paphlagonians' oath of loyalty to Augustus is the most detailed.[184] We read there: 'And if I do anything contrary to the oath... I invoke a complete curse of destruction...upon myself, my body and spirit, my life and my children and all my seed (to be born) to the last generation of mine and my descendants, and may the land and sea not accept my corpse or the corpse of my progeny'.

176. See Weidner, *Pol. Dok.*, p. 68.48ff. Cf. *ibid.* p. 74 line 13ff. (reverse) and see the curses and blessings in PRU IV, pp. 80ff. In the treaties between Šupiluliuma and Mattiwaza the series of blessings and curses is longer. See Weidner,] *Pol. Dok.*, p. 54.44ff.

177. יצרו אלהן...ומן...ליצר...יהפכו...אלהן...אש[א] הא וביתה ואל ירת שר[ש]ה אשם (I C.15f.).

178. In the ancient Near East as well as in Greece the oath (Akk. *māmītu*, Hittite *lingai*, Phoen. Heb. אלה) [signifies the covenant which is basically an obligation, and as in Akk. *(māmīte)* and Aramaic (עדיא, עדן) (cf. עדות IIeb.) so in Greek the concept appears in plural forms even though only one covenant is intended and not many. See my article in *JAOS* 93 (1973), p. 191, No. 9; 192, No. 47.

179. For reference see above note 129.

180. τὸμ μὴ ἐμμένοντα τούτοις τοῖς ὁρκίοις ἀλλὰ παρβεῶντα καταλείβεσθαί νιν καὶ καταρρὲν ὥσπερ τὸς κολοσός, καὶ αὐτὸν καὶ γὸνον καὶ χρήματα, τοῖς δέ ἐμμένοισιν τούτοις τοῖς ὁρκίοις ... ἦμεν πολλὰ καὶ ἀγαθὰ καὶ αὐ[τοῖς καὶ γό]νοις.

181. Bengtson II, No. 297, pp. 68–72, 87–90.

182. *OGI*, 229, 69, 78.

183. Bengtson III 468.21–23 and cf. 476–89f; 463.12f; II 263.34f; 308.5f. and in the oath of loyalty to Caligula from Assos.

184. *OGI* 532.

In the Latin oath of loyalty to Gaius Caligula from Aritium: 'If consciously I swear falsely...may Jupiter...and all the immortal gods punish me *and my children* with loss of country, safety and all my fortune'.[185]

The feature common to all of these curses is that they threaten the descendants of the treaty breaker, an idea expressed clearly in Rabbinic literature: 'For all transgressions in the Torah he alone is punished, but here (a false oath) he and his family (*b. Shebu.* 39a).[186]

In the ancient Hebrew and Greek Blessing and Curse formulae stress is laid upon *seed* and offspring in the broad sense: '*the fruit of the womb, of the soil and of the flock*'.

Thus for example we read in the Blessing and Curse section of the Deuteronomic covenant:

> 'Blessed shall be the fruit of your womb, the fruit of your soil and the fruit of your cattle, the calving of your herd and the lambing of your flock' (28.4) and the exact opposite in the curse section (28.18).

More elaborate are the formulae found in the prologue to Deuteronomy (7.12ff.):

> And if you do obey these rules and observe them faithfully, the Lord your God will maintain for you the gracious covenant...he will bless the fruit of your womb, the fruit of your soil, your new grain and wine and oil, the calving of your herd and the lambing of your flock...there shall be no sterile male or female among you or among your livestock. The Lord will ward off from you all sickness.

These formulae and especially the reference to sickness and sterility actually have their roots in the ancient epilogue to the Covenant Code.[187]

> You shall serve the Lord your God, and he will bless your bread and your water. And I will remove sickness from your midst. No woman in your land shall miscarry or be barren. (Exod. 23.25–26)

Striking parallels to the cited formulae are to be found in the old Greek oaths. Thus we find in the amphictyonic oath quoted by Aischines:

> that their land bear no fruit, that their wives bear no children...that their flocks yield not their natural increase...and that they perish utterly themselves, their houses, their whole race... (Aisch. 3.111)

185. Si s[cie]ns fallo...tum me liberosque meos...: omnes di immortales expertam patria incolumitate fortunisque omnibus faxint. M. Dessau *Inscript. Latinae* Vol.1. 190, 13.

186. And cf. Herodotus VI 86(3): 'Yet an oath has a son, nameless, without hands or feet, but swift to pursue until he has seized and destroyed utterly the race and house of the perjured but the one who keeps his oath, his children are happier'. The last sentence ἀνδρός δ'εὐόρκου γενεὴ μετόπισθεν ἀμείνων appears verbatim in Hesiod's *Opera et Dies* in connection to an oath (ll. 283–285) and apparently Herodotus borrowed from there. For the curse as pursuing and overtaking cf. Deut. 28.45: 'All these curses shall befall you, they shall pursue you and overtake you until you are destroyed'. This concept of the curse which pursues, overtakes, and speedily destroys is found in Mesopotamian sources and appears in the Hittite treaties. See M. Weinfeld, *DDS*, pp. 108–109.

187. For the dependence of Deut. 7 upon Exod. 23.20ff. cf. Weinfeld, *DDS*, pp. 46ff.

And in the oath of the Athenians against the Barbarians:

> if I keep what is written in the oath, let my polis be without sickness...and my land shall bear (fruit)...the women shall bear children...and the cattle shall bear.[188]

The curse of not burying a treaty-breaker's body, which is found in the Paphlagonians' oath is also found in the vassals' oath to Esarhaddon (VTE): 'may the dogs and pigs drag your bodies around in the squares of Ashur and may the earth not accept them (for burial)' (ll. 483–484). This curse is actually found in the most ancient documents. For example, among the curses found at the end of the inscription of Yaḫdun-lim, King of Mari, we find: 'and may the dead not accept (him)' (*mūti aj imḫur*, *Syria* 32 [1955], p. 17, V 22).

P. *Dramatization of the Curses*

In the ancient world it was customary to accompany the curses with dramatic acts intended to illustrate the curses. Thus, for example, in the oath of the Hittite soldiers[189] wax is melted to illustrate the melting of an infringer of the treaty, salt is scattered to illustrate the stoppage of his seed, barley is ground while threats are made that this is how the treaty-breaker's bones are to be ground,[190] women's clothes, a spindle and a mirror are displayed so as to illustrate the fate of the treaty-breaker – that he shall turn into a woman; a blind and a deaf man are brought and threats are made that this will be the fate of the infringer, and so on.

In the Aramaic Sefire treaty[191] we hear about illustrations of curses such as: burning wax figurines in fire, breaking bows and arrows, gouging out eyes from wax figurines, cutting up a calf, etc.

In the vassal oaths to Esarhaddon we also find in the curses use of wax figurines, breaking bows, gouging out eyes, and displaying a spindle, but they are supplemented by other illustrations.[192]

In the Assyrian treaty between Ashurnirari V and Matti'el of Arpad the head of a calf is broken off to demonstrate the severity of punishment of a treaty infringer.[193]

In the biblical covenant we hear primarily about cutting up animals in the covenant ceremony (Gen. 15; Jer. 34), this being done in order to show what will happen to anyone who breaks the treaty: 'so I will make you like the calf (reading כעגל)[194] of the covenant when they cut it into two and passed between the pieces'. (Jer. 34.18) Such an activity is mentioned in the Sefire treaty: '[As] this calf is cut up, thus Matti'el and his nobles shall be cut up'.[195]

188. Cf. for text and discussion: P. Siewert, *Der Eid von Plataiai* (1972), pp. 6ff.

189. See n. 5 above.

190. Cf. VTE 445–46.

191. I.A 35ff.

192. Line 530 etc.

193. E. Weidner, *AFO* 8 (1932–33), pp. 16ff.

194. For this reading cf. A. Ehrlich, *Randglossen zur Hebr. Bibel* IV, p. 331

195. [w'yk ży] ygzr ʿgl' znh kn ygzr mt''l wygzrn rbwh (I A 39–40). It is interesting that the verb גזר is used here, it being the same verb used for making a covenant: גזר עדיא Cf. Jer. 34.18: הברית אשר כרתו לפני העגל אשר כרתו לשנים.

The custom of cutting up an animal in a covenant ceremony, apparently reflected in the expressions כרת ברית (Hebrew), כרת אלת (Phoenician), גזר עדן (Aramaic),[196] was prevalent in Greece and there as well the expression for making a treaty is to 'cut an oath' ὅρκια τέμνειν.[197] In the Laws of Plato, we even find explicit mention of passing through the pieces while making a commitment[198] (electing a candidate) (753^{d}).[199]

In the dramatization of curses found in the covenants and oaths from the east, the use of wax and wax figurines is most prominent. For example, we find in the oath of the Hittite soldiers: 'Just as this (after it is put in the pan) melts, may anyone who breaks the treaty melt'[200] (I.40–II.5). In the first curse in the Sefire treaty:[201] 'As this wax figurine[202] is consumed by fire, thus Arpad…shall be consumed… As this wax is consumed by fire, thus Matti'el shall be consumed by fire'. And in the vassals' oath to Esarhaddon: 'Just as one burns a wax figurine (*ṣalmu ša iškuri*) in fire…so may they burn your figure in fire' (ll. 608–611). Such a curse and its illustration are found in the pact between the people of Thera and the settlers of Cyrene which were inscribed on a stela.[203] We read here that the people of Thera and Cyrene made a covenant (ὅρκια ἐποιήσαντο)[204] and cursed those who infringe (παρβεῶντας) the covenant and do not heed it… They moulded wax figurines and burned them, and all those gathered, men, women and children recited curses: 'May those who do not heed the words of the covenant and infringe them, melt and perish like this figurine, they and their seed, and their property…'[205] (see above p. 25).

Q. *Covenantal Sacrifices*

Sacrifices in connection with covenant making were very widespread in Greece[206]

196. Even so, we must admit to the possibility that the verb *gzr/krt* in this connection may indicate deciding or determining. Cf. E. Kutsch, 'Verheissung und Gesetz', *BZAW* 131 (1973), p. 47ff.

197. See J. Priest, *JNES* 23 (1964), 48ff., and my article *JAOS* 93 (1973), p. 192, No. 47.

198. διὰ τομίων πορευόμενος. Concerning the τόμια at an oath ceremony see P. Stengel, *Hermes* 49 (1914), p. 95ff.

199. For a Hittite ceremony in which the soldiers pass through pieces of animals and a cut man see O. Masson, *RHR* 137 (1950), pp. 5–25, however there the ceremony is not necessarily connected to a covenant. And see my article Addenda to *JAOS* 90, *JAOS* 92 (1972), p. 469 to pp. 196ff. The origin of the rite itself seems to be anchored in some kind of protective ceremony, see E. Bikerman, *Arch. d. Hist. d. Droit Orient.* 5 (1950–51), p. 133f. On the other hand the ceremony adds some sacred force to the pledge (*ibid.*). Cf. also Th. Gaster, *Myth, Legend and Custom in the OT* (1969), pp. 140ff.

200. For refer. see n. 5.

201. איך זי תקד שעותא זא באש כן תקד ארפד... (I. A. 35–38).

202. That a figurine is spoken about may be learned from the continuation: ואיך זי יער גבר שעותא 'and just as a man of wax is blinded'.

203. See references above, n. 129.

204. Compare ὅρκους ποιήσασθαι in connection with Josiah's covenant in Josep. *Antiq.* 10.63, cf. too Arist. *Athen.* 3,3.

205. This parallel has been noticed by E. Bikerman, *Arch. Hist. Droit Orient.* 5 (1950–51), pp. 146–47, cf. also C. Picard, *Rev. Arch.* (1961), p. 85f. However in the meantime the clause from Esarhaddon's treaty has been discovered.

206. P. Stengel, *Die Griech. Kultusaltertümer*^{3}, Handbuch der Klassischen Altertumswiss., Vol. 3 (1920), pp. 136–37; M. Nilsson, *Gesch. D. Griech. Religion*^{3} (1967), Band I, pp. 139ff.

as well as in the Mesopotamian and Hittite world[207] and in ancient Israel (Exod. 24.5ff, cf. Ps. 50.5 כרתי בריתי עלי זבח)[208] However, in Mesopotamia and Israel we hear of these sacrifices in documents pertaining to the second millenium BCE while there is no testimony for such in first millenium documents.[209]

In the covenant ceremonies involving sacrifices, the blood has a special function and this is attested in Israel, Greece and Arabia.[210] Thus we find in Exodus 24 that in the course of the covenant ritual, sacrificial blood is sprinkled on the people entering the covenant and the blood is called דם ברית 'blood of the covenant' (v. 8; Zech. 9.11). A like phenomenon is found in Aeschylus (Seven Against Thebai, 42–48). Here, the warring princes obligate themselves by oath to destroy Thebai: they slaughter a bull and collect its blood and swear.[211] Covenant ceremonies involving blood are known from the Arabs[212] and Herodotus[213] also mentions it.

In Israel and in Greece three separate animals were chosen for covenantal sacrifices, in Greece (τριττύες),[214] a bull, goat, and a boar, or bull, ram, and boar, and in Genesis: a calf, a goat, and a ram.[215] It should also be pointed out that touching the sacrifice while making the oath – which is well attested among the Greeks[216] – is found as well in Mesopotamia[217] and it resembles the holding of a sacred object while taking an oath[218] which is known from Talmudic literature (= נקיטת חפץ) (*b. Shebu.* 38b).

R. *Eternal Validity of the Oath*

The binding force of the oath is expressed in Mesopotamia, in the Bible and in Greece by means of identical terms. Thus we find in Mesopotamia *māmītu/arratu rabîtu* = the big oath/curse, *adê rabûti.* (Streck, *Assurbanipal* p. 78, IX72) and also the NAM. ÉRIM (*māmītu) dannu* or *nīš ilim dannu* 'strong (= valid) oath' (See *CAD* D *dannu*). Identical terms are found in the Greek sources: ὅρκος μέγας (Il. 1; 239; 19, 113; Odyss. 4.746; 10.381), ὅρκος μέγιστος (Thuc.5.18.8) on the

207. Cf. Weinfeld, *DDS*, pp. 102–103.

208. For sacrificial elements in the 'covenant between the pieces' in Gen. 15 see Loewenstamm, *VT* 18 (1968), pp. 500–506.

209. For the gradual diminishing of the sacrificial element in the covenant see E. Bikerman, *art. cit.* 155f and cf. Weinfeld, *DDS*, 102ff.

210. This is in contrast to Mesopotamia and Egypt, and see McCarthy, *JBL* 88 (1909), pp. 166ff.

211. This parallel is discussed by E. Kutsch, *VT* 23 (1973), pp. 25ff., cf. also Xen. *Anab.* II 2,9.

212. W. Robertson Smith, *The Religion of the Semites*^{2} (1972), pp. 314ff., 481f.

213. 3.8 and comp. 1.74.

214. P. Stengel, *Die Griech. Kultusaltertümer*^{3} (1920), p. 119 n. 17, 137.

215. The birds were not cut up, as we may see from v. 10.

216. The holding of the ἱερά and the σπλάγχνα: see P. Stengel, *Hermes* 49 (1914), pp. 95ff.

217. The Akkadian expression is *nikissa lapātu* (*RA* 18 [1921], 25 II.10; Šurpu III.35) = to touch the slaughtered, and cf. (*puḫada lapātu*), 'to touch the lamb'. See *CAD* L, p. 85, 2.

218. M.P. Nilsson, *Geschichte der griech. Religion*^{3} (1967), I. pp. 140ff. Cf. also Bikerman, *Arch. D.Hist.d.Droit Orient* 5, p. 146. Compare also the phrase in the Elamite documents: 'they have sworn, they have touched the head of their god' (cf. *CAD* L *lapātu* 1 b) and the oath taken by the members of the private shrine at Philadelphia (see above n. 105) accompanied by touching the inscribed stela (ll. 55ff.).

one hand, and ὅρκος ἰσχυρός (Antip. V 11; VI 25), ἀρὰ ἰσχυρά (Aeschines 2.115; 3.109), ὅρκος καρτερός (Il 19.108) on the other.

In a context similar to that of Aeschines (amphictyonic oath) we find in Judg. 21.5 השבועה הגדולה 'the great oath'.

The eternal validity of the oath found in Mesopotamian, Phoenician, Aramaic and biblical sources (ברית עולם) is also expressed in the Greek sources εἰς τὸν ἅπαντα χρόνον, τὸν ἀει χρόνον etc. (cf. *JAOS* 93 [1973], pp. 198–99).

S. *Erecting Monuments in Commemoration of the Covenant*

Commemoration of a pact by erecting stelas is already attested in Mesopotamia in the third millenium BCE (cf. the stela of the vultures, S.N. Kramer, *The Sumerian* 310 f) and is known from the Bible (Gen. 31.45, 51–52; Exod. 24.4), the Aramaic documents (Sefire stelas) and the Greek sources (cf. e.g., Thuc. 5.18.10; 23.5.)

All of the above-mentioned finds indicate that there is a common, formal basis to loyalty oaths, treaties and general adjurations in the ancient world. The formal similarity between oaths and treaties in East and West is so great that it seems to be impossible not to assume an eastern influence on the west (Greece and Rome) in this area. Even were we to assume a chance independent formation of the formulae and ceremonies we would be forced to admit that the oriental treaties have much in common with the occidental ones and this common background can help us to clarify various problems involved.

Even before the ancient oriental material became known there were those scholars who claimed an oriental origin for the treaties and loyalty oaths of the West and especially the loyalty oaths to Caesar.[219] The discovery of many Hittite and Assyrian documents attesting the various types of loyalty oaths and covenants, has strengthened this claim. In order to become fully aware of the connection between the oriental fealty oaths and the oaths of loyalty to the Roman Emperor, let us examine the oath of the Paphlagonians which is the longest and most complex of these oaths and we will see that every one of its elements is already known from the loyalty oaths of the ancient Near East.

1. The oath opens with a stereotyped formula ὀμνύω Δία Γῆν Ἥλιον 'I swear by Zeus, earth and sun', followed by θεοὺς πάντας καὶ πάσας 'all of the gods and goddesses', formulae discussed along with their Near Eastern parallels above in paragraph M. It should be pointed out that in distinction to the Hittite treaties where the divine witnesses appear at the end,[220] in Esarhaddon's adjuration of the vassals and in the Sefire treaty the witnesses appear in the beginning just as in the Greek and Roman oaths.

2. καὶ αὐτὸν τὸν Σεβαστόν 'and by Augustus himself'[221] – Swearing by the

219. Especially F. Cumont, *Rev. Ét. Gr.* 14 (1901), p. 44f.

220. An exception is the treaty with the Kaskeans cited above in note 163.

221. Swearing by the king *himself* was of special importance, cf. Sifrē Num. Sec. 153 (Horowitz ed. p. 199). מה הפרש נדרים לשבועות? בנדרים כנודר בחיי המלך,בשבועות כנשבע במלך עצמו. Concerning נדר meaning swear see S. Liebermann, *Greek in Jewish Palestine* p. 117f, where he cites the Tosephta (Sotah 6.1): שאין אדם נודר בחיי המלך אלא אם כן אוהב את המלך *ibid.*, p. 118, No. 21 אוהב here means loyal, see above, Sec. A.

king (ὅρκος βασιλικός) was very common in Ptolemaic Egypt[222] but is also known from other Hellenistic kingdoms.[223] The oath in the treaty between Smyrna and Magnesia is of particular interest to us since at the end of the list of divine witnesses we find the τύχη of the King Seleucus[224] (cf. the oath by the *genius* of Caesar).[225]

In ancient Near Eastern political documents the king is not mentioned among the divine witnesses but, as in Ptolemaic Egypt, he appears in private documents from the Assyrian and neo-Babylonian periods. There we find an oath by the *adê* of the king and the gods Bēl and Nabû.[226] Swearing by the life of the god and king together is actually known from the beginning of the second millenium BCE[227] and it seems that swearing by the τύχη,[228] the δαίμων[229] and the *genius* of the king in the Hellenistic and Roman periods is only a continuation of the custom of swearing by the life of the king in Egypt and in Mesopotamia.[230]

It appears from the evidence before us that it was not usually the custom[231] to include the king in the list of divine witnesses to loyalty oaths and political treaties. The inclusion of Augustus in the list of divine witnesses should then be viewed against the background of the Emperor cult which crystallized in Rome (even though the roots of this cult are in the Near East).

3. εὐνοήσειν (Καίσαρι) 'to be loyal' or 'to be well disposed' to Caesar Augustus, and in the parallel clause in the oath of loyalty to Tiberius from Palaipaphos

222. E. Seidl, *Der Eid im ptolomäischen Recht* (1929); *idem*, Ptolomäische Rechtsgeschichte (1962).

223. P. Hermann, *Kaisereid*, pp. 46–47.

224. *OGI* 229.61.

225. On Genius Caesaris cf. S. Weinstock, *Divus Julius* (1971), p. 250f.

226. See reference in *CAD* A *adû* B. The dictionary distinguishes between *adê* meaning oath (= A) and *adê* meaning power or majesty (= B), however Deller found that occasionally the scribe will write TI.MEŠ (= LIFE) in place of *adê* in this connection (*Wiener Zeitschrift f. Kunde d. Morg* 57 [1961], pp. 31ff.) and therefore there is no justification for this distinction in meaning (see also R. Frankena, *Oudt St.* 14 [1965], p. 134). *Adê* is therefore equivalent in meaning to *nīšu* (= life).

227. In documents from the time of Sin-idinnam of Larsa (1849–1843 BCE) (A. Goetze, *JCS* 4 [1950], 97.18) mu ^{d}Nanna ^{d}Šamaš u ^{d}Sin-i-di-nam in-pàd-eš, 'They swore by Nanna (the moon god), by Šamaš and by Sin-idinnam'. And in a document from Cappadocia. *nīš Aššur nīš rubā'im tamā'um* 'to swear by the life of Ashur and the life of the prince'. (F. Hrozny, *Inscriptions cunéiformes du Kultépé*, I (1952), No. 32; cf. J. Lewy, *HUCA*, 27 [1956], pp. 10ff.). For Elam cf. P. Koschaker, *Orientalia* 4 (1935), pp. 46ff.

228. Most instructive is the oath of a woman from the period of Bar-Cochba by the τύχη of the emperor. See H.J. Polotsky, *IEJ* 12 (1962), p. 260.

229. It seems to me that swearing by one's נפש (Amos 6.8; Jer. 51.14) is like swearing by one's daimon or tyche; for נפש as external soul see Saggs, *JSS* 19 (1974), 1f, and for the relationship between δαίμων and τύχη see E.R. Dodds, *The Greeks and the Irrational* (1951), p. 58, No. 80; M.P. Nilsson, *Gesch. d. Griech. Rel.* II^{3}, pp. 200ff.

230. For the oath by the life of the king of Egypt see J. Wilson, 'The Oath in Ancient Egypt', *JNES* 7 (1948), pp. 129ff. and for the oath by the life of king and god in Mesopotamia see *nīš ilim / šarrim zakāru* and see n. 227 as well as references in *CAD* A *adû* B, and cf. in the Bible 'By the life of Y. and life of my lord the king'. חי ה׳ וחי אדוני המלך (2 Sam. 15.21) and 'he will curse by God and by his king', וקלל באלהיו ובמלכו (Isa. 8.21).

231. Except the oath by the τύχη – cited above from the treaty between Smyrna and Magnesia which stems from the military character of the obligation, see P. Herrmann, *Kaisereid*, p. 47.

also: σεβάσεσθαι 'to fear'/'revere'.[232] In Latin this would be expressed by having *pietas*[233] which equals εὐσέβεια, a word paired with εὐνοία (*Syll.*[3] 814.1). In paragraph A, we discussed εὐνοήσειν and its parallels in the oriental treaties but σεβάσεσθαι/εὐσεβεῖν = to fear, is also found in oriental treaties. Thus, for example, in Esarhaddon's adjuration of the vassals: 'their sons and their sons' sons will fear him (*lipluḫu*)' (line 390).[234]

4. καὶ τοῖς τέκνοις ἐγγόνοις τε αὐτοῦ 'and to his sons and to his progeny'. Loyalty to the king's dynasty and progeny has been discussed in paragraph D.

5. πάντα τὸν τοῦ βίου χρόνον 'for all the days of the life'. This expression appears in the loyalty oath to Ashurbanipal,[235] in the oath of the vassals of Esarhaddon: 'as long as we, our sons and our grandsons live' (ll. 507–509), in the covenant of the plains of Moab in the book of Deuteronomy, 'in order that they may learn to fear Me as long as they live on earth' (Deut. 4.10; cf. Deut. 31.13)[236] and in the loyalty oath of the people of Megiddo in Egyptian documents (see Appendix A).

6. καὶ λόγωι καὶ ἔργωι καὶ γνώμηι 'by word, by deed and by thought'. Compare in the oath quoted by Andocides: καὶ λόγω? καὶ ἔργω? (I 97) and in the oath of Colophon (Bengtson II 145.46).

7. φίλους ἡγούμενος οὕς ἂν ἐκεῖνοι ἡγῶνται ἐκχθρούς τε νομίζων οὕς ἂν αὐτοι κρίνωσιν 'considering as friends those whom they consider (friends) and to consider as enemies those whom they consider (enemies)'. We discussed this formula above in paragraph I. The oriental origin is very clear and it was noticed by classical scholars immediately after the discovery of the Hittite treaties.[237]

8. μήτε σώματος φείσεσθαι μήτε ψυχῆς μήτε βίου μήτε τέκνων ἀλλὰ... πάντα κίνδυνον ὑπομενεῖν 'To spare neither body nor life nor children but...to stand up to any danger'. Cf. paragraph B above.

9. ὅτι τε ἄ[ν αἴσ]θωμαι ἢ ἀκούσω ὑπεναντίον τουτ[οις λε]γόμενον ἢ βουλευόμενον ἢ πρασσόμενον, τοῦτο ἐγμηνύσειν τε καὶ ἐχθρὸν ἔσεσθαι τῶι λέγοντι ἢ βουλευομένωι ἢ πράσσοντί τι τούτων 'If I discern or hear anything being said or planned or done against them I will report it and I will be the enemy of him who says, plans or does any of those things'. This clause has formal resemblance to the corresponding part in the loyalty oath of the people of Chersonesus Taurica (*Syll.*[3] 360):

(a) καὶ εἴ τινά κα συνωμοσίαν αἴσ[θω]μαι...ἐξαγγελῶ τοῖς δαμιοργοῖς 'and if I discern a plot... I will report to the magistrates'. (ll. 46f.)
(b) καὶ πολέμιος ἐσσῦμαι τῶι ἐπιβουλεύοντι 'and I will be an enemy to him who plots...'.

232. T.B. Mitford, *Jour. of Roman St.* 50 (1960), p. 75 line 13.

233. Cf. S. Weinstock, *Divus Julius*, pp. 256f.

234. For other instances see my book *Deuteronomy*, p. 83 n. 6. Cf. also the biblical covenant with its command to *love* God on one hand and *fear* him on the other.

235. Waterman, *RCAE,* No.1105 v. 32f.

236. Weinfeld, *DDS*, p. 358.

237. W. Schwahn, Symmachia, *Real-Encyclop.* IV 1109.

The clause about uncovering traitors and rebels and reporting anything which one might see or hear is known to us – as we saw in paragraph F – from treaties and loyalty oaths in Akkadian, Hittite, Aramaic and Greek and has even penetrated into the Bible in the covenant of the Plains of Moab (Deut.13).[238]

10. 'I will pursue...by land and by sea with arms and with iron...' The formula calling for total vengeance (by arms, by sword, on sea and on land) approximates a similar condition in Esarhaddon's adjuration of his vassals in which he commands his vassals to avenge Ashurbanipal, to spill the rebels' blood and eradicate their name and seed from the earth (cf. above, paragraph G).

11. *The curse* – We discussed the curse above in paragraph O and there we showed that the curse of non-burial of a treaty-infringer appears in the treaties and oaths from the ancient Near East. This threat is apparently connected to the presence of the gods of the netherworld as witnesses to the covenant (above, paragraph N).

We discussed also the curses about 'bearing fruit' in the Israeli and Greek curses. A striking resemblance to the curse in the oath of the Paphlagonians is to be found again in the oath of the people of Chersonesus Taurica: καὶ μήτε γῆ μοι μήτε θάλασσα καρπὸν φέροι 'nor earth nor sea bear fruits for me'.

12. The last section of the Paphlagonians' oath speaks about the participation of the entire population of the city and province in the oath ceremonies held in the temples, and this matter was discussed above in paragraph K.

It is difficult to contend that such a full overlapping with the Near Eastern loyalty oaths is purely coincidental, and it is our opinion that the oath of loyalty to the Roman Emperor has its roots in an ancient Near Eastern tradition, as was already conjectured by F. Cumont.

It also seems that the ancient Near Eastern royal tradition is reflected in the titles granted to Julius Caesar by the Senate.[239] ἱερὸς καὶ ἄσυλος, πατὴρ πατριδος, εὐεργέτης, προστάτης.[240]

We know of five titles granted to the king in Egypt at the time of his coronation, and it seems that this custom was also practised in Israel[241] (cf. the titles in Isa. 9.5 פלא יועץ אל גבור אבי עד שר שלום[242]). 'Father' as a royal title is known from the ancient Near East,[243] and we also know from the East of titles

238. Weinfeld, *DDS*, pp. 91ff.

239. According to Suetonius the emperor was granted, by decision of the Senate, *omnia simul divina atque humana*, 'all of the markings of gods and man'. (Caesar 2.84) and cf. Appian, *Bella Civilia* II, pp. 601–602.

240. Compare Dio Cassius 1, 49: πατήρ, ἀρχιερεύς, ἄσυλος, ἥρως, θεός.

241. A. Alt, 'Jesaia 8.23–9.6, Befreiungsnacht und Krönungstag', *Kleine Schriften* II, pp. 206–255.

242. There have been many claims that the fifth epithet in Isa. 9 was deleted accidentally and traces of it may be found in לם at the beginning of Verse 6. According to K.D. Schunk (*VT* 23 [1973] p. 108f.) the restored fifth title should be: שופט עולם

243. Cf. Codex Hammurapi XXV 20–21 'Hammurapi...who is like a real father to the people' and in the inscription of Azitawada King of the Danunites: פעלן בעל לדננם לאב ולאם. 'And Baal made me as father and mother to the Danunites' (Donner-Röllig *KAI* 26.3), and cf. Gen. 45.8 וישימני לאב לפרעה ולאדן לכל ביתו 'he has made me a father to Pharaoh, lord of all his household'.

similar to those attributed to Caesar, such as: divine hero,[244] benevolent king,[245] etc. Perhaps it is not a coincidence that Suetonius and Dio Cassius speak about five titles, the number of titles known in Egypt and perhaps in Israel as well.

II

The Loyalty Oath to the God of Israel

The elements of the loyalty oath as we have surveyed them thus far are actually contained in the covenant of the Plains of Moab and they are apparently in the background of the Sinaitic covenant (Exod. 24.3–8) and Joshua's covenant at Shechem (Josh. 24.24–26) albeit in a less clear form than is seen in the covenant of Deuteronomy.[246]

It is, however, most surprising to find these motives in the Recitation of the שמע (including אמת ויציב, see below) which, as is well known, is the basic confession of the Jewish Faith[247] and called by the Rabbis קבלת עול מלכות שמים, 'taking upon oneself the yoke of the kingdom of heaven'.[248] קבלה in this context implies an oath[249] and in the שמע confession the believer actually swears to be

244. *ilu* UR-SAG, cf. Seux, *Épithetes Royales Akkadiennes et Sumériénnes* (1967), p. 108.

245. *Šarru damqu*, Cf. Seux, *ibid.* p. 67.

246. Cf. Weinfeld, *DDS* etc. pp. 65ff.

247. For שמע as an ancient confession of faith see I. Elbogen, *Studien zur Gesch. des Jüdischen Gottesdienst* (1907), p. 13ff. In a liturgy from the Manual of Discipline (1QS 10.10ff.) we find 'the entering into the Covenant of God' in a passage which sounds like an introduction to the שמע prayer, cf. Talmon *RevQ* 2 (1960), pp. 475ff.

248. *M. Ber.* 2.2. Israel's acceptance of the yoke of the kingdom of heaven down on earth is made an example of the angels' acceptance of the yoke in heaven (cf. 'They (=angels) all take upon themselves the yoke of the kingdom of heaven' וכולם מקבלים עליהם עול מלכות שמים in the Qedushah of the morning prayer). Both of them receive the kingdom of God upon themselves by oath (see below). Note also the juxtaposition of the oath and the yoke of kingdom in the עלינו prayer: כי לך תכרע כל ברך תשבע כל לשון...ויקבלו כולם את עול מלכותך 'to you every knee must bend, every tongue must swear (loyalty)...may they all accept the yoke of your kingdom'.

A loyalty oath of the heavenly retinue to the head of the pantheon is known to us from the Babylonian creation epic – *Enūma Eliš*. We are told that the gods swear by oil and water and proclaim that Marduk's kingship is exclusive and that he has no rival (VI 95ff.). In the continuation we read: 'Let it be done on earth as has been done in heaven' (line 112), and in the Mesopotamian documents we hear indeed about human bearing of the divine yoke (W.G. Lambert, *BWL*, p. 84.240: 'he that bears god's yoke never lacks food' and the heavenly retinue who break the yoke (W.G. Lambert and A.R. Millard, *Atra-ḫasīs*, [1969], p. 44 K 10082.2) on the other. Concerning the Qedushah which is an 'acceptance of the yoke of the kingdom of heaven' by the angels and its connection to heavenly enthronement ceremonies in the ancient Near East, see S.N. Kramer, M. Weinfeld, *Beth Miqra* 19 (1974), pp. 136ff. (Hebrew).

249. See S. Lieberman, *JBL* 71 (1952), p. 200. The pledge of שמע is connected to the enthronement of God and acceptance of his exclusivity (see previous note). Cf. the response ברוך שם כבוד מלכותו לעולם ועד 'blessed be the name of the glory of his kingdom forever', said after שמע ישראל as well as the blessing preceding the recitation of the שמע found in the Genizah fragments: אשר קדשנו...להמליכו בלבב שלם וליחדו בלב טוב ובנפש חפצה 'who has sanctified us...to acclaim his kingship wholeheartedly and to acclaim his unity with a satisfied heart and willing soul'. J. Mann, *HUCA* 2 (1925), p. 286. And see E.A. Urbach, *The Sages* (1975), p. 402. It should be pointed out that

loyal to the King of the Universe just as the subjects of a corporeal king swear to their king. The expression עול מלכות 'yoke of the kingdom' is well known from Mesopotamian documents[250] having the connotation of submission and subjugation to the kingdom.[251]

In the mystery-religions of the Hellenistic-Roman period we also find the concept of 'carrying the yoke' which signified in particular, entry into the religious sect and accepting its authority. The new initiate's oath was considered a *sacramentum* and was like a soldier's oath of loyalty to his commanding officer, the members of the mystery sect being called *militia*.[252] We are told by Apuleius who describes the words addressed to him during his rite of initiation into the mystery-sect of Isis.[253] 'Make yourself one of this holy order to which you have recently been adjured and submit yourself to our religion and accept upon yourself a voluntary[254] yoke of worship'.[255]

the expression כבוד מלכותו 'the glory of his kingdom' of the refrain mentioned, which was also said in the temple after blessings, is found verbatim in Mesopotamian texts (*melam šarrūti*) in connection to both gods and kings. See references s.v. *melammu*, von Soden, *AHw*. For the equation of כבוד and *melammu* see my article in *Tarbiz* 37 (1968), p. 132, and my article 'Presence Divine', *EJ*.

250. *nīr belūti/šarrūti* (references under *nīru*, von Soden, *AHw*) and cf. the *juqum* under which the submissive was brought. Livy III 28; IX 6.

251. Very enlightening in this matter is the passage in *2 Chron*. 12.8 וידעו עבודתי ועבודת ממלכות הארצות 'they will know (the difference) between serving me and serving the rulers of lands'.

252. Cf. F. Cumont, *Les Religions Orientales dans le Paganisme Romain*[4] (1929), pp. X, 207 No. 5. (I am grateful to Professor D. Asheri for lending me this edition of the book). In his opinion, these concepts were borrowed from political-military loyalty oaths customary in the Near Eastern kingdoms. A more detailed discussion of *sancta militia* is found in R. Reitzenstein, *Die Hellenistischen Mysterienreligionen*[3] (1927), pp. 194ff.

253. Da nomen sanctae huic militiae, cuius non olim sacramento etiam rogabaris, teque iam nunc obsequio religionis nostrae dedica et ministerii iugum subi voluntarium (Apuleius, *Metamorph.* XI 15, cf. XI 30; iugum subeo). Similar concepts stand behind the Qumran sect which views itself as צבאות אל – the legions of God (1QM 4.11) and furthermore they are also called the army of גורל אל 'the divine lot' (1QM 13.5) which apparently means the heavenly army (see Y. Yadin, *The War of the Sons of Light* etc. (1962), p. 241 similar to Στρατιῶται τῆς εἱμαρμένης in Vettius Valens, *Antholog.* (Libri V, 2 p. 22 ed. Kroll). Concerning the military basis of the mystery religion of Mithra and its Iranian origins, see G. Widengren, *Religionen Irans* 224f. Apuleius also tells about a member of *cohorte religionis unus* who gives him his coat (*Metamorph.* XI 14. Cf. 1 Kgs 19.19). Very important in this respect is the passage in Eph. 6.11–13 that has rightly been seen as parallel to the War of the Sons of Light and the Sons of Darkness (see K.G. Kuhn, πανοπλία, *ThWBNT* V 297f.). This epistle is full of contacts with the Qumran Literature and Jewish literature in general. See for example τέκνα φωτός = בני אור in 5.8 and cf. 1.18 with Manual of Discipline 2.3; 4.2 (see D. Flusser, *Scripta Hierosyl.* 4 (1958), p. 263, No. 164, 250 n. 121) and we may add 6.6–7: ποιοῦντες τὸ θέλημα τοῦ θεοῦ ἐκ ψυχῆς, μετ' εὐνοίας δουλεύοντες 'who do the will of God with their (whole) mind and serve him with loyalty' (for εὔνοια = loyalty, see above par. A) to which we may cf. 1 Chron. 28.9 ועבדהו בלב שלם ובנפש חפצה 'and serve him with whole heart and willing mind' and 2 Macc. 1.3–5 ποιεῖν αὐτοῦ τὰ θελήματα καρδιᾳ μεγάλῃ καὶ ψυχῇ βουλομένῃ 'to do his will with broad heart and willing mind'. For the passage in Maccabees and its parallel in the קדושה דסדרה see D. Flusser, *Festschrift Michel* (1963), p. 143f.

254. Cf. ומלכותו ברצון קבלו עליהם 'and they took upon themselves his kingdom willingly', in the אמת ואמונה liturgy of the evening prayer. It is interesting to note that Augustus too says that the whole of Italy swore to him by their own will (sponte sua). See above n. 137.

This phenomenon elucidates well Philo's conception of Israel's entry into the covenant. The entrance into the covenant in Deut. 29.11–14 is understood by Philo to be like an initiation into a mystery-sect (μυσταγωγῶν).[256]

Philo's conception of the covenant as an initiation into a mystery is quite relevant, especially against the background of the religious sects at the second temple period. The congregation of the exultants קהל הגולה and the various Jewish sects in the later period were like the Hellenistic mysteries: closed associations that preserved their uniqueness by carefully observing their specific rules and therefore very strict in the policy of accepting new members. (Cf. the 'oath' אמנה in Neh. 10;[257] Ezra 9–10; Neh. 9.2; 13.1–3). An instructive case in this respect is an edict of Ptolemy IV Philopater according to which all the members of the mystery of Dionysus had to gather in Alexandria in order to present in a written form their sacraments: τὰ ἵερα. Everybody had to prove from whom he received the sacraments. This had to be checked three generations back. The assembled had to submit 'the holy document' τὸν ἱερὸν λόγον with the name signed on it.[258] This reminds us of the situation of the exultants קהל הגולה whose members were required to show their written genealogy in order to be admitted into the congregation (Ezra 2.59; Neh. 7.61; cf. Neh. 7.5).[259] Checking three generations back reminds us of the law of Deut. 23.8–9 according to which only the third generation of an Egyptian or an Edomite could enter 'Yahweh's congregation'.

The Qumran sect and apparently the Pharisees[260] were also based on the same principle as the mysteries. Let us bring up some common salient features:

255. For 'carrying the yoke' see Ben-Sira 51.17, 23ff. (and cf. 6.30; 40.1), Mt. 11.25ff. On these passages and their context, cf. the typological study with comparison to the Mystery literature by E. Norden, *Agnostos Theos* (1913), pp. 277ff.

256. Virt. 33, 178, and see the discussion of H. Wolfson, *Philo I*, pp. 43ff. Transfer of children to Moloch was thought of in the Hellenistic Jewish literature as dedication to a pagan mystery religion (See my article 'The Worship of Moloch and of the Queen of Heaven and its background', *Ugarit Forsch.* 4 (1972), pp. 133ff. After finishing that article I found that at initiation to mysteries the children were carried between two men keeping torches, see Nilsson *HTR* 46 [1953], p. 197f.). Cultic deviations in general were considered by Hellenistic Judaism to be intercourse with idolatrous mystery-religions. Cf. e.g. LXX to Num. 25.3: ויצמד ישראל לבעל פעור. καὶ ἐτελέσθη Ἰσραηλ τῷ βεελφέγωρ 'and Israel *consecrated* themselves to Baal Peor' (τελεσθῆναι is a technical term for the entrance into the Dionysus mystery-religion) cf. *ibid.* v. 5 and Ps. 106.28, as well as the addition to the LXX to Deut. 23.18. See the cited article in *Ugarit Forsch.* 4 (1972), p. 143. On the relationship of Hellenistic Judaism to the mystery religions see J. Gutmann, *The Beginnings of Jewish- Hellenistic Literature*, Vol. 1 (1958), p. 144 (Hebrew). On the existence of religious mysteries in Mesopotamia see A.L. Oppenheim, *History of Religions* V, 2 (1966), p. 250f. It seems that the 'seventy men' preparing incense in darkness in Ezek. 8 constitute some sort of pagan mystery. Cf. Th. C. Vriezen, *Symbolae F.M.T. de liagre Böhl* (1973), pp. 390–91.

257. For a comparison of Nehemiah's אמנה to the rules of the religious associations in the Persian and Hellenistic period, see my article *VT* 23 (1973), pp. 72ff.

258. A papyrus published by W. Schubart in *Amtliche Berichte der Königl. Kunstammlungen* 38 (1916–17), pp. 189ff. And cf. R. Reitzenstein, *ARW* 19 (1916), p. 191f. M.P. Nilsson, *Gesch. D. Griech. Rel.* II^3, p. 162.

259. Cf. Ezek. 13.9 בסוד עמי לא יהיו ובכתב בית ישראל לא יכתבו 'they shall have no place in the council of my people, they shall not be entered in the roll of Israel'.

260. At the time of the existence of the חבורה, see S. Liberman, *JBL* 71 (1952), pp. 200ff.

1. In the mysteries as well as in the Jewish sects the admission into the group was involved with a pledge or oath (see above).
2. Entrance was conditioned by baptizing and observance of purity regulations (cf., e.g., Apuleius, *Metam.* XI 1, 21, 23).
3. The sect was organized as a military unit (see above).
4. Members of the sect experienced revelations of divine mysteries (IQS 9.18; 11.4, 19; M 4.27; 7.27, etc.).
5. Uncovering of the secrets of the group was strictly prohibited in the Qumran sect (S 4.6; M 5.11, 25 etc.) and in the Hellenistic mysteries (cf. Apuleius *Metam.* XI 23).
6. Participating in the heavenly sphere.[261]
7. Hymns and thanksgiving psalms proclaimed for the revelation of the divine truth (see especially Hodayot).[262]
8. Polemics with other groups.[263]
9. The concept of redemption (σωτηρία).
10. The common meal.
11. Humble life and ascetic ideal.
12. Drive for 'knowledge of God' (γνῶσις τοῦ θεοῦ).[264]

The pledge of loyalty by the Jewish believer is composed of two parts:

i. the demand of loyalty – והיה אם שמוע,שמע.
ii. the loyalty oath – אמת ויציב.[265]

261. Cf. Y. Yadin, *The War of the Sons of Light* etc., p. 240f.

262. Cf. Apuleius' hymn at the end of the induction into the mystery of Isis (XI 25).

263. Compare רזי פשע and סוד שוא in the scrolls and see. K. Prümm, 'Zur Phänomenologie des Paulinischen Mysterion', *Biblica* 37 (1956), pp. 135ff.

264. For all these motifs in the mystery religions, see, R. Reitzenstein, *Die Hellenistischen Mysterienreligionen* and M.P. Nilsson, *Geschichte der Griechischen Religion*^{3}, II (1974), pp. 581ff. The features not found in the Jewish sects are (1) apotheosis; (2) death and resurrection of the god; (3) use of magic; (4) symbolic or real sexual intercourse. Clearly the similarity to the mystery religions is not in content but only in form. That common to all of the mystery-religions from a formal standpoint is the desire to attain 'knowledge of god' γνῶσις θεοῦ, which entails religious, cultic, moral, and intellectual values, see most recently A. Böhlig, *Mysterion und Wahrheit* (1968), p. 72.

265. The אמת ויציב prayer was already common in the Second Temple period. See *m. Tamid* 5.1 and according to R. Yehudah (*b. Ber.* 21a) it is 'biblically' commanded. On the antiquity of the text of this prayer see I. Elbogen, *Der Jüdische Gottesdienst*, etc. (1931), pp. 22–23.

The polarity of adjuration and oath or command and affirmation is found frequently in the liturgy. Cf., e.g. שמע ישראל ה׳ אלוהינו ה׳ אחד before the Torah reading and the response after it אחד הוא אלהינו. In the blessing for the Haphtarah; in the words of the Maphtir: האל הנאמן... המדבר ומקים, 'the faithful God…who speaks and fulfills', and in the congregation's reply: נאמן אתה...ונאמנים דבריך 'Faithful are you…and faithful are your words' (see *Tract. Soferim* 13.10–14, Higger edition, p. 245) and cf. as well in the Qedushah of the Musaf service שמע ישראל...ה׳ אחד and the refrain after it אחד הוא אלוהינו. For reverse of the order in the response (אחד אלוהינו) see Liebermann, *Sinai*, Nissan-Iyyar (1975), pp. 1–3. This dialectic appears as well in a section of the Mechilta in connection with the *nwṭryqwn* of אנכי. See S. Abramson, *Sinai*, Tishrei-Heshwan 1974 and S. Libermann, *Sinai*, art.cit.

a. The שמע portion includes: (1) the demand to recognize the uniqueness of deity,[266] i.e. the kingdom of god (Deut. 6.4). (2) the demand to love God with the entire heart and soul (v. 5). (3) the demand to teach the sons and educate them toward loyalty (v. 7).

The והיה אם שמוע portion also includes the demand to love God with the entire heart and soul (Deut. 11.13), the demand to teach the sons (*ibid.* v. 19) and, in addition, it presents a *blessing and curse* (*ibid.* vv. 14–17) which we have met in the above listed oaths of loyalty.

According to the ancient tradition the שמע prayer was once preceded by the Decalogue,[267] thus indicating the connection between 'taking upon oneself the yoke of the kingdom of heaven' and the ancient Sinaitic covenant.

b. The oath of loyalty which is actually an affirmation[268] of the demand of the first part includes:

1. A formal affirmation of the divine demands: 'It is true, firm, established and confirmed…this word upon us, אמת ויציב ונכון וקים הדבר[269] הזה עלינו.

2. A declaration about the kingdom of god: …אמת אלהי עולם מלכנו 'It is true, he is the God of the universe, our king'.

3. A declaration of the validity of the obligation on coming generations: 'Upon us, our children and our (next) generations' עלינו על בנינו ועל דורותינו.

266. For the meaning of ה׳ אחד cf.: והיה ה׳ למלך על כל הארץ ביום ההוא יהיה ה׳ אחד ושמו אחד 'then the lord shall become king over all the earth, on that day the lord shall be one and his name one' (Zech. 14.9). That the שמע ישראל contains the idea of the kingdom of god may be seen from the fact that this verse appears among the verses of the Malkuyot section of the Musaf service for New Year. אחד implies uniqueness and exclusivity. See, for example, in Ugaritic literature: *ʾḥdy dymlk ʾl ilm* = 'I alone will have sway over the gods' (*CTA* 4 VII: 49–50). In the continuation we read *dymrʾu ilm wnšm*, which is interpreted: 'who rules (*mrʾu* = officer) over gods and men…', and perhaps this alludes to imposing the yoke of kingship upon them similar to what was found in the *Enūma Eliš* (see above n. 248). Cf. as well the proclamation about Enlil in a Sumerian dedication inscription = ^{d}*Enlil an-ki-šu lugal-ám, aš-ni lugal-ám*, 'Enlil is the lord of Heaven and Earth, he is king alone (literally: his oneness) (A. Poebel, *Historical and Grammatical Texts*, [1914], p. 66 I.1–3) and cf. the proclamations of the Mysteries: *Isis quae es omnia; Hermes omnia solus et unus*; Εἷς Ζεὺς Σάραπις. Compare also the Samaritan inscription of Emaus: ΕΙC ΘΕΟC (M. Lidzbarski, *Handbuch*, pp. 117, 440). For all this cf. E. Peterson, Εἷς θεός *FRLANT* NF 24 (1926), pp. 227ff., and see recently A. Negev, *EI* 12 (1975), pp. 136ff. in connection with the inscriptions of Wadi Haggag.

267. See *m. Tamid* 5.1 and cf. the Nash Papyrus and the Qumran texts. Cf. A.M. Haberman and Y. Yadin, *Eretz Israel* Vol. 9 (1969), pp. 60ff. It seems to me that the recital of the Decalogue involved with a pledge of loyalty (שמע) is reflected in the record of Pliny (ep. Ad Trajan X, 96,7) about the Christians who used to gather before dawn and take upon themselves by oath (*sacramentum*) not to steal, commit adultery, or break faith. After the confession they gathered for the meal. The reflection of the Decalogue in this text has been seen by some scholars but because they could not explain the *sacramentum* within the context of the letter, their proposal was rejected, cf. Sherwin-White, *Pliny*, pp. 706ff.

268. And see I. Elbogen: 'אמת ויציב ist eine Bestätigung des Glaubensbekenntnisses' (*Der jüdische Gottesdienst* etc., p. 22).

269. For דבר meaning agreement and obligation see my article in *Leshonenu* 36 (1972), pp. 8ff. All of the sixteen attributes in the אמת ויציב prayer relate to הדבר הזה, which is the imposition of the yoke of the kingdom of heaven.

The two elements noticed in the liturgy of the שמע: the demand for loyalty by the sovereign and the affirmation of the demand by the vassal, are both found in Esarhaddon's adjuration of his vassals. The demand appears in ll. 266ff.:

> If you do not love Ashurbanipal, King of Assyria, as you do your own lives…if you do not instruct your sons, grandsons, your offspring, your descendants who will live in the future (concerning this covenant)… Let this word be acceptable and good to you… Do not set over yourselves another king, another lord.

Here the three demands of the שמע portion are incorporated:

1. sole recognition of the authority.
2. love of heart and soul.
3. instructing the sons.

The vassals' affirmation of these demands appears in ll. 494ff., a paragraph already cited above in which we found, as in the אמת ויציב liturgy (see Appendix C):

1. an oath of obligation.
2. a declaration of the exclusivity of the divine kingdom.
3. obligation for the future generations.

Especially worthy of note are the sentences: 'if, as long as we, our sons and our grandsons live, the crown prince designate Ashurbanipal will not be our king and lord, if we place another king, another prince over ourselves', which are striking in their similarity to: אלהי עולם מלכנו... על בנינו ועל דורותינו...מלכנו מלך אבותינו...אין אלהים זולתך. 'The God of the universe is our King…upon our children and (next) generations…our King and King of our ancestors…there is no god besides you'.

The formulae contained in the אמת ויציב prayer belong to the legal realm of treaties and contracts: אמן and אמת are known to be formulae authorizing validity.[270] An identical term is attested in the Greek and Hellenistic documents: ἀληθῆ ταῦτα, which occurs as a formula which approves the preceding commitment.[271]

יציב as a term approving the validity of an agreement and contract is known to us from the Elephantine papyri: זנה ספרא...הו יציב[272] an expression which literally translates the Akkadian (*ṭuppu*) *dannu*.[273] In Dan. 6.13 we find יציבא מלתא which is literally analogous to דבר...יציב in the אמת ויציב prayer and alludes there to the non-controvertible decree of the king. The Greek term parallel to יציב which also appears in connection with the authorization of a treaty and obligation

270. אמן means firmness and hence אמנה which means a firm and valid document and the same applies to Akkadian *dannatu* (√ *danānu*) and Nabatean *tqp* (cf. *tqp* in Est. 9.29), see *Leshonenu* 36 (1972), pp. 10–11, No. 49.

271. Bengtson, *Staatsverträge* II, 145.51, 264.23; III 545–29, and E. Seidl, *Der Eid in Ptolom. Recht*, p. 29.

272. E.G. Kraeling, *The Brooklyn Museum Aramaic Papyri* (1953), No. 10.16–17.

273. For references see *CAD dannu*, p. 95 and cf. *Leshonenu* 36 (1972), p. 101 n. 49 concerning the meaning of *dannu*.

is κύριος ἔστω[274] and is identical to שריר וקים ‘firm and reliable’ from later Jewish documents.[275]

וקים עלינו found in the אמת ואמונה prayer (in the evening שמע recitation)[276] expresses obligation like that found in the book of Esther: קימו... עליהם ועל זרעם (9.27 cf. v. 31),[277] in Nehemiah: והעמדנו עלינו מצות (10.33), and in the Qumran scrolls הקים על and קים על such as: ...ואשר יקים בברית על נפשו (S 5.10).[278] Of interest in this connection is a segment of a Nabonidus inscription[279] which tells about two of the king’s officers, one of whom prostrates and one of whom stands before the king while they ‘confirm the royal dictum, stand by his words, they (even) bare their heads[280] and pronounce the oath...’[281] In *Lev. Rabah*[282] we read something similar referring to the recitation of the שמע: ‘Like a king who sent out his decree (פרוסתגמא) to a city. What did the people of the city do? They rose to their feet, uncovered their heads and read it in awe, fear, trembling and trepidation. In the same way the Holy One, blessed be He, said to Israel it is the recitation of the שמע which is my decree...’

נכון, like אמת expresses reliability and validity just as in Deut. 13.15.[283] ‘It is true, the fact is established’ והנה אמת נכון הדבר (cf. 17.4), and this is the meaning

274. See, for example, Thucydides 5.12.47 and see in the index to Bengtson, *Staatsvertr*. III. For the formula in the Egyptian Hellenistic documents see L. Mitteis, *Reichsrecht u. Volksrecht* etc. (1891), p. 178.

275. Cf. A. Gulak, *Das Urkundenwesen im Talmud im Lichte der griechisch aegyptischen Papyri* (1935), 26f. J.J. Rabinowitz, *Jewish Law* (1956), p. 199, claims that the Aramaic formula gave rise to the Greek formula but this supposition is groundless. See R. Yaron, *The Law of the Elephantine Documents*, Jerusalem 1961 (Hebrew) p. 151. Furthermore, the rest of the formulae cited by Rabinowitz are also not of Aramaic origin since they are attested in Assyrian documents. Thus סגן ומרא who will be powerless to cancel the document, and the Greek parallel brought by Rabinowitz μήτε στρατηγὸν μήτε ἄρχων appear in Assyrian documents: *u lū šarru u lū rubû ša pī dannite šuatu ušannu* = ‘and if it is a king or a prince who will violate (what is written) in this valid document’ (*ADD* 646.65; 647.26; 651.8–10). Cf. J.N. Postgate, *Neo-Assyrian Grants* (1969), for these documents. The same is true for ספר חדת ועתיק (Rabinowitz, *ibid.*, p. 118), as well, to which we have found a parallel in Mesopotamia: *leʾu labiru u leʾu eššu ana muḫḫišu šaṭir* (*CT* 22 204.11), cf. Ebeling, *Neubabyl. Briefe* (1949), p. 111.

276. כל זאת ‘all this’ in the אמת ואמונה prayer of the evening recitation of the שמע is also connected to formulae of covenant affirmation, cf. the pact of Nehemiah: ובכל זאת אנחנו כורתים אמנה (Neh. 10.1).

277. לקים דבר in place of להקים דבר is already found in Ezek. 13.6 and cf. Ruth 4.7.

278. Cf. Est. 9.31 וכאשר קימו על נפשם. For קים in the Qumran scrolls see M.Z. Kadari, החיוב בלשון המגילות (1968), p. 244. Compare also קים על in the letters of Murabba‘t *DJD* II 24 C 18, p. 182, 26.2, p. 137.

279. S. Smith, *Babylonian Historical Texts* (1942), p. 86, V: 22–27.

280. *qaqqada paṭāru* in the document at hand means to uncover the head. See von Soden, Ahw *paṭāru* 5a and cf. the translation of the document by B. Landsberger, Th. Bauer, *ZA* 37, p. 93. Concerning baring the head during prayer see 1 Cor. 11.4 (and see Strack, Billerbeck, *Kommentar zum* NT, III, pp. 423ff).

281. *ukannu pû šarri ušzazzu amassu, ipaṭṭaru qaqqassunu, izakkaru māmīt kî. kî* after *māmīt* marks the opening of the oath. *ušzazzu amassu* is literally corresponding to יקימו דברו.

282. 27.6 and see M. Margalioth edition for additional references. As for the פרוסתגמא and the entire matter see S. Liebermann, *JQR* 35 (1944–45), pp. 6ff.

283. Cf. Weinfeld, *DDS*, p. 93, No. 9.

of Akkadian *kunnu* as is seen clearly in the conclusion of Esarhaddon's treaty with Baal of Tyre: *ṭuppu adê kunnu* (*ša Baalu*) = 'the authorized tablet of the treaty (of Baal)'.[284] In the sentence from the Nabonidus inscription cited above the Akkadian word translated as 'confirm' is *ukannu*, the same root (*kunnu*) found in the text cited from the treaty with Baal of Tyre.

ישר 'right' appears in the VTE in the form *tarīṣu* (right/straight) alongside *banītu* (nice) and *ṭābtu* (good), approximating the combination of these expressions in the אמת ויציב prayer (and see below).

נאמן is to be classified with אמת אמונה discussed previously. אהוב וחביב ונחמד ונעים 'beloved, precious, sweet and pleasant' – we have already discussed terms of love indicating faithfulness.[285] נורא ואדיר 'fearful and glorious' – express admiration[286] and respect out of fear, a concept common in the realm of treaties.[287]

מתוקן expresses by Aramaic influence the Biblical נכון. Therefore, in Ps. 89.38, יכון which is parallel to נאמן there is translated by the Targum: מתקן and is parallel there to מהימן. In Judg. 16.26, נכון is also translated by מתקן.[288]

ומקבל וטוב ויפה הדבר הזה – this formula – as we have already seen – appears in VTE (11 266ff.): 'let this word be acceptable, good and proper to you'.[289] Just as in the אמת ויציב prayer where ומקבל וטוב ויפה is followed by the declaration of kingship, אמת אלהי עולם מלכנו, so in the Esarhaddon treaty, 'let this word be acceptable etc'. is followed by the demand to enthrone Ashurbanipal alone. This juxtaposition of ideas occurs once more in the על הראשונים[290] paragraph. Here as well, after דבר טוב וקים ... אמת ואמונה 'good thing and firm, true and faithful', we find a declaration about the exclusivity of the divine kingdom: אמת שאתה הוא מלכנו... אין... זולתך.

The attributes ישר,טוב, יפה, נחמד (נעים) are found primarily in the VTE,[291] while דבר טוב in the על הראשונים paragraph appears both in the Bible and in Aramaic documents with the meaning of covenant and agreement.[292]

284. R. Borger, *Die Inschriften Asarhaddons* (1956), p. 109, IV 20.

285. See also *Leshonenu* 36 (1972), pp. 91ff. For נעים in covenantal context see H.L. Ginsberg apud Bickerman, *Amer. Journ. Philol.* 73 (1952), p. 8 No. 16.

286. For אדר meaning admire, see Exod. 15.11 and Ben Sira 43.11.

287. See above p. 31.

288. תיקון העולם in the Mishnah (*Giṭ*. 4.2,3) means establishing world order on a strong basis and cf.: לתקן עולם במלכות שדי in the עלינו prayer meaning to establish the world in the kingdom of the Lord.

289. According to Borger's reading: *abūtu annītu ina pānikunu lū maḫrat ina muḫḫikunu lū ṭābat*. (Cf. The translation of E. Reiner in *ANET*[3]). If Wiseman is right in reading *lu da-ri* rather than *lu ṭ[a-bat]* (cf. text No. 36 plate 10 where the sign *ri* is visible and not *bat*, and see as well the reading in *CAD* AII, p. 35), we will have to translate: 'this thing will be accepted by you for generations', a formula which also has parallels in אמת ויציב ... ומקובל...הדבר הזה עלינו לעולם ועד... על .בנינו ועל דורותינו

290. The formulae על הראשונים ועל האחרונים expresses the continuity over the generations of the obligation to keep the covenant: the fathers of those present, those actually present, and the sons who will appear in the future, and cf. above p. 17.

291. The expressions are: *tarīṣu* 'right', *banītu* 'nice', *damiqtu* (SIG_5-tu) 'proper', *ṭābtu* 'DÙG.GA-tu) 'good', and see ll. 67, 73, 108, 125, and others (cf. the variants in the different texts).

292. See my article in *Leshonenu* 36 (1972), pp. 10ff.

חוק ולא יעבור (אמת ואמונה) 'a law that none transgresses' – this formula is known primarily from the second temple period and expresses the absolute force of the obligation. We find, for example, in Est. 1.19: ויכתב בדתי פרס ומדי ולא יעבור 'Let it be inscribed in the laws…never to be transgressed' and in 9.27: קימו… עליהם … ולא יעבור 'they took upon themselves…never to be transgressed' and in Aramaic כדת מדי ופרס די לא תעדא 'according to the law of the Medes and Persians that is not to be transgressed' (Dan. 6.9, 13). If the recitation of שמע implies the imposition of the yoke of the kingdom of heaven, then אמת ויציב expresses the acceptance of the yoke which is the confirmation by oath of the imposition[293] and it thus entails the 'we shall do and listen' נעשה ונשמע of the Sinai Covenant (Exod. 24.7; cf. 19.8; Josh. 24.24).[294]

Appendix A

The Loyalty Oath in the Egyptian Documents

No treaties and fealty oaths have been discovered so far in ancient Egypt. However, from various Egyptian documents one may learn that the Egyptians too used to demand loyalty oaths from their subjects and vassals, and, similarly to the oaths surveyed in this study they contain the following pledges:

1. that the vassals observe loyalty to the Egyptian sovereign during their whole life
2. that their children will keep loyalty too
3. to inform whatever one sees or hears (cf. above).

1. Thus we read in the Barkal stela of Thutmose III that the king administered an oath of fealty (*sḏf tryt*) to the people of Megiddo with the words: 'we shall not repeat any evil thing against Mn-ḫpr-r' during our lifetimes' (*Urkunden* IV 1235.16).
2. Amenhotep II tells us that after defeating Kadesh, he adjured the people and their sons to keep loyalty (*Urkunden* IV 1304.2).
3. In a papyrus from the time of Ramses III, we read that Pharaoh administered an oath of fealty to one of his subjects that he will not hear or see anything without informing (his master) about it (Edgerton, *JNES* 10 [1951], p. 141).

293. Professor S. Liebermann suggested to me (in a letter of November 4, 1974) that the confirmation formulae (לשונות קיום) in the אמת ויציב prayer refer to the שמע and the Decalogue as well (see above and n. 267) since both were recited in the temple (*m. Tamid* 5.1) and cf. his article in *Sinai*, Nisan-Iyyar (1974), pp. 1–3. On the basis of my interpretation of אמת ויציב he now reads in the new discovered passage of the *Mekhilta* (S. Abramson, *Sinai* Tishrei-Heswan [1974], p. 8) אמרין נאמנים [כנים] יפים. This is the *nwt[ryqwn]* (in a reverted form) of אנכי of the Decalogue, which actually constitutes the response of Israel to God's proclamation opened with אנכי.

294. I wish to thank Professors A. Fux, M. Amit and R. Meridor for being helpful in connection with this article.

For the above, compare W. Helck, *Die Beziehungen Ägyptens zu Vorderasien im 3. und 2. Jahrtausend v. Chr.*[2] (1971), p. 246, and for *sḏf* see recently D. Lorton, *The Juridical Terminology of International Relations in Egyptian Texts through Dyn. XVIII* (1974), p. 132.

APPENDIX B

The Oath of the Paphlagonians, 3 BCE
(W. Dittenberger, Orientis Graeci Inscriptiones Selectae*, no. 532)*

Ομνύω Δία, Γην, Ηλιον, Θεοὺς πάντα[ς καὶ πᾰ-]
σας καὶ αὐτὸν τὸν Σεβασ[τ]ὸν εὐνοή[σειν Καί-]
σαρι Σεβαστῶι καὶ τοῖς τ[έκ]νοις ἐγγό[νοις τε]
αὐτοῦ πάν[τ]α [τ]ὸν τοῦ [βίου] χρόνον κ[αὶ λό-]
γωι [κ]αὶ ἔργωι καὶ γνώμ[ηι, φί] λους ἡγού[μενος]
οὓς ἂν ἐκεῖνοι ἡγῶντα[ι] ἐκχθρούς τε ν[ομίζων]
οὓς ἂν αὐτοὶ κρίνωσιν, ὑπέρ τε τῶν τ[ούτοις]
διαφερόντων μήτε σώματος φείσεσθ[αι μή]τε
ψυχῆς μήτε βίου μήτε τέκνων, ἀλ[λὰ παν-]
τὶ τρόπωι ὑπερ τῶ[ν] ἐκείνοις ἀνηκό[ντων]
πάντα κίνδυνον ὑπομενεῖν. ὅτι τε ἂ[ν αἴσ-]
θωμαι ἢ ἀκούσω ὑπεναντίον τούτ[οις λε-]
γόμενον ἢ βουλευόμενον ἢ πρασσό[μενον,]
τοῦτο ἐγμηνύσειν τε καὶ ἐχθρὸν ἔσ[εσθαι τῶι]
λέγοντι ἢ βουλευομένωι ἢ πράσσο[ντί τι τού-]
των οὕς τε ἂν ἐχθροὺς αὐτ[ο]ὶ κρίν[ωσιν, τού-]
τους κατὰ γῆν καὶ θάλασσαν ὅπλο[ις τε]
καὶ σιδήρωι διώξειν καὶ ἀμυνεῖσ[θαι.]
Ἐὰν δέ τι ὑπεναντίον τούτωι τ[ῶι ὅρκωι]
ποήσω ἢ μὴ στοιχούντως καθὼ[ς ὤμο-]
σα, ἐπαρῶμαι αὐτός τε κατ' ἐμοῦ καὶ σ[ώμα-]
τος τοῦ ἐμαυτοῦ καὶ ψυχῆς καὶ βίου κα[ὶ τέ-]
κνων καὶ παντὸς τοῦ ἐμαυτοῦ γέν[ους]
καὶ συνφέροντος ἐξώλειαν καὶ παν[ώλει-]
αν μέχρι πάσης διαδοχῆς τῆς ἐ[μῆς καὶ]
τῶν ἐξ ἐμοῦ πάντων, καὶ μήτε σ[ώματα τὰ]
τῶν ἐμῶν ἢ ἐξ ἐμοῦ μήτε γῆ μ[ήτε θάλασ-]
σα δέξαιτο μηδὲ καρπαὺς ἐνέγ[κοι αὐτοῖς.]
Κατὰ τὰ αὐτὰ ὤμοσαν καὶ ἐ[ν τῆι χώραι]
πάντες ἐν τοῖς κατὰ τὰς ὑ[παρχίας Σε-]
βαστήοις παρὰ τοῖς βωμοοῖ[ς Σεβαστοῦ]

APPENDIX C

The אמת ויציב *Prayer*

אמת ויציב ונכון וקים וישר ונאמן ואהוב וחביב ונחמד ונעים ונורא ואדיר ומתקן ומקבל וטוב ויפה הדבר הזה עלינו לעולמ ועד. אמת אלהי עולם מלכנו, צור יעקב מגן ישענו. לדר ודר הוא קים ושמו קים, וכסאו נכון ומלכותו ואמונתו לעד קימת, ודבריו חיים וקימים, נאמנים ונחמדים, לעד ולעולמי ועולמי עולמים, על אבותינו ועלינו, על בנינו ועל דורותינו, ועל כל דורות זרע ישראל עבדיך.

על הדאשונים ועל האחרונים דגר טוכ וקים לעולם ועד, אמת ואמונה, חק ולא יעבר. אמת שאתה הוא ה׳ אלהינו ואלהי אבותינו, מלכנו מלך אבותינו, גאלנו גאל אבותינו, יוצרנו צור ישועתנו, פודנו ומצילנו, מעלם שמך נו גאל אין אלהים זולתך.

The version of the Genizah:

אמת ויציב ונכון וקיים וישר ונאמן וטוב הדבר הזה עלינו על אבותינו על בנינו ועל דורותינו ועל כל דורות זרע ישראל עבדיך, על הראשונים ועל האחרונים לעולם ועד חק ולא יעבור.

(S. Schechter, *JQR* 10 [1897–98], p. 656)

Chapter 2

The Heavenly Praise in Unison

The adoration offered by the *seraphim* in Isa. 6.3, which forms the basis of the Qedushah liturgy[1], is described as follows: וקרא זה אל זה ואמר קדוש etc. The translation 'and one would call to the other "Holy" etc.' (the Jewish Publication Society of America, Philadelphia, 2nd edn, 1978) is hardly satisfactory. *The New English Bible* (Oxford University Press, Cambridge University Press, 1970) translates 'they were calling ceaselessly to one another', but this is not reflected in the Hebrew text. The targum ומקבלין דין מן דין ואמרין 'and they received one from another and say' corresponds to the Midrashic concept about the angel of lower rank taking permission to sing from the higher one.[2] It is also possible that 'receiving' one from the other here expresses the alternate singing of two choirs as we find in ספר הרזים עומדים מחצה במחצה,חצים משוררים וחצים עונים אחרימו:[3] 'they stand half against half, one half singing, the other half chanting in antiphon'. This interpretation is indeed applied to Isa. 6.3 by S.D. Luzatto in his commentary on Isaiah.[4] וקרא זה אל זה 'they lifted their voice in unison', together, like the phrase: (תהום אל תהום קורא (לקול צנוריך which means: *the deeps sound their voices in unison*, and the meaning of זה אל זה is one opposite the other (one facing the other); similarly תהום אל תהום means deep opposite deep (deep facing deep).

This interpretation appears to be the most plausible. One should add that the phrase לעמת found in the context of Ezek. 3.13f., which constitutes a basic part of the Qedushah liturgy, actually means 'facing one another'. We read there: קול כנפי החיות משיקות אשה אל אחותה וקול האופנים לעמתם 'the sound of the wings of the חיות beating against one another and the sounds of the אופנים facing them'.[5] The חיות and the אופנים appear here as two choirs sounding an

1. For a discussion of the liturgy see I. Elbogen, *Der jüdische Gottesdienst in seiner geschichtlichen Entwicklung* (1931), pp. 61–66. For an up to date discussion see J. Heinemann in the Hebrew translation of this work (1972), pp. 52–53.

2. Cf. *ARN* (ed. S. Schechter), newly corrected edition, N.V. (1967), ch. 12 (Version 1), p. 52. Compare the Yoṣer Liturgy (S. Singer, *Standard Prayer Book* (*SPB*) (1943), p. 46: להקדיש ליוצרם נותנים רשות זה לזה 'and they give authority (permission) to each other to hallow their creator'. In the first part of this liturgical phrase: וכולם מקבלים עליהם עול מלכות שמים זה מזה the words זה מזה should be omitted (they crept in by influence of ומקבלין דין מדין), see E. Fleischer, *Tarbiz* 38 (1969), p. 267 n. 46 (Hebrew).

3. M. Margalioth, *Sepher Ha-Razim* (1966), p. 90, ll. 179–180. Cf. also J. Gruenwald, in *A. Schalit Memorial Volume* (1980), p. 461 n. 11. Compare also Rashi to Isa. 6.3.

4. S.D. Luzatto, ספר ישעיה מתורגם איטלקית ומפורש עברית, Padova 1855 *ad loc.*

5. The sounds of the wings and of the wheels (אופנים) were considered voices of praise-song.

antiphon.[6] Both groups appear elsewhere in Ezekiel and there too in the position of facing each other (1.20; 10.19; 11.22). The terms לעמת and נגד refer elsewhere to two groups arranged in choirs, as for example in Neh. 12.24:...וראשי הלויים ואחיהם לנגדם להלל...משמר לעמת משמר 'and the chiefs of the Levites...with their brethren opposite them to praise...division opposite division'.[7] In 2 Chr. 7.6 we hear indeed about two choirs composed of Levites and priests respectively: the Levites with musical instruments and the priests opposite them with their trumpets (והכהנים מחצצרים נגדם). The harmony between the singers (the Levites) and musicians (the priests) is perfect as is explicitly stated in 2 Chr. 5.12–13:

> And all of the Levitical singers...were standing...with cymbals, harps and lyres; with them stood one hundred and twenty priests blowing the trumpets. The trumpeters and singers join in harmony to sound forth in praise with one voice (ויהי כאחד למחצצרים ולמשוררים להשמיע קול אחד להלל).

Singing in unison is expressed in other instances by יחד.[8] Thus we find in Job 38.7 in connection with the praise of the morning stars and the divine retinue: ברן יחד כל כוכבי בקר ויריעו כל בני אלהים 'when the morning stars sang *in unison* and all the divine beings shouted aloud'.[9] יחד in the sense of 'unison' is clearly reflected in Isa. 52.8: 'Hark, your watchmen raise their voices' (נשאו קול), 'they sing out in unison' (יחד ירננו) and in Ps. 98.8: 'the mountains sing out in unison' (יחד הרים ירננו). About the heavenly retinue arrayed in a choir, we hear in Ben Sira 42.16ff:

> The brilliant sun shines forth upon everything,
> The glory of God fills his creation. His angels
> were unable to completely recount all his wonders...
> all in pairs, one opposite the other.
> (כולם שנים שנים זה לעומת זה)[10]

Cf. my forthcoming study on the *Qedushah* in Qumran. (See provisionally my article in *Studies in the Bible and the Ancient Near East*, Festschrift S.E. Loewenstamm [1978], p. 177 n. 43).

6. In the conventional Qedushah liturgy which combines Isa. 6.3 with Ezek. 3.13f. the two choirs are: Seraphim chanting קדוש on the one hand and the Chayoth and Ophanim chanting ברוך on the other. In order to express the antiphon here too לעמת is used: לעומתם ברוך יאמרו (see S. Singer, *SPB*, p. 55).

7. Cf. W. Rudolph, *Esra und Nehemia*, HAT (1949), *ad loc.*

8. יחד is rendered in the Aramaic Targums by כחדא which equals the Hebrew כאחד used in 2 Chr. 5.13, just quoted. כאחד is a calque of יחד (Cf. E. Kutscher, *Tarbiz* 33 [1964] p. 122 [Hebrew]) formed by the influence of Aramaic and therefore attested only in second temple literature, cf. Isa. 65.26 ירעו כאחד (cf. in the parallel in Isa. 11.6: ימראו כאחד [Qumran]), Eccl. 11.6; Ezra 2.64; 6.20; Neh. 7.66.

9. In the Qumran Targum of Job this is rendered: במזהר כחדא כוכבי צפר ויזעקון כחדה כל מלאכי אלהא 'when the morning stars *shone* together and all of God's angels shouted in unison' (cf. van der Ploeg, van der Woude, *Le Targum de Job de lat grotte XI de Qumran* [1971], Col. XXX: 4–5). The 'shining' of the stars expresses their adoration as the 'voices' of the angels. On the luminaries as angels cf. chapter 5 below.

10. Cf. Y. Yadin, 'The Ben Sira Scroll from Masada' *Eretz-Israel* 8 (Sukenik Volume) (1967), p. 29, see the reconstruction of ll. 14–15.

As in Isa. 6.3 and Ezek. 3.13f. where the antiphon of the divine creatures is expressed by זה אל זה and לעמת here too we find the angels, together with the shining sun, praising God's wonders in two choirs, one opposite the other: זה אל זה.

That the angelic song was understood to be offered in full harmony may be learned from Enoch 47.2: 'In those days the holy ones who dwell above in the heavens *shall unite with one voice*...and praise and give thanks...' and from En. 61.10–11: 'He will summon all the host of the heavens...shall raise *one voice* and bless and glorify and exalt...'

In order to achieve 'one voice' the choirs must be arranged according to rank and ability. Indeed in the angelic song of Qumran, the so-called '*Shirat 'Olat Hashabath*'[11] we read that, 'all of them [the angels] were singing mustered each according to his rank' (ורננו כל פקודיהם אחד אחר במעמדו). The angels are the Lord's servants and must fulfil their duties, everybody according to his place in the hierarchy.

Similar concepts are attested in Mesopotamian hymns concerning the *Annunaki* and the *Igigi*, which overlap in many ways the angels in the Israelite tradition.[12] Thus we read in a hymn to the goddess Ištar.[13]

> Everyday the gods assemble to her
> the *Annunaki* to council[14]
> the *Igigi* encircle her that she assign
> their functions and that they receive
> their orders,[15] the goddesses of the peoples[16]
> bow down to her, they pray to her in unison
> (*mithariš*), bow beneath her.

The Muses in the Greek tradition, which functionally and typologically also resemble the angels,[17] are said to sing to Zeus in unison (φωνῇ ὁμηρεῦσαι =

11. Cf. J. Strugnell 'The Angelic Liturgy at Qumran, 4Q Serek širot Olat Haššabat', *SVT* 7 (1960), p. 337 (4Q 403 24.9).

12. This is discussed in chapter 5, below.

13. Cf. W.G. Lambert, in *Zikir šumin, Festschrift F.R. Kraus* (1982), p. 202.

14. The angels in the Bible constitute, as is well known, the heavenly council, cf. Chapter 5.

15. Compare Ps. 103.19–21 and see the Sumerian parallels adduced in my article in *Beth-Mikra* 57 (1974), pp. 136–37 (Hebrew).

16. These are the *Annunaki* and the *Igigi* who like the angels in Israel are considered the princes of the nations (cf. e.g. Daniel 10.20f.).

17. The Muses appear in several functions, recalling the various functions of the angels:
   1. Compare, for instance, המלאך הדבר in Zech. 1.9 who transmits the vision to the prophet, with the Muse who communicates the oracle to the poet, the spokesman; for a discussion of this in Old Greek literature see E.R. Dodds, *The Greeks and the Irrational* (1951), p. 82 and the references there.
   2. The Muses are, as known, omniscient; cf. 2 Sam. 14.17.
   3. They appear from the mist (Hesiod, *Theogony* 9); cf. the smoke and the cloud in connection with the divine entourage in Isa. 6.4; Ezek. 1.4–5.
   4. The angel that struck Jacob in Gen. 32 finds its parallel in the *Iliad* II 594ff., where the Muses maim (περὸν θέσαν) Thamyris who tries to compete with them in singing.

'consenting voice').[18] The perfect harmony in the heavenly praise of the Lord comes to clear expression in the Hekhalot literature. Here we read: 'They all stand in purity and holiness, offering songs and hymns, praise and jubilation…their voice being one voice…one mind, one melody. וקולם בקול אחד...בדעת אחת ובנעימה.[19] Elsewhere in the Hekhalot literature we find that the angel who disrupts the harmony is pushed into the fire: בגזירה שוה, בפה אחד, שם נורא מוציאין...והמערב קולו בחבירו בשם כשיעור נימה של שיער, מיד נדחף ואש להבה.[20]

Men sing in unison with the angels

The belief that the earthly worshippers praise the Lord as do the angels of heaven is alluded to already in the hymns of the OT.[21] However, the notion that men *join the angels* in their praise is first made explicit in the writings of the Qumran sect. Thus the author of the Thanksgiving Hymn in 1QH: 3.20ff. tells us how he was lifted 'to the height of the universe' (לרום עולם)[22] 'in order to stand among the ranks[23] of the host of the holy ones and to join together in the assembly of the sons of heaven' (להתיצב במעמד עם צבא קדושים ולבא ביחד עם עדת בני שמים). He goes on to say that God has 'cast man's eternal lot' (גורל עולם) among 'the spirits of knowledge' (רוחות דעת)[24] to praise his name harmoniously in song (להלל שמכה ביחד רנה).

Similarly, we read in 1QH 11.11f.:

> You have cleansed man from sin…to be united (להיחד) with the children of your truth and in the lot (גורל) of your saints…*to stand in rank* (להתיצב במעמד) *before you*

18. Hesiod, *Theogony*, 39.

19. Cf. סדר רבה דבראשית in מדרשי הגניזה בתי מדרשות Vol. I (ed. A. Wertheimer, 1958), p. 47, and see also G. Scholem, *Jewish Gnosticism, Merkabah and Mysticism*, p. 29f.; D. Flusser, 'Sanktus und Gloria', *Festschrift O. Michel*, p. 134. Compare in the *Yoṣer Qedushah*: משמיעים ביראה יחד בקול 'and they proclaim with awe in unison aloud' (*SPB*, p. 45).

20. I. Gruenwald, קטעים חדשים מספרות ההיכלות, *Tarbiz* 38 (1969), pp. 364–65 (Hebrew).

21. Cf. my forthcoming study on the *Qedushah* in Qumran.

22. The expression appears in the *Yoṣer Qedushah* (*SPB*, p. 45) as well as in 1QSb 5.23 and in the Hebrew book of Enoch in the form ברום ערבות; see H. Odeberg, *3 Enoch* (1928), 7.1; 18.6; 27.2; 35.1; 42.2 (the latter parallel shows that עולם has to be understood in the spatial, cosmic sense). Compare also in the *Geullah* Benediction: ברום עולם מושבך (*SPB*, p. 52) and see the discussion of the term רום עולם in H.W. Kuhn, *Enderwartung und gegenwärtiges Heil* (1966), pp. 56–58.

23. Cf. 1QH 11.13: ולהתיצב במעמד לפניכה and 1QH frag. 7.11, מעמד means 'rank order', cf. e.g. 1QS 2.22f. (איש בית מעמדו) in connection with the order of the members of the sect and 1QM 2.3 (איש במעמדו) in connection with the priestly order. In IQM we find the phrase התיצב על מעמד in the military sense, cf. 8.3, 17; 16.4; 17.11. The angels were also mustered according to their ranks, cf. 4QS 40, 24.9: (ו)רננו כול פקודיהם אחד אח(ד) במעמ(ד), see above. For a discussion of the term מעמד cf. H.W. Kuhn *Enderwartung etc.*, pp. 70–71.

24. Compare in the 'Qedushah' liturgy in Apost. Constit. VII, 35 (ed. F.X. Funk, 1905) 'and the spirits of knowledge (πνεύματα νοερά) say to Palmoni' (cf. Dan. 8.13), on דעת 'knowledge' in connection with the angels and the creation, see below.

> *together with eternal hosts and the spirits of* (*knowledge*)[25] to be renewed with all that came into being[26] and *together* with those who have knowledge (ידעים) *harmoniously in song* (ביחד רנה).[27]

In 1QH 11.25–26:

> Your name will be praised by the mouth of all; they will praise you in accordance with their knowledge (כפי שכלם)[28] *and with the sons of heaven will proclaim in unison the voice of song* (ועם בני שמים ישמיעו יחד בקול רנה).[29]

And in 1QH fragment 1.6–7:

> and we gathered together with those who have knowledge…with your mighty ones (גבוריכה)[30] *and will declare in unison the wonders* (ובהפלא נספרה יחד).[31]

Cf. also 1QH 18.23; 1QH fragment 2.6f.; 5.3f.

As is clear from the first example, the angels and the men not only sing praises together, they also have a common lot. Indeed we find the common lot (גורל) of the members of the sect and the angels is expressed in three ways:

1. joining in praise, as quoted above
2. having a common fate with the heavenly beings, which means to share in eternal life, as may be learned for example from Lk. 20.36: 'for they cannot die anymore, because they are equal to angels'. Thus we read in 1QS 11.7f.: 'Those whom God has chosen he has established as an eternal possession (אחוזת עולם); he made their inheritance (וינחילם) in the lot (גורל) of the holy ones, with the sons of heaven he united their assembly for a council of community…for an eternal plant…'. Compare also 1QH 6.13–14; 1QH frag. 2.9ff.; 1QSb 4.25f.; Wis. 5.5; En. 39.4; Acts 20.32; 26.18; Eph. 1.11; Col. 1.12, etc.
3. taking part in the holy war side by side with the host of heaven (1QM 7.6; 12.4).

25. Restored according to 3.22. See J. Licht, מגילת ההודיות *ad loc.* Kuhn, *Enderwartungen* p. 79 n. 4. suggests רוחות עולם, cf. Holm-Nielson, *Hodayot* (1960), p. 187.

26. ולהתחדש עם כול...נהיה. This refers to the new creation in the eschatological sense, see Kuhn, *Enderwartung*, pp. 50ff., 75. For the 'new creation' see also 1QH 13.12; 18.27 and cf. 'the day of creation' in Jub. 1.27 (the word 'new' seems to be a gloss, cf. Charles, Pseudepigrapha, *ad loc.*) with the 'day of creation' יום הבריה in the Temple Scroll 29.9 (Yadin, The Temple Scroll, Vol. II, p. 129). For the reading יום הבריה and not יום הברכה, as read by Yadin, see E. Kimron, *Shnaton* IV (1979–80), p. 25349(Hebrew). Cf. also, Enoch 45.4; 72.1; 91.16.

27. For the relationship between 1QH 3.20ff. and 1QH 11.11ff. see Kuhn, *Enderwartung*, 78ff.

28. For this idiom cf. 1QH, frag. 10.4: לפי שכלם וכפי דעתם which is followed there by ואנחנו יחד נועדנו ועם ידעים...עם גבוריכה ובהפלא נספרה יחד (11.6–7) which will be discussed presently.

29. For the restoration cf. Kuhn, *Enderwartung*, p. 96 n. 3.

30. For the angels as גבורים, cf. Ps. 103.20.

31. The angels praise God's wonders ויודו שמים פלאך (Ps. 89.7).

These three understandings of the communion of men with the angels actually intermingle. Those who join the angels in praise feel that they cast their lot with them, thus achieving eternal life, and the same applies to those who fight in battle together with the heavenly beings.

Thus, for example, those who were lifted to the height of the universe in order to stand among the ranks of the angels in praise (1QH 3.19f.) are said to have been redeemed from the grave and to have attained hope for an eternal fellowship (לסוד עולם). Similarly, those who stand in rank together with the eternal host praising God (1QH 11.13–14) realize that they share their lot (גורל) with the holy ones and are raised from the worms of the dead (תולעת מתים) to an eternal fellowship (11.12).

The notion of the spiritual-eschatological share (גורל, חלק, נחלה) of those who serve God properly is already attested in the Psalms (16.5–6; 73.26; 142.6).[32] But its association with the heavenly beings is characteristic of the post-exilic literature (cf. Zech. 3.7; Mal. 2.7; Dan. 7.18ff.[33] and the references noted above). Though this concept of a share with the angels is not common in Rabbinic literature it is reflected in the Jewish liturgy which has affinities with Qumran liturgical texts in other respects as well. In one of the morning prayers[34] recited before an early *Shema'* proclamation (*SPB*, p. 9)[35] we read:

> It is, therefore, our duty to praise...and sanctify (לקדש)...Happy are we, how good is *our portion* (חלק) how pleasant is *our lot* (גורל) and how beautiful *our heritage* (ירושה). Happy are we who early and late, morning and evening, twice every day declare.[36] 'Hear, O Israel' etc.

The *Shema'* is connected with the *Qedushah* ritual: *Shema'* on earth is said in unison with the angels who proclaim the *Qedushah* in heaven.[37] No wonder then that as in the Qumran texts so also here, by reciting *Shema'*, Israel feels itself taking share (חלק, גורל, ירושה) among the holy ones and proclaim their happiness over such. For חלק in the eschatological sense in Rabbinic literature cf. כל ישראל יש להם חלק בעולם הבא in *m. Sanh.* 10.1. The dictum there is based on Isa. 60.21: לעולם ירשו ארץ, which implies that ירושה also has an

32. Cf. G. von Rad, *Gesam. Studien*, pp. 241ff. See Kuhn, *Enderwartung*, pp. 72–75 for a discussion of these concepts.

33. Cf. especially the Aramaic verb חסן (which equals Hebrew נחל) in connection with the kingdom given to קדישי עליונין (vv. 18,22) or to the עם קדושי עליונין 'the people of the holy ones of the most high'.

34. As will be shown elsewhere it is especially these prayers which have their counterparts in the Qumran liturgy.

35. The prayer is found in *Tanna debe Eliahu* (ed. M. Friedman) (1904), ch. 19 (p. 118). A fragment of this prayer, זרע אברהם אוהבך,בני יחידך יצחק,עדת יעקב בנך בכורך, is quoted in *Mekhilta Širah*, sec. 10 (ed. Horowitz-Rabin, p. 150) in connection with Exod. 15.18 (kingship of the Lord).

36. Compare in the *Musaf Qedushah* (*SPB* p. 228): המיחדים שמו ערב ובקר בכל יום תמיד פעמים באהבה שמע אומרים.

37. Cf. my forthcoming study of *Qedushah* in Qumran.

eschatological connotation. As has been indicated גורל,חלק have an eschatological meaning already in the Psalmodic literature (see n. 32).

The idea of the congregation on earth joining the angels in their praise stands behind the whole pattern of the Qedushah liturgy and has penetrated the ancient Christian liturgy. Thus we read in 1 Clem. 34.7, after the Trishagion: 'let us, gathered together in awareness of our concord (ὁμονοίᾳ), as with one mouth (ὡς ἐξ ἑνὰς στόματος) shout with zeal'.[38] Before the Trishagion there we find a kind of proem which reads: 'let us think of the whole host of angels, how they stand by and serve his will'. This, as has already been seen by D. Flusser,[39] parallels the poems of the *Qedushah* in the Jewish liturgy: 'let us sanctify your Name in this world, even as they sanctify it in the heavens above', and the other similar openings of the *Qedushot*. This notion of emulating heavenly powers in connection with the *Qedushah* is also reflected in the Apostolic Constitutions, which as already shown by Bousset,[40] preserved in a most genuine manner the Jewish *Qedushah*. Thus we find there, [41] after the two basic constituents of the *Qedushah*, Isa. 6.3 and Ezek. 3.12: 'Israel, your ecclesia on earth...emulating the heavenly powers night and day'.[42] Similarly, we read there in Book VIII 12.27, that: 'the cherubim together with ten thousand times ten thousand of angels'[43] say 'Holy, holy, holy' etc. and 'let all the people say it with them together' (καὶ πᾶς ὁ λαὸς ἅμα εἰπάτω).

The liturgy of the *Qedushah* is thus founded on the notion that the members of the congregation on earth can join in the angelic song, and, in unison, as if in a single chorus, sing out praise to their Creator. Indeed, the custom of lifting one's heels when reciting the *Qedushah* is rooted in just this idea.[44] Lifting of one's heels during prayer said in unison is attested in ancient Christian sources, cf.

38. Compare also Ignatius, *Ephesians* 4.1f.: 'harmonizing in concord (ὁμονοία) you present the divine tone in unison praising with one voice (Ἓν φωνῇ μιᾷ), see D. Flusser, 'Sanktus und Gloria', *Festschrift O. Michel*, p. 133.

39. Art. cit., pp. 135f., see also E. Werner, *HUCA* 19 (1945), p. 197f. and his reference there to the statement of Clement of Alexandria that 'we ever give thanks to God, as do the creatures (ζῶα) who praise him with hymns of whom Isaiah speaks in an allegory' (*Stromateis* VII 12: PG IX 512).

40. *Nachrichten der Ges. Wiss. Göttingen*, Phil. Hist. Kl. (1915), pp. 435ff.

41. F.X. Funk, *Didascalia et Constitutiones Apostolorum* (1905), Book VII, 35.34 (p. 430).

42. Compare in the *Musaf Qedusha*: 'who evening and morning...proclaim constantly the uniqueness of his name' (*SPB*, p. 228).

43. See also the Epistle to the Corinthians of Clement of Rome 34.7: 'Ten thousand times ten thousand were doing service to him crying out Holy, Holy, Holy etc'. This is to be compared with passages of the Yoṣer-Qedushah from the Genizah published by S. Schechter in *Gedenkbuch zur Erinnerung an D. Kaufmann*, 1900 p. 54 יוצר משרתים אשר משרתיו אלף אלפי אלפים עומדים לפניו,רבי רבבות סובבים את כסאו and the Genizah passage published by S. Asaf, *Festschrift B. Dinaburg* (1949), p. 120: אשר משרתיו אלף אלפי אלפים עומדים ברום עולם. These are of course influenced by Dan. 7.10 and Ps. 68.18.

44. For various explanations of this custom in Rabbinic literature see I. Gruenwald, art. cit., p. 477 n. 101.

Clement of Alexandria, *Stromateis* VII, vii, 40.1: 'So also we raise the head and lift the hands to heaven, and stand up on the tiptoes at the closing prayer said in unison, following the eagerness of the spirit to direct itself toward the spiritual sphere'.

Chapter 3

PRAYER AND LITURGICAL PRACTICE IN THE QUMRAN SECT

Discussion on the Qumran Sect is usually centred on those aspects distinctive to the sect. In contrast to this, we shall try to point up the features this sect has in common with other sections of Judaism. Although in the second temple period orthodoxy, such as that which developed under the Pharisees after the destruction of the second temple, was not yet in existence, there were, nevertheless, certain norms concerning the way of life and the worship of God which were the common inheritance of the various streams of Judaism during this period. In this paper we shall deal with this common inheritance.

In the Judaism of the second temple period, there existed a wealth of religious and social obligations that were self-evident, even though they were not prescribed in the Torah. Among these are matters for which the Pharisees laid down rules in the Oral Law. However, there are also others for which there are no definitive rules laid down in the Mishnah based on the Oral Law, and which remain within the bounds of sanctified customs, as we shall see below. In fact, it is difficult to know exactly when specific customs began to crystallize. For example, the obligation to recite a Benediction upon seeing a rainbow in the cloud, which appears in *t. Ber.* 6.5[1] is already found in *Ben Sira* 43.11: 'Behold the rainbow and bless its Maker'.[2] In addition to those, there are religious customs that do not originate in Judaism, evidence for which exists in ancient Eastern religions. For example, the 'Enjoyment Benedictions' (ברכות הנהנין *m. Ber.* 6) which are not clearly explained in the Bible[3] and for which the Rabbis sought scriptural support,[4] were, in fact, common practice in the ancient East from earliest times. The Babylonian poem of the righteous sufferer dating to the first half of

1. 'He who sees the rainbow in the cloud says: "Blessed is He who is faithful to His covenant, who remembers the covenant" '. On the variations of formulae in the Rabbinic sources, see S. Lieberman, *Tosefta Ki-Fshutah*, A Comprehensive Commentary on the Tosefta, Order *Zera'im*, Part I (New York, 1955), pp. 108–109 (Hebrew).

2. *The Book of Ben Sira. Text, Concordance and an Analysis of the Vocabulary*, (The Academy of the Hebrew Language and Shrine of the Book; Jerusalem, 1973) (Hebrew).

3. The Mishnah does not prescribe the Benediction, but rather asks: 'What Blessings are said?' (*Ber.* 6.1). The obligation to say the Benediction is a self-understood assumption.

4. 'It is forbidden for a man to enjoy anything of this world without a Benediction...whoever enjoys anything of this world without a Benediction is like someone who enjoys of things consecrated to heaven, since it says: "The earth is the Lord's and all that it holds" ' (*b. Ber.* 35a).

the first millenium BCE[5] refers to the wicked man who 'ate without invoking his god'.

The Thanksgiving Benedictions (called ברכת הגומל, the Benedictions of Deliverance) were instituted for four situations in which people are required to offer thanksgiving: the sick person recovered from an illness, the prisoner set free, the sea voyager upon reaching dry land, and the traveller in the desert upon reaching his destination.[6] These appear in a Babylonian hymn from the first half of the first millenium BCE[7] and evidence also exists of pagans in the Hellenistic period who conducted thanksgiving ceremonies for similar situations.[8]

In this paper an attempt will be made to analyse certain prayers and religious customs which struck roots in Judaism, traces of which are found in the Qumran Scrolls, and will be examined under the following headings: (1) *Shema'*; (2) The *Qedushah* and Benediction of the Lights; (3) Prayers for the Sabbath and Festivals; (4) The Morning Prayer; (5) The Prayer of Supplication (תחנון); (6) The Prayer before Setting Forth on a Journey; (7) The Benediction on Performing the Marriage Ceremony; (8) Grace after Meals; (9) The *Minyan* (quorum of ten); (10) The Precedence of the Priest in Matters of Holiness; (11) The Canon and (12) *Tĕfillin* and *Mĕzuzot*.

Shema'

Let us begin with the recitation of the *Shema'* with which the Mishnah opens.[9] In the song from the *Manual of Discipline*, which has a hymn-like, liturgical character, the poet says that he enters the 'covenant of God' morning and evening: 'With the coming of the day and night I will enter the covenant of God (אבואה בברית אל) and when evening and morning depart I will recite His ordinances'.[10] This idea of *entering into the covenant* morning and evening is none other than the *Shema'* proclamation which is *defined as the acceptance of the*

5. W.G. Lambert, 'The Poem of the Righteous Sufferer' (*ludlul bēl nēmeqi*), *Babylonian Wisdom Literature* (*BWL*) (1960), p. 38, line 19: 'had eaten his food without invoking his god' (*ilšu lā izkur ekul akalšu*). This can be interpreted in the sense that he ate that which belonged to the god; (see Lambert, 'The Poem of the Righteous Sufferer', p. 289), similar to the reason given for saying a Benediction in Rabbinic literature (above n. 4): he enjoys of things that belong to heaven.

6. The Benedictions of Thanksgiving to be said by those who have been delivered from calamity appear in Ps. 107, which serves as a scriptural support in rabbinic writings for the obligation to say the Thanksgiving Benedictions (*b. Ber.* 54b).

7. For the text, see Lambert, 'The Poem of the Righteous Sufferer', p. 130. For a discussion of this, see M. Weinfeld, 'A Comparison of a Passage from the Šamaš Hymn (ll. 65–78) with Psalm 107', *Archiv für Orientforschung*, Beiheft 19 (1982), pp. 275–79.

8. See *m. 'Abod. Zar.* 1.3; *Tosefta* 1.4 and see A.D. Nock, *Conversion* (1933), pp. 83ff.

9. Here also, as in the Enjoyment Benedictions (above n. 3) the Mishnah assumes that the fact of the obligation to recite the *Shema'* is known, and that one only needs to determine the exact time of the recitation: 'From what time may one recite the *Shema'* in the evening?' (*Ber.* 1.1).

10. Cf. P. Wernberg-Moller, *The Manual of Discipline* (1QS X 10) (1957), p. 37.

yoke of the kingdom of heaven,[11] in the words of the Pharisees (קבלת עול מלכות שמים or קיבול עול מלכות שמים)[12] whose meaning is obligation with an oath, as has been explained by S. Lieberman.[13] In another place in this scroll we find that the expression 'entering into the covenant of God' (ביאה בברית אל), is parallel to committing oneself with a binding oath (5.8): 'Whoever...shall enter the Covenant of God...and shall undertake by a binding oath...' (אשר יבוא בברית אל...ויקם על נפשו בשבועת איסר)

What is most instructive for our subject is the fact that this section on the entering into the covenant is preceded by the Song of the Lights which we shall discuss below. This fact shows us that in the Qumran prayers as in the conventional Jewish liturgy, the Benediction of the Lights is conjoined with the recitation of the *Shema'*.[14]

The Qedushah *and the Benediction of the Lights*

A surprising congruence can be found between the hymn of the creation of the luminaries and the [song] of the angels from Qumran Cave 11,[15] and the liturgical *Yoṣer* hymns in the conventional prayers, and those from the Geniza, as I have shown above.[16] The theme of the establishing of the luminaries in wisdom and knowledge into which is interwoven the sanctification formulae recurs from time to time: '*Great and Holy...from generation to generation*' (גדול וקדוש... לדור ודור), which run like a thread through the various texts on *Qedushah* in Jewish liturgy of all the periods.[17] Other themes, such as the throne of glory (כסא כבוד) or the divine chariot (מרכבה), which have as their foundation (מכון), faithfulness (חסד), justice (משפט), truth and mercy (רחמים, אמת), also occur. Around the throne or the divine chariot, the angels stand singing,[18] and all this occurs at the hour at which the luminaries appear, and the gates of darkness and light are opened.[19] Even more instructive is the fact that in the Qumran Scroll (11QPS^{a} XXVI 9–12) the song of the angels comes immediately after Psalm 150. This coincides with the conventional Jewish prayers, in which

11. *m. Ber.* 2.2.
12. *Sifrē Num*, Section 101 (ed. Horowitz, 1917).
13. S. Lieberman, 'The Discipline in the So-Called Dead Sea Manual of Discipline', *JBL* (1952), pp. 199–205 and see ch. 1, section 1. On the recitation of the *Shema'* as *qlws* (acclamation) and the manner of its recitation in public, see. I. Knohl, 'A Parasha Concerned with the Accepting of the Kingdom of Heaven' (Hebrew with English abstract) *Tarbiz* 33 (1984), pp. 11–32.
14. See my article, 'The Prayers of Knowledge and Forgiveness in the 'Eighteen Benedictions' – Qumran Parallels, Biblical Antecedents, and Basic Characteristics' (Hebrew with English abstract), *Tarbiz* 48 (1978–79), pp. 192–93.
15. J.A. Sanders. *The Psalms Scroll of Qumran Cave 11 (11QPs.^{a}), DJD* 4 (1965), p. 47 (on XXVI 9–12).
16. See chapter 2
17. *Ibid.*
18. *Ibid.*
19. See my article, 'Prayers for Knowledge and Forgiveness', pp. 192–93.

the *Yoṣer Qedushah* is adjacent to the Psalms of the morning service ('פסוקי דזמרה') which conclude with Psalm 150.[20]

The liturgy of *Qedushah* was usually recited on Sabbath days, as E. Fleischer has shown[21] and indeed, a liturgical composition called Song for the Sabbath *Olah* (שירת עולת השבת)[22] has been preserved in Qumran which centres around the mystical idea of the joining of the congregation of Israel in the singing of the angels in the heavenly temple.[23]

Prayers for the Sabbath and Festivals

In the scrolls from Cave 4, edited by Baillet,[24] many fragments of prayers for the Sabbath and Festivals have been found in which appear Benedictions for the selection of the people of Israel and the establishing of certain days for *rest, rejoicing and enjoyment*, such as the prayer:

> 4Q503, 24–25: 'they will bless...[Blessed be the God of Israel] who has chosen us from all the nations...(and has given us) rest and delight (מנוח ותענוג) (p. 111).
> 4Q503, 37–38: 'Holiness and rest' (קדוש מנוח) (p. 118)
> 4Q503, 40–41: 'Rest and holiness' (מנוח קודש) (p. 119)

Formulae such as these are found in the *Amidah* recited on Sabbaths and Festivals. In connection with this, one should note that the liturgical formula known to us today from the prayers of the Festivals 'You have chosen us from among all the peoples' (אתה בחרתנו מכל העמים), is not distinctive to Festival days alone, for it was normally recited in the *Amidah* prayer for Sabbaths before the formula 'Moses will rejoice' (ישמח משה), became firmly implanted, and attached to it we find the formula 'and You gave us...this day of rest (ותתן לנו...את יום המנוח הזה)...'.[25]

Similar formulae are found in the *Book of Jubilees*:

> And the Creator of all things blessed it (the Sabbath), but He did not sanctify all peoples and nations to keep Sabbath thereon, but Israel alone...and (He) blessed this day which He had created for blessing and holiness and glory...(2.31–32).

Parallel formulae have also been found in the prayer for the Sabbath in the

20. See chapter 2, 'Traces of Qedushat Yoṣer...', pp. 23–26.

21. E. Fleischer, 'The Diffusion of the Qedushot of the Amidah and the Yoṣer in the Palestinian Jewish Ritual' (Hebrew with English abstract) *Tarbiz* 38 (1968), pp. 255–84.

22. C. Newsom, *Songs of the Sabbath Sacrifice: A Critical Edition* (Harvard Semitic Studies 27; Atlanta, 1985).

23. See Chapter 2.

24. M. Baillet, *Qumran Grotte 4*, III (4Q482–4Q520) *DJD* 7 (1982).

25. See N. Wieder, 'The Controversy about the Liturgical Composition "ישמח משה" – Opposition and Defense' (Hebrew), *Studies in Aggadah, Targum and Jewish Liturgy in Memory of Joseph Heinemann* (ed. J.B. Petuchowski and E. Fleischer, 1981), pp. 75–99, and see recently, J. Yahalom, 'Piyyut as Poetry', *The Synagogue in Late Antiquity* (ed. Lee I. Levine, 1987), pp. 115–16.

Geniza fragment TS NS 1604[26] in which election (or 'love') appears in juxtaposition with attributes of the Sabbath, similar to those found in the *Book of Jubilees*:

> And out of Your love (מאהבתך) O Lord our God, for us who have loved Your people, the House of Israel...you gave us...the seventh day...for holiness, for rest and for thanksgiving...and for glory (ולתפארת)...[27]

In fact, in the *Amidah* prayer for the Sabbath morning that is currently recited, the formula of the selection of Israel found in the *Book of Jubilees* and the prayers of Qumran, is also included:

> And You did not give it (the Sabbath), O Lord, our God, to the nations of other lands...but to Your people Israel You gave it in love, to the *seed of Jacob whom You choose* (לזרע יעקב אשר בם בחרת). The people that hallow the seventh day, even all of them, shall be satiated and delighted...with Your goodness...(*SPB*, p. 201).

Another formula found in the prayers of Sabbaths and Festivals in the Qumran Scroll edited by Baillet[28] is that which appears in 4Q509, fragment 3 (p. 186): 'And You gathered [our (men) dispersed for the time of...] and our scattered [for the season of] You [regathered (them)...(ואספת[נדחינו] למועד [... ונפו]צותינו [ת]קבץ לתקופ[ת])' and is congruent with the conventional text in the prayers of the additional service (מוסף) for Festivals: 'Bring our scattered ones from among the nations near to You and gather our dispersed from the ends of the earth' (ונפוצותינו כנס מירכתי ארץ) (*SPB* p. 339).

It is interesting to note that the idea of the ingathering of the exiles in connection with a Festival appears in the Septuagint translation of Jer. 31.8 (LXX 38.8). This verse, which in the MT reads as: 'Behold I will bring them in from the northland, gather them from the ends of the earth, *the blind and the lame among them* (בם עור ופסח), those with child and those in labour' is read by the Greek translator as: 'Behold I will bring them from the north and will gather them from the end of the earth at the *feast of the passover* (ἐν ἑορτῇ φασεχ = במועד פסח),[29] an idea that is anchored in the liturgy mentioned above, in which the ingathering of the exiles is adjacent to a festival and which is based on the midrash:

> R. Joshua says, 'In (the month of) Nisan they were delivered, in (the month of) Nisan they will be delivered in the time to come' (*b. Rosh Hash.* 11b).

A Qumran fragment in which we find formulae congruent with those in the prayers for Rosh Hashanah and Yom Kippur is 1Q27.5–6 (*DJD*, 1, p. 103) in which we read:

26. See N. Wieder, 'The Controversy about the Liturgical Composition "ישמח משה"', p. 13 (see n. 25).

27. Compare the Benediction After the Reading of the Torah: 'We thank Thee...for this Sabbath day, which Thou hast given us, Lord our God, *for holiness and rest, for glory and honour*' (*SPB*, p. 215).

28. *DJD* 7.

29. E. Tov, *The Text – Critical Use of the Septuagint in Biblical Research* (1981), pp. 238–39.

> *When the descendant of iniquity will be shut up* (בהסגר מולדי עולה) Wrong will depart before Right as darkness departs before light; *and as smoke disappears* (וכתום עשן ואיננו) and is no more, so will Wrong disappear for ever and Justice will appear like the sun…

These words are parallel to the section of a prayer from the service of the High Holy Days:

> …while iniquity shall close her mouth (ועולתה תקפץ פיה) and all wickedness shall be wholly consumed like smoke (כעשן תכלה); when you make the domination of arrogance to pass away from the earth (*SPB* 351).

The incarceration of the outcome of iniquity in the Qumran passage is analogous to iniquity closing her mouth, just as the image of the disappearance of wrong like smoke in the Qumran passage parallels the idea of wickedness being wholly consumed like smoke, in the conventional prayer.

On the basis of this perception, David Flusser suggested seeing in the passage a part of the sect's Rosh Hashanah service (in his lecture at the Ninth World Congress of Jewish Studies in Jerusalem, 1985).

In the fragments opening with '*the prayer for Yom Kippur*' (תפילה ליום כיפורים) found in Qumran (1Q34^{bis} 2+1.6; *DJD*, 1, p. 153; 4Q508 2.4; *DJD*, 7, p. 179) there are also points of contact with the Confession for the Day of Atonement in the conventional Jewish liturgy. In 4Q508 2.4 we find the formula: 'אתה ידעת הנסתרות והנגל[ות]' 'and You have known things hidden and revealed'. This is similar to the formula: 'הלא כל הנסתרות והנגלות אתה יודע – Do You not know all things, both hidden and revealed?' in the conventional confessions for Yom Kippur (*SPB*, p. 384). In the same text from Qumran we find the expression 'הרשענו' 'we were lawless' (4Q508 3.1) which appears in the present-day prayer for Yom Kippur in proximity with 'Do You not know all things both hidden and revealed?' 'כי אמת עשית ואנחנו הרשענו – for You have acted faithfully *but we were lawless*' (*SPB*, p. 384).

The text 1Q34^{bis}, which is connected with the Day of Atonement, has points of contact with the conventional *ne'ilah* (closing) prayer for Yom Kippur. Thus we read in the Qumran prayer:

> *For you do not desire* (כי לא תחפוץ) (iniquity) and wickedness…*But You have chosen* a people in the time of Your favour…*in separating them* (להבדל לך) as a holy thing from all people (1Q34^{bis} 3ii 4–6).

This text is very similar to the conventional *ne'ilah* prayer for Yom Kippur:

> *You have set* mortal man *apart* (אתה הבדלת) from the very beginning and have given him the privilege to stand before You…*For You do not desire* (כי לא תחפוץ) the destruction of the world.

However, there is a difference. In its emphasis on separation the Qumran text stresses the chosen people, whereas in the conventional prayer, 'אנוש' 'mortal man' and 'עולם' are spoken of at a universal level.

Another text with a motif identical to that of the first Benediction of the *Amidah* is the fragment from the Genesis Apocryphon, which refers to the shield

(מגן) of Abraham. There we read words which go beyond the framework of the Targum to the verses: 'I am a shield to you' (Gen. 15.1): '...and I shall be to you both support and strength (סעד ותקף) I (shall be) a shield over you and a buckler for you (ואספרה לך)[30] against one stronger than you' (XXII 30–31). It appears that we have before us here a liturgical formula reflected in the first Benediction of the *Amidah* 'shield of Abraham', 'brings a redeemer to their descendants, a King, a Helper, a Savior and a Protector' (מלך עוזר ומושיע ומגן) (*SPB*, p. 54). And indeed, the expression, 'Your protecting shield' (מגן עזרך) in Deuteronomy 33.29 is rendered in Targum Onkelos as '*the strength of your support*' (תקוף בסעדך, in contrast to the Neophyti and Pseudo Jonathan Targums, which retain the biblical metaphor). The Benediction of the Shield of Abraham should also be compared with the Benediction of the *Ge'ula* which comes before the *Amidah*: 'עזרת אבותינו אתה הוא מעולם, מגן ומושיע לבניהם בכל דור ודור – *Helper of our Fathers* you are from eternity, Shield and Saviour for their descendants after them every generation' (*SPB*, p. 52).

The Morning Benedictions (ברכות השחר)

The Morning Benedictions, which appear to be marginal in the conventional liturgy, have ancient roots. In the *Psalms Scroll* of Qumran Cave 11[31] we have found Songs and Thanksgiving with elements congruent with the Morning Benedictions of the conventional liturgy. The liturgy from Cave 11, which the editor has named 'Plea for Deliverance'[32] is none other than the Morning Thanksgiving, which opens by praising God for the return of breath after the night's sleep and is interwoven with a Blessing to God who performs loving kindness toward his created beings. This is followed by a request for forgiveness for iniquities and for deliverance from afflictions (פגע) and temptations from Satan and the evil inclination (יצר הרע), just as we find in the conventional prayers, for which there is evidence in the Babylonian Talmud (*Ber.*60, b) and the Jerusalem Talmud (*Ber.* 4.2; 7d), as well as in the prayers from the Geniza.[33] Similar prayers can be found in the *Psalms of Solomon* as well as in fragments from the *Thanksgiving Scroll* from Qumran.[34]

The return to life, as it were, after sleep, arouses associations with resurrection from the dead, a subject which finds expression in the Morning Prayer of the Jerusalem Talmud, which concludes with the words: 'Blessed are You who raise the dead'[35] and indeed, in the conventional prayer,[36] as well as in the Thanksgiving

30. It appears that 'sprk' is a loanword from Persian, where *spr* means a shield. See J.A. Fitzmyer, *The Genesis Apocryphon* (1971), p. 182.

31. J.A. Sanders, *The Psalms Scroll of Qumran Cave 11*.

32. *Ibid.*, pp. 75–76.

33. J. Mann, 'Geniza Fragments of the Palestinian Order of Service', *HUCA* 2 (1925), pp. 278ff.

34. See ch. 8.

35. *TJ Berakhot* 4.2; 7d.

36. See in the Prayer 'אלהי נשמה', 'But Thou wilt restore it unto me hereafter', *SPB*, p. 5.

Psalms of Qumran, awakening in the morning is accompanied by eschatological expectations: union with the world above, etc.[37]

The Prayer of Supplication (תחנון)

As M. Lehmann[38] has observed, the long prayers of supplication named *Dibrei Hamĕ'orot* (דברי המארות) from Qumran Cave 4 are parallel to the text of the prayer of supplication (תחנון), recited on Mondays and Thursdays in the conventional prayers. However, he did not note that a very clear distinction must be drawn between the personal, private part of the prayer of supplication, which is called נפילת אפים (prostration)[39] and the supplication of the public prayer, which opens with the words: 'And He is merciful, and will atone for iniquity'(והוא רחום יכפר עון) recited while standing on Mondays and Thursdays.[40] This public prayer of supplication is composite, comprising fragments and parts of verses taken from the public confessions found in Dan. 9; Neh. 9; Ezra 9; Joel 2.17 and Isa. 63.7–64.11. The public prayers of supplication in Qumran and in Judaism belong typologically to the category of national confessions, as do the above biblical fragments. Indeed, these confessions and supplications are clearly reflected in both the prayer of supplication for Mondays and Thursdays of the conventional prayers[41] and in the *Dibrei Hamĕ'orot* (דברי המארות) from Qumran. Compare:

a. 'let Your wrathful fury turn back'. ('ישוב נא אפכה וחמתכה') (cf. Dan. 9.16) in 4Q504 1–2, II 11, VI 11 and the Prayer for Mondays and Thursdays in the conventional prayer book.[42]

b. 'With You, O Lord, is the right' ('לך אדני הצדקה') (cf. Dan. 9.7) in 1Q504 1–2, VI3 and the Prayer for Mondays and Thursdays.[43]

c. 'For Your Name is attached to Your city and Your people' ('שמך נקרא על עירך ועמך') Dan. 9.19, see also v. 18 'and the city to which Your Name is attached' ('העיר אשר נקרא שמך על יה') in 4Q504 1–2, II 12 and the Prayer for Mondays and Thursdays.[44]

d. 'Because of our sins and the iniquities of our fathers' ('בחטאינו ובעונות אבותינו') (Dan. 9.16) in 4Q504, 1–2 VI 5 and the Prayer for Mondays and Thursdays.[45] (Cf. Neh. 9.2 and also Lev. 26.39).

37. See M. Weinfeld, review article of B.P. Kittel, *The Hymns of Qumran* (1981) in *Bibl. Orientalis* 41 (1984), pp. 712–13 and in my book: *Early Jewish Liturgy* (2004) (Hebrew), introduction, pp. טז–כב.

38. Manfred R. Lehmann, 'A Re-Interpretation of 4Q Dibrei Ha-Mĕ'oroth', *RevQ* 5 (1964), pp. 106–110.

39. I. Elbogen, *Der jüdische Gottesdienst in seiner geschichtlichen Entwicklung* (1931), pp. 73–77.

40. Elbogen, *ibid.*, pp. 77–79. On the obligation of standing during the prayer see *Beth Yoseph, Joseph Karo, 'Oraḥ Ḥayyim'* Par. 134.

41. Dan. 9.15–19 is included in its entirety in the Prayer of Supplication; see Y. Baer, *Siddur Avodat Israel* (1868), p. 113.

42. Y. Baer, *ibid.*, p. 113.

43. Y. Baer, *ibid.*, pp. 114–15.

44. Y. Baer, *ibid.*, pp. 113, 115.

45. Y. Baer, *ibid.*, p. 113.

The dominant motif in both *Dibrei Hamĕ'orot* and the Prayer for Mondays and Thursdays is the *remembering of the covenant with the patriarchs*.

Compare:

Prayers for Mondays and Thursdays	*Qumran*
And remember for our benefit the Covenant of our fathers (Baer, p. 113) (וזכר לנו את ברית אבותינו)	Remember the desolate sons of Your Covenant (זכור בני בריתך השוממים) (4Q501 1.2)
Have mercy upon us for the sake of Your Covenant (Baer, p. 114)	And remember Your Covenant, You Who brought us out in the eyes of the nations (4Q504 1–2, V 9–10)

In connection with the remembering of the covenant of the patriarchs one mentions the gathering of the exiles, and here again, we find parallels:

Give grace to the nation that waits Your Name (חון אום לשמך מקוה) (Baer, p. 117).	and did not leave us among the Nations. *You have been gracious* to *Your people*, Israel in all the countries whither You have banished them (4Q504 1–2, V 10–12)
And gather our exiles from the four corners of the earth (Baer, p. 113)	And deliver *Your people, Israel*... out of all the countries, near and far whence You banished them. (4Q504 1–2 VI 12–13) (cf. Dan. 9.7)

Prayer Before Setting Forth on a Journey (תפילת הדרך)

The editor of text 4Q158 1–2[46] calls this fragment a paraphrase of a number of passages from the books of Genesis and Exodus. However, one should question how the request for deliverance from violence: 'ויצילכה מכל חמס...עד היום הזה ועד דורות עולם' – 'And let him deliver you from all violence from this day and forever' is connected to the story of Jacob and how what occurred to Jacob at Penuel is connected to the journey of Aaron to meet Moses after the incident at the night encampment (Exod. 4.27). We find however that in the prayer before setting forth on a journey mentioned in the Babylonian Talmud (*Ber*. 29b) (תפילת הדרך) there are interwoven verses from the story of Jacob's setting out on his journey in the context of his encountering the angels of God (Gen. 32.2). This combination is now comprehensible to us in the light of the fragment from Qumran, which includes biblical verses referring to Jacob's going on his way (וילך לדרכו Gen. 32.2) and the wrestling with the angel and prevailing over him on the one hand (Gen. 32.25–33) and the encounter of Moses and Aaron after the destroying angel sought to kill him at a night encampment (Exod. 4.23–27), on the other hand. Both these incidents, connected with the encountering of assailants while on a journey and deliverance from them, are most suitable for prayers and requests in which one asks for deliverance from the perils of a journey.

46. John M. Allegro, *DJD* 5, p. 1.

Benediction on Performing the Marriage Ceremony

Baillet[47] correctly named Scroll 4Q502 'Rituel de Mariage', for, as can be seen from the parallels presented here, there is a close similarity between the traditional Benediction on performing the marriage ceremony and the fragments under discussion in this text from Qumran. One should note that the traditional Benediction of the Marriage Ceremony centres around three principal subjects: (1) The creation of man coming from the power of procreation whose original source comes from Adam and Eve who are mentioned in the Benediction for the Marriage Ceremony, (2) The rejoicing of the groom and bride against the background of *love, companionship and friendship* connected with this, (3) The rejoicing of Jerusalem in whose streets a cry of joy and gladness bursts forth.

Although today we are accustomed to the seven Benedictions in the order of the marriage service, we know that there existed a difference of opinion between the communities of Babylon and Palestine and that the Palestinian Jews used to recite only three Benedictions during the marriage ceremony.[48] It appears that in Palestine these three Benedictions centred around the three above-mentioned themes, whereas, in the conventional formulation of seven Benedictions there is a duplication of these themes.[49] Traces of the three themes can be found in Qumran 4Q502 mentioned above (see Appendix). Baumgarten[50] attempted to refute the claim that the scroll refers to the Benediction for the Marriage Ceremony on the basis of the allusion to *old men and women* in this text. He claimed that the text apparently refers here to old men who joined the sect, basing his claim on the description of the therapeutai in Philo the Alexandrian. However, he did not consider the fact that in the prophetic description of Jerusalem, reinhabited and teeming with life, from which the expressions in the Benediction for the Marriage Ceremony are drawn (such as Jer. 33.10–1), there are also found expressions which refer to *old men and women* such as: 'There shall yet be old men and women in the squares of Jerusalem', which is juxtaposed to 'and the squares of the city shall be crowded with boys and girls playing in the squares' (Zech. 8.4–5). The reference to *lulavim* (palm branches) found here[51] is reflected in the custom of bringing myrtle to the *hupa* and reciting a Benediction over them,[52] a custom mentioned in the *b. Shab.* 110.[53]

47. *DJD* 7, pp. 81–105.

48. M. Margulies, *The Differences Between Babylonian and Palestinian Jews* (1938), pp. 83, 143–45. Cf. recently M. Bar-Ilan, ברכת "יוצר האדם",מקומות הופעתה, תיפקודה ומשמעותה, *HUCA* 56 (1985), pp. כח–ט.

49. 'Creator of man' (יוצר האדם) twice; 'who makest the bridegroom and bride to rejoice' (משמח חתן וכלה), alongside 'who makest the bridegroom to rejoice with the bride' (משמח חתן עם כלה).

50. J.M. Baumgarten, '4Q502, Marriage or Golden Age Ritual?', *JJS* 35 (1983), pp. 125–36.

51. 4Q502, 99.2, *DJD* 7, p. 94.

52. See *Siddur R. Saadja Gaon* (ed. I. Davidson, S. Assaf and B.I. Joel, 1941), p. 13 (Hebrew): 'and sanctifies her with a cup of wine and a myrtle branch'.

53. There the Sabbath is likened to a bride whom they go out to meet with bundles of myrtle (מדאני אסא).

Grace After Meals

A division of opinion existed among the Tannaim over whether the three Benedictions should be recited only after eating bread, or whether it was necessary to say the Benedictions also after eating the fruits with which the land of Israel was blessed (*m. Ber.* 6.8). According to R. Gamaliel, the commandment 'And you shall eat and be satisfied and you shall bless' (ואכלת ושבעת וברכת) (Deut. 8.10), refers to all the seven species of the blessed land mentioned in Deut. 8.8 and not only to 'bread' (לחם) mentioned in v. 9, whereas according to the Sages, the word 'land' (ארץ) in v. 9 interrupts the matter, and therefore the Benediction mentioned in v. 10 refers only to the word 'land', which is connected to 'bread' in v. 9. It is interesting that in the Qumran fragment (4Qdeut^{n}) in which the biblical verses under discussion appear,[54] there is a space of one line between the words 'a land of wheat and barley, of vines etc.' (v. 8), and the verse 'a land where you may eat bread without stint' (v. 9). Stegemann, who first edited this fragment,[55] was surprised by this line space between the verses and was unable to explain it. It would appear that the space can only be explained against the background of this difference of opinion among the Sages. The scribe of the scroll before us wished to make it known that the Benediction in v. 10 belonged to the section in which bread is mentioned and had no connection to the fruits mentioned in v. 8.[56]

It is possible that the very existence of this fragment standing by itself, a fact that surprised Stegemann,[57] could be explained in terms of its liturgical function.

Minyan

In the *Manual of Discipline* we find the fixed order of the quorum of ten men for prayer (1QS 10.14). We learn also that in the Benediction at the Messianic Banquet ten men were required (1QS^{a} 2.22) and according to the *Damascus Covenant*, it appears that for the matter of reading the Torah, ten men were also mandatory (CD 13.2–7). These three situations: official prayer, grace after a communal meal (when invoking the name of God) and also the reading of the Torah require the *Minyan* in conventional Jewish Halakhah.

54. *Scrolls from the Wilderness of the Dead Sea* 63 (Smithsonian Institute, Washington, published by the Trustees of the British Museum, 1965), plate 19, p. 20.

55. M. Stegemann, '4Q Mit Exzerpten aus Deuteronomium', *RevQ* 6 (1967–1968), pp. 224–29.

56. The Sages regulated that one Benediction, an abstract of the three (מעין שלש), should be said over fruit, rather than three Benedictions such as one recites after the eating of bread. (See *m. Ber.* 6.8).

57. In his article, '4Q Mit Exzerpten aus Deuteronomium', pp. 224–25. It is interesting to note that in another text from Qumran (4Q378) in which the people's satisfaction with the land, rather than their eating of its fruit is emphasized, the hemistich 'a land where you may eat food without sting' 'ארץ אשר לא במסכנת תאכל בה לחם' is omitted. See C. Newsom, 'The Psalms of Joshua from Qumran Cave 4', *JJS* 39 (1988), p. 65.

The Precedence of the Priest in Matters of Holiness

In the Qumran sect the priest took priority in leadership, in religious ceremonies, in judicial matters and at communal meals. For example, the priest passes at the head of the procession of the entering into the covenant (1QS 2.19–20), the priest is the first to offer a Benediction before and after a communal meal (1QS 4.4–5 cf. Josephus, *War* 2.131), judicial matters are decided according to the priest's verdict (1QS 9.7) and 'where the ten are there shall never be lacking a Priest learned in the Book of *Hagu*' (CD 13.2–7). As I have mentioned elsewhere,[58] the priest was considered as the leader in the Qumran sect, at least in a formal way. So also in Pharisaic law, we find a preference for the priest in similar matters: the priest is the first to begin the reading of the Torah, the first to recite a Benediction at a communal meal, and not only after the meal, but also before it (see below), and in general, the priest appears as first in things concerned with holy matters, as can be learned from the Bĕraitha of the School of R. Ishmael: 'וקדשתו' 'and you must treat him as holy' (Lev. 21.8): to wit [give him precedence] in every matter involving holiness, to open proceedings, to bless first and to take his portion first (*b. Giṭ.* 49b, *Ned.* 64, *Mo'ed Qat.* 28b, *Hor.* 12b).

The Canon

Although members of the sect wrote literary compositions beyond that permitted according to the conventional Pharisaic criterion of sacred books, they also believed that there was a series of sacred books, a canon consisting of the Torah and Prophets: the law of Moses and the books written by the servants of the Lord, the prophets. In this matter they were of the same mind as other streams of Judaism, especially the Pharisees who speak of: (a) the law of Moses, (b) that which is passed on by your servants, (c) the words of Your Holy One (דברי קדשך). This triple sense of canonical writings is reflected in the liturgy of Rosh Hashanah: (the references to)... Kingdom, Remembrances and Shofars (מלכויות זכרונות ושופרות). The liturgy is divided into three sections: verses from the Torah; writings which were said 'by Your Servants, the Prophets'; verses from the writings: 'by the words of Your Holy One'.[59] The expression 'דברי קדשך' 'the words (of the Spirit) of Your Holiness' is also found in the writings of the sect (1Q34 11.6) although their context is not clear.

The threefold division of the canon also appears in the Greek introduction to Ben Sira[60] and in the Gospel of Luke (24.44), where the categories, the Law of Moses, the Prophets, and the Psalms (probably representative of the third division),

58. M. Weinfeld, *The Organizational Pattern and Penal Code of the Qumran Sect* (Novum Testamentum et Orbis Antiquus 2; 1986), pp. 19–21.

59. See *t. Rosh Hash.* 4 (2), 6: 'One begins with [verses from] the Torah and ends with [verses from] the Torah; he recites [verses from] the Prophets and [verses from] the Writings in the middle'.

60. On 'the Torah, the Prophets and the rest of the Writings' see M.Z. Segal, *The Complete Book of Ben Sira* (in Hebrew) (1953), p. א.

are enumerated. However, the New Testament also refers to a twofold division consisting of the Law of Moses and the Prophets in Lk. 16.29–31; 24.27 and Acts 24.14.[61]

Tĕfillin And Mĕzuzot

The discovery of *Tĕfillin* at Qumran with their containing capsules, and the arrangement of the sections in them, reveals a close similarity to the conventional Halakhah with respect to the writings of phylacteries. Furthermore, even the division of opinion in medieval Judaism over the methods of Rashi and Rabenu Tam is reflected in Qumran.[62]

In conclusion, customs known to us from Pharasaic Halakhah were current in the Qumran sect. These customs, however, were based upon the Judaism of the second Temple period.

APPENDIX

References to the Various Paragraphs

Jewish Conventional Prayers	*Qumran*
1. *Shema'*	
בשכבנו ובקומנו נשיח בחוקיך (before the *Shema'* of evening) (*SPB*, p. 131)	עם מבוא יום ולילה אבואה בברית אל ועם מוצא ערב ובוקר אמר חוקיו (1QS 10.10ff.)
2. *The Qedushah and Benediction of the Lights*	
לדור ודור...כי מלך גדול וקדוש אתה. אתה קדוש...וקדושים בכל יום יהללוך (*SPB*, p. 55)	גדול וקדוש ה' קדוש קדושים לדור ודור
יוצר אור...ובורא חושך אל...גדול דעה הכין ופעל זהרי חמה...פנות צבאיו קדושים מספרים כבוד אל (*SPB*, pp. 44-45)	מבדיל אור מאפלה שחר הכין בדעת לבו אז ראו כל מלאכיו וירננו
חסד ורחמים לפני כבודו, זכות ומישור לפני כסאו (*SPB*, pp. 187–188)	חסד ואמת סביב פניו, אמת ומשפט וצדק מכון כסאו (11QPS[a] 26.9–12)

61. In connection with the combination of Torah and Prophecy in Qumran, see G. Brin, 'Explicit Quotations from the Torah and the Writings of the Dead Sea Scrolls', *Dor le-Dor: from the End of Biblical Times up to the Redaction of the Talmud* (Studies in Honor of Joshua Efron; Tel Aviv, 1985), pp. 105–112 (Hebrew).

62. *DJD* 6, 4Q 128–155, pp. 48–85 and cf. Y. Yadin, 'Tefillin (Phylacteries) from Qumran (Qphy 1 1–4)', *Eretz Israel*, 9 (1969) (W.F. Albright Volume), pp. 60–85.

באופיע מאורות מזבול קודש
בהתחדשם...ואות למפתח חסדי עולם
(1QS X 1–8)

מאורות נתן סביבות עזו...
(*SPB*, p. 45)

המחדש בטובו...כי לעולם חסדו
(*SPB*, pp. 46–47)

ברוך אל ישראל...בצאת השמש להאיר
על הארץ דגלי ערב...גורלי חשך...
שערי אור...אור כיומם
(4Q503)

פותח שערים...גולל אור מפני חושך וחושך
מפני אור
(*SPB*, p. 130)

3. *Prayers for the Sabbaths and Festivals*

ברוך...אשר בחר בנו מכל העמים למועד
מנוח ותענוג...שמחים.

אתה בחרתנו מכל העמים...ותתן לנו את
יום המנוח הזה מועדים לשמחה ולששון.
(*SPB*, pp. 327–328)

ואספת [נדחינו] למועד...[ונפוצ]ותנו
תקבץ לתקופ[ת]...
(4Q507–509)

וקרב פזורנו מבין הגוים ונפוצותינו כנס
מירכתי ארץ
(*SPB*, p. 335)

Prayer for Yom Kippur

אתה ידעת הנסתרות והנגל[ות]...הרשענו
כי לא תחפוץ בעולה ורשע...ותבחר לך
עם...להבדיל לך...
(1Q34^{BIS} 3 ii 4–6)

ואנחנו הרשענו... הלא כל הנסתרות
והנגלות אתה יודע
(*SPB*, p. 384)
אתה הבדלת אנוש מראש...כי לא תחפוץ
בהשחתת עולם
(*SPB*, p. 412)

4. *The Morning Prayers*

חי חי יודה לכה נשמת כל בשר אתה נתתה
ברוך ה' עושה צדקות
מעטר חסידיו חסד ורחמים

למוות הייתי בחטאי ועוונותי לשאול
מכרוני.
ותצילני ה' ברוב רחמיכה...סלחה ה'
לחטאתי וטהרני מעווני רוח אמונה ודעת
חונני
אל אתקלה בעווה
אל תשלט בי שטן ורוח טמאה מכאוב ויצר
רע אל ירשו בעצמי
(11QPS^{a} 19)

אלהי נשמה שנתת בי...ואתה עתיד לטלה
ממני ולהחזירה בי לעתיד לבוא מודה אני
לפניך...ברוך...גומל חסדים טובים.
(*SPB*, pp, 5,8)
חטאתי לפניך ואם גרמו עוונותי הצילני מכל
דבר עוון
(Genizah)
הבינני דעה
(Genizah)
ואל תביאנו לידי עברה...ולא אכשל
בעוון...ואל תשלט בנו יצר הרע...שתצילני
מפגע רע ומשטן המשחית ...
(*SPB*, p. 8)

5. *The Prayer of Supplication (Taḫanun)*

ולמען בריתכה
ישוב נא אפכה וחמתכה מעמכה ישראל
ותזכור בריתכה
עשה נא כגדול כוחכה
ולשמכה הגדול
לכה אתה אדני הצדקה כיא אתה עשיתה
את כל אלה והצילה את עמכה ישראל

למען בריתך
ישב נא אפך וחמתך מעירך ירושלים
זכור לנו ברית
עשה עמנו כרוב רחמיך
שמך הגדול
לך ה' הצדקה עושה נפלאות בכל עת

מכול הארצות הקרובות והרחוקות	וקבץ נפוצותינו מארבע כנפות הארץ
(4Q504–506 DibHam)	(*SPB*, pp. 70–76)

6. *The Prayer before Setting Forth on a Journey*

ויברך אתו שם ויאמר לו יפרכה	ותצילנו מכף אויב ואורב ותשלח ברכה...
ה'...ויצילכה מכול חמס...וילך	ויעקב הלך לדרכו ...
לדרכו...אל אהרון לאמור לך...לקראת	
(4Q158)	

7. *The Benediction on Performing the Marriage Ceremony*

האדם ואשתו לעשות זרע	יוצר האדם
	אשר יצר את האדם והתקין לו ממנו בנין
בת אמת...רעייתו, אחים ואחיות	...
אשישיהם ונערים...מועד	אהבה אחווה ורעות בערי יהודה וחוצות
לשמחתנו...זקנים וזקנות...ובתולות.	ירושלים קול ששון וקול שמחה...נערים
נערים ונערות	
מעין לפרי בטן אשר שמחנו ...	שמח תשמח רעים האהובים...משמח חתן
לולבים לפניו כל שבעת ימים...ברוך אל	וכלה
ישראל שמחת יחד...אני הנערה	(*SPB*, p. 444)
(4Q502)	

8. *Grace After Meals*

4QDeut^{n}

... ארץ חטה ושעורה וגפן תאנה ורמון. ארץ זית שמן ודבש
ארץ אשר לוא במסכנות תאכל בה לחם ולוא תחסר כול בה ...
ואכלת ושבעתה וברכתה את ה' אלהיך על הארץ הטובה אשר נתן לך.

9–10. *The Minyan and the Precedence of the Priest in Matters of Holiness*

ואברכנו תרומת מוצא שפתי במערכת אנשים (1QS X 14)
ובמקום עשרה אל ימש איש כהן מבונן בספר ההגו (CD XIII 2)
ויחד יואכלו ויחד יברכו...ובכול מקום אשר יהיה שם עשרה אנשים...אל ימש מאתם איש כוהן ... (1QS VI 3–4)
והיה כי יערוכו השולחן לאכול או התירוש לשתות הכוהן ישלח ידו לרשונה להברך ... (1QS VI 4–6)
ואם לשלחן יחד יועדו...[אל ישלח] איש את ידו ברשת (=בראשית) הלחם והתירוש לפני הכהן כי[א הוא י]ברך את רשית הלחם...[ואחר יבר]כו כול עדת היחד. (1QS^{a} II 17–21)
וכחוק הזה יעשו לכול מע[רכת]...עד עשרא אנשים (1QS^{a} II 17–22)

11. *The Canon*

לעשות הטוב והישר לפניו כאשר צוה ביד משה וביד כול עבדיו הנביאים (1QS I2–3)
אשר צוה ביד משה...וכאשר גלו לו הנביאים ברוח קדשו (1QS VIII 15–16)
אשר כתב משה ועבדיכה הנביאים (4Q504 III 1–2)

Chapter 4

The Day of the Lord: Aspirations for the Kingdom of God in the Bible and Jewish Liturgy

'From thine abode, our King, appear and reign over us *for we wait for thee* (כי מחכים אנחנו לך). When wilt thou reign in Zion? Speedily, in our days, do thou dwell there forever. Mayest thou be exalted and sanctified in Jerusalem thy city throughout all generations and to all eternity. May our eyes behold thy kingdom, as it is said in thy glorious Psalms by thy truly anointed, David: "The Lord shall reign forever, thy God, O Zion, for all Generations. Hallelujah"'.[1]

'They (the Jews) assemble, according to their customs...on the Sabbaths, New Moon days and festivals...to prostrate...calling in the Hebrew language: "on which day will you come? at what time will you reveal yourself? because we are expecting your coming...Do not tarry, even if you tarry we shall wait"'.[2]

The passage from the Sabbath and festival morning *Qedushah* liturgy[3] adduced above actually continues the biblical tradition of 'longing (אוה) for the day of the Lord' (Amos 5.18). 'Looking for' (צפה) and 'expecting' (יחל) (Mic. 7.7, cf. 7.4). 'Waiting' (חכה) and 'hoping' (קוה) for the Lord (Isa. 8.12, cf. Zeph. 3.8). Daniel continues this tradition into the second temple period with his exclamation: 'Happy is the man who "waits"' (המחכה; 12.12).

Prophets and people alike anticipate the future revelation of God's majesty, which will entail divine judgement. (The people long for this judgment, assuming that it will be followed by vengeance upon Israel's enemies and the redemption of Israel, while the prophets insist that judgement will encompass Israel as well as her enemies). Revelation (=salvation) of the Lord in fact occurred also in the past, at the dawn of Israel's history, at Sinai. Indeed the liturgical passage cited above begins 'From thine abode (ממקומך), our King, appear (תופיע)', a phrase

1. *Qedushah* liturgy: cf. Rev. S. Singer, *The Standard (Jewish) Prayer Book* (1943), p. 199 (referred to below as *SPB*). Biblical and liturgical texts in this article reflect the author's adaptations of various English translations.

2. From Shenoute, Abbot of Athribis in Egypt, in the 4th century; cf. E. Amélineau, *Oeuvres de Schenoudi II* (1914), pp. 379–80. I owe this reference to Professor Shisha-Halevy of the Hebrew University.

3. The various elements of this passage are quite ancient, appearing in the Prayer Book of Amram Gaon, Maimonides, and Yemenite Jewry. In Byzantine Palestine the *Qedushah* was recited only on Sabbaths and festivals (see E. Fleischer, 'The Diffusion of the *Qedushah* of the *Amidah* and the *Yoṣer* in the Palestinian Jewish Ritual', *Tarbiz* 38 [1969], pp. 256–57) and therefore the more elaborate form of the *Qedushah* is now said only on these occasions, while the contemporary daily *Qedushah* is much simpler. For the ancient roots of the *Qedushah* see Chapter 2.

borrowed from ancient Israelite tradition, according to which God appears from his abode, Sinai (Deut. 33.2) or Zion (Ps. 50.2) to save Israel (Judg. 5.4; Hab. 3.3, *et al.*).[4] Similarly, the other phrases in the *Qedushah* passage: 'Speedily, in our days do thou dwell there forever. Mayest thou be exalted and sanctified…', are rooted in the prophetic tradition, according to which the day of the Lord is *near or coming speedily* (Obad. 15; Joel 4.14; Zeph. 1.14, *et al*; see below), and in the belief that on that day the name of the Lord will be exalted and sanctified (Ezek. 38.18–23). These hopes for revelation/salvation can be found in texts from all sorts of biblical literature, and refer to events spanning all of biblical history. They are expressed most fully in the prayer of Ben Sira (Eccl. 36, see below) and in the liturgy of the Jewish people until today. However, although the anticipation of a future revelation spans all of Jewish history, each period, each prophet, and every author expressed it in his own way.

We shall attempt here to clarify this idea of the anticipation of divine revelation and the establishment of God's kingdom, beginning with the prophetic concept, 'the day of the Lord', which epitomizes most of Israel's eschatological hopes. Amos is the first prophet to refer to the Day of the Lord: 'Ah, you *who long for the day of the Lord!* Why should you want the day of the Lord? It shall be darkness, not light…blackest night without a glimmer' (Amos 5.18, 20). The prophet here refers to a future era, which the people look forward to as the era of salvation, but which the prophet insists will be not of salvation, but of retribution. It is likely that Amos himself coined the term 'Day of the Lord',[5] but the idea is clearly more ancient and well-rooted in Israelite religion.

The Term 'Day of the Lord'

The word 'day' (יום) is not to be taken literally here – it means rather 'the time/period'. This is true often of the word 'day' in biblical Hebrew. Deut. 16.3 refers to 'the *day* of your coming out of Egypt', for which Mic. 7.15 has 'the days of your coming out of Egypt'. In either case, 'time/period' is meant. Compare Gen. 2.4: 'on the day (ביום) of the Lord God's creating heaven and earth', which means: *when* God created heaven and earth (see translations). The same applies to the phrase in Gen. 2.17: 'on the day (ביום) you eat of it, you shall die', where ביום has to be rendered: 'the moment' or 'as soon as' (cf. *JPSV* translation); Adam did not die on the very day he ate from the tree of knowledge. Cf. also Exod. 10.28; 32.34 *et al.* In Akkadian as well, *ūm ša* (lit. 'the day that') means simply 'when'. 'Then', in Akkadian, is expressed with the phrase *ina ūmi, inūma,* 'on the day'.[6]

4. Many verses speak of God coming forth (יצא) from his abode (Judg. 5.4; Isa. 26.21; Mic. 1.3) or shining forth (זרח Deut. 33.2). Cf. the Kuntillet 'Ajrud inscription quoted below, p. 79 and n. 41. 'Coming forth' (יצא) connotes also 'shine forth' (זרח) (cf. H.O. Preuss, 'יצא', *TWAT* III [1981], col. 797), or 'sprout forth' (יעא in Aramaic means 'to shoot', cf. Isa. 11.1). See also S. Morag, 'ומתערה כאזרח רענן' (Ps. 37.35), *Tarbiz* (1971), pp. 4–6, and the various references there to the connection between the semantic field 'shining' and that of 'shooting forth' in the Semitic languages.

5. M. Weiss, 'The Origin of the Day of the Lord Reconsidered', *HUCA* 37 (1966), pp. 45–48.

6. W. von Soden, *Grundriss der Akkadischen Grammatik* (1952), §174 (p. 229).

יום ('day'), עת ('time') and קץ ('destined hour')[7] are, in fact, synonymous. All three are used in Ezekiel 7, a chapter that bears the character of a Day of the Lord prophecy.[8] There we read in vv. 6ff.: 'the destined hour is coming (בא הקץ), the time is coming (בא העת), the day is near (קרוב היום). Similarly, in Ezek. 21.30ff., which deals with the prince of Israel who will undergo judgement in the future, we also find these three terms: 'his day (יום) has come, at the time (עת) of his destined hour (קץ) of punishment'. The passage goes on to describe the humbling of the haughty, which is reminiscent or Isaiah's Day of the Lord prophecy: 'Then man's haughtiness shall be humbled and the pride of man brought low' (Isa. 2.17).

In Habakkuk we find in the same eschatological context the term מועד ('appointed time') as a parallel to קץ ('destined hour'): 'For there is still (עוד) a vision for the appointed time (מועד), a יפח for the destined hour (קץ)' (2.3). From the discoveries at Ugarit it is clear that יפח means 'witness',[9] and therefore one should amend עֵד ('still') to עֵד ('witness', reading: 'The vision is a witness (עֵד) for the appointed time (מועד), a witness (יפח) for the destined hour (קץ). Even if it tarries, wait for it still, it will surely come, without delay.' Compare Zeph. 3.8: 'For wait for me – says the Lord, for the day when I arise as a witness (עֵד)'. Here, as in Habakkuk, we hear of anticipating the day of the accusing witness (עֵד).[10]

Daniel also refers to 'the destined hour of the appointed time (מועד קץ)', the hour of salvation and doom. In biblical poetry we also find מועד with reference to the future revelation of God in judgement: 'I seize the appointed time (מועד), and then I judge (mankind) with justice' (Ps. 75.3). Just as in the prophecies of the Day of the Lord, this judgement is also set against a background of natural upheavals: 'when the earth dissolves, with all its inhabitants' (v. 4). Two other Day of the Lord motifs are found in the continuation of the psalm: 'For God judges: lifting one man up, bringing another down. For the Lord has a cup in his hand, with foaming wine fully mixed; from this He pours; all the wicked of the earth drink, draining it to the very dregs.' The humbling of the haughty ('he brings down one man') is familiar to us from the Day of the Lord prophecy in Isa. 2.9 (cf. Ezek. 21.31), while the metaphor of the cup of poison is found in the doomsday prophecy of Jer. 25.15ff. We cannot then limit our discussion of the Day of the Lord phenomenon to prophecies which specifically refer to the 'Day of the Lord'. The phrase יום ה׳ itself is not the criterion. Some prophecies refer to the day not as יום ה׳, but rather as יום נקם לה׳, יום לה׳ צבאות ('day of vengeance for the

7. Cf. M. Greenberg (*Ezekiel 1–20* [*AB*, 1983], p. 147) who points out correctly that קץ means properly 'term, measure of time' whence evolves the sense 'time's end' (I would rather translate 'running of time', *Ablauf* in German). In the Qumran writings קץ has the meaning of 'time', cf. M. Wagner, 'קץ', *TWAT* II, 663, and the references there.

8. For the linguistic affinities of this chapter to the prophecy of the Day of the Lord in Isa. 13, cf. M. Greenberg (above, n. 7), pp. 159–60.

9. S. E. Loewenstamm, *Comparative Studies in Biblical and Ancient Oriental Literatures* (AOAT, 204, 1980), pp. 137–45.

10. For עד as a witness and accuser cf. I.L. Seeligmann, 'Zur Terminologie für das Gerichtsverfahren', *Hebräische Wortforschung* (*SVT*, 16; Festschrift W. Baumgartner [1967]), pp. 262ff.

Lord'), or simply 'on that day'. Often, terms such as מועד, קץ and עת take the place of יום. Our criteria for determining which passages belong to the 'Day of the Lord' category are the specific motifs which characterize the day of the theophany. These include, on the one hand, cosmic phenomena: clouds, darkness, thick mist, eclipses, earthquakes and the dissolution of mountains – and on the other hand, military motifs: battle array, arming the hosts, the sword and blood.[11] The following two examples illustrate these motifs. In Zeph. 1.14–16 we read:

> The great day of the Lord is approaching, approaching most swiftly. Hark – the day of the Lord! It is bitter. There a warrior shrieks. That day shall be a day of wrath, a day of trouble and distress, a day of calamity and desolation, a day of darkness and deep gloom, a day of densest clouds. A day of horn blasts and alarms, against the fortified towns and the lofty corner towers.

The passage combines natural and military motifs. Similarly, in Isa. 13.4–6:

> Hark! – a tumult on the mountains as of a mighty force. Hark! an uproar of kingdoms, nations assembling! The Lord of hosts is mustering a host for war. They come from a distant land, from the end of the sky – the Lord with the weapons of his wrath – to ravage all the earth! Howl! For the day of the Lord is near. It shall come like a havoc from Shaddai.

This military metaphor is followed by a description of cosmic upheaval (vv. 9–10):

> Lo! the day of the Lord is coming with pitiless fury and wrath, to make the earth a desolation, to wipe out the sinners upon it. The stars and constellations of heaven shall not give off their light. The sun shall be dark when it rises, and the moon shall diffuse no glow.

What is the source of these motifs? Modern scholarship, in dealing with the Day of the Lord question, concerned itself primarily with its *Sitz im Leben*. The roots of the Day of the Lord are sought in a literary model that had originated in public life. We will now turn our attention to this subject in more detail.

The Day of the Lord in Jewish Liturgy

According to Mowinckel,[12] the New Year festival celebrated the coronation of God as king of all the earth (as is indeed reflected in Jewish liturgy even today), and the New Year festival was the *Sitz im Leben* of the Day of the Lord theme in Israelite literature.

Mowinckel, alone among non-Jewish scholars, made use of Jewish tradition (e.g. *m Rosh. Hash.* 4.5) in order to understand the nature of the New Year festival. He noticed that the New Year prayers, especially those connected with the blowing of the shophar, centre around the themes of מלכויות (God's kingship), זכרונות (God's remembrance of the deeds of mankind, in his capacity as judge),

11. See M. Weiss (above, n. 5), table A.
12. S. Mowinckel, The *Psalms in Israeli Worship*, I (1962), pp. 106ff.

and שופרות (shophar blasts in theophanies past and future). God once again becomes king of all the earth, just as at the creation and at Sinai he became king over Israel.[13] Shophar blasts celebrate this coronation just as when human kings ascend the throne (cf. 1 Kgs 1.39; 2 Kgs 9.13). The Day of the Lord prophecies indeed describe theophanies amid shophar blasts (e.g. Joel 2.1) and these theophanies involve God's ascending the cosmic throne to judge the universe, just as in the New Year liturgy. In fact, all the New Year's prayers, not only those contained in the three thematic sections cited above, are composed of elements which also appear in the Day of the Lord prophecies, as can be seen from the following table:

	Rosh Hashanah Prayer Book	*'Day Of The Lord' Prophecy*
1. *Anticipation of divine rule in Zion*	Thou shalt reign over all whom thou hast made, in Zion thy holy city... Blessed art thou, O Lord, holy king. *(SPR 351.361)*	And the Lord shall be king over all the earth. For liberators shall march up on Mount Zion...and kingship shall be the Lord's. (Obad. 1.21)
2. *Universal acknowledgement of God's rule*	Now Lord our God, put thy awe upon all whom thou hast made, and thy dread upon all whom thou hast created; let thy works revere thee; let thy creatures worship thee. May they all blend into one brotherhood to do thy will with wholeheartedness. (*SPB* 350) May every existing being know thou hast made it; may every creature realize thou hast created it. (*SPB* 353,365)	None but the Lord shall be exalted that day... On that day men shall fling away the idols of silver and the idols of gold...and they shall enter the clefts... before the dread of the Lord (Isa. 2.11; 20–21: cf. Mic. 5.11–12) For I will make the peoples pure of speech so that they may all invoke the Lord by name and serve Him with one accord. (Zeph. 3.9)
3. *Theophany in glory and splendour*	Reign over all the universe in thy glory, be exalted over all the earth in thy grandeur, shine forth in thy splendid majesty (הדר גאון עזך) over all the inhabitants of thy world. *(SPB* 353, 365)	...before the dread of the Lord and his splendid majesty (הדר גאנו) when he comes forth to overawe the earth. (Isa. 2.19, 21) They shall behold the glory of the Lord, the splendour of our God (Isa. 35.2) The glory of the Lord shall be revealed (ונגלה כבוד ה׳) and all mankind shall see it. (Isa. 40.5)

13. On God's coronation at creation, Sinai and in the future universal redemption, see my book *Social Justice in Ancient Israel and in the Ancient Near East* (1995), pp. 179ff.

4. *The abolition of evil and tyranny*	Iniquity shall shut its mouth, wickedness shall vanish like smoke, when thou wilt abolish the rule of tyranny (זדון) on earth. (*SPB* 351,360)[14]	I will put an end to the pride of the arrogant (זדים), and humble the haughtiness of tyrants. (Isa. 13.11; cf. Ezek. 7.24)

Mowinckel finds support for his theory in the juxtaposition of passages in Amos.[15] Amos' Day of the Lord prophecy (5.18–20) is followed directly by a passage in which God rejects the Israelite festivals (5.21–25). According to Mowinckel, this passage deals with the New Year rites, which in ancient times encompassed the harvest festival 'at the turn of the year' (cf. Exod. 34.22), as well as New Year's Day (first day of Tishrei) itself.

However, even if we grant that the Day of the Lord is bound up with the New Year liturgy, it remains to be seen whether the New Year ritual gave rise to the anticipation of the Day of the Lord, or whether these hopes, born of general nationalistic and religious circumstances, are simply reflected in the New Year service. In fact, the motifs cited above are not specific to the New Year service. They are found as well in the *daily* Jewish liturgy.

1. *The anticipation of divine rule in Zion* is found in every component of Jewish liturgy from the ancient core of the daily service (the *Amidah* or 'eighteen benedictions') to the personal prayers of Talmudic sages now appended to the public service:

'Restore our judges as at first...*reign thou alone over us* (some rites add *speedily*), O Lord' (daily *Amidah, SPB* 58).

'May our eyes behold thy return in mercy to Zion, Blessed art thou, O Lord, who restores the divine Presence to Zion' (daily *Amidah, SPB* 62).

'The Lord shall reign for ever, thy God, O Zion, for all Generations. Hallelujah' (Ps. 146.10, the conclusion of the *Qedushah*. Cf. the introductory passage cited at the beginning of this article).[16]

'Glorified and sanctified be God's great name throughout the world which he has created according to his will. May he establish his kingdom...within the lifetime of the entire house of Israel, speedily and soon' (*Kaddish, SPB* 80, recited a number of times during every service).[17]

'May they all accept the yoke of thy kingdom, and do thou reign over them speedily forever and ever. For thine is the kingdom, and to all eternity wilt thou reign in glory, as is written in thy Torah: "The Lord shall be king forever and ever" (Exod. 15.18). And it is said: "The Lord shall be king over all the earth, on

14. Cf. the Qumran passage in 4Q417, 1.5–6: 'when the progenitors of iniquity (עולה) will be stopped and the wickedness will be expelled before the righteousness...and just as smoke vanishes so shall wickedness vanish forever'. See D. Flusser, 'Sefer Megilat Harazim and the Prayer of the High-Holidays', *FS E. Fleisher* (1994), pp. 3–20.

15. Mowinckel (above, n. 12), p. 116.

16. Cf. above. n. 3.

17. On the *Kaddish* and its affinities to the 'Lord's Prayer' (Mt. 6.4–13) cf. D. de Sola Pool, *The Old Jewish-Aramaic Prayer, the Kaddish* (1909).

that day there shall be one Lord with one name" (Zech. 14.9)' *(Aleinu prayer, SPB* 94).[18]

The theme of the revelation of God's kingdom is the climax of the Jewish service. *Kaddish* is recited in full at the end of each service, as is the *Aleinu* prayer (see preceding quote). Similarly, we find (in ancient rites) at the conclusion of the evening prayer,[19] after the second Benediction of the evening *Shema'* (*Hashkibenu* – 'Grant us to lie down in peace'), a messianic prayer[20] which reads:

> O God who art in heaven, assert the unity of thy name and establish thy kingdom forever; do thou reign over us forever and ever. May our eyes behold, our heart rejoice, and our soul exult in thy salvation, when it will be said in Zion, 'Your God is king'. The Lord is king, the Lord was king, the Lord shall be king forever and ever. For thine is the kingdom, and to all eternity wilt thou reign in glory. Blessed art thou, O Lord, glorious king, who wilt reign over us and over all thy creatures forever and ever (*SPB* 137–138).

The function of this prayer is to bring the day to a close with eschatological aspirations for the divine kingdom on earth.

The personal meditations appended to the public liturgy also express the longing for the establishment of God's kingdom. The original version of the *'Elohai neṣor* prayer said privately after the recital of the *Amidah* (*SPB* 60; cf. *b. Ber.* 17a) contained such a petition: 'Our king and God, unite thy kingdom on earth, rebuild thy city, establish thy house and restore thy temple'.[21] Similarly, the petitions[22] following the core of the Grace after Meals begin with requests for the divine kingdom and universal acknowledgement of God's kingship. The 'Lord's prayer' (Mt. 6.9–13; Lk. 11.2–4), which begins with the sanctification of God's name and the wish for his kingdom likewise belongs to this genre of personal prayer.[23] Jewish and Christian liturgies alike ended with short formulae petitioning the coming of the redeemer *('Marana-tha'* and parallels: see below, p. 88).

2. *Universal acknowledgement of God's rule and the eradication of idolatry,* so prominent in Isaiah's Day of the Lord prophecy (2.19ff.) are expressed in the second paragraph of the *Aleinu* prayer:

'We hope, therefore (על כן נקוה), Lord our God, soon to behold thy majestic glory, when idols (lit., abominations) shall be removed from the earth and false

18. On the antiquity of this prayer, which today concludes every service, and was part of the *Malkuyot* section of the New Year prayer (תקיעתא דבי רב) cf. below, n. 24.

19. As is well known, the evening '*Amidah* prayer' (eighteen benedictions) is not obligatory. The standard evening service then concludes with the *Shema'* and its accompanying Benedictions.

20. Cf. I. Elbogen, *Der jüdische Gottesdienst in seiner geschichtlichen Entwicklung* (Frankfurt, 1931), pp. 102–105.

21. Cf. Elbogen, *ibid.* 59–60 on the prayer מלכנו אלהינו יחד שמך found in the prayer books of Amram Gaon and Saadya Gaon (9–10th centuries).

22. The number of the petitions which open with הרחמן: 'May the merciful…' vary in the different rites. Most contain, however, the basic elements found in the 'Lord's prayer': the kingdom of the Lord, his reign on heaven and earth, the request for daily livelihood and for deliverance from evil by implanting fear and love of the Lord, cf. E.D. Goldschmidt, *On Jewish Liturgy, Essays on Prayer and Religious Poetry* (1978), pp. 70–71 (Hebrew).

23. I will deal elsewhere with the nature of these personal meditations, including the 'Lord's Prayer'.

gods exterminated; when the world shall be perfected under the reign of the Almighty, and all mankind will call upon thy name' (*SPB* 93–94).[24]

This paragraph is an essential part of the New Year liturgy, and is in fact known as the *shophar* liturgy of the school of the third century Babylonian scholar Rab (תקיעתא דבי רב). However, this does not justify the assumption that it was originally composed in the third century CE. Most scholars today consider it an ancient prayer, from the second temple period.[25] The phrase, 'and the false gods exterminated' (והאלילים כרת יכרתון) in the section of על כן נקוה is a resonance of the phrase והאלילים כליל יחלוף 'and the idols shall vanish completely' in the Day of the Lord prophecy in Isa. 2 (v. 18).

3. *Revelation of God's glory and splendour.* So characteristic of the Day of the Lord prophecy, this is likewise prominent in the second paragraph of the *Aleinu* prayer cited above: 'We hope...soon to behold thy majestic glory'.[26] Similarly, in the Musaf prayer for festivals: 'Reveal the glory of thy kingship to us and appear and be exalted above us in the sight of all the living',[27] and in the prayer *Al hakkol* said before the reading of the Torah (*SPB* 216): 'Let his kingship be revealed and seen over us speedily and very soon' *(Tractate Soferim* 14.1).[28]

4. *The abolition of evil and tyranny,* a theme prevalent in the Day of the Lord prophecies and in the New Year service, is likewise found in the daily *Amidah:* 'Do speedily uproot and crush the arrogant kingdom (מלכות זדון תעקר)',[29] in the paragraph following the petition for the restoration of the ideal judiciary, wherein we find the request: 'Reign thus alone, over us, O Lord' (*SPB* 58).

The inclusion of eschatological motifs, and especially the notion of concluding a prayer with such motifs, is found in biblical hymns and prayers. The Song

24. The two paragraphs of the *Aleinu* prayer*: Aleinu* and *Al ken neqawweh* form an integrated unit. In the *Aleinu* paragraph God is extolled for separating Israel in the present from idol worshippers while in the *Al ken neqawweh* paragraph the hope is expressed that in the future the idol worshippers will abandon idolatry and accept the belief in the true God. The combination of these two ideas is indeed attested in the liturgical pericope of Jer. 10.1–16. On the one hand the idea of the particular religious inheritanceof Israel is brought to expression: 'the idols are vanity…not like these is the Lot (= God) of Jacob, for it is he who created all things (לא כאלה חלק יעקב כי יוצר הכל הוא)' (vv. 15–16); on the other hand, hope is expressed that 'the gods who did not make heaven and earth will perish' (vv. 11, 15). (For the integrity of Jer. 10.1–16 cf. M. Margalioth, 'Jeremiah X.1–16: A Re-examination', *VT* 30 [1980], pp. 295–308). On the affinities of the *Aleinu* prayer to Jer. 10.1–16 cf.:

Jer. 10.15–16	*Aleinu*
הבל המה...לא כאלה **חלק** יעקב כי **יוצר הכל** הוא	**לאדון הכל**... **ליוצר** בראשית... שלא שם **חלקנו** כהם... משתחווים **להבל**

25. See J. Heinemann, *Prayers in the Talmud: Forms and Patterns* (1977), pp. 173–75, and cf. recently E.E. Urbach, *The Halakhah* (1984) (Hebrew).

26. On עז תפארת as parallel to כבוד in the theophanic descriptions, cf. my article 'כבוד', *TWAT*, vol. IV (1982), cols. 28–29.

27. *SPB* 339, mentioned in *Tractate Soferim* 19.5 (ed. Higger, p. 327). The prayer is close in wording to the New Year's *Amidah* prayer מלוך על כל העולם, mentioned above.

28. *Ibid.,* 260.

29. In some versions we find also the phrase 'and let all wickedness perish as in a moment'. For the variants of the Benediction cf. I. Elbogen (above, n. 20), pp. 51–52.

of the Sea concludes: 'The Lord shall reign forever and ever' (Exod. 15.18). Psalm 29 concludes with the establishment of God's kingdom on earth (v. 10). Psalm 68 concludes with a call to all the kingdoms of the earth to acknowledge God's majesty. The doxology following the second book of Psalms concludes 'Let his glory fill the whole world. Amen and Amen' (72.19, cf. Num. 14.21). Psalm 22, a psalm of thanksgiving for salvation from distress, likewise ends with the hope that the whole world will acknowledge the divine salvation: 'Let all the ends of the earth pay heed and turn to the Lord, and the peoples of all nations prostrate themselves before you, for kingship is the Lord's and he rules the nations' (vv. 27–28 [Heb. 28–29]). Mesopotamian prayers also tend to end with an eschatological petition. The hymn to the god Shamash ends: 'May they bear your tribute...the wealth of the lands in sacrifice...may your throne-dais be renewed...whose utterance cannot be changed'.[30]

This tradition of eschatological prayer is continued in the book of Ecclesiasticus. In the prayers of Ben Sira (Ecclesiasticus 36), we find many eschatological elements later incorporated into the Jewish liturgy:

> Save us thou God of all, put thy awe upon all nations (שים פחדך על כל הגוים). Raise thy hand against the heathen and let them see thy power. As you became holy among us before their eyes so be honoured with us before our eyes. Let them learn, as we also have learned, that there is no God but thou... Hasten the destined hour (קץ) and remember the appointed time (מועד). For who can tell thee what to do? Gather all the tribes of Jacob (vv. 1–11).

The beginning of the prayer is echoed in the opening of the New Year *Amidah* liturgy (*SPB* 350, 360): 'Put thy awe upon all your creatures' (תן פחדך על כל מעשיך), while the continuation: 'be honoured with us' is echoed in the following section of this New Year prayer: 'Grant honour, O Lord, to thy people (תן כבוד לעמך)' (*ibid.*). The formula 'Raise thy hand against the heathen' (v. 3) is reflected in the abridged form of the daily *Amidah* (*SPB* 67): 'Raise thy hand against evildoers',[31] and 'Let them learn that there is no God but thou' (v. 5) parallels the second paragraph of *Aleinu:* 'May all the inhabitants of the world realize and know[32] that before thee every knee must bend' (*SPB* 94).

'Hasten the destined hour (קץ), remember the appointed time (מועד)' refers to the era of salvation, and we have already seen that these two words are used in Day of the Lord prophecies. The motif of the ingathering of the exiles, which follows, is also an integral part of the daily *Amidah* (*SPB* 58) and Jewish eschatology in general.

The prayer of Ben Sira continues:

30. W.G. Lambert, *Babylonian Wisdom Literature* (1960), p. 138, ll. 196–199; see M. Weinfeld, 'A Prayer to Shamash' *Shnaton* 2 (1977), p. 248 (Hebrew).

31. *b. Ber,* 29a. Cf. *y. Ber,* 4.3, 6a; see L. Ginsberg, *A Commentary on the Palestinian Talmud* (1941), p. 329.

32. 'Realize and know' יכירו וידעו occurs a number of times in the liturgy, and is apparently an ancient formula. It is attested in the *Aleinu* liturgy, in the morning prayer אתה הוא ה' (*SPB* 10) found in *Tannā dĕbē Eliahu* cited below, and in the *Amidah* of the afternoon service of Sabbath: 'let thy children realize and know that their rest is from thee' (*SPB* 257).

> Show mercy to the city of thy sanctuary, Jerusalem, city of thy dwelling place. Fill Zion with thy majesty; fill thy tabernacle with thy glory. Give acknowledgement to Your creation at the beginning; and fulfil the vision which has been spoken in thy name (vv. 13–15).

Here we find the motif of glorious revelation which is attested in both the daily and New Year liturgy. The rebuilding of Zion and Jerusalem are described as the fulfilment of prophecy. This idea is echoed in the daily *Amidah:* 'Return in mercy to thy city Jerusalem and dwell in it as thou hast promised (דברת)' (*SPB* 59). The 'glory' which is to fill Zion is identical with the 'divine Presence' (שכינה), which according to the *Abodah* Benediction of the *Amidah* (*SPB* 61–62) is to be restored to Zion: 'Be appeased, Lord, our God, and dwell in Zion (ושכון בציון)'.[33] All these are to be traced back to the prophecy of Zechariah (2.14; 8.2).

Both the prayer of Ben Sira and the daily *Amidah* are rooted in the eschatological hopes of the prophets. As I have elsewhere pointed out,[34] these aspirations are likewise to be found in Mesopotamian prophecies, but without the ideological-religious element of the elimination of idolatry. As in Israelite prophecy and Jewish liturgy, where we find expressions of aspiration for the ingathering of the exiles, the restoration of ideal justice, the end of evil, and the establishment of a cultic centre, so Mesopotamian prayers ended with eschatological petitions; as in Israel, both prayer and prophecy reflected eschatological hopes. It is likely that, as in many other cases, prophecy adapted liturgical material to its own purposes, and not vice versa. Although in later liturgy, verses from the prophets were incorporated into prayer, the original desire for the revelation and God's kingdom predates classical prophecy. It lies behind the expectations of the people as described by Amos (5.18–20).

Mowinckel correctly realized that the Day of the Lord theme is echoed in the Jewish prayer of the New Year. But he was incorrect in pinpointing the New Year service as the *Sitz im Leben* of this theme. The New Year's day, which is the day of creation and the day of the divine coronation, is especially appropriate for prayers regarding the future divine kingdom, but this need not lead to the conclusion that these aspirations first arose in this context, especially since they are reflected in the daily prayer as well. These hopes always existed, and were a dominant theme of Israelite religion from its inception. They were simply expressed most forcefully on God's coronation day.

The Day of the Lord as a Day of War

Until now we have dealt with the positive aspirations associated with the Day of the Lord. However, the prophets tell us that the Day of the Lord will have negative aspects as well: 'The Day of the Lord shall be darkness, not light' (Amos

33. This is the oldest version of the Benediction (*Lev. Rab.* 7.2 [ed, M. Margulies], p. 151); cf. the version in the Palestinian Genizah (J. Mann, 'Genizah Fragments', *HUCA* 2 [1925], p. 306). The conclusion of the Benediction today is 'who restores his *Shekinah* to Zion'.

34. M. Weinfeld, 'Mesopotamian Eschatological Prophecies', *Shnaton* 3 (1979), pp. 268–70 (Hebrew).

5.18), a day of war and retribution. This provided the basis for G. von Rad's position as to the *Sitz im Leben* of the Day of the Lord.[35] He took note of the war imagery associated with the Day of the Lord and concluded therefrom that the *Sitz im Leben* of the prophecies was the 'holy war', an Israelite institution dating from the conquest of Canaan. War in ancient Israel was a sacred undertaking; the Israelites purified themselves beforehand, the ark of the Lord was marched into battle, and fasts, sacrifices, and sacred assemblies were held (e.g. Judg. 20.26–27). The war imagery associated with the Day of the Lord suggested to von Rad that we are dealing with an ancient belief, from the time of the conquest, that God marches into battle with Israel. The Day of the Lord is the day on which God is victorious over his, and Israel's, enemies.

The Day of the Lord prophecies do indeed include martial motifs, such as declaration of war by horn blast (Zeph. 1.16), battle array (Isa. 13.4), or Jeremiah's elaborate description:

> Get ready buckler and shield, and move forward to battle! Harness the horses, mount, you horsemen! Fall in line, helmets on! Burnish the lances, don your armour!... Let not the swift get away. Let not the warrior escape. In the north, by the river Euphrates, they stagger and fall...That day shall be for the Lord God of Hosts... (46.3–10).

We also find there the ban (חרם), confusion, slaughter (Isa. 34.5–6), impossibility of escape, etc. The fact that the Day of the Lord theme is found primarily in prophecies to the nations, in conjunction with war, suggests to von Rad that the Israelite holy war is the birthplace of the theme. However, even before his research into the Day of the Lord, von Rad wrote about the Israelite holy war, and greatly exaggerated the centrality of this institution in Israelite thought.[36] In fact, all over the ancient world, war was seen as divine judgement, and there is nothing novel in the Israelite approach.[37] It must be admitted, however, that to counterbalance Mowinckel it was necessary to stress this neglected aspect of the Day of the Lord. Noteworthy in this regard is Ezek. 13.5: 'You did not enter the breaches and repair the walls for the House of Israel that they might stand up in battle on the Day of the Lord'. Ezekiel refers to a past Day of the Lord, the time of the destruction of Jerusalem. 'Your prophets, O Israel, have been like jackals among the ruins' (v. 4). The prophets of Israel did not do enough to 'repair the breaches' on that 'Day of the Lord', the day of the fall of Jerusalem.

The same applies to the author of Lamentations who looks back on the fall of Jerusalem and defines it as the 'day of the Lord's anger' (1.12; 2.22).[38] Isaiah too, speaks of the Day of the Lord as a day of war and destruction in the Valley of Vision. 'For my Lord God of Hosts has a day of tumult and din and confusion in the Valley of Vision' (22.5). Compare Jer. 46.10, with reference to the battle of Carchemish between Egypt and Babylon: 'But that day shall be for the Lord God

35. G. von Rad, 'The Origin of the Concept of the "Day of Yahweh" ', *JSS* 4 (1959), pp. 97–108.

36. *Idem*, *Der heilige Kreig im alten Israel* (1951).

37. See M. Weinfeld, 'Divine Intervention in War in Ancient Israel and in the Ancient Near East', in *History, Historiography and Interpretation, Studies in Biblical and Cuneiform Literatures* (ed. H. Tadmor and M. Weinfeld, 1983), pp. 121–47.

38. Cf. A.J. Everson, 'The Days of Yahweh', *JBL* 93 (1974), pp. 329–37.

of Hosts a day when he exacts retribution from his foes. The sword shall devour, it shall be sated and drunk with their blood. For the Lord God of hosts is preparing a sacrifice in the northland, by the river Euphrates.' The war is here described as God's sacrifice, as in Isa. 34.6:

> For YHWH holds a sacrifice in Bozrah; a great slaughter in the land of Edom.

And in 13.3:

> I have summoned my purified guests to execute my wrath; behold, I have called my stalwarts, my proudly exultant ones.

'Purified' guests are normally invited to partake of a sacrificial meal. Similarly, in Zeph. 1.7, we read:

> Be silent before my Lord God, for the Day of the Lord is approaching; for the Lord has prepared a sacrificial feast, has bidden his guests purify themselves.[39]

Meir Weiss[40] correctly contested von Rad's theory. According to Weiss, the two most important Day of the Lord prophecies, Amos 5 and Isaiah 2, contain no references to war: hence war alone cannot be seen as the *Sitz im Leben* of the Day of the Lord. However, even if war is not the only institution that gave rise to the Day of the Lord prophecies, one can hardly deny completely the connection between war and the Day of the Lord, in light of the above-cited references. An inscription recently discovered in Kuntillet 'Ajrud yields the following reference to war theophany: 'When God shines forth...mountains will be dissolved on the day of wa[r]'.[41] This proves that the idea of God's appearing in war was already prevalent in the days of Ahab and Jehoshaphat.

In fact, both Mowinckel's and von Rad's theories contain a kernel of truth.[42] The Day of the Lord is connected with Israelite aspirations for triumph and the establishment of God's kingdom, but as the occasion of the enthronement of the God of Israel, God of Justice, this is also the day on which evildoers are requited for their deeds. This, in turn, is bound up with divine war. One cannot therefore disregard the blacker aspect of the Day of the Lord, a day of judgement and war.

The Day of the Lord as The Day of Divine Revelation

It seems that the attempt to find the *Sitz im Leben* of the Day of the Lord is in vain: it is impossible to pinpoint a concrete institution or set of circumstances which gave rise to this concept. We are dealing with the belief in the advent of God to save Israel and mankind. This salvation involves both the eradication of evil through cosmic war and the establishment of cosmic redemption. It is only natural

39. For the development of the term זבח ('sacrifice') in the prophecies of the Day of the Lord, see M. Weiss (above, n. 5), pp. 54ff.

40. *Ibid.*

41. ובזרח...אל וימסן הרם בים מלח[מה] (cf. n. 4 above, and see my article: 'The Kuntillet 'Ajrud Inscriptions and their Significance', *Studi Epigrafici e Linguistici* 1 (1984), p. 126.

42. Cf. F.M. Cross, 'The Divine Warrior in Israel's Early Cult', *Biblical Motifs* (ed. A. Altmann; 1966), pp. 11–30.

that the people see in this day of divine theophany the promise of national redemption through which, in their view, the God of Israel's kingship will be manifested. This hope found expression in Psalm 47, which is nowadays recited before the blowing of the shophar on the New Year (cf. *Tr. Soferim* 18.11, ed. Higger, 322) and which is among the most important of the enthronement psalms, of which the *Sitz im Leben,* according to Mowinckel, is the New Year festival:

> All you peoples, clap your hands, raise a joyous shout to God. For the Lord Most High is awesome, great King over all the earth. He subjects peoples to us, sets nations at our feet. He extends[43] our inheritance for us, the pride of Jacob (גאון יעקב), whom he loved. Selah. God ascends midst acclamation; the Lord, to the blasts of the horn… God reigns over nations; God is seated in His holy throne…

'The pride of Jacob' (v. 5) parallels the greater Israelite heritage, which involves the subjugation of nations. Amos (6.8) opposes this pride in material greatness and says: 'I loathe the pride of Jacob, and I detest his fortresses'. Thus it is natural that Amos should stress the retribution of the Day of the Lord, which will be the lot of those who stress 'the pride of Jacob' at the expense of divine justice. For these people, the Day of the Lord is a day of darkness. They would do better to cease their sacrifices and see to the establishment of justice: 'I loathe, I spurn your festivals…If you offer me burnt offerings, or your meal offerings, I will not accept them… Spare me the sound of your hymns…but let justice well up like water, righteousness like an unfailing stream' (5.21–24). These verses directly follow the prophecy of 'the Day of the Lord'.

Isaiah likewise stresses the retribution aspect of the Day of the Lord. The Day of the Lord symbolizes for him the end of idolatry, which is the end of human pride: 'then man's haughtiness will be humbled, and the pride of man brought low. None but the Lord shall be exalted that day' (2.17). This is the purpose of God's future revelation according to Isaiah. There is no room in this new redemption for narrow-minded national interests: for soaring towers, mighty walls, ships of Tarshish or gallant barks. On this day, rather, what is important is the triumph of justice and God's kingship over humanity. The future redemption will bring retribution to each individual, and to every nation that violates the principles of justice: 'For the Lord of Hosts has ready a day against all that is proud and arrogant, against all that is lofty – so that it may be brought low: against the cedars of Lebanon, tall and stately… None but the Lord shall be exalted that day' (vv. 12–17). Retribution will strike every man, and then all will acknowledge their impotence and God's greatness.

It is impossible to apply the same standard to all the prophets. There is an important difference between, on the one hand, Amos and Isaiah – who lived during an era of prosperity and thus directed their ire against national pride and stressed an abstract concept of redemption, and on the other hand, Jeremiah, Ezekiel and others – who lived during the low point of Israelite history when vengeance on the nations became the central aspiration of the Day of the Lord. No two prophets have quite the same conception of the Day of the Lord.

43. Read ירחב instead of יבחר; cf. I.L. Seeligmann, 'Psalm 47', *Tarbiz* 50 (1981), p. 32 (Hebrew).

One should not seek a concrete *Sitz im Leben* for the Day of the Lord. It is the day on which God will appear to save his people and the entire world, i.e., to rule over the whole earth as he ruled over Israel during the Exodus and the revelation at Sinai, and as he revealed himself to save Israel in its wars. God arrives to save Israel, from the hand of the Canaanites or any other nation. In biblical theophanies, God leaves his holy place in order to do battle on Israel's behalf. In the blessing of Moses: 'the Lord came from Sinai; He shone upon them from Seir; He appeared from Mount Paran' (Deut. 33.2), which connects with the end of the blessing: 'Thus Israel dwells in safety; untroubled is Israel's abode, in a land of grain and wine, under heavens dripping dew' (33.28). In Deborah's song, God leaped forth from Edom to save Israel from the Canaanites: 'O Lord, when You came forth from Seir, advanced from the country of Edom, the earth trembled, the heavens dripped, yea, the clouds dripped water. The mountains quaked – before the Lord, Him of Sinai, before the Lord, God of Israel' (Judg. 5.4–35). Similar are Habakkuk 3 and Psalm 68.

The prophets also describe God as leaving his abode,[44] not necessarily to save, but to judge Israel and the nations. Thus, Mic. 1.3–4: 'For lo! the Lord is coming forth (יצא) from His dwelling place. He will come down and stride upon the heights of the earth. The mountains shall dissolve[45] under him and the valleys burst open.' This is in order to punish Samaria for her sin; God appears to exact vengeance from his enemies. Nahum (1.3–5) states: '...He travels in whirlwind and storm and clouds are the dust on His feet. He rebukes the sea and dries it up, and he makes all rivers fail. Bashan and Carmel languish and the blossoms of Lebanon wither. The mountains quake before him, and the hills melt. The earth heaves before him, the world and all that dwell therein.' The mythic vengeance against the sea is here combined with historical retribution: 'mountains quake because of him...who can stand before his wrath? Who can resist his fury?' (vv. 5–6).

The prophets make use of conventional symbols in describing God's salvation, but sometimes there is a surprise twist in that the enemies against whom God sets forth are not the enemies of Israel but Israel itself. Theophany motifs take on a negative air when used by the prophets, in order to advance their goals. Thus Amos speaks of darkness as opposed to light, even though darkness and light together symbolize God's advent in biblical theophanies: for example, in David's victory song, 2 Sam. 22 (= Psalm 18), where all the 'Day of the Lord' motifs appear in a description of national salvation.

> Then the earth rocked and quaked, the foundations of heaven shook...He mounted a cherub and flew; He was seen on the wings of the wind. He made pavilions of darkness about him, dripping clouds, huge thunderheads, in the brilliance before Him blazed fiery clouds. The Lord thundered forth from heaven, the Most High sent forth his voice. He let loose bolts, and scattered them; lightning, and put them to rout... (2 Sam. 22.7–15)

44. See J. Jeremias, *Theophanie* (WMANT, 10, 1965), p. 97f.

45. Cf. in the Kuntillet 'Ajrud inscription: 'The mountains shall dissolve'; see above, nn. 4, 41.

Here we find both darkness and brilliance together. The brilliance is of course the divine fire, enveloped in clouds, darkness and thick mist.[46] Amos plays a game with these symbols. He says, as it were: You expect brilliance in God's appearance, but don't forget that there is also darkness and clouds, which symbolize catastrophe.[47]

Ezekiel, Joel and Zechariah used the Day of the Lord motifs in order to describe the final 'war to end all wars' which will lead to the glorification of God's name. All nations assemble near Mount Zion, in Jerusalem, or in the Valley of Jehoshaphat, and the Lord judges them. This trial leads to Israel's redemption. Ezekiel and Zechariah stress that all nations will thus be led to recognize God's greatness: 'And the Lord shall be king over all the earth. On that day the Lord shall be one and his name one' (Zech. 14.9). 'Thus I will manifest my greatness and my holiness...and they shall know that I am the Lord' (Ezek. 38.23). The same idea, with less nationalistic zeal and without the assembly of the nations is expressed in the simple statement of Isaiah: 'As for idols, they shall vanish completely' (2.18). This idea is also central to the *Aleinu* prayer: '...when the false gods will be exterminated; when the world will be perfected under the reign of Shaddai, and all mankind will call upon thy name' (*SPB* 94).

The symbols which typify the Day of the Lord reflect no concrete *Sitz im Leben,* but are rather literary conventions for describing theophany. The revelation and the giving of the Torah at Sinai are also accompanied by thunder and lightning, horn blasts and trembling mountains – clouds and darkness on the one hand, and a burning fire on the other – the same symbols used to describe God in battle.

Von Rad's assumption that war lies at the heart of the Day of the Lord concept provides no explanation of the revelation at Sinai, where God appears under similar circumstances, without any reference to a holy war. Mowinckel indeed takes Exod. 19 into account in his discussion of Day of the Lord imagery. According to him the revelation at Sinai is likewise a reflection of the New Year celebration, at which the people accept God's laws. But this is, of course, only a hypothesis.

In fact, the theophany of the Day of the Lord is no different from any other theophany in the Bible, or, for that matter, in ancient Near Eastern literature. These images are not the clue to the *Sitz im Leben* of the Day of the Lord. They are literary conventions employed in describing theophany, whether for the purpose of war, judgement, or law-giving. It has been suggested that a volcanic eruption lies behind the Sinai imagery in Exod. 19,[48] but this theory is erroneous. The natural upheavals depicted in the theophany are too literary conventions for theophany descriptions in the ancient world.[49] When Amon, the Egyptian god, sent forth his voice, the earth trembled. When Zeus sat upon his throne, Olympus quaked (*Iliad* VIII, 442–443). Therefore, there is no basis for Gunkel's claim that descriptions

46. The notion of the כבוד of YHWH appearing in a cloud in the Israelite priestly literature is actually based on such concepts; cf. my article 'כבוד' (above, n. 26) cols. 32–34.

47. See M. Weiss (above, n. 5), p. 51.

48. Cf. e.g., R. de Vaux, *The Early History of Israel,* I (trans. D. Smith, 1978), pp. 433–39.

49. Cf. my article cited above, n. 37.

of natural upheaval (other than those connected with the sea) are based on the Sinai imagery, which is the archetype of such motifs in the prophetic books. The Sinai theophany itself is rooted in the ancient belief that when God appears the earth trembles.[50]

Furthermore, if we investigate ancient Near Eastern theophanies we find even closer parallels to the Day of the Lord descriptions, involving both war and judgement. Thus we read of Ishtar in Mesopotamia: 'Ishtar, torch of heaven and earth, splendour of the entire universe...a burning fire which devours the enemy... when your name is mentioned heaven and earth tremble. You judge men with justice and righteousness...You turn to the oppressed and exploited and justify him daily'.[51]

We have here descriptions of both a military and a judicial nature. It seems that the fact that the God of justice (e.g. of Sinai) has the same characteristics as the God of war, both in Israel and in Mesopotamia, is due to the fact that the 'judge', especially in Israel (compare the 'judges' in the book of Judges), functions not only as magistrate, but as warrior as well. The two tasks are in fact identical: the salvation of oppressed individual from oppressor and of the oppressed nation from the oppressive nation. In Israel and the ancient Near East, the king was both supreme commander of the army and supreme judge. These tasks were combined most naturally, and this natural combination is reflected in the identical theophany imagery employed at war and in justice.[52]

Especially significant as far as ancient Near Eastern parallels are concerned is the Day of the Lord prophecy in Isaiah 2, which exhibits many points of comparison to the theophany of Psalm 29. These two passages deal not with war, but with the revelation of God's glory, or, in Isaiah's words, the fear (פחד) of the Lord and the splendour (הדר) of his majesty' (2.19). This strange juxtaposition of 'fear' (פחד) and 'splendour' can be explained on the basis of Akkadian *pulḫu melammu*, which we find in reference to both divine revelation and the presence of a human king. *pulḫu* is fear, *melammu* is splendour. The two expressions are a *hendiadys* that describes the theophany as simultaneously splendid and terrifying. Hence the *splendour and fear* of the verse in Isaiah. Elsewhere I have dealt with biblical parallels to *pulḫu melammu*;[53] here we shall confine our discussion to Isaiah 2.

In Mesopotamia we find a text in which *pulḫu melammu* appears in a context similar to that of Isaiah 2: men are judged and requited by the goddess *Inanna*, who appears in terror and splendor. Furthermore. The *Anuna*, a type of lesser divinity, hide from Inanna's splendour in crevices of the rocks, like bats. In this text, called *The Exaltation of Inanna* from the end of the third millennium BCE, we read: 'As men appear before your fear and glory they are requited as they

50. See S.E. Loewenstamm, 'The Trembling of Nature during Theophany', *Comparative Studies in Biblical and Ancient Oriental Literatures* (AOAT, 204; 1980), pp. 173–89; J. Jeremias (above. n. 44), pp. 97ff.

51. E. Ebeling, *Die Akkadische Gebetserie 'Handerhebung'* (1953), p. 130, ll. 20ff.

52. Cf., M. Weinfeld, *Social Justice* (above, n. 13), pp. 189–90.

53. M. Weinfeld, 'כבוד' (above, n. 26), cols. 27–31.

deserve…the *Anuna* (lesser divinities) fly to and fro as bats and flee from you to the crevices of rocks. These dare not stand before your fear and splendour.'[54]

These sentences are typologically parallel to Isaiah 2.12–21:

> For the Lord of hosts has (ready) a day against all that is proud and arrogant…And men shall enter caverns in the rock and hollows in the ground – Before the fear of the Lord and the splendour of his majesty, when he comes forth to overawe the earth. On that day men shall fling away to the flying foxes and the bats, the idols of silver and the idols of gold which they made for worshipping. And they shall enter the clefts in the rocks and the crevices in the cliffs, before the fear of the Lord and the splendour of his majesty, when he comes forth to overawe the earth.

The similarity is, of course, only in the form and expressions used to describe the theophany, not in the content and purpose. In Isaiah, God appears in order to lay low man's pride, which attaches divine value to human handicraft. Idolatry, for Isaiah, symbolizes power and the worship of power. When God reveals himself, all men will know that he alone is exalted, and will abandon the idols of their own handicraft that they now worship.

It can hardly be expected that these ideas would be found in Babylonian literature, but the very idea of the terror that results from the theophany is expressed identically in Israel and in Babylonia. The conventions are similar; the ideas are thoroughly different.

Theophanies similar to that of Isaiah 2 and its Babylonian parallel are found also in the revelations to Moses and Elijah at Horeb. Both stood in a cave or rock when God appeared. Regarding Moses: 'As my Presence passes by, I will put you in a cleft of the rock' (Exod. 33.22), and regarding Elijah: 'When Elijah heard, he wrapped his mantle about his face and stood at the entrance of the cave' (1 Kgs 19.13). Compare also Exod. 3.6, 'And Moses hid his face, for he was afraid to look at the Lord'. Even more interesting are God's words to Job out of the whirlwind. Here we find a hitherto undiscussed parallel to Isaiah. There, in reference to man's impotence as opposed to God's omnipotence, we read: 'Deck yourself now with grandeur and eminence (גאון וגבה),[55] clothe yourself in glory and splendour (הוד והדר). Scatter wide your raging anger; see every proud man and bring him low. See every proud man and humble him, and bring them down where they stand. Bury them all in the earth; hide their faces in obscurity' (Job 40.10–13). Here we find all the elements familiar to us from Isaiah 2: (1) splendour and anger appearing simultaneously; (2) the humbling of the arrogant; (3) hiding in the dust – all of which are the result of God's appearing in the whirlwind. One can hardly consider these elements in Job as parts of a Day of the Lord prophecy.

In all the above cases we have a conventional model of ancient theophany. However, in the ancient Near East, the god sheds some of his glory and majesty on the king, and therefore the appearance of the king in battle is similar to that of the gods. Even the motif of hiding occurs in such a context. In the Sennacherib

54. W. W. Hallo, J. J. A. von Dijk, *The Exaltation of Inanna* (1968) 16, ll. 21ff.

55. For these expressions being synonymous with הדר/כבוד, cf. my 'כבוד' (above, n. 26), cols. 28–29.

inscriptions we read: 'Great kings leave their dwellings (in the face of *pulḫu melammu*) as bats in caves fly alone to abandoned places'.[56] We might add, in reference to Isaiah 2, that the motif of throwing away gold and silver in order to depend upon the Lord alone recurs in Zeph. 1.17–18: 'I will bring distress upon the people and they shall walk like blind men, because they sinned against the Lord...Moreover, their silver and gold shall not avail to save them on the Day of the Lord's wrath'. Compare also Ezek. 7.19: 'They shall throw their silver into the streets, and their gold shall be treated as something unclean. Their silver and gold shall not avail to save them on the Day of the Lord's wrath to satisfy their hunger or to fill their stomachs, for they made them stumble into guilt.' It would not be justified to speak of direct influence of Zephaniah on Ezekiel, or vice versa. We are dealing with expressions typical of a certain genre: one of the motifs of the Day of the Lord prophecy is the futility of gold and silver in the face of God's majesty. This motif is found as well in Proverbs, a completely neutral book as far as prophecy is concerned: 'Wealth is of no avail on the day of wrath (ביום עברה)' (11.4). This is obviously the same conception, applied by the prophets to the Day of the Lord.

The Sanctification of the Divine Name and the Establishment of the Divine Kingdom

In light of the above, it seems likely that the belief in a future redeeming revelation lies at the heart of the Day of the Lord prophecies, and is expressed in the prayers of the people. Although the people are aware, and the prophets constantly remind them, that this revelation is bound up with a last judgement in which even Israelite evildoers will not be spared, the central aspect of the revelation is the sanctification of God's name and the establishment of the God of Israel as King of the earth. This is expressed in Ezekiel's prophecy (38.18–23) regarding Gog: 'On that day...a terrible earthquake shall befall the land of Israel...I will punish him (the enemy) with pestilence and bloodshed...hailstones and sulphurous fire...Thus will I manifest my greatness and my holiness, and make myself known in the sight of many nations', and in the prophecy of Zechariah (14.3–9): 'The Lord will come forth and make war on those nations...there shall be a continuous day only the Lord knows when – of neither day nor night... And the Lord shall be king over all the earth...the Lord will be one and his name one'. Compare also the passage in Isa. 5.16–17: 'And the Lord of Hosts is exalted in judgement: the Holy God sanctified by righteousness', a passage which belongs to Isaiah's Day of the Lord prophecy in ch. 2.[57] These motifs of sanctification of God's name and the establishment of his kingdom became dominant in the liturgy. We have cited above references to God's kingdom in the liturgy: to these must be added references to the sanctification of his name.

56. D.D. Luckenbill, *The Annals of Sennacherib* (1924), p. 24; i.18.

57. Verses 15–16 interrupt the flow of Isa. 5 and their style belongs rather to 2.6ff. (see Commentaries).

The *Amidah* prayers of the New Year contain references to the sanctification of God's name along with reference to his kingship: After the petition 'Rule over us thou alone speedily', we find 'Thou art holy and thy name is awesome (קדוש אתה ונורא שמך)' (*SPB* 351,361), in connection with which Isa. 5.16, 'And the Lord of Hosts is exalted by judgement; the Holy God sanctified with righteousness', is cited. A Benediction regarding the sanctification of God's name (קדושת השם) is contained in the daily *Amidah as* well (*SPB* 55) and according to ancient sources (*Sifre*, *Deut.*, 343) and Geniza texts,[58] this Benediction also contained the above-mentioned phrase 'Thou art holy and thy name is awesome', now recited only on the New Year. The juxtaposition of God's holy name and his kingship is a dominant motif in all Jewish liturgy. The congregation must recite seven times daily the *Kaddish*,[59] which begins with the sanctification of God's name and the establishment of his kingdom. Although its origins are unclear, the *Kaddish* has very ancient roots and it expresses the Israelite aspiration of the Day of the Lord.[60]

The 'complete *Kaddish*' is recited at the end of each service, and is the summit of all the prayers. Similarly, the *Aleinu* prayer is recited toward the end of each service. This poetic Hebrew prayer expresses the hope that idolatry will pass from the earth, that the world will be perfected in the kingdom of the Almighty and that all will accept the yoke of God's kingship. As we have pointed out, it is accepted in modern scholarship that this prayer is from second temple times. It is in fact the credo recited by the worshipper at the end of the service.

Other prayers which combine the sanctification of the divine name and the establishment of the divine kingdom, include the prayer before the reading of the Torah, cited in *Tractate Soferim* 14.1: 'Magnified and hallowed, praised and glorified...be the name of the supreme King of Kings...in the world which he has created...according to his desire...May his kingdom be revealed and seen by us' (*SPB* 210), which is in fact a Hebrew version of the Aramaic *Kaddish.* Compare also the Lord's prayer: 'Hallowed be thy name. Thy kingdom come: thy will be done on earth as in heaven (=throughout the world)' (Mt. 6.9–10; Lk. 11.2). Compare also the prayer in the preliminary morning service, cited in the Midrash *Tanna debe Eliahu:* 'Reveal thy holiness to those who sanctify thy name...let all mankind realize and know that thou alone art God over all the kingdoms on earth; gather them that hope for thee from the four corners of the earth...who among all thy creatures can say unto thee: what dost thou?...' (*SPB* 10). This liturgy has much in common with the prayer in Ecclesiasticus 36 quoted above; especially salient are the parallels in the motifs of sanctification of the Lord: the realization of all the inhabitants of the world that there is no god besides YHWH; the hope of the ingathering of the exiles, coupled with the idea of absolute sovereignty of God ('who can say to God: what dost thou?').

58. See, e.g., S. Schechter, 'Genizah Specimens', *JQR* 10 (1898), pp. 656–57; see also below chapter 5, pp. 91–93.

59. Cf., e.g., ערוך השולחן (by J.M. Epstein), אורח חיים, par. 54.

60. See above, n. 17.

Coming of the Day of the Lord – Soon and Speedily

The anticipation of the divine kingdom and the wish that it be revealed 'speedily and soon' (בעגלא בזמן קריב, *Kaddish*), is also rooted in the prophecies of the Day of the Lord:

> The great day of the Lord is approaching…most swiftly (קרוב ומהר מאד) (Zeph. 1.14).
> The time has come; the day is near (קרוב היום) (Ezek. 7.7).
> For a day is near. A day of the Lord is near (Ezek. 30.3).
> For the day of the Lord has come. It is close (קרוב) (Joel 2.1).
> For the day of the Lord is close (קרוב) in the valley of decision (Joel 4.14).
> Yea, against all nations, the day of the Lord is close (קרוב) (Obad. 15).
> For the vision is a witness (read עֵד; see above p. 70) for the appointed time…even if it tarries, wait for it still. It will surely come, without delay (Hab. 2.3).

Compare the following liturgical passages:

> Rebuild it (the Temple) *soon, in our days* (בקרוב בימינו) (*Amidah*, *SPB* 59).
> Speedily cause the offspring of thy servant David to flourish (*Amidah*, *SPB* 60).
> May his kingdom be revealed very soon (prayer before the reading of the Torah; *SPB* 83).
> *We hope…soon to behold thy majestic glory* (*Aleinu*, *SPB 94*).
> May he establish his kingdom…speedily and *soon* (*Kaddish*, *SPB* 94).
> Speedily in our days, in our lifetime do dwell there forever (Sabbath morning *Qedushah, SPB* 199).

Compare also the following verses from the Gospel of Luke:

> …they thought that the reign of God will reveal itself at any moment (Lk. 19.11).
> …you may know that the kingdom of God is near (ἐγγύς) (Lk. 21.31).
> The kingdom of God has come close (ἤγγικεν) to you (Lk. 10.9).
> The kingdom of God has come close (ἤγγικεν) (Lk. 10.11).

The closeness of the Day of the Lord must encourage the people to repent. Thus Isa. 56.1: 'Observe what is right and do what is just, for soon my salvation shall come…'; cp. 51.4–5: 'Hearken to me my people. The triumph I grant is near, the salvation has gone forth'; Mt. 3.2: 'Repent for the kingdom of heaven is close to you (ἤγγικεν)', and Mk. 1.15: 'The time has come, the kingdom of God is close to you. Repent.'

The Hope for Salvation

The 'longing' for the Lord that comes boldly to expression in the words of the prophets (compare above in the beginning of this study) continues in the liturgy of the second temple period. Thus we read in the Qumran prayer devoted to Zion:[61] 'Great is your hope, O Zion…those who desire (המתאוים) the day of your salvation will rejoice in your plentiful glory…How they hoped for your salvation… Your hope will never die, O Zion, and your aspiration will never be

61. J.A. Sanders, *The Psalm Scroll of Cave 11* (11QPs.^{a}), *DJD* IV (1965) cols. 22; 2ff.

forgotten... Take the vision which speaks of you...'. This is reminiscent of the formula in the prayer for the Davidic kingdom in the daily *Amidah:* 'For we have hoped for your salvation all day' (*SPB* 60). 'Take the vision which speaks of you' can be compared to Ecclesiasticus 36.15: 'Fulfil the vision spoken in thy name'.

Anticipation of the divine kingdom was considered especially meritorious. Thus Dan 12.12 'Happy is the man who waits', and Isa. 30.18: 'Happy are all who wait for him'. The Gospels also hold those who wait for the Lord in special esteem: 'Joseph of Aramithea...a man who waited for the kingdom of God' (Mk. 15.43; Lk. 23.51).

In the Aramaic Targumim, one who anticipates the divine kingdom is called מחמד, a 'desirer', thus in the Targum to Jer. 31.5: 'Those who desire (מחמדיו) the years of consolation (נחמתא) to come, who say: when will we arise and go up to Zion to be seen before our God'. In the Targum to 2 Sam. 23.4. 'And it shall be well with you who desired (מחמדיו) the years of consolation (נחמתא) to come'. 'Consolation' (נחמתא) as a term for the redemption is ascribed in the Talmud[62] to Simeon ben Shetah and Judah b. Tabbai (first century BCE): 'may I not live to see the consolation if...(לא אראה בנחמה)'. These rabbis lived during the second temple period, and thus the consolation is not necessarily the rebuilding of the temple but rather all eschatological hopes. In Targum Pseudo-Jonathan to Gen. 1.21 we read that Leviathan and his partner are ready for 'the day of consolation', i.e., the feast of the redemption. (This feast is referred to in the Apocrypha, cf. 1 Bar. 29.4, and the gospels, cf. Mt. 8.11; 26.29; Lk. 13.29–30; 14.15; 22.18.) Compare the reference to consolations (נחמתא) in the *Kaddish,* and the rabbinic statement that the day of consolation is hidden from man (*b. Pes.* 54b).

One should mention in this context the liturgical exclamations *marana tha* (= master, come) at the end of 1 Corinthians (16.21) and at the end of Revelation (22.20). There, Jesus says: 'Yes, I am coming soon', to which the response is 'Amen, come, Lord Jesus'. The same response *marana tha* is found at the end of the Grace of the Meal at Didache (10.6), which encompasses eschatological petitions such as 'Hosanna (save us), God of David'.[63] This is to be compared with the prayers at the end of the Jewish grace after meals: 'May the merciful one send us Elijah the prophet...' (*SPB* 429), 'Make us worthy of the days of the Messiah' (*SPB* 430). The eschatological aspirations of Judaism were then adopted by the early Christians, but the object of the aspirations changed from 'Lord God' to 'Lord Jesus'. See below p. 118.

In addition to the above-cited eschatological petitions at the closing of various liturgies, we have the אין כאלהינו prayer at the end of the Jewish service (*SPB* 238), whose acrostic reads אמן בא ('Amen, come'), similar to the Christian formulae.[64]

62. *b. Mak.* 5b and parallels.

63. G. Alon, *Studies in Jewish History,* I (1967), p. 290 (Hebrew).

64. E. Werner, 'The Doxology in Synagogue and Church, A Liturgico-Musical Study', *HUCA* 19 (1945–46), p. 302, n. 89.

To sum up: The belief in a final revelation of God to save the world thus unites all Israelite sources, from the prayer of Moses to the contemporary liturgy. This salvation involves the abolition of evil; hence the dim aspects of the Day of the Lord prophecies (compare the phrase, 'the birthpangs of the Messiah', in later Judaism.) The details differ in the various sources, and the 'day' takes on different characteristics in Amos from those in Jeremiah, Ezekiel or Daniel. Daniel in turn differs from the zealots of the Roman period in that he speaks of a redemption 'without hands': באפס יד (8.25), די לא בידין (2.45). What is similar in the prophecies and in the beliefs of the people in all generations is the conviction that the redemption will indeed come, and that God's name will be sanctified on earth. All generations are united in the belief that the redemption is coming 'soon', though exactly in what manner was always subject to various interpretations.

Chapter 5

THE ANGELIC SONG OVER THE LUMINARIES IN THE QUMRAN TEXTS

There are in the Qumran Psalms Scroll (11QPs[a]), in addition to the psalms themselves, fragments of other hymns and prayers the nature and essential characteristics of which have so far not been investigated. In this study we shall analyse the so-called 'Hymn to the Creator' (col. 26.9–15).[1]

The 'Hymn to the Creator' appears in the scroll immediately after Ps. 150.[2] In this hymn we find in 26.12 the angels singing at the very phenomenon upon which the *Yoṣer Qedushah* of the morning[3] is based and which, as we shall see, is further reflected in the books of Ben Sira and Jubilees.

1. J.A. Sanders, *The Psalms Scroll of Qumran Cave 11 (11QPs.[a]), Discoveries in the Judean Desert* (=*DJD*) vol. 4 (1965); J.A. Sanders, *The Dead Sea Psalms Scrolls* (1967). See *DJD* 4.40, 47, 76–79, 89–91.

2. On the importance of this position see chapter 2.

3. For the *Yoṣer Qedushah* cf. recently J. Heinemann in I. Elbogen, התפילה בישראל בהתפתחותה ההיסטורית (1972), pp. 52–53. The argument that the *Yoṣer Qedushah* does not appear in the Genizah documents is now refuted by the significant number of Genizah fragments which contain *Yoṣer Qedushah* liturgies (cf. e.g. the fragments listed by J. Heinemann, *ibid.*, 53). Very instructive are the passages from the Genizah published by S. Schechter, *Gedenkbuch zur Erinnerung an D. Kaufmann* (1900), p. 54 (Hebrew) and S. Asaf, 'מסדרי התפילה בארץ ישראל' *Sefer Dinaburg* (1949), p. 120 (Hebrew). The former reads: יוצר משרתים אשר משרתיו אלף עומדים לפניו: רבו רבי רבבות סובבים את כסאו. כלם אהובים... The latter reads אשר משרתיו אלף אלפי אלפים עומדים ברום עולם ומשמיעים... These passages, influenced by Dan. 7.10 and Ps. 68.18, are very close to the liturgical passage in the Epistle to the Corinthians of Clement of Rome 34.7: 'Ten thousand times ten thousand were doing service to him crying out "Holy, Holy, Holy, Lord Sabaoth, the whole creation is full of His Glory" ', and Apostolic Constitutions VIII xii 27: 'Say together the thousand times ten thousand of angels, incessantly and with constant and loud voices, and let the people say it with them: "Holy, Holy, Holy, Lord of Hosts, heaven and earth are full of His glory" ' (*Didascalia et Constitutiones Apostolorum* [ed. F.X. Funk, 1905], vol. I). On the reflection of the Jewish *Qedushah* liturgy in 1 Clem. and Ignatius to the Ephesians see D. Flusser, 'Sanktus und Gloria', *Festschrift O. Michel* (1963), pp. 132ff. For the Jewish *Qedushah* liturgy and especially the *Yoṣer Qedushah* embodied in the Apostolic Constitutions, Book VII, ch. 35, see W. Bousset, 'Eine jüdische Gebetssamlung im siebenten Buch der apostolischen Konstitutionen', *Nachrichten von der Gesellschaft der Wissenschaften zu Göttingen*, Phil. Hist. Kl., 1915, 435ff. It should be admitted that the angelic praise is an independent unit interpolated into the *Yoṣer* Benediction. The formula המחדש בטובו בכל יום תמיד מעשה בראשית with which the benediction closes (S. Singer, *The Standard Prayer Book*, [1943] =*SPB*) 46–47) is almost identical to the opening phrase ובטובו מחדש בכל יום תמיד מעשה בראשית (*SPB*, 45), creating a *Wiederaufnahme*, bringing us back to the original theme the continuity of which has been interrupted. (On this phenomenon in biblical literature see C. Kuhl, 'Die 'Wiederaufnahme' – ein literarkritisches

The Qumran Text and its Parallels in Common Jewish Liturgy

Not only do we find in the Qumran passage that God's establishing of the luminaries of heaven is associated with the song of the angels; the very language of the hymn attests to its affinity to the various forms of the *Qedushah*, mainly to the *Amidah Qedushah* and the *Yoṣer Qedushah*. Let us analyse the text.[4]

Great and holy is the Lord the holiest of holy ones for every generation.	גדול וקדוש ה׳ קדוש קדושים לדור ודור.
Majesty precedes Him, and following Him is the rush of many waters.	לפניו הדר ילך ואחריו המון מים רבים.
Grace and truth surround His presence; truth and justice and righteousness are the foundation of His throne.	חסד ואמת סביב פניו אמת ומשפט וצדק מכון כסאו.
He separates light from darkness, by the knowledge of His mind He established the dawn.	מבדיל אור מאפלה שחר הכין בדעת לבו.
When all His angels had witnessed (it) they sang aloud, for He showed them what they had not known.	אז ראו כל מלאכיו וירננו כי הראם את אשר לוא ידעו.
He clothes the mountains with produce, good food for every creature.	מעטר הרים תנובות אוכל טוב לכול חי.

A.
The opening line גדול וקדוש ה׳ קדוש קדושים לדור ודור is clearly reflected in the various forms of the *Qedushah* and the Benediction of *Qedushat Hashem*:

1. לדור ודור המליכו לאל כי מלך[5] גדול וקדוש אתה recited daily, according to the *Seder Rav Amram Gaon;*[6]
2. לדור ודור נגיד גדלך ולנצח נצחים קדושתך נקדיש (*SPB*, 55), designated for the Reader only in most rites;

Prinzip?' *ZAW* 64 [1952], pp. 1–11). However, even if it is an interpolation (see also Flusser, *ibid.*, 140 n. 1), this has no bearing on the dating and liturgical use of the interpolation. It is quite possible that the phrase quoted was repeated because the angelic-song section, itself ancient, disrupted the continuity of the benediction, rendering it necessary to compose an ending similar to the beginning; see L. Ginzberg, פירושים וחידושים בירושלמי, 4.156 (New York: JTS, 1941). The extensive material collected by A. Büchler, 'La Kedouscha du Yocer chez les Gueonim' (*REJ* 53 [1907], pp. 220–30) affirms that this liturgy itself was well known and accepted, but that some authorities held that it was not to be recited by the private worshipper, just as is the case with the *Amidah Qedushah* (Maimonides, *Hilkot Tefillah* 7.17). This led to the *Qedushah* being entirely omitted from the benediction in the *Siddur R. Saadia Gaon* (ed. Mekiṣe Nirdamim, 13).

4. J.A. Sanders, *DJD* 4, 26.9–12. The translation is from Sanders' 1967 edition.
5. For the place of enthronement (המלכה) in the *Qedushah*, cf. my forthcoming study on the biblical and ancient Near Eastern background of the *Qedushah*.
6. *Seder Rav Amram Gaon* (ed. D.E. Goldschmidt, 1971), p. 24.

3. אתה קדוש ושמך קדוש וקדושים בכל יום יהללוך סלה (*SPB*, 55), recited by the individual worshipper; and, in two Genizah versions;

4. אתה קדוש ושמך קדוש ולך יאמרו קדושים קדוש[7]

5. לך יאמרו קדושים קדוש ברוך אתה ה׳ האל הקדוש[8]

In the morning *Amidah Qedushah* for the Sabbath and holidays, according to the Ashkenazic rite, the reading is תתגדל ותתקדש... לדור ודור ולנצח נצחים (*SPB*, 199). At the conclusion of the *Qedushah* of the *Musaf* service for the New Year and Day of Atonement: כי מקדישיך כערכך (בקדשתך or) קדשת, נאה לקדוש פאר מקדושים.[9] Finally, in an ancient version found in the *Qedushah* songs of the Hekhalot literature, יתקדש שמך קדושתך יתגדל בגדולה לנצח עד סוף כל הדורות כי גבורתך לנצחי נצחים.[10]

All the components of the Qumran version – גדול וקדוש, לדור ודור, קדוש קדושים[11] – are thus present in the various forms of the benediction of *Qedushah Hashem* and in the *Qedushah* itself.

That גדול וקדוש was considered an essential element of the *Qedushat Hashem* benediction may be learned from the version of the *Amidah* found in a Cambridge Genizah fragment published by E. Fleischer,[12] which reads: נקדש את שמך... ויאמר והיה ה׳ למלך... צהלי ורני יושבת ציון כי גדול בקרבך קדוש ישראל... ברוך אתה ה׳ האל הקדוש. Since the publication of this version, E.S. Rosenthal has shown[13] that the passage in *y. Ber.* 1.5, 3d (=*Ta'an.* 2.3, 65c): 'As for those who say צהלי ורני etc. (Isa. 12.6), this is not considered a 'verse-benediction', deals with the recitation of a verse of scripture as part of the benediction of *Qedushat Hashem* like the custom reflected in the Genizah passage. We may conclude, therefore, that the formula גדול וקדוש, 'Great and Holy', was an accepted portion of the benediction of *Qedushah* in the period of the Palestinian Talmud.

Recently, N. Wieder has pointed out[14] that the same verse, צהלי ורני (Isa. 12.6), appears in the description of the *Amidah* in a Genizah fragment from the

7. J. Mann, 'Genizah Fragments of the Palestinian Order of Service', *HUCA* 2 (1925), p. 296.

8. *Ibid.*, p. 335 n. 134. The Qumran text shows that קדוש קדושים is an epithet related to God.

9. Appearing as early as the poems of Yannai, see *Piyyuṭei Yannai* (ed. M. Zulai, 1938) 2.336. For a discussion on this passage and those accompanying it, see E.D. Goldschmidt, מחזור לימים הנוראים, vol. 1, *Rosh Hashanah* (1970), p. 43.

10. A. Altmann, 'שירי קדושה בספרות ההיכלות הקדומה', *Melilah* 2 (1946) 23 (58a, ll. 16ff.). The *Qedushah* occurs very often in *Hekhalot* literature, cf. P. Schäfer (ed.), *Synopse zur Hekhalot-Literatur* (1981); see recently M. Bar-Ilan, 'קווי יסוד להתהוותה של הקדושה וגיבושה', *Daat* 2 (1980), pp. 10–14.

11. קדוש קדושים is congruent in meaning and construction with אדיר אדירנו which is found in the *Musaf Qedushah* on the festivals and High Holy Days (see Elbogen, 66, 521). The pleonastic type of the construct state of two nouns of the same root encountered in קדוש קדושים and אדיר אדירנו is especially prevalent in later literature; cf. Y. Avishur, *The Construct State of Synonyms in Biblical Rhetoric* (Jerusalem: Kiryat Sefer, 1977) (Hebrew), p. 83, 175 (for קדוש קדושים see the reference there to פיוטי ינאי).

12. E. Fleischer, 'לנוסחה הקדום של קדושת העמידה', *Sinai* 63 (1968), pp. 240–41.

13. E.S. Rosenthal, 'Two Comments', *Tarbiz* 41 (1972), p. 450 (Hebrew).

14. N. Wieder, 'On an Obscure Passage in the Palestinian Talmud', *Tarbiz* 43 (1974), pp. 46–52 (Hebrew). On צהלי ורני in the *Qedushah* of the Karaites, see Bar-Ilan (above, n. 10), pp. 15–16.

Adler collection after לדור ודור. Wieder thus demonstrates a connection between the formula גדול וקדוש and לדור ודור, and the verse צהלי ורני which contains the words 'Great and Holy'. Now it becomes evident that גדול וקדוש was recited together with לדור ודור already in the Qumran liturgy.

Alongside גדול וקדוש in the *Qedushah* benediction we find also קדוש ונורא, 'holy and awesome': קדוש אתה ונורא שמך.[15] The triplet גדול,נורא,קדוש is attested, in fact, in the liturgy of the Bible itself. In the enthronement psalm (Psalm 99), in which a triple '*Qedushah*', in the form of three separate refrains echoes throughout (vv. 3, 5, 9), we read: יודו[16] שמך גדול ונורא קדוש הוא, 'Let them praise Your name, Great and Awesome One! Holy is He!' The formula גדול וקדוש, then, existed alongside that of קדוש ונורא found in the *Sifre*,[17] and it was the former which became normative in the Qumran service and has remained so ever since.

The combination of גדול,קדוש, and ונורא appears again in the formal responsive prayer chanted prior to the reading of the Torah (*SPB*, 216). As part of this prayer it is customary to recite the *Shema'* followed by the verses beginning רוממו ה' אלהינו from Psalm 99 (vv. 5, 9) just quoted. It thus appears that the refrains of this psalm, יודו שמך and the two רוממו verses, provide a basis for a liturgy, combining *Shema'* with *Qedushah*.[18]

The verse with which the 'Hymn to the Creator' opens thus constitutes a formula of the *Qedushah* type and shows that the *Qedushah* rite was already existent in the second temple period.[19]

B.

לפניו הדר ילך ואחריו המון מים רבים, 'Majesty precedes Him and following Him is the rush of many waters'. Such imagery is known to us from the various biblical descriptions of theophanies. 'Glory and splendour' (הוד/הדר) precede God in Ps. 96.6, while the sound of 'many waters' accompanying his appearance is well known from the description of the heavenly chariot in Ezek. 1.24 and especially 43.2. The latter verse describes the glory (כבוד) of God coming from the east while its sound is like the sound of 'many waters', and the earth shone with his glory: והנה כבוד אלהי ישראל בא מדרך הקדים וקולו כקול מים רבים והארץ האירה מכבדו. This is similar to what we find in the hymn discussed here.

15. *Sifre Deut.* 343 (ed. Finkelstein, 395), cf. *Pirqe de-Rabbi Eliezer* 31 and the Genizah versions: J. Mann, 'Genizah Fragments of the Palestinian Order of Service', *HUCA* 2 (1925), pp. 269–338; S. Schechter, 'Genizah Specimens', *JQR* 10 (1898), pp. 656–59; Asaf, *Sefer Dinaburg*, p. 117.

16. Taking יודו as jussive, as vv. 5 and 9 are imperative.

17. For a combination of both formulae cf. המלך הגדול והגבור והנורא קדוש הוא in the *Yoṣer Qedushah* (*SPB*, 46).

18. On the combination of the *Shema'* unit with the *Qedushah* see my book, *Early Jewish Liturgy* (2004), xxii–xxvi (Hebrew).

19. Therefore, the origin of גדול וקדוש in 11QPs[a] is not to be sought in linguistic association with Pss. 149–150, as proposed by P.W. Skehan, 'A Liturgical Complex in 11QPs[a]', *CBQ* 35 (1973), p. 203.

In this hymn as well the coming glory (הדר)[20] is accompanied by the rush of 'many waters'[21] and following its appearance comes the light (ll. 11–12). Moreover, like the theophany of Ezekiel, which revolves around the throne and chariot (chs. 1, 10), so also here we find next to the 'many waters', the throne (מכון כסאו) and its attributes (v. 3). The image of God's throne upon the waters[22] which occurs in Rev. 4.6 and *b. Hag.* 12b–13a indeed belongs to the *Merkabah* tradition, incipient in the book of Ezekiel,[23] and may be traced back to more ancient times.[24] Moreover, the 'many waters' in Ezekiel come to illustrate the rush and sound of angels' wings (1.24; 10.5), and it seems that in our hymn also the rush of the 'many waters' in v. 2 already anticipates the angels of v. 5. According to the Targum of Ezek. 43.2 'the sound of many waters' actually constitutes the angels' praise: 'the voice of those blessing his name' (קל מברכי שמיה). This view is already found in 1.24 where בקול מים רבים is explained by the Targum as the sound of angels praising the Lord and קול המולה בקול מחנה is interpreted as the voice of the camp of heavenly angels (בקול משרית מלאכי מרומא). An identical explanation is given by the Targum for the קול רעש גדול in Ezek. 3.12.[25] The same conception lies behind the LXX translation of Ezek. 43.2. וקולו בקול מים רבים is rendered καὶ φωνὴ τῆς παρεμβολῆς, ὡς φωνὴ διπλασιαζόντων πολλῶν, 'and the sound of *the camp* like the sound of many redoubling (their shouts)'. The *camp* which is added here is based on Ezek. 1.24 whereas the *redoubling* draws upon the tradition that the angels continually praise the Lord (cf. Rev. 4.8).[26] The notion that the wings of the angels are, as it were, their instruments for singing is reflected in the 'Angelic Liturgy' of Qumran: והמון רנה ברום כנפיהם, 'and there is a roar of singing as they lift their

20. הדר is synonymous with כבוד and constitutes an identical concept; see my article כבוד in *TWAT* (ed. H. Ringgren and G.S. Botterweck, 1982), vol. IV, cols. 25–27.

21. המון מים in Jer. 10.13; 51.16 and מים רבים in Jer. 51.13 are associated with rain and, therefore, are irrelevant for the context of vv. 2–3 of the hymn where theophany and God's throne occur (contra Sanders in his edition and Skehan, 204).

22. 'The sound of many waters', שאון מים רבים in Isa. 17.12–13 is paralleled there by the sound of the roaring seas, בהמות ימים, and according to the *Merkabah* traditions God's throne is upon the sea. Cf., e.g., the Moslem tradition of Ibn Ṣayyād taken from the *Merkabah* literature: 'I see a throne upon the sea (var. upon the water) and around it *al-Ḥayyat*'. For the latter see D.J. Halperin, 'Ibn Ṣayyād Traditions and the Legend of al-Dajjal', *JAOS* 96 (1976), p. 217.

23. This view is correctly illustrated by D.J. Halperin, 'The Exegetical Character of Ezek. X 9–17', *VT* 26 (1976), pp. 129–41.

24. For the biblical roots of this idea, see my article 'Divine Invervention in War in Ancient Israel and in the Ancient Near East', *History, Historiography and Interpretation* (ed. H. Tadmor and M. Weinfeld, 1983), pp. 121–47.

25. '...קל זיע דמשבחין ואמרין בריך יקרא', 'a great roaring sound of those who praise and say "Blessed"...'

26. Cf. Apost. Constit. VIII xii 27: 'ten thousand times ten thousand of angels *incessantly*...say: "Holy, Holy, Holy"...' (see above, n. 3). For Rabbinic parallels and for an analysis of the LXX version of Ezek. 43.2 see D.J. Halperin, 'Merkabah Midrash in the Septuagint', *JBL* 101 (1982), pp. 351–53. According to Halperin, this concept goes back to Ps. 68.18 where שנאן is derived from שנה, 'repeat'. Ps. 68.18 is incorporated in the *Qedushah* pasage of Apost. Constit. VII xxxv 3 and in the Genizah (see n. 3).

wings'.[27] The same conception prevails in the rabbinic sources (*b. Hag*. 13b; *Gen. Rab*. 65.21 [ed. Theodor-Albeck, 737–40] and parallels). It should be remembered that in Isa. 6.4 we find that the doorposts shook from the sound of the praising angels: וינעו אמות הספים מקול הקורא. It is therefore not impossible that the above interpretation in Ezekiel reflects a kernel of authentic interpretation.

That the 'sound of the many waters' has been associated with the *Yoṣer* liturgy may be learned from a Genizah fragment of the *Yoṣer* benediction. Here we read: בא מדרך הקדים וקולו כקול מים רבים והארץ האירה מכבודו, קומי אורי כי בא אורך וכבוד ה׳ עליך זרח בא״י יוצר המאורות, 'He comes from the way of the East, and His sound is like the sound of many waters; the earth shines from His glory. Arise, shine, for your light has come and the Glory of the Lord has shone upon you. Blessed are You…Creator of the luminaries'.[28] This passage is a combination of two verses, one taken from the theophany in Ezek. 43.2 and the other taken from Isa. 60.1. As has been argued by S. Lieberman (see below), the latter seems to correspond to the morning prayer of the Essenes as described by Josephus (*War*. 2.128). As will be shown below, the Isaianic verse incorporated in the *Yoṣer* benediction reflects the eschatological concept implied in the praise of the renewal of the luminaries which is prevalent in the sectarian literature.

C.

חסד ואמת סביב פניו,אמת[29]ומשפט וצדק מכון כסאו, 'Grace and truth surround His presence, truth and justice and righteousness are the foundation of His throne'. As has been indicated, the throne of God is part of the theophany presented here, and the theme of the throne is indeed prominent in the various *Yoṣer* hymns. Thus we find in the famous *El Adon* hymn[30] (*SPB*, 187–88) a glorious description of the Lord's chariot,[31] and, as in the Qumran hymn, it is associated there with grace, justice and uprightness.

11QPs^{a}	*El Adon*
חסד ואמת סביב פניו	חסד רחמים (מלא) כבודו
(אמת) ומשפט וצדק מכון כסאו	זכות[32] ומישור לפני כסאו

27. C. Newsom, *Songs of the Sabbath Sacrifice – A Critical Edition* (1985), p. 315.

28. Cf. Mann, 292.

29. אמת in this hemistich seems to be redundant; cf. Skehan, p. 203 n. 26.

30. On the early date of this poem see E. Fleischer, 'The Diffusion of the Qedusha of the *Amidah* and the Yoṣer in the Palestinian Jewish Ritual', *Tarbiz* 38 (1969), p. 270 (Hebrew).

31. המתגאה על חיות הקדש ונהדר בכבוד על המרכבה, 'Who rises high on the holy Chayoth, majestic in glory on the chariot'. The throne occurs also in another *Yoṣer* hymn of the Sabbath liturgy, לאל אשר שבת, where we read: ביום השביעי נתעלה וישב על כסא כבודו, 'on the seventh day He exalted himself and sat upon the throne of His glory' (*SPB*, 188).

32. צדק has been transformed into זכות as a result of the late Hebrew use of זכות. Cf., for example, Gen. 15.6: ויחשבה לו צדקה, Targums: וחשבה לה לזכו (*Tg. Onq. and Tg. Ps.-J.*); 2 Sam. 19.29: ומה יש לי עוד צדקה, Targum: ומה אית לי עוד זכו. The well-known Mishnah in *Mak*. 3.15 so interprets Isa. 42.21: רבי חנניא בן עקשיא אומר רצה הקדוש ברוך הוא לזכות את ישראל לפיכך הרבה להם תורה ומצוות שנאמר ה׳ חפץ למען **צדקו** יגדיל תורה ויאדיר. צדקה in the quoted verse served as the basis for the idea of זכות. I owe this last observation to Dr. Baruch Schwartz.

11QPs[a]	*El Adon*
Grace and truth surround His presence (Truth) and justice and righteousness (are) the base of His throne	Grace and compassion are before His glory Justice and uprightness (are) before His throne[33]

This theme has its origin in Ps. 89.15,[34] 'Righteousness and justice are the base of Your throne, grace and truth stand before You', צדק ומשפט מכון כסאך חסד ואמת יקדמו פניך. The hymnic part of this psalm, which preserves an ancient angelic liturgy,[35] shows affinities to the *Yoṣer Qedushah* pattern in other respects as well. Thus we find there at the beginning a section (vv. 1–5) which revolves around the formula לדור ודור (vv. 1,5), found in line 1 of the Qumran hymn and discussed above in connection with the benediction of *Qedushat Hashem*. Then comes the praise of the angels (vv. 6–9) followed by the creation theme (vv. 10–15) in which the throne associated with grace, truth and justice appears (vv. 15). The next verse speaks about the 'light' of God's presence, אור פניך (vv. 16). Now the question is: what is the meaning of the grace in the cosmic angelic context found here?

Cosmic Renewal as Grace, Truth, Righteousness and Compassion

A characteristic feature of the hymns and prayers of the *Yoṣer* liturgy is the various expressions of benevolence, grace and truth that occur so often there:

1. המאיר לארץ ולדרים עליה ברחמים[36] ובטובו מחדש בכל יום (תמיד) מעשה בראשית, 'He Who brings light to the earth and to them that dwell upon it with *compassion*, and in His *goodness* renews each day (always) the work of creation' (*SPB*, 45).

2. הכין ופעל זהרי חמה **טוב** יצר כבוד לשמו, 'He has established and made the rays of the sun and thus has formed *goodness*, glory to His name' (*SPB*, *ibid.*, the hymn of אל ברוך).

3. ומאיר לעולם כולו וליושביו שברא **במדת רחמים**, 'Who brings light to the whole universe and its inhabitants whom He has created with *the measure of compassion*' (*SPB*, 187, the poem הכל יודוך).

33. Similar descriptions are found in the Hebrew book of Enoch, H. Odeberg, *3 Enoch* (1928), ch. xxxi, 106 (Hebrew, 48), and in various midrashim; cf., for example, בתי מדרשות אותיות דרבי עקיבא in II [ed. A. Wertheimer, Jerusalem: Mosad HaRav Kook, 1952], p. 343.

34. The expression in 11QPs[a] 'surrounding his presence', סביב פניו, recalls also Ps. 89.8,9: סביבותיך,סביבו.

35. See my forthcoming study mentioned in n. 5.

36. Compare in the eucharistic prayer of Addai and Mari: 'Who created the world and its inhabitants in His lovingkindness'. This prayer is considered 'the most ancient Christian eucharistic composition to which we can have access today' (L. Bouyer, *Eucharist, Theology and Spirituality of the Eucharistic Prayer* [1966], p. 147). According to G. Dix (*The Shape of the Liturgy* [London: 1945], 186) it is to be dated to later second or early third century. Cf. also J. Vellian, 'The Anaphoral Structure of Addai and Mari compared to the Berakoth Preceding the *Shema'* in the Synagogue Morning Service', *Le Museon* 85 (1972), pp. 201–223. (This article refers constantly to the second benediction before *Shema'* as 'ahubah', but it should be called 'ahabah').

4. גדלו וטובו מלא עולם...זכות ומישור לפני כסאו חסד ורחמים לפני כבודו,טובים מאורות שברא אלהינו, ‘His greatness and *goodness* fill the universe... *Justice and uprightness* are before His throne, *grace and compassion* are before His glory. *Good* are the luminaries which our God created...’ (*El Adon* Hymn, *SPB*, 187–88).

5. דרש הכין והתקין חמתו... פועלי צדקו קרובי רחמיו שיר תשבחות שוררו למלכם, ‘He sought, established and made the radiance of His sun... Those who perform His *righteousness*, those who are close to His *mercy*, sang a song of praise to their king’ (אשר ברוב חכמה of the Genizah, see below).

6. אשר מאמרו ברא שחקים וברוח פיו כל צבאם,חוק וזמן נתן להם שלא ישנו את תפקידם...פועל אמת פעלתו אמת, ‘Who created the heavens by His command and all their hosts by the breath of His mouth; He has given them fixed statute and season so that they should not alter their task..., the One who performs *truth*, Whose work is *true*’ (benediction over the New Moon, *SPB*, 437).

In a Qumran passage to be cited below, in which God’s knowledge (דעת) is associated with the luminaries, the divine attributes of justice, צדק, and mercy, רחמים, are also mentioned (1QS 10.11–12): ‘I shall call God ‘my righteousness’ (צדקי) and the Most High ‘establisher of my goodness’ (מכין טובי), ‘fountain of knowledge’ (מקור דעת)’.[37] The *goodness* and *grace* of the Lord in all these passages may be explained in the following manner. The rising of the sun is due to the gracious force of the Creator: המחדש בטובו בכל יום (תמיד) מעשה בראשית, ‘Who renews *through his goodness* the creation every day continually’ (*Yoṣer* liturgy, *SPB*, 45, 46; cf. *b. Hag.* 12b). This notion is in fact expressed in the continuation of the Qumran hymn discussed here: ‘He clothes the mountains with produce, *good* food for every living creature’, מעטר הרים תנובות אוכל טוב לכול חי (line 6). With the rise of the dawn everything is, as it were, newly created. Angels as well as men praise God for the renewal of creation and especially for the regeneration of the luminaries (cf. the benediction יוצר המאורות). חסד and אמונה/אמת in this context express the benevolent, constant creation of God as found in *Gen. Rab.* 78.1 (ed. Theodor-Albeck, 915): ‘It is written (Lam. 3.23) “They are new every morning, great is Your truth” (lit. ‘steadfastness = ’אמונתך’)’,[38] חדשים לבקרים רבה אמונתך. ‘Because You renew us every morning, we know that great is Your truth to redeem us/to revive our dead.’[39] The juxtaposition of awakening in the morning with awakening in the afterlife is

37. For דעת and צדק associated with the heavenly bodies, cf. 1QM 17.8: ושמח צדק במרומים וכול בני אמתו יגילו בדעת עולמים, and see Y. Yadin, *The Scroll of the War of the Sons of Light against the Sons of Darkness* (1955) (Hebrew), p. 259 n. 8.

38. The preceding verse speaks about God’s uninterrupted grace and compassion: חסדי ה׳ כי לא תמנו כי לא כלו רחמיו, which is echoed in the *Modim* benediction of the *Shemoneh Esreh*, the main topic of which is thanks to God for his wondrous deeds every day. There we read: הטוב כי לא כלו רחמיך והמרחם כי לא תמו חסדיך, ‘You are the Beneficent One for Your compassion has never ceased, You are the Compassionate One for Your grace/kindness has never ended’ (*SPB*, 63).

39. Cf. the parallels in *Lam. Rab.* And *Midrash Tehillim* for which see Theodor-Albeck, *Gen. Rab.* 915–16. Compare also the prayer מודה אני recited upon waking from sleep: ‘I thank You...Who restored my soul within me mercifully, great is Your steadfastness’. For the history of this prayer cf. A. Berliner, *Randbemerkungen zum täglichen Gebetbuch* (1909), p. 31.

likewise expressed in the אלוהי נשמה prayer and in the hymns of the Qumran Hodayot.[40]

Regeneration of the lights in the morning, described as the 'eternal grace' of the Lord, is found in the song about changing seasons in 1QS 10.1–4:

'When the luminaries shine forth from the holy height...when they are being renewed (בהתחדשם)...a sign...for eternal grace' (חסדי עולם;ll. 3–4).

Renewal of creation linked to the praise of the angels, as in the *Yoṣer* prayer, is actually found in the Hodayot Scroll (1QH 1.3–14):

'I thank you my God, that you have dealt wondrously with dust[41] to raise from the dust of the worms of the dead (להרים מעפר תולעת מתים) to the everlasting foundation (לסוד עולם)...to stand in Your presence together with the eternal hosts...to be renewed together with the whole creation' (להתחדש עם כל נהיה).[42]

'Raising from the dust of the worms of the dead' in this context is to be associated with the idea of revival from death in the morning.[43] The 'renewal' here is the renovation of creation every morning when men and angels unite together to praise the Lord, a union which has eschatological overtones, as indicated above.

The rebirth of the luminaries associated with the idea of 'truth' and combined with eschatological revival is clearly expressed in a Jewish prayer to be said at the appearance of the new moon.[44]

> Blessed be You, O God...Who created the heavens...(and) all their host. He assigned to them order and season...They are glad and rejoice to do the will of their Master (ששים ושמחים לעשות רצון קונם),[45] the Worker of truth Whose work is true (פועל אמת שפעולתו אמת);[46] He commanded the moon to renew itself (שתתחדש) as a crown of glory to those carried from the womb (לעמוסי בטן) who likewise are destined to renew themselves and to glorify their Creator.[47]

The 'work of truth' here has been rightly understood by Rashi on *San.* 42a: שאינם משנים את סדרם, 'that they do not change their course'. That concept is

40. Cf. Chapter 8.

41. For this idea in the morning prayers of the cited Qumran sect as well as those of the conventional Jewish prayers, see chapter 8.

42. For נהיה, cf. 1QS 3.15: כל הויה ונהיה which means 'whatever exists', i.e., the whole universe. See J. Licht, מגילת הסרכים (1965), p. 90 and the references there.

43. See Chapter 8.

44. Quoted in *b. San.* 42a and *Tractate Soferim* 19.10 (ed. M. Higger, *Massechet Sopherim* [1937], pp. 337–38); cf. *SPB*, p. 437.

45. For such phrases in the *Qedushah* liturgy cf. the *El Adon* hymn (*SPB*, 188): שמחים בצאתם וששים בבואם עושים באימה רצון קונם, 'They (the luminaries) rejoice in their going forth and are glad in their returning, they perform with awe the will of their master'. For the heavenly host performing the will of its master, cf. in the *Yoṣer* liturgy (*SPB*, 45): 'and all of them in awe and fear do the will of their master', וכלם עשים באימה וביראה רצון קונם. Cf. Slavonic Enoch 6.4: 'The heavenly host...stand before God and perform His will'.

46. An alternative formula: פועלי אמת שפעולתם אמת, ascribes the work to the luminaries themselves. A variant in a Schechter manuscript reads: פעלו צדק. See Higger, *Massechet Sopherim*, p. 338, n. 76.

47. In *Maḥzor Vitry* (ed. S. Hurvitz; Nürenberg, 1889 [2nd edn, 1923]), p. 183: להתחדש ולפאר יוצרם כמותם, 'to renew themselves and to glorify their Creator *like them*' (i.e., like the luminaries).

actually expressed in the prayer itself: שלא ישנו את תפקידם, 'that they should not change their tasks', to which compare Ben Sira 39.31: בצותו אותם ישישו ובחקם לא ימרו פיו, 'they are glad to (carry out) his order and they do not disobey the laws'.[48]

The notion of eschatological renewal is here clearly expressed and it is quite possible that this idea, which was originally linked to the sun and associated with the *Yoṣer* liturgy, was shifted to the moon and the moon blessing because of opposition to Essene practice.[49] In fact, the original tradition in which an eschatological motif was appended to the morning liturgy may be discerned in the concluding section of the *Yoṣer* benediction. As indicated above, S. Lieberman[50] has observed that the Genizah fragment of the *Yoṣer* benediction which reads: קומי אורי כי בא אורך וכבוד ה׳ עליך זרח, בא״י יוצר המאורות,'Arise, shine, for your light has come and the glory of the Lord has shone upon you. Blessed are You, O Lord, Who created the luminaries',[51] seems to reflect a liturgical custom similar to that of the Essenes.[52] We may add that in light of what has been said before about the eschatological aspect of the renewal of the luminaries in the Qumran writings, Lieberman's view gains strength, especially since the verse quoted in the Genizah fragment is taken from an explicitly eschatological chapter (Isa. 60). This tradition has indeed penetrated the prevalent *Yoṣer* liturgy which contains at the end a clear eschatological address:אור חדש על ציון תאיר ונזכה כלנו במהרה לאורו, 'Cause a new light to shine on Zion, so that we may all soon have a share in its light'.[53] In spite of the objections raised to the inclusion of this formula,[54] it could not be eliminated, apparently because of its strong roots.

In addition to this prayer for 'new light' we find at the end of the *Yoṣer* benediction other formulae found in the Qumran liturgies associated with the luminaries. After המחדש בטובו בכל יום תמיד מעשה בראשית, and before the prayer אור חדש, we find the verse לעושה אורים גדולים כי לעולם חסדו (Ps. 136.7). This verse actually stands behind the liturgical passage quoted above from the Manual of Discipline: בהתחדשם... גדול לקודש קודשים ואות למפתח חסדי עולם. The Qumran exegetes interpreted כי לעולם חסדו of Ps. 136.7 in an eschatological

48. Cf. also 1 En. 2.1–3 and *Sifre Deut.* 306 (ed. Finkelstein, 332); see recently the discussion of M. Kister, 'Metamorphoses of Aggadic Traditions', *Tarbiz* 60 (1991), pp. 196–97 (Hebrew).

49. Josephus, *War* 2.128.

50. S. Lieberman, 'Light on the Cave Scrolls from Rabbinic Sources', *PAAJR* 20 (1951), pp. 398–99.

51. Mann, 292. This comes after the verse וקולו כקול מים רבים והארץ האירה מכבדו that is reflected in the Qumran hymn under study (see above). It is therefore not impossible that behind the Genizah fragment lies a liturgical tradition consisting of elements similar to those of the Qumran hymn.

52. According to Lieberman the...קומי אורי, said at dawn, could have been taken by Josephus as a real invocation of the sun, 'as if entreating it to rise' (ὥσπερ ἱκετεύοντες ἀνατεῖλαι).

53. In some of the Genizah fragments the phrase נר משיחך תאיר לנו is appended to the אור חדש formula; cf. Elbogen, 15. For other forms of this formula see E. Fleischer, *The Yoṣer, Its Emergence and Development* (Jerusalem: Magnes Press, 1984), pp. 35–36 (Hebrew).

54. It was especially Saadiah Gaon who fought against the inclusion of the formula, see Elbogen, *ibid.*, p. 15.

sense, as did the composer of the *Yoṣer* liturgy who attached the אור חדש to the verse לעושה אורים גדולים כי לעולם חסדו.[55]

The notion of the creation of new luminaries in the eschaton was prevalent in the sectarian literature. Thus we read in the book of Jubilees that when God builds the new temple in Zion,[56] '*all the luminaries will be renewed* for the salvation, peace and blessing of all the chosen of Israel' (1.29). Similarly, in 1 En. 91.16 we find that the heavens will change, a new firmament will appear, and *the host of the heavens will shine sevenfold.*

The renovation of the luminaries in the recreated world is attested also in rabbinic literature.[57] It occurs likewise in the blessing said at the appearance of the new moon quoted above. As in Jub. 1.29, where it says that the luminaries will be renewed for the salvation of the chosen of Israel, so we find here that the moon will be renewed as a crown of glory for those who have been carried from the womb (=the chosen ones): שתתחדש עטרת תפארת לעמוסי בטן (*SPB*, 437). By the same token the *perfect light* (אורתום) mentioned in 1QH 18.29 (cf. 4.6) alludes to the *light* reserved for the righteous and the chosen in the future life (1 Enoch 58) and to the light of the seven days (אור שבעת הימים) known from rabbinic literature.[58]

The joy (שמחה) and gladness (ששון) of the luminaries while fulfilling their function, found in the *El Adon* prayer (שמחים בצאתם וששים בבואם) quoted above, as well as in the blessing said at the appearance of the new moon (ששים ושמחים לעשות רצון קונם), is also reflected in Qumran literature. In 1QM 17.8 we read that the archangel Michael will be sent to help the holy warriors with eternal light (באור עולמים) to illuminate *with joy* the house of Israel for peace and blessing to those of the divine lot (שלום וברכה לגורל אל),[59] and that צדק will rejoice in heaven (ושמח צדק במרומים), which undoubtedly refers to the luminary which represents justice (compare שמש צדקה in Mal. 3.20).[60] Joy caused by the luminaries is clearly expressed in the phrase which concludes the *Yoṣer* liturgy (Sephardic version): והתקין מאורות משמח עולמו אשר ברא, 'and He established luminaries to gladden the world that He created'.[61]

D.

Creation of the luminaries through knowledge (דעת), followed by the song of the angels, is a characteristic feature of the *Yoṣer* liturgies.

55. Cf. Elbogen, *ibid.*

56. *Ibid.*, pp. 15–16.

57. Cf. L. Ginzberg, *The Legends of the Jews*, I (1967), pp. 23–24.

58. Ginzberg, *ibid.*

59. Cf. Jub. 1.29 quoted above: 'the luminaries will be renewed for salvation, peace and blessing for all the chosen of Israel'.

60. For the identification of the light with צדק cf. 1 En. 58.4 concerning the righteous in the world to come: 'they will look for light and will find justice'.

61. Cf. Elbogen, p. 15.

11QPs[a]	*El Barukh (SPB, 45)*
מבדיל אור מאפלה[62] שחר הכין בדעת לבו אז ראו כל מלאכיו וירננו	אל ברוך גדול דעה[63] הכין ופעל זהרי חמה טוב יצר... מאורות נתן סביבות עזו פנות צבאיו קדושים... מספרים כבוד אל וקדושתו
Separating light from darkness *by the knowledge* of His mind *He established the dawn* When all *His angels* had witnessed it, they *sang aloud*	Blessed God, great in *knowledge He established* and made *the rays of the sun*... He set luminaries round His glory The chiefs of His host, *the holy ones*... They *recount the Glory* of God and His holiness

El Adon (*SPB*, 188)	Genizah[64]
טובים[65] מאורות... יצרם בדעת בבינה בהשכל... פאר וכבוד נותנים לשמו... שבח נותנים לו כל צבא מרום...	אשר ברוב חכמה גדולה דרש הכין והתקין זיו חמתו,פועלי צדקו קרובי רחמיו שיר תשבחות שוררו למלכם
Good are the luminaries... *He has formed them with knowledge*, understanding and insight...they give glory and honour to His name...*all the hosts of heaven give Him praise*...	the One Who with great wisdom has explored, *established* and made the *radiance of His* sun, those who perform His righteousness *those close to His mercy sang* to their King songs and praises

The idea of the creation of light and the luminaries through knowledge is frequently attested in the writings of Qumran,[66] especially those which speak explicitly of the following section of a prayer on the changing of the seasons.

At the departure of the night and the coming of the day, unceasingly, at the birth in time of all the established...through the course of the seasons	למוצא לילה ומבוא יום תמיד בכל מולדי עת יסודי קץ...ותקופת מועדים
in their order appointed by their signs, for the whole of their rule...*for the God of knowledge has established it.*[67]	בתכונם באותותם לכל ממשלתם... אל הדעות הכינה

62. This formula recalls אור עולם באוצר חיים אורות מאפל אמר ויהי which opens the *Yoṣer* benediction in today's rite on the high holy days only, but which, according to the Palestinian tradition, is to recited daily; see Mann, p. 295.

63. The acrostic here matches that of the *El Adon*: אל אדון=אל; ברוך מברך=ברוך; גדלו וטובו=גדול; דעת תבונה=דעה. See Z. Jawitz, *Mekor Haberakhot* (=*Die Liturgie des Siddur und ihre Entwicklung* [1910], p. 53).

64. The acrostic for *ṭet* and *yod* matches in *El Baruch*: טוב,יצר (*SPB*, 45).

65. Mann, 323; I. Levi, 'Fragments de rituels de prières provenant de la gueniza du Caire', *REJ* 53 (1907), p. 241.

66. On the concept of דעת in the writings of the sect, see W.D. Davies, 'Knowledge in the Dead Sea Scrolls and Matthew 11.25–30', *HTR* 46 (1953), pp. 113–40; J. Licht, מגילת ההודיות (1957), pp. 42–43; H.W. Kuhn, *Enderwartung und gegenwärtiges Heil* (1966), pp. 139ff.

67. For translation see S. Holm-Nielsen, *Hodayot, Psalms from Qumran* (1960), *ad loc.*

In a prayer from the Manual of Discipline,[68] which represents a similar liturgical tradition,[69] we encounter, immediately after a list of the changes of time – day and night, seasons of the year, Sabbatical and Jubilee years – the words אזמרה בדעת, 'I will sing of knowledge',[70] followed later by references to the recitation of the morning and evening prayers: עם מבוא יום לילה אבואה בברית אל ועם מוצא ערב ובקר אמר חוקיו...ברשית ידי ורגלי אברך שמו,בראשית צאת ובוא לשבת וקום,ועם משכב יצועי ארננה לו, 'With the coming of day and night I shall enter God's covenant[71] and when evening and morning appear I shall recite His laws...[72] When I begin to send forth my hands and my feet I will bless His name; at the beginning of my going and coming when I sit down or rise, when I lie down on my bed I will sing unto him'.[73] In another passage from the War Scroll (10.15–16) we read: מועדי קודש ותקופות שנים וקצי עד...אלה ידענו מבינתכה, 'holy festivals, seasons of the years and endless epochs...*these we have come to know from Your wisdom*'. This last phrase appears again in 1QH 1.21: אלה ידעתי מבינתכה. In the same hymn we find the words (line 11): מאורות לרזיהם כוכבים לנתיבותם, 'luminaries by their mysteries, stars in their courses', and in the concluding passage dealing with the establishment of seasons and epochs *through God's knowledge* (ll. 18–19): למספר דורות עולם ולכל שני נצח...ובחכמת דעתכה הכינותה תעודתם... אלה ידעתי מבינתכה. 'To numerous generations and eternal years...by Your skillful knowledge You did establish their function...*These I have come to know from Your wisdom*'.

Since in the writings of the sect the struggle between good and evil is compared to the war of light and darkness, it is no wonder that the expression 'God of knowledge', אל הדעות, appears in connection with the separation of truth from falsehood: מאל הדעות כל הויה ונהייה ולפני היותם הכין כול מחשבתם... וישם לו שתי רוחות...האמת והעול במעין אור תולדות האמת וממקור חושך תולדות העול.[74] 'From the God of knowledge exists all that is and will be; before they came into being He established their entire design...And He made for Himself two spirits...truth and perverseness. From a spring of light come the generations of truth, but from a fountain of darkness come the generations of perverseness.'

Especially telling is the fact that in most of these passages that speak of the creation of the luminaries through knowledge, the verb used is הכין,[75] 'institute,

68. 1QS 10.9–14.

69. See S. Talmon, 'The "Manual of Benedictions" of the Sect of the Judean Desert', *RevQ* 2 (1960), pp. 475ff; cf. Licht's discussion in his מגילת הסרכים (1965), pp. 204–208.

70. אזמרה בדעת וכל נגינתי לכבוד אל (1.9). The subject here is *divine* knowledge; see Licht in his commentary, *ad loc.*

71. In this context, entering into the covenant refers to reciting the daily *Shema'* which is associated with the *Qedushah*. On the *Shema'* and its connection with the covenant see chapter 5, p. 93 n. 18.

72. Cf. בשכבנו ובקומנו נשיח בחוקיך in the Evening Prayer (*SPB*, 131): the reading is identical in the Genizah; see Mann, p. 307.

73. Cf. Talmon, 'Manual of Benedictions', pp. 475–500, on morning, afternoon, and evening prayers reflected in this passage and the parallel passage in the Hodayot scroll.

74. 1QS 3.15–19.

75. Cf. the LXX's addition to Solomon's prayer (1 Kgs 8.12) [v. 53 in LXX]: ἥλιου ἐγνώρισεν ἐν οὐρανῷ, 'He acknowledged the sun in the heavens'. Scholars tend to assume that the translator

establish'. In 11QPs[a]: שחר הכין בדעת לבו; Hodayot 13.10: כי אתה הכינותמה, the poem *El Barukh*: גדול דעה הכין הכין; the Genizah Hymn: אשר ברוב חכמה הכין והתקין זיו חמתו. Significantly, the use of הכין in connection with the heavenly bodies appears in Ps. 74.16: אתה הכינות מאור ושמש, though there is no mention of wisdom or knowledge.

The image of God as ordering seasons and separating light from darkness through wisdom and knowledge is in fact incorporated in the Evening Service in the המעריב ערבים benediction: בחכמה פותח שערים ובתבונה משנה עתים ומחליף את הזמנים...ומבדיל בין יום ובין לילה, '*In wisdom* He opens the gates and *in understanding changes* the seasons...and distinguishes between day and night' (*SPB*, 130). This distinction between light and darkness linked to knowledge finds its clearest expression in the liturgy in the prayers אתה חוננתנו למדע תורתך and ותודיענו recited at the close of the Sabbath, the former when a weekday follows (*SPB*, 140), the latter when a festival commences (*SPB*, 328).[76] Both these prayers begin with the theme of דעת and proceed to enumerate the distinctions between holy and profane, light and darkness, Sabbath and weekday. The rabbis, at least as far as the first of the two is concerned, prescribed its recitation as part of the Benediction of Knowledge, אתה חונן...דעת (*m. Ber.* 5.2).[77]

The ability to discern and to make distinctions, which originates in the possession of knowledge,[78] refers not only to the distinction between light and darkness, holy and profane, but also to the distinction between Israel and the gentiles, the clean and the unclean.[79] Such ideas bring us again to the Dead Sea sect, for whom such distinctions between light and darkness symbolized the difference between truth and falsehood, righteousness and evil.[80]

misread (הבין(בשמים for הכין. If this were so, this would be another case of the use of הכין in a cosmological context. But הכין is never translated by γνωρίζειν and there is thus no place for assuming the reading הכין in this verse. On the contrary, the association of דעת with the creation of the luminaries is likely to increase the possibility that the reading שמש הודיע is original.

76. Called by the rabbis; מרגניתא בבבל, 'the jewel (=precious prayer) of Babylonia, *b. Ber.* 33b.

77. The expression חנן דעת appears in 1QH 14.25: ואני עבדך חנותני ברוח דעת, which follows upon הסולח לשבי פשע (line 24). In the preceding passage (14.8–22), we find מתן בינה (line 8) followed by הגשה and קרבה (ll. 13–14), all of which recall the benediction triplet of: דעת, תשובה (repentance) and סליחה (forgiveness) which open the petitionary part of the *Shemoneh Esreh*. On דעת, קרבה and תשובה as a basic pattern in the Qumran prayers, see my article, 'The Prayers for Knowledge, Repentance and Forgiveness in the "Eighteen Benedictions" – Qumran Parallels, Biblical Antecedents, and Basic Characteristics', *Tarbiz* 48 (1979), pp. 186–200 (Hebrew).

78. Cf. the rabbis' incisive statement, אם אין דעת הבדלה מנין, 'Without knowledge, whence distinction?', *y. Ber.* 5.2 9b. The association of הבדלה with דעת is evident also in the Damascus Covenant: ולהבדיל בין הטמא לטהור ולהודיע בין הקדש לחול (6.17–18; 12.19–20). The influence of Ezek. 22.26 is apparent, which in turn draws upon Lev. 10.10–11; however, in the latter source the verb ידע does not appear in the parallelism.

79. Cf. *b. Pes.* 104a, as well as in the Genizah (Mann, p. 323); N. Wieder, 'The Old Palestinian Ritual – New Sources', *JJS* 4 (1953), pp. 30–37.

80. דעת is essentially the power enabling man to distinguish between good and evil, to identify the seasons and time periods. It thus has both cosmic and moral associations. On the relation of the concept of דעת to the Greek (γνῶσις) in Hellenistic religions, see Chapter 1, 'Loyalty Oath in the

The concept of ‘distinction’ in both the cosmic and the religious spheres is well known from the other religions of the first century CE. We read, for example, in the oath of allegiance of a Mystery[81] (first and third century CE papyri) that the oath is to be sworn by ‘the god who has separated heaven from earth, darkness from light, day from night, rising from setting of the luminaries, death from life, black from white, dry from wet, hot from cold, bitter from sweet, and body from soul’.[82]

The luminaries, and the changes of time associated with them, originate in the highest, peculiarly divine knowledge. Thus, the Qumran liturgy dealt with here closes by saying: כי הראם את אשר לא ידעו, ‘for He showed them what they did not know;’ the angels acquire the revelation of secret things by their closeness to God. Indeed, the very same sentence is found in 1QH 13.1–2 in which we find the idea of revealing רזי פלאים, ‘wondrous mysteries’ (cf. 1.21), and the host of God’s spirits and the assembly of his holy ones, צבא רוחיך ועדת קדושיך. At the end of the hymn we find the proclamation: יספרו כבודך בכל ממשלתך כי הראיתם את אשר לא [ידעו], ‘Let them recount Your glory throughout Your dominion, for You did show them that which no other [flesh] had seen before’.[83] The entire thanksgiving hymn (13.1ff.), it should be noted, bears many similarities to the first hymn of the Hodayot quoted above in connection with luminaries, knowledge, and time changes.

Angels, Luminaries and Knowledge

Angels as possessors of ‘knowledge’ is a very common motif in Qumran literature and especially comes to the fore in the context of heavenly praise dealt with here. Thus, in Hodayot 3.22–23 the praising angels are called רוחות דעת, ‘spirits of knowledge’, while in 11.14 and in fragment 10.6 they are called ידעים. Most important in this respect is text 4Q400 frag. 2 from cave 4.[84] There we read that

Ancient Near East’. On דעת in the apocalyptic-visionary sense, cf. I. Gruenwald, ‘Knowledge and Vision’, *Israel Oriental Studies* 3 (1973), pp. 63–107.

81. See M.P. Nilsson, *Geschichte der griechischen Religion* (2nd edn, 1974), II, pp. 695–96 for additional references and the Greek text.

82. Compare the הבדלות in *b. Pes.* 104a: (1) קדש וחול (2) אור וחושך (3) ישראל ועמים (4) יום השביעי וששת ימי המעשה (5) טמא וטהור (6) ים וחרבה (7) מים עליונים ותחתונים. These appear in the old Palestinian *Havdalah* (Mann, 323; Wieder, 36). It is interesting that while the Greek document enumerates ten distinctions, the rabbis limited the הבדלות to seven, apparently due to a tendency to make use of a typological number. For the religious significance of הבדלה, cf. the Nabatean text: פילען פרש לילא מיממא מן די ינפק יתהם לעלם, ‘and let the one who separates day from night curse forever those who will remove them’ (the bodies from the sepulchre). See J.C. Greenfield, ‘Studies in the Legal Terminology of the Nabatean Funerary Inscriptions’, ספר זכרון לחנוך ילון (1974), pp. 64–83.

83. In light of the parallel from the Psalms Scroll, it would appear that the hymn here speaks of angels, not members of the sect. It remains difficult to be certain, however, for the members of the sect see themselves as partners of the angels in God’s revelation (see below).

84. Cf. Newsom, *Songs of the Sabbath Sacrifice*, p. 110.

God's glory is praised by אלי דעת,[85] 'angels (lit. divine beings) of knowledge', 'while standing in their abodes' (במעוני עומדם), and that they praise the Lord's glory together with men, according to their knowledge, אלוהים ואנשים יספרו הוד מלכותו כדעתם.[86] In a fragment from the Benediction of the Chief Priest ($1QS^b$ 4.22–28)[87] we read that the chief priest is like the מלאך פנים, 'angel of the presence',[88] in the holy abode (במעון קודש) who serves in the 'king's palace' (היכל המלך)[89] and that he shares his lot with the 'angels of the presence', as a result of which he becomes 'the great luminary of the world of knowledge' (למאור גדול לתבל בדעת). This text identifies, then, the chief priest with the 'angel of the presence' (who has direct access to the Lord)[90] as well as with the great luminary (i.e., the sun) of knowledge.[91]

This latter identification of the chief priest with the great luminary should not surprise us. As has been indicated above, the angels are paralleled with the morning stars in Job 38.7, a view which is also reflected in Psalm 148 where (v. 3) we find the sun, moon and the כוכבי אור (bright stars or morning stars)[92] together with the angels and the Lord's host (מלאכיו,צבאיו). The identification of the luminaries with the angels is most clearly expressed in the book of Job in the passages about the culpability of angels and men. In the verses in which men are

85. Compare קרובי דעת in fragment 1 of the same text (line 7) and צבא דעת in 1QH 18.23.

86. The passage is fragmentary and runs as follows: להלל כבודה **באלי דעת** ותשבוחות מלכותה בקדושי ק[דשים ... המה נכבדים בכל מחני אלוהים ונוראים למוסדי אנשים פ[לא] ... מאלוהים ואנשים יספרו הוד מלכותו **כדעתם** ורוממו [... שמי מלכותו ובכול מרומי רום תהלי פלא לפי כול [... כבוד מלך אלוהים יספרו במעוני עומדם ... נרוממה **לאלוהי דעת**] [ק]ודש **ובנתו** ככול ידעי ...

87. For this passage and the identification of the blessed there with the chief priest, cf. Licht, מגילת הסרכים, pp. 282–83.

88. Cf. the blessing to Levi in Jub. 31.14: 'And may the Lord cause you and your descendants from among all flesh to approach him to serve in his sanctuary as the *angels of the presence and as the holy ones*'. מלאך פנים occurs in 1QH 6.13. For מלאך פנים in apocryphal literature, cf. Licht, *Hodayot*, p. 284 and Holm-Nielsen, *Hodayot*, p. 14 n. 110.

89. For this term denoting temple, cf. Ben Sira 50.2,8.

90. See 1QH 6.13 where the members of the sect are compared with the מלאכי פנים who do not need any mediator or intercessor (מליץ בֵנים).

91. Cf. also Test. Levi 4.2–3 where it is said that Levi will serve before the Lord and will spread 'the light of knowledge' upon Jacob, being like the sun for Israel. The comparison of the priests with the angels and luminaries seems to support the thesis first suggested by J. Maier, 'Zum Begriff יחד in den Texten von Qumran', *ZAW* 72 (1960), pp. 148–60, that the notion of the communion of the sect with angels is rooted in 'Tempelsymbolik'. Cf. also K.G. Kuhn, *RGG*[3], V (1961), pp. 748–50 and Kuhn, *Enderwartung*, pp. 66–70. For a comparison of the priests with angels cf. y. Ber. 1.1, 2c: אמר רב הונא זה שרואה את הכהנים בבית הכנסת בברכה ראשונה צריך לומר ברכו ה׳ מלאכיו. The idea of the priests being like the luminaries because of their association with the shining Urim and Thumim occurs also in 4QpIsa[a] in the Pesher to Isa. 54.12, 'As to that which is said: 'And I will make as a gate all your pinnacles (שמשתיך)', this refers to the twelve (priests) who give light by the judgement of the Urim and Thumim...which shine forth from them like the sun in all its radiance'. See J.M. Baumgarten, 'The Duodecimal Courts of Qumran, Revelation, and the Sanhedrin', *JBL* 95 (1976), pp. 61–62. Cf. n. 10 there referring to Rashi regarding the association of שמשתיך with אלף...ישמשונה in Dan. 7.10.

92. אור may be rendered 'morning', cf. Job 24.14; Neh. 8.3 and hence M. Dahood's proposal (*Psalms*, III, *AB*, 1970, 353) to consider כוכבי אור in Ps. 148 as synonymous with כוכבי בקר in Job 38.7.

compared to angels, by way of *a minori ad majus*, there is an interchange of מלאכים and קדושים (4.18; 15.15) with the moon and the stars (25.5):

Even His servants He distrusts
charges His angels with errors
how much more those who dwell in clay houses (4.18)

Even His angels he distrusts
The heavens are not pure in *His sight*
How much more a man…
(15.15)

Even the moon is not bright
Nor the stars pure in His sight
How much more a man…
(25.5)

That the celestial bodies constitute God's host may be learned too from Isa. 40.25–26 (cf. also 1 En. 18.13; 21.3), and the same view is found in the first hymn of the Hodayot:

> You have stretched out the heavens to Your Glory…(put) the strong winds according to their ordinances into angels of holiness before they were created, into eternal spirits over their dominions, bodies of light according to their mysteries, stars according to their courses…[93]

Besides the equation of angels with luminaries we find here the angels equated with winds and spirits (cf. 13.8: צבא רוחיך), a phenomenon encountered also in Ps. 104.2–3): 'He makes the winds his messengers/angels' (עשה מלאכיו רוחות), and in the heavenly vision in 1 Kgs 22 where the רוח appears as one of the members of the divine council.

That the luminaries fulfil a role identical with that of the angels may be learned from the way the position of both in the heavenly abode is described in the Qumran writings. Thus, in 1QM 12.1–2 we read that the hosts of the angels are stationed in the 'holy habitation', מזבול כבודכה/בזבול קודשכה/במעון קודשכה. The same is said about the luminaries: 'In the morning they shine forth from the holy habitation (מזבול קודש) and in the evening they enter into the glorious abode (למעון כבוד)' (1QS 10.2–3; cf. 1QH 12.5–7).

The overlapping function of the luminaries with that of the angels is clearly attested in 1 En. 41.7 and in the *El Adon* hymn. In both sources the luminaries, like the angels, praise the Lord and extol him. In 1 Enoch: 'They (sun and moon) praise and extol and do not cease'.

In the *El Adon* hymn.

מלאים זיו מפיקים נגה   נאה זיום בכל העולם
שמחים בצאתם ששים בבואם   עושים באימה רצון קונם
פאר וכבוד נותנים לשמו   צהלה ורנה לזכר מלכותו

'Full of splendour and emanating radiance, their splendour shines over the whole world. Joyous at their rising and glad at their setting, they perform with fear the will of their Master. They give honour and glory to His name, jubilation and exultation at the mention of His kingdom.'

93. For translation and comments see Holm-Nielsen, *Hodayot*, pp. 17, 21.

And in the poem לאל אשר שבת:

> Lights You have created will praise You. מאורות אשר יצרת (עשית) יפארוך[94]

The connection between angels and knowledge is to be traced back to the literature of the first temple period. Thus we read in 2 Sam.14.17 that the king is like a *divine angel to discern between good and evil* or that he has wisdom *like the divine angel to know everything on the earth* (*ibid.*, v. 20). Similarly, we read in Prov. 9.10 and 30.3 about דעת קדושים, ‘knowledge of the angels’ (cf. LXX), a ‘knowledge’ reflected in Job 15.8 where reference is made to the myth about man’s stealing wisdom from the divine council.[95] A similar background lies behind Gen. 3.5, ‘You will be like divine beings who know good and evil’,[96] והייתם כאלהים ידעי טוב ורע, and Gen. 3.22, ‘Now that the man has become like one of us, knowing good and evil’,[97] a tradition which may be linked to the story of Ezekiel 28 about an angel or cherub ‘full of wisdom’ (מלא חכמה) in charge of the garden of God (v. 12).

Finally, we should refer to Mal. 2.7. Here, as in 1QS^b 4.22–23 quoted above, the priest is compared to the angel of the Lord of hosts who imparts knowledge and Torah: ‘For the lips of a priest guard knowledge and men seek instruction from his mouth, for he is a מלאך of the Lord of Hosts’, כי שפתי כהן ישמרו דעת ותורה יבקשו מפיהו כי מלאך ה׳ צבאות הוא. Here we find the priest, the angel and knowledge combined as in Qumran with the only exception being that no luminary is mentioned.

In the Qumran writings, as well as in other Jewish contemporaneous circles, there existed a correlation between angels, knowledge and luminaries. It seems that the idea of celestial bodies endowed with mind and knowledge found in the Pseudepigrapha,[98] Philo,[99] and various midrashic legends,[100] was already prevalent in Jewish circles of pre-Christian times. Maimonides follows the same line when stating:

> All the stars and planets are endowed with soul, wisdom and insight, and they live and exist and recognize the One Who spoke and the world came into being. All of them, everyone according to its eminence and rank, praise and extol their Creator like the angels.[101]

94. See *Seder Rav Amram Gaon* (ed. Goldschmidt), p. 71; cf. A. Rofé, *Israelite Brief in Angels* (Dissertation Hebrew University, 1969), pp. 53ff. (Hebrew).

95. See the commentary of N.H. Tur-Sinai (Torczyner), *The Book of Job, A New Commentary* (1957).

96. Cf. Tg. Ps.-J.: ותהוון כמלאכין רברבין דחכמין למנדע בין טב לביש, ‘And you will be like the great angels that know to distinguish between good and evil’ and cf. Neofiti Targum.

97. Cf. *Gen. Rab.* 21, 5 (ed. Theodor-Albeck 200): ‘Rabbi Pappias expounded “the man has become like one of us”, as one of the serving angels’.

98. See Pss. Sol. 18.10–12 (considered a separate psalm); cf. the blessing for the new moon (b. San. 42a) and Syriac Apocalypse of Baruch 48.9.

99. Plant. 3.12; Opif. 24.73; Somn. 1.135. It should be noted, however, that by expressing this opinion he might refer to the prevalent view and is not necessarily speaking in his own name; cf. H.A. Wolfson, *Philo*, I (1947), pp. 363–85.

100. Cf. Ginzberg, *Legends of the Jews*, I, pp. 100, 112.

101. הלכות יסודי התורה, 3.9. Cf. *Guide for the Perplexed*, II, 5. Maimonides is here influenced by

The last sentence about the rank and hierarchy in the divine choir accords with the above-mentioned statements from Qumran about the rank and order of the angels in praise (cf. 1QH 3.20–23; 11.13; 4Q 405 20 II–21–22, line 14).[102]

The Angels' Praise in Ben Sira

The angelic song, associated with the appearance of the luminaries and the changes of time, appears in Ben Sira also, here again connected with divine knowledge. A song of praise of God and his creations reads there as follows (42.16–20):

The brilliant sun shines forth upon everything, And God's Glory fills His creations.	שמש זהרת[103] על כל נגלתה וכבוד אדני מלא מעשיו
God's Holy ones were unable to completely recount His wonders,	לא השפיקו קדשי האל לספר כל נפלאותיו
The Lord has strengthened His hosts To stand firm before His glory…	אמץ אדני צבאיו להתחזק לפני כבודו…
For the Most High knows everything and observes the eternal signs,	כי ידע [ע]ליון כל [דעת] ומביט אותיות עולם
Discloses past and future,	מחוה חליפות נהיה
and reveals secret things,	ומגלה חקר נסתרות
Knowledge does not escape Him…[104]	לא נעדר מפניו שכל

Here we see both stylistic and thematic similarity to the Qumran passages we have quoted,[105] from which we may conclude that the prayers we are dealing with are indeed all quite early and do reflect ancient versions of a sort of *Yoṣer* prayer.

The idea expressed in the Ben Sira passage, that the angels are unable to sufficiently recount God's wonders, appears as well as in 1QH 12.29–30: וגבו[רי פל]א המה לא [יוכלו] לספר כל כבודכה, 'and the wondrous mighty ones, they cannot recount Your full glory', and in frag. 1.1–4: מלאכי קודש אשר...בשמים ...והם לא יוכלו...ולא יעצורו לדעת בכל...',[106] '[the holy] angels…in heaven… they cannot…they are not able to know all…'.

The passage from Ben Sira above also helps to determine the sense of a passage from Qumran cave 6[107] which reads: [מל]אכי צדק י]חזקו ברוח דעת...

Neoplatonic thought, especially by Plotinus; see A.L. Ivri 'Neoplatonic Currents in Maimonides' Thought', *Perspectives on Maimonides, Philosophical and Historical Studies* (ed. J.L. Kraemer, 1991), pp. 115–40.

102. Cf. Newsom, *Songs of the Sabbath Sacrifice*, p. 303.

103. Cf. זהרי חמה in the prayer אל ברוך גדול דעה and זיו חמה in the Genizah passage אשר ברוב חכמה quoted above.

104. According to the version found at Masada 5.3–9 = 42.16–20; see Y. Yadin, 'The Ben Sira Scroll from Masada', *EI* 8 (Sukenik Memorial Volume; 1968), pp. 27–28 and J. Strugnell, 'Notes and Queries on "The Ben Sira Scroll from Masada"', *EI* 9 (Albright Volume; 1969), p. 116 (English section).

105. Yadin, *ibid.*, p. 27.

106. Restoration according to Licht, מגילת ההודיות, p. 219.

107. 6Q 18, Fragment 5, *DJD*, III, p. 134.

[לעו]למים לא... יכלו, 'the righteous angels that strengthen themselves with the spirit of knowledge forever cannot'. Just as in Ben Sira 42.16–20, we have here the strength of the angels, and at the same time their inability to praise God fully. What is true in heaven is all the more obvious of man, as we see in the apocryphal Psalm 151 from the Qumran Psalms Scroll: כי מי יגיד (אדון הכל) את מעשי ומי ידבר ומי יספר, 'For who can proclaim, who can tell, who can recount the Lord's works?'[108] as well as in Ben Sira 18.4–5, 'For who can fully[109] recount His works, and who can trace His great deeds? No one can measure His majestic power and who can tell in full all His mercies?'

The same theme recurs in the so-called Benediction of the Song (ברכת השיר), the *Nishmat* prayer (*SPB*, 182–182; see *b. Pes.* 118a), which according to Genizah versions, was recited daily.[110] אילו פינו מלא שירה כים ולשוננו רינה כהמון גליו ושפתותנו שבח כמרחבי רקיע... אין אנו מספיקים להודות לך...ולברך את שמך על אחת מאלף אלפי אלפים ורבו רבבות פעמים הטובות שעשית..., 'Though our mouths were full of song as the sea, and our tongues of exaltation as the multitude of its waves, and our lips of praise as the widely extended firmament..., we should still be unable to thank You and bless Your name for one thousandth of a thousand thousands...of the bounties which You have bestowed...[111]

An identical *topos* is found in the Hekhalot literature in connection with the praise of the angels.[112] כי מי יכול להגיד אחת מאלף אלפי אלפים ורבי רבבות גבורתיך מלך מלכי המלכים... שהחיות נצבות לפניך... מלך גדול וקדוש אתה שיכול לדעת את מעשיך ולחקור את גבורתיך..., 'Who is able to recount one thousandth of a thousand thousands...of the marvellous deeds of the King of

108. Cf. Sanders, *The Psalms Scroll of Qumran Cave 11*, 28.6–7. According to the verse division of A. Hurwitz, 'Adon Hakkol', *Tarbiz* 34 (1965), 224, we should read: ומי יספר את מעשי אדון הכול. F.M. Cross, 'David, Orpheus, and Psalm 151.3–4' (*BASOR* 231 [October 1978), pp. 69ff., who reads in ll. 5–6 *lu* instead of *lo*, understands מי here in parallel with *lu* as 'would that someone (tell)', arguing that a different rendering, viz., the mountains cannot tell, would be 'nonsense in a biblical or early Jewish context' (p. 70 n. 6). However, the problem is one of exhausting the praise and not the mere telling of it: although the mountains etc. praise God (cf. Ps. 148.9–10, rightly adduced by Cross), they are not able to recount all his praises; cf. Ps. 106.1–2: 'Praise the Lord...who can tell the mighty acts of the Lord, proclaim *all* His praises', and cf. also Ps. 40.6: 'You, O Lord...have done many things... I would rehearse the tale of them but they are more than can be told'. The passage from Ps. 151 of 11QPs[a] should then be thus translated: 'The mountains do not witness to Him, nor do the hills. The leaves of the trees do not recount my words, nor does the flock my deeds. For who can tell...' For the reading 'leaves of the trees', cf. Skehan, *CBQ* 25 (1963), pp. 407–408. This reading may be supported by a liturgical fragment from the Genizah: 'Your praise supercedes in number the dust of the earth...more than every plant, every leaf and seed...'. (TS NS 198.20).

109. ἐξεποίησεν has to be translated as הספיק as may be learned from 42.17 where the Hebrew has השפיק and LXX ἐξεποίησεν.

110. Cf. Mann, 279, 325.

111. For a parallel in Mandaic liturgy, cf. J.C. Greenfield, 'A Mandaic "Targum" of Psalm 114', *Studies in Aggadah, Targum and Jewish Liturgy in Memory of Joseph Heinemann* (1981), p. 29: 'If our mouths would be like the sea, and our lips like the waves, and our tongues like steep mountains'.

112. Cf. *Pirke Hekhalot Rabbati, Bate Midrashot* I (ed. A.J. Wertheimer, 1950), p. 111. Cf. P. Schäfer, *Synopse zur Hekhalot Literatur* (1988), p. 276.

Kings...when the angels stand before You...because You are a King great and Holy that one may know Your deeds and explore Your mighty acts...'.

This *topos* is already attested in the Homeric literature. Thus, we read there in connection with naming the ships and the troops that participated in the war at Troy,

> Tell me now, you Muses...for you are goddesses and...know all things..., who were the captains of the Danaans..., but the common folk I could not tell, nor name, not *though ten tongues were mine and ten mouths and a voice unwearing...*
> Homer, *The Iliad* II 485–494.

Here the muses (=the angels)[113] who know everything can recount the story but not men. Similarly, we find in Virgil's Aeneid (vi 625–627):

> Nay, had I a hundred tongues, a hundred mouths and a voice of iron I could not sum up all the forms of crime.

This topic is also found in the hymn of Lucius to Isis:

> My voice has no power to utter that which I think of your majesty. No, not if I had a thousand mouths and many tongues and were able to continue forever...(Apuleius, *Metamorphoses*, XI, 25).

Most recently a Greek inscription was discovered in Ḥammat Gader that has on it a poem by the Empress Eudocia (fifth century CE). Here we read:

> In my life many and infinite wonders have I seen. But who, however many his mouths, could proclaim...your strength.[114]

The Praise of the Angels in the Book of Jubilees

P.W. Skehan[115] has shown that Jub. 2.2–3 parallels 11QPs[a] 26.4–5. Furthermore, the verbal congruency between the passages led him to the conclusion that the Qumran hymn influenced the book of Jubilees.

Jubilees	*11QPs[a]*
He created...day and dawn[116] which He established in the *knowledge of His heart*. Thereupon we *saw His work and praised Him...*	He established the dawn by the *knowledge of His heart*. Then *all His angels saw and were jubilant*.

Although both sources speak about creating *dawn* and not the luminaries, as in the liturgies quoted before, this should not be viewed as a different tradition since

113. For the muses functioning as angels see ch. 2, pp. 42–48.

114. J. Green and Y. Tsafrir, 'A Poem of the Empress Eudocia', *IEJ* 32 (1982), pp. 79–80. Cf. the parallel to this *topos* adduced by A. Scheiber, 'Parallels to a Topos in Eudocia's Poem', *IEJ* 34 (1984), pp. 180–81.

115. P.W. Skehan, 'Jubilees and the Qumran Psalter', *CBQ* 37 (1975), pp. 343–47.

116. Following the Greek version of Epiphanius (Skehan, p. 345).

the light created on the first day was considered identical with that of the heavenly bodies (cf. *b. Hag.* 12a).

Conclusion

The Hymn to the Creator in 11QPs[a] 26.9–15 contains the basic elements of the *Qedushah* liturgy in the conventional Jewish morning prayer (*Yoṣer* liturgy) as well as in the book of Jubilees and in Ben Sira. The opening sentence of the Hymn to the Creator: גדול וקדוש ה׳ קדוש קדושים לדור ודור, 'Great and holy is YHWH the holiest of holy ones for every generation', overlaps the conventional and the Genizah formulae of the Benediction of the *Qedushah*.

Furthermore, the basic formula of the Qumranic hymn: שחר הכין בדעת לבו, 'He established the dawn (=the light) by the knowledge of his mind', occurs in the book of Jubilees 2.2–3, in Ben Sira 42.16–20, and in the *Yoṣer* liturgy; cf. especially גדול דעה הכין ופעל זהרי חמה, '(the God) great in knowledge formed and established the rays of the sun'.

The cosmic renewal of the luminaries accompanied by grace, truth, and justice is found both in the Qumran literature and in the *Yoṣer* liturgy.

Chapter 6

GRACE AFTER MEALS IN QUMRAN

The so-called ברכי נפשי hymns, found in the fourth cave of Qumran, and published in *DJD* XXIX, consist of six scrolls: 4Q434 to 439. Usually they open with the phrase ברכי נפשי, 'Bless, O my soul' and they contain praises to God for the salvation of the pious and for giving them a pure heart that will keep them away from temptation and enable them to understand the divine secrets. Compare, for example, 4Q434: 'Bless, O my [soul], the Lord, for all his wonders…, and let his name be blessed because he saved the poor…and did not forget the trouble of the needy…he opened their eyes to see his ways…and circumcised the foreskins of their heart…and revealed to them the message of peace and truth…'.

ברכי [נפשי] את אדוני על כל נפלאותיו...
וברוך שמו כי הציל נפש אביון...
ולא שכח צרת דלים...
ויפקח עיניהם לראות את דרכיו...
וימול עורלות לבם...
ויגל להם תורות שלום ואמת...

Among the fragments ascribed to 4Q434 material was found (frag. 2 [PAM 43.513]) that has nothing to do with hymns and in fact, as we shall see, constitutes a blessing after the meal at the mourner's house. The existence of such a liturgical practice at Qumran has been suggested by me on a previous occasion in an analysis of a passage from 4QDeut^{n} (the so-called All Souls scroll)[1] containing Deut. 8.5–10, which mentions blessing God after eating from the bounty of the good land. The appearance of this passage as a separate unit next to Deut. 5.1–6.1 – that is, the Decalogue and its frame, so often copied at Qumran has not found any explanation. It seems therefore that the function of this passage, like the function of the Decalogue next to it, is liturgical, since it serves as the basis for the grace after meals in Judaism. What we have, then, in 4QDeut^{n} is a scroll for a liturgical purpose: the recital of the Decalogue, next to the blessing after meals.

The affinity of the Decalogue (and *Shema'*) with the blessing after meals may be explained by the common meal (ἀγάπη) that followed the prayer.[2] This custom

1. See S.A. White, 'A Critical Edition of seven manuscripts of Deuteronomy: 4QDt^{a}; 4QDt^{c}; 4QDt^{d}. 4QDt^{f}: 4QDt^{g}; 4QDt^{i} and 4QDt^{n}' (dissertation, Harvard University, 1990; see also her article '4QDt^{n}: Biblical Manuscript or Excerpted Text?', in *Of Scribes and Scrolls: Studies on the Hebrew Bible, Intertestamental Judaism and Christian Origins, Presented to John Strugnell on the Occasion of his Sixtieth Birthday* [ed. H.W. Attridge, J.J. Collins and T.H. Tobin, 1990], pp. 13–20).

2. For the connection of ἀγάπη with the communal religious meals in Pharisaic Judaism, see

is reflected in the epistle of Pliny the Younger to Trajan (10.96) about the group of Christians who used to get up before dawn (like the Essenes; see Josephus, *War* 2.8.5 §128–29); after their singing of hymns (a kind of פסוקי דזמרא),[3] they recited a *sacramentum* (that is, the pledge of the Decalogue) not to steal, not to commit adultery, and so on, and then assembled to partake of food.[4] At any rate, the morning prayer, which contains the Decalogue with the *Shema'* and the blessing after meals, represents the liturgical order of the day, and this is reflected in the All Souls Scroll (4QDeut^{n}).

Another scroll of the same nature is 4QDeut^{j}, recently investigated by J. Duncan.[5] There we find material from Deuteronomy 5–6 (= Decalogue and *Shema'*); 11; Exod. 12–13; Deut. 8.5–10; and Deuteronomy 32. Now, all this material belongs to Jewish liturgical practice. The phylacteries found at Qumran[6] contain the Decalogue (Deuteronomy 5), the *Shema'* (Deut. 6.4–9), והיה אם שמוע (Deut. 11.13–21), sections that contain injunctions about educating children, and the phylacteries in Exodus 13 – the so-called parashiyot of קדש (vv. 1–10) and והיה כי יביאך (vv. 11–16).[7] Deut. 8.5–10 reflects, as shown above, the grace after meals, whereas Deuteronomy 32 is known as a liturgical text which used to be recited by the Levites in the temple on the Sabbath (*b. Rosh Hash.* 31a; *y. Meg.* 3.6, 74b). Deuteronomy 32 was also recited at the temple service of the מעמדות.[8] The so-called מעמד constituted a group of representatives designated to accompany the daily services of the temple with prayers.

For our purpose it is now clear that Deut. 8.5–10 stands out as an autonomous text in two scrolls of Qumran, 4QDeut^{n} and 4QDeut^{j}, undoubtedly because of its liturgical function: the blessing after meals. That Deut. 8.5–10 served a liturgical function may be learned from the vacant line between v. 8 and v. 9 in 4QDeut^{n}. H. Stegemann, who first edited this text, was surprised by the *vacat* between the two verses (see photo appended here) and did not know how to explain it.[9] An

G. Alon, *Studies in Jewish History: In the Times of the Second Temple, the Mishna and the Talmud* (1957), I, p. 288 (Hebrew).

3. The recital of psalms in the morning prayers can be traced back to Ben Sira and the Qumran sect; see M. Weinfeld, 'Traces of *Kedushat Yoser* and *Pesukey de-Zimrah* in Qumran Literature', *Tarbiz* 45 (1976), pp. 16–26.

4. See M. Weinfeld, 'The Uniqueness of the Decalogue and its Place in Jewish Tradition', in B.Z. Segal and G. Levi (eds.), *The Ten Commandments in History and Tradition* (1990), pp. 31–32.

5. J. Duncan, 'A Critical Edition of Deuteronomy Manuscripts from Qumran Cave IV: 4QDt^{b}, 4QDt^{e}, 4QDt^{h}, 4QDt^{j}, 4QDt^{k}, 4QDt^{l}' (dissertation, Harvard University, 1989).

6. See J.T. Milik, *Qumran Grotte 4: II. Tefillin, Mezuzot et Targums 4Q128–4Q157* (*DJD* 6/2, 1977), pp. 48–85; see also Y. Yadin, *Tefillin from Qumran*: *(XQ Phyl 1–4)* (Jerusalem Israel113Exploration Society, and Shrine of the Book, 1970), p. 44, pl. XX.

7. See *Mechilta D'Rabbi Ishmael:* פסחא (ed. H.S. Horovitz and I.A. Rabin; Jerusalem: Whahrmann, 1970), p. 66 sec. 17; *Sifre Deut.* (ed. L. Finkelstein, 1969), p. 63 sec. 35.

8. See E.E. Urbach, 'Mishmarot and Ma'amadot', *Tarbiz* 42 (1973), pp. 304–327. The Song of Moses in Deuteronomy 32 was divided into seven sections for the seven days of the week. These formed an acrostic- הזיו לך = 'the glory is yours': האזינו (v. 1), זכר (v. 7), ירכבהו (v. 13), וירא (v. 19), לו (v. 29), כי (v. 40).

9. H. Stegemann, 'Weitere Stücke von 4Q Psalm 37, von 4Q Patriarchal Blessings und Hinweis

explanation can now be given in the light of rabbinic divergences concerning the duty of the blessing after meals based on the reading of these verses.

There existed a division of opinion among the Tannaim whether one should recite the three mandatory benedictions after food (for the food, for the land, and for Jerusalem and the Davidic dynasty) only after eating bread, or whether it was necessary to recite the benedictions also after eating the fruits with which the land of Israel was blessed (*m. Ber.* 6.8). According to R. Gamaliel, the commandment 'and you shall eat and be satisfied and you shall bless' (ואכלת ושבעת וברכת Deut. 8.10) refers to all of the seven species of the blessed land mentioned prior to it in 8.8 and not only to 'bread' (לחם) mentioned in v. 9. But according to the sages, the word 'land' (ארץ) in v. 9 interrupts the sequence (הפסיק הענין), and therefore the benediction mentioned in v. 10 refers only to the word 'land', which is connected to 'bread' in v. 9 (cf. *b. Ber.* 44a). Now the space of one line between the words 'a land of wheat and barley, of vines etc' (v. 8) and the verse 'a land where you may *eat bread* without stint' (v. 9) can be explained only against the background of this difference of opinion among the sages. The scribe of this scroll wished to make it known that the blessing in 10 belonged to the section in which bread is mentioned and not to the fruits mentioned in v. 8. According to the conventional halakhah, after wine and the other fruits of the land one has to bless God with a short blessing (מעין שלש) but is not obliged to recite the full blessings as after the meal containing bread.

But the discovery of fragment 4Q434, frag. 2 (PAM 43.513) adduces clear evidence about the existence of the grace after meals at Qumran, not only in general cases but even in the specific case at the house of the mourner.

As is well known, the blessings after meals were supplemented with special liturgies in both cases: the mourner's house (*b. Ber.* 46b) and the bridegroom's house (*b. Ketub.* 8ab). Indeed, in frag. 2 of 4Q434 we find not only the elements of the grace after meals that according to the rabbis are mandatory but even the specific formulas applying to the mourner. The text is fragmentary, but sufficient phrases were preserved in order to identify its nature.

Transcription

Text

1]כה[ ]כה להנחם על אבלה עניה ה°[[
2 גיים ל[ש]חת ולאומים יכרית ורשעים °[ ]חדש
3 מעשי שמים וארץ ויגילו וכבודו מלוא[כל הארץ כער אש]°מתם
4 יכפר ורב {{טו}} טוב ינחמם טוב הש°[ ]°ם לאכול
5 פריה וטובה *vacat*] *vacat*[
6 כאיש אשר אמו תנחמנו כן ינחמם בירושל[ים כחתן]על כלה עליה
7 לעו]לם ישכו[ן כי]א כסאו לעולם ועד וכבודו °[ ]וכל גוים

auf eine unedierte Handschrift aus Höhle 4Q mit Exzerpten aus Deuteronomy', *RevQ* 6 (1967), pp. 193–227.

8]]לו והיה בו צב[א]ים ו[ ]רצם חמדה
9]]עד תפאר[ת]ש[ ]ך אברכה את
10]]ברוך שם עליו[ן *vacat*[
11]] ברכי[ ]חסדך עלי
12]]לתורה הכנותה
13]]ך סכר חוקיך

Translation

1. [ ]°*kh*[ ]*kh* to be comforted for the poor in mourning *h*°[ ]
2. to [de]stroy peoples and cut down nations and wicked °[ ] renew
3. the works of heaven and earth and let them rejoice, and his glory to fill[all the earth] to atone [for] their [guil]t.
4. And the one abounding in goodness (God) will comfort. Goodness *hš*°[ ]°*m* to eat
5. its fruit and goodness *vacat*
6. as a mother comforts her son, so will he comfort them with Jerusal[em as a bridegroom on a bride
7. will dwel[l forev]er [fo]r his throne forever and until his glory *y*°[ ] and all peoples
8. [ ]*lw* and it was *bw ṣb*[ ]*ym* and their desirable [l]and
9. [ ]'*d* glor[y] *s*[ ]*d* I will bless
10. [ ]Blessed be the name of the highe[st] *vacat*
11. [ ] Bless[ ]your grace upon me
12. [ ]for the Torah you established
13. [ ] *k* the book of your laws

Notes to the Text

Line 1. להנחם על אבלה עניה. Cf. Isa. 54.11: עניה...לא נחמה. The term אבלה applied to Jerusalem, not found in the Bible, is attested in the prayers of mourning for the ninth of Ab in *y. Ber.* 4.38a: רחם... על ירושלים...ועל העיר האבלה, 'have mercy…upon Jerusalem…upon the city in mourning'.

Line 2. For the parallel of גוים and לאמים, see Isa. 34.4; 43.9; Ps. 2.1; 44.3, 15; 149.7.

Line 3. חדש מעשי שמים וארץ ויגילו. Cf. Isa. 65.17–18: כי הנני בורא שמים חדשים וארץ חדשה...וגילו עדי עד, 'for behold, I am creating a new heaven and a new earth…rejoice forever'.

Lines 3–4.]בעד אש[מתם יכפר. Cf. 1QS 9.4: לכפר על אשמת פשע; 1QM frag. 2.13: לכפר אשמה.

Line 4. ורב טוב ינחמם. The word רב in the expression רב טוב appears in the Bible as an attribute of טוב = vast bounty (Isa. 63.7; Ps. 31.20; 145.7; Neh. 9.35). Here, however, it is applied to God, the possessor of bounty: 'great in goodness', like רב חסד, 'great in kindness' (Exod. 34.6; Num. 14.18; and parallels).

Lines 4–5. לאכול פריה וטובה. Cf. Jer. 2.7; Neh. 9.36.

Line 6. [כחתן] על כלה. Cf. Isa. 62.5; cf. 61.10.

Lines 6–7. עליה [לעו]לם ישכו[ן]. Cf. Deut. 33.12: ידיד ה׳ ישכן לבטח עליו, 'beloved of the Lord, he dwells securely on him'; other instances have: 'dwell in' (שכן ב...לעולם, Ezek. 43.9; 1 Chr. 23.25, וישכן בירושלים לעולם).

Line 7. כסאו לעולם ועד. Cf. 2 Sam. 7.16; Ps. 45.7; Prov. 29.14; 1 Chr. 17.14 in reference to the king; cf. Ps. 93.2; Lam. 5.19 in reference to God.

Line 10. ברוך שם עליו[ן]. Cf. שם אל עליון in IIQBer 1–2; see A. S. van der Woude, 'Ein neuer Segensspruch aus Qumran (11QBer)', in *Bibel und Qumran* (ed. S. Wagner; Berlin: Evangelische Haupt Bibelgesellschaft, 1968), 252–58. See the review by J. Strugnell in *RB* 77 (1970), 267–68.

Line 12. לתורה הכינותה. The verb הכין in Qumran literature implies creation; see 1QH 1.14, 20; 1QS 3.15–16.

The text opens with consolation of the poor mourner (להנחם על אבלה עניה...), having in mind Jerusalem in its mourning. The most important common element in the Qumran fragment and in the conventional Jewish grace after meals in the mourner's house is the verse from Isa. 66.13: 'as a mother comforts her son so I will comfort Jerusalem'. This verse appears both in the conventional Jewish blessings[10] after meals at the mourner's house and in the Qumran passage discussed here. In the Qumran text the consolation of Jerusalem is juxtaposed with the joy of the bridegroom with his bride. Similarly in the Jewish conventional liturgy, the Benediction of Jerusalem at Blessings of Marriage overlaps the Benediction at the Blessing of the Mourner's House. In both cases the conclusion of the third blessing was 'Blessed be YHWH...who consoles his people in his city'.[11] This is rooted in the prophecies of Deutero-Isaiah (49.19–21; 61.2–3; 62.4–5; 65.19–20; 66.10–11).

The next line (2) in the fragment of 4Q434, which mentions the destructions of peoples and nations: (גיים ל[ש]חת ולאומים יכרית), also belongs to the pattern of grace after meals. It seems to be associated with the land taken away by the Lord from other nations and given to Israel. This may be reflected in the Palestinian Talmud (*y. Ber*. 1.9, 3d) in connection with land and Torah, which are to be mentioned in the second benediction of the grace after meals. There we read: 'Rabbi Simon said in the name of Rabbi Yehoshua ben Levy: "Whoever did not mention Torah in the Benediction for land has to read [the Benediction] again. What is the reason for this? (it is written) 'he gave them the lands of nations (ויתן להם ארצות גוים), they inherited the wealth of peoples (ועמל לאמים יירשו) that they might keep his laws (חקיו) and observe his teachings (ותורתיו)' " (Ps. 105.44)'. Indeed both חוקים and Torah are mentioned explicitly in the fragment from Qumran (ll. 12–13; see below).

However, since the next sentence speaks about the renewal of creation (ll. 2–3), there is a possibility that the destruction of peoples and nations and the wicked is to be associated here not with the inheritance of the land but with the messianic future, when peoples and the wicked will be judged and punished. The next

10. See סדר רב עמרם גאון (ed. D.S. Goldschmidt, 1971), pp. 187–88 par. 158 (Hebrew).

11. See S. Lieberman, תוספתא כפשוטה, I (1955), p. 52.

sentence in the Qumran fragment (line 3) brings up the idea of the renewal of creation, an idea that is widespread in the second temple period, beginning with Isa. 65.18[12] (cf. 66.22) and continuing with 1 Enoch 45.4; 91.16; Jub. 1.29; 1QH 13.11–12; 11QTemple 29.8–10; 2 Cor. 5.17; Rev. 21.1; etc. Messianic expectations are included in the third benediction of the grace after meals (see especially the phrase 'the kingdom of the house of David, your Messiah' and the wish 'that Elijah, the prophet and the Messiah come soon')[13] but are also mentioned at the end of the grace after meals, where all kinds of personal wishes occur:

> May the merciful send us Elijah, the prophet, ...
> who shall bring us good tidings, salutation and consolation ...
> May, the merciful make us worthy of the days of the
> Messiah and of the life of the world to come.[14]

This is to be compared with the *Didache* (*Teaching of the Twelve Apostles*) ch. 10 in connection with the grace after meals: 'Gather it [the church] together... to your kingdom which you prepared for it. Let grace come and let this world pass away. Hosannah to the God of David'.[15]

The next phrase in the Qumran fragment (ll. 3–4) is [בעד אש]מתם יכפר, 'he will forgive for their guilt'. This undoubtedly refers to the deceased, whose sins are expiated by their death. This is also reflected in the Jewish blessing after meals for mourners: 'Blessed be YHWH our God...the God of truth, who judges truly...and takes away souls in justice' (דיין אמת...לוקח נפשות במשפט) (*b. Ber.* 46b). This actually constitutes an acknowledgment of divine justice (צידוק הדין), which is recited at the Jewish burial service and whenever one sees graves (see *b. Ber.* 58b; *t. Ber.* 7.6).

A salient motif of the conventional grace after meals is the goodness of God (טובו) by providing food to all his creatures: 'who feeds the world with his goodness' (הזן את העולם...בטובו). Actually a separate benediction was established for God 'who is good and does good' (הטוב והמיטיב) with all, and as has been shown by C. Albeck and A. Büchler this is an old blessing from before the destruction of the temple.[16] There were, however, disputes among the Tannaim whether this benediction should be said in the mourner's house. Only after the great disaster at Bethar (in Bar Kokhba's time), when the very possibility of burying the dead was considered a miracle, it was decided by all to preserve this blessing even at the mourner's house. הטוב והמיטיב was then interpreted: הטוב ('is good') that the bodies of the slain were not decomposed, and והמיטיב ('does

12. Note the juxtaposition of rejoicing (גיל) with the new creation in Isa. 65.17–18 and in the Qumran fragment under discussion (ll. 2–3).

13. See סדר רב עמרם גאון, 45; see also E.D. Goldschmidt, *On Jewish Liturgy* (1978), p. 161 (Hebrew).

14. The *Standard Prayer Book* (ed. Rev. S. Singer, 1943), pp. 429–30.

15. K. Lake, *The Apostolic Fathers* (LCL, 1977), pp. 1–325.

16. C. Albeck, 'Die vierte Eulogie des Tischgebets', *MGWJ* n.F.42 (1943), pp. 430–37; A. Büchler, 'The History of the Benediction הטוב והמיטיב in the Grace after meals', in *Abhandlungen zur Erinnerunig an H.P. Chajes* (Vienna: A. Kohut Memorial Foundation, 1933), pp. 137–67 (Hebrew).

good') that they were given for burial. הטוב והמיטיב occurs also in the short blessing after eating fruits of the seven species (*b. Ber.* 44a).

This formula, הטוב והמיטיב, is actually reflected in the Qumran fragment discussed here. Thus in line 4 we read 'and the one great in goodness (ורב טוב) will console them...the good one' (טוב...הש[).[17] The motif of goodness in connection with the land is actually mentioned in the prayer of Nehemiah: 'they ate and were satiated...by your great goodness (בטובך הגדול, Neh. 9.25); 'And with your great goodness (בטובך הרב) that you gave them, and the ample and rich land (הארץ הרחבה והשמנה) that you put at their disposal' (9.35). There we also find the phrase 'to eat its fruit and goodness' (לאכול את פריה ואת טובה, 9.36), which occurs in the Qumran fragment (ll. 4–5) as well as in the conventional shortened blessing after eating the fruits of the land of the seven species (Deut. 8.8); see *b. Ber* 44a.

The words in line 7 לעו[לם ישכו[ן]... כסאו לעולם ועד וכבודו, 'dwell forever...his throne forever and his glory' refer either to David's throne or to God's throne. In fact both should be taken into account here, as stated in *b. Ber.* 49a: 'since he mentioned David's kingdom it is inappropriate not to mention the kingdom of heaven'. Indeed, the kingdom of God is mentioned thrice in the fourth blessing: מלך העולם, מלכנו,המלך הטוב. The messianic element is indispensable in the grace after meals, as stated in *b. Ber* 48b: 'Whoever did not mention the Kingdom of David in the Benediction over Jerusalem did not fulfil his obligation'.

Another element that must be mentioned in the grace after meals is ארץ חמדה טובה ורחבה (*b. Ber.* 48b), 'the pleasant, good, and ample land'. This is reflected in the Qumran fragment in line 8: [אר]צם חמדה, 'their pleasant land'. The same applies to the obligation to cite ברית and תורה, 'covenant and Torah', mentioned in *b. Ber.* 49a. This is found in ll. 12–13 of our fragment: לתורה הכינותה, 'You have established for the Torah' and ספר חוקיך, 'the book of your laws'. The laws and the Torah are mentioned in the passage from *y. Ber* 1.9.3d, quoted above.

We find then in the Qumran fragment all the elements of the blessings after meals practised in Judaism, although not in the conventional order, that is: (1) food for all creatures (2) the land (3) Jerusalem and the messianic line (4) the good one who does good. The fixed order of these blessings is apparently of later times. This may be deduced from the grace after meals in early Christianity. In the *Didache* (second century CE) we read about the prayer after meals (ch. 10)[18] (I do not quote the christological material inserted into this prayer):

1. 'We give thanks to you...for the knowledge[19] and faith...etc'. (land is omitted). This parallels the blessing for Torah and covenant in the conventional Jewish blessing.

17. The...טוב הש in line 4 may reflect the formula of הטוב והמיטיב.

18. See Alon, *Studies in Jewish History*, I, pp. 286–91.

19. On דעת = 'knowledge' in the sense of divine instruction (תורה), see my article 'The Prayers for Knowledge, Repentance and Forgiveness in the Eighteen Benedictions', *Tarbiz* 48 (1979), pp. 186–200 (Hebrew).

2. 'You created everything...and gave food to men...and blessed them with spiritual food and drink and eternal light'. This parallels the first blessing.

3. 'Remember, Lord, your community *(ekklesia)* to deliver it from all evil... and gather it together from all the corners of the earth to your Kingdom. Let grace come and let this world pass away. Hosannah to the God of David'. This overlaps the mention of Zion and the Davidic-messianic kingdom in the conventional grace after meals (see above). The 'kingdom of God' mentioned here is actually prescribed in *b. Ber.* 49a as a mandatory element in the grace after meals. 'The God of David' mentioned here is prominent in the Palestinian form of the third blessing in the grace after meals (see *y. Ber.* 4.5, 8c; *y. Rosh Hash.* 4.6, 59c).[20]

The Qumran fragment contains all of the basic elements of the grace after meals that were also common in rabbinic Pharisaic Judaism. Although we do not find in the Qumran fragment the common liturgical-hymnic formulas such as ברוך אתה ה׳ found at the end of each blessing in the conventional Jewish benedictions after meals, there are traces of them here. Thrice we find in the fragment the root ברך: 'I will bless' (אברכה, line 9); 'Blessed be the name of the most high' (ברוך שם עליון, line 10); 'Bless, O [my soul]' (ברכי [נפשי], line 11). The second phrase, ברוך שם עליון, is close in form to the conventional Jewish formula ברוך (אתה) ה׳. Furthermore, the blessing of the 'Name' in the Qumran fragment is a characteristic feature of postexilic biblical prayers as well as of the Qumran prayers.[21] The same applies to the epithet עליון, which was introduced in postbiblical prayers.[22]

The difference between the two traditions is in two things: (1) the order of the blessings and the lack of formal rigidity in the Qumran fragment and (2) that the Pharisaic benedictions were not permitted to be written *(b. Shab.* 115b) whereas the Qumran benedictions exist in a written form. This applies, of course, to the notion of *oral Torah*, which has not been adopted by the non-Pharisaic tradition.[23]

20. Cf. Rödelheim, סדר עבודת ישראל, 1868 (ed. S. Baer, 1957), pp. 96–97 (Hebrew).

21. See A. Hurvitz, *The Transition Period in Biblical Hebrew* (1972), pp. 97–100 (Hebrew),

22. See A. Hurvitz, 'Observations on the Language of the Third Apocryphal Psalm from Qumran', *RevQ* 5 (1965), pp. 225–32.

23. This study has been prepared at the Institute for Advanced Studies of the Hebrew University of Jerusalem during my stay as a member of the Qumran Research group in 1989–1990. I am indebted to the institute for the help given to me for the preparation of this study. I am thankful to Professor John Strugnell (also a member of the group at the Institute) for making available to me the photocopies and the transliteration of the manuscript discussed here.

Appendix

Grace after Meals in the Mourner's House
The Jewish Tradition and Rabbinic Sources

ברוך מנחם אבלים שאכלנו משלו ובטובו חיינו.

Blessed be (our God) who comforts the mourners, he of whose bounty we have partaken and through whose goodness we live

סדר ברכת המזון: ברכת הזן (ובטובו, ובטובו הגדול,מטיב לכל).

(who feeds) with his goodness…with his great goodness, who does good to everybody…

ברכת הארץ: (על שהנחלת לאבותינו ארץ חמדה טובה ורחבה; על בריתך...על תורתך שלמדתנו)

(we thank you)…for you gave us an inheritance to our fathers a good, a desirable and ample land as well as for the covenant…and for the Torah which you taught us

כל מי שלא הזכיר תורה בברכת הארץ מחזירים אותו,'ויתן להם ארצות גוים ועמל לאומים יירשו. בעבור ישמרו חקיו ותורתו ינצרו' (תה׳ קה,מה).

whoever did not mention Torah in the Benediction for land has to read (the Benediction) again, for it is written: 'he gave them lands of nations, they inherited the wealth of peoples that they might keep his laws (חקיו) and observe his teachings (תורותיו)' (Ps 105.44; y. *Ber.* 1.9, 3d).

בונה ירושלים: (על ציון משכן כבודך) ועל מלכות בית דוד משיחך.

give grace…to Israel…Jerusalem, Zion the abode of your glory, and the kingdom of David your anointed

כל שלא אמר ארץ חמדה ורחבה בברכת הארץ ומלכות בית דוד בבונה ירושלים לא יצא ידי חובתו (ברכות מח ע''ב).

whoever did not mention 'the good desirable and ample land' in the Blessing for the land nor the Kingdom of David in the Blessing for building Jerusalem did not fulfill his obligation *(b. Ber.* 48b).

כל שלא אמר ברית ותורה בברכת הארץ לא יצא ידי חובתו (ברכות מט ע''א)

whoever did not mention covenant and Torah in the Blessing for the land did not fulfill his obligation *(b. Ber.* 49a).

בבית האבל: נחם ה׳ אלהינו את אבלי ירושלים ואת האבלים המתאבלים באבל הזה. נחמם מאבלם... כאמור : 'כאיש אשר אמו תנחמנו כן אנכי אנחמכם ובירושלים תנחמו'. (ישע׳ ס''ו 13)

In *the mourner's house:* Comfort" you, our God, the mourners of Jerusalem and the mourners who mourn this mourning, console them…as it is written: 'as a mother comforts her son so I will comfort you, you shall find comfort in Jerusalem' (Isa. 66.13).

ברוך אתה ה'...המלך החי, הטוב והמיטיב, אל אמת, דיין אמת...ולוקח נפשות במשפט...(ברכות מו ע''ב).

Blessed be you our God...the living God, the good, who does good... the God of truth, who judges truly...and takes away souls in justice... *(b. Ber.* 46b)

ברכה לאחר שבעה מינים: ועל ארץ חמדה טובה ורחבה שהנחלת לאבותינו לאכול מפריה ולשבוע מטובה רחם ה' אלהינו...על ירושלים עירך ועל ציון משכן כבודך...כי אתה טוב ומיטיב לכל (ברכות מד ע''א).

Grace after wine and fruits of the seven species (Deut. 8.8): Blessed be...for the good desirable and ample land which you gave as an inheritance to our fathers to eat of its fruits and to be satiated with its goodness. Give grace...to Jerusalem and Zion the abode of your glory because you are good and do good for all...(*b. Ber,* 44a).

Synopsis of Grace after Meals at Mourner's House

Qumran (4Q434 frag. 2)	*Pharisaic-Rabbinic*	
בעד אש]מתם יכפר	ולוקח נפשות במשפט...(בברכות מו ע''ב)	
ורב טוב...טוב	ברכת הזן (ובטובו, ובטובו הגדול, מטיב לכל) הטוב והמיטיב (הוא הטיב, הוא מטיב, הוא ייטיב לנו)	סדר ברכת המזון:
ארץ חמדה	ברכת הארץ (ארץ חמדה טובה ורחבה; על בריתך...	
לתורה...ספר חקיך	על תורתך שלמדתנו	
כי]א כסאו לעולם ועד וכבודו	בונה ירושלים: (על ציון משכן כבודך ועל מלכות בית דוד משיחך).	
להנחם על אבלה עניה כאיש אשר אמו תנחמנו כן ינחמם בירושל[ים]	בבית האבל: נחמם מאבלם...כאמור: כאיש אשר אמו תנחמנו כן אנכי אנחמכם ובירושלים תנחמו	
גיים...ולאומים יכרות לאכול פריה וטובה.	ברכה לאחר שבעה מינים: ועל ארץ חמדה טובה ורחבה שהנחלת לאבותינו לאכול מפריה ולשבוע מטובה-רחם ה' אלהינו...על ירושלים עירך כי אתה טוב ומיטיב לכל (ברכות מד ע''א)	

Chapter 7

מנחה *MINḤAH*

The term מנחה, 'gift, present', early acquired the specialized meaning of a sacrifice or offering which was to be a 'pleasing odour' (ריח נחוח) to the deity and was to soothe its senses. Thus David says to Saul: 'If it is Yahweh who has stirred you up against me, then give him a מנחה to smell (רוח, hiphᶜil)' (1 Sam. 26.19). This pleasing smell of the sacrifice's fragrance is also implied even if the term מנחה is not explicitly mentioned. Thus it also happens that when Noah makes an offering to Yahweh after the deluge, and Yahweh smells its pleasing fragrance (וירח ה׳ את ריח הניחח), he pledges not to curse the earth a second time (Gen. 8.21): cf. negatively Lev. 26.31: 'I will no longer smell the fragrance of your sacrifices'; Amos 5.21: 'I take no pleasure in smelling your solemn assemblies'.

And indeed, the מנחה constitutes that part of the ritual which creates the fragrance: corn, flour, baked bread, or cakes mixed with oil and frankincense and presented before Yahweh (Lev. 2.14f.). The מנחה constitutes the high point of the sacrificial ritual, since it ensures that God is able to smell the pleasing fragrance of the offering.

Although the term *minḥah* frequently occurs in connection with or parallel to עולה,זבח it usually constitutes a fixed ritual together with the קטרת and the incense offering (לבונה) cf. Isa. 1.13: 'It is futile to bring me מנחה*;* incense (קטרת) is an abomination to me'. Isa. 43.23: 'I have not burdened you with מנחה, or wearied you with frankincense (לבונה)' (cf. also Neh. 13.5–9; Isa. 66.3; Jer. 17.26; 41.5). The tandem מנחה and לבונה also appears in the Elephantine papyri, indeed exclusively in this combination.[1]

Ps. 141.2 is of significance regarding the association of מנחה (especially the evening מנחה) with the incense offering: 'Let my prayer be counted as incense before thee, and the lifting up of my hands as an evening *minḥah* (cf. discussion below).

The מנחה, mixed with oil and frankincense, was blended from flour or meal and could be offered by anyone, independent of animal sacrifice (cf. Lev. 2). Indeed, the מנחה and the incense offering (קטרת, לבונה) developed into a kind of universal ritual; cf., e.g., Mal. 1.11: 'For from the rising of the sun to its setting my name is great among the nations, and in every place incense (מוקטר) is offered to my name, and a pure מנחה'.

1. Cf. *AP*, 30.21, 25; 31.21; 32.9; 33.10f.; cf. also Vogt, 107.

Reference should be made also to the eighty men who go up to Jerusalem bringing מנחה and לבונה (Jer. 41.5).

Offerings of the מנחה type are attested throughout the ancient Near East. Thus in a Kassite votive inscription we read: 'For Adad…he libated from seeds and… roots, he caused incense to go up in smoke' (*i-na* ŠE.NUMUN *ù ḫir-ṣa-ti qut-ri-nam ú-ša-aq-ti-ir*).[2] In Mesopotamia we also find fragrant offerings whose odour is meant for the deity: 'Without you [Šamaš] the great gods of heaven and earth cannot smell the incense offerings' (*ul iṣ-ṣi-nu qut-rin-nu*).[3]

In the official cult, however, the מנחה was normally connected with animal sacrifice, something already attested by ancient Israelite sources. Gideon takes for his offering a kid and unleavened bread baked from an ephah of flour (Judg. 6.19); Manoaḥ, the father of Samson, takes a kid and a מנחה (Judg. 13.19: cf. v. 23); Hannah, the mother of Samuel, prepares a thankoffering consisting of three bulls (LXX and 4QSam: 'a three-year-old bull'), an ephah of flour and a skin of wine (1 Sam 1.24). The Priestly Document provides precise instructions concerning the quantities of grain or flour for such offerings. The מנחה consists of a tenth of an ephah of fine meal (סלת) to lamb offering, two tenths for a ram offering, and three tenths for a bull offering (cf. Num. 15.1–15; 28; 29).

It should be pointed out that, in contrast to the usual interpretation, this סלת does not strictly speaking mean 'fine flour', but rather 'meal', i.e., ground, pulverized grain (cf. Akk. *siltu,* and *b. Shab.* 74b: *s l t slty,* 'cut into pieces, cut evenly'; cf. Akk. *salātu*), which – one assumed – was more finely sifted than flour and contained no husks.[4]

In his temple vision, Ezekiel mentions other quantities for the מנחה: 'one ephah for a ram, one ephah for a bull, and for a lamb as much as he has at hand' (Ezek. 46.4; cf. 45.24). The determination of such recipes for the preparation of ritual sacrifices is also regulated in Mesopotamia: 'three sheep…three *ṣimid*-measures (=סאים) of grain'.[5] The proportions of grain/flour per animal sacrifice derive from current customs at the court or among the populace for the preparation of meals and feasts. Accordingly, Abraham prepares as a hospitality meal for his guests one calf and three measures (סאים) of meal (סלת) (Gen. 18.6f.). Similarly, a list for deliveries to soldiers found at Ugarit reads: 'one lamb and a *lth* of flour'.[6] One *lth* (cf. Heb. לתך, Hos. 3.2) corresponds roughly to one tenth of an ephah (2.2 1. [2.3 qt.]),[7] which in Israel accompanied a lamb offering.

2. *Designation of Time.* Since the מנחה together with frankincense constituted the high point of the sacrificial ritual, namely, the presentation of the 'pleasing fragrance' (ריח נחוח), the time of this offering was viewed as the most favourable time of the day. Thus Elijah offers his prayer to God at the time of the מנחה

2. *BM* 92699; E. Sollberger. 'Two Kassite Votive Inscriptions', *JAOS*, 88 (1968), pp. 191–95.
3. J. Nougayrol, 'Textes Religieux (I)', *RA* 65 (1971), p. 162, 3.
4. See recently J. Milgrom, *Leviticus 1–16.* (*AB*; 1991), p. 179.
5. T.G. Pinches, *The Babylonian Tablets of the Berens Collection* (1915), p. 110.8.
6. *KTU*, 4.751.
7. Cf. Heltzer.

offering (בעלות המנחה, 1 Kgs 18.36), and his prayer is answered (vv. 38ff.). Ps. 141.2 also attests that the hour of the מנחה and of the incense offering was viewed as the most favourable time of the day: 'Let my prayer be counted as incense before thee, and the lifting up of my hands as an evening מנחה'. In fact, the expression 'favourable time' is itself attested in the Psalms: 'But as for me, my prayer is to thee, Yahweh, at a favourable time (עת רצון). O God, in the abundance of thy steadfast love, with thy faithful help answer me' (Ps. 69.14[13]). This verse is recited in the synagogue at the מנחה prayer on the Sabbath,[8] a tradition that seems to go back very far. Here, too, the petitioner uses the formula עננו, 'answer me', which goes back to Elijah's evening prayer. It is of further significance that the prayer of fasting days 'עננו' is recited only in connection with the מנחה prayer.[9] The burning of incense offerings within the context of liturgy is also reflected in Isaiah's inaugural vision (Isa. 6). The angels' trishagion is accompanied by the filling of the temple with smoke, directly recalling the smoke ascending from the incense altar (v. 6). Solomon's prayer of consecration in 1 Kgs 8.12ff. should probably also be understood against this background (cf. the description of the cloud in the temple in vv. 10f.), namely, as a prayer accompanied by an incense offering (cf. Lev. 16.2,13).

The literature from the period of the second temple as well as rabbinic writings richly attest this understanding of the time of the מנחה as the appropriate time for prayer. It is said that Ezra offered his penitential prayer (in connection with the problem of mixed marriages) at the time of the evening מנחה (Ezra 9.5). Similarly, the angel Gabriel reveals himself at just this time to Daniel (Dan. 9.21) or to the priest Zechariah (Lk. 1.9f.). As was the custom, the people prayed 'outside the house of God' while the priests presented the incense offering. This is picked up in a regulation in the Mishnah (*Tamid* 4.3; *Kelim* 1.9), according to which the people were not permitted to enter the area between the porch and the altar (בין האולם ולמזבח) while the priest presented the incense offering. The people assembled in the outer court (עזרה) for prayer. Finally, Judith prays in the house of God at the time of the evening מנחה (Jth. 9.1).

It is said that the Hasmonean high priest John Hyrcanus received his revelation at the time of the incense offering (Josephus *Antiq.* xiii 282f.).

The Targum understood the various references to incense and offering fragrance in Cant. 4.11–16 as if they were referring to the incense offering in the temple, whereby the priests and people prayed: 'May God, my beloved, enter the temple and readily accept the offerings of his people' (Targ. to vv. 11,16). The blessing of Isaac in Gen. 27.27f. ('Ah, the smell of my son is like the smell of a field that Yahweh has blessed') was similarly interpreted with an eye on the incense offering in the temple (cf. further the apocryphal Life of Adam and Eve 29; *T. Levi* 3.5f.).[10]

All these examples illuminate the rabbinic designation '*minḥah* prayer' (תפילת מנחה) as the afternoon prayer. Although the מנחה was also presented in the

8. Cf. I. Elbogen, *Der jüdische Gottesdienst in seiner geschichtlichen Entwicklung* (1913), p. 118.

9. *Ibid.*, p. 55.

10. Cf. D. Kellermann, 'לבונה lᵉḇōnâ', TDOT VII, pp. 441–47.

morning as a cereal offering, the actual time of prayer was associated with the evening offering at which the people were assembled. This מנחה worship took place at the ninth hour (3 p.m.), when the evening offering, the cereal offering, and the incense offering were presented (cf. m. *Pesaḥ* 5.1; Acts 3.1; 10.3,30).

Ezra's penitential prayer (Ezr. 9.5) showed that the time of the מנחה was also the most appropriate time for confession, a custom continued later. On the eve of the Day of Atonement the confession of sin was spoken shortly before darkness (עם חשכה; *t. Kippurim* 4.14). A similar confession over the tithe was spoken at the מנחה offering at the Passover Festival (*m. Ma'as. Sh.* 5.10; cf. Lev. 2). The Talmud also sees in מנחה the appropriate time for prayer (בעי רחמי) (cf. *b. Ta'an.* 12b and *passim*). Midrash Psalms even views the confession of sin and the מנחה prayer as the continuation of the presentation of the burnt offering in the period without temple and priest.[11]

11. Cf. A. Jellinek, בית המדרש: *Sammlung kleiner Midraschim und vermischter Abhandlungen aus der älteren jüdischen Literatur* (1967), IV, 104ff. [Heb.; Ger. intro.).

Chapter 8

The Morning Prayers (*Birkhoth Hashachar*) in Qumran and in the Conventional Jewish Liturgy

As is well known, the so-called 'Blessings of the Morning' *Birkhot Hashachar* (the standard Prayer Book, translated by Rev. A. Singer = *SPB*, 1943, pp. 4–11) in the Jewish liturgy are not part of the official prayers. They rather constitute private benedictions that are recited by the individual before the official public prayers.[1] However, in spite of their private nature the overall system of these blessings and prayers has not changed since the beginning of their appearance in liturgical texts. Furthermore, all the elements of *Birkhot Hashachar* are already attested in the rabbinic sources and in the Genizah texts and, as we shall try to show, they can be traced back to the Qumran liturgies.

As will be demonstrated, the *Birkhot Hashachar* contain two basic constituents: praise for giving life and soul (after sleep) on the one hand and apotropaic prayers[2] at the beginning of the day on the other. The apotropaic prayers were not destined for the morning only, they were used before sleep (*SPB*, p. 438), at the beginning of the week (cf. below, p. 129), at the beginning of the month (*SPB*, pp. 219–20), in the prayers on the New Year (cf. below, p. 129), and on other occasions. All of them have, as will be seen, a common typology, but the *Birkhot Hashachar* are the most elaborate and reveal a clear systematic pattern. This is quite understandable. The beginning of the day is the more appropriate occasion for such prayers. As will be shown below, the morning apotropaic prayers could be recited either before the official morning prayer or after it.

Let us analyse the traditional pattern of the *Birkhot Hashachar*.

1. *Basic elements of the* Birkhot Hashachar

1. *Praise of God for restoring the soul after sleep*. The benediction, which is to be said after one awakens from sleep, runs as follows:[3]

1. Cf. e.g. Maimonides, *Mishneh Torah*, Hilkhot Tefilah 7.9. For the *Birchot Hashachar*, see I. Elbogen, *Der jüdische Gottesdienst in seiner Geschichtlichen Entwicklung*[3] (1931), pp. 87–92.

2. For this definition, cf. D. Flusser, 'Qumran and Jewish Apotropaic Prayers', *Israel Exploration Journal* 16 (1966), pp. 194–205.

3. Cf. *b. Ber.* 60b. For the textual variants of this prayer, see A.L. Gordon, סדור אוצר התפלות (1914).

> 'O my God, the soul (נשמה) which You gave me is pure, You created it (בראתה), You formed it (יצרתה'), You breathed it into me, You watch it within me, and You will take it from me but will restore it unto me hereafter. So long as the soul is within me, I will give thanks unto You, O Lord my God and God of my fathers. Sovereign of all creatures, Lord of all souls. Blessed be You, O Lord, who restores souls unto dead bodies' (*SPB*, p. 4).

During sleep, the body is lifeless and awakening is therefore considered as coming back to life, hence the conclusion: 'Blessed be You, O Lord, who restores souls unto dead bodies' (המחזיר נשמות לפגרים מתים) in the Bablyonian custom (*b. Ber.* 60b) and 'Blessed be You, O Lord, who revives the dead' (מחיה מתים) in the Palestinian custom (*y. Ber.* 4.2, 7d).

2. Associated with this is *the blessing for the creation of man*: ברוך... אשר ברא את האדם (בצלמו) in the Genizah documents[4] and: ברוך...אשר ברא את האדם (בחכמה) in the traditional rites.[5] The benedictions for returning the soul and for creating man actually express one and the same idea: creation of human body and soul. Man, then, thanks God in the morning for creating body and soul as if he were born anew.

In the *Hodayot* of Qumran, which, in our opinion, follow the pattern of the morning prayers discussed here, this combination of thanks for creating the body (out of dust) and the soul is very common (see below, p. 133)

3. *Blessing over the Torah*. Selection of the created, i.e. created as a Jew and not as a gentile is reflected in the gift of the torah, the special heritage of Israel. No wonder then that in the context of the morning benedictions the 'new created man' blesses God for choosing the people of Israel and teaching it the Torah: 'Blessed are you YHWH who has chosen us from all the peoples and gave us his Torah...' 'Blessed are you YHWH who teaches the Torah to his people Israel' (המלמד תורה לעמו ישראל, *SPB*, p. 4, cf. ברוך אתה ה׳ למדני חקיך in Ps. 119.12). In the Palestinian versions of this Benediction we read: 'Blessed are You who has chosen his flocks... and made known to them the ways of his will (אשר בחר בעדרו והודיעם דרכי רצונו);[6] 'Blessed are you YHWH who gives Torah from the heaven and eternal life[7] in the heights' (הנותן תורה מן השמים וחיי עולם במרומים);[8] 'Blessed are you who has chosen this Torah and sanctified it and has

4. See J. Mann, Genizah Fragments of the Palestinian Order of Service, *HUCA* 2 (1925), p. 277; S. Asaf, מסדר התפילה בארץ ישראל, B.Z. *Dinaburg Festschrift*, 1949, p. 121. The identical benediction at the wedding feast (*SPB*, p. 44) is influenced by the morning blessing, cf. L. Ginsberg, פירושים וחידושים בירושלמי, III N.Y. 1941, p. 228f.

5. Cf. *b. Ber.* 60b. The אשר יצר benediction is associated with healing. This is based on the assumption that the body is constantly exposed to sickness and malfunction and it is through God's wonders that the body functions properly. The concluding formula of this benediction מפליא לעשות is attested often in the *Hodayot* when speaking about the creation of body and soul, cf. 1QH 11.3. הפלתה עם עפר וביצר חמר הגברתה, 1QH. Fr. 3.3–5 ועם בשר להפליא...ביצר עפר מהתפרר *et al.*

6. S. Asaf, *FS Dinaburg* (see n. 4), p. 123.

7. The same notion is expressed in the blessing after the recital of the Torah (*SPB*, 84: 'who gave us the Torah of truth and planted eternal life in our midst'= אשר נתן לנו תורת אמת וחיי עולם נטע בתוכנו), cf. *Tractate Soferim* 13,s (ed. Higger, 244). For this blessing cf. *John* 5.39 'You search the scriptures in which you think you have eternal life', see my remark in the article quoted in n. 10, *Tarbiz* 48 (1979), p. 194 n. 44 (Hebrew.)

8. J. Mann, *HUCA* 2 (1925), 293; cf. *Tractate Soferim* 13.6 (ed. Higger, p. 243).

chosen those who observe it' (אשר בחר בתורה הזאת וקידשה ורצה בעושיה).[9] Similar blessings are attested in the Qumran liturgical hymns and especially in the hymn of 1QS X, I–XI, 22 which constitutes – to our view – a morning prayer. Here we read:

> 'Blessed are you, my God who opens the heart of Your servant to knowledge (דעת = Torah)[10], direct...his actions... as You have chosen to the elected of men to stand before You forever' (1QS 11.15–16).

The idea of God's gift (the Torah) bestowed upon his people – thus making them like children of heaven and like an eternal plantation – found in the above Palestinian versions of the Benediction over the Torah is clearly expressed in the hymn in 1QS 11.7–8.

After enumerating the various spiritual gifts bestowed upon the chosen group, the author of the hymn proclaims:

> 'Those whom God has chosen he has established as an eternal possession; he has bestowed upon them a share in the lot of the holy ones and with the sons of heaven he has united them... for an eternal plantation'. (למטעת עולם) (1QS 11.7–8).

4. *A prayer for deliverance from sin, temptation, evil inclination and Satan*[11]

> 'O lead me not into the power of sin or of transgression or iniquity or of temptation...'
> ואל תביאני... לידי עבירה ועוון ולא לידי נסיון
> 'let not evil inclination (יצר הרע) rule over me (subdue my inclination that it may submit to You)'.[12]
> ואל תשלט בי יצר הרע (וכף את יצרי להשתעבד לך)

This negative formulation is supplemented by a positive one: 'make me cleave to the good inclination', ודבקני ביצר הטוב.

The positive formulation is indeed predominant in the morning prayer of the Palestinian rite as preserved in *y. Ber.* 4.2, 7d on behalf of the school of Yannai:

> 'May it be your will... that You give me a good heart, a good character (חלק טוב)[13] a good inclination (יצר טוב), a good companion[14]... a good soul... and a humble spirit'.

On the other hand, the Palestinian Talmud has also preserved a negative formulation of this prayer by Rabbi Tanhum Scholasticus[15]:

> 'May it be Your will... that You break and remove the yoke of the evil inclination (יצר הרע) from our heart'. (*y. Ber.* 4.2, 7d)

9. For this version and other versions of the Benedictions over the Torah see J. Heinemann, *Prayer in the period of the Tanna'im*, etc.[2] Jerusalem 1966, pp. 106ff. (Hebrew.)

10. For 'knowledge' as Torah, see my article 'The Prayers for Knowledge, Repentance and Forgiveness in the "Eighteen Benedictions" – Qumran Parallels, Biblical Antecedents and Basic Characteristics', *Tarbiz* 48 (1979), pp. 186–200. (Hebrew.)

11. *SPB*, pp. 7–8, cf. *b. Ber.* 60b.

12. Following the version in *b. Ber.* 60b.

13. For such interpretation of חלק, see L. Ginsberg, פירושים וחידושים בירושלמי, III, p. 236.

14. Read חבר instead of the printed סבר, cf. L. Ginsberg, *ibid.*, p. 231.

15. This title was found on an inscription from the synagogue at Sepphoris: see ספר הישוב, I (ed. S. Klein), 1939, p. 138, no. 90.

The traditional rite also includes a prayer, ascribed in *b. Ber.* 16b to R. Judah Hanasi', which he used to say after the official service. In this prayer he asks deliverance from arrogant men, from evil men, from bad companions as well as from mishap, evil inclination and the Satan who destroys: מפגע רע מיצר רע... ומשטן המשחית. The combination of פגע, יצר הרע or שטן is found in other personal apotropaic prayers. Thus in the prayer recited after the official service by Mar the son of Rabina, according to *b. Ber.* 17a, we read: ותצילנו מפגע רע, מיצר רע ומאשה רעה ומכל רעות המתרגשות לבא לעולם with the conclusion 'and other evils which break forth to enter the world'.[16] Here the 'wicked woman' stands for temptation as may be learned from Ben Sira 22.27ff.

In another prayer to be said before retiring to sleep at night יצר הרע is also coupled with פגע and afflictions: ואל ישלוט בי יצר הרע ותצילני מפגע רע (*b. Ber.* 60b). The same applies to the השכיבנו benediction of the evening prayer (*SPB*, pp. 135–36) where one asks to be saved from Satan as well as from enemy, pestilence, sword, famine and sorrow: והסר מעלינו אויב דבר חרב רעב ויגון והסר שטן מלפנינו ומאחרינו. The Palestinian formulation of this prayer in the Genizah is: ופחד וצרה ושטן בלילות אל ימשול בנו, 'fear, trouble, and Satan in the nights shall not rule over us'.[17] Similarly, in the prayers for the beginning of the week according to the Sephardic rite we have: 'save us from the bad Satan, from any bad mishap', הצילנו משטן רע, מפגע רע.[18] The same pattern occurs in the New Year prayer attached to the Modim Benediction.[19] כלה דבר וחרב ורעב ומשחית ומגפה ויצר הרע...וכל גזירה רעה, as well as in the אבינו מלכנו litany according to the Sephardic and Yemenite rites: כלה וחרב ורעב... ומשחית ומגפה ויצר רע וחלאים רעים.[20] In the Ashkenazic rite of the אבינו מלכנו litany we also find 'rid us of every oppressor and adversary', כלה כל צר ומשטין, attached to כלה דבר,חרב,רעב, 'rid us of pestilence, sword (=war), famine… destruction' (*SPB*, p. 68)

In the Qumran prayers (11QPs^{a} XIX, XXIV), which will be analysed below, we also find next to the deliverance from שטן and יצר הרע the deliverance from 'pain' (מכאוב)[21] which is identical with פגע or נגע.[22] In Ps. 155 (11QPs^{a} XXIV, 3–17) which belongs to the genre of personal apotropaic prayers, we hear about deliverance from temptation and sin along with purification from bad affliction (טהרני מנגע רע). Temptation next to פגע appears in Ben Sira 36.1: ירא ה' לא יפגע רע כי אם בניסוי ישוב ומלט, 'the man who fears the Lord, mischance will not strike him, in times of temptation he will be rescued again and again'.

16. For this phrase התרגש לבא לעולם, cf. *y. Ber.* 5.1, 8d. The *hithpa*ʿ*el* of רגש is not found in the Bible. It is attested, however, in Qumran (1QH II, 12: III, 16).

17. Mann, *HUCA* 2 (1925), p. 304 n. 83 (Codex Turin 51); S. Abramson, *Sinai* 81 (1977), p. 216 (Ms. Leningrad 122).

18. Cf. e.g. E.D. Goldschmidt, *On Jewish Liturgy, Essays on Prayer and Religious Poetry*, Jerusalem 1978, pp. 200, 294, 308 (Hebrew).

19. Cf. *Seder R. Amram Gaon* (ed. E.D. Goldschmidt), p. 136.

20. Cf. e.g. שיבת ציון,תכלאל, III, 1952, p. 76.

21. Compare in the short prayer '*hbynenw*' (*b. Ber.* 29a): ורחקנו ממכאוב = 'keep us far from pain'.

22. The traditional usage of פגע instead of נגע, מכאוב was influenced by 1 Kgs 5, 18 אין שטן ואין פגע רע.

5. *Asking for grace*

> 'Let me obtain this day and everyday grace, favour and mercy in Your eyes and in the eyes of all who behold me[23] and bestow lovingkindness upon me'.
> ותנני היום ובכל יום לחן ולחסד ולרחמים בעיניך ובעיני כל רואנו ותגמלני חסדים טובים

This prayer concludes with the benediction: 'Blessed be… the Lord who bestows lovingkindness' (גומל חסדים טובים)[24] which parallels the blessing in the Qumran prayer 'Blessed be the Lord who does righteous deeds and crowns his pious with lovingkindness and mercy' (11QPs[a] 29.7–8): ברוך ה׳ עושה צדקות מעטר חסידיו חסד ורחמים. Finding mercy before the Lord is included in the 'Plea of Deliverance' (11QPs[a] 29.17) the plea that the family of the supplicant rejoice by God's grace.

After the private individualistic prayers and before passing to the official public prayers, we find in the traditional custom of *Birkhot Hashachar* two more liturgies:

6. *Self-abasement declaration as a motivation for forgiveness*

> 'Sovereign of all worlds, not because of our righteousness do we lay our supplications before You but because of Your abundant mercies… What are we? What is our life? What is our righteousness? What shall we say before You? Are not all the mighty men as naught before You, the men of renown as though they had not been… for most of their works are void and the days of their lives are vanity before You, and the preeminence of man over beast is nought, for all is vanity'.
>
> רבון כל העולמים לא על צדקותינו אנחנו מפילים תחנונינו לפניך כי על רחמיך הרבים, מה אנחנו, מה חיינו, מה צדקותינו...מה נאמר לפניך?...הלא כל הגבורים כאין לפניך ואנשי השם כלא היו...כי רב מעשיהם תהו וימי חייהם הבל לפניך ומותר האדם מן הבהמה אין כי הכל הבל (*SPB*, pp. 8–9)

The first sentence of this prayer לא על צדקותינו... is taken from Dan. 9.18 where it is followed by the request for forgiveness: אדני שמעה אדני סלחה. Indeed, the prayer רבון כל העולמים appears in *b. Yoma* 87b as a formula of Yom Kippur confession.[25] The continuing phrases: מה אנחנו, מה חיינו also occur in *b. Yoma* 87b as a confession for Yom Kippur and indeed belong to the concluding penitential service (תפילת נעילה) of Yom Kippur until our days (*SPB*, p. 412).[26] Furthermore, both formulae, לא על צדקותינו as well as מה אנחנו, מה חיינו are

23. For such wishes and their parallels in ancient Near Eastern literature see ch. 17.

24. The words לעמו ישראל are a later addition (non-existent in *Seder R. Amram Gaon*, Maimonides, etc.) and indeed look strange in the group of individual-private prayers. Some versions have לבריותיו 'to his creatures' instead of לעמו ישראל, see e.g. S. Baer, סדר עבודת ישראל *ad loc.*

25. According to Rashi the prayer רבון העולמים in *Yoma* 87b, considered there as a confession for Yom Kippur, is identical with the liturgical declaration discussed here.

26. A similar overlapping between the daily personal prayer and that of Yom Kippur is found in connection with the liturgy of self-abasement:

'O my God, before I was formed I was worth nothing, and now that I have been formed I am but as though I had not been formed. Dust I am in my life, how much more in my death. Behold, I am before You as a vessel filled with shame and confusion'.

This prayer, which the Amora Rabba used to say after the official prayers according to *b. Ber.* 17a, was recited by R. Hamnuna Zutah after confession on Yom Kippur, and so it is recited in our days.

recited in the various penitential prayers (סליחות) associated with confession on Yom Kippur as well as on weekdays.[27] All this clearly indicates that the liturgy of self-abasement רבון כל העולמים, etc., actually belongs to confession of sin and plea for forgiveness.

Indeed, in the Palestinian tradition the *Birkhot Hashachar* open with a confession: 'My Lord, I have sinned before You' רבוני חטאתי לפניך (*y. Ber.* 4.2, 7d). In the Genizah: רבון כל העולמים אל תוציא עלי גזירות מוות... ואם גרמו לי עוונותי תהא מיתתי כפרה, 'Sovereign of all worlds, do not decree upon me a decree of death… and if my sins have caused it to me… let my death be an atonement'.[28] In the continuation of the Genizah prayer, we find the verse from Dan. 9.18–19: ...לא על צדקותינו אנחנו מפילים, included in the רבון כל העולמים liturgy of the traditional rite dealt with here. However, whereas in the conventional formulation of רבון כל העולמים only the self-abasement formula of Dan. 9.18–19 is quoted (לא על צדקותינו) and Dan. 9.19, where we find the plea for forgiveness אדני שמעה אדני סלחה is omitted, in the Genizah liturgy the whole passage Dan. 9.18–19 is quoted. Furthermore, in the Genizah the verses from Dan. 9.18–19 are preceded by an explicit plea for forgiveness: וסלח ותמחול ותכפר לעונתי ולעונות אבותי, etc.[29]

It seems that the omission of the confession in the conventional רבון כל העולמים before the service was motivated by the fact that the תחנונים after the *Amidah* gradually took over the confession[30] and thus all confessions during the service were transferred to that section.[31] Indeed, *Seder R. Amram Gaon* preserved the רבון כל העולמים – after the *Amidah* – together with the confession of sins.[32] Attached to it is the Palestinian prayer of R. Yannai (*y. Ber.* 4.2, 7d) which is to be recited after awakening in the morning. This indicates that the רבון כל העולמים adduced there (*Parag.* 65) actually belongs to the *Birkhot Hashachar* but was transferred to its present position because of the prevailing (Babylonian?) custom to confess after the *Amidah*.

Self-abasement is also characteristic of biblical prayers, as e.g. Gen. 18.27 in the intercession of Abraham for Sodom: 'Here I venture to speak to my Lord, I who am but dust and ashes (ואנכי עפר ואפר)' and similarly David before thanking the Lord for his promise: 'What am I, O Lord God, and what is my family that You have brought me thus far?', מי אנכי...ומי ביתי כי הביאתני עד הלם (2 Sam. 7.18).[33]

27. Cf. *Seder R. Amram Gaon*, p. 37; שיבת ציון,תכלאל, I, p. 34, III, p. 130 (1952); E.D. Goldschmidt, מחזור לימים נוראים, II (1970), pp. 26, 47, etc.

28. Mann, *HUCA* 2 (1925), p. 278; Asaf, *Dinaburg Festschrift* (see n. 4), p. 121.

29. Compare the confession formula for Yom Kippur in *y. Yoma* 8, 9, 45c: רבוני חטאתי...שתכפר לי על כל עוונותי ותמחל לי על כל פשעי. Cf. also *Lev. Rab.* 3.3 (p. 61, ed. Margalioth).

30. Cf. *t. Ber.* 3.6.

31. For the development of this custom, see E.D. Goldschmidt, *On Jewish Liturgy* (see n. 18), 1978, pp. 369–71.

32. Ed. E.D. Goldschmidt, p. 37.

33. Verse 21 there also contains a self-abasement formula, read with 1 Chron. 17.19 בעבור עבדך וכלבך but vocalizing *wēkalbeka* instead of *ukelibka*: 'For your slave and your dog have You done

Self-abasement declarations are also very common in secular petitions (to kings and princes) in ancient Israel[34] and in the ancient Near East.[35]

7. *Salvation*. The last element in the traditional rite of *Birkhot Hashachar* appended to the first verse of שמע is sanctification of the Lord's name as a result of which his people will be gathered and salvation will come.

> 'You were the one ere the world was created, You have been the one since the world has been created, You are the one in this world and you will be the one in the world to come. Sanctify Your name… in Your world… O, gather them that hope for you from the four corners of the earth. Let all inhabitants of the world recognize and know that You are the God, You alone, over all the kingdoms of the earth. You have created heaven and earth… Our father in heaven, deal with us graciously…and fulfill for us…that which is written "at that time I shall bring you home… I will make you a name and a praise among all the peoples of the earth" (Zeph. 3.20) …'[36]

In the Palestinian morning prayers, as will be shown, we also encounter eschatological prayers. However, there it is not ingathering of the exiles which is stressed but restoration of Zion. This is quite understandable. For the Babylonian Jews the ingathering of the exiles was the most important thing in redemption while for the Palestinian it was restoration of Zion. For the same reason the השכיבנו/נשכבה benediction of the Palestinian evening service concludes with *spreading the tent of peace over Jerusalem*, פורש סוכת שלום על ירושלים, whereas in the Babylonian rite it concludes with שומר עמו ישראל לעד = 'who guards his people Israel forever'. For Sabbaths and festivals some of the Babylonians adopted the Palestinian formula הפורש סוכת שלום... ועל ירושלים but most of them retained the usual form שומר עמו ישראל לעד.[37]

In the Qumran liturgy the eschatological element – as will be seen – is represented by the so-called 'Apostrophe for Zion' (11QPs[a] 22).

2. *Qumran Morning Liturgy*

The so-called *'Plea of Deliverance'* in 11QPs[a], col. 29 contains, like the morning pleas we have just discussed, the following themes:

1. *Self-abasement* – 'I am (humble) and destitute', [עני] ודל אנכי.[38] This occurs before praise, and therefore should be seen as a topos of self-abasement

this great thing'. For 'dog' as self-abasement, cf. 2 Sam. 9.8; 2 Kgs 8.13, and the Amarna letters. See especially, N.H. Tur Sinai, פשוטו של מקרא, II (1964), p. 200.

34. See e. g.1321 Sam. 18.18 מי אנכי ומי חיי, 2 Sam. 9.8, cf. Lachish letters *KAI* 192.2, 3, 5; 195.4; 196.2–3.

35. Especially in the Amarna letters. On the problem in general, see G.W. Coats, *Self-Abasement and Insult Formulas, Journal of Biblical Literature* 89 (1970), pp. 14ff.

36. The beginning of this prayer is alluded to in the Palestinian Talmud (according to B. Ratner, אהבת ציון וירושלים, p. 199) and is attested in the Genizah Fragments (Mann, *HUCA* 2 (1925), pp. 281, 283).

37. Cf. J. Mann, *HUCA* 2 (1925), p. 305.

38. For this phrase which is missing in 11QPs.[a], cf. J. van der Ploeg, *Fragments d'un manuscript de Pasumes de Qumran (11QPs.[b]), Revue Biblique* 74 (1967), p. 408f.

and not as motivation for help[39] as the ones found in the psalmodic complaints: Ps. 40.18; 70.60; 86.1 and 109.22.

2. *Praise for returning life and soul:*

Surely a maggot cannot thank You
Nor a graveworm recount Your lovingkindness
But the living can praise You
all those who stumble can praise You
In revealing Your kindness to them
and by the righteousness You enlighten them
For in Your hand is the soul of every living soul
the breath of all flesh You have given.

כי לא רמה תודה לכה   תספר חסדכה תולעה
חי חי יודה לכה   יודו לך כל מוטטי רגל
בהודיעך חסדכה להמה   וצדקתך תשכילם
כי בידכה נפש כל חי   נשמת כל בשר אתה נתתה

(11QPs[a] 29.1–4)

As we have seen above, the first Blessing in the morning liturgies contains praise for returning life after sleep. In the Palestinian rite this Blessing opens with 'Blessed are you… the Lord of praises' (אל ההודאות) and concludes with 'Blessed are you… who revives the dead' (מחיה מתים), whereas in the Babylonian rite it concludes with: 'who returns the soul to dead bodies'. The passage under scrutiny covers the same theme: the praise (הודיה) for not letting man die and for giving him breath (נשמה). The wording נשמת כל חי אתה נתתה is indeed reflected in the אלהי נשמה liturgy (*SPB*, p. 5, see above, p. 482). There we read נשמה (טהורה) שנתת בי and here נשמת כל בשר אתה נתתה. In the *Hodayot* of Qumran which contain the motifs of the morning prayers discussed here, we find even more connections with אלהי נשמה. In 1QH 3.19ff. we hear the supplicant praising the Lord for redeeming him from the pit and the Sheol, giving hope to what he created from dust (לאשר יצרתה מעפר) and purifying the soul (ורוח נעוה טהרתה) which is close to נשמה שנתת בי טהורה היא אתה יצרתה 'The soul which You gave me is pure, You created it'.

3. *Benediction for Grace*. The Benediction: ברוך יהוה עושה צדקות, מעטר חסידיו חסד ורחמים, 'Blessed be YHWH who establishes righteousness, crowning His pious with kindness and mercy' (11QPs[a] 29.7–8) parallels – as indicated – גומל חסדים טובים 'who bestows lovingkindness' in the traditional morning prayer. The phraseology is taken from Ps. 103.4, 6 and interestingly enough המעטרכי חסד ורחמים comes there after הגואל משחת חייכי 'who redeems your life from the pit' not unlike our Qumran passage where the Benediction follows the concept of being saved from the graveworm.

After the Benediction comes a prayer in the first person singular starting again with an individual praise for being saved from death and Sheol (11QPs[a] 29.8–13). The supplicant here declares that he actually deserves death for his sins (למות הייתי ועוונתי לשאול מכרוני) but has been saved by God's mercy and righteousness (cf. above p. 487).

39. In contrast to van der Ploeg (art. cit. in previous note) who puts on one and the same level both the phrase in the Qumran liturgy and the other phrases in the Psalms.

Next come the pleas:

4. *For forgiving sins* (11QPs^{a} 29.13–14), which is characteristic of the Palestinian morning rite (see above) : 'Forgive my sin O YHWH and purify me from iniquity' (סלחה יהוה לחטאתי וטהרני מעווני).

5. *To be granted 'the spirit of faith and knowledge'*, רוח אמונה ודעת חנני.[40] This is identical with the plea in Ps. 155 (11QPs^{a} 24.8) הבינני יהוה בתורתכה ואת משפטכה למדני[41] and parallels the plea for giving Torah in the traditional Jewish prayers (see above, no. 3)

6. *For deliverance from sin and temptation*: 'let me not stumble in iniquity', אל אתקלה בעויה (11QPs^{a} 29.14–15). This phrase has an Aramaic flavour (cf. Dan. 4.24 חטא / עויה) and would be rendered in Classical Hebrew אל אכשלה בעוון or in later Rabbinic Hebrew (אל אכשל בעבירה).[42] The equivalent of this plea in the traditional rite is: אל תביאני לידי עבירה ועוון (see above, p. 128). In the *Hodayot* which contains – as indicated – prayers of the kind discussed here we find similar pleas: בעד עבדך מחטוא לך ומכשול בכול דברי רצונך [ותסוך?], 'You (will spare) your servant from sinning against you and from stumbling in all the words of your will' (IQH 17.23).[43]

7. *For deliverance from Satan and evil spirits*: 'let not Satan rule over me nor an impure spirit, neither let pain nor evil inclination rule[44] over myself' אל תשלט בי שטן ורוח טמאה,מכאוב ויצר רע אל ירשו בעצמי (11QPs^{a} 19.15–16). As already indicated above, p. 129, the combination of Satan, evil inclination (יצר רע) with affliction (פגע, נגע, מכאוב) and sickness, pestilence, etc. (חלאים רעים,דבר, מגפה) is characteristic of personal prayers. The association of Satan identifiable with יצר רע and the angel of death מלאך המוות[45] is the one who causes sickness, death and pestilence.[46]

In a fragment of *Hodayot* scroll (4.3–20) which mentions morning (בוקר) and deals with forgiving sin and self-abasement motifs characteristic of morning prayers we read: 'you rebuke every Satan, destroyer' (תגער בכל שטן משחית), a phrase also found in fragment 45 there: כול שטן ומשחית. שטן parallels here 'impure spirit' רוח טמאה (cf. Zech. 13.2). The equation of Satan and impure spirit may be discussed in Mk. 3.20–23 where we find the accusation that Jesus is

40. This is to be compared with the *Amidah* Benediction (*SPB*, p. 56): 'You grant man knowledge…grant me knowledge, understanding' (אתה חונן לאדם דעת...חונני דעה והשכל) and cf. Ps. 119.29 תורתך חנני and the prayer אתה חוננתנו למדע תורתך. (*SPB*, p. 440) see my article 'The Prayers for Knowledge, Repentance and Forgiveness in the "Eighteen Benedictions"', *Tarbiz* 48 (1979), pp. 186ff. (Hebrew).

41. For the identification of דעת and תורה in Qumran literature, cf. my article (previous note).

42. For this translation, cf. J. Goldstein, *JNES* 26 (1967), p. 307; R. Polzin, *HTR*, p. 60 (1967), p. 469.

43. Compare the confession in *1QS* 11.12: ואם אכשול בעוון בשר.

44. For רשה and its correct interpretation, see J.Goldstein, *JNES* 26 (1967), p. 301; R. Polzin, *HTR* 60 (1967), pp. 469–70.

45. Cf. *b. B. Bat.* 16a: הוא שטן, הוא יצר הרע,הוא מלאך המוות.

46. These three demonic forces combine together in 1 Chr. 21. The Satan is the one who *incites* (ויסת) David to count the children of Israel (1 Chr. 21.1), and the punishment for the sin is executed by המלאך המשחית (v. 15 there), which according to the Rabbis is identical with Satan.

controlled by the 'impure spirit' (πνεῦμα ἀκάθαρτος,v. 30). Jesus however reacts by saying: 'How can Satan drive out Satan' (v. 25). In other words: how can an impure spirit drive out impure spirit, which clearly implies that Satan and 'impure spirit' are the same.

As D. Flusser has recognized[47] the phrase אל תשלט בי שטן is found in the prayer of Levi in the Aramaic *Testament of Levi* אל תשלט בי שטן [48] and both overlap ואל תשלט בי יצר הרע in the rabbinic prayers.

In the prayers from the Genizah we also find the form: אל ימשול בנו שטן as for example in the evening prayer: ושטן בלילות אל ימשול בנו.[49] The roots of this formula are to be found in Ps. 119.113b: ואל תשלט בי כל עון (cf. Ben Sira 23.6 and see above).

8. *For finding grace in the eyes of man* : 'Let my brothers rejoice with me and the house of my father, who are confounded,[50] by your grace… I will rejoice with you' ישמחו אחי אמי ובית אבי השוממים בחינכה... אשמחה בכה (11QPs^a 19.17–18). The rejoicing of his 'brothers' with him and his family with the grace of God is tantamount to finding grace in the eyes of man and the eyes of God, a motif found in the traditional morning prayer (ותנני לחן ולחסד בעיני כל רואי) mentioned above. A similar prayer is found in *b. Ber*. 28 b: וישמחו בי חברי... ואשמח בהם which is parallel to *y. Ber*. 4.2, 7d: 'I shall not be angry with my friends' (שלא אקפיד כנגד חברי).[51]

9. *Restoration of Zion and its salvation* appears in the Qumran Psalms scroll as a separate prayer, in the so-called '*Apostrophe to Zion*' (11QPs^a 22). The hope is expressed there that the prophetic visions on Jerusalem will be fulfilled: 'Accept the vision spoken of you and the dream of the prophets' קחי חזון דובר אליך וחלומות נביאים (11QPs^a 22.13–14, compare 11QPs^a 22.5–6). This is associated with the longing of the pious for its salvation: גדולה תקותך ציון ושלום ותוחלת ישועתך לבוא 'Great is your hope, Zion, that peace and longed for salvation will come' (11QPs^a 22.2–3). 'How they hoped for your salvation', כמה קוו לישועתך (11QPs^a 22.8), 'those who yearn for the day of your salvation', המתאוין ליום ישעך (11QPs^a 22.4).

Similar wishes are found in the Ben Sira prayer (cf. 36.20–21): 'Fulfil the testimony of the beginning of creation, establish the vision spoken in your name, give reward for those who hope for you, prove your prophets trustworthy'

תן עדות למראש מעשיך להקם חזון דבר בשמך
תן את פעלת קוויך ונביאיך יאמנו

47. 'Qumran and Jewish "Apotropaic" Prayers', *Israel Exploration Journal* 16 (1966), pp. 194ff.

48. Cf. J.T. Milik, 'Le Testament de Levi en Araméen', *Revue Biblique* 62 (1955), pp. 398–406.

49. Cf. J.Mann, *HUCA* 2 (1925), p. 304 n. 83; S. Abramson, *Sinai* 81 (1977), p. 216 (Hebrew).

50. The verb 'שמם' has been chosen here in order to form the antithesis with 'שמח' by similar sounds, cf. *b. Yoma* 76b: זכה משמחו,לא זכה משממו, 'if a man is good if (the wine) means joy to him, if not it means confounding'.

51. Cf. L. Ginsberg, פירושים וחידושים בירושלמי III, p. 221–22. Cf. S.Abramson, *Sinai* 81 (1977), Leningrad Ms. 103 1a, p. 205.

The elements found in the traditional morning prayer,

1. praise of God for restoring the soul after sleep,
2. blessing for giving knowledge of Torah,
3. deliverance from Satan and temptation,
4. benediction for grace,
5. self abasement,
6. plea for forgiveness of sins,
7. salvation and restoration of Zion;

are thus attested in 11QPs^{a} col. 19 and, as we shall demonstrate in a forthcoming study, the same elements are found in the *Hodayot* and other hymns of Qumran.[52]

52. Cf. provisionally my review article in *Bibliotheca Orientalis* 41 (1984), pp. 712–13.

Chapter 9

The Biblical Origins of the *Amidah* Prayer for Sabbath and Holy Days

1. *Obligatory Prayer*

We first encounter an obligation on Israelite men to recite prayer to a pre-set formula in Deut. 26.5–11 (the first fruits) and 13–15 (the acknowledgement of presenting of the tithe). Both passages begin, 'And you shall declare before the Lord your God…' i.e. 'You shall recite as follows…'. It is no coincidence that such obligation should be found in Deuteronomy, for it is this book that embodies the transition from a religion of cult to a religion of book and prayer, as the religion of the synagogue came to be.[1] The elimination of the provincial cultic sites accomplished by Josiah's reform, and reflected in the book of Deuteronomy discovered during his reign, broke the hitherto inseparable connection between religion and the temple cult. From then on, the Israelites' religion drew its inspiration from spiritual meditation and exhaustive textual study. The destruction of the first temple reinforced this spiritualizing tendency by giving rise to fixed forms of prayer intended for a national congregation. These fixed forms had three main motifs: (a) the exclusivity and oneness of God, creator of heaven and earth; (b) the maintenance of God's gracious covenant that he swore to the patriarchs;[2] (c) acknowledgement of God's greatness and mighty deeds, i.e. of the complete submission of the universe to his providence. These motifs are subject to variation, but on the whole we find all three in the openings to the fixed prayers, as we shall see.

A. An early declaration embodying all three elements is found in Deuteronomy, put into the mouth of Moses:

> Behold, the heaven and the heaven of heavens belongs to the Lord your God, the earth also with all that is on it. Only the Lord took delight in your fathers to love them, and he chose their seed after them, from all peoples', as it is this day […] For the Lord your God

1. See M. Weinfeld, *From Joshua to Josiah* (1992), pp. 173–79 (Hebrew). cf. M. Weinfeld, *DDS 1–11* (*AB*, 1991), pp. 16–17.

2. For the identity between the terms (ברית) שמר and (ברית) זכר see M. Weinfeld, '"Covenant and Grace (הברית והחסד)": The terms and their development in Israel and the Ancient World', *Leshonenu* 36 (1971–72), pp. 96–98. For 'keeping the covenant' and 'showing kindness to the Patriarchs' see *ibid.* pp. 97–98 (Hebrew).

> is God of gods, the Lord of lords, a great God, a mighty, and awesome (הגדול,הגיבור והנורא) (10.14–17)[3]

We have here the idea of the God of Israel's exclusive control, his election of the patriarchs, and acknowledgement of his *greatness and might* (cf. Moses' prayer, *ibid.* 3.24: '...for what God is there in heaven or in earth who can do according to Your works, and according to Your might?')[4]

B. The redactor of the great historiographic deuteronomic enterprise working around the time of the destruction of the first temple, kept up this practice of putting prayers – hymns, in effect – containing these three elements into the mouths of the nation's leaders. For example, he ascribes to David the following:

> Therefore You are great, O Lord God; for there is none like You, neither is there any God besides You [...] And who is like Your people Israel, a unique nation on earth, whom God went and redeemed as His people [...] doing *great awesome things*. (2 Sam. 7.22–23)

This passage contains only two of the three elements – God's exclusive power and his *greatness and might*.

C. The opening of the deuteronomistic Solomon's prayer[5] runs:

> ...the Lord God of Israel, there is no God like You, in the heaven above or in the earth beneath, who keeps covenant and kindness with Your servants who walk before You with all their heart; who has kept with Your servant David, my father, that which You promised him.
>
> (1 Kgs 8.23–24)

Here too we find only two of the three elements – God's exclusive control and the covenant with the patriarchs.

D. The same elements appear in Jeremiah's prayer, after its deuteronomistic redaction:

> Oh Lord God! Behold, You have made the heaven and the earth by Your great power and out-stretched arm [...] You show kindness to thousands [...] O great and mighty God! (32.17–18).

This time all three elements are present – God's creation of heaven and earth, the great favour shown to the patriarchs, and God's *greatness and mighty* deeds.[6]

E. The liturgy of the second temple period continued the deuteronomistic pattern, although sometimes parts of it were omitted:

3. The titles 'Great, Mighty and Awesome' open all forms of the *Amidah* and the Sages considered that it was the Great Assembly that inaugurated this opening usage (*b. Ber.* 33b and parallels).
4. For the deuteronomic character of this prayer, see M. Weinfeld, 1992 (Hebrew) (n. 1 above), p. 221.
5. *Ibid.*, pp. 220–21.
6. *Ibid.*, p. 222.

> ...O Lord, the great and dreadful God, keeping covenant and kindness to those who love Him, and to those who keep His commandments
>
> (Dan. 9.4)

> ...O Lord God of heaven, the *great and awesome* God, who keeps covenant and kindness to those who love him and keep his commandments...
>
> (Neh. 1.5)

F. The Chronicler put into David's mouth a long prayer concerning Solomon's coronation and this too follows the deuteronomistic mould:

> ...Blessed be You, Lord God of Israel, our father, forever and ever.
> Yours, O Lord, is the *greatness and the power* [...] for all that is in heaven and earth is yours, yours is the kingdom, O Lord, and You are exalted as head above all. [...] You reign over all and in Your hand is power and might [...] O Lord God of Abraham and Yitzhak and of Yisrael, our fathers, keep this forever [...]
>
> (1 Chr. 29.10–19)[7]

Here we have the concept of God's exclusive power alongside an evocation of His *greatness and might*, and at the conclusion of the prayer God is besought to keep (= remember) for ever the patriarchs of Israel. As we shall see, the standard Jewish liturgy joined this passage with the prayer in Neh. 9.5ff. This prayer is the starting point for understanding the composition of the *Amidah,* and at the conclusion of the Palestinian version of the *Amidah,* the two passages are recited together.

G. Jehoshaphat's prayer in Chronicles contains the same three elements that we have been discussing:

> O Lord God of our fathers! Are not You God in heaven? And do You not rule over all the kingdoms of the nations? And in Your hand is there power and might so that none is able to withstand You.
>
> (2 Chr. 20.6)

The measure of almost exact repetition in these two prayers from Chronicles is remarkable; 'You reign over all and in Your hand is power and might' (1 Chr. 29.10–19); 'And You rule over all the kingdoms of the nations; And in Your hand is there power and might' (2 Chr. 20.6).

The prayers that I have been quoting from appear in the Bible in a range of contexts:

(A) is part of Moses' leave-taking from the people; (B) is from David's thanksgiving for an everlasting kingdom; (C) is from the inauguration of the temple; (D) belongs to the time of the Babylonian siege of Jerusalem; (E) relates to the

7. The word 'all, everything' (כול), with and without preposition ('in all', 'to all' etc.), occurs ten times in this prayer, emphasizing the unity of the passage. The Sabbath song of the *Yoṣer* Benediction is a prime example of this usage: 'He makes peace and creates *everything* [instead of 'and creates evil' in Isa. 45.7], *everything* thanks You, and *everything* lauds You, and *everything* says 'There is no holy one like God', and *everything* exalts You, Selah, Creator of All'.

desolation of Jerusalem and the rebuilding of her walls; (F) concerns Solomon's becoming king; and (G) relates to the war against Ammon, Moab, and Edom.

Different from all these is the prayer in Neh. 9.5ff., where the setting is a gathering called for the purpose of public prayer for its own sake, prayer that, together with the Bible reading, constitutes the chief component of the synagogue service of worship. It is in Neh. 8–9, indeed, that we have first mention of public prayer and Bible readings. In Chapter 8 the occasion is a gathering of the people in the square before the Water Gate, called for the purpose of reading from the Bible. Ezra, with others placed to his left and right, stands atop a tall wooden structure and opens the scroll in the face of the standing congregation. He blesses the Lord God, the people responding 'Amen, Amen', raising their hands and then prostrating themselves. The recited Bible text is both translated and interpreted (v. 8). Later, we are told that during the Succoth festival there was a daily public Bible reading (v. 18). All these are customs that can be found in synagogues to this day.[8]

Chapter 9 informs us that the people came together again on the twenty-fourth of the month to pray and listen to readings. One of the four quarters of the day was devoted to Torah reading. During another quarter the people prostrated themselves and made confession, and it was in this session that the people were ceremonially called on to pray. The wording of this call to prayer, 'Rise up and bless the Lord your God from everlasting to everlasting' (v. 5), overlaps the blessing put into the mouth of David in 1 Chron. 16.36 and 29.10: 'Blessed be You, Lord God of Israel (our father), forever and ever'.[9] The Torah reading too, as is familiar in every synagogue, has its formal summons: 'Blessed be the Lord who is to be blessed' and Ezra indeed blesses the Lord, the great God, after he has opened the scroll of the Torah (Neh. 8.6).

The key finding in the text of this public prayer is a series of affirmations that parallel the first four blessings of the *Amidah* for Sabbath and Festivals in the commonly accepted liturgy. Here we have the first instance in the Bible of public prayer recited to a fixed order and formula. Its elements are as follows:

a. Acknowledgement of God, the sole creator of heaven and earth (v. 6), in the words of the prayer: 'the creator (*qoneh*) of heaven and earth' (Palestinian version);[10] '...the great, the mighty and the awesome God who keeps covenant and kindness...' i.e. remembers his great favour towards the patriarchs (9.32);

b. Acknowledgement of God as the giver of life to all creation, that is, he maintains the universe and all that is in it (9.6);

c. The heavenly host (=the angels) bowing down before God (9.6);

d. The choice of Abraham (v. 8);

8. For Neh. 8.4–5 as the origin of the practice of raising up the scroll, see D. Sperber, *The Customs of Israel: Origins and History* (1989), pp. 78–81 (Hebrew).

9. Many are of the opinion that we should read 'Blessed are You, O Lord our God, from everlasting to everlasting', in Neh. 9.5 . See H.G.M. Williamson, 'Structure and Historiography in Nehemiah', *Proceedings of the Ninth World Congress of Jewish Studies*, Panel Sessions, Jerusalem, 1988 pp. 117–31.

10. See N. Wieder 1976, 'The form of the *Amidah* prayer in the Early Babylonian Jewish Community', *Sinai* 78 (1975–76), pp. 97ff. (Hebrew).

The descent of God to Mt. Sinai to give the Torah and commandments (v. 13)
The giving of the Sabbath (v. 14).

For some reason the first blessing, the essence of whose content is the creation of the world and the divine favour shown to the patriarchs, is split into two – the creation is recalled in the opening but '...the great, the mighty and the awesome God who keeps covenant and kindness...' is not mentioned until the close (v. 32), i.e. the prayer's conclusion completes its opening. Other prayers of this period place the favour to the patriarchs at the very beginning: '... O Lord God of heaven, the great and awesome God, who keeps covenant and kindness to those who love him and keep His commandments...' (Neh. 1.5); 'O Lord, the great and awesome God, keeping covenant and kindness to those who love Him, and to those who keep His commandments...' (Dan. 9.4).

The prayer in Neh. 9 thus contains two basic motifs from the *Amidah* – which are found there in the benediction on the patriarchs and the benediction on God's mighty works: (a) אבות – the creation of heaven and earth and divine favour to the patriarchs; (b) mighty works 'גבורות' of which the most important are his providence over all life and the provision of its needs ('sustains the living with kindness'). However, the *Amidah* prayer adds a third element – the Holiness of the Name – whose main concern is with the holy ones (=the angels) praising and sanctifying the name of God, and thus paralleling the actions of the Children of Israel on earth. This same dualism also occurs in the biblical hymns and songs to the Lord, especially in Ps. 148, half of which is devoted to praise of things celestial, 'Praise the Lord from the heavens: praise him in the heights. Praise him all his angels: praise him all his hosts' (v. 1ff.), and the other half to praise of beings earthly, 'Praise the Lord from the earth[...] kings of the earth and all peoples; princes and all judges of the earth' (v. 6ff.). The idea that the people of Israel join their song to that of the angels and together extol the Lord (=Holiness) is a very common one in the Qumran literature.[11] This is an element missing from the prayers of the leaders of Israel that I cited earlier and the reason would seem to lie with the principled opposition to angelology that is characteristic of Deuteronomy.[12]

These same elements of the *Amidah* for Sabbath and festivals appear in a Qumran text: 'I will bless Him for his wondrous activity. I will meditate upon his mighty work (בגבורתו) and upon his kindness (חסדיו). I shall rely[...] land He has bequeathed them the portion of the holy ones and with the Sons of Heaven he has joined together their Assembly for the Council of the Community' (1QS 10.16; 11.8)[13] we have here: mighty works, the favour shown to the patriarchs[14] and forming one congregation with the angels in heaven (holiness). We find

11. See chapter 2.
12. See M. Weinfeld (n. 1 above) pp. 141–42, 218.
13. J. Licht, *The Manual of Discipline* (1965), pp. 218–30.
14. For parallels to the 'great favour to our forefathers' and to 'mighty works' in the *Amidah* see S. Talmon, 'The "Manual of Benedictions" of the Sect of the Judean Desert', *Revue de Qumran* 2 (1960), pp. 475ff.

similar parallels in the Thanksgiving Scroll: 'I thank You, my God[...] and put Your thanksgiving in my mouth[...] and make my lips a place for songs of praise[15], and I shall sing Your *great favours* and of Your *mighty works* I shall discourse all the day.. and of the portion of Your *Holy Ones*... and to assemble ranked before You with the host of eternity[...] to be renewed with all our longing and all singing known songs' (11.3–14)[16]. Again we find the divine favour and mighty works (in the same order as in the *Amidah*) and convocation with the eternal host in heaven.

In today's standard liturgy the blessings begin, as we know, with the word 'You': 'Blessed are You [...] O Lord our God', 'You are mighty to eternity', 'You are holy', 'You have chosen us', and so also in Nehemiah's prayer: '*You* are Lord alone, *You* have made the heavens[...] and *You* preserve them all[...] and *You* are the Lord God who chose Abram' (9.6–7).

As scholars have already noted, the blessing of the quickening of the dead belongs to the category of the Lord's mighty works and in its origin did not refer to any eschatological raising of the dead but to the restoration of life to those on the threshold of death. We now have new evidence for this in the Assyrian expression *mīta muballiṭ*.[17] The expression *muballiṭ* means 'who saves people from mortal danger' and in Assyrian too figures as one of a list of titles extolling the god's mighty works, such as: 'supports the falling, loosens the bound, quickens the dying' in a parallelism with the blessing of the mighty works in the Jewish liturgy.[18]

As for the 'the host of heaven bow down before You' (Neh. 9.6) this element without doubt belongs to the liturgy on Holiness, which itself is extremely ancient.[19] With respect to the heavenly host bowing down before the Lord, we have Ps. 29.2: 'bow to the Lord in the beauty of holiness' (cf. 96.15; 97.7) and LXX Deut. 32.43, and also in the DSS.[20]

Nehemiah's prayer in Neh. 9 next recalls the election of Abraham (vv. 7–9), the Exodus from Egypt (vv. 9–12), the giving of the Torah on Sinai (v. 13) and the giving of the holy Sabbath (v. 14). It is noteworthy that this is the first and only occasion that the Hebrew Bible includes the gift of Torah and Sabbath in the list of the Lord's favours. Observance of the commandments is a duty not a

15. Identical to 'Lord, open You my lips and my mouth will give forth Your praise' (Ps. 51.17), which are the opening words of the *Amidah*. See also: G. Glazov, 'The invocation of Ps. 51.17 in Jewish and Christian morning prayer', *JJS* 26 (1995), pp. 167–82.

16. J. Licht, *The Thanksgiving Scroll* (1957), pp. 161–63.

17. See M. Weinfeld (n. 1 above), pp. 226–27 and *ibid.*, n. 122.

18. *Ibid.*, pp. 226–27. See also the Qumranic text: E. Puech, '4Q521 Une apocalypse messianique', *Revue de Qumran* XV (1992), pp. 475–519; also: D. Flusser, 'A Qumran fragment and the mighty works of the *Amidah*', *Tarbiz* 64 (1994), pp. 331–34 (in Hebrew). The formulation Flusser quotes from Qumran is: 'loosens the bound, opens the eyes of the blind, straightens the bent, just as He heals the injured and quickens the dying, heartens the oppressed'.

19. M. Weinfeld and S.N. Kramer, 'Sumerian literature and the Book of Psalms, Part 2', *Bet Miqra* 57 (1974), pp. 136–60 (in Hebrew).

20. P.W. Skehan and E. Ulrich. 'Qumran Cave 4, IX', in: E. Ulrich and F.M. Cross (eds.) *Deuteronomy, Joshua, Judges, Kings* (*DJD*, XIV, 1995), p. 141.

privilege, one of the obligations laid on Israel and the commandments themselves are not deemed to be acts of favour. (Cf. Num. 20.15–16; Deut. 26.5–9; Josh. 24.2–13; 1 Sam. 12.7–11). Beginning from the time of Nehemiah, however, the Sabbath and the commandments are numbered with the acts of the Lord's loving kindness to Israel. Indeed, the Lord's choice of Israel to be his people is henceforward summed up in his gift to them of Torah and Sabbath. The blessing that precedes the Torah reading runs: 'who chose us from all peoples and gave us His Torah', and in similar vein in the blessing of the Holiness of the Day in the *Amidah:* 'You have sanctified the seventh day [...] sanctify us with Your commandments and grant us our portion in Your Torah', and in the *kiddush* of the day over the wine: 'You have chosen us [...] and have given us this Sabbath/ appointed day', '...sanctified us with His commandments and took pleasure in us and gave us His holy Sabbath as an inheritance[...] for us [...] You have chosen and sanctified us from all nations and have given us in love and favour Your holy Sabbath/appointed day as an inheritance'. Thus the election of Israel is expressed in the gift of the Sabbath and the appointed times and in the imposition of the commandments. In confirmation of this, the central blessing of the *Amidah* for Sabbath and Holy Days, called 'The Holiness of the Day', opens with the act of election ('You have chosen us from among all peoples...'), with the gift of the holy day (Sabbath or one of the great Festivals), and with the gift of the commandments ('...sanctified us with His commandments'). The same three motifs form part of the *kiddush* over the wine with which the Sabbath and the Holy Days commence: '..who has chosen us from all peoples [...] and sanctified us with His commandments and given us this day of [...]'.

N. Wieder has shown that the middle blessing of the *Amidah* had a similar opening not only on Holy Days but on the Sabbath too, but that at a later juncture excerpts of *piyyuṭ* (liturgical poetry) were introduced: for the Sabbath Eve prayer: 'You have sanctified...', for the morning service: 'Moses rejoiced...', and for the afternoon service: 'You are one...' etc.[21]

The wording closest to that of Neh. 9 is that of a copy of the *Musaf* service for the three pilgrimage festivals found in the Cairo Genizah: 'You have chosen Israel as Your people from all the peoples [...] and in love You brought them to Mount Sinai and gave them right judgements and true teachings [...] and You have given us this day of [...]' etc.[22] (cf. Neh. 9ff. 'You are the Lord God who chose Abraham [...] and You came down on Mt. Sinai and spoke with them from heaven, and gave them right judgements and Your true teachings[...] and made known to them Your holy Sabbath'.)

The same liturgy, tying the choice and sanctification of Israel to the gift of the Sabbath is found as early as the book of Jubilees: 'Hereby I have singled out a

21. N. Wieder, 'Moses rejoiced in the gift of his portion: resistance and defense', *Studies in Israelite Aggadah, Targums, and Prayers in memory of Y. Heinemann* (1984), pp. 75ff. (Hebrew).

22. See E. Fleischer, *Israelite Prayer and Liturgical Practice during the Genizah Period* (1987), pp. 95–96 and the references. Also: L.J. Liebreich, 'The impact of Neh. 9.5–37 on the Liturgy of the Synagogue', *HUCA* 32 (1961), pp. 234–35.

people for myself from amongst all the peoples and by their observing the Sabbath I have sanctified them to me as a people [...] and He did not sanctify all peoples and nations to rest on that day but Israel alone [...] and He blessed [...] that day for blessedness, holiness, and glory' (2.31–32).[23]

This wording is reflected in the piyyuṭic version[24] of the sanctification of the Day blessing in the *Amidah* of the Sabbath morning service: 'And You did not give it, O Lord our God, to the nations of the lands, nor did you make it the inheritance, our King, of the worshippers of graven idols, but to Israel Your people You have given it in love to the seed of Jacob, whom You chose'.

In fact we can also trace the roots of this linking of the sanctification of the people to the gift of Sabbath, Torah, and commandments back into the priestly sections of the Bible: 'Verily my Sabbaths shall you keep, for it is a sign between me and you throughout your generations, that you may know that I am the Lord who sanctifies you' (Exod. 31.13). From here the idea passed into Ezekiel's prophecy.[25]

'Also I gave them my Sabbath [...] that they might know that I am the Lord who sanctifies them' (Ezek. 20.12). This passage in Ezekiel comes immediately after reference to the giving of laws and judgements to Israel (v. 1) so that we see in Ezekiel too the same linkage of the sanctification of Israel to the gift of Torah and Sabbath, with the difference that in Ezekiel there is no explicit statement that the gift of Sabbath is the result of God's choice and favour.

We also find the combination of the choice of Israel and the gift of the Sabbath and the Holy Days in the Qumranic festival prayers: 'Blessed is the God of Israel who has chosen us from among all peoples[...] for rest and enjoyment' (מנוח ותענוג) (4Q503 1.24–25). This motif of the enjoyment of the Sabbath is also central to the *Amidah* for Sabbath and festivals in its Genizah version, as E. Fleischer has shown: 'A day of enjoyment you gave for this people'.[26]

To return to Neh. 9, after the formal prayer comes a long, national-historical confession, a sort of prayer of supplication (תחנון). The book of Baruch confirms that it was the custom to make confession on festivals and appointed days, saying with respect to a book that Baruch ben Neriyah had sent: 'Read the book that we sent you for confession in the House of the Lord on holy days and appointed days' (1.14)[27]

23. Cf. the early version of the Benediction of the sanctification of the Sabbath: 'And from Your love for us, O Lord our God [...] You have given us, O Lord our God, the seventh day [...] for its greatness, mightiness, and glory...etc.' See also: E. Fleischer (*op. cit.*), p. 22 and the Haftarah blessing: 'For the Torah and for Your worship and for the prophets and for this Sabbath day that You have given us, O Lord our God, for its holiness and rest, for honour and splendour'.

24. On the piyyuṭic form of the sanctification of the Day Benediction in the Sabbath service see: A. Mirsky, 'Yesod Kerova', *Sinai* 57 (1965), pp. 127–32 (Hebrew); J. Yahalom, 'Piyyut and Poetry', in L.I. Levine (ed.), *The Synagogue in Late Antiquity* (1987), pp. 111–26; also Liebreich (n. 22 above).

25. M. Greenberg, *Ezekiel 1–20* (1983), pp. 366–67.

26. Fleischer (see above n. 22), p. 31.

27. E. Tov (ed. and trans.), *The Book of Baruch* (1975).

It is remarkable that the description of the liturgical ceremonies in the book of Nehemiah, ceremonies held from 1st to the 24th of the month of Tishri, contains not a single mention of the temple or of temple services of worship, and this the month of the most important holy days, when the people made pilgrimage to the temple to offer the special festival sacrifices (cf. Ezra 3.4–6). The explanation might be that the author's objective is to describe the prayers and Torah readings for which people assembled, i.e. in the synagogues, and that these had nothing to do with the temple services conducted by the priesthood. This would also explain the absence of any mention of the sounding of the Shofar at the New Year[28] for the Shofar call was essentially part of the temple service, and also the absence of any mention of the Day of Atonement, since we know that the ritual of the Day of Atonement was almost entirely confined to the temple and to the High Priest, the people remaining passive onlookers. The author's interest being focused on the worship taking place outside the temple precincts, he also ignores the special New Year and Succot sacrifices.[29]

It was this disconnection of the synagogue worship from the temple cult that characterized its liturgy. The synagogue was a house of prayer. Another instance of this disconnection is the confession which follows after the prayer service (Neh. 9) and which carries echoes of Solomon's prayer in 1 Kgs 8 (cf. vv. 32, 34, 36, 39, 43): 'and You heard them from the heavens and delivered them according to Your mercies' (Neh. 9.28), 'and in the time of their trouble when they cried to You and You heard them from heaven' (v. 27). The contrast between Neh. 9 and these passages from 1 Kings – which, although redacted by the Deuteronomist, are by their context recited by Solomon at the inauguration of the temple – is that in Nehemiah there is not the smallest reference to the temple.

It is the synagogal context of Nehemiah's prayers that probably also explains the absence of the *Amidah*'s three last blessings – those on the Worship (עבודה), Thanksgiving, and the Blessing of the Priests, that formed part of the temple liturgy: 'And they recited three blessings: worship, thanksgiving, and the blessing of the priests' (*Tamid* 5.1). The 'worship' referred to is the offering of sacrifice in the temple, and indeed the priests blessed the service on completion of the daily *Tamid* offering (*ibid.*), just as the High Priest blessed the Day of Atonement service when he had ended his part in the ritual of that day (*Yoma* 7.1), and just as the King did after he had read the king's section (*Soṭa* 7.8). The original closing of the Service of Worship Blessing was either: 'and we shall worship in awe You alone' (*y. Soṭa* 7.6, 22a) or: 'and You alone we shall worship and fear' (*ibid.* 7.1, 44b) and not as today '…who restores his divine presence to Zion'.

The Priestly Blessing was also originally part of the temple service, as was the Thanksgiving Blessing, which is never mentioned except in conjunction with the Priestly Blessing and the Service Blessing (*Rosh Hash.* 4.5 and elsewhere).

To the thanksgiving Blessing was usually linked the praise for some topical event, be it from the past (e.g. the Hasmonean victory over the Greeks and its

28. See G. Alon, 'Philonic halakha', *Tarbiz* 6 (1935), pp. 452–59 (Hebrew).

29. See Y. Kaufmann, *History of Israelite Belief* 8 (1956), Jerusalem – Tel-Aviv 1956, pp. 324ff. (Hebrew).

associated Blessing of the Miracles [על הניסים])or of the present, e.g. thanksgiving for the victory of King Jonathan recently discovered in a scroll from Qumran Cave 4 (4Q448).[30] The antiquity of the Thanksgiving Blessing is attested by the idioms occurring in it which have survived unchanged for hundreds of years. In the Qumran Thanksgiving for King Jonathan we have:

> 'On King Jonathan and all the congregation of Your people Israel who are dispersed at the four winds of heaven – peace on them all, and on Your kingdom may Your name be blessed'.

This language is reflected in the Thanksgiving Blessing in the *Amidah:* 'We thank You [...] for our lives and for Your miracles [...] for all these may Your name be blessed and exalted, our king, continually for ever and ever'. Also in the blessing after the Torah and Haftarah reading (from the Prophets) we hear: 'For the Torah, the service of worship and for the prophets [...] for all [...] we thank You and bless You, may Your name be blessed in the mouth of every living thing always and forever'. Again in the Grace after meals: 'We thank You O Lord our God [...] for all and we thank You and bless You. May Your name be blessed in the mouth of every living thing always and forever'.

The expression 'We thank You' (מודים אנחנו לך) from the Thanksgiving Blessing (see Sifre 34) [Finklestein p. 395]; *y. Ber.* 1.5, 3d; *b. Soṭa* 40a) is found once and once only in the Bible, in King David's prayer in 1 Chr. 29.13, and even the idea of the 'kingdom' is one element of it (v. 11), as it is in the Thanksgiving for King Jonathan from Qumran quoted above. In David's prayer too the word 'all' כול, הכול occurs ten times. We should also note that the words from the Thanksgiving for Jonathan 'all the congregation of Your people Israel who are dispersed at the four winds of heaven' are also echoed in the *Modim* (thanksgiving) of the Rabbis (מודים דרבנן) from the *Amidah:* 'We thank You [...] blessings and thanks are due to Your name [...] for You have given us life and sustained us [...] and gather our exiles to the courtyards of Your sanctuary'. And as D. Flusser has shown, the motif of the ingathering of the exiles appears in the Epistle of Judah the Maccabee to the Jews of Egypt as well as in the Apostles (Didache) in the Grace after Meals there.[31]

It goes without saying that the *Amidah* Blessing on Jerusalem and the kingdom of David originates with the temple service, cf. Ben Sira 51: 'Give thanks to Him who built His city and Temple [...] give thanks to Him who raised up the House of David [...] give thanks to him who chose Zion'.

The eschatological aspirations of the *Amidah* are reflected in the classical prophecy of the end of days.[32] These blessings for the nation were recited in the

30. See H. Eshel, E. Eshel and A. Yardeni, 'A Qumran Composition Containing part of psalm 154 and a prayer for the Welfare of King Jonathan and his kingdom', *IEJ* 42 (1992), pp. 199–229. Vermes proposes that the Jonathan referred to is Judah the Maccabee's brother; see: G. Vermes 'The so-called King Jonathan Fragment', *JJS* 44 (1992), pp. 294–302.

31. See D. Flusser, 'Note on the prayer for the welfare of King Jonathan', *Tarbiz* 61 (1991), pp. 299 (Hebrew).

32. See M. Weinfeld 'Mesopotamian prophecy of the end of days', *Shnaton, Biblical and Ancient Eastern Studies Yearbook* 3 (1979), pp. 263–76 (Hebrew).

temple and their topics include: the fertility of the soil, the ingathering of Israel's exiles, God's establishment of justice and righteousness, the eradication of evil and the practice of informing, the strengthening of the righteous, the rebuilding of Jerusalem and the prosperity of the House of David.

I. Elbogen[33] has already hinted at the eschatological nature of these blessings but for some reason has ascribed them to Ezekiel 'and I shall gather you in from the lands in which you are scattered' (20.34, 41) when in fact this formulation belongs to other prophets. The blessing 'Sound the great Shofar for our freedom' comes from Isa. 27.13: 'And it shall come to pass on that day that a great Shofar will be blown and they shall come who were lost in the land of Ashur and the outcasts in the land of Egypt', whereas for the ingathering of the exiles cf. *ibid.* 11.12: 'and he shall set up a banner for the nations and shall assemble the outcasts of Israel and shall gather together the dispersed of Judah from the four corners of the earth'. For the blessing 'Restore our judges', cf. *ibid.* 1.26: 'And I will restore your judges as at the first and your counselors as at the beginning' and for its closing words: 'who loves righteousness and judgement' cf. *ibid.* 61.8: 'For I the Lord love judgement...' For 'May all Your enemies be cut off' in the Blessing against Heretics, cf. Mic. 5.8: 'and all your enemies shall be cut off'. For the Rebuilding of Jerusalem: 'And to Jerusalem your city may You return in compassion and dwell in it as You have said', cf. Zech. 1.16: 'I have returned to Jerusalem with mercies, my house shall be rebuilt in it', and also *ibid.* 2.14: 'for lo, I come and I shall dwell in the midst of you'. For the blessing 'The offspring of David', cf. Jer. 33.16: 'In those days and at that time I shall cause an offshoot of righteousness to grow up for David' and *ibid.* 23.5: 'I will raise to David a righteous offshoot', and see also Zech 6.12: 'Behold a man whose name is Zemakh who shall grow up out of his place and he shall build the temple of the Lord...'

Expressions of national aspiration like the above also formed part of the prayers recited daily before the Hittite king and queen and their subjects:

> 'Grant to the king and queen and to the princes of their land long life; recovery from illness; fertility of the soil; corn and the fruit of the vine; sheep and cattle and their offspring [...], May the enemies of their land fall under their feet [...] remove from the land the fear of pestilence and famine [...] (*KUB* XXIV 1).[34]

Petitions even closer to those of the *Amidah* are found in Mesopotamian literature,[35] the petitions containing assurances of fertility and plenty; justice and righteousness in the king's dealings with his subjects, including the eradication of evil and the strengthening of the righteous; the ingathering of exiles; the coming of the prince-redeemer and the establishment of temple and cult. Even more remarkable,

33. See I. Elbogen, *The History of Prayer in Israel* (trans. Y. Amir; ed. Y. Heinemann, 1972), p. 54.

34. A. Goetze, in J.B. Pritchard (ed.), *Ancient Near Eastern Texts Related to the Old Testament* (1969), p. 397; R. Lebrun, *Hymnes et prières hittites* (1980), pp. 180–87.

35. See M. Weinfeld (n. 32 above).

a Mesopotamian prophetic text, in which the *mīšarum* – i.e. justice and righteousness for the people – occupies a central place,[36] contains, in addition to the *mīšarum* and the call for the ingathering of exiles, an explicit wish for the eradication of informers and the strengthening of the righteous just as we find in the *Amidah:* 'The announcement from the fire (comes) [...] the land hears the voice of the gates of heaven, Anu commands Enlil to make *mīšarum. Mīšarum* will be performed [...] the exiles will be ingathered [...] the righteous will be firmly established [...] informers will be struck down'.[37] The announcing fire is the fire beacon called 'the golden torch' which announces the declaration of liberty, in a manner parallel to the announcement of the year of liberty in Israel by a blast of the Shofar (Lev. 25.9–10).[38] Thus, the beacon is the heaven-sent herald of freedom similar to the sounding of the heavenly Shofar in the blessing 'Sound the Shofar' which also heralds liberty, the ingathering of exiles, and the establishment of justice, this last being associated with the eradication of informers, on the one hand, and, on the other, with the strengthening of the righteous.[39]

Expressions of national desires also occur in Greek prayer, as Y. Ba'ar[40] and E.A. Bickermann have noted.[41] We find there pleas for the fertility of earth and man; for good political leadership, for justice and right dealing, and for the establishment of divine worship. Considering all the evidence presented here, the conclusion must be that the eschatological aspirations of the *Amidah* did not originate in the second temple period and were certainly not the fruit of Greek influence; their roots are to be traced back to the national aspirations of first temple-period prophecy and similar expressions in Mesopotamian and Ancient Greek liturgies.

It would be my opinion that the four Benedictions constituting the synagogal

36. On the *mīšarum* and its Israelite parallels see: M. Weinfeld, *Social Justice in Ancient Israel and in the Ancient Near-East* (1995), p. 75ff.

37. R.D. Biggs, 'More Babylonian Prophecies', *Iraq* 29 (1967), pp. 117ff. ('*saphutum ipaḫḫura[...] kinātum uktannama[...] mubiršunu* GAZ.MES-*ma*').

38. On the raising up of the 'golden torch' on the proclamation of freedom in Mesopotamia, see M. Weinfeld (n. 36 above), p. 73.

39. In the *Amidah* blessings on Righteousness and Justice, the elimination of Heretics and Informers, the blessing of the righteous and the devout, Flusser detects reference to the three sects, Saducees, Essenes, and Pharisees. See D. Flusser, 'MMT and the Blessing Against Heretics', *Tarbiz* 61 (1993), pp. 366–74. It is indeed more than likely that the Blessing of the righteous and the devout is directed towards the Pharisees. The phrase 'the remnant of the scribes' preserved in the Ashkenazi version, tends to confirm Flusser's opinion on this point. It is well known that the phrase occurs in the Ta'anit Scroll (Lichtenstein, p. 347) where it refers to the Pharisees who fled to Syria from the wrath of Alexander Yannai. Cursing heretics, informers, apostates and suchlike quite possibly targets the Essenes too. Flusser's idea that is the hardest to accept is that the Restoration of our Judges blessing refers in part to the Saducees. The content of this blessing is the establishment of righteousness and justice in Israel, namely social equality, for which evil must be eradicated and the hand of the righteous empowered (see M. Weinfeld [n. 36 above] p. 29). Furthermore, why devote a blessing to the Saducees? After all, perceived by the authors of the blessing as belonging with the other categories of secessionist groups, they were lumped with all such secessionists in the statement against heretics and other evildoers.

40. Y. Ba'ar, *Israel among the Peoples* (1955), pp. 32ff.

41. E.A. Bickermann, 'The civic prayer for Jerusalem', *HTR* 55 (1962), pp. 163–85.

core of the *Amidah* for Sabbath and Holy Days – on the Patriarchs, God's Might, the sanctification of God's Name, the Election of Israel and the gift of the Sabbath – originated in Babylon, for the reason that it was Ezra and Nehemiah who led these prayers. It is also possible, however, that they took shape in Judah during the time of the post-destruction Exile. On the return of the exiles to Jerusalem, these four blessings were supplemented with the blessing on the Temple Service, the blessing of Thanksgiving, and the Priestly Blessing, all borrowed from the temple liturgy. Evidence for this opinion is that just as no roots in temple liturgy can be traced for the earliest synagogue prayer service, so no synagogal roots can be found for the blessings recited in the temple. The latter contain not a hint of blessings on the patriarchs, God's mighty works, or the sanctification of God's name that formed part of the earliest synagogue liturgy.[42] Over time, the two sources were combined[43] to produce the seven blessings for Sabbaths and Festivals and the eighteen for weekdays.

A most instructive instance for the theme of this paper is the seven-part prayer that forms part of the Apostolic Constitutions and which is very similar to the seven-part prayer of the Jewish liturgy that is still recited today.[44] The Constitution, as it is known today, was formulated in the fourth century CE, but its original core is known to reach back to the first century CE. i.e. to a time before Judaism and Christianity finally disassociated themselves. It opens with an invocation of the God of Abraham, Isaac and Jacob, the sole creator and redeemer, and the opening ends with the words 'Blessed be the shield of the seed of Abraham'. Then comes a blessing on God's mighty works recalling God's great feats of creation: 'Creator of clouds to feed his creation' (echoes the 'causes the rain to fall' and 'sustains life' in the parallel Blessing on God's Mighty Works in the *Amidah*), and 'quickens the dying'. The third blessing is the Holiness of God's name, which here refers essentially to the angels in heaven extolling the Lord in song together with the Children of Israel on earth. At this point come the liturgical verses 'Holy, holy, holy etc'. from Isa. 6.3 and 'Blessed be the glory of the Lord from His place' from Ezek. 3.12. The fourth blessing, the sanctification of the Day, praises the Sabbath as a day of rest, enjoyment, and reflection on Torah. The fifth blessing evokes the promises of the prophets concerning Jerusalem and the House of David. The sixth is the blessing of thanksgiving: 'For all we thank You, master of all'.

We do not know when the two liturgies, of synagogue and temple, began to be combined. But it is at least clear from Neh. 8–9 that during the Babylonian exile a liturgy was in use unconnected with the temple cult and that we see it today in the four first blessings of the seven in the *Amidah* for Sabbath and Festivals.

The fact that the form of the blessings in Neh. 9 was the starting point for the evolution of the *Amidah* may explain the custom of the Palestinian congregations

42. These blessings are reflected in the Qumran texts, as I have shown above.

43. On the special character of the three middle blessings, Knowledge, Repentance, and Forgiveness see M. Weinfeld, 'The blessings on Knowledge, Repentance, and Forgiveness in the *Amidah*', *Tarbiz* 48 (1979), pp. 186–200.

44. See D.A. Fiensy, *Prayers alleged to be Jewish: an examination of the Constitutiones Apostolorum* (1985), pp. 143ff.

first pointed out by E. Fleischer, to conclude their various *Amidah*'s with a passage from Neh. 9.6–8.[45] Does this represent a faint memory of the *Amidah* as recited by the people referred to in this passage from Nehemiah? Perhaps for the same reason it was decided that 'And David blessed… etc.' from 1 Chr. 29.10–13 (that came to be attached to Neh. 9.6–8 in the *pesukei d'zimra*) would not be recited when there are less than ten persons in the service communion, a custom also attested by Fleischer.[46]

The early Christians recited the Ten Commandments and the *Shema'* in their daily morning Sacramentum[47], that is, they swore a loyalty oath to God, as S. Lieberman has shown.[48] And now we learn from the Apostolic Constitutions that they also recited the *Amidah* (see above). Hence, it is clear that the Lord's prayer, 'Our Father who is in heaven…' (Mt. 6.9–13; Lk. 11.2–4), was not intended to replace the public prayer that was already obligatory and which was recited by the early Christians too, but to be a private prayer. Furthermore, we have located all the component motifs of the 'Lord's prayer' in various private prayers that were appended to public prayer services (see below). This proves that it was intended for private prayer, as were the prayers from which it originated, which were recited either before or after the public prayer service, after the benediction of שומע תפילה[49], or after the Grace After Meals, or before going to sleep, etc.[50]

2. *Private Prayer*

Those who claim a late date for the *Amidah* quote R. Eliezer: 'He who makes his prayers a fixed form, his entreaties will not be heard' (*m. Ber.* 4.4)[51] as evidence that, at first, i.e. in the second temple period, there was no public prayer conducted to a fixed structure and fixed formulae. As against this, the Sages bear witness that, from the days of Ezra and Nehemiah on, blessings and prayers were formally inserted into the service of worship by the members of the Great Assembly (*b. Ber.* 33a). We have also seen that Neh. 9 contains a series of public prayers arranged in the same order as the four first blessings of today's *Amidah* for Sabbath and Holy Days – the Patriarchs, God's Might, the Holiness of God's

45. Fleischer (see n. 22 above), pp. 43, 90.

46. *Op. Cit.*

47. See M. Weinfeld, 'The Ten Commandments: their unique role and place in Israelite tradition', in B. Segal (ed.) *The Ten Commandments Down the Ages* (1985), p. 25.

48. S. Lieberman, 'The discipline in the so-called Manual of Discipline', *JBL* 71 (1952), pp. 199–200.

49. On the blessing 'A God who hears prayer' as the last blessing of the Amidah, see: S. Safrai, 'Gathering in the synagogues on festivals, sabbaths, and weekdays', in R. Hachlili (ed.), *Ancient Synagogues in Israel: Third- Seventh Century* CE. *Proceedings of a Symposium at the University of Haifa, May 1987* (BAR international Series, 499, 1989), p. 13.

50. See Ch. 8.

51. See Y. Malkhi, 'Brief prayer and travelers' prayers', *PAAJR* 58.1–13; for private prayer among the early Christians see: J. Stadlhuber, 'Das Studengebet des Laien im Christlichen Altertum', *Zeitschrift für katholische Theologie* 71 (1949), pp. 129ff.

Name, and the Holiness of the Day. The Qumran scrolls add further proof that on Sabbath and Festivals a fixed service of prayer was the norm, and that it included the Patriarchs and God's Might blessings.[52]

The only reservation possible about the fixed nature of prayer concerns personal or private prayer which always existed alongside public prayer. R. Eliezer says that a person praying alone should not use the fixed forms of public prayer, which does not mean that he did not take as given that public prayer in fixed forms existed. The fact that there was a liturgy that demanded the presence of a *Minyan* – Torah reading, *Kiddush*, *Kaddish* and the *Amidah* recited aloud – demonstrates that a clear distinction was drawn between public prayer, that had its fixed formulation, and private prayer, which necessarily changed according to circumstance. And if R. Eliezer was opposed to fixed forms he was referring only to private prayer.

3. *Personal Petitionary Prayer*

At least from the time of Rabban Gamaliel in Yavneh, on the fringes of formal public prayer services, with their fixed order of blessings in their authorized formulations, there was also a place for personal private prayers. Mostly, these were said before the public morning service (comprising the *Shema'* and its accompanying blessings and the *Amidah*) and went by the name of the 'Morning Prayers'.[53] This was the most usual and the most extended occasion for private prayer, but such prayer might also be said at the end of the public service, i.e. after the *Amidah*, after the blessing 'A God who hears prayer',[54] or at night before sleep.[55] The Morning Blessings usually comprised: (a) thanksgiving to God for restoring to the sleeper his spirit (sleep was considered to be a form of death). This section usually concluded, in the Jerusalem Talmud version, with the words: 'Blessed [...] who quickens the dying', and in the Babylonian Talmud version, 'Blessed [...] who restores the spirit to dead corpses'; (b) a blessing for the re-creation of the person praying – to some extent a continuation of the thanksgiving for being awakened from 'death';[56] (c) a petition to be granted a heart capable of understanding Torah; (d) thanksgiving to God for the Torah that he had conferred on Israel;[57] (e) apotropaic prayer against sin, temptation, the evil instinct and Satan;[58]

52. See above. The fact is made especially evident in the liturgy of *DJD* Vol. VII. See M. Baillet, *Qumran Grotte 4, III (4Q482–520)*, *DJD*, VII, Oxford 1949, pp. 111ff., where we find the blessing 'You have chosen us' for sabbaths and festivals. See also M. Weinfeld, 'The Qumran Liturgy', in M. Broshi *et al.* (eds.) *The Dead Sea Scrolls: Forty Years of Research* (1991), p. 163.

53. See ch. 8.

54. See n. 49 above.

55. See ch. 8.

56. See M. Bar Ilan, 'the blessing 'Creator of Man': occurrences, functions and meanings', *HUCA* 56 (1988), pp. 15–17 (Hebrew).

57. See ch. 8.

58. *Op. Cit.*, pp. 74–75.

(f) a petition to find favour with God and with other people;[59] (g) a petition for redemption – the revelation of God's kingdom on earth; (h) a petition for forgiveness of sin; (i) a petition to be provided the means to a livelihood; (j) a petition to be saved from evil, affliction, and pain.

Since we are dealing with private prayer, individuals did not keep strictly to the known formulae nor was there any obligation to recite every one of the above possible components. Most known variations, however, included the following: thanksgiving to God for restoring to the sleeper his waking spirit, a petition to be granted a heart capable of understanding Torah; a petition for protection against evil and the evil instinct, a petition for forgiveness of sin, a petition to be provided the means of livelihood, and the aspiration to the redemption that will come with the establishment of God's kingdom on earth.

The Psalms Scroll from Qumran (11QPSa) has been found to contain prayers that are part of the Morning Blessings, as they are still recited in our day.[60] Column XIX of the Scroll contains what its editor terms a Plea of Deliverance[61], comprising petitions to be saved from affliction and disease, from the evil instinct and from Satan. Longer and more complex versions of the same petitions have been found in the Cairo Genizah.[62] As in the Morning Blessings recited today, the Qumran petitioner pleads for divine protection from pain, Satan and the instinct to do evil: 'Let not Satan and the unclean spirit prevail over me. Let not pain and the evil instinct (יצר רע) hold sway over me'.[63] The petitions found in the Genizah fragments are closer to the Qumran formulae than to the present-day ones, for example:

> [Blessed are You O lord our God, God of thanksgiving {...} who loosens the bonds of sleep {...} save us from every evil thing[64]] let my tongue not be accustomed to deceit and let me not have need for the gifts of the flesh whose gifts are few and whose shame is large... O lord, rescue my soul from lying tongues and deceiving words. May it be Your merciful will, O Lord our God, and God of our forefathers that Your city be soon rebuilt in our days and Your temple be established in our time, so that you may give us consolation in it and joy within its walls, as You have said and promised us. Blessed are You, O Lord our God who rebuilds Jerusalem in mercy, Amen.

The petitions in their Genizah formulation thus open with a plea to be rescued from the decree of death, which is then followed by petitions for revivification, knowledge, forgiveness from sin, livelihood, acknowledgement of man's lowliness, rescue from affliction, the instinct to evil and Satan, the creation of man in the divine image and the rebuilding of Jerusalem.[65]

59. On this topic see Chapter 17.

60. See ch. 8.

61. J.A. Sanders. *The Psalms Scroll of Qumran Cave 11* (Discoveries in the Judean Desert of Jordan, IV, 1965), pp. 76–79.

62. J. Mann, 'Genizah fragments of the Palestinian order of service', *HUCA* 2 (1925), p. 277; S. Assaf, 'the order of the service in the Land of Israel', in *On the 50-year Jubilee of B.Z. Dinur* (1949), p. 121 (Hebrew).

63. See ch. 8.

64. Textual restorations by Mann (see n. 62 above).

65. Assaf (n. 62 above) pp. 120–21.

The Plea for Deliverance from Qumran opened likewise (the opening has not survived but can be reconstructed from the context) with the petition that the petitioner not be condemned to death. The surviving text begins with the words: 'For a worm cannot praise You', taken from King Hezekiah's prayer in Isa. 38.18–19: 'For She'ol cannot praise You, death cannot celebrate You [...] the living, the living he shall praise You'. There follows a plea for pardon from transgression: 'Pardon O Lord my sins and cleanse my offences', a plea for knowledge: 'Bestow on me the spirit of faith and knowledge', and lastly the apotropaic petition: 'Let not Satan and the evil instinct have power over me'.

The apocryphal psalm in the same scroll (Psalm 3, 'the Syrian') has corresponding elements: (a) gift of a heart capable of understanding Torah: 'Give me understanding of Your Torah, O Lord, and teach me Your judgments'; (b) forestall evil fate: 'Do not give me to forces stronger than me', a formula that corresponds in content to the plea not to let Satan and the evil instinct have power over the petitioner; (c) forgiveness from sin: 'The sins of my youth keep distant from me and do not recall to me my crimes'; (d) deliverance from afflictions: 'Cleanse me, O Lord, from the afflictions of evil and let them not revisit me'.

We find these and other similar elements in the Lord's prayer of the New Testament: (a) provision of a daily livelihood (Τὸν ἄρτον ἡμῶν ἐπιούσιον δὸς ἡμίν σήμερον);[66] (b) forgiveness from sin; (c) forestall temptation and trial;[67] (d) rescue from evil.[68]

Just as Jewish petitionary prayer does not observe a uniform wording and order (see below), nor do the pleas for deliverance found in the various Christian Gospels. Mt. 6.9–13 comprises seven petitions, of which the first three envision

66. For the various possible translations see: G. Dalman, *Die Worte Jesu*, I (1930), pp. 321ff. The main comparison must be with the private prayer 'The needs of your people Israel are numerous[...] may You provide each one his livelihood [...] enough of want' (*y. Ber.* 4.4, 8b; *b. Ber.* 29b; *t. Ber.* 3.7 [Lieberman, p. 34]. It is of interest that this prayer occurs in the order of service of R. Amram Gaon with the concluding words 'and do what is right in Your eyes', a formula already familiar to us from R. Eliezer's prayer (*t. Ber.* 3.7), which itself has points of contact with Jesus' prayer. See *The Prayer Service of Rav Amram Gaon* (D. Goldschmidt Edition, 1972), p. 183. (Hebrew). See also: J. Heinemann, *Prayer in the Period of the Tannaim and Amoraim* (1964), p. 196; Y.D. Gilat, *The Mishna of R. Eliezer ben Horkanos and its Place in the History of Halakha* (1968), p. 86. I agree with Dalman that the expression ἄρτον [...] ἐπιούσιον in Jesus' prayer reflects a petition that the needs of today and tomorrow be provided for. See also: J.A. Fitzmyer, *The Gospel According to Luke (X–XXIV)* (*AB*, 1985), pp. 896–901. In this passage from a 'Christian' Gospel, albeit borrowed from a Hebrew source, Hieronymos detected behind the term '*maar*' the Hebrew מחר. If he is right then it is plausible to read the passage as referring to the needs of today and tomorrow. Indeed, Hebrew prayers are known containing the petition to have needs met before the need actually arises, 'before we have the need for it', e.g. the prayer attached to the 'A God who hears prayer' blessing: 'Provide me with my portion of bread [...] my food before I have need for it' (see: *Siddur Otzar Hatfilot*, pp. 176–77).

67. For a comparison between 'Do not subject me to temptation and trial' from conventional Jewish prayer and 'Do not subject me to forces stronger than me' as in the Syrian Psalm' from Qumran see: D. Flusser, 'Qumran and Jewish apotropaic prayers', *IEJ* 16 (1966), pp. 194–205.

68. Cf. in the Genizah version immediately after the blessing on the passing of sleep: 'deliver me from all evil things' (Mann [n. 61 above], p. 278). For a detailed discussion of the meaning of ἀλλὰ ῥῦσαι ἡμας ἀπὸ τοῦ πονηροῦ in Mt. 6.13 see Dalman (n. 66 above), pp. 347ff.

an ideal future (the end of days) and the last four present wishes concerning the individual's current needs: (a) sanctification of the name of God; (b) the realization of his kingdom; (c) May His will be done in heaven and on earth; (d) giving each his daily bread according to his needs; (e) forgiveness from sin; (d) not to let the petitioner be tempted by evil; (g) deliverance from all evil. Luke 11.2–4 in contrast includes only five petitions: (a) sanctification of the name of God; (b) the realization of his kingdom; (c) giving each his daily bread according to his needs; (d) forgiveness from sin; (e) not to let the petitioner be tempted by evil.[69]

In effect, we also find the same petitions in the post-*Amidah* private prayers quoted in *b. Ber.* 16b–17a. For instance the prayer of R. Eliezer contains petitions for: (a) the establishment of peace and friendship; (b) a portion in Paradise; (c) the restoration of the instinct for good and a heart full of divine awe; (d) contentment (i.e. satisfaction of one's virtuous desires). Rav's prayer has: (a) life; (b) peace; (c) livelihood; (d) love of Torah and awe of heaven; (e) fulfilment of virtuous desires. Rabbi's prayer has (compare it to today's Morning Blessings) (a) deliverance from evil affliction; (b) deliverance from the evil instinct and from Satan the Destroyer. Rav Safra prays for: (a) peace among both the heavenly and earthly hosts, and (b) Torah study for its own sake. Mar Bar deRabina (in the prayer 'My God, guard my tongue') prays for: (a) the eradication of hatred and slander; (b) the opening of the heart to Torah and the commandments; (c) deliverance from evil affliction, and (d) deliverance from the instinct to do evil.

In our day, Mar Bar deRabina's prayer is conventionally placed at the end of the *Amidah.* In Rav Amram Gaon's order of service it is inserted into a long series of petitions that comprises most of the motifs found in the private prayers from Qumran quoted above. Furthermore, Rav Amram's service opens with a petition for the realization of God's kingdom on earth that recalls Jesus' 'Our father'. I give here an abridged version of the Rav Amram prayer:

> Our King and God, make Your kingdom in Your world as one and Your name in Your world as one [...]
> O Merciful One, grant us to see the days of the Messiah and life in the world to come [...]
> In Your manifold mercies grant absolution for my sins [...]
> And deliver me from evil men and from the evil Satan and from evil times [...]
> Open my heart to Your Torah and may Your commandments pursue my soul [...] and
> open for me the gates of wisdom, the gates of Torah [...] the gate of life and sustenance and livelihood [...][70]

The components of the prayer are, as we see: (a) God's kingdom on earth; (b) forgiveness for sin; (c) deliverance from Satan and from evil experience; (d) opening the heart to knowledge; (e) livelihood and sustenance – in other words the same elements as are found in the 'Our Father' and the Qumran prayers.

The *Amidah* concludes, as we know, with 'He who makes peace in his heights, may he make peace upon us and on all Israel' a petition that is also echoed in the

69. See Fitzmyer (n. 66 above), pp. 896–901.
70. See The Prayer Service of Rav Amram Gaon (n. 66 above), p. 28. (Hebrew).

'Lord's Prayer': 'May Your will be done on earth as it is in heaven'[71], in the prayer uttered by R. Eliezer the Great: 'May Your will be done in the heavens above and grant contentment to those that fear You',[72] and in the Rav Safra prayer quoted earlier: 'May it be Your will before You, O Lord our God, that You establish peace in the heavenly as in the earthly hosts'.

The same private petitions as we have been considering also occur in a prayer from the school of R. Yannai:

> 'I have sinned before You [...] may You grant me a good heart, a good instinct [...] and give me not into the power of the gifts of the flesh [...] and give us our share in Your Torah to those that do Your will. Rebuild Your house and the palace of Your city and rebuild Your Temple speedily in our days' (*y. Ber.* 4.2, 7d).

The petition for the rebuilding of the temple is nothing less than a wish that the divine kingdom be realized on earth. When the temple still stood the same aspiration was expressed by the plea for the deliverance of Zion and the restoration of her glory. Indeed, in the Qumran Psalms Scroll we find a special petition devoted entirely to this matter (col. 22.1–15), and it would seem that this petition fills the role of the petition for the realization of the divine kingdom that was, as we have seen, a common feature of individual petitionary prayer, but which seemed, on the face of it, not to feature in the Qumran prayers.

A similar thing seems to happen in today's standard liturgy. After the recitation of the evening *Shema'* the 'Lay us down to sleep' blessing is said, which is in fact a petition for protection, similar in content to the apotropaic petitions made at dawn before the public morning service (see above). It is followed by a blessing, the whole of which is an appeal for the realization of God's kingdom in Israel and in all its deeds, accompanied by a petition for the revelation of God's kingdom in Zion: 'May our eyes see [...] when Zion is told "Your god has become king" '. This appeal has two parts. The first part commences with the doxologies from the book of Psalms: 'blessed be the Lord forevermore, Amen, Amen' (Ps. 89.53), 'Blessed be the Lord out of Zion, He who dwells at Jerusalem' (*ibid.* Ps. 135.21), 'Blessed be His glorious name forever and let the whole earth be filled with His glory, Amen and Amen' (*ibid.* Ps. 72.19). It concludes with the plea: 'Our God who is in Heaven, exalt the unity of Your name and establish Your kingdom forever and rule over us forever and ever'. This is a very similar petition to that in the opening sentence of the petitionary private prayer, placed in the R. Amram Gaon order of service after the end of the *Amidah:* 'Our King and God, make Your kingdom and Your world as one and Your name in Your world as one [...]'. The second part of the appeal: 'May our eyes see and our heart rejoice...' closes with the blessing 'the King in his glory will always reign over us forever and ever and over all his deeds' and in the Roma version: 'the King and God lives forever and exists for eternity'. The petitions of this appeal should

71. For the connection between this blessing and the establishment of peace in heaven and earth (cf. Lk. 2.14 and the translation into Aramaic of Isa. 6.3 inserted into the *Kedusha Desidra*) see: D. Flusser, 'Sanktus und Gloria', *Abraham Unser Vater, Festschrift O. Michel* (1963), pp. 149ff.

72. *t. Ber.* 3.7 (Lieberman Edition, p. 34).

be regarded as an extension and conclusion to the apotropaic blessings in the 'Lay us down to sleep' blessing – to sleep and wake in peace, to be defended against foes and delivered from everything evil (see above, n.68), for Satan to be removed from before and behind, and to be preserved from night-time fears.[73] And last of all – the realization of God's kingdom.

Even on the margins of the Grace after Meals there is also to be found a series of petitionary prayers. After the obligatory blessings comes a series of pleas, formulated differently in each liturgical tradition, and Aboudraham has declared with regard to this: 'Every one will recite the Harakhaman as he wishes and according to what he wishes for'. In the Sepharadi tradition we find a series of seventeen petitions each introduced by the invocation '*Harakhaman*!' I list here those already mentioned in the course of this paper:

> *Harakhaman*, may he rule over us forever and ever
> *Harakhaman*, may he be blessed in heaven and earth
> *Harakhaman*, may he sustain us in honour
> *Harakhaman*, may he plant his Torah and his love in our hearts

These are four of the five petitions of Jesus in the Lord's prayer:

> The kingdom of God on earth
> God being blessed in heaven and earth
> Livelihood at need
> Opening the heart so that it shall not be tempted to sin

We may conclude from all the foregoing that the petitions for deliverance, defence and the revelation of the divine kingdom that are found in the Qumran scroll and in the 'Lord's prayer' belong to a category of private petitions that supplemented the formal liturgy but did not replace it. The rabbinic texts teach us that such prayers were usually said on rising in the morning, or at night before sleep, or at the conclusion of the *Amidah* or after the Grace after Meals. Occasionally they were also attached to the blessing 'A God who hears prayer'.

73. See chapter 8.

Part II

The Qumran Scrolls

Chapter 10

The Temple Scroll or 'The Law of The King'

In his publication of the Temple Scroll[1] Y. Yadin has gone beyond what is commonly done in preparing the editio princeps of a manuscript. Not only did he decipher the document, join sections and fragments of manuscripts, and even supply what was missing when necessary, but he also explained the text and analysed its contents, a task which requires comprehensive knowledge of many fields and the most comprehensive philological training. Yet the editor has accomplished all this and has presented a magnificent work.

This scroll, the longest of the Qumran Scrolls discovered to date, provides us with much new information about the structure and appurtenances of the Temple, the festivals regulated by the calendar, holy donations, the law of the king and his relationship to God and the people, the unique views of the sect on ritual, laws of holiness and purity, and other laws, especially those in Deuteronomy. History shines through all this, that is, the time of the Hasmonean kings is reflected in the Scroll as the editor has correctly determined. But above all, the Scroll provides us with new information about Second commonwealth hermeneutics, that is, the way in which the author came to crystallize its laws, and on this subject I wish to begin my discussion.

Aside from the laws relating to the Temple and its appurtenances, sacrifices, and festivals in the Scroll, especially laws from Deuteronomy, the scroll interprets and harmonizes them with the other laws in the Pentateuch by making stylistic changes. That is, the laws quoted here are not attributed to Moses as in Deuteronomy, but to God himself. This change we shall discuss extensively below. It is interesting that, like the Scroll which is basically a commentary on Deuteronomy, Deuteronomy itself is a commentary and exposition of the four preceding books of the Pentateuch. This has been already observed by the medieval commentators when they wrote that the passage 'Moses undertook to explain this law' (Deut. 1.5) indicates laws which were already mentioned and Moses 'repeats in order to interpret and look for new meanings in them' according to the Nachmanides in his commentary upon Deut. 1.1 or as Abraham Ibn Ezra writes: 'And Moses began to explain to the children who were born in the desert what happened to

1. The Temple Scroll, edited with an introduction by Yigael Yadin; Vol. I: *Introduction*; Vol. II: *The Text and its Meaning*; Vol. III: *Tables and Text* (Israel Exploration Society, The Institute of Archaeology of the Hebrew University, the Shrine of the Book, Jerusalem; English edition, 1983).

their fathers and told them all the commandments...which their fathers heard from the LORD so that they too will hear from a reliable messenger' (Commentary on Deut. 1.5).[2]

Indeed both the Temple Scroll and Deuteronomy are a sort of midrashic commentary on the earlier books of the Pentateuch[3] and both employ a similar method. Y. Yadin[4] characterized the method of the author of the Scroll by showing that he usually

a. adds Halakhic expositions
b. standardizes laws (harmonization)
c. puts together laws which deal with the same subject. I shall adduce several examples of this.

A. *Halakhic expositions*

The author of the Scroll adds to the law of a beautiful captive woman (Deut. 21.10–14): 'And she shall not touch your purity for seven years, and she shall not eat of the offering of well-being until seven years have passed (afterward she may eat)' (63.13–15).

1. To the law on eating the tithe (Deut. 26.14), he adds, 'You will eat it on festivals' (43.15–16).

2. With the law on the setting aside of special areas for lepers and gonorrheics (cf. Num. 5.2), the Scroll conflates the law on the allocation of places for cemeteries (48.11–14).

3. To the law 'You shall not kill both her and her young in one day' (Lev. 22.28) is added a law, peculiar to the sect, not to sacrifice a pregnant animal (52.5).[5]

4. Sometimes the author of the Scroll adds a commentary on the wording rather than a halakhic explanation, e.g. 'But if in the open country a man comes upon a young woman who is betrothed' (Deut. 22.25), he adds, 'in a place distant and hidden from the city' (56.4–5).

B. *Harmonization of laws*

1. The author of the Scroll harmonizes the law of the seduced virgin in Exod. 22.15–16 with the law of the 'virgin who is seized' in Deut. 22.28–29 (66.8–11) thereby doing away with difficulties and discrepancies with which the author of Deuteronomy grappled.[6]

2. Based on the edition of Asher Weiser (1978). On the limitations of this edition, see U. Simon, *Kiriyat Sefer* 51 (1976), pp. 646–54.

3. Weingreen terms Deuteronomy Proto-Mishnaic, see J. Weingreen *Proceedings of the fifth World Congress of Jewish Studies* (1969), I, pp. 27ff.

4. *Temple Scroll*, I, pp. 73ff.

5. On this subject see my article: 'The Genuine Jewish Attitude Towards Abortion', *Zion* 47 (1977), pp. 129–42 (Hebrew).

6. Actually, the author of Deuteronomy interprets the law in Exod. 22 and explains it in his own way, and see M. Weinfeld, *DDS* (1972), pp. 284ff. And see Yadin, vol. I, pp. 368ff.

2. In order to harmonize the law on the pouring out of the blood of an animal in Deut. 12.16, 24 with the law in Lev. 17.13, the author of the scroll adds the passage 'and cover it with dust' to 'you shall pour it out upon the earth like water' (52.12; 53.5–6).[7]

C. *Combination of Laws dealing with the same subject*

1. The mention of the vows in Deut. 12.26 is followed by the law of the payment of the vow in Deut. 23.22–24 and the laws of vows in Num. 30ff. (53.9–54.5).

2. To the prohibition against sacrificing blemished animals in Deut. 17.1 the author of the Scroll adds the prohibition from Lev. 22.28: 'You shall not kill both her and her young in one day' as well as the law which we mentioned above concerning the sacrifice of a pregnant animal (52.4–7).

It can be shown that Deuteronomy applied the same methods to laws which were in its source material.

A. *Explanations*

1. Deuteronomy, which quotes almost *verbatim* the law in Exod. 21.1–11 on the obligation to set a slave free (cf. Exod. 21.2 with Deut. 15.12), and is dependent on this law in the matter of the boring of the ear of a slave, differs from the original law about the difference between a male slave and a female slave, and adds stipulations that do not appear in the Book of the Covenant, e.g. the obligation of setting free a slave and furnishing him 'liberally' (Deut. 15.13, 18).[8]

The ancient law, which apparently refers to primitive Hebrews of the *Habiru* type,[9] is here made to fit the new situation when the Hebrew is truly a 'brother': 'your brother, a Hebrew man or a Hebrew woman' (Deut. 15.12).[10]

7. According to Lev. 17, there is no place for the covering of the blood of an ox and a lamb since the slaughter of every ox and sheep must be done in the tent of meeting, and the blood sprinkled there upon the altar (vv. 1–7). Only the blood of a beast and a bird which is not brought to the altar must be covered with dust (vv. 13–14). Deuteronomy, in permitting the free consumption of meat for food did away with the custom of placating the blood and therefore says, 'you shall pour it out on the ground like water'. See M. Weinfeld *DDS* (1972), pp. 213–19. The author of the Scroll harmonized Lev. 17 and Deut. 12, and added the duty of covering up the blood to the law in Deuteronomy. The Pharisaic method did not make this harmonization, and thus an anomaly was created: the blood of an ox and of a lamb is poured out without being covered up, according to Deut. 12, while the blood of a beast or a bird is covered, in keeping with the law in Lev. 17. We need scarcely add that this is illogical. Why was the blood of cattle spilled out while the blood of a beast and a bird was covered? Is the blood of a bird redder?

On the difficulties of the concept of the pharisaic halakha on this subject see the Nachmanides' deliberations and commentary on Deuteronomy 12.22, and on a similar attempt of interpretation as the Scroll see Jacob Minaa in *b. Ḥul.* 84a.

8. See Weinfeld, *DDS*, pp. 282ff.

9. On the connection between the law of the slave in Exod. 21 and the Nuzi documents on the subject of the *Habiru*, see S. Paul, *JNES* 28 (1969), pp. 48–53.

10. Jeremiah draws a far-reaching conclusion and applies the law of the Hebrew slave to 'a Jew, his brother' (34.9), see my study: *Social Justice in Ancient Israel and in the Ancient Near East* (1995), p. 155.

2. In the law in Exodus it says, 'If you meet your enemy's ox or his ass going astray, you shall bring it back to him' (23.4). This law is accorded a lengthy explanation in Deuteronomy which adds that a lost possession must be taken care of if the owners are not found. In addition, it elaborates upon the application of the concept of the lost possession: be it a garment or any other object which may have been lost (22.1–3).

3. In Leviticus 19.9 it says, 'nor shall there come upon you a garment of clothes made of two kinds of stuff (שעטנז)'. It is not stated what שעטנז is so this work was apparently known to the listener. The author of Deuteronomy explains שעטנז by adding 'wool and linen together' (22.11).

B. *Harmonization (Unification of the laws)*

1. In the laws of the Book of the Covenant in Exodus, the festivals of unleavened bread and the Passover are separate. Thus, for example, in Exod. 23.15 we read: 'You shall keep the feast of unleavened bread; ...you shall eat unleavened bread for seven days'. Later, in v. 16 the subject of the verse changes to the feast of the first fruits and the feast of the ingathering, while the Passover is mentioned at the end: 'You shall not offer the blood of my sacrifice with leavened bread or let the fat of my feast remain until the morning'[11]. The same applies to its parallels in the Minor Book of the Covenant in Exodus 34 in v. 18 'the feast of unleavened bread you shall keep', while at the end, 'You shall not offer the blood of my sacrifice with leaven; neither shall the sacrifice of the feast of the Passover be left until the morning' (v. 25). We found a similar instance in the Priestly Code in Exodus 12. In verses 1–14, the law of the Passover concludes with the closing formula typical of the Priestly code: 'You shall observe it as an ordinance forever'. Later comes the section about the festival of the unleavened bread (vv. 15–20) which is independent and contains no indication of a Passover sacrifice and the festival of the Passover. The same is true of the calendar of the appointed feasts in Leviticus 23. Here we read: 'In the first month, on the fourteenth day of the month in the evening, is the LORD's Passover' (v. 5), and only later, 'And on the fifteenth day of the same month is the feast of unleavened bread to the LORD' (v. 6), as well as in the list of additional festival sacrifices in Num. 28.16 17. Thus in these sources there is a complete separation of the festival of unleavened bread and the passover, as if there were no connection between the two. On the other hand, Deuteronomy attempts to conflate the two festivals and create from them a single festival as was accepted in later Judaism. In order to do this, Deuteronomy cuts the law of the Passover sacrifice in its source material and inserts the law of unleavened bread, thereby artificially creating a single unit. Thus we read:

> And you shall offer the Passover sacrifice to the LORD your God...You shall eat no leavened bread with it; seven days you shall eat it with unleavened bread...No leaven shall be seen with you in all your territory for seven days; nor shall any of the flesh which you sacrifice on the evening...remain all night until morning.

11. See M. Haran, *Tequfoth umosadoth baMiqra* (1977), p. 108f (Hebrew).

The verses 'you shall eat no leavened bread with it', 'nor shall any of the flesh...remain...until the morning' seem to be a citation of the laws of the Passover sacrifice as found in the Book of the Covenant in Exod. 23.18 and 34.25. But while there they follow immediately upon each other, here they have been separated in order to insert the law regarding the eating of unleavened bread which is also taken from Exodus.[12] Indeed, if we remove the section on the law of eating unleavened bread (16.3–4) (from 'seven days you shall eat it' to 'no leaven shall be seen with you...seven days'), we obtain a continuous and uninterrupted treatment of the Passover sacrifice just like that in the Book of the Covenant.

C. *Joining of the laws dealing with the same subject*

In Deuteronomy 14 three subjects follow immediately upon each other which in the Pentateuchal laws appear separately, namely the prohibition against cutting and making any baldness on the forehead for the dead (vv. 1–2), eating unclean animals and carrion (3–21a), and boiling a kid in the milk of its mother (21b). The first prohibition appears in the Book of Holiness in connection with the holiness of priests and Israelites (Lev. 21.5; 19.27–28); the second begins the section containing the laws of uncleanness and purity in Lev. 11–15, while the third, boiling a kid in the milk of its mother, appears in the Major and the Minor Books of the Covenant in the context of the ceremonies of the appointed feasts (Exod. 23.19; 34.20). The author of Deuteronomy detached these laws from their natural context and made them a single unit for he considers them all customs not befitting the people of Israel. Indeed he twice added the reason: 'For you are a people holy to the LORD your God' (Deut. 14.2, 21).

Therefore, we may say that like Deuteronomy that interprets ancient laws and associates them in accordance with his views, the author of the Scroll interprets the laws of Deuteronomy and associates them according to his taste. For this reason he is a transitional link with the halakhic interpretations in the oral tradition.

To be sure, despite the fact that Deuteronomy and the Scroll employ the same exegetical methods, they differ as we indicated, in the style of address and commandment. In Deuteronomy Moses is the speaker, whereas in the Scroll it is God himself. In Deuteronomy Moses presents issues in his own name or as his explanation. He emphasizes his personality which acts as the intermediary in the formula which is repeated about forty times in Deuteronomy: 'which I have commanded you this day', evidence that it is he who commands[13] – albeit in the name of the Lord – on the occasion of the covenant in the plains of Moab. (Deut. 1–30 constitutes a long farewell address by Moses in the first person). On the other hand, outside Deuteronomy we found this formula only once, in Exodus 34.11: 'Observe what I command you this day', but contrary to the formulae in Deuteronomy where the commander is Moses, here the commander is God and the laws are those of the covenant which was renewed after it had been violated in the episode of the

12. Exod. 23.15, cf. 34.18 and 13.3–4,7, and see in M. Haran, *op. cit.*, p. 125f.

13. The passages in which God speaks in the first person (Deut. 7.4; 11.13–15; 17.3; 28.20) were analysed by A. Klostermann, *Pentateuch* NF (1907), pp. 186ff. and proved to be corrupt.

worship of the calf. The formula 'Observe what I command you this day' in Exodus 34.11, after which come the commandments of the renewed covenant (vv. 12–26 = the Minor Book of the Covenant) is appended to God's announcement about the making of the covenant. This announcement is accompanied by God's promise of the elevation of Israel's status: 'Behold, I make a covenant. Before all your people I will do marvels such as have not been wrought in all the earth or in any nation'.[14] It is interesting that the single place in the book of Deuteronomy in which the formula 'command you this day' is attributed to God and is linked to observation of the laws as in Exodus 34 is the place in which we find the establishing of the covenant and the promise to elevate the horn of the people of Israel:

> This day Yhwh your God commands you to do these laws and judgments; you shall keep and do them...you have proclaimed Yhwh this day to be for you a God...and Yhwh has proclaimed you this day to be for him a peculiar people[15] to make you high over all the nations (Deut. 26.10–19).

Actually, there is an obvious relationship between the beginning of the Minor Book of the Covenant in Exodus 34 and the verse from Deuteronomy 26 which we have cited. In both places the author connects the giving of the laws 'this day'[16] to the covenant between God and Israel and the promise of preserving the supremacy and uniqueness of Israel, except that in Exodus 34, this subject serves as the introduction to the laws of the renewed covenant, whereas in Deuteronomy it constitutes their conclusion. So it is surprising that the Temple Scroll begins with the subject of making the covenant which is taken from Exodus 34.[17] As Y. Yadin

14. See Exodus 33.16: 'Is it not in your going with us so that we are distinct, I and your people, from all other people that are upon the face of the earth?' And see the Rashbam's commentary upon 33.18: 'Here, too, Moses asked for the making of a covenant and (God) agreed... "*behold I make a covenant. Before all your people I will do marvels*" as you have requested "*that we are distinct, I and your people*"', etc. In the opinion of many commentators, this paragraph belongs in 33.14–16 after 34.9. See S.R. Driver, *Exodus* (Cambridge Bible), pp. 361, 368 and his references to the other scholars.

15. The subject here is the declaration of the text of the covenant (verba solemnia) on the part of the two parties. The people of Israel caused the Lord to say, 'I shall be your God', while God caused Israel to say, 'I shall be a people for your own possession', and cf. Hosea 2.20 after the betrothal of Israel to the Lord: 'and I will say to Not my People, "You are my people"; and he shall say, "You are my God"'. Indeed in Mishnaic Hebrew the marriage declaration is called 'to act verbally' (עשה בה מאמר) (*m. Yebam.* 2.1; 3.6, etc.). On acting verbally in the sense of entering into a covenant, see Tur-Sinai's lengthy treatment in *Peshuto shel Miqra* on Deut. 26.3–4.

16. On 'today' as a legal formula in various kinds of documents and contracts, see Weinfeld, *JAOS* 90 (1970), p. 190 n. 55, and references. At the same time we should note that 'today' and 'this day' carry great rhetorical weight, see Weinfeld, *DDS*, pp. 173ff.

17. The formula 'Observe what I command you this day' (Exod. 34.11) has, to be sure, not been preserved there (Y. Yadin, Vol. II, p. 1), but from this we need not conclude that it was omitted or not available to the author in the text of Exodus 34 from which he copied the written sources. In Yadin's opinion column two, line 1 does not have enough space for the beginning of Exod. 34.11, but it is possible that in the text of the Scroll was written, 'Observe what I command you' (the Syriac omits 'you' לך and the Septuagint omits 'this day'), so this short formula could be fitted into this line in addition to the space which Yadin reconstructs here.

rightly observes (col. 2, l.1), the author of the Scroll begins with the covenant renewed in Sinai which is attached to the building of the Tent of Meeting just as the first covenant (Exod. 19–24) immediately precedes the ordinances concerning the building of the Tent of Meeting (Exod. 25ff.). But why does he begin with the second covenant? The author of the Scroll wants to begin with the covenant renewed after the incident of the golden calf rather than with the chapters describing the former covenant which was violated.[18]

This tendency actually exists already in Deuteronomy itself. In contrast to the source of Exodus, which attributes to Moses the giving to Israel of the laws of the Book of the Covenant (Exod. 21–23 and cf. 24.3) after the revelation in Sinai (Exod. 19–20), the author of Deuteronomy tells us that only the ten commandments were given to Israel on Mt. Sinai, while the rest of the laws were given to Moses already in Sinai (Deut. 5.28), but not until the people arrived at the plains of Moab were they given to Israel. The sin of the calf caused the violation of the covenant and therefore all the obligations before that episode are no longer binding. The ten commandments are rewritten on Mt. Sinai (Exod. 34; Deut. 10.4), but the rest of the covenant is given to Israel in the plains of Moab where the covenant is made (Deut. 28.69; 29.9ff.). According to this view, the Book of the Covenant (Exod. 21–23), which was pronounced before the sin of the calf, is no longer binding; instead, there is the book of Deuteronomy which was the subject of the renewed covenant in the plains of Moab.[19]

On the other hand, the author of the Scroll, for whom all the laws of the Lord originated in Sinai – a dominant view in second temple Judaism – transfers the laws of the covenant from the plains of Moab back to Sinai. Accordingly, he changed the form of address in Deuteronomy so that, just like the laws in the Sinai covenant, the laws of the plains of Moab are said by God and not by Moses as is found in our version of Deuteronomy.[20] In fact, in principle he does not change the basic tradition of Deuteronomy, since the author of Deuteronomy, too, admits that the laws of Deuteronomy were given to Moses in Sinai (5.28), but were given to Israel as a covenant only in the plains of Moab. Yet while Deuteronomy tells us that the contents were given to Israel by Moses in the plains of Moab, the author of the Scroll relates the contents in the form in which they were given by the Lord on Mt. Sinai: spoken by God in the first person to Moses.

18. The importance of this new covenant in Sinai in the traditional Jewish view is evident from the fact that according to the Masora, the line 'observe what I command you this day' requires the beginning of a page in the book of the Torah next to six other acrostic verses whose first letters are ביה שמו as in ספר התגין and see M. Kasher, תורה שלמה, *Genesis*, Vol. I, p. 1, note to paragraph ה.

19. On Deuteronomy which reworked the Book of the Covenant according to its own view, see M. Weinfeld, *DDS*, pp. 282ff. On Deuteronomy which places itself instead of the book of the covenant in Exodus 20.22–23, 33, see the discussion in O. Eissfeldt, *Einleitung in das AT*^{3}, 1964, pp. 292ff.

20. See below, chapter 12.

The Definition of the Scroll and its aim – the law of the king

The main laws in the Scroll, aside from those having to do with the temple and its appurtenances, stem from Deuteronomy. What is the reason for this? It seems to me that the author chose Deuteronomy as his point of departure because this book is 'the law of the king' which the author of the Scroll was interested in unfolding. Deuteronomy is intended for a king and a monarchical regime as the following facts demonstrate:

a. Of all the books in the Pentateuch, the law of the king is mentioned only in Deuteronomy,[21] and this law also has a positive attitude towards the idea of a dynasty.[22]

b. According to the law in Deuteronomy 17, the king is commanded to make a copy for himself of 'this law', that is, Deuteronomy,[23] 'from that which is in charge of the levitical priests' (Deut. 31.9, 25–26), and 'to read in it all the days of his life' (17.19).

c. According to Deuteronomy 31.11–12, the reader must read Deuteronomy before all Israel at the end of the sabbatical year, the year of release, and the second temple tradition rightly interprets the reader of the law as being the king (see below).

d. Only in this book do we find a national constitution with the background of a monarchical regime: a king, a supreme court (17.6–13), army commanders (20.9), mobilization (24.5), etc.

e. It is about 'this book'[24] that Josiah made a covenant, so we may assume that the laws in this book guided him in his royal religious activities (2 Kings 23) and that his scribes were engaged in copying it (cf. Jer 8.8).[25]

The tradition that Deuteronomy was a guide for a royal regime continued into the second temple period, as we learn from the fact that *m. Soṭa* 7.8 terms some chapters of Deuteronomy 'the section on the king' (פרשת המלך). We may assume that this tradition gained impetus during the Hasmonean monarchy which is reflected in our Scroll.

'The section on the king'

The term פרשת המלך found in *m. Soṭa* 7.2,8 in connection with the reading of the law at the end of the seventh year, does not refer to the law of the king in Deuteronomy 17 in the limited sense, i.e. a law which relates solely to the conduct of the king, but rather to the Deuteronomic laws in general which he must read before the people. The Mishnah interprets the content of פרשת המלך as follows:

21. The king is mentioned also in Deut. 28.36: 'The LORD will bring you, and your king'.

22. 'So that he may continue long in his kingdom, he and his children, in Israel' (Deut. 17.20) and see Weinfeld, *DDS*, p. 168f.

23. The expression 'this law' is found only in Deuteronomy and with reference to this book only, see Weinfeld, *DDS*, p. 107.

24. On the identity of 'the book of the law' in 2 Kgs 22–23, see my article 'Josiah', *Encyclopaedia Judaica*, Vol. 10, col. 288–293.

25. See Weinfeld, *DDS*, pp. 167ff.

> How was the 'section on the king' recited?...The prefect gave to the Priest...the book of the law...and the King received it standing up and read it sitting... He read from the beginning of Deuteronomy to 'Hear, [O Israel!] 'שמע' (6.4)...'*it shall come to pass if you shall hearken*'... (11.13) and you shalt surely tithe...(14.22) and '*When you have finished tithing*' (26.12)...and the section on the king [in the restricted sense]...the Blessings and Curses until the end (7.8).[26]

In *t. Soṭa* 7.17 we read:

> He reads from the beginning of '*These are the commandments*' to '*Hear, O Israel!*' (Deut. 6.4) And...*when you shall hearken* (והיה אם שמע תשמעו) (Deut. 11.13), *you shall surely tithe (*Deut. 14.28) and '*When you have finished taking a tithe*' (Deut. 26.12). R. Judah said: There was no obligation to start from the beginning of the book but (be start) *Shema',* when you shall hearken, you shall surely tithe, When you have finished taking a tithe and the section on the king until he finishes it all and the paragraphs [var 'expositions'] that are commentaries on it (ופרשות הנדרשות בה) and he completes it.[27]

The contents of the sections on the king as defined here overlap with those of our Scroll. Aside from the Deuteronomic laws whose obligation to be read is implicit in the Mishnah and Tosefta which we quoted (cf. 'until he finishes it all' or 'and he completes it'), there is special emphasis on what the Rabbis have to say about 'You shall surely tithe (עשר תעשר)', 'the section on the king' and 'blessings and curses', issues which appear with more than usual prominence in the Scroll. The tithe is discussed at length in the scroll (col. 43–44, for which see also pp. 182ff. below); 'the law of the king' takes up approximately four columns in the Scroll with the 'blessings and curses' appended to it. This shows that 'blessings and curses' which in Mishnah Soṭa are appended to the law of the king are also appended in the Scroll to the law of the king as could also be learned from the Tosefta. In the latter, 'blessings and curses' are not mentioned; instead we find 'the sections which are commented upon (הפרשות הנדרשות)' in the law of the king are the subjects which are interpreted by the supplementary law of the king in the Scroll (col. 57–59): (1) the organization of the army and its commanders; (2) the royal bodyguard; (3) the king's council; (4) the administration of justice; (5) mobilization procedures and those for waging war; 6. cursing and blessing of king and people in connection with the observation of these laws. As we know, these topics do not appear in the Old Testament in the section on the king, so they are therefore homiletical interpretations or 'sections' which are commented upon 'הפרשות הנדרשות' in the law of the king in Deuteronomy. The absence of blessings and curses in the Tosefta may be explained by the fact that they are included in 'the sections which have been interpreted' as we find in the supplementary law of the king in the Scroll.

26. In the Palestinian versions of the Mishna, 'the section on the king' is not mentioned, cf, the Mishnah in the Palestinian Talmud, the version of Maimonides, etc. In the opinion of S. Lieberman, the words 'the section on the king' were inserted into the Mishnah from the Tosefta, see *Tosefta Kifshutah*, Soṭa, Part 8, p. 684.

27. According to S. Lieberman (*ibid.*) R. Judah's words end with 'the finishing of the tithe' whereas 'the section on the King' goes back to the words of the first Tanna.

In S. Lieberman's opinion[28] 'the sections which are commented upon' refer to the passages about 'the assembly' and 'assemble' in Deut. 31.12, 28 but it seems to me that the subject here is not the biblical passages which are connected to the reading by the king as Lieberman thinks, but rather to homiletical interpretations of the law of the king. That is, they are a kind of homiletical interpretation of the verses and are not explicit in the verses themselves.

Indeed we also hear from Philo[29] about 'the sections which are commented upon' which are supplementary to the law of the king in Deuteronomy. After citing the Deuteronomic laws relating to the election of a king, the inadmissability of crowning a foreigner king, the accumulation of excessive wealth, and sending the people out of Israel,[30] he dwells upon the writing of Deuteronomy[31] by the king[32] and then quotes a kind of declaration of the king's obligation:

> I wrote these things...in order to inscribe them upon my heart and if I rely on holy laws, I shall earn equality because pride and arrogance belong to a small soul (of limited understanding...) I shall walk the king's road (the middle road) a leader who respects equality, who does not take bribes and administers justice will live long... He will choose for himself advisers who will help him rule in governing and in judgment...select...helpers who eschew pride...(the king) will administer justice to resident alien, orphan and widow...

The subjects which appear here are also found in the law of the king in the Scroll. (1) To administer justice (169, see 57.19); (2) Never to accept bribes (169, see 57.20); (3) To appoint aides and advisors who will help the king carry out his duties (170, see 57.11–15); (4) To further equality (165–166, see 57.14). We should add that these subjects appear as a literary unit appended to the law of the king in Deuteronomy similar to the supplementary unit in the Temple Scroll which also includes such subjects, and we may consider it a 'paragraph which is commented upon', thereby eliminating the puzzlement of the scholars with regard to the origin of the additional warnings to the king in Philo.[33] In fact, we find such additions also in Josephus. In presenting the law of the king (*Antiquities* IV 223f.) he adds that the king must ensure the administration of justice and consult the council of elders and the high priest.

In the Mishnah, too, we find an expanded law of the king which partially overlaps with that in the Scroll: laws of the Sanhedrin (=council) (*Sanh.* 1.6; Scroll 57.11–15); marital laws applicable to the king (*ibid.* 2.2 = Scroll 57.15–19); waging of war and division of the spoils (*ibid.* 2.4 = Scroll 58.11–15). The

28. See Lieberman, *ibid.*, p. 684.

29. *Spec. Leg.* IV 160ff.

30. This is how he comments upon the words, 'And he will not return the people to Egypt', etc.

31. In Philo's own words. τὴν ἐπινομίδα κεφαλαιώδη τύπον 'an appendix in the form of a precis', i.e. a brief summary of the laws. For this use of Deuteronomy see *Quis Rerum* 162, 250.

32. Philo emphasizes that the king should write with his own hand αὐτοχειρία γράψαι (160, and see 162) by contrast with the Scroll which reads 'and they should write for him' (instead of 'and he should write' in the Masoretic text), and cf. *Tg. Ps. J.* 'and the elders should write for him'. The Rabbis explain לו as 'for him', see *Sipre* 160, and *m. Sanh.* 2.4.

33. See e.g. J. Heinemann, *Philons griechische und judische Bildung* (1932), pp. 183–84, and the discussion in H.A.Wolfson, *Philo* II^4, 1968, p. 336.

parallel between the Scroll and the laws of the king in the Mishnaic literature is very instructive: both of them contain laws from Deuteronomy; in both, royal affairs and the tithe are emphasized and both begin with an affirmation of faithfulness to the covenant; the Scroll begins with the covenant renewed after the episode of the golden calf, containing the verse, 'What I command you this day' (Exod. 34.11), while the law of the king opens, according to Rabbi Judah, with '*Hear, O Israel...And if you obey*' where we also find 'what I command you [sing] this day' (Deut. 6.6), 'what I command you [pl.] this day' (11.13).

Moreover, as in the Temple Scroll in which the author joins subjects from various paragraphs relating to the same issue, so also regarding the law of the king we learn that when reading 'you shall tithe' in Deuteronomy 14, they would go on to 'when you have finished paying all the tithe' in ch. 26, and afterwards return to the law of the king in Deuteronomy 17 in order to join the laws and regulations of tithing to each other.[34] Indeed in the Scroll too, the regulations on tithing from Deuteronomy 14 are joined to the regulations on tithing from Deuteronomy 26 (col.43), as Yadin noted.[35]

The law of the king in the Scroll

The law of the king is the second most important subject in the Scroll next to the Temple regulations. We could explain this phenomenon in light of my assumption that the entire Scroll was intended to be a sort of guide for the king in his carrying out of the laws relating to national life. However, in the Scroll the law of the king relating to the organization of his kingship is unique. Yadin has already compared it to 'the rule of the kingship' in 1 Sam. 10.25 (Vol. I, p.264) and it seems to me that the law of the king in the Scroll can indeed illuminate this chapter. In 1 Sam. 10.25 we read of 'the rule of kingship' (משפט המלוכה)[36] which Samuel *wrote* in a book and laid up before the Lord. S. Lieberman has shown that the expression 'written and laid up' (כתוב ומונח), means published and sanctified.[37] And indeed, it does seem that 'he wrote...and laid it up' (ויכתב...ויניח) in Samuel means that he published and sanctified it. We do not know what was in the book which Samuel wrote and laid up before the Lord, although by all indications, it was a mutual agreement between the king and the people which we heard about in 2 Kgs 11 in connection with the covenant of Jehoiada (v. 17).[38] So it seems to us that in the law of the king in the Scroll, traces have been preserved

34. Cf. Rashi on the Mishnah in *b. Soṭa* 41a.

35. Vol. I, p. 114.

36. By contrast with 'the custom of the king' (משפט המלך περὶ βασιλέιας) in 1 Sam. 8.9, meaning the *custom* of the king with his people. In 'the custom of the king' in 1 Sam. 8 the prophet Samuel brings up the not necessarily legal practice of kings whose custom was to enslave their subjects, and in this way he wants to dissuade the people from pressing its request for a king. The 'rule of kingship' on the other hand, is the written, binding agreement between the two parties, cf. 'the rule of redemption' and 'the rule of inheritance' in Jer. 32 which is connected to a written, binding document (vv. 7–8).

37. S. Lieberman, *Hellenism in Jewish Palestine*[2] (1962), p. 86.

38. See Z. Ben Barak, 'the custom of the King and the custom of Kingship' (dissertation submitted to the Hebrew University of Jerusalem, 1972).

of a mutual agreement of a type which was probably common in the Hasmonean period. The obligations which appear in this law of the king, but which are not written down in Deuteronomy 17 include the people's duties to the king such as the muster for army, the constitution of the royal bodyguard, the donation of the tithe to the king on the one hand, and the king's duties to the people on the other hand, for example, that of heeding the advice of his council, dealing honestly, and administering justice to his people.

To these mutual obligations are added blessings and curses which are a kind of divine sanction which generally accompanied covenants in the ancient Near East.[39] Indeed we hear of such mutual obligations between a king and his people from the ancient historians. Xenophon[40] tells us that in Sparta the king used to obligate himself to act in accordance with the laws of the state,[41] while the people obligated itself to maintain the stability of the kingship.[42] Josephus describes the covenant between the king and the people in the time of Jehoiada: the king assembled the people and soldiers in the temple and made them swear an oath to be faithful to him and to ensure his welfare and the existence of his kingship, while the king was made to swear that he would honour the Lord and not transgress the laws of Moses (*Antiq.* 9.153).

It is surprising indeed that from the Ptolemaic kingdom there has been preserved the royal swearing-in ceremony whose details and circumstances remind us of the covenant of Jehoiada and show us that coronation customs remained unchanged for centures. Polybius' description of the crowning of Ptolemy V in Egypt reminds us of the crowning of Jehoash by Jehoiada. Sosibius, the guardian of the orphan boy Ptolemy, gathered the bodyguard around the platform, then placed the crown on the boy's head and made him king and made the army officers swear an oath to be loyal to the king and preserve his kingship. Later he relates that they made the people swear an oath as they were accustomed to do by proclaiming the king (Polybius 15.25).

Such a mutual agreement seems to have been preserved in a description of the appointing of Simon the Maccabee as the leader in a large assembly of the priests and the people, heads of the people, and elders (1 Macc. 14.25ff.) This text mentions a document which was inscribed on bronze tablets and displayed on a pillar on Mt. Zion (v. 26). As was common in covenants in the ancient world,[43] this document begins with an historical introduction (vv. 29–40), then reports the people's decision[44] to accept Simon the Maccabee as their prince. Simon the prince

39. For more on this subject, see chapter 1.

40. Rep. Lacedaemon 15.7.

41. κατὰ τοὺς τῆς πόλεως κειμένους νόμους βασιλεύσειν.

42. αστυφέλικτον τὴν βασιλείαν παρεξεῖν.

43. V. Korošec, *Hethitische Staatsverträge* (1931), pp. 12ff.

44. εὐδόκησαν (v. 41 cf. 46) overlaps the Greek ἔδοξε which introduces resolutions and agreements (cf. e.g. 1 Macc. 15.2 with reference to a treaty with the Romans). This expression recurs when the subject is the other party, i.e. Simon, who is deciding to take upon himself the office of high priest and prince: καὶ ἐπεδέξατο...καὶ εὐδόκησαν (v. 47) which seems to me to reconstruct 'took it upon themselves' as in Est. 9.27 (cf. *ibid.*, v. 23). For קבלה in the sense of pledge by an oath, see S. Lieberman, *JBL* 71 (1952), p. 200.

obligates himself to maintain the temple, the army, and the safety of the country, while the people obligate themselves to obey him, not to assemble against him, nor to rebel against him (vv. 41–47). The covenant was inscribed on bronze tablets and laid up in the precinct of the sanctuary, while the copy of the covenant was deposited in the treasury so that Simon and his sons 'might have them' (v. 49), a custom which is known from the drawing up of contracts in the ancient Near East.[45] The laying up (θέσθαι) of the copy in the temple parallels the laying up (הניח) of the rule of kingship by Samuel in 1 Sam. 10.25, and likewise therefore (see above) it shows that it is given validity by being published.

We may, therefore, assume that also in the case of John Hyrcanus and Alexander Jannaeus, mutual agreements were kept which are reflected in the 'law of the king' in the Scroll. That the 'supplementary' law of the king in the Scroll reflects the covenant between the king and the people at the time of the coronation we may learn from the fact that it goes into effect: 'on the day on which you shall make him king' (57.2).

The law of the king in Israel and the ancient Near East

Despite the fact that the law of the king peculiar to the Scroll reflects a custom which was common in the establishment of the relationship between the king and his people, in its present form it is more ideal than real, for this is an attempt to educate and guide the king. Indeed the literary genre of books of guidance for the king or 'law of the king' was widespread in the ancient world from early times until the Middle Ages. In ancient Egypt, especially in the Middle Kingdom, we found instructions in the form of a king's testament to his son. These are in fact the ethical instructions of a wise man who wrote an educational guide for the young king.[46] Here we find instructions on the subject of royal councillors, the administration of justice, and the organization of the army – subjects which appear in the Scroll as well as in laws of the king (περὶ βασιλέιας) from the Hellenistic period (see below).

45. See G. Kestemont, *Diplomatique et droit internationale en Asie Occidental* (1974), p. 123. For evidence from the Hellenistic period see F.M. Abel, *Les livres des Maccabees* (1949), pp. 262 (to vv. 48–49).

46. See M. Lichtheim, *Ancient Egyptian Literature* (1975), I, pp. 9f., 97ff.; P. Hadot, 'Fürstenspiegel', *Realexikon in Antike und Christentum* VIII, 1972, 555ff. At the beginning of his article he surveys the Egyptian instructions but does not distinguish between general wisdom and ethics and ethical instruction designated personally for the king, which guide him in the performance of his functions. This failure to distinguish is also reflected farther on in the article. It includes in the discussion confessions of the king which is a genre in its own right (cf. Ps. 101), royal psalms which are also a separate literary genre, and the like. In Hellenistic literature, too, we must distinguish between a philosophical description of a royal ideal, and concrete instructions intended to guide the king in the performance of his duties.

Thus for example, we find in the testament of the Egyptian king to his son Meri-Ka-Re (A, 42ff.):

> *Officials and courtiers* – 'Advance your great men, so that they may carry out your laws...Valiant is the king possessed of courtiers'.
>
> *Justice* – 'Do justice whilst you endure upon the earth...do not oppress the widow; supplant no man in the property of his father...'
>
> *Army* – 'Fill your people with an army; see your city full of young men twenty years old...'[47]

In Mesopotamia too we find documents containing advice to kings regarding the conduct of their kingship. In the library of Ashurbanipal, King of Assur (seventh century BC) there is a text which scholars call 'Advice to a Prince' in which we read:[48]

> If a king does not heed justice, his people will be thrown into chaos, and his land will be devastated.
>
> If he does not heed his nobles, his life will be cut short.[49] If he does not heed his adviser, his land will rebel against him.[50]
>
> If citizens of Nippur are brought to him for judgment, but he accepts a present (bribe) and improperly convicts them, Enlil, lord of the lands, will bring a foreign army against him...
>
> If he takes the silver of the citizens of Babylon and adds it to his own coffers,... Marduk...will give his property and wealth to his enemy...
>
> If he mobilizes the whole of Sippar, Nippur, and Babylon, and imposes forced labour on the people, exacting from them a corvée at the herald's proclamation, Marduk... will turn his land over to his enemy so that the troops of his land will do forced labour for his enemy...[51]

Here we find the same three subjects as in the Egyptian instructions: administration of justice, attentiveness to advisors, and mobilization of the army, with the addition of warnings against accepting bribes and coveting the property of others. The latter two subjects are found together with the first in the Temple Scroll: 'And he will not accept a bribe to pervert justice, nor will he covet a field and vineyard or any fortune, house, or חמוד in Israel' (57.20–21). Most instructive is the fact that at the end of the Assyrian text which we quoted, there is a colophon in which

47. Lichtheim, *op. cit.*, pp. 100ff. Mobilization into the army at age 20 is found in our Scroll as well as in Diodorus' description of the conscription of the Egyptian royal bodyguard (see below).

48. W.G. Lambert, 'Advice to a Prince', *Babylonian Wisdom Literature* (1960), p. 110.

49. Cf. the curse which will come upon the king and his people in the Scroll: 'And in all this, their towns will be a waste, a hissing, and a desolation and their enemies will cause desolation in them' (59.4–5).

50. This was the end of Rehoboam who did not follow the advice of the elders (1 Kgs 12).

51. Sippar, Nippur and Babylon were cities with special privileges including exemption from the duty to mobilize. See H. Tadmor, 'The Temple City and the Royal City in Babylonia and Assyria' (Hebrew), 'City and Community', XIIth Convention of the Historical Society of Israel, December 1966, Jerusalem 1967, p. 194.

Ashurbanipal says,[52] '(this) in tablets have I written, checked,[53] and collated...[54] for constant reading I have established it in my palace'. The obligation of constant reading[55] here parallels the law of the king in Deuteronomy 17.19: 'And he shall read in it all the days of his life' and parallels what is written by Moses to Joshua (who represents the type of a king): 'This book shall not depart out of your mouth, but you shall meditate on it day and night' (Josh 1.8) (and see below).[56] Furthermore like the Deuteronomic texts the Assyrian texts were canonized. E. Reiner has shown[57] that the quoted text from Assurbanipal's library was canonical in Mesopotamia and is actually cited in a Middle Babylonian text from the twelfth century BCE. It says there that the ancestors handed down tablets where it is written that the people of Nippur, Babylon and Sippar should not be mistreated. In a recently discussed letter to Essarhaddon, King of Assyria, the auther cited the rights of the cities Sippar, Nippur and Babylon and says: 'Let the Lord of the Kings...look at the tablets: "If the King does not give heed to justice"' which actually constitutes the beginning of the Advice to the Prince mentioned above.

We should note that we found similar colophons in Assyrian ritual texts,[58] a fact which shows that the Assyrian king, like the Israelite, was obligated to read aloud not only the books concerning kingship, but also writings concerning religious matters and the cult in general. But this need not surprise us, since the king was the chief person responsible for religious and cultic procedures in his state, and as we shall see below, also for the administration of justice, the army, and the cult. These constituted the three main spheres of the king's concern. Thus we see that the king of Assyria, too, used to read (so to speak) properly collated tablets which were deposited in his archives (see below), tablets in which were written laws regarding the king and those which had to do with religion and ritual.

Egypt in the Late Period

Diodorus Siculus who describes practices of the kings of ancient Egypt, quoting from Hecataeus of Abdera,[59] also relates that the practices of the kings of Egypt

52. See I.M. Diakonoff., *Landsberger Festschrift* (AS 16, 1965), p. 349 n. 24. The Akkadian (A Babylonian Political Pamphlet from about 700 BC) text reads: *ina tuppāni ašṭur, asniq, abrêma ana tāmarti šitassija* (Gtn) *qereb ēkallija ukīn* (H. Hunger, *Babyl. U. Assyr. Kolophone* (AOAT 2, 1968), no. 319.7–8, p. 98.

53. The basic meaning of *sanāqu* is 'to compare, to straighten out' and hence 'to check the correctness'. Indeed, instead of *sanāqu*, *ašāru* sometimes appears, cf. the colophon *ašra bariā šalmâ*, 'checked, collated, and is correct'. See Hunger, *Kolophone*, no. 63 (p. 34).

54. Cf. Hebrew הגהה from the root נגה meaning 'to make shine, to see'; thus also *bārû* in Akkadian.

55. *Šitassija* is from *šasû*, 'to recite' with the *tan*-infix indicating constant repetitive action.

56. The Rabbis also interpret the book of the law here as Deuteronomy, see *Gen. Rab.* VI (ed, Albeck, p. 49): 'Rabbi Shimon Ben Yohai said, "The Book of Mishneh torah was a *signum* to Joshua when the Holy One, Blessed be He, revealed Himself to him, he found him sitting down with the Book of Mishneh Torah in his hand. He said to him, 'Joshua, be of good courage, this book will not depart from your mouth, etc.!"'

57. 'The Babylonian Fürstenspiegel in practice', *Societies and Languages in the Ancient Near East, Festschrift I. M. Diakonoff* (1980), pp. 320ff.

58. Cf. Hunger, *op. cit.*, no. 318–319, pp. 97–98; M. Streck, *Assurbanipal*, I, pp. 354–75.

59. Book I, 70.

were laid down in the laws and that the latter included not only matters relating to administration, but also customs of the king's day-to-day life.

In his description we find:

1. A blessing and a curse by the high priest for the king with the blessing stipulated in the administration of justice for his subjects (cf. the blessing and the curse in the law of the king in the Scroll).
2. Good deeds will lead the king to fear the god and practise the ways of right conduct, a feature which reminds us of the passage in the law of the king in Deut. 17.19 'that he may learn to fear the LORD his God, by keeping all the words of this law…'
3. A priest-scribe will read from the holy books before the king about the outstanding deeds of the praiseworthy men so that he will learn from them (compare the reading of the book of the law by the king and see the Epistle of Aristeas, parag. 283, and below, p. 176ff.).

However, the most instructive subject has a surprising parallel in the law of the king in the Temple Scroll. We shall present this paragraph side by side with that which overlaps it in the Scroll.

The Scroll	*Diodorus*[60]
(And they should take a census) of Israelites who are twenty years old to sixty years old… and he should select a thousand from each tribe so there should be twelve thousand warriors[62]	As for the guard (θεραπεία)[61] (of the kings of Egypt) none was a purchased slave or born in a home, but all were sons of the most distinguished priests, twenty years old and older and better

60. See the explanation by A. Burton, *Commentary on Diodorus Siculus*, I, 1972, pp. 209f.

61. θεραπεία indicates a guard in the broadest sense, cf. e.g. Polybius (15.25) in connection with Ptolemy V and his coronation by Sosibius his guardian, a fact which reminds us of the coronation of Joash in 2 Kgs 11 which we mentioned above. Sosibius assembles the bodyguard (shield bearers = υπασπιστάς cf. Maccabees 4.3, 12) and the guard (θεραπεία), the commanders over the army and the commanders over the horsemen. Agathocles and Sosibius place the crown on the boy's head and proclaim him king. The members of the θεραπεία play an important role during the rebellion and revolution and the king's bodyguard were only a part of this body. On the term θεραπεία during the Hellenistic period see P.M. Fraser, *Ptolemaic Alexandria*, 1972, Vol. II, p. 152 n. 224.

62. Yadin compares the selection of 12,000 men here to Num. 31.3 but does not mention the selection of 12,000 men at the advice of Ahitophel in 2 Sam. 17.11 and the 12,000 horsemen with Solomon (1 Kgs 10.26) (cf. *ibid.* 5, 6). We should note that in connection with the latter passage, Josephus quotes a detailed description of the king's bodyguard (*Antiq.* VIII, 184ff.), a description which reminds us of King Aristobulus' escort (*Antiq.* XIV, 45). (See A. Shalit's note in *Antiq.* Vol. 2, p. קל״ג, n. 248). These passages may help to fill in the realistic background to the Hasmonean royal bodyguard which is apparently behind the command in the Temple Scroll (see Yadin, Vol. 1, pp. 348–349). At the same time, we must admit that in Numbers 31 we find 'one thousand from each tribe' as in the Scroll 'one thousand of the tribe' (11.5–6). Also in Num. 31 we find 'men of war' (vv. 28 and 49) and in the Scroll 'man of war' (1.9). To be sure, Num. 31 does not speak about the king's bodyguard, but this chapter does have some connection with the description of the royal bodyguard in 2 Kings 11, cf. 'the captains' in 2 Kgs 11.4, 15, 19 with Num. 31.14, 43 and 'the captains who were set over the army' in 2 Kgs 11.15 with Num. 31.14: 'the officers of the army, the commanders of thousands and the commanders of hundreds'. It is possible that Jehoiada the priest

The Scroll	*Diodorus*[60]
who will not leave him alone… and all the select ones[63] whom he will select will be trustworthy men who fear the Lord, hate unjust gain, and valorous warriors, and they will be with him always day and night and guard him from all sin[65] and from the foreign people so he will not be captured by them (57.9–11).	educated than the other Egyptians so that the king, by having the nobles caring for his person and guarding him[64] night and day, will not err and commit a sinful deed.

The similarities between the two documents consist of the following details:

1. Each of the parallel passages begins a description of royal practices.
2. The guard which is described in both has a double function: physical and moral protection of the king.
3. The members of the guard must be select[66] and have a superior education.
4. They must be over twenty years old.[67]
5. They guard him day and night.

We should add that the section on the royal bodyguard was quoted only as an example of permanent regulations regarding royal practices. Therefore, this is a subject that belonged to the king's law in Egypt, and typologically is one of the treatises 'on kingship' (περὶ βασιλέιας) which we hear of so often during the Hellenistic period (see below).

Some maintain that Diodorus' description reflects common practice in Egypt in the Hellenistic period, although in my opinion this assumption is not warranted. E. Meyer[68] is correct in saying that although this was written by a Greek and from the Greek viewpoint, the author intends to depict Egypt as it really was

who commanded the commanders of hundreds who were to be set over the army (2 Kgs 11), embodies the figure of Pinchas the son of Eleazar the priest who commanded the commanders of thousands and hundreds in Num. 31. For the parallel between the description of the bodyguard in the Scroll and the description of the bodyguard in 2 Kgs 11, cf. 'and they shall be with him always day and night: with 'Be with the king when he goes out and when he comes in' in 2 Kgs 11.8.

63. For the meaning of the term see Yadin, *The Temple Scroll*, Vol. 2 p. 257 ad line 85. And cf. *y. Qidd.*: 'Anyone you appoint over you shall be only from the chosen (ברורין) among your brethren' (4.5, 66a).

64. προσεδρευεῖν meaning 'to surround and closely guard'.

65. This defective written spelling (חט) is found elsewhere in the Scroll: חט משפט מות (64.9) where it was corrected by the addition of a supralinear *aleph*, and see Yadin, *op. cit.* in his commentary on line 20.

66. In Egypt they must be of priestly descent. We should add that according to Plato (*Politeia* 290 d), the Egyptian king himself must be of priestly descent.

67. Cf. the instructions of Meri-Ka-Re quoted above.

68. E. Meyer, 'Gottesstaat Militärherrschaft und Standewesen in Ägypten', *Sitzungsberichte der preussischen Akademie der Wissenschaften*, 1928; Philos. – *histor. Klasse*, pp. 529f. and cf. also F. Jacoby, *Realencyl.* Pauly Wissowa, VII, 2764.

in its most flourishing period. However, for our purposes it does not matter whether the practice reflects the Ptolemaic monarchy or an earlier period. What is important is the fact that outside Israel we have found a royal ideology similar to that of the Temple Scroll in a source from a neighbouring kingdom, a source which was written in the period closest to that of the composition of the Scroll.

It would seem that what we have here are ideas which were common in 'laws of the king' in the ancient Near East and that religious functionaries developed these ideas in order to formulate their law of the king. It is interesting that despite the fact that the law of the king in the Scroll does not require the guard to be composed of priests – unlike the case in Egypt – the author of Chronicles and following him Josephus (*Antiq*. 9.143f.) tells us that the guard of Joash was composed of priests and levites (2 Chron. 23), a fact which is not mentioned at all in 2 Kings 11. Quite the contrary – in the latter source we find Carites (and the courtiers) who are generally thought to be foreign mercenaries.[69] We should mention that the author of Chronicles makes the men of the guard levites in order to have the events conform to his view that foreigners are forbidden to enter the temple courtyard (see v. 6).[70] At the same time, it is not impossible that along with the tendency to harmonize at the time of the author of Chronicles, the idea gained general acceptance that the royal bodyguard had to be composed of priests, as in Egypt.

Personal instructions to the king

Along with the instructions in the socio-political sphere which are a recurrent theme all through the law of the king which we detailed above, we also find instructions in the sphere of personal ethics. Thus for example, in Proverbs 31 we find a moral guide for the king in which are instructions of the king's mother to her son, king of Massa. The instructions comprise three principles:

1. 'Give not your strength to women' (v. 3).
2. 'It is not for kings…to drink wine, or for rulers to desire strong drink' (v. 4).
3. 'Judge righteously, maintain the right of the poor and the needy' (v. 9).

The warnings against women and wine are given because they are liable to make the king forget his duties to administer justice and care for the poor. Such instructions appeared mostly in instructions to kings from the Hellenistic period onwards.

A personal guide for the king is in fact actually a part of the law of the king in Deuteronomy 17 where the king is forbidden to multiply horses (v. 16), wives (v. 17), and silver and gold (v. 17) for himself. Hence the reasons given for these things is the fear that the multiplication of these luxuries will cause the king's heart to turn away and be lifted up above his brethren (vv. 17, 20).

69. Whether we retain the reading כרי in which case the reference is to the 'Carites' of Asia Minor, or we correct it to כרתי and see *Encycl. Biblica*, vol. 4, col. 310f. (Hebrew), s.v. כרי.

70. W. Rudolph, *Chronikbücher*, HAT, 1955, pp. 271f.

The personal aspect of the Temple Scroll is expressed in the prohibition against the king's taking more than one wife[71] and in the warning not to covet any field or vineyard nor any property and house or any חמוד in Israel.[72]

The law of the king in the Hellenistic period

In the period of Alexander and apparently under the Eastern influence, the literary genre of the περὶ βασιλέιας 'on kingship' developed. Sages, scribes, and philosphers wrote guidebooks for kings. Cicero testifies that he possessed books of counsel and guidance which had been written by Aristotle and Theopompus for Alexander of Macedonia συμβουλευτικὰ πρὸς Ἀλέξανδρον.[73] It was also related that Demetrius Phalerus told Ptolemy that he must read the books of περὶ βασιλέιας, for what friends dare not say, they write in a book.[74] This literary tradition continued through the period of the Roman empire,[75] through the Sassanian period[76] until the Islamic period[77] when these works are attributed to Aristotle who taught his doctrine to Alexander the Great. In these works we find instructions on all the subjects which we mentioned previously and which are also found in the law of the king in the Scroll. Thus, for example in the crystallized laws of the king of Ecphantus, Diotogenes, and Sthenidas[78] we find instructions in the following areas:

1. Preservation of righteousness and justice[79]
2. Preservation of brotherhood and equality[80]
3. Rejection of covetousness and amassing of wealth[81]

71. It is possible that the prohibition against marrying two women, which appears in the law of the king in the Scroll, applies to the king only, as does the duty to marry a woman from his father's household which was taken from the law of the high priest (see Yadin, Vol. 1, pp. 354–55).

72. Cf. 1 Sam. 12.3 where Samuel justifies himself as a judge by saying that he has not taken anyone's property, defrauded anyone or taken a bribe, after his declaration that he has 'walked before', i.e. served the people all his life. Thus we should consider the giving of these details as a reflection of 'the king's instructions' of the type which we have been discussing and also cf. Moses' speech in Num. 16.15. It is interesting to note that the Septuagint and the Samaritan Pentateuch have חמוד instead of חמור, 'ass' in Num. 16.15 a version which apparently influenced the author of the Scroll, as Yadin has already noted in his commentary, *loc. cit.*

73. *Epist. Ad Atticum* XIII, 28.

74. Plutarch, *Apophtheg*, 198.

75. See mainly Seneca's *de Clementia*, which is directed at Nero.

76. M. Grignachi, 'La *Siyāsatu – 'ammiya*', *Acta Iranica* 6, Monumentum H.S. Nyberg (1975), p. 237f. He proves that this piece originated in the time of the Sassanids.

77. See G. Richter, *Studies zur Gesch. des ältern arabischen Fürstenspiegel*, *LSS* NF 3 (1932); Bosworth, *JNES* 29 (1970), pp. 25ff.

78. For the protracted controversy among scholars as to whether to attribute these works to the early Hellenistic age or to the second century AD, see R.E. Goodenough, 'The Political Philosophy of Hellenistic Kingship', *Yale Classical Studies* (1928), pp. 55ff. See also the discussion in L. Delatte, *Les traités de la royauté d'Ecphante, Diotogéne et Sthenidas* (1942), pp. 125ff. (assigning a late date to the works). At any rate, even if the compositions are late, doubtless as far as the subjects are concerned, they preserve material from the early Hellenistic period.

79. See the discussion in Delatte, *Les traités*, etc. pp. 251ff.

80. *Ibid.*, pp. 241ff.

4. Control of the natural urges[82]
5. Fear of the God[83]
6. Showing charity towards subjects.[84]
   In the law of the king in Philo we found similar instructions. Here too, the administration of justice, equality and the subjugation of pride, hatred of ill-gotten gain, and care for the underprivileged are emphasized. (Laws IV, 165f.). The choice of subjects and their formulation greatly resembles the Hellenistic law of the king, although in light of the law of the king in the ancient Near East, we are not justified in saying that Philo derived all this from Greek literature.

We encounter the same problems regarding the advice of the Jewish elders to Ptolemy in the symposia in the letter of Aristeas.[85] Here we find almost all the political and personal instructions mentioned above:

1. Preservation of justice (189, 209, 279, 291–292).
2. Rejection of the reliance upon power and wealth (193–196 and cf. Deut. 17.16–17, 20)[86]
3. Hatred of ill-gotten gain (209, cf. Temple Scroll 57.9)
4. Heeding advice of good counselors (264, cf. 190)
5. Guarding of the king by men who hate evil and are outstanding in heroism and righteousness (270, 280–281, cf. Temple Scroll 57.7–11 and Diodorus I, 70; see p. 173ff. above).
6. Reading books (283 and see D. Mendels, *Aegyptus* 59 [1979] [see n. 85], pp. 127–36).
7. Fostering equality; the subjugation of pride (191, 263 cf. Deut. 17.20)
8. Avoidance of frivolous pleasures (245, cf. Prov. 31.4–5).
9. Clearheadedness = avoidance of drunkenness (νήφειν, 209).

Here, too, the ideas have been developed and formulated in the spirit and style of Hellenistic philosophy, but the ideas themselves already existed in Jewish ethics and traditions of the ideal king. Especially instructive is a series of proverbs in connection with the king in Ben Sira (Sirach) 10: 1f. Here we find preaching in connection with the judge of the people, and its advocate. The poet warns

81. *Ibid.*, pp. 256ff.
82. *Ibid.*, pp. 253ff.
83. *Ibid.*, pp. 263ff.
84. *Ibid.*, pp. 269ff.
85. See D. Mendels, 'On Kingship in the "Temple Scroll" and the Ideological Vorlage of the Seven Banqets in the "Letter of Aristeas to Philocrates" ', *Aegyptus* 59 (1979), pp. 127–36.
86. Compare Ps. 33.16, 17: 'A king is not saved by his great army, a warrior is not delivered by his great strength, the war horse is a vain hope for victory and by its great might it cannot save'. Cf. also Ps. 20.8: 'Some boast of chariots, and some of horses; but we boast of the name of the LORD our God'. The advice to call upon the name of the god instead of relying upon military might is found in paragraph 193 in the letter of Aristeas ἀλλὰ τὸν θεόν ἐπικαλοῖτο διὰ πάντων. Negation of the reliance upon military power is found in Egyptian as well as Israelite sources, cf. M. Weinfeld, *Early Jewish Liturgy* (2004), pp. 66–67 (Hebrew).

especially against the pride of the king seeing that 'To-day a King, and to-morrow he shall fall!' (v. 10); he also warns against contempt for the poor and the destitute (21.22–23) while on the other hand praising a God-fearing leader (v. 20).

A written book of the law for the guidance of the king

We have seen that in the ancient Near East and the Hellenistic world it was common to write books of guidance for kings, although what was unique in Israel was that the book written for the king contained guidance not only for the king and court but also laws applicable to the king as the leader of the nation, laws which the king must take care to execute; as we indicated, Deuteronomy is such a book. Members of the Qumran sect made sure that the book for the king should reflect the spirit of their religious law and our Scroll represents such a book of laws.

There are explicit laws of ancient origin as to the king's duty to keep a book of the law at hand, deposited in his archive. Thus in *m. Sanhedrin* 2.4:

> He must write out a scroll of the Law for himself; when he goes forth to the battle he shall take it forth with him, and when he returns he shall bring it back with him; when he sits in judgment it shall be with him and when he sits at meals it shall be before him, for it is written, '*It shall be with him and he shall read therein all the days of his life*'.

It is surprising that the evidence for the existence of such a book of the law with a king was found only concerning King Jannaeus who ruled at the time of the composition of the Scroll, in Yadin's opinion. In *Tractate Soferim* we find:

> It happened with the law of the book of Alexander [i.e. Jannaeus] all of whose *tetra grammata* (אזכרותיה) were written in gold, and that the affair came to the sages and they said that it should be hidden.[87]

Moreover, according to *t. Sanhedrin*, this law was supposed to be proofread in the court of priests, levites and notables of Israel advising the priesthood.[88] This component of priests, levites, and notables we also find in a council with which, according to the Scroll, the king had to consult on every important matter. Yadin considers this council of thirty-six men as half the seventy-one members of the *Sanhedrin*,[89] so it is interesting that according to the Palestinian Talmud and Midrash Tannaim to Deuteronomy, the law of the king must be proofread before the court of seventy-one.[90]

To our great surprise, we found a similar procedure in the books of the king in the court of Ashurbanipal. In colophons of texts from the library of Ashurbanipal which we mentioned above, we read that the tablet was written, collated and

87. *Tractate Soferim* (Higger ed., pp. 105–106, and cf. *ibid.*, *Tractate Soferim* 2.1.7 (p. 376), *Tractate Sefer Torah* 1.7. On the writing of the law in gold, cf. the letter of Aristeas 176 and *Antiq.* 12.89. And see also S. Lieberman, Hellenism in Jewish Palestine (1950), p. 206 n. 25.

88. *t. Sanh.* 4.7 (ed. Zuckermandel, p. 421).

89. *Temple Scroll*, Vol. 1, p. 351.

90. *y. Sanh.* 2.7, 20d; מדרש תנאים (ed. Hoffman), p. 105 and see Sipre (ed. Finkelstein) paragraph 160.

checked before the assembly of the sages (=a council of the king)[91] and deposited in his palace to be read and consulted.[92]

C. *The Name of The Scroll According to the Sect*

Yadin[93] would identify the Scroll with the ספר ההגי/ההגו which is mentioned several times in the Qumran Scrolls and with the 'Book of the Second Law' which we found among the writings of the Qumran *pesharim*. These assumptions are confirmed on the basis of my argument that what we have here is the law of the king. ספר ההגו in my opinion is the book which the leader and the king were obligated to meditate upon day and night as we saw in Josh. 1.8: 'This book of the law shall not depart out of your mouth, but you shall meditate (והגית) on it day and night'.

There is no doubt that here Joshua represents a king-like leader who carries out what is written in the law of the king:

> He shall write for himself in a book a copy of this law, and it shall be with him, and he shall read in it all the days of his life (Deut. 17.17, 18).

The meditation in Joshua is the reading in Deuteronomy 17; the two verbs being identical, as we learn from the parallel in the verse: 'Let the *words* of my mouth and the *meditation* of my heart be acceptable in your sight' (Ps. 19.15). '*Meditation* of my heart' parallels here '*words* of my mouth'.[94] Also 'shall not depart out of your mouth' in our quotation from Joshua shows that the continuation 'and you shall meditate on it' implies speech.[95]

Joshua plays the role of a king[96] in assembling the people and reading the book of the law before them as found in Josh. 8.31–35 and indeed also in the command about congregating the people in Deut. 31.9f. which follows the summoning of Joshua in verses 7–8; the command is in the singular: 'Assemble the people' (v. 12) being addressed to Joshua.[97] And indeed according to Josh. 8.34–35 Joshua reads the book of the law 'before all the assembly of Israel, and the women, and

91. It seems to me that the subject is *bīt mummu* which was a sort of academy where wise men and their students sat, like the Sanhedrin (*m. Sanh.* 4.3–4). The *bīt mummu* is appealed to on various religious and cultic questions which only experts 'who know secrets' could solve. Thus, for example, we read that Nabunaid, King of Babylon, gathered scribes and wise men 'Those who sit in the *bīt mummu*, guardians of secrets of the great gods (*nāṣir pirišti ilāni rabûti*), and consults them regarding the foundation inscription of the temple. S. Langdon, *Neubabyl. Königsinschriften* (1912), p. 255, 32f. The Sanhedrin fulfilled similar functions in the לשכת הגזית.

92. *tuppu šuātu ina tapḫurti ummāni aštur, asniq abrēma, ana tāmarti šarrūtiya qereb ēkalliya ukîn* (H. Hunger, *Kolophone* 1968, no. 318.608).

93. Vol. 1, pp. 393ff.

94. The root הגה means 'to mumble, mutter' (cf. Ps. 115.10; Isa. 38.14; 59.11, etc. as in Aramaic and Arabic.

95. 'לב' in many sources means 'the throat', see H.L. Ginsberg, 'Hebräische Wortforschung, Festschrift W. Baumgartner', *Suppl. Vet. Test.* 16 (1967), p. 80.

96. Philo speaks a great deal about Moses and Joshua as embodiments of the ideal characters of a king and see the discussion in H.A. Wolfson, *Philo* II (1947), pp. 325ff.

97. See Weinfeld, *DDS*, p. 65, n.1.

the little ones, and the sojourners who lived among them'. This is identical with the command to Moses to assemble the people and to read before them the Torah in Deut. 31.12. The tradition, it is true, carried on this ideology and assigned the role of reader to the king (*m. Soṭa* 7.8). We should note that in the Manual of Discipline from Qumran, the ספר ההגו which includes 'the laws of the covenant' and 'their rules' (col. 1.7–8) comes after the opening paragraph in which is described the gathering of the assembly (1.1–5). According to the Manual, at this gathering all 'the laws of the covenant' 'and their rules' (1.5) must be read; this would support our assumption that the ספר ההגו is identical to the section that the king reads at the gathering of the congregation.

The idea of meditating upon the law day and night is also found in Ps. 1.2: 'but his delight is in the law of the LORD, and on his law he meditates day and night'; scholars have already hypothesized[98] that this is a reference to the king who is the subject in Psalm 2 (which has no heading and which, according to *b. Berakot* 9b and Qumran Scroll constitutes together with Psalm 1 a single psalm.

Another designation for the Scroll which Yadin has suggested is 'The Book of the Second Law' (ספר התורה השנית) which we found in the writings of the sect,[99] coinciding with the Greek concept, and therefore, the reference is to Deuteronomy which is the heart of the Scroll. At any rate, here the subject is the book of the law of the men of the sect about which apparently the men of the 'Wicked Priest' spoke evil, as we see from the rest of the *pesher*: 'it is the book of the second law which [...] his advisors and they spoke evil of'. In the *pesher* on Ps. 37.32–33[100] we find that the Teacher of Righteousness sent a *torah* to the Wicked Priest and for this reason apparently he wanted to kill him. Yadin[101] correctly suggests that this law is the Scroll which is also called 'the Book of the Second Law', ספר התורה השנית. Presumably the Teacher of Righteousness sent to one of the Hasmonean kings a *torah* so that he should read it and conduct himself in accordance with it, but the king refused to accept it.

D. *The Ordinances of the Temple*

The ordinances of the temple with which the author of the Scroll deals at such length can also explain the setting of the law of the king. According to Deuteronomy and contra the law of the tent of meeting in Leviticus 17, before 'the place which the LORD your God will choose' was fixed, every Israelite did whatever was right in his own eyes in worshipping the Lord (Deut. 12.8f.) and only when they had come to the 'rest and the inheritance' which God gave them from their enemies round about, i.e. during the reigns of David and Solomon[102] was the time

98. See the discussion in T. Mettinger, *King and Messiah*, 1976, pp. 289ff.

99. See 'the Chain of the *pesharim*' in the section commenting upon Hos. 5.8, *DJD* V, 177 (Catena A), pp. 67ff., ii, 13–14.

100. *DJD* V 171, pp. 42ff., col. IV, 11, 6–8.

101. Vol. 1, pp. 396–97.

102. See 2 Sam. 7.1; 1 Kgs 5.17–18.

suitable for building the first temple. The building of the first temple is conditional, therefore, upon the crowning of a king, and as the Rabbis appropriately said:

> 'When the Israelites entered Israel they were given three commands: they were commanded to appoint a king over themselves, to build the temple and to exterminate the seed of Amalek'. (*t. Sanh.* 4.5)

Yadin[103] cites the Midrashim which discuss the *plan of the temple* which was given to David by Samuel. But as is well known, Samuel laid down 'the rights and duties of the kingship' before the LORD in the time of Saul (1 Sam. 10.25), and thus it happens that the law which was given to the first king by Samuel included two important subjects – the temple and kingship which occupy the most important place in the Scroll. The primary importance of the temple in the time of the Hasmoneans and especially at the consolidation of their rule and the making of the covenant with the people, we may see from the covenant between Simon the Hasmonean and the people which has been mentioned above (p. 169f.), that was apparently the prototype of covenants between the Hasmonean kings and the people made in the time of Yohanan and Jannaeus. In the covenant between Simon and the people we hear that Simon obligated himself to take care of the temple ὅπως μέλῃ αὐτῷ περὶ τῶν ἁγίων (1 Macc. 14.42, 43)[104] while preserving security in the country.

This royal obligation to ensure the regular functioning of the cult is not unique to Israel. Aristotle bases the obligations of the king upon three things: (1) Leadership in war; (2) Provision of sacrifices; (3) Administration of justice.[105] Diotogenes also explicitly maintains in his law of the king: 'the functions of the king are three: military leadership, judgment and the cult.[106] Similarly, Cicero holds that the princeps, like the king, must ensure the administration of justice, the army, and the cult.[107] Centuries earlier we hear of the king's role as judge in ancient Israel. The people which demand a kingship from Samuel ask for a king who will govern them and fight their battles (1 Sam. 8.20), while in the time of David and Solomon, the king assumed the third role connected with the temple.

Ezekiel's ordinances

The lengthy descriptions of the temple with all its installations and procedures which we find in the Scroll (the temple and its courtyards, the altar, the sacrifices, and festivals) remind us of Ezekiel's vision in chs. 40–48. Here, too, we find (at the beginning of the plan as in the Scroll), the law of the temple in detail (40.1–43.12), a description of the altar and the ceremony of the seven-day consecration of priests (43.13–27; cf. the Scroll 12.15–16), the offerings for the festivals

103. Volume 1, pp. 396–97.

104. The subject appears twice there, apparently because of a corruption, see J. Goldstein, *Maccabees*, *AB* (1976), ad.loc.

105. Aristo., *Politica* III 14,7 (1285 b9).

106. See Delatte, *Les traités*, etc. Diotogene 263,20, p. 37.

107. See Delatte, *op. cit.*, p. 249.

(45.18–25; cf. Scroll 17–30) and the procedures for cooking the sacrifices for the priests and the people (46.19–24; cf. Scroll 37). Both in the Scroll and in Ezekiel's plan the prince who shall arise in the future is assigned a law of the king. Ezekiel's plan was, to be sure, written in detail like the Scroll since the prophet was commanded not only to make known the plan but also to write down 'all its ordinances and its whole form and all its laws' (43.11)[108] In Ezekiel's vision, the kings of Israel are responsible for building the temple (43.7–19)[109] and supplying the additional sacrifices on the festivals, new moons, and Sabbaths (45.16–19).

In both the Scroll and Ezekiel's vision there is a detailed law of kingship[110]: the prince-king is commanded not to defraud his people, but to execute 'justice and righteousness'[111] (45.8–12), while for its part, the people is commanded to give its offerings and tithes to the prince (45.13–16). On the one hand, the prince is warned not to take any land from the inheritance of the people (46.18); on the other hand, there is the concern for the rights of the prince: the lands which he grants his servants revert to him in the year of liberty (46.16–17).[112] In the ordinances, the sacral rights of the king are determined (44.1–13; 46.1–3). It seems therefore, that like Ezekiel's ordinances, our scroll was intended to guide the leader in the establishment of the cultic procedures, justice, and kingship, and both of them are laws of the king.

E. *The Feast of Booths, Tithes and Reading of the Law before the People*

Already Rashi in his commentary on the Mishnah which discusses the section on the king in the Talmud (*b. Meg.* 41a) writes that 'the king reads out loud' '*you shall tithe*' (עשר תעשר) (Deut. 14.22), '*when you have finished paying all the tithe*' (כי תכלה לעשר) (26.12) because it is the time of the ingathering and gifts for the poor, and of dedication of offerings and tithes. This tradition is in fact reflected in the reading of the law on the eighth day of the Feast of Booths in the land of Israel. According to the *baraita* in *Megilla* 31a one should read on the last day of the Festival (i.e. Succot).[113] 'commandments, laws and first-born' (Deut. 15.19ff.), and in the *haftarah* '*Now as Solomon finished offering all this prayer…*' (1 Kgs 8.54ff.). Rashi (*Meg.* 31a) comments: 'But they begin from '*You shall tithe every year…*' (Deut. 14.22) because that portion contains many commands and laws which pertain to the Festival at this time which is the time of the ingatherings', etc.[114] As for the *haftarah*, Rashi says, they read 1 Kgs 8.54ff.: 'Because *on the eighth day he (Solomon) sent the people away*' (1 Kgs 8.66).

108. See M. Haran, *Tarbiz* 44 (1975), p. 34 and n. 12.

109. See Y. Kauffmann, תולדות האמונה הישראלית, Vol. 3, p. 579.

110. Y. Kauffmann, *ibid.*, p. 569f.

111. Cf. M. Weinfeld, *Social Justice in Ancient Israel and in the Ancient Near East* (1995), p. 55.

112. For a Mesopotamian parallel see J. Lewy, *Eretz-Israel* V, Mazar Vol., 1958, pp. 23ff.

113. 'Every first born' seems to be an addition. See J.M. Epstein, מבוא לנוסח המשנה, p. 539 n. 9.

114. See the *Vitry Maḥzor* (Hurwitz ed., 1893), pp. 445–46. The reading of 'you shall tithe' on the Festival of Booths is reflected in the *piyyuṭim* of HaKallir of Palestine, see E. Fleischer, *Tarbiz* 36 (1967), pp. 196ff.

It seems that according to the tradition reflected in this *baraita* Solomon fulfils the commandment of assembling the people on the eighth day.[115] Indeed in 2 Chronicles 6–7 where a solemn assembly on the eighth day is explicitly mentioned (7.9), Solomon offers up his prayer while standing on the bronze platform before all the assembly of Israel[116] which reminds us of the pulpit on which Josiah stands when he reads the law before the whole people (2 Kgs 23.3),[117] and the 'wooden pulpit' on which Ezra stood when he read the law (Neh. 8.4).

In our Scroll which in our opinion may be considered the 'parashah of the king' which must be read aloud on the Festival of Booths (indeed the Festival of Booths and the tithe serve as the focal points), in fact help us to understand the literary structure of the entire Scroll. The Scroll consists of three parts. The first contains instructions for the building of the temple and keeping of the festivals with their sacrifices, and ends with the *Festival of Booths* and the solemn assembly on the eighth day, mentioning in passing the covenant that was made with Jacob in Bethel on the Feast of Booths as well as the new temple in the end of days[118] which is well known to us from the book of Jubilees 32.10f; 1.26f. and makes a festive conclusion to the first part. In the book of Jubilees (32.10f.) there occurs the second tithing incidental to the revelation to Jacob in Bethel; and indeed the laws connected with the appointed times for the first fruits in this first part (col. 18–22), is actually the fixing of the tithe year for every kind of produce as we find on col. 43.4f., and as we also found in the book of Jubilees in the context of the revelation to Jacob at Bethel.

The second part of the Scroll deals with the structure of the temple and its courtyards (30–43), and concludes with a long discussion of the building of booths on the third floor of the structures in the temple courtyard, followed immediately by the laws of the tithe, its redemption, and consumption in the courtyard.

The third part, which begins on col. 94 is closely associated with Deuteronomy and the instructions regarding the allocation of separate chambers for the priests, levites, and Israelites, and the laws of purity which come afterward are actually bound to Deuteronomy 14. After its conclusions of the treatment of this subject, it mentions the rest of the laws of Deuteronomy by the method of association and linkage.

In light of the close relation between the Feast of Booths and the laws of the tithe in the Scroll, it is clear to us why 'you shall tithe' and 'when you have finished paying all the tithe' appear at the beginning of the laws which are read in the parashah of the king.

115. For this reason Ecclesiastes is read at the solemn assembly on the eighth day, see *Vitry Maḥzor*, p. 441: 'They read Ecclesiastes… '*Give a portion to seven*' (Eccles. 11.2); these are the seven days of the Festival, '*or even to eight*' which is the eighth day of the Festival; Kohelet (Ecclesiastes) because of '*they assembled to King Solomon at the feast in the month of Ethanim*' (1 Kgs 8) and that is when Solomon said it'.

116. For the blessings accompanying the law of the king which resemble the blessings of the high priest, see *m. Soṭa* 7.8 (end).

117. And see Epstein, *op. cit.*, p. 540.

118. And see Yadin, Vol. 1, pp. 184–85.

F. *Summary*

In the ancient world, in Mesopotamia as well as in Egypt, there is a literary genre which can be termed 'the law for the king'. This law comprised various instructions for the conduct of the king in the sphere of relations with his subjects as well as his personal life. These instructions were written in a book and intended to be constantly read aloud before the king.

In Israel this custom is reflected in the law of the king in Deut. 17.14–20. According to this law, the king is commanded to behave modestly in his court and is also required to write the 'copy of this law' in a book and read it all the days of his life so that he 'may *learn to fear the LORD his God*' (vv. 18–19). Moreover, in Israel the king as leader of the people was required to teach this law to his people and for this purpose in Deut. 31.10–13 he was commanded to assemble men, women and children at the end of the Sabbath year and to read the laws aloud before them so that they, too, like the king would learn to fear the Lord (v. 13). We hear about the carrying out of this law in *m. Soṭa* 7.8 according to which the king reads the section on the king at the end of the seventh year. This section comprises primarily passages from Deuteronomy such as 'Hear, O Israel' (6.4) and 'if you will heed' (11.13), 'you shall tithe' (Deut. 14.22–29), 'when you have finished paying the tithe' (26.12–15), the section on the king (17.14–20), blessings and curses (v. 28), as well as other parts of Deuteronomy.

In my opinion, the 'Temple Scroll' belongs to this literary genre. Except for laws of the temple and its appurtenances which occupy a great deal of space in the Scroll, the Scroll comprises an introduction dealing with the renewed covenant in Sinai, laws concerning the tithe, festivals, and sacred gifts, a law of the king which is expanded with the addition of blessings and curses, as well as other sections from Deuteronomy. Thus what we have is a framework resembling that of the 'parashah of the king' in the Mishnah.

The sole exception is the part of the laws on the temple and its sacred objects. We can explain this in the setting of the period of the Hasmonean kings who had to carry out the repair of the temple and the performance of cultic procedures, compare for example 1 Macc. 14 where Simon takes it upon himself to take care of the temple as part of his obligations to the people. The matter of worship in the temple was especially important to the Qumran sect which had its own special calendar and laws of purity in relation to the temple and the holy city, a fact which prevented their associating with the priests of Jerusalem. We should add that the instructions for the king (περί βασιλέιας) from the Hellenistic period, the care of the temple and its cult are described as one of the primary functions of the king. Yadin has already hypothesized that the Temple Scroll may be identical to the law which the teacher of righteousness sent to the Wicked Priest (*pesher* on Ps. 37.32–33), an hypothesis which is reinforced by our assumption concerning the character of the Scroll. We learn of the books of the law of the Hasmonean kings from Rabbinic literature which speaks of 'the torah of King Jannaeus'.

Lastly, we should note that the Festival of Booths at which the king read the book of the law before the people every Sabbatical year as well as the laws of the tithe with which the king begins the legal part of the treatise of the king ('you shall tithe', 'when you have finished paying all the tithe') constitute the focal points of the Scroll. The first part of the Scroll (col. 1–29) concludes with the Festival of Booths and the solemn assembly, while the second part (30–43) ends with instructions for building booths on the roofs of the structures in the temple courtyard and on the eating of the redeemed tithe. Only in the third part does the author of the Scroll proceed to quote laws from Deuteronomy using his unique method.

Chapter 11

The Royal Guard According to the Temple Scroll

The law of the king[1] in the Temple Scroll (col. 57, 1ff)[2] prescribes that twelve thousand men, one thousand from each tribe[3], should be chosen for guarding the king. These guards called ‘selected ones’ (ברורים)[4] must be truthful, fearing God, hating gain and valiant in war (גבורי חיל למלחמה). Their task is defined as follows:

> and they shall be with him (the king) always day and night in order to keep him away from any sinful thing (דבר[5] חט) and from a foreign people (גוי נכר) that he might not be caught in their hand (11.9–11).

1. On the king's law in the Temple Scroll and its relationship to the *Fürstenspiegel* in the ancient world see Chapter 10.
2. Y. Yadin, מגילת המקדש, Jerusalem, 1977, Vol. II, p. 179f.
3. Yadin, *ibid.*, Vol. 1, p. 267, compares the selection of the twelve thousand men here to Num. 33.3f. but fails to note the selection of the twelve thousand in Absalom’s revolt and the twelve thousand *parashim* of Solomon (1 Kgs 10.26, comp. v. 6). It is noteworthy that Josephus in his accounts related to Kgs 5.6f., tells us that Solomon was surrounded by riders ‘most delightful to see…they let their hair hang down to a very great length and were dressed in tunics of Tyrian purple… With these men about him dressed in armour and equipped with bows, the King himself was accustomed to mount his chariot…’ (*Antiq.* VIII, 185). This information has no support at all in the OT, and seems to be influenced by court customs of the second temple period. A similar description is indeed found in connection with Aristobulus who was accompanied, in his appearance before Pompey, by ‘young swaggerers, who offensively displayed their purple robes, long hair…’ (*Antiq.* 14.45). Cf. A. Schalit in his notes to three Hebrew translations of *Antiquities,* Vol. II, p. 133 n. 248. All this might serve as realistic background for the king's guard as depicted in theTemple Scroll. This is especially important since the background of the Temple Scroll is Hasmonean (cf. also Yadin, Vol. I, pp. 267–68).

   Although Num. 31 has no reference to the royal guard it does have some affinities to the description of Joash's guard in 2 Kings 11; cf. especially שרי המאיות vv. 4, 15, 19 with Num. 31.14,53 and פקודי החיל in v. 15 with Num. 31.14. Indeed Jehoiada, the priest, who organized the guards of Joash, shares certain qualities with Pinchas, the priest, who commands the officers of hundreds and thousands in Num. 31

   For a parallel between the description of the bodyguard in the Temple Scroll and that of 2 Kgs 11, cf. והיו עמו תמיד יום ולילה in the Scroll and והיו את המלך בצאתו ובבואו in 2 Kgs 11.8.
4. For the meaning of this term cf. Yadin, מגילת המקדש Vol. II, P. 180 (11,5,8), Comp *y. Qidd.* 4.5, 66 a: כל שתמנהו...לא יהיו אלא מן הברורין שבאחיך (see above p. 174).
5. Deficient spelling like this is found also in col. 64 1.9 חט משפט מות, but there it was corrected by adding the Aleph above the line, see Y. Yadin, *ibid.*, line 10.

The juxtaposition of 'valiant warriors' and 'men fearing God'[6] is unusual but more strange is the combination of physical guard with moral-spiritual supervision; Yadin (Vol. 1, pp. 267–68) tentatively suggests that the specification of the moral qualities reflects a reaction against the Hasmonean kings who used foreign mercenaries for their bodyguard.

However, new light is shed on the whole matter by the description of the Egyptian royal guard by Diodorus Siculus[7] who drew upon Hecataeus of Abdera. Diodorus tells us that the behaviour of the Egyptian kings was regulated by prescriptions set forth in laws (LXX, 9). The observance of these should lead the king to fear the gods (LXX, S. Comp. Deut. 17.19). Furthermore, the sacred scribe *recited* some of the proper counsels and deeds of the most distinguished men[8] *publicly* (παρανεγίνωσκε) out of the sacred books, 'in order that he who held the supreme leadership should first contemplate in his mind the most excellent general principles…' (LXX, 9). This reminds us in general of the law of the king in Deuteronomy.

The clause of Diodorus' passage most pertinent to our subject (= the Temple Scroll) is the beginning paragraph, describing the conduct of the kings in ancient Egypt.

It reads:

> In the manner of their guard (θεραπεία)[9], for instance, not one was a slave, such as had been acquired by purchase or born in the home, but all were sons of the most distinguished priests, over twenty years old and the best educated of their fellow-countrymen, in order that the King, by virtue of his having the noblest men to care for his person and to attend him throughout both day and night, might not follow low practices.

The regulations found in Diodorus Siculus and those of the Temple Scroll share the following features:

i. the instructions about the bodyguard open the set of regulations about the King's rule and his behaviour.
ii. a guard with a double function is presumed – both physical care and moral supervision are imposed.

6. As Y. Yadin noted the writer is here influenced by Exod. 18.21, However אנשי חיל in Exodus means 'capable men' (Comp. JPS translation), like the ones mentioned in Gen. 47.6, whereas the writer of the Scroll changed אנשי חיל into גבורי חיל למלחמה to make it clear that it means 'warriors'.

7. Book 1, 70, cf. the recent commentary of A. Burton, *Diodorus Siculus, A Commentary* (1972), pp. 209ff.

8. Comp. *PS. Aristeas,* 283, and see D. Mendels, *Shnaton 3* (1978), p. 249 (Hebrew).

9. θεραπεία designates homeguard in the broad sense, see e.g. Polybius on the coronation of Ptolemy V, an account which shares much in common with the description of the coronation of Joash in 2 Kgs 11. Sosibius gathers the bodyguard (= the bearers of the shields ὑπασπιστάς, cf. *4 Macc.* 3.12), the homeguard (θεραπεία) the military officers and the officers of the horsemen. Agathocles and Susibius then put the crown upon the child and proclaim him king. Then they demand an oath of loyalty from the military officers and also adjure the people as was customary at such occasions (XV, 25). The θεραπεία was very active during revolutions and court rebellions, and the bodyguard was only a part of it; see P.M. Frazer, *Ptolemaic Alexandria* (1972), Vol. II, p. 152 n. 224.

iii. The guards should be selected[10] and of best education.
iv. The guards should be above twenty years of age.
v. The king should be watched day and night.

Some scholars have expressed their doubts concerning the authenticity of the information of Hectaeus cited by Diodorus.[11] For our purpose the dating or the very existence of the institution described in the passage by Diodorus is of no importance. Suffice it to say that an ideology like that of the Temple Scroll has been found in a contemporaneous source of a neighbouring country. The two sources apparently reflect royal ideologies prevalent in Judah and Egypt in the Hellenistic period.[12]

10. According to the Egyptian regulations the guards should be of priestly origin. According to Plato (*Politicus* 290 d) the Egyptian king himself should be of priestly descent.

11. For arguments against this scepticism see E. Meyer, *Gottesstaat, Militärherrschaft und Standewesen in Ägypten, Sitzungsberichte der preussischen Akademie der Wissenschaften* (Jg. 1928), Philos. hist. Klasse, pp. 529ff. See also F. Jacoby, Realencycl. Pauly-Wissowa, VII, 2764.

12. For such ideologies embedded in the περὶ βασιλείας, treatises which served as manuals for the king in the Hellenistic period, see my article mentioned in n. 1.

Chapter 12

God Versus Moses in the Temple Scroll 'I Do Not Speak on My Own but on God's Authority' (*Sifre Deuteronomy.* Sec. 5; John 12.48f.)

As is well known, the author of the Temple Scroll changed the words of God in the book of Deuteronomy from the third person to first person. As Y. Yadin already noted, by this change the author wanted to make clear that the Torah of Deuteronomy was delivered as the direct speech of God and not paraphrased by Moses, as it appears in the canonical book of Deuteronomy. Here are a few examples

Temple Scroll	*MT Deuteronomy*
ועשיתה הטוב והישר לפני,אני ה׳ אלוהיכה	כי תעשה הטוב והישר בעיני ה׳ אלהיך
'You will do what is good and right before me; I am YHWH your God'	'for you will do what is good and right in the eyes of YHWH your God'

The substitution of לפני instead of בעיני does not matter here since both are equal in meaning, compare e.g. מצא חן בעיני (Esther 7.3) with מצא חן לפני (Esther 8.5),[1] similarly in Akkadian the Sumerogram IGI indicates 'eye' (*īnu*) as well as 'face' (*pānu*) and also 'before' (*maḫar*).

What matters is the person speaking: God and not Moses. Since v. 28 ends the parasha (*sĕtumah*), the ועשיתה הטוב והישר לפני looks awkward as a conclusion and therefore the author added אני ה׳ אלוהיכה, a conclusion common in the priestly literature. By this addition he avoided the omission of the clause ה׳ אלהיך:

TS	*Deut.*
כי דרוש אדורשנו מידכה	כי דרש ידרשנו ה׳ אלהיך מעמך
'for I will require it of you' (53.11)	'because YHWH your God will require it of you' (23.22)
כי משנה אנוכי אתכמה	כי מנסה ה׳ אלהיכם אתכם
'for I am testing you' (54.12)	'for YHWH your God is testing you' (13.4)

According to the book of Deuteronomy only the Decalogue was delivered directly to the people of Israel at Sinai, whereas the rest of the law was delivered

1. Cf. Chapter 17 p. 244.

by Moses to the people not at Sinai but at the plains of Moab (5.28). This is in contrast to the other sources according to which all the laws were delivered by Moses at Sinai (Exod. 21–23; 24.3, Lev. 26.46,34)[2] and a covenant was concluded only there.

In Deuteronomy Moses presents the laws in his own name as they were revealed to him and hence the term: *torat Moshe* 'the Torah of Moses' in the Deuteronomic literature (Josh. 8.31; 23.6; 2 Kgs 14.6 compare Mal. 3.22). Furthermore the Torah of Deuteronomy is considered in the book of Deuteronomy itself as secondary. It is named here *mishneh hatorah* (Deut. 17.18, cf. Josh. 8.32) which means 'repeated law' or 'second law' and thus alludes to the fact that Deuteronomy is a (revised) repetition of the main Sinaitic laws of the Tetrateuch. Indeed Deuteronomy is dependent on the previous traditions of the Tetrateuch but was revised according to the principles of the Hezekianic-Josianic reforms. Thus, for example, the laws of tithe, of the year of release (שמיטה), liberation of slaves, the first-born animals, the Passover offering and the three festivals (Deut. 14.22–16.17) are all ancient laws (cf. Exod. 21.1–11; 22.28–29; 23.10–11, 14–19; 34.19–26). They appear however in Deuteronomy in a new form adjusted to the principles of centralization of cult. There was thus an awareness of this book being secondary.[3]

A similar categorization of stabilized canonic tradition versus extraneous or secondary added tradition is found in Mesopotamia.[4] There we find the term *šanû* (second/another)for sacred literary material distinct from the original canonic material. An Akkadian term which overlaps *šanû* is *aḫu* (=external), an expression which equals late Hebrew חיצון, for which one is to compare the expression ספרים חיצונים 'extraneous books',[5] which defines non-canonical literature (see *m. Sanh.* 10.1). In the Qumran literature we find the term ספר התורה שנית referring apparently to a non-canonical Torah (4Q177, *Catena*[a] II, 14, *DJD* V p. 68).

In Deuteronomy Moses appears as the 'law giver'. He emphasizes this role about 40 times in the constant recurring address: 'which I command you this day' (אשר אנכי מצוך היום) – although in the name of YHWH. Deuteronomy indeed constitutes one long farewell speech by Moses which is formulated in the first person. The involvement of Moses is clear not only in the hortatory parts of the book but also in the law itself (see 18.15–16). The formulation אשר אנכי מצוך היום is found in the Tetrateuch only once i.e. in Exod. 34.10 'observe that which I command you this day' (שמור לך את אשר אנכי מצוך היום) yet in contrast to the formulation in Deuteronomy wherein the 'lawgiver' is Moses, here the lawgiver is God, who gives the covenantal commandments anew after it had been violated by the worship of the golden calf. The formulation 'observe that which I command

2. Only the laws of the division of land and of the conquest (Num. 26.3–65; 33.50–34.29; 36.1–13) were delivered in the steppes of Moab.

3. See Ibn Ezra in his comment to Deut. 1.5, and Nahmanides to Deut. 1.1.

4. Cf. F. Rochbeg-Halton, 'Canonicity in Cuneiform Texts', *Journal of Cuneiform Studies* 36 (1984), pp. 140–44.

5. Compare the term ברייתא, derived from בר = outside, in Rabbinic literature which refers to extraneous tradition not included in the Mishnah.

you this day' in Exod. 34.11 after which come the commandments of the renewed covenant (vv. 12–26, which parallels Exod. 23.10–19) is linked to the announcement of God which proclaims the elevated status of Israel:

> Behold I make a Covenant; before all your people of Israel I will make wonders (נפלאות), such as have not been done in all the earth nor among all the nations.

This corresponds to 33.16:

> If you go with us we shall be distinguished (ונפלינו), I and your people, from all the people that are upon the face of the earth.

Indeed, according to many commentators the proper position of Exod. 33.14–16 is right after 34.9.[6]

Now, it is interesting that the single place in the book of Deuteronomy, in which the formula 'I command you this day' is attributed to God and is linked to observation of the laws as in Exod. 34, is the place in which we find the establishing of the covenant and the promise to elevate the status of the people of Israel:

> *This day YHWH your God commands you* (מצוך היום) to do these laws and judgments; you shall keep them...you have proclaimed YHWH this day to be for you a God...and YHWH has proclaimed you this day to be for him a peculiar people (עם סגלה)...to make you high over all the nations which he has made, in praise, in name and in honour (Deut. 26.16–19).

There exists a clear connection between Exod. 34.10 and the paragraph that we just quoted from Deuteronomy 26. In the latter the author connects the giving of the laws 'this day' to the covenant between God and Israel and to the promise of Israel's elevated status and distinction; in Exod. 34 this subject serves as an opening to the laws of the renewed covenant, while in the book of Deuteronomy it serves to conclude them. As Yadin has pointed out (vol. 2, p. 1) the Temple Scroll writer opens with the renewed covenant at Sinai as it adjoins the building of the Tabernacle just as the first covenant (Exod. 19–24) also is joined to the commandments concerning the building of the Tabernacle (Exod. 25ff.).

Why does the Temple Scroll open with the second covenant? The Temple Scroll writer is concerned to begin at the covenant that was renewed after the golden calf incident and not in the chapters that describe the preceding covenant which was annulled. This objective already exists in the book of Deuteronomy itself. In contrast to the sources in the book of Exodus that attributes to Moses the passing on of the Covenant Code laws to Israel (Exod. 21–23; 24.3) after the revelation at Sinai (Exod. 19–20) the writer of Deuteronomy tells us that only the Ten Commandments were announced to Israel at Mt. Sinai, and, although the remainder of the laws were given to Moses also at Sinai (Deut. 5.28), they were passed on to Israel only upon the establishing of the covenant in the Wilderness of Moab. The transgression of the golden calf caused the annulment of the covenant and accordingly all of the obligations and affirmations that were in force prior to

6. See S.R. Driver, *Exodus* (Cambridge Bible), pp. 361, 368; see also Rashi on 33.16ff. and Rashbam on 33.18.

that transgression and repentance were no longer binding. The Ten Commandments were written anew at Mt. Sinai (Exod. 34; Deut.10.4) but the remainder of the words of the covenant were given to Israel in the Moab wilderness and there was a covenant cut with them (Deut. 28.69; 29.9ff). According to this outlook there was no more validity to the Covenant Code (Exod. 21–23) that was announced prior to the golden calf transgression and in its stead came the book of Deuteronomy upon which was cut a renewed covenant in the Moab wilderness.[7]

In contrast to this the Temple Scroll writer, for whom all the laws of God have as their source Mt. Sinai (a point of view representative of second temple Judaism), transfers the laws of the Moabite wilderness covenant once again to Sinai. In accordance with this he shifts the style of address that is in the book of Deuteronomy; as are the laws of the Sinai covenant so are the laws of Deuteronomy spoken in the mouth of God himself and not in the mouth of Moses, as we find in our book of Deuteronomy. This is not actually a major divergence from the tradition of the Deuteronomic writer since he also acknowledges that the laws of Deuteronomy were spoken to Moses at Sinai (Deut. 5.28), only they were transmitted to Israel in the covenant at Moab. However, while the book of Deuteronomy renders the words in the form in which they were transmitted to Israel by Moses in the Wilderness of Moab, the Temple Scroll writer gives us the words in the form in which they were given by God at Mt. Sinai: from the mouth of God in the first person to Moses.

In this matter the author of the Temple Scroll follows the view of the priestly code in the Pentateuch. In the priestly code every legal section opens with the phrase: 'YHWH spoke to Moses as following' (וידבר ה׳ אל משה לאמר) in order to ascertain that Moses spoke on behalf of God and that the words proclaimed are not his own. Indeed, when the author of the Temple Scroll quotes from the priestly code he leaves the commandments of God in the third person since in the opening phrase it was already stated that these are the words of the Lord.[8] According to the priestly code all the laws were given to the Israelites at Sinai (Lev. 7.38; 25.1; 27.34) and only the laws concerning the division of the land and its inheritance were given at the plains of Moab (Num. 26.3; 33.50; 35.1, see above n. 3).

It seems that the fact that Deuteronomy was styled as a sermon of Moses could give room for the argument that the contents of the sermon are of Moses himself and not of God. In order to prevent the rise of such arguments the author of the Temple Scroll changed the divine address from third person to first person.

The same sensitivity is felt in Rabbinic sources and in the Targums and hence the repeated statements concerning Deuteronomy: 'I (Moses) do not speak on my own authority but on God's authority'. In the verse in Deut. 1.6: 'YHWH our God spoke to us in Horeb as follows'. Midrash Sifrei adds: 'he said to them: I do not speak on my own but from the mouth of the Holy One I speak to you': אמר להם: לא מעצמי אני אומר לכם אלא מפי הקדוש (*Sifrei* sec. 5). Furthermore, whenever we find Moses saying ואומר לכם 'I said to you', *Midrash Sifrei* explains: 'I

7. On Deuteronomy as substitute for the Covenant Code see O. Eissfeldt, *Einleitung in das Alte Testament*[3] (1964), 292ff.

8. Cf. Y. Yadin, *The Temple Scroll*, vol. 1, 72.

don't speak on my own etc.' (sections 9, 19, 25). Pseudo-Jonathan follows this system and adds to Deut. 1.6. ולא אנא באנפי נפשי: (ה׳ אלהינו דבר: אלינו בחרב לאמר) 'and not I by myself'.

By the same token, Targum *Neophyti* adds אמר משה 'said Moses' to the passages which are undoubtedly the words of Moses himself like: 'and YHWH said to me', 'and YHWH gave to me', and YHWH listened to me' (2.2, 9, 17, 31; 3.2; 5.19, 25; 9.10, 11, 12, 13, 19; 10.1, 4, 10, 11; 18.17) in order to make clear that all the other words in Deuteronomy are from God and not from Moses.

The term: 'I do not speak on my own etc'. in the Targum and in the Rabbinic sources comes to confirm the truth of the prophetic message, cf. e.g. the words of Jeremiah referring to the false prophets: חזון לבם ידברו לא מפי ה׳ 'they speak from their own minds, not from the mouth of YHWH'(23.16).

Interestingly enough this term is found in the Gospel of John concerning the prophecies of Jesus: 'not on my own that I spoke', ἐγὼ ἐξ ἐμαυτοῦ οὐκ ἐλάλησα 12.49, compare 7.17–18; 14.10). Before this statement we read: 'the word that I have spoken, that is what will condemn him on the last day'. This seems to reflect the Targum's rendering of אנכי אדרש מעמו concerning the false prophet who speaks on his own in Deut. 18.19, not 'I will take vengeance on him' but 'my word (*rēma*) will take vengeance on him' מימרי יפרע מינה (*Tg. Onq.*), מימרא יפרע מינה (*Tg. Ps. J.*) אנא במימרי אתפרע מינה (*Tg. Neof.*).[9]

It seems that the term *the Torah of Moses* coined by the Deuteronomist (Josh. 8.31; 23.6; 2 Kgs 14.6; compare Mal. 3.12), which could be misunderstood as *Moses' own law,* motivated the retroversion from Moses to God as well as the specific statements that it was not Moses speaking on his own but on behalf of God.

9. Cf. M.E. Boismard, 'Les Citations Targumiques dans le quatrième Évangile', *Revue Biblique* 66 (1959), pp. 376–78. See also Raymond E. Brown, *The Gospel According to John I–XII* (*AB*, 1966), pp. 491–92.

Chapter 13

SARAH AND ABIMELECH (GENESIS 20) AGAINST THE BACKGROUND OF AN ASSYRIAN LAW AND THE GENESIS APOCRYPHON

U. Cassuto[1] interpreted the gifts Abimelech gave to Abraham (Gen. 20.16) and Pharaoh's 'favour' to Abram (Gen. 12.16) according to the law which states that a man who takes a married woman on a (trade?) journey[2] with him, without knowing that she is married, must make an oath to that effect and give two talents of tin to the woman's husband (Middle Assyrian Laws, I, sect. 22).[3] Pharaoh, and also Abimelech, did not know that Sarah was married and were thus obligated – according to Cassuto – to make an oath and give compensation, as determined in the Assyrian law.[4]

Cassuto's comparison, however, is not complete, since the texts speak – in regard to both Pharaoh and Abimelech – of gifts and favour, but not of any oath. He did, in fact, assume, in view of the Assyrian parallel, that declarations by oath were made by the two kings. Such an oath, however, is not mentioned in the text. Cassuto's assumption, then, remained but a conjecture.

A number of years after the appearance of Cassuto's *Commentary* (1944), the apocryphal Genesis scroll of Qumran was published,[5] wherein we find, to our surprise, evidence which may nevertheless confirm Cassuto's hypothesis. We read there in connection with Sarai and her leaving Pharaoh's house:

וימא לי מלכא במומה די לא...
ויהב לה מלכא [כסף וד]הב...
ולבוש שני בוץ וארגואן...

1. U. Cassuto, *A Commentary on the Book of Genesis*, II (1964), pp. 357–58 (translated from the Hebrew by J. Abrahams).

2. In Akkadian: *ḫarrāna ultaṣbissi*, apparently referring to a trade journey, cf. *ḫarrāna epēšu* and *ḫarrāna alāku*, both meaning to go on a trade journey, see *CAD*, H, pp. 110–11; 4, E, p. 218, and so also עשות דרכיך in Isa. 58.13 and הלך בדרך מרחוק in Prov. 7.19–20; see my comments in *MAARAV* 3/1 (January 1982), pp. 44–45.

3. See G.R. Driver and J.C. Miles, *The Assyrian Laws* (1935), p. 392, II.105–111; G. Cardascia, *Les Lois Assyriennes* (1969), pp. 138–41 (translation and notes).

4. Cassuto, n. 1 above.

5. N. Avigad and Y. Yadin, *A Genesis Apocryphon, A Scroll from the Wilderness of Judea* (1956), and recently, J.A. Fitzmyer, *The Genesis Apocryphon of Qumran Cave 1, A Commentary*^{2} (1971).

'And the king swore an oath to me that [he had] not [touched her?][6]
...and the king gave to him[7] [silver and go]ld,
many garments of fine linen and purple'.[8]

We thus find here explicitly both an oath and monetary compensations as in the Assyrian law. This practice of an oath of purification required of a man accompanied by a married woman without his knowing that she was married, and also the compensation owed in such a case to the woman's husband for his wife's being kept for a certain time by another,[9] was apparently prevalent in the ancient Near East[10] (as Cassuto assumed), and is not necessarily characteristic of Assyria. The fact that this practice is found in a law code from the middle of the second millenium BCE[11] on the one hand, and in a Qumran scroll from the first century BCE or CE[12] on the other, presents a historical problem (see the end of this article). Nevertheless, we can assume that we have here a practice widespread over the ancient Near East for a period of more than a thousand years, without assuming any dependence or influence of one source on another.

Cassuto's explanation of the problem should therefore be accepted, but not as he presented it in detail, for the following reasons:

1. Cassuto assumes, in view of the comparison with the Assyrian law, that both Pharaoh and Abimelech proclaimed that they did not touch Abraham's wife.[13] Against this, it should be noted according to the Assyrian law it is clear that the man did not make an oath concerning his not approaching the woman, but concerning *not knowing* that she was married.[14] Indeed, from the Assyrian law it is not at all clear what the relations were between the man and woman on

6. N. Avigad and Y. Yadin reconstruct: 'that cannot [be changed?]' – שאין [לשנותה?], apparently under the influence of the formulas (וקים) די (מלכא יהקים) לא להשניא in Dan. 6.16 (cf. v. 9). This should really be translated '(an oath) which cannot *be broken*', see my comments in *Shnaton – Annual for Biblical and Ancient Near Eastern Studies* 1 (1976), p. 89 n.1 (Hebrew). Fitzmyer (n. 5 above) reconstructs: 'that [he had] not [touched her]', but see our discussion below.

7. It is possible to translate 'and gave to her' (i.e., to Sarah), as does Fitzmyer, *ibid.*, p. 142, since Abraham speaks of himself in the first person.

8. Similar to Esther when Ahasuerus bestowed favour on Mordechai for her sake and dressed him in fine linen and purple (Est. 8.15); see on this matter J. Finkel, 'The Author of the Genesis Apocryphon Knew the Book of Esther', in C. Rabin and Y. Yadin (eds.), *Essays on the Dead Sea Scrolls in Memory of E.L. Sukenik* (1961), pp. 178–79.

9. Cf. *Tg. Ps. J.*, the *Frg. Tg.* and *Tg. Neof.* on Gen. 20.16: חלף דאתכסית מן בעליך ליליא חדא – 'because you were hidden from your husband for one night'.

10. A monetary compensation for keeping someone else's wife is found in English law; see Miles' comment in Driver-Miles (n. 3 above), p. 72 n. 5.

11. The Middle Assyrian law code was committed to writing in the days of Tiglath-Pileser I (1112–1074 BCE) as proven by E. Weidner, 'Das Alter der mittel-assyrischen Gesetzestexte', *Archiv für Orientforschung* 12 (1937), pp. 48ff., but the laws themselves are ancient and reflect the middle of the second millenium.

12. For the dating of the Scroll see recently J.A. Fitzmyer and D.J. Harrington, *A Manual of Palestinian Aramaic Texts* (1978), p. 206.

13. *Ibid.*, p. 244.

14. Cf. the text of the law: *kî aššat a'īlini lā idî itammama*, i.e., he shall make an oath that he did not know she was married, and see the translations and treatments of the law by the commentators of the Assyrian law (see n. 3 above and also Th. S. Meek, *ANET*^{2}, p. 181).

the journey.[15] Actually, even if there were no relations between them, the deed is considered as a wrong that has to be righted. If the man knew that the woman accompanying him on a journey was a married woman and took her with him without the consent of her husband – even if he did not touch her – this constitutes a trespass. This is the case for Pharaoh and Abimelech: if they had known that she was married and took her into their palaces, even if they did not touch her, they were committing a trespass. In order to be cleared of the guilt they are obliged in such cases to make an oath that they did not know that she was married. On the other hand, if the man *did not know* that she was married, it makes no difference *from the legal standpoint* whether he slept with her or not, as is clear from Section 14 of the Assyrian law which states that a man who slept with a woman not knowing that she is married is exempt from punishment. It is thus likely that, according to the analogy of the Assyrian law, the presumed oath of Pharaoh and Abimelech would necessarily entail a proclamation of not knowing that Sarah was married. Such a proclamation inheres in fact to Abimelech's words בתם לבבי ובנקיון כפי עשיתי זאת – 'my heart was blameless and my hands were clean' (Gen. 20.5).

It is correct that according to the author of the scroll and also to Philo (*On Abraham* 98), Josephus (*Antiq.* I.161–165), and Rabbinic literature,[16] Pharaoh did not touch Sarai since it was inconceivable that the saintly Abraham could take her back if she had been defiled.[17] However, such a view does not derive from the text of Genesis 12 itself. The author of the scrolls and the midrashim transferred what was said of Abimelech, 'Abimelech had not approached her' (Gen. 20.4) to Pharaoh, though this is not the plain meaning of the text there.

2. Cassuto's explanation also cannot be accepted concerning the gifts that Pharaoh gives to Abraham. According to the text of ch. 12, Pharaoh bestows his gifts on Abraham when he takes Sarai and not when he lets her go. The gifts to Abraham thus bear the character of a dowry or bridal gift.[18] Things are different in the episode of Sarah and Abimelech in ch. 20, where Abimelech gives his gifts to Abraham when he lets her go (vv. 14–16). According to the plain meaning of the text,[19] the function of the gifts in ch. 12 must thus be distinguished from that in

15. See the discussion in Driver-Miles (n. 3 above), p. 72.

16. Cf. A. Shinan and Y. Zakovitch, *Abram and Sarai in Egypt, Gen. 12.10–20 in the Bible, the Old Versions and the Ancient Jewish Literature* (Research Projects of the Institute of Jewish Studies, Monograph Series 2, 1983), pp. 87ff. (Hebrew).

17. See J.C. Greenfield, 'The Genesis Apocryphon – Observations on Some Words and Phrases', in G.B. Sarfatti, P. Artzi, J.C. Greenfield and M. Kaddari (eds.), *Studies in Hebrew and Semitic Languages Dedicated to the Memory of Prof. E.Y. Kutscher* (1980), pp. XXXIV–V.

18. Cf. *Pirqe R. El.* sect. 26: 'Pharaoh transferred to her by a marriage deed (שטר כתובה) all of his capital…and Hagar his daughter…for a handmaiden. In the continuation of the story it is said, to be sure, 'so that I took her as my wife?' – ואקח אתה לי לאשה (v. 19)'. Cf. also *Tg. Ps. J.* On 16.1 and Genesis Rabbah (ed. Theodore Albeck), p. 448 with the parallels noted there. In the Genesis Apocryphon also Pharaoh gives Hagar to Abram (col. XX, line 32), though like the other gifts this also was given upon Abram's sending away.

19. And not as some commentators have endeavoured to do by understanding Abimelech's gift to Sarah in v. 16 as referring to the past; see, e.g., Rashbam on Gen. 20.16.

ch. 20. Only in ch. 20 do we hear of gifts, after the fact, as learned from the continuation of the passage: 'This will serve you as a covering of the eyes', that is, the payment Abimelech makes has the character of compensating for the injury done[20] and demonstrates his good intentions in what he had done.[21] הנה נתתי אלף כסף should be understood as in other places in the Bible, 'I herewith give', and not 'I gave' in the past tense.[22]

The author of the Genesis Apocryphon projected the situation described in the story of Abimelech in ch. 20 onto the Pharaoh story in ch. 12 and transferred the gifts from the beginning of the account to its end in order to present Pharaoh's favours and gifts as compensation – and not as dowry, similar to what Cassuto did. This rearrangement, however, is doubtless a tendentious midrash.

The analogue with the Assyrian law thus concerns and is most pertinent to the story of Sarah and Abimelech. However, the author of the scroll transferred it to the story of Sarai and Pharaoh. Nevertheless, it should be admitted that by the very mention of the oath, the scroll adds an important element to the picture and further substantiates the analogy with the Assyrian law which Cassuto proposed.

In summary: the connection between the Assyrian law and the biblical account of Sarah in Abimelech's house, as pointed out by Cassuto, is indeed strengthened by the version of the Genesis Apocryphon from Qumran though we still do not know how to connect a practice of the middle of the second millenium BCE with sources dating 1,500 years later. Do we have here a custom that was prevalent in a region for such a long period of time? Or perhaps the author of the scroll knew of the ancient practice of the Mesopotamian region – maybe written Assyrian laws survived with which he was familiar – and he attributed them to the kings of Egypt? Moreover, does the biblical narrator indeed assume that besides the

20. כסות עינים lit. 'eye-covering', means 'ransom', whose purpose is to atone for guilt. Cf. the covering of the face of the judge in Job 9.24 done by the evil person: 'he covers the eyes of its judges' – פני שפטיה יכסה. The bride indeed blinds the eyes of a judge (Exod. 23.8; Deut. 16.19), i.e., covers the eyes of the judges in order that they should not see the guilty one. Cf. also Gen. 32.21: אכפרה פניו במנחה – 'I will wipe off his (angry) face' and see Prov. 16.14. In Akkadian as well we find the expression, 'wipe off the face' – *pāna kuppuru*. The face and eyes often interchange, and so also in Akkadian.

The Septuagint translates ταῦτα ἔσται σοι εἰς τιμὴν τοῦ προσώπου σου which has the meaning of restoring honour to the face of the woman, a meaning found also in Targum Onkelos: הא הוא ליך כסות דיקר – 'it is for you a cover of honour'. For the text of theTargum see A. Sperber, *The Bible in Aramaic*, I (1959). My student, Galen Marqus, pointed out to me that τιμή also translates כסף 'money' (cf. Septuagint to Gen. 44.2: ואת כסף שברו), and that the Greek translator understood כסות עינים as 'face-money' (cf. τιμὴ αἵματος – 'blood-money' in Mt. 27.6). According to Liddell-Scott-Jones, τιμή also means 'compensation', and if so, the Septuagint has well understood כסות עינים as a present offered in compensation for the wrong which has been done.

21. And see the comments of Rashi and Rashbam.

22. Cf. Gen. 1.29; 9.13; 15.18; 17.20; 23.11; 48.22 *et al.* This form, called *Koinzidenzfall*, usually comes with promises of legal character as similarly נשבעתי (Gen. 22.16; Jer. 22.5) and אמרתי in 2 Sam. 19.30, which means 'I declare herewith'. On this form in other Semitic languages see recently W. Mayer, *Untersuchungen zur Formensprache der Babylonischen Gebetsbeschwörungen* (1976), pp. 187ff. Rashbam understood נתתי as past tense and was thus forced to assume a reference to a dowry, like with Pharaoh.

monetary compensation Abimelech gave Abraham, he also made an oath? Such an oath may be inherent in Abimelech's words to God: 'My heart was blameless and my hands were clean' (Gen. 20.5). It is difficult to decide the issue. In any case, both external sources, the Assyrian laws on the one hand, and the Genesis Apocryphon on the other, shed new light on the story of Sarah and Abimelech.

Part III

THEOLOGY AND IDEOLOGY

Chapter 14

THE COVENANTAL ASPECT OF THE PROMISE OF THE LAND TO ISRAEL

Two types of covenants are found in the Old Testament: the obligatory type reflected in the covenant of God with Israel and the promissory type reflected in the Abrahamic and Davidic covenants.[1] The nature of the covenant of God with Israel has been thoroughly investigated and recently clarified by a comparison with the treaty formulations in the ancient Near East.[2] The nature of the Abrahamic-Davidic covenants, however, is still vague and needs clarification. This chapter suggests a new way of understanding the character of the Abrahamic-Davidic covenants by means of a typological and functional comparison with the grant formulae in the ancient Near East.[3]

Two types of official judicial documents had been diffused in the Mesopotamian cultural sphere from the middle of the second millenium onward: the political

1. See, e.g., D.N. Freedman, 'Divine Commitment and Human Obligation', *Interpretation* 18 (1964), pp. 419–31, and R.E. Clements, *Abraham and David* (Studies in Biblical Theology, 2nd, Series 5; 1967). Cf. Also N. Lohfink, *Die Landverheissung als Eid* (Stuttgarter Bibelstudien, 28; 1967) and F.C. Fensham, 'Covenant, Promise and Expectation in the Bible', *Theologische Zeitschrift* 23 (1967), pp. 305–22.

2. Cf. G.E. Mendenhall, 'Covenant Forms in Israelite Tradition', *Biblical Archaeologist* 17 (1954), pp. 50ff.; K. Baltzer, *Das Bundesformular* (Wissenschaftliche Monographien zum Alten und Neuen Testament 4; 2nd edn, 1964); D.J. McCarthy, *Treaty and Covenant*[2] (Analecta Biblica, 21a; 1978); M. Weinfeld, *DDS* (1972).

3. A. Poebel, *Das Appositionell Bestimmte Pronomen der 1 Pers. Sing. In den westsemitschen Inschriften und in A.T.* (Assyriological Studies 3, 1932). Poebel suggested that the promise to the Patriarchs bears the character of an oral 'Belehnungsurkunde'. His suggestion was based on the syntactical function of the phrase 'I am the Lord' preceding the promise of the land. According to his view, the phrase 'I am the Lord' is a typical opening phrase of royal documents in the ancient Near East, which has to be connected with and understood as the following: 'I am the one who does so and so, etc.', and not 'I am the Lord' as an independent phrase of self-introduction. This assumption, which seems to be correct, is not sufficient to bear out the thesis about the identity of the Abrahamic-Davidic covenant with the grant. We must, however, give credit to Poebel for his penetrating glance into the nature of the covenant in Israel, which, although expressed in one sentence, antedated Mendenhall (see n. 2) by twenty-two years. Cf. his summation of the syntactical discussion, 'Wir sahen auch, dass in jedem einzelnen Fall die Anwendug der dem Herrscher und Urkundestil entlehnten Formell durchaus der Situation angemessen war, weil die Verheissung, den Nachkommen der Erzväter das Land Kanaans zu verleihen, gewissermassen eine mündliche Belehnungsurkunde ist und auch die Bundesschliessung Gottes mit Israel nach der Absicht der Erzähler ahnlich wie der Abschluss eines Bundnisses zwischen politischen Staaten oder Herrschern unter dem Gesichtspunkt eines rechtlichen Staatsaktes betrachtet werden soll' (p. 72).

treaty, which is well known to us from the Hittite empire,[4] and the royal grant, the classical form of which is found in the Babylonian *kudurru* documents (boundary stones)[5] but which also occurs among the Hittites[6] in the Syro-Palestine area[7] and in the neo-Assyrian period.[8] The structure of both of these types of documents is similar. Both preserve the same elements: a historical introduction, border delineations, stipulations, witnesses, blessings, and curses.[9] Functionally, however, there is a vast difference between these two types of documents. While the 'treaty' constitutes an obligation of the vassal to his master, the suzerain, the 'grant' constitutes an obligation of the master to his servant. In the 'grant', the curse is directed toward anyone who violates the rights of the king's vassal,[10] while in the treaty the curse is directed toward the vassal who violates the rights of his king. In other words, the 'grant' serves mainly to protect the rights of the *servant*, while the treaty protects the rights of the *master*. In addition, while the grant is a reward for loyalty and good deeds already performed, the treaty is an inducement to future loyalty.

The covenant with Abraham and the covenant with David indeed belong to the grant type and not to the vassal type of document. Like the royal grants in the ancient Near East, the covenants with Abraham and David were gifts bestowed upon individuals who excelled in loyally serving their masters. Abraham is promised the land because he obeyed God and followed his mandate (Gen. 26.5; cf. 22.16, 18), and David is given the grace of dynasty because he served God with truth, righteousness, and loyalty (1 Kgs 3.6; cf. 9.4; 11.4, 6; 14.8; 15.3). The

4. Cf. E. Weidner, *Politische Dokumente aus Kleinasien: Die Staatsverträge in akkadischer Sprache aus dem Archiv von Boghazköi, Boghazköi Studien* 8 (1923); J. Friedrich, *Staatsverträge des Hatti Reiches in hethitischer Sprache, MVAeG* 31 (1926); 34 (1934).

5. L.W. King, *Babylonian Boundary Stones and Memorial Tablets* (1912). Cf. also F.X. Steinmetzer, *Die babylonischen Kudurru (Grenzisteine) als Urkundenform* (Studien zur Geschichte und Kultur des Altertuns, 11; 1922).

6. Cf. H. Güterbock, 'Siegel aus Bogazköy', AfO, *Beiheft* 5 (1940), especially pp. 47–55, which deal with the 'Landschenkungsurkunden'; K. Riemschneider, *Die hethitischen Landschenkungsurkunden* (Mitteiulungen des Instituts für Orient-forschung, 6, 1958), pp. 321–81.

7. Cf. the gift-deed of Abban to Yarimlin in D.J. Wiseman, *The Alalah Tablets*, no. 1* (London, 1954), complemented by the tablet ATT/39/84 published by Wiseman in 'Abban and Alalah', *JCS* 12 (1958), pp. 124ff., for which see also: A. Draffkorn, 'Was King Abba-AN of Yamḫad a Vizier for the King of Ḫattuša?', *JCS* 13 (1959), pp. 94ff., and the Ugaritic donation texts in *PRU* 2 and 3.

8. Cf. J. Kohler and A. Ungnad, *Assyrische Rechtsurkunden*, No. 1–30 (1913); J.N. Postgate, *Neo-Assyrian Royal Grants and Decrees* (1969).

9. For the structure of the Hittite treaties, cf. V. Korošec, *Hethitische Staatsverträge* (1931), and for the structure of the *kudurru* documents, cf. F.X. Steinmetzer, *Kudurru* (No. 5).

10. Cf. the *kudurru* inscriptions in L.W. King, *BBSt* (No. 5) and the neo-Assyrian grants in Kohler-Ungnad, *ARu*. No. 1–30 (n. 8); J.N. Postgate, *Royal Grants* (n. 8), No. 1–52. A peculiar threat occurs in an Old Babylonian grant from Hana, *bāqir ibaqqaru…kupram ammam qaqqassu ikkappar* ('whoever challenges the gift, his head will be covered with hot pitch'), in M. Schorr, *Urkunden des altbabylonischen Zivil-und Prozessrechts*, VAB 5, No. 219 (1913), pp. 17–24. At times the donor takes upon himself a conditional self-curse as, for instance, in the grant of Abban, where Abban takes the following oath: *šumma ša addinukummi eleqqû* = '[may I be cursed] if I take back what I gave you' (Wiseman, *AT* [n. 7] 1*, pp. 16–20). For the conditional oath sentences, see W. von Soden, *Grundriss der akkadischen Grammatik* (Analecta Orientalia, 33; 1952), 185g,i.

terminology used in this context is indeed very close to that used in the Assyrian grants. For example, in the grant of Aššurbanipal to his servant *Balṭaya* we read:

> I am Aššurbanipal...who does good (*ēpiš ṭābti*)...who always responds graciously[11] to all the officials who serve him and returns kindness to the servant (*pālihi*) who keeps his royal command, whose heart is devoted [lit., is whole] to his master, served me [lit., stood before me] with truthfulness, acted perfectly [lit., walked in perfection] in my palace, grew up with a good name and kept the charge of my kingship. I took thought of his kindness and I have established his gift...[12] Any future prince from among the kings my sons...do good and kindness to them and their seed. They are friends and allies (*bēl ṭābti, bēl dēqti*) of the king their master.[13]

The gift comes as a reward for the 'good and kindness' shown by the official to his master, the king, and is considered itself as 'good and kindness (*ṭābtu damiqtu*)'.[14]

This is very similar in concept to the gifts bestowed upon Abraham and David, the faithful servants.[15] Like the Assyrian king who, prompted by the kindness of his servant, promises 'good and kindness' (*ṭābtu damiqtu*) to his descendants, so does YHWH to the offspring of Abraham.

> Know, therefore, that...your God...keeps his gracious covenant (שׁמֵר הבּרית והחסד) to the thousandth generation of those *who love him and keep his commandments.* (Deut. 7.9)[16]

Although this verse is taken from Deuteronomy, which was written relatively late, its basic formula goes back to the more ancient sources, such as Exod. 20.6 (cf. Deut. 5.10):

> The God who does kindness (עֹשֶׂה חסד; cf. *ēpiš ṭābti*, above) to the thousandth generation of those *who love me and keep my commandments,*

and also,

11. *it-ta-nap-pa-lu ina damqāti*. The reading *apālu* ('to answer') and not *abālu* ('lead, direct') is supported by the vassal treaties of Esarhaddon, ll. 98, 236 (D.J. Wiseman, 'The Vassal Treaties of Esarhaddon', *Iraq* 20 [1958]) where R. Borger ('Zu den Asarhaddon – Verträgen aus Nimrud', *ZA* 20 [1961], pp. 177, 182) reads correctly: *ina kināte tarṣāti lā ta-ta-nap-pal-šu-ú-ni* ('if you do not respond with truth'). In a similar context we read in 1 Kgs 12.7: ועניתם ודברת אליהם דברים טובים, which means: 'you will respond graciously'; in other words, 'comply with their requests'. See my article 'The Council of the "Elders" to Rehoboam and Its Implications', *Ma'arav, A Journal for the Study of the NorthWest Semitic Languages and Literatures* 3 (1982), pp. 25–54.

12. For this reading cf. my article 'Covenant Terminology in the Ancient Near East and its Influence on the West', *JAOS* 93 (1973), p. 195, n. 77.

13. Postgate, *Grants* (no. 8) No. 11, pp. 1–13, 42–45.

14. *ṭābtu damiqtu* is a hendiadys, which denotes covenantal relationship; see my article 'Covenant Terminology' (n. 12), *JAOS* 93 (1973), pp. 191ff.

15. For Abraham and David as Yahweh's servants see Gen. 26.24; Ps. 105.6, 42; 2 Sam. 3.18, 7.5, etc.

16. 'Who love him and keep his commandments' refers to the Patriarchs (like most of the Commentaries, cf. M. Weiss, 'Some Problems of the Biblical "Doctrine of Retribution"', *Tarbiz* 32 (1963–64), pp. 4ff. (Hebrew) and thus parallels the phrase in the Aššurbanipal grant, 'returns kindness to the reverent who keeps his royal command'.

> Who keeps kindness (נֹצֵר חסד) to the thousandth generation. (Exod. 34.7)

The kindness (חסד) of God to David is likewise extended to the future generations as may be seen from 2 Sam. 7.15 and 22.51; 1 Kgs 3.6 and 8.23; and Ps. 89.34f. Furthermore, as the official of Aššurbanipal is called *bēl ṭābti bēl damiqti* 'friend and ally' (lit., 'man of kindness and favour') so are Abraham and David 'the lovers' and 'friends of God'.[17]

The phrase found in the grant of Aššurbanipal, 'who returns kindness to the reverent (lit., 'the one who fears') who keeps his royal command', which is parallel to 'keeps/does kindness to those who love me/him and keep my/his commandments' in the quoted verses, is also found in reference to God's followers in general. Thus we read in Ps. 103.17–18.

> But the kindness of YHWH is from everlasting to everlasting upon them that revere (lit., fear) him (יראיו) and his righteousness to children's children to those who keep his covenant (לשֹׁמרי בריתו) and remember his commandments (ולזֹכרי פקדיו) to do them.[18]

The phrase *ṭābtašu ahsusma* 'I took thought of his kindness' in Aššurbanipal's address to his loyal servant reminds us of God's words to Israel in Jeremiah's prophecy. 'I took thought of (זכרתי לך) the kindness (חסד) of your youth... following me[19] in the desert ' (Jer. 2.2). The 'kindness' referred to is the one that Israel did with her God for which she was granted the land (cf. v. 7 and Jer. 31.1f.). However, unlike the promise to David, where the imagery is taken from the royal sphere, in Jeremiah the imagery is borrowed from the familial sphere. A similar typology is actually found in legal documents of a marital nature. For example, in a gift deed from Elephantine we read, 'I took thought of you...(עשתת לבי)...and have given it to...in affection (ברחמן)[20] since she took care of me...'[21] The gift by the father is then motivated as in Jeremiah by the devotion of the donee, his daughter.

God's promises to Abraham and David and their descendants are motivated by loyal service and are typologically parallel to the 'royal covenantal grants' of the

17. *Ibid.*, and see also Isa. 41.8: אברהם אוהבי. David is called חסיד in Ps. 89.20. (Read לחסידך with manuscripts and versions; the reading לבחירך in 4Q Ps. 89 [J.T. Milik, 'Fragment d'une source du Psautir [4Q Ps. 89] et fragments des Jubilés, de Document de Damas, d'un phylactère dans la grotte 4 de Qumran', *RB* 73 [1966], p. 99; cf. also E. Lipinski, *Le Poème royal du Ps. 89, 1–5, 2–38* [1967], pp. 70ff.] is not original and was influenced – in my opinion – by verse 4a). Compare also תמיך ואריך לאיש חסידך (should perhaps be read as: לאיש חסדך) in Deut. 33.8. Here the term is ascribed to Levi who, like David, was devoted to God and therfore was granted priesthood (see below, pp. 262–64). The phrase *bēl ṭābti bēl damiqti* equals the Hebrew חסיד/איש חסד; cf., e.g., *bēl dāmi* with איש דמים in Hebrew. As is the Akkadian *bēl ṭābti/damiqti*, so the Hebrew חסיד / איש חסד is not a man who is shown kindness but the one who shows kindness, i.e., practices חסד and fulfills the demands of loyalty. Cf. N. Glueck, *Ḥesed in the Bible* (1967), pp. 66–69.

18. Compare Ps. 119.63: לכל אשר יראוך ולשמרי פקודך, which exactly parallels the Assyrian phrase dealt with.

19. הלך אחרי in Hebrew and *alāku arki* in Akkadian are legal formulae of the marital and political spheres; cf. my 'Covenant Terminology',*JAOS* 90 (1973), p. 196, n. 83.

20. Cf. the discussion of the term in Y. Muffs, *Studies in the Aramaic Legal papyri from Elephantine* (Leiden, 1969), pp. 40ff., 132f.

21. E.G. Kraeling, *The Brooklyn Museum Aramaic Papyri*, No. 9 (1953), pp. 16–17.

Hittites and Assyrians. Also, as will be shown, the analogy goes even further. Hittite and Assyrian grants are similar to God's covenants with Abraham and David even in their formulation of the commitment *to keep the promise to the descendants* of the loyal servants.

A Hittite grant typologically similar to the grant of dynasty to David is the decree of Hattušili concerning Middannamuwa, his chief scribe.

> Middannamuwa was a man of grace (*kaniššanza* UKÙ-*aš*)[22] to my father...and my brother Muwatalli was kindly disposed to him, promoted him (*kanešta...para huittiyat*)[23] and gave him Hattuša. My grace (*aššul*) was also shown to him...I committed myself for (*šer memiyahhat*) the sons of Middannamuwa...and you will keep (*pahhašdumat*)...and so shall the sons of my son and the grandsons of my son keep. And as my son, Hattušili, and Puduhepa, the great queen, were kindly disposed (*kanešta*) towards the sons of Middannamuwa so shall be my sons and grandsons...And they shall not abandon the grace (*aššulan anda lē daliyanzi*) of my son. The grace and their positions shall not be removed (*ueh-*).[24]

Like Hebrew חסד/טובה, Akkadian *ṭābtu/damiqtu*, and the Aramaic טבת, the Hittite *aššul* and *kannešuwar* connote kindness and covenantal relationship. [25] As in the case of David, in the Hittite grant the promise is to be 'kept'[26] to the future generations of the devoted servant, i.e., 'the man of grace'.[27] The most striking parallel to the promise to David is the last sentence: 'they shall not abandon the grace...their position shall not be removed'. The language (*anda*) *daliya*, equivalent to the Akkadian *ezēbu* and the Hebrew עזב, which is often employed in connection with חסד/חסד ואמת, and *weh* ('turn away', remove) is equivalent to the Hebrew סור, which appears in 2 Sam. 7 in a phrase similar to that of the Hittite grant וחסדי לא יסור ממנו – 'and my grace shall not turn away from him' (v. 15).

The formulations concerning the promises to Abraham and David are overlapping. Thus we read in Gen. 26.4–5, 'I will give to your descendants all these lands...inasmuch as Abraham obeyed me (שמע בקלי)[28] and kept my charge (וישמר משרתי), my commandments, my rules and my teachings',[29] a verse

22. For clarification of this term, cf. A. Goetze, *Ḫattušiliš* (*MVAeG* 29/3, 1924, 1925), pp. 64–65.

23. The verbs in question correspond to נטה and משך in Hebrew (*kaniniya* = Akk. *kanāšu* = Hebr. נטה, and *ḫuittiya* = Akk. šadādu = Hebr. משך), both employed with חסד: נטה חסד (Gen. 39.21), משך חסד (Jer. 31.3, Ps. 36.11; 109.12). Goetze (*ibid.*) related *kaneššuwar* to *rēma rašû* in Akkadian and correctly remarked that the object corresponding to *rēmu* in Hittite gradually became superfluous since it had been implied in the verb itself. The same equation has to be made, in my opinion, in regard to the Hebrew משך חסד / נטה חסד and also מצא = *rāšû*.

24. A. Goetze, *Ḫattušiliš (MVAeG* 29/3, 1925), pp. 40–44; (*Kbo* 4, 12).

25. *aššul* = SILIM *–ul* (SILIM = *salīmum*). *kaneššuwar* is synonymous with *aššul*; see Goetze, *Ḫattušiliš* (no. 24), pp. 64–65.

26. *paḫš* = Akk. *naṣāru* = Hebr. נצר / שמר, verbs employed in connection with keeping the promise.

27. It occurs to me that *kaneiššanza* UKÙ-*aš* is equivalent to the Hebrew איש חסיד and the Akkadian *bēl ṭābti/damiqti* appearing frequently in the context of grants.

28. Cf. in the Amarna letters, *amur arda ša išme ana šarri bēlišu* (behold, the servant who obeys the king, his Lord) (*EA* 174, 48f.).

29. This verse is not necessarily Deuteronomic; שמע בקול, along with other terms expressing obedience, is very frequent in the Deuteronomic literature, which stresses loyalty to the covenant, but

preserving verbally the notion of keeping guard or charge (*iṣṣur maṣṣarti*) found in the Assyrian text. The notion of 'serving perfectly' found in the Assyrian grants is also verbally paralleled in the Patriarchal and Davidic traditions. Thus, the faithfulness of the Patriarchs is expressed by 'walk(ed) before me' (התהלך לפני – Gen. 24.40; 48.15 = JE; 17.1 = P), which is equivalent to the expression *ina mahriya ittalak/izziz* in the Assyrian grant. The P source adds to התהלך לפני the phrase והיה תמים (Gen. 17.1), which conveys the idea of perfect or loyal service expressed in the Assyrian document by (*ittalak*) *šalmiš*.[30] According to P, not only Abraham but also Noah was rewarded by God (Gen. 9.1–17) for his loyalty, which is expressed by the very phrase used to describe Abraham's devotion: התהלך את אלהים,היה תמים (6.6, 9).[31]

David's loyalty to God is couched in phrases that are closer to the neo-Assyrian grant terminology. Thus the terms 'who walked before you in truth, loyalty[32] and uprightness of heart' הלך לפניך באמת ובצדקה ובישרת לבב (1 Kings 3.3, 6); 'walked after me with all his heart הלך אחרי בכל לבבו (14.8); and 'a whole heart (like the heart of David)' לב שלם (כלבב דוד) (15.3)[33] are the counterparts of the Assyrian terms 'with his whole heart' *libbašu gummuru*; 'stood before me in truth' *ina mahriya ina kināti izizuma*;[34] and 'walked with loyalty

this does not mean that the terms were coined by the Deuteronomic school. The combination of חקים ותורות ('laws and teachings') is never found in the Deuteronomic literature. Deuteronomy always uses Torah in the singular and usually with the definite article התורה ('the law'). On the other hand, this combination is attested to in JE (Exod. 18.16, 20). The origin of שמר משמרת is not Deuteronomic; see my *DDS* (n. 2), Appendix A.

30. Cf. Mal. 2.6 – בשלום ובמישור הלך אתי – which means 'he served me with integrity and equity'; see Y. Muffs, *Aramaic Papyri* (No. 20), pp. 203–204 (following H.L. Ginsberg). This phrase occurs in connection with the grant of priesthood to Levi (see below). For the interpretation of *ittalaku šalmiš* as 'served with integrity' and not as Kohler-Ungnad translates – 'in good or peaceful condition (wohlbehalten)' – see Y. Muffs, *ibid.*, p. 203. *alāku/atalluku šalmiš* is equivalent to הלך בתם ('walk with integrity') (Prov. 10.9) and to התהלך בתם לבב, which in Ps. 101.2 in connected with בקרב ביתי (within my house/palace).

31. However, in contradistinction to the JE source, where the loyalty of the Patriarchs is a matter of the past, in the priestly source it is anticipated.

32. צדקה here means loyalty and faithfulness, as does צדק in a similar context in the Panamuwa inscriptions (*KAI* 215.19; 216.4–7; 218.4), where בצדק אבי ובצדקי הושבני מראי ... על כרסא אבי has to be understood as: 'because of my father's and my own loyalty, the king has established me on the throne of my father'. Virtually the same idea is expressed in 1 Kgs 3.6: 'You have done grace with your servant David my father as he walked before you in truth, loyalty and uprightness of heart and you kept your grace (promise) and gave him a son to sit upon his throne as at present'.

33. Cf. Also 2 Kgs 20.3.

34. As in Hebrew התהלך / הלך לפני, so also in Akkadian *ina pāni alāku/atalluku* is similar in connotation to עמד לפני = *ina pāni uzzuzu*, but the latter seems to have a more concrete meaning – praying, interceding, worshipping and serving – whereas the former is more abstract. Cf. Jer. 18.20. For discussion of these terms, cf. F. Noetscher, *'Das Angesicht Gottes schauen', nach biblischer und babylonischer Auffassung* (Würzburg, 1924), pp. 83ff., 112f. A phrase identical with הלך לפני...בצדקה may be found in the Hittite *A-NA PA-NI DINGIR, MEŠ para ḫandandatar iya-* (cf. A. Goetze, *Ḫattušiliš* (No. 22) 1.48, *MVAeG* 29/3 (1924), p. 10, and his note on pp. 52–55 there), which means, 'to walk before the gods with righteousness/loyalty', *ḫandai* is equivalent to the

(perfection)' *ittalaku šalmiš*, which come to describe the loyal service as a reward for which the gift was bestowed.[35]

In the grants from Ugarit the loyalty of the donee is expressed by terms such as 'he exerts himself very, very much for the king his lord'.[36] Similarly, in a deed from Susa conveying a gift from a husband to a wife we read, 'it is given her as a gift because she took care of him and worked hard for him'.[37] The same motivation occurs in a deed from Elephantine quoted above: 'I took thought of you (עשתת לכי) during my lifetime and have given you part of my house...I Anani have given it to Yehojišma my daughter in affection since she took care of me (supported me) (לקבל זי סבלתני) when I was old in years and unable to take care of myself'.[38] The verb *anāhu*, expressing the exertion of the vassal to his

Akkadian *kunnû*, and *ḫandandatar* is rendered by NÍG.SI.SÁ-*tar* (NÍG.SI.SÁ = *mīšarum*), which also supports our analogy. Instances of *para ḫandandatar* in which the gods show *para ḫandandatar* in distress, war, etc. (cf. Goetze, *Ḫattušiliš* (No. 22) 1.45; 2.15, 45; 3.18, 23) might be put in the proper light by the biblical צדקה, which also connotes salvation. For the saving acts of God by means of צדקה, see, e.g., Ps. 31.2; 71.2; 143.11; *para ḫandandatar* is revealed by the gods (A. Goetze, *Die Annalen des Muršiliš*, MVAeG 38 [1933], p. 46.15), and the same is said about God in Israel in Isa. 56.1 and Ps. 98.2. Even the phrase in the introduction to the Apology of Hattušili, *ŠA* ^{d}*IŠtar para ḫandandatar memaḫḫi* (l. 5), may be better understood on the basis of biblical parallels. Reciting or telling God's צדקה is very common in the Old Testament and is clearly attested in the ancient poem of Judg. 5 (v. 11).

As in the Assyrian documents, in Hittite the idiom 'to talk in righteousness/loyalty before RN', in the sense of serving locally, is attested in the treaties (cf. A. Kempinski and S. Košak, 'The Išmeriga-Vertrag', *Die Welt des Orients* 5 [1970], p. 192.13). The idiom seems to have been rooted in the royal sphere and then projected onto the divine realm.

35. The close affinities to the neo-Assyrian phraseology in these verses may be understood in light of an identical chronological and cultural background. All of these verses appear in a Deuteronomic context, which means that they were styled in the seventh century, a period in which the above-mentioned documents were written. On the affinities of the Deuteronomic literature to the neo-Assyrian literary tradition, see my *DDS* (n. 2) (1972).

36. *Ana šarri bēlišu aniḫ danniš dannišma, PRU* 3, 14.27–30; cf. a*na šarri aniḫ/ītanaḫ, PRU* 3, 84.24; 141.29; 108.16; 110.7. Cf. the Barrakib inscription, ובית אבי [ע]מל מן כל ('and my father's house exerted itself more than anybody else', *KAI* 216.7–8), which occurs in a passage expressing the loyalty of Barrakib to Tiglath-Pileser (see above, n. 32). Two different interpretations have been given to the phrase ובית אבי [ע]מל מן כל, but neither of these is satisfactory. F. Rosenthal (*ANET*^{2}, p. 501), following H.L. Ginsberg (*Studies in Koheleth* [1950], p. 3, n. 2a) translates, 'the house of my father has profited more than anybody else', but this does not fit the immediate context, which is concerned with loyalty to Tiglath-Pileser. The same argument applies to B. Landsberger's translation, 'the house of my father was more miserable than any body else' (*Sam'al, Studien zur Entdeckung der Ruinenstätte Karatepe* [1948], p. 71), which is diametrically opposed to Rosenthal's translations. Besides, Landsberger's translation is contradicted by the Panammuwa inscription (*KAI* 214.9), a fact of which Landsberger was aware (*ibid.*, No. 187). Donner's translations, which we have adopted, is the most satisfactory and is now supported by the Akkadian parallels. It seems that עמל is the semantic equivalent of *anāḫu*. Similarly *manaḫātu* means 'results of toil', as does the Hebrew noun עמל; for the Hebrew עמל in this sense, cf. H.L. Ginsberg, *Qohelet* (1961), pp. 13–15 (Hebrew).

37. *aššum ittišu īnaḫu dulla ill*[*ika*] *nadišši qiš*[*ti*], *MDP* 24, 379;7f.; for an analysis of this document, see J. Klima, 'Untersuchungen zum elamischen Erbrecht', *Archiv Orientální* 28 (1960), p. 39.

38. E. Kraeling, *The Brooklyn Museum Aramaic Papyri* (No. 21) (1953), p. 9.16–17.

lord and the wife to her husband, actually means to toil, to suffer, but in our context they denote exertion and devotion. The notion of exertion is sometimes completed by the verb *marāṣu* ('to be sick'), as, for instance, in a letter from El-Amarna where the vassal says, 'behold I exerted myself to guard the land of the king (*ētanhu ana nāṣar māt šarri*) and I am very sick' (*marṣāku danniš*).[39] In fact, the verb *marāṣu* in Akkadian has also the meaning of 'to care for', as does the Hebrew חלה.[40] Held pointed out the correspondence of the Hebrew סבל to the Ugaritic *zbl* ('to be sick').[41] The same correspondence exists between the expressions *anāhu* and *marāṣu* on the figurative level. The notion of exerting oneself for the suzerain is also expressed in the Akkadian inscription of Idrimi, the king of Alalah, in the middle of the second millennium BCE.[42] 'I sent a messenger to the lord and told him about the exertion of my forefathers (*adbub manahāte ša abūtēya*) for them...and they had made a sworn valid alliance (*māmītu*) with me. On the account of our vassal service (exertion, *manahāte*) he received my tribute (*šulmu*)...I made many offerings'[43] (ll. 41–55).

In light of all this, we may properly understand Psalm 132.1 זכר לדוד את כל ענותו which the Septuagint and the Syriac misunderstood by reading '*anwātō* ('his humility'), which does not fit the context. In line with what we have seen above, it has to be understood as 'his submissiveness[44] or devotion'. To introduce God's promise to David, the psalmist depicts the devotion of David to God, which found expression in his deep concern for the ark. This is what is meant by the opening prayer, 'Remember to David all his submissiveness'.[45] זכר ל here is the semantic equivalent of עשת ל in the quoted Aramaic gift deed, which means 'to take favorable thought'.[46] The Akkadian *hasāsu*, the equivalent of the Hebrew זכר,[47] likewise means 'to think about' or 'to consider'[48] and, in fact, occurs in

39. EA 306.19–21.

40. Cf. especially 1 Sam. 22.8 – ואין חלה מכם עלי ('and nobody cares about me') – in the context of loyalty to the king. Cf. also Amos 6.6, ולא נחלו על שבר יוסף ('They do not care about the breach of Joseph'), and Jer. 22.13, זרעו חטים וקוצים קצרו נחלו לא יועילו ('They have sown wheat and have reaped thorns, they exerted themselves but did not profit').

41. M. Held, 'The Root ZBL/SBL in Akkadian, Ugaritic and Biblical Hebrew' (Speiser Memorial Volume), *JAOS* 88 (1968), p. 93.

42. Cf. E.L. Greenstein and D. Marcus, 'The Akkadian Inscription of Idrimi', *The Journal of the Ancient Near Eastern Society of Columbia University* 8 (1976), pp. 59–96.

43. The reference to the covenant with the ancestors of the suzerain and the sending of gifts to him was a stereotype in the oath of the vassals; see my 'Initiation of Political Friendship in Ebla', in H. Hauptmann and H. Waetzoldt (eds.), *Wirtschaft und Gesellschaft von Ebla* (Heidelberger Studien zum Alten Orient, 2, 1988), pp. 345–48.

44. Cf. וענ אנכ ארצת עזת ('I subjugated mighty countries') in the Azittawada inscription (*KAI* 26.18); cf. the Mesha inscription (*KAI* 181.5) and Exod. 10.3: עד מתי מאנת לענת מפני, which has to be rendered, 'how long will you refuse to surrender before me'. Cf. also Gen. 15.13; 16.6; Exod. 1.11; Num. 24.24; 2 Sam. 7.10; 1 Kgs 11.39; Nah. 1.12.

45. The notion that the promise of dynasty to David is to be seen as a reward for his devotion seems to lie behind the juxtaposition of 2 Sam. 6–7.

46. Cf. H.L. Ginsberg, 'Lexicographical Notes', *Hebräische Wortforschung: Festschrift W. Baumgartner* (Suppl. *VT* 15, 1967), pp. 81–82.

47. See, e.g., *EA* 228.18–19: *lihsusmi* glossed by *yazkurmi*; cf. M. Held, 'Studies in Comparative

this sense in the neo-Assyrian grant quoted above. After describing the loyalty of his servant, upon whom he bestows the grant, the Assyrian emperor says, *ṭābtašu ahsusma ukîn ši-ri-*[*ik*]*-su*[49] (I took thought of his kindness and established his gi[ft])'. The establishing of God's grant to the Patriarchs is expressed by הקים, which is the semantic equivalent of *ukîn* in the Assyrian grant.[50]

David's exertion, for which he was granted dynasty, is expressed in Psalm 132 by ענה, which corresponds to the discussed *anāhu*, *marāṣu* and עמל.[51]

In the Deuteronomic historiography, however, David's devotion is expressed, as in the neo-Assyrian grants,[52] in a more abstract way – 'walking in truth', 'acting with wholeheartedness and integrity', etc. The phraseological correspondence between the Deuteronomic literature and the neo-Assyrian documents is very salient in the description of the benevolence of God toward the Patriarchs and toward David. Thus the Assyrian king, before announcing the grant, says, 'I am the king...who returns kindness to the one who serves in obedience (lit., to the reverential) and (to the one who) guards the royal command'.[53] This phrase is close to the biblical phrase, 'the God...who keeps his gracious promise (הברית והחסד) to those who are loyal to him (lit., who love him) and guard his commandments' (Deut. 7.9–12), which appears in connection with the fulfillment of God's promise to the Patriarchs. A similar phrase occurs in the context of the promise of dynasty to David: 'who keeps his gracious promise (הברית והחסד) to your servants who serve you wholeheartedly' (ההלכים לפניך בכל לבם, 1 Kgs 8.23; cf. 3.6). The grant par excellence is an act of royal benevolence arising from the king's desire to reward his loyal servant.[54] It is no wonder, then, that the gift of the land to Abraham and the assurance of dynasty to David were formulated in the style of grants to outstanding servants.

The grant and the treaty alike are named ברית, a word which conveys the general idea of an obligation involving two parties, similar to *riksu* in Akkadian and *išhiul* in Hittite. However, in the more developed and therefore more reflective stage of Deuteronomy one can find a distinction between the term for grant and the term for treaty. As we have seen, the Deuteronomic sources refer to the Abrahamic and Davidic covenants as הברית והחסד ('the gracious covenant'), in

Semite Lexicography', *Studies in Honor of B. Landsberger on his Seventy-Fifth Birthday* (Assyriological Studies, 15; 1965), p. 399. On the root *zkr* cf. P.A.H. de Boer, *Gedenken und Gedächtnis in der Welt des A.T.* (1962); B.S. Childs, *Memory and Tradition in Israel* (1962); W. Schottroff., *'Gedenken' im Alten Orient und im Alten Testament* (1967).

48. See Y. Muffs, *Aramaic Papyri* (No. 20), p. 134.

49. See n. 12.

50. Compare the Latin *foedus firmare* ('to establish a pact'), cf. J.J. Rabinowitz, *Jewish Law* (1956), pp. 1–2.

51. See n. 36. For the correspondence of עמל to ענה, see Gen. 41.51–52; Deut. 26.7, etc.

52. See n. 34 above.

53. *ana pāliḫi nāṣir amāt šarrūtišu utirru gimilli dumqi*, Postgate, *Royal Grants* (n. 8), numbers 9–11.

54. Cf. F. Thureau-Dangin, 'Un acte de donation', *RA* 16 (1919), p. 118: 'Ces titres de propriété sont généralement des actes royaux de donation dont le bénéficiare est, soit un enfant de roi, soit un prêtre temple, soit quelque serviteur que le roi veut récompenser'.

contradistinction to the covenants of Sinai and the Plains of Moab, which referred to ברית only.

The Unconditional Gift. Although the grant to Abraham and David is close in its formulation to the neo-Assyrian grants and therefore might be late, the promises themselves are much older and reflect the Hittite pattern of the grant. 'Land' and 'house' (dynasty), the objects of the Abrahamic and Davidic covenants, respectively, are indeed the most prominent gifts of the suzerain in the Hittite and Syro-Palestinian political reality, and like the Hittite grants, the grant of 'land' to Abraham and the grant of 'house' to David are unconditional. Thus we read in the pact[55] of Hattušili III (or Thudhalya IV) with Ulmi-Tešup of Tarhuntašša.[56] 'After you, your son and grandson will possess it, nobody will take it away from them. If one of your descendents sins (*waštai-*) the king will prosecute him at his court. Then when he is found guilty...if he deserves death he will die. But nobody will take away from the descendents of Ulmi-Tešup *either his house or his land* in order to give it to a descendent of somebody else'.[57] In a similar manner Muršili II reinforces the right of Kupanta-Kal to the 'house and the land in spite of his father's sins'.[58] A similar wording occurs in the royal decree of Tudhaliya IV and Puduhepa for the descendants of Šahurnuvaš, a Hittite high official, where we read:[59] 'Nobody in the future shall take away[60] this house from

55. In fact, this document can also be considered as a grant and, according to V. Korošec ('Eininge juristische Bemerkungen zur Šahurunuva-Urkunde', *Münchener Beiträge zur Papyrusforschung und antiken Rechtsgeschichte* 35 [1945], p. 221, No. 5), is something between a grant and a treaty. Cf. also E. von Schuler, 'Staasverträge und Dokumente hethitischen Rechts', *Historia*, Einzelschriften 7 (1964), p. 40.

56. *KBo* 4.10, obv. 8-14; cf. the treaty with Tarhuntašša between Thudhalya IV and Kurunta, written on a bronze tablet and edited by H. Otten, *Die Bronzetafel aus Boğazköy* (Studien zu den Boğazköy-Texten Beiheft, 1; 1988), Par. 20. The connection between this treaty and the Davidic covenant has been seen by R. de Vaux, 'Le roi d'Israël, vassal de Yahve', *Mélanges E. Tisserant* 1 (1964), pp. 119–33.

57. Cf. (*KBo* 4.10), Rev. 21ff.: 'Now as for what I, the sun, have given to Ulmi-Tešup... I have engraved on an iron tablet and in future no one shall take it away from any descendant of Ulmi-Tešup, nor shall any one litigate with him about it; the king shall not take it, but [it shall belong] to his son. To another man's descendant they shall not give it'. It seems that this iron tablet was the original gift-deed.

58. J. Friedrich, *MVAeG* 31 (No. 4) (1926), No. 3.7–8 (pp. 112–15), 21–22 (pp. 134–37).

59. *KUB* 26, 43 and 50. Cf. V. Korošec, 'Einige juristische Bemerkungen' (see n. 55) for analysis of this document.

60. *ziladuuwa arḫa lē kuiski dāi*; cf. the same formula in *KBo* 4.10, obv. 11. Cf. *urram šerram mamman la ileqqê ištu qāti* PN in the grants from Ugarit written in Akkadian (PRU 3 passim), and *šḥr. 'lmt bnš bnšm* (or *mnk mnkm* = whoever you are) *l' yqḥnn. bd* PN in the Ugaritic version of the grants. Compare the conveyance formula from Elephantine, מחר או יום אחרנ לא יהנצל מנכי למנתנ לאחרננ ('on a future day I will not take it away from you in order to give it to the others'). (A.E. Cowley, *The Aramaic Papyri of the Fifth Century B.C.* (1923), pp. 7.18–19. On the correspondence between *urram šerram* and מחר או יום אחר, see J.J. Rabinowitz, *Jewish Law* (No. 48) (1956), p. 161. The Hebrew מחר and therefore יום אחרון also mean future; cf. Gen. 30.33; Exod. 13.14; Deut. 6.20; Josh. 4.6, 21; 22.24, 27 for מחר, and Isa. 30.8 for יום אחרון. Cf. also the neo-

U-manava (or Tešup-manava), her children, her grandchildren and her offspring. When anyone of the descendents of U-manava provokes the anger of the king…whether he is to be forgiven[61] or whether he is to be killed, one will treat him according to the wish of his master but his house they will not take away and they will not give it to somebody else'.[62]

A striking parallel to these documents is found in a will of Nuzi,[63] where it says: 'Tablet of Zigi…in favour of his wife and his sons… All my lands…to my wife Zilipkiashe have been given…and Zilipkiashe shall be made parent of the sons.[64] As long as Zilipkiashe is alive the sons of Zigi shall serve/respect her (*ipallahšunuti*).[65] When Zilipkiashe dies the sons of Zigi shall receive their inheritance portions, each according to his allotment.[66] Whoever among my sons will not obey Zilipkiashe, Zilipkiashe shall put him in the house of de[tention],[67] their mark (on the head) shall be applied to him and (they) will be put in (their) fetters,[68] but (their) right shall not be annulled[69]…and Zilipkiashe shall not give away anything to strangers'.

Assyrian formula *ina šerta ina lidiš* ('some time in the future'); see Y. Muffs, *Aramaic Papyri* (No. 20), pp. 206–207.

61. *duddunu* means 'to forgive'; cf. A. Goetze, 'Critical Reviews of *KBo* 14 (by H.G. Güterbock)', *JCS* 18 (1964), p. 93. Cf. also F. Imparati, 'Conassione de Terre', *RHA* 32 (1974), pp. 96ff.

62. Cf. the Abban deed from Alalah, *ana šanim ul inaddin* ('he shall not give it to any one else', D.J. Wiseman, 'Abban and Alalah', *JCS* 12 [1958] p. 1.63), and the Nuzi deed *mimma ana nakari la inandin* ('she shall not give anything [from the inheritance] to strangers', HSS 5 73.27–28). Compare the deed from Elephantine quoted above (No. 60): למנתנ לאחרנ ('to give it to the others').

63. *Excavations at Nuzi I*, HSS 5 73.1–28; cf. E.A. Speiser, 'New Kirkuk Documents', *AASOR* 10, No. 20 (1930), pp. 51–52.

64. Read *a-na a-bu-ti ša mārē īteppuš* (ll. 10–11), with P. Koschaker, 'Review of Scheil, *MDP XXII*', *OLZ* 35 (1932), pp. 399f.

65. *ipallaḫšunūti* has to be translated as 'she shall respect them', but as Speiser pointed out (see., e.g., *Introduction to Hurrian, AASOR* 20 [1941], pp. 206f.) this grammatical confusion is characteristic of the Hurrian scribes (cf. also Speiser, 'A Significant New Will from Nuzi', *JCS* 17 [1963], p. 66 to ll. 21f.).

66. *u mārū ša Zigi attamannu kī emūqišu zitta ileqqû* (lit., 'and the sons of Zigi, *whoever you are*, shall receive his inheritance portion according to his allotment'. *attamannu* here is the equivalent of the Ugaritic *mnk* (mn + ka) quoted in n. 58. Cf. the Canaanite and Aramaic inscriptions: *KAI* 13.3 (מיאתה), 225.5 (מנאת), 259.2 (ומנ זיאת), and Zech. 4.7: מי אתה הר הגדול לפני זרבבל למישר ('whoever you are big mountain before Zerubbabel, you will become a plain').

67. *ina bit nu-*[*pa-ri*] *inandin*; cf. E. Cassin, 'Nouvelles données sur les relations familiales à Nuzi', *RA* 57 (1963), p. 116, and M. Burrows and E.A. Speiser (eds.), *One Hundred New Selected Nuzi Texts, AASOR* 16 (1935–36) (1936), p. 3, line 40: *ina (bīt) nupāri ittadanni*; p. 12, line 12: *bīt nupāri; nupāru* occurs in parallel with *bīt kīlī* in texts from Nuzi; see E. Cassin, 'Nouvelles données', *RA* 57 (1963), p. 116.

68. *abbutašunu umaššaršu u ina kurṣišunu* (GIR-*šu-nu*) *išakkan*. On the meaning of *abbutu* in this context, see E. Cassin, 'Nouvelles données', *RA* 57 (1963), p. 116; E. Cassin, 'Pouvoir de la femme et structures familiales', *RA* 63 (1969), pp. 133f.; E. Speiser, 'New Will from Nuzi' (n. 65), *JCS* 17 (1963), pp. 65ff.

69. *kirbana lā iheppe* (lit. 'lump [clod] of earth [symbolizing tablet of rights] will not be broken'); cf. E. Cassin, 'L'influence babylonienne à Nuzi', *JESHO* 5 (1962), p. 133; M. Malul, *Studies in Mesopotamian Legal Symbolism*, AOAT (1988), pp. 80ff.

The same concept lies behind the promise of the house to David and his descendants in 2 Sam. 7.8–16 where we read: 'I will establish the throne of his kingdom forever, I will be his father and he shall be my son, when he sins I will chastise him with the rod of men and with human afflictions but my grace will not be removed...your house and your kingdom will be steadfast before me forever, your throne shall be established forever'. The phrase 'I will be his father and he shall be my son' is an adoption formula[70] and actually serves as the judicial basis for the gift of the eternal dynasty. This comes to the fore in Psalms 2 where we read, 'he (God) said to me: you are my son, this day[71] have I begotten you. Ask me and I will give you nations for your patrimony and the ends of the earth for your possession' (vv. 7–8).

Similarly we read in Psalm 89:[72] 'I have found David my servant...with whom my hand shall be established, my arm shall hold him אשר ידי תכון עמו אף זרועי תאמצנו[73]...I will smash his adversaries before him and will defeat his enemies... he will call me 'you are my father'[74] my God...and I will make him as my first born, the highest of the earthly kings. I will keep my grace forever and my covenant shall endure for him. Should his children forsake my law and will not follow my decrees...I will punish their rebellion with the rod and their sin with afflictions. But I will never annul my grace with him and shall not betray my pact (ולא אשקר באמונתי)[75] (with him). I will not profane my covenant and alter what came out of my lips'.

'House' (dynasty), land, and peoples are then given to David as a fief, and as was the rule in the second millennium this gift could be legitimized only by

70. Cf. C. Kuhl, 'Neue Dokumente zum Verstädnis von Hos. 2.4–15', *ZAW* 52 (1934), pp. 102ff.

71. *hywm* ('this day') indicates the formal initiation of a legal contract; cf. Ruth 4.9–10, 14; Gen. 25.31, 33; see G.M. Tucker, 'Witnesses and "Dates" in Israelite Contracts', *CBQ* 28 (1966), pp. 42–45. Compare S.E. Loewenstamm, 'The Formula *mĕ 'attā wĕ'ad 'ōlām*', *Comparative Studies in Biblical and Ancient Oriental Literatures* (AOAT, 204, 1980), pp. 166ff., for the formula *ištu ūmi annīm* (from today) in the Akkadian documents from Alalah and Ugarit.

72. On the relationship of this Psalm to Nathan's oracle, see N.M. Sarna, 'Psalm 89: A Study in Inner Biblical Exegesis', in A. Altman, ed., *Biblical and other Studies* (Philip W. Lown Institute of Advanced Judaic Studies, Brandeis University, 1963), pp. 29–46.

73. חזק and אמץ, verbs connoting strength (cf. the pair חזק and ואמץ), when intensified by Hiph'il or Pi'el, express the concept of keeping and holding; cf. Ps. 80.18 – תהי ידך על איש ימינך על בן אדם אמצת לך ('May your hand be on the man at your right, upon the man you held with you'); cf. also Isa. 41.10 – אמצתיך אף עזרתיך בימין צדקי ('I have taken hold of you and helped you. I kept you with my victorious right hand'). For an understanding of אמץ in Ps. 80.18 and Isa. 41.10 I am indebted to the late Professor H.L. Ginsberg.

74. Cf. Jer. 3.4, 19, and see below.

75. Cf. Sefire, p. 3, line 7 – שקרתם בעדיא אלן ('You will have been false to this treaty'); see W. Moran, 'Recensiones, G.W. Ahlström, *Psalm 89*', *Biblica* 42 (1961), p. 239. אמונה here and in v. 50 has the same meaning as אמנה in Neh. 10.1 (cf. J.C. Greenfield, 'Stylistic Aspects of the Sefire Treaty Inscriptions', *Acta Orientalia* 29 [1965], p. 8). אמונה in 2 Kgs 12.16 and 22.7 also, in my opinion, means pact or contract, and the reason for not calling to account the people in charge of the work was that they were bound by the oath to deal honestly. On the loyalty oath of craftsmen, see D.B. Weisberg, *Guild Structure and Political Allegiance in Early Achaemenid Mesopotamia* (1967).

adoption.[76] That this is really the case here may be learned from the treaty between Šupilluliuma and Mattiwaza.[77] Mattiwaza (or Kurtiwaza), in describing how he established relations with Šuppiluliuma, says: '(The great king) grasped me with [his ha]nd...and said: when I will conquer the land of Mittanni I shall not reject you, I shall make you my son,[78] I will stand by (to help in war) and will make you sit on the throne of your father...the word which comes out of his mouth will not turn back'.[79] A similar adoption imagery is to be found in the bilingual of Hattušili I.[80] In this document, which actually constitutes a testament, we read.[81] 'Behold, I declared for you the young Labarna: He shall sit on the throne, I, the king called him my son';[82] 'he is for you the offspring of my Sun' (he is for you the offspring of his majesty).[83] On the other hand, when he speaks of his rejected daughter he says, 'She did not call me father, I did not call her "my daughter",'[84] which reminds us of Ps. 89.27: 'He will say to me: "you are my father...and I will appoint (נתן) him as my first born"' (compare Jer. 3.4, 19).

Hattušili I himself is similarly described as adopted and legitimized by the sun goddess of Arinna: 'She put him into her bosom, grasped his hand and ran (in battle) before him'.[85] According to Psalm 89, David is also grasped and held by God's hand, as a result of which he succeeds in the battles with his enemies (vv. 22–26).[86] If the emendation of Ps. 2.7 is correct, then the idea of the heir placed

76. Cf., e.g., Yarimlim of Alalah, who is named son of Abban (see Wiseman, *AT* 444a, [n. 7] seal impression) but actually was the son of Hammurabi (*AT* 1.9; cf. *444b). According to A. Alt, 'Bemerkungen zu den Verwaltungs-und Rechtsurkunden von Ugarit und Alalach', *Die Welt des Orients*, Band 3, Heft 1–2 (1964), pp. 14ff., Abban adopted Yarimlim in order to create the legal basis for installing him as king of Haleb.

77. Weidner, *Politische Dokumente* (No. 4), No. 2, ll. 24ff. (pp. 40–41).

78. *ana mārūtija ēppuškami. ana marūti epēšu* means to adopt as a son; cf. E.A. Speiser, 'New Kirkuk Documents Relating to Family Laws', *AASOR* 10 (1930), pp. 7ff. Cf. also below.

79. *amātu ša ina pīšu uṣṣa ana kutallišu ul itār.*

80. F. Sommer and A. Falkenstein, *Die hethitisch-akkadische Bilingue des Hattušili I (Labarna II)*, Abhandlungen der bayerischen Akademie der Wissenschaften, Phil.-hist. Abt. N.F. 16 (1938).

81. *u a-nu-um-ma* TUR-*am la-ba-ar-na* [*aq-b*]*i-a-ak-ku-nu-ši-im šu-u li-it-ta-ša-ab-mi* LUGAL-*ru* [*al*]-*si-šu-ma* DUMU (?)-*am* (in Hittite, [*nu-uš-ma-aš* TUR-*la-an*] *la-ba- ar-na-an te-nu-un* [*a-pa-a-aš-ua-aš-ša-an e-ša-ru* LUGAL-*ša-an-za*] DUMU-*la-ma- an hal-z-ih-hu-un* (1/2; 2–4). The Akkadian *qabû* is equivalent to the Hittite *te* and the Hebrew אמר. In this context they have the same connotation as אמר אלי in Ps. 2.7, 'proclaim' or 'declare'. The newly appointed king is not the real son of Hattušili, but the son of his sister, who is being adopted.

82. Compare 1/2.37: 'Behold, Muršili is now my son'.

83. 2.44: NUMUN ^{d}UTU^{si} .KU .NU. Compare the Akkadian *ana marūti nadānu* in the sense of adopting; see S.M. Paul, 'Adoption Formulae', *Eretz Israel* 14, *H.L. Ginsberg Volume* (1978), p. 32 (Hebrew).

84. 3.24–25.

85. *ana sūnišu iškunšu u qāssu iṣbatsu, ina pānišu irtup alakam, KBo* 10,1 vv. 13–14 (cf. H. Otten, 'Keilschrifttexte', *MDOG* 91 [1958], p. 79 and A. Goetze, 'Review of *KBo* X', *JCS* 16 [1962], p. 125). For the corresponding Hittite restoration (*KBo* 10, 2 Vs. 1.28–30), see H.A. Hoffner, 'Birth and Name-Giving in Hittite Texts', *JNES* 27 (1968), p. 201 n. 27.

86. According to H.L. Ginsberg (private communication), Isa. 41.9ff., which also deals with grasping the hand and helping against enemies, refers to the election of Abraham (cf. end of v. 8),

into the bosom of his adoptant also occurs in connection with David.[87] It is also not without significance that the promise of Šupilluliuma to Kurtiwaza, as well as God's promise to David (v. 35), are accompanied by the declaration that the suzerain will not alter his word. Psalms 132.12 also says that 'the lord swore to David in truth from which he will not turn away'.

The notion of sonship within the promise of dynasty comes then to legitimize the grant of dynasty. It has nothing to do with mythology; it is a purely forensic metaphor. The metaphor is taken from the familial sphere,[88] as may be seen from the quoted Nuzi will. In this document, the father decrees that in case of disorder the rebellious son might be chained and confined but his inheritance rights will not be cancelled. The same concept is reflected in 2 Samuel 7, where the phrase הוכח בשבט ('chastening with the rod') is used, which in other places occurs in a didactic context (cf., e.g., Prov. 13.24; 23.14). Furthermore, on the basis of the comparison with the familial documents from Nuzi, the phrase 'rod of men' (אנשים) and afflictions of the sons of man (בני אדם) may now be properly understood. In the so-called *tuppi šīmti* documents from Nuzi published[89] and analysed by Speiser,[90] we find often, in connection with the provisions about obedience to the adoptive father,[91] phrases such as 'If PN_1 (the adopted child) fails to show respect for PN_2 (the adoptive father) then just as a man treats his son too shall PN_2 treat PN_1'.[92] Another document says that 'just as one treats the citizen of Arrapha, so should PN_1 treat PN_2; he shall put fetters upon his feet, place a mark on his hand, and put him in the house of detention.[93] The intention is clear: the

which supports our view about the common typology of the Davidic and Abrahamic covenants. On 'grasping the hand' in Deutero-Isaiah and the corresponding neo-Babylonian royal imagery, see S. Paul, 'Deutero-Isaiah and Cuneiform Royal Inscriptions', *JAOS* 88 (1968), p. 182, n. 19.

87. אספה אל חיקי,אמר אליו ('I will gather him to my bossom, I will say to him') instead of אספרה אל חק,ה׳ אמר אלי ('I will recite the law, YHWH said to me'). Cf. H. Gunkel, *Psalmen* (HKAT; Göttingen, 1929) *ad loc.*, which follows Torczyner. For אסף in the sense of adoption, see Ps. 27.10.

88. Cf. Ruth 4.6 and see Hoffner, 'Birth', etc., *JNES* (no. 85). We must admit however, that putting into the bosom as such does not necessarily indicate adoption; it may just as well signify care and protection. T. Jacobsen ('Parerga Sumerologica', *JNES* 2 [1943], p. 120) denies that nourishing by the goddess or placing on her knee in Sumero-Akkadian literature implies adoption. Similarly, giving birth on one's knees in the Old Testament (Gen. 16.2; 30.3; 50.23) does not necessarily imply adoption; see J. Tigay, 'Adoption', *Encyclopedia Judaica* 2, cols. 298–301.

89. E.R. Lacheman, *Excavations at Nuzi VIII: Family Law Documents* (1962).

90. E.A. Speiser, 'A Significant New Will from Nuzi', *JCS* 17 (1963), pp. 65–71; cf. also E. Cassin, 'Nouvelles données sur les relations familiales à Nuzi', *RA* 57 (1963), pp. 113–19.

91. This means, of course, anybody who assumes parenthood of the children (*ana abbūti*) as, for instance, the wife or the daughter of the one who draws the will.

92. *šumma* PN_1=PN_2 *lā* [*ipal*]*laḫšu u kīme awēlu māršu huddumumma ippuš kinannama huddumumma ippuš* (JEN 572.26–31). Cf. the analysis of this passage by Speiser (n. 90), pp. 68–69. According to Speiser, *huddumumma epēšu* means to discipline. Cassin (n. 90), p. 116 translates it as 'enfermer'.

93. *kīme māršu ša awīl Arraphe ippušu, kinannama* PN_1-PN_2 *ippuššuma, kurṣâ ina šēpešu išakkan, abbuta ina qaqqadišu išakkan, ina bīt kīlī inandin (Nuzi VIII*, HSS 19, 39.16–23) (n. 89); cf. Speiser (n. 90), p. 69; E. Cassin, 'Pouvoir', *RA* 63 (1969), p. 134 (n. 68).

son given into adoption has the duties of a son (i.e., respecting his parents) but has also the privileges of a son: he has to be treated like the son of a free citizen and not like a slave. This is implied in another document of this collection, where the father says that the adoptive parent 'may act as though she were I'.[94] This kind of privilege for the adopted can be traced back to the Old Babylonian period. In a document of adoption by manumission, the master of the manumitted slave says, 'If Zugagu will say to his father Sinabušu 'you are not my father' they will impose upon him the punishment of the free born',[95] i.e., he will not be enslaved but disciplined as the son of a free citizen.[96]

What is meant, then, in 2 Sam. 7.14, is that when David's descendants sin they will be disciplined like rebellious sons by their father,[97] but they will not be alienated. One must say that this lenient approach toward rebellious sons was not the rule in familial relationship in the ancient Near East. On the contrary, in most cases rebelliousness brought about the dissolution of sonship, be it sonship by birth or by adoption.[98] Among the quoted adoption documents from Nuzi we find that the adoptive parent may chastise the disobedient son but may also disinherit him if he wants.[99] Similarly, we find that the Hittite suzerain did not always grant land unconditionally. In a land grant of Muršili II to Abiradda, the Hittite suzerain guarantees the rights of DU-Tešup, Abiradda's son, to throne, house, and land, only on the condition that DU-Tešup will not sin (*waštai-*) against his father.[100]

94. *k*[*īma*] *yâši eteppuš* (*Nuzi VIII*, HSS 19, 19.31–32) (n. 89); cf. Speiser, 'New Will from Nuzi' (n. 90), p. 70 and n. 22 for the grammatical problem involved.

95. PN *ana* PN *abišu ula abi atta iqabbīma, aran mārū awīlē immidūšu* (M. Schorr, *Urkunden* [No. 10], 1913, 23.23–27, p. 46).

96. Contrary to Schorr (*ibid.*), who understands it as deprivation of freedom, i.e., enslavement.

97. B. Jacob ('Das hebräische Sprachgut im Christlich-Palästinischen' (*ZAW* 22 [1902], pp. 91–92) interprets בשבט אנשים בנגעי בני אדם 'Schlage wie sie die Kinder vom Vater erhalten d.h. aus Liebe und daher mit Maassen', which generally fits our understanding of the phrase. However, his interpretation of אדם and אנשים as 'parents', literally (on the basis of the Palestinian Syriac *'nšwt'*), is not warranted. It might as well be understood as 'human' (cf. Hos. 11.4, בחבלי אדם אמשכם בעבתת אהבה ('I drew them with human cords, with bands of love').

98. Cf., e.g., CH, 168–69 and the discussion in G.R. Driver and J.C. Miles' *The Babylonian Laws* 1 (1952), pp. 348–49, 395–405. These laws apply to the real son as well as the adopted, as may be learned from a Nuzi document (*Nuzi I*, HSS 5 [No. 63], p. 7), where it is stated that the adopted son might be disinherited following repeated trials (11.25ff.), which is similar in attitude to CH, 168–69, according to which the son is to be disinherited only after being brought up before the judges for the second time. Compare Deut. 21.18–21, where the rebellious son is to be condemned to death only after being previously chastised. For dissolution of sonship as a result of disobedience, cf. also RS 8.145 (F. Thureau-Dangin, 'Trois contrats de Ras-Shamra', *Syria* 18 [1937], pp. 249–50).

99. PN *kurṣi inandinšu abbuta umaššarsu, ina bīt kīlī inandin, šumma hašihšu kirba*[*na*] *iheppe u ukaššašu k*[*īma*] *yâši eteppuš* ('PN may put fetters upon him, apply the slave mark to him, put him in the house of detention or, if it pleases her, break the clump of clay to disinherit him [*kuššudu*], she may act as though she were I' (*Nuzi VIII*, HSS 19, 19.28–32) (n. 89).

100. F. Hrozny, *Hethitische Keilschrifttexte aus Boghazköi* (Boghazköi Studien, 3, 1919), pp. 142–44, vv. 2.10–18; J. Friedrich, 'Aus dem hethitischen Schrifttum, 2 Heft', *Der Alte Orient* 24.3 (1925), p. 20, ll. 10–18; cf. also E. Vavaignac, 'L'affaire de Iaruvatta', *RHA* 6 (January 1932), p. 196; H. Klengel, 'Der Schiedsspruch des Muršili II', *Orientalia*, NS 32 (1963), pp. 35–36, 41–42.

The unconditional promise is therefore a special privilege and apparently given for extraordinarily loyal service.

In connection with David, this privilege is also reflected in that David is given the right of the first born. As is now known to us from Nuzi, Alalah, Ugarit and Palestine,[101] the father had the right to select a 'firstborn' as well as to make all his heirs share alike,[102] and was not bound by the law of primogeniture.[103] Needless to say, the selection of the firstborn elevated the chosen son to a privileged position in the family and thus entitled him to a double share in the inheritance. Indeed, the phrase בכור אתנהו (Ps. 89.28) means 'I will *appoint* him or make him firstborn', which speaks for a given right and not one acquired by nature. The titles 'son' and 'firstborn' are also attested among Mesopotamian kings; see M.J. Seux, *Épitètes royales Akkadiennes et Sumériennes*, pp. 42–44.

In fact, not only David is named the firstborn to God; Israel itself is called by God 'my son the firstborn Israel' (Exod. 4.22; cf. Jer. 31.8), and as the adoption of David is supposed to legitimize the inheritance of nations, i.e., the Davidic empire, the adoption of Israel by God is supposed to validate the gift of land. Though this is not expressed explicitly in the Pentateuch it is clearly indicated in a prophetic text (Jer. 3.19), where we read, 'I said I will surely[104] put you among the sons (I will adopt you as a son, ואנכי אמרתי איך (אך) אשיתך בבנים)[105] and give you a pleasant land, the goodliest heritage of the host of nations, and I said you shall call me my father[106] and you will not turn away from me'. The phrase אשיתך בבנים ('I will put you among the sons') undoubtedly alludes to adoption, as Ehrlich indicated, and as such anticipates the inheritance of the land.[107]

101. Cf. I. Mendelsohn, 'On the Preferential Status of the Eldest Son', *BASOR* 156 (December 1959), pp. 38–40 and the references there.

102. Cf., e.g., *ina libbišunu ša māriya rabi yānu* ('there is none among them who shall be the oldest'), *Nuzi VIII* (No. 89) HSS 19 23.5–6; cf. 17.12–13; see Speiser, 'New Will from Nuzi', *JCS* 17 (1963), p. 66 (No. 65) and the discussion on p. 70.

103. This is prohibited in the Deuteronomic Code (21.15–17). The Deuteronomic Law stands in clear contradiction to Gen. 48.13–20, where Joseph, the son of the loved woman Rachel, is given the double share, while Reuben, the son of the 'unloved' Leah (cf. Gen. 29.33 – שנואה), is repudiated as the firstborn.

104. Read אכה instead of איכה; cf. A. Ehrlich, *Randglossen zur hebr. Bibel, ad loc.*

105. Cf. the new JPS translation of *The Torah* (1978): 'I had resolved to adopt you as my son'. Cf. in the Azitawadda inscription, *w'p b'bt p'ln kl mlk* ('and every king made me his father [his suzerain]'); see N.H. Tur-Sinai (Torczyner), *The Language and the Book II* (2nd edn, 1964), p. 76 (Hebrew). The Greek *poieīsthai* (the Hebrew פעל, the Akkadian *epēšu*) or *thesthai* (the Hebrew שים,שית) are the verbs used for adoption. וישימו בנים in Ezra 10.44 implies adoption (cf. S. Feigin, 'Some Cases of Adoption in Israel', *JBL* 50 [1931], pp. 196ff., though we do not accept his restoration). For the Akkadian *ana abbūti epēšu* as adoption see the discussion by S.M. Paul, 'Adoption Formulae' (n. 83), pp. 33, n. 23.

106. Inheritance of land in connection with divine sonship (בני אל) occurs in Deut. 32.8 (Septuagint and Qumran). Compare the cone of Enmetena of Lagash, 'Enlil, the king of all the lands, the father of all the gods, marked off the boundary for Ningirsu (god of Lagash) and Shara (god of Umma) by his steadfast word' (Cone A, 1–7); cf. F. Thureau-Dangin, *Die sumerischen und akkadischen Königinschriften* (1907), p. 36; J.S. Cooper, *Presargonic Inscriptions* (1986), p. 55.

107. Cf. above, p. 212.

The use of familial metaphors to express relationships belonging to the royal-national sphere should not surprise us, since the whole diplomatic vocabulary of the second millenium BCE[108] is rooted in the familial sphere. For instance, the relationship between the states is defined as *abbūtu* = fathership (suzerainty); *mārūtu* = sonship (vassalship); *ahhūtu* = brotherhood (parity relationship). The phrase *itti nakrīya lū nakrāta itti salmīya lū salmāta*, 'with my enemy be an enemy, with my friend be a friend', which is so common in the Hittite-Ugaritic treaties,[109] is already found in the Elamite treaty of the third millennium BCE.[110] This phrase is found in an Old Babylonian marriage contract in which we read *zenî ša* PN_1 PN_2 *izenni salāmiša isallim* = 'PN_2 (the second wife) will be angry with whom PN_1 (the first wife) will be angry, she will be on good terms with whom PN_1 will be on good terms.'[111] Similarly, we read in a Mari adoption document, *damaqišuni idammiq lemenišunu ilemmin* ('their joy will be his joy, their sorrow will be his sorrow').[112] The close relationship of familial and political alliances has also been seen long ago by N. Glueck,[113] who says, 'Allies had the same rights and obligations as those who were blood relatives'.

Thus, the gift of land to Abraham and the gift of kingship to David are formulated in the way Hittite grants used to be formulated, particularly those grants bestowing gifts upon privileged vassals. Contrary to the prevalent law in the Hittite kingdom,[114] in Ugarit,[115] and in Alalah,[116] according to which the property of the condemned is to be confiscated, in the cited documents the property of the condemned cannot be taken away.

It was the Deuteronomist, the redactor of the book of Kings, who put the promise of David under a condition (1 Kgs 2.4; 8.25; 9.4f.), as did Deuteronomy

108. Cf. J. Munn-Rankin, 'Diplomacy in Western Asia in the Early Second Millennium B.C.', *Iraq* 18 (1956), pp. 68ff.

109. Cf. *PRU* 4, pp. 36, 49 passim. From the Hittites it passed to the Greeks; see my article 'Covenant Terminology' (n. 12) *JAOS* 93 (1973), p. 198 and n. 103.

110. Cf. W. Hinz, 'Elams Vertrag mit Naram-Sin von Akkade', *ZA* 24 (1967), pp. 66ff. See also the text in *Baghdader Mitteilungen* 2 [1963], p. 54, which according to F.R. Kraus, *Bibliotheca Orientalis* 22 [1965], p. 289) is part of a treaty, where we read: [*lu a-n*]*a-ki-ir* [*is-l*]*i-mu lu-u a-sa-li-im*.

111. M. Schorr, *Urkunden des altbabylonischen Zivil – und Prozessrechts* (VAB, 5; Leipzig, 1913), 4.21–23; cf. 5.7–8; Schorr's translation is wrong and Ungnad's is incorrect; see p. 11 there. Cf. *CAD* v. 21 (Z) *zenû* b.

112. ARM 8 1.4–5. R. Yaron, 'Varia on Adoption', *Journal of Juristic Papyrology* 15 (1965), pp. 173–75, discussed this text in the context of some of the above-mentioned texts and reached similar conclusions.

113. *Hesed in the Bible* (n. 17) (1967), p. 46.

114. Cf., e.g., Friedrich, *Staatsverträge* (n. 4), No. 3, 7C.13–17 (pp. 112ff.); V. Korošec, 'Juristische Bemerkungen' (No. 53), pp. 218ff., although the different attitudes toward the condemned do not reflect a historical development, as Korošec puts it, but might be explained as a double standard: to the privileged on the one hand and to the unprivileged on the other.

115. *PRU* 3, 16.249.22–29 (pp. 97–98); 16.145 (p. 169, *bēl arni*).

116. *AT* No. 17 (p. 40 – *bēl mašikti*). See S.E. Loewenstamm, 'Notes on the Alalah Tablets', *Comparative Studies in Biblical and Ancient Oriental Literatures* (AOAT, 20; 1980), pp. 23–26.

with the promise to the Patriarchs.[117] The exile of Northern Israel, the destruction of Jerusalem, and the disruption of the dynasty refuted, of course, the claim of the eternity of the Abrahamic and Davidic covenants, thereby necessitating a reinterpretation of the covenants. This was done by making them conditional, i.e., by asserting that the covenant is eternal only if the donee keeps his loyalty to the donor. It is true, even in the predeuteronomic documents, that the loyalty of David's sons and the sons of the Patriarchs is somehow presupposed,[118] but it is never formulated as the condition for national existence as in Deuteronomic literature. In the JE source, Israel is never threatened with destruction for violating the law. The non-observance of the covenant will certainly bring punishment (Exod. 33.33; 34.12) but no annihilation. Even the parenetic section of Exodus 19.5–6, which sounds like a condition, is in fact a promise and not a threat: 'If you will obey me faithfully and keep my covenant you shall be a treasured possession (סגלה).[119] Indeed all the earth is mine but you shall be to me a kingdom of priests and a holy nation'.[120] The observance of loyalty in this passage is not a condition for the fulfillment of God's grace, as in Deuteronomy (cf. 7.12f.; 11.13f.), but a prerequisite for high and extraordinary status.

The Priestly Code also, in spite of the curses and the threat of exile in Leviticus 26, does not end with the breach of the covenant; on the contrary, it has God saying: 'Even when they are in the land of their enemies I will not reject them or spurn them so as to destroy them, violating my covenant with them (להפר בריתי אתם). I will remember in their favour[121] the covenant with the ancients (וזכרתי להם ברית ראשנים)' (Lev. 26.44–45). Deuteronomy, however, concludes chapter

117. It is significant that in spite of frequent references to the promise of the Patriarchs, Deuteronomy never mentions the eternity of this promise (עד עולם,לדורותם,ברית עולם), in contrast to JE and P; see below.

118. Cf. Gen. 18.19. This is an expectation and not a condition.

119. For the meaning of סגלה and its Akkadian equivalent *sikiltum*, see M. Greenberg, 'Hebrew *segullā*: Akkadian *sikiltu*', *JAOS* 71 (1951), pp. 172ff. Cf. now *PRU* 5, 60 (18.38), 11.7–12 (p. 84), where the Ugaritic vassal is called the *sglt* of his suzerain, which is rendered by C. Virolleaud as *propriété*. The *sglt* in the Ugaritic text now elucidates the סגלה in the Pentateuch. It seems that *sglt* and סגלה belong to the treaty and covenant terminology and that they are employed to distinguish the special relationships of the suzerains to their vassals. On the basis of Ugaritic, biblical and also Alalahian evidence (cf. the seal impression in D.J. Wiseman, *AT*, p. 3, where the king Abban is said to be the *sikiltum* of the goddess), we may safely say that the basic meaning of the root *sakālu* is to set aside a thing or certain property either with good intention (as Israel is set aside form other nations) or with an evil purpose, as in CH 141 and other Babylonian sources. Cf. the discussion by M. Held, in 'A Faithful Lover in an Old Babylonian Dialogue', *JCS* 15 (1961), pp. 11–12. For the Ugaritic text, cf. also H.B. Huffmon and S.B. Parker, 'A Further Note on the Treaty Background of Hebrew *yada'*', *BASOR* 184 (1966), pp. 36ff.; S.E. Loewenstamm, *'Am Segulla', Hebrew Language Studies Presented to Z. ben-Hayyim* (1983), pp. 321–28.

120. As a reward for her loyalty, Israel will in turn be God's most precious possession – she will be God's priesthood. A similar idea is indeed expressed in the consolation prophecy in Isa. 61.6: 'And you shall be called the priests of YHWH. You will be named servants of our God, you shall eat the wealth of nations and in their splendor you shall excel'. For a thorough discussion of this passage see W.L. Moran, 'A Kingdom of Priests', in J. McKenzie (ed.), *The Bible in Current Catholic Thought* (1962), pp. 7–20.

121. Cf. above, pp. 207–208.

28 with the threat that the people will be sent back to Egypt, and no allusion to the grace of the covenant is made.[122]

The Covenant with Abraham in Genesis 15[123]

In light of our analysis we properly understand the nature of the covenant in Genesis 15: God as the suzerain commits himself and swears, as it were, to keep the promise.[124] It is he, accompanied by a smoking kiln and a blazing torch (תנור עשן ולפיד אש),[125] who passes between the parts as though he were invoking the curse upon himself.

A similar oath occurs in the Abban-Yarimlim deed, where Abban, the donor, takes the oath by cutting the neck of a lamb (*kišād 1 immeru iṭbuh*), saying '(may I be cursed) if I take back what I gave you'.[126] In another document, which completes the data of this gift, we read: 'On that day Abban in exchange for Irridi gave the city... On that day Yarimlim delivered (or brought up) to Ištar...',[127] which seems to reflect a situation similar to that of the covenant in Genesis 15, i.e., that the inferior party delivers the animals while the superior swears the oath.

In Alalah as in Genesis 15 the animals slaughtered at the scene of the covenant are considered sacrificial offerings.[128] That the act of cutting the neck of the animal is of sacrificial nature may be learned from another covenantal description

122. Deut. 30.1–10 and 4.29–31 are of a later origin and revolve around the Deuteronomic doctrine of return to God; cf. H.W. Wolff., 'Das Kerygma des deuteronomistischen Geschichtswerks', *ZAW* 73 (1961), pp. 180ff., and recently M. Weinfeld, *DDS 1–11* (*AB*, 1991), pp. 216–17.

123. See the bibliography in C. Westermann, *Genesis* (I BK 14, 1979), pp. 247–50.

124. On the covenant with Abraham in Gen. 15 as representing an oath, cf. Lohfink, *Die Landverheissung* (n. 1), pp. 11–23.

125. Compare the Sinaitic theophany where God appears in fire and smoke; cf. Exod. 19.18, 'for YHWH had come down upon it in fire (אש) and the smoke (עשן) rose like the smoke of a kiln'. In the commentary of the Syrian church father Ephrem (quoted by T. Zachariae; see J.C. Greenfield, 'An Ancient Treaty Ritual and its Targumic Echo', *Salvacion en la Palabra, Targum – Derash – Berith: Homenaje al Profesor A. Diez Macho* [1985], p. 395, we find the tradtion 'that the Chaldeans would solemnize a pact by passing through the dissecting parts holding torches'.

126. D.J. Wiseman, 'Abban and Alalah', *JCS* 12 (1958), p. 126, ll. 39–42; cf. n. 10 above. In the continuation Abban states that if Yarimlim betrays him he will forfeit his territory, thus making the gift conditional. We must, however, keep in mind that the deed of Abban to Yarimlim is not a deed of grant but rather of exchange. Alalah was given to Yarimlim in place of the destroyed Irridi. The gift of Alalah is therefore not a reward for loyal service as is the case in grants, but part of a political arrangement between two parties.

127. *ina ūmišu Yarimlim*...[*ana*[d]]*Ištar ušēlî*, reading with *CAD* E, p. 130. According to Lohfink (*Landverheissung* [n. 1], pp. 93ff.) the tradition of Gen. 15.7ff. reflects an incubation dream in a sanctuary (Hebron or Shechem). If true, this might be an additional parallel with the Alalah covenant.

128. Cf. *Jubilees* 14.9ff.; Pseudo-Philo, *Biblical Antiquities* 23.6–7; Apocalypse of Abraham 9–15; Josephus, *Antiq*. I, 183–85; see C.T. Begg, 'Rereadings of the 'Animal Rite' of Gen. 15 in Early Jewish Narratives', *CBQ* 50 (1988), pp. 36–46. For the sacrificial nature of the offerings brought to the ceremony in Gen. 15, see E. Loewenstamm, 'Zur Traditionsgeschichte des Bundes zwischen den Stücken', *VT* 18 (1968), pp. 500ff. (in English in *AOAT* 204, [1980], pp. 273–80). *VT* 18 (1968), pp. 500ff. (in English in *AOAT* 204, [1980], pp. 273–80). However, in view of the evidence presented here, we cannot accept his opinion that the sacrifice is a late element in the tradition of Gen. 15.

in Alalah, where we read, 'the neck of a sacrificial lamb was cut in the presence of PN the general'.[129] A later Alalahian covenantal text[130] tells us about offerings[131] in connection with the oath of the vassal Idrimi to his Hurrian suzerain.[132] The ancient covenant in Exodus 24 is wholly based upon sacrifices, and the secular Patriarchal covenants are also ratified by sacrifices (Gen. 21.27).[133]

In Greece, too, sacrifices were offered at the covenant ceremony.[134] Thus we read in the *Iliad* 3.103–07 that for the covenant with the Achaeans the Trojans bring two lambs and a ram and prepare libations (3.268ff.). Furthermore, as in Genesis 15.9, in Greece three animals (*trityes*), a bull, a ram and a boar, were usually taken for the covenantal rite.[135] The offerings of the *lustrum* in Rome also consisted of three animals (*souvetaurilia*), a boar, a sheep and a bull (*sus, ovis, taurus*), and according to Dionysus of Halicarnassus, the triple sacrifice consisted of a bull, a ram and a goat,[136] as in Genesis 15.9.

This tradition of covenantal sacrifices goes back to the third millennium BCE. In the treaty between Lagash and Umma, recorded on the stele of the vultures, we hear about sacrificing a bull[137] and two doves.[138] The doves remind us of the

129. AT* 54.16–18: GÚ SILÁ *a-sa-ki* IGI PN UGULA UKÚ.UŠ *ṭa-bi-ih* (cf. A. Draffkorn 'King Abba-AN' (No. 7), *JCS* 13 (1959), p. 95, No. 11). The presence of the general at this transaction may be paralleled with Gen. 21.22f. and the Yahwistic counterpart in 26.26ff., where the covenant between Abimelech and Abraham and Isaac, respectively, is made in the presence of Phicol the general. For אחזת מרעהו, who joins פיכל in 26.26, cf. Jonathan D. Safran, 'Ahuzzath and the Pact of Beer-Sheba', in M. Cogan (ed.), *Beer-Sheva 2: Presented to S. Abramsky on his Retirement* (1985), pp. 121–30 (Hebrew). According to Safran, מרעהו is equivalent to *merhum* in Mari, who is in charge of the pasture lands.

130. S. Smith, *The Statue of Idri-mi* (1949); for a thorough investigation of this inscription see E.L. Greenstein and D. Marcus, 'The Akkadian Inscription of Idrimi', *The Journal of the Ancient Near Eastern Society of Columbia University* 8 (1976), pp. 59–76.

131. See ll. 55–56 – SISKUR (*niqê*) *ušarbi* (I multiplied offerings); cf. ll. 89–90.

132. E. Szlechter, 'Les tablettes juridiques datées du règne d'Abî-ešuh̲ conservées au Musée d'art et d'histoire de Genève', *JCS* 7 (1953), p. 92, 5.16–17; A. Goetze, 'Critical Review of S. Smith *The Statue of Idri-mi*', *JCS* 4 (1950), p. 228, n. 20.

133. We are told there that Abraham gave seven lambs to Abimelech as a 'witness' (עדה) or as Speiser (*Genesis*, *AB*, *ad loc.*) translates, a 'proof' for his rights on the well. A similar procedure is found in an old Babylonian act of partition where one of the partners gives to the other two lambs as a proof of the agreement (E. Szlechter, *JCS* 7 [1953], p. 92, 5.16–17). Cf. also A. Goetze, *JCS* 4 (1950), p. 228, n. 20.

134. Cf. P. Stengel, *Die griechische Kultusaltertümer* (1920), p. 119, n. 7; 137; M.P. Nilsson, *Geschichte des griechischen Relgion*, I^3 (1967), pp. 139ff.; W. Burkert, *Griechische Religion* (1977), pp. 133ff.

135. Cf. P. Stengel, *Griechische Kultusaltertümer* (n. 134), pp. 119, 137f.

136. It was pointed out that the later Greeks sometimes performed such sacrifices and the knowledge of such sacrifices may have misled the scribe of the work of Dionysius; see E. Cary, *Dionysius Halicarnasseusis* (Loeb Classical Library, 1939), pp. 338–39.

137. Rev. 1.37–40, *Utu lugal ni-sig$_{10}$-ga-ra larsam (ki) e-babbar NINDÁ + GUD-še an-ku*, which is translated by E. Sollberger (*Le système verbal dans les inscriptions 'royales' presargoniques de Lagaš* [1952], example 161), a Utu, le roi étincelant, à Larsa dans L'Ebabbar, j'y ai fait le sacrifice (alimentaire). Compare *idem*, *Inscriptions royales Sumériennes et Akkadiennes* (1971), p. 54. The passage is not altogether clear; some scholars take the phrase to mean that the doves were offered *like*

pigeon and the turtledove in Genesis 15, whereas the NINDA + GUD (fattened bull), which equals Akkadian *bīru*, is in many cases three years old[139] and may therefore be paralleled with Gen. 15.9. An offering of a similar kind, though in a different context (lustration), is found in Lev. 14.4, 49, where two birds are taken, along with cedar wood, crimson stuff, and hyssop.

Release of birds for lustration is very common is Mesopotamia and Anatolia.[140] Especially instructive are the Hittite lustrations, where we find, as in Leviticus, cords of red wool, etc., put on the head of the substitute like a crown.[141]

In the covenantal ceremony of Genesis 15, as in the treaty between Lagash and Umma, it is very difficult to distinguish between the sacrifice proper and the lustration; we may have a combination of both here. Indeed, the rite of passing between the pieces of the victims originated in Asia Minor and had been propagated in the sphere of Hittite influence; cf. E.J. Bickerman, 'Couper une alliance', *Archives d'histoire du droit Oriental* 5 (1950–51), pp. 141ff. Cf. Also S. Henninger, 'Was bedeuted die rituelle Teilung eines Tieres in zwei Hälften?' *Biblica* 34 (1953), pp. 344–53. Especially interesting for our discussion is the case in which a man, a goat, a puppy, and a little pig were cut, and the soldiers had to pass between the pieces (see O. Masson, 'A propos d'un rituel Hittite pour la lustration d'une armée: le rite de purification par le passage entre les deux parties d'une victime', *RHR* 137 [1950], pp. 5–25). An oath accompanied by passing between the pieces is found in Greece: electing a candidate for office is done by passing between the pieces of the sacrifice while walking toward the altar (Plato, *Laws* 753d).

In Mari we encounter a ritual accompanying the covenant (*ARM* 2.37) that also does not look sacrificial. For the covenant between the Haneans and the land

sacrificial bulls (see J.S. Cooper, *Presargonic Inscriptions* [1986], p. 36 and the references there, pp. 33–34), but in the other paragraphs the doves are being released and not sacrificed. Cf. also G. Steiner, 'Der Grenzvertrag Zwischen Lagaš und Umma', *Acta Sumerologica* 8 (1986), pp. 219ff. C.T. Begg ('The Covenantal Dove in Ps. 84.19–20', *VT* 37 [1987], pp. 78–80), interprets Ps. 84.19–20, where *twr* (dove) is mentioned next to *bĕrit* (covenant), on the basis of Gen. 15.9, 17.

138. 'Two doves on whose eyes he had put kohl (and) on whose heads he had strewn cedar he released them to Enlil at Nippur (with the plea): "As long as days exist…if the Ummaite…breaks his word…"'

139. Cf. *bīru* B, *CAD* B, p. 266. The three-year-old bull in 1 Sam. 1.24 (Septuagint and Qumran) and the three-year-old animals in Gen. 15 do not therefore reflect precisely a Shilonite tradition, as Loewenstamm contends (loc cit). It seems that the three-year-old-animal was considered of good quality in general; cf., e.g., *1 immeru ša šullušītu damqu* ('one three-year-old sheep of good quality', C.J. Gadd, *Tablets from Kirkuk, RA* 23 [1926], p. 154, No. 47.15); *šullušīta enza* ('a three-year-old she-goat') in connection with a feast (*Anatolian Studies* 6 [1956], p. 152.15, 44); *1 alpu šuluššu ešru sa*…PN *ana Ebabbara iddinu* ('the three-year old ox, the tithe which PN has given to Ebabbara') (J.N. Strassmaier, *Inschriften von Nabonidus, König von Babylon* [1889], No. 1071.1). For cattle and sheep and their ages in Mesopotamia, cf. *MSL* 5 Vol. 1 and esp. p. 67 there. For the age adjective *šuluššu*, cf. also עגלת שלשיה (Isa. 15.5; Jer. 48.34) and see Mishnah *Parah* 1.1 שלשית.

140. Cf. David P. Wright, *The Disposal of Impurity: Elimination Rites in the Bible and in the Hittite and Mesopotamian Literature* (1986), pp. 80–83.

141. *Ibid.*, p. 56.

of Idamaraṣ, the provincial tribes brought a young dog and a she-goat, which the king of Mari did not permit but gave the command to use a donkey foal (*hayaru*) instead. The 'killing of a donkey foal' (*hayaram qatālum*) for a covenant ceremony was so common that this phrase was tantamount to 'making a covenant'.[142] In the ceremony of Genesis 15, the passing between the parts symbolizes the self-curse, similar to the act of 'seizing the throat', but this does not nullify the sacrificial nature of the ceremony. On the contrary, the ritual adds solemnity to the oath. It is only in the covenantal ceremonies of the first millennium that the sacrificial element gradually disappears and gives way to the dramatic act. Thus, the neo-Assyrian treaty and the Deuteronomic covenant become binding and valid not by virtue of the treaty ritual but by the oath-imprecation (the *māmītu*)[143] that accompanies the ceremony. The ritual itself – if it was performed – served only a symbolic and dramatic end: to tangibly impress upon the vassal the consequences that would follow inevitably should he infringe the covenant. The treaty between Ashurnirari V and Mati'ilu of Bit-Agusi[144] even states explicitly that the ram is brought forward in the treaty ceremony not for sacrificial purposes but to serve as a palpable example of the punishment awaiting the transgressor of the treaty (Drohritus): 'This ram was not taken from its flock for sacrifice (UDU.SISKUR), it has been brought to conclude the treaty of Ashur-nirari, king of Assyria, with Mati'ilu, if Mati'ilu [shall violate] the covenant and oath to the gods, then just as this ram, which was taken from its flock and to its flock will not return, and not behold its flock again, so Mati'ilu with his sons (ministers), the men of his land, shall be taken from his land, and to his land he shall not return, and not (behold) his country again' (col. 1, ll. 10ff.).

Like Saul, who cut a yoke of oxen into pieces and proclaimed, 'Whoever does not come after Saul and Samuel, so shall it be done to his oxen' (1 Sam. 11.7),[145] Bar Ga'yah declared in his treaty with Mati''el, '[As] this calf is cut apart so shall Mati''el be cut apart'.[146] Zedekiah's covenant with the people on the manumission of the slaves (Jer. 34.8–22) is to be understood in an analogous manner. Hence, those passing between the two parts of the calf (v. 18) must have accepted the consequences ensuing from a violation of the oath-imprecation: 'So may it befall me if I shall not observe the words of the covenant'.[147] Dramatic

142. Cf. M. Held, 'Philological Notes on the Mari Covenantal Rituals', *BASOR* 200 (1970), pp. 32–40.

143. Cf. M. Weinfeld, *DDS* (1972), pp. 102–104.

144. See E. Weidner, 'Der Staatsvertrag Aššurnirāris VI von Assyrien mit Mati'ilu von bit Agusi', *AfO* 8 (1932), pp. 17–34; E. Reiner, *ANET*^{3}, pp. 532–33; R. Borger, 'Assyrische Staatsverträge', in O. Kaiser, *Texte aus der Umwelt des Alten Testaments*, Band 1 Lieferung 2 (1983), pp. 155–58; S. Parpola and K. Watanabe, *Neo-Assyrian Treaties and Loyalty Oaths* (State Archives of Assyria, 2, 1988), pp. 8–13.

145. Compare the Mari letter (*ARM* 2, 48), where it is proposed to cut off the head of a culprit and circulate it among the cities of Hana so that the troops may fear and quickly assemble.

146. [*w'yk zy*] *ygzr 'glh znh kn ygzr mt''l*; see J.A. Fitzmyer, *The Aramaic Inscriptions of Sefire*, I (1967), A.39–40.

147. See W. Rudolph, *Jeremia* (HAT, 2nd edn, 1985), p. 205.

acts of this sort were not, however, performed only with animals. In the Sefire treaty,[148] in the vassal treaties of Esarhaddon,[149] and in Hittite military oath-taking ceremonies,[150] similar acts were performed with wax images and other objects.[151] Generally speaking, however, it appears that this was not a requisite part of the ceremony. Many Hittite and Assyrian treaties make no mention of such acts, and neither does the book of Deuteronomy. Apparently the oath-imprecation, which was recorded in the treaty document, was believed to be enough to deter the treaty party from violating the stipulations of the treaty.

Distinction should therefore be made between the covenant in Genesis 15 (which, like the covenants of Alalah and Mari, preserves the sacrificial element alongside the symbolic one), and the covenant in Jeremiah 34, in which the ceremony, although performed before God, seems to be nothing more than a self-curse dramatized by a symbolic act. Another difference between Genesis 15 and Jeremiah 34 is that while in Genesis 15, as in the Abban deed, it is the superior party who places himself under oath, in Jeremiah 34, as in the treaty of Ashur-nirari V, the vassals are the parties who commit themselves to their masters.

The Legal Formulae in the Covenant with Abraham

It has already been indicated that the legal formulae expressing the gift of land to Abraham are identical to the legal formulae of conveyance of property in the ancient Near East.[152] Especially instructive in this case are the formulations of conveyance in perpetuity. For example, the formulae, 'for your descendants forever' (לזרעך עד עולם – Gen. 13.15) and 'for your descendants after you throughout their generations' (לזרעך אחריך לדרתם[153] – Gen. 17.7–8)[154] are identical to

148. 1A.35–42.

149. D.J. Wiseman, *Vassal Treaties* (n. 11), ll. 608–11.

150. J. Friedrich, 'Der hethitische Soldateneid', *ZA* 35 (1924), p. 163, 1.41–45; 2.1–3; see now N. Oettinger, *Die militärischen Eide der Hethiter* (Studien zu den Bogazköy Texten, 22, 1976).

151. This type of symbolism was also employed in Babylonian magic; see E. Reiner, *Šurpu: A Collection of Sumerian and Akkadian Incantations* 3, *AfO* 11 (1958); pp. 60–112.

152. Cf. J.J. Rabinowitz, *Jewish Law* (1956), pp. 130–31; *idem*, 'The Susa Tablets', *VT* 11 (1961), pp. 55ff.

153. As Loewenstamm indicated in his article 'The Divine Grants of Land to the Patriarchs', *JAOS* 94 (1971), pp. 509–10 (AOAT 204 [1980], pp. 423–25), there are two types of legal declarations in the grant formulae: (1) the land is given to the patriarch and to his seed (Gen. 13.15; 17.8; 26.3; 28.4, 13; 35.12), and (2) the land is given to the patriarch's seed (Gen. 12.7; 15.18; 24.7; 48.4). The former type represents the standard formula of the royal grant, but it is inappropriate in Genesis, where the patriarchs are sojourners in the land and only their descendants are the legal possessors of it. On the formulation of the land promise in the Priestly code versus the one in the Deuteronomic source, see M.Z. Brettler, 'The Promise of the Land of Israel to the Patriarchs in the Pentateuch', *Shnaton* 5–6 (1981–82), pp. VII–XXIV.

154. דור (*dūru*) with the pronominal suffix is also attested in old Babylonian documents pertaining to conveyance in perpetuity. Cf., e.g., *eqlam ana dūrišu idna* ('give the field as his permanent property') (TCL 7, 16.13; cf. F.R. Kraus, *Briefe aus dem British Museum* [*Altbabylonische Briefe*], in *Umschrift und Ubersetzung* 7 [Leiden, 1977] to which one might cf. Lev. 25.30, 'that house shall be established forever to him that bought it throughout *his generations*' לדרתיו (i.e., for his permanent property).

the conveyance and donation formulae from Susa,[155] Alalah,[156] Ugarit[157] and Elephantine.[158] In Assyria and Babylonia proper we meet with different clichés in this context, such as *ana arkat ūmē*[159] or *ana ṣāt ūmē*,[160] which, though not as close to עד עולם or לדרתם as the expressions of the peripheral documents (*adi dāriš*,[161] etc.), nevertheless render the same idea of perpetuity.

The proclamation of the gift of land in Genesis 15 is also styled according to the prevalent judicial pattern. In the gift-deed of Abban to Yarimlin we read, 'On that day (*ina ūmišu*) Abban gave the city…'. Similarly, we read in Gen. 15.18, 'On that day (ביום ההוא) Yahweh concluded a covenant with Abraham saying: "To your offspring I give this land".' The phrase 'on that day' in these instances certainly has legal implications.[162] The delineation of the borders and the specification of the granted territories in vv. 18–21 indeed constitute an important part of the grant documents in the ancient Near East.[163]

The formulation of the Priestly covenant with Abraham, 'to be unto you a God' (להיות לך לאלהים – Gen. 17.7,8) and the priestly formulation of the covenant with Israel, 'I will be your God and you shall be my people' (והייתי לכם לאלהים ואתם תהיו לי לעם – Lev. 26.12; Exod. 6.7; cf. Deut. 29.12), is taken from the sphere of marriage/adoption legal terminology,[164] as is its Davidic counterpart in 2 Sam. 7.14.[165]

155. Cf. *ana dūr u pala ana šêršêri…kīma abu ana māri išâmu,* PN *ana darāti išâm* (*MDP* 22, 45.10–21) ('forever and for all times, for the offspring…like a father, who bequeathes to his son, so shall PN bequeath forever'.

156. *mārmārišu ana dāria marianni*: 'his descendants will have the status of *mariannu* forever' (*AT* 15.8–9); cf. S. Smith, 'A Preliminary Account of the Tablets from Atchana', *The Antiquaries Journal* 19 (1939), p. 43.

157. Cf. *PRU* 3, p. 160, 16.132.27–38: *u ittadinšu ana* ^{m}*Adalšeni* [*u*] *ana mārēšu adi dārīti* ('and gives it to Adalšeni and his sons forever'); cf. 16.248.14 (p. 48: *ana dāri dūri*), 16.182 + 199.9 (p. 148: *ana dārīti/ana dāri dūri*) 16.146.10–12 (p. 146: *eqlatu ṣāmid ana dārīti*). In Ugaritic the formula is *wlbnh 'd 'lm* (*PRU* 2, 16.382, pp. 20–21).

158. Cf. A. Cowley, *The Aramaic Papyri of the Fifth Century B.C.* (1923), 8.9, p. 22: *ʾnty šlyṭh bh mn ywmʾ znh wʿdʿlm wbnykyʾhrykyʾ* ('you have rights over it from this day forever and your children after you'); *ibid.*, 25.9, p. 85. Cf. R. Yaron, *The Law of the Elephantine Documents* (1961), p. 82f., 165 (Hebrew).

159. F. Steinmetzer, 'Die Bestallungsurkunde Königs Šamas-šum-ukîn von Babylon', *Archiv orientální* 7 (1935), pp. 314–18, 2.9.

160. *ana ṣāti irenšu* ('he granted to him in perpetuity'), *BBSt* 8 (n. 5), 1;13; cf. also 34.6.

161. Cf. *CAD* D, p. 198.

162. Cf. n. 71 above.

163. Cf. *BBSt* (no. 5) (passim) and also Cowley, *Aramaic Papyri* (n. 158), 8.3ff.; 13.13f.; 25.4f. On this point see my *DDS* (n. 2), pp. 69ff.

164. Cf. Y. Muffs, 'Studies in Biblical Law IV (The Antiquity of P)', Lectures at the Jewish Theological Seminary (1965). For the use of *verba solemnia* in marriage and adoption in Mesopotamia see S. Greengus, 'The Old Babylonian Marriage Contract', *JAOS* 89 (1969), pp. 514ff. On the prophetic vs. pentateuchal imagery of the covenantal relationship between God and the people, see my *DDS* (n. 2), pp. 81ff.

165. The tradition of the covenant with Abraham is very ancient and reflects the covenant customs in Mari and Alalah, but the literary formulation of this covenant is more recent and seems to be from

The covenant with Abraham and the covenant with David are indeed based on a common pattern, and their literary formulation may have the same historical and literary antecedents.[166] The promise of the land to Abraham is preceded by the promise of progeny (Gen. 15.4–5), and the latter is formulated in the way the promise of the dynasty is phrased in 2 Sam. 7.12: אשר יצא ממעיך. Similarly, the promise of a great name to Abraham (ואגדלה שמך – Gen. 12.2) sounds like 2 Sam. 7.9: 'David will have a name like the name of the great ones of the earth' (כשם הגדלים אשר בארץ). As I have shown elsewhere,[167] the greatness of the name has political significance,[168] which also finds expression in the Genesis traditions apparently crystallized under the impact of the united monarchy.[169]

The priestly source in Genesis goes even further and combines the promise of land with the promise of dynasty. To the promise of progeny he adds, 'Kings shall come out from you' (17.6,16; 35.1), which sounds like a promise of dynasty.

The Grant of Hebron to Caleb

On the basis of the grant typology, discussed here, we may properly understand the nature of some other promises and bestowals in the Old Testament. Thus, the accounts of the conquest inform us about the gift of Hebron to Caleb (Josh. 14.13–14; Judg. 1.20; cf. Num. 14.24; Deut. 1.36).[170] The reason for the gift was the faithfulness of Caleb during his mission with the spies: 'Because he filled up after the lord' (יען כי מלא אחרי ה׳ אלהי ישראל – Josh. 14.14; cf. vv. 8, 9 and Num. 14.24; 32.11–12; Deut. 1.36), a phrase which is semantically equivalent to היה תמים (be perfect, i.e., wholly devoted) of the Abrahamic covenant and היה שלם of the Davidic covenant. Furthermore, as in the Abrahamic-Davidic covenants and in the grants of the ancient Near East, in the Caleb gift we also find the conventional formulae of conveyance in perpetuity: 'to you and your descendants forever' (לך...ולבניך עד עולם – Josh. 14.9).

Granting a city or a territory to the one who excelled in the king's expedition is indeed very common in the *kudduru* documents,[171] and the case of Caleb has

the time of the United Monarchy; cf. R.E. Clements, *Abraham and David* (Studies in Biblical Theology, 2nd Series 5; 1967).

166. Cf. K. McCarter, *II Samuel* (*AB*, 1984), p. 205.

167. 'Political Greatness: The Realization of the Promise to the Patriarchs', *Eretz-Israel* Vol. 24 (1993), A. Malamat volume.

168. Cf. *šumam rabêm* in connection with military victories in ARM 1, 69.14–16.

169. The extent of the promised land in Gen. 15.19–21, and especially the Kenites, Kenizzites and Kadmonites mentioned there, also point to a Davidic background; cf. B. Mazar, 'Historical Background of the Book of Genesis', *JNES* 28 (1969), pp. 79f.

170. Joshua is secondary in this tradition (cf. Num. 14.24; Deut. 1.36). The promise of land to Joshua was incorporated later, when the conquest was nationalized and the original account of spying out the south (to Hebron and the Valley of Eshkol, Num. 13.22–23) was expanded by an alleged excursion to the northern part of the country (to Rehob at Lebo-hamath, v. 21). See Commentaries and J. Liver, '*Caleb*', in *Encyclopedia Miqra'it* 4, cols. 106–110 (Hebrew).

171. Cf., e.g., King, *BBSt* (n. 5), pp. 31ff., 43ff., 96ff.

therefore to be considered as a grant, although we do not know whether the grant reflects an authentic historical fact of the times of the conquest or is rather a back projection of later times. Granting a city to a vassal who proved loyal to the overlord is found in connection with the city *Ṣiqlag*, which was given to David by Achish, the Philistine king (1 Sam. 27.6).[172]

Clements[173] suggested that Hebron was the birthplace of the traditions of the Abrahamic and Davidic covenants. The tradition about the grant to Caleb is certainly rooted in Hebron. It therefore seems plausible that the tradition of the grant of Hebron to Caleb had been transmitted by the same circle that transmitted the tradition of the Abrahamic-Davidic covenants.

The Grant of Priesthood and Priestly Revenues

The documents of grant in the ancient Near East also include grants of status – *maryannu*–ship,[174] priesthood,[175] etc. The priesthood of Aaron in Israel had also been conceived as an eternal grant. Thus we read in Num. 25.12–13: 'Phinehas, son of Eleazar son of Aaron the priest, has turned back my wrath from the Israelites by displaying among them his passion for me...say, therefore, I grant him my pact of friendship (ברית שלום). It shall be for him and his descendants after him a pact of priesthood forever (ברית כהנת עולם)'. As in other grants, here the grant is given for showing one's zeal and devotion for the master; and like the other grants, the gift of priesthood is given in perpetuity.[176] In biblical texts that do not follow the rigid distinction (of the Priestly Code) between priests and Levites but rather adopt the Deuteronomic attitude of priests and Levites being one group, the grant applies to the whole tribe of Levi. Thus, we read in Mal. 2.4f.: 'that my covenant might be with Levi...my covenant was with him of life and well being (חיים ושלום)'. In the continuation, an indication of the loyalty and devotion of Levi is also found, which is similar in its phraseology to the descriptions of the loyalty of Abraham and David.[177] 'he walked with [he served me] with integrity and equity' (בשלום ובמישור הלך אתי – v. 6).[178] The eternal covenant with Levi is also mentioned alongside the covenant with David in Jer. 33.17ff.

Priestly revenues in the ancient Near East were also subject to grants and royal bestowals. This is also reflected in Israel. The holy donations assigned to the Aaronide priesthood are formulated in the manner of royal grants:[179] 'All the

172. Cf. J. Tigay, 'Psalm 7.5 and Ancient Near Eastern Treaties', *JBL* 89 (1970), p. 183.

173. See n. 1.

174. Cf. S. Smith, *The Antiquaries Journal* 19 (1939), ATT/8/49 (p. 43): *mār mārēšu ana dāria maryanni u šangi ša Enlil* ('his grandsons in perpetuity are [will be] *maryannu* and priests of Enlil').

175. Cf., e.g., Schorr, *Urkunden* (no. 10), VAB 5, No. 220; F. Thureau-Dangin, 'Un acte de donation de Marduk – zâkir – šumi', *RA* 16 (1919), pp. 141ff., and the Alalah text in the previous note.

176. Cf. above.

177. Cf. above.

178. See n. 30 above.

179. Following the translation of *The Torah*, Jewish Publication Society of America (1962).

sacred donations of the Israelites, I grant them to you and your sons as a prerequisite,[180] a due for all time' (לכל קדשי בני ישראל לך נתתים למשחה ולבניך לחק עולם – Num. 18.8; cf. Lev. 7.34ff.), and in slightly different formulations, 'all the sacred gifts that the Israelites set aside for YHWH I give to you, to your sons...as a due forever, it shall be as everlasting salt covenant...for you and your offspring as well' (v. 19).

Similarly, the tithe, which according to Num. 18.21f., belongs to the Levites, was also given to them as a grant for the services that they perform (חלף עבדתם אשר הם עבדים). Grants of the tithe of a city to royal servants are actually known to us from Ugarit, as we read, for instance, in the grant of Ammištamru II.[181] '(From this day) Ammištamru granted everything whatsoever (that belongs to the city) to Yaṣiranu...forever for his grandsons: his grain, and his wine of its tithe'. Yaṣiranu receives here the right to collect the tithe.[182]

The connection of the Aaronites and the Levites to Hebron has been pointed out,[183] and we may therefore suppose that the 'Sitz im Leben' of the grant to Aaron and the Levites is rooted in Hebron, as are the other grant traditions discussed.

As has been shown, the grants to Abraham, Caleb, David, Aaron, and the Levites have much in common with the grants from Alalah, Nuzi, the Hittites, Ugarit, and middle-Babylonian *kudurru*'s, i.e., in documents from the second half of the second millennium BCE. This fact and the possible link of the mentioned Israelite grants to Hebron, the first capital of David's kingdom, may lead us to the contention that it was Davidic scribes who stood behind the formulation of the covenant of grant in Israel.

180. On the priestly revenue as a royal grant see Y. Muffs, 'Joy and Love as Metaphorical Expressions of Willingness and Spontaneity in Cuneiform, Ancient Hebrew and Related Literatures', in J. Neusner (ed.), *Christianity, Judaism and other Greco-Roman Cults: For Morton Smith at Sixty*, 3 (1975), pp. 14ff.

181. GN *qadu gabbi mimmi šumsiša iddin ana* PN*...ana dāriš ana mārē mārēšu: šêšu, šikarsu ša ma'šarišu* (*PRU* 3, 16.153): 4–11 (pp. 146–47). As in Ugarit, in Israel the tithe is taken from grain and wine (and also oil).

182. Cf. M. Heltzer, *The Rural Community in Ancient Ugarit* (1976), pp. 50–51.

183. Cf. the dissertation by M.D. Rehm, 'Studies in the History of the Pre-Exilic Levites', announced in the *Harvard Theological Review* 61 (1968), pp. 648–49. Cf. also B. Mazar, 'Cities of Priests and Levites', *SVT* 7 (1959), pp. 197ff.

Chapter 15

THE DAY OF ATONEMENT AND FREEDOM (*DEROR*): THE REDEMPTION OF THE SOUL

The freedom proclaimed on the Day of Atonement (Lev. 25.10) underwent a process of spiritual metamorphosis during the second temple period, so that the proclamation of freedom brought about not only the physical liberation of slaves and of land, but also the liberation of the soul and its restoration to its pure source. Thus, for example, Philo of Alexandria says in connection with the Day of Atonement:[1] 'We find it (the number ten)[2] in Jubilee (ἄφεσις), in the complete freedom of the soul, which shakes off (ἀποσειομένης = שמט) from its misleading (ways) and returns to its heritages'.

This concept of Yom Kippur as proclaiming freedom to the soul – that is, the return of the soul to its pure source by means of abandoning sin – appears in the Qumran scrolls:[3] 'And that which is said, "in this year of jubilee, each of you shall return to his holding"...and called to them freedom, that they may abandon [the burden] of all their sins' (1.1–6).

It seems, indeed, that the motif of forgiveness and atonement in the Day of Atonement liturgy was influenced more than a little by the erasing of debts and sins in the declaration of 'freedom' and amnesty. In the Hellenistic period, the royal amnesties opened with the forgiving of errors and deliberate sins (ἀγνοήματα, ἁμαρτήματα),[4] expressions which later found their way into the religious realm (Tob. 3.4).[5] Indeed, the prayers and confessions of Yom Kippur ask forgiveness for both deliberate and unwitting transgressions.[6]

1. *De congressu pruditionis gratia*, 107–108; cf. *Quod deferior potiori*, 63; *De Congressu*, 89.
2. That is, on the tenth of Tishrei, i.e., the Day of Atonement of the Jubilee year.
3. See J.T. Milik, 'Milki-ṣedeq et Milki-rešaᶜ dans les anciens écrits juifs et chrétiens', *JJS* 23 (1972), pp. 95–109 (11 Q. Melch).
4. Cf. my *Social Justice*, pp. 147–48.
5. Compare Ben-Sira 23.2. These expressions penetrated into Christian theological literature in connection with the atonement of sins. See, for example, Eusebius, concerning Jesus, who forgives errors and deliberate sins: λύσιν τε καὶ ἄφεσιν τῶς πριν ἀγνοημάτων καὶ ἁμαρτημάτων ὑπιοχνουμενος *Evangelica Demonstratio* IV, 10. Cf. The discussion of this in L. Koenen, *Eine Ptolemäische Königsurkunde* (*Pap. Kroll*) (1957), pp. 5–6.
6. The one confessing must say: 'I have sinned (חטאתי), I have done iniquities (עויתי), I have transgressed (פשעתי)' based upon the verse, 'And he shall confess over it all the iniquities (עונות) and transgressions (פשעיהם) of the Israelites, whatever their sins (חטאתם)' (Lev. 16.21). According to Rabbinic interpretation, עונות alludes to deliberate sins, פשעים to rebellious acts, and חטאים to unintentional errors (*t. Kippurim* 2.1; *b. Yoma* 36b; *y. Yoma* 3.7, 40d).

The statements concerning the erasure of transgressions and sins in Isaiah 44.22[7] are made against the background of the proclamation of freedom.[8] An analogy to this may be seen in Sargon's declaration of freedom:[9] 'Their iniquities will be no more, their transgressions will be reduced, their sin will be erased, their violations will be an abomination'.[10]

Together with the erasure of sin, one finds in Isa. 43.25 the refusal to remember – that is, the forgetting of sin: an expression widely used in Greek in connection with the proclamation of liberation (*amnestia*); it also occurs in Akkadian (*mašûtu*).[11] The most concrete example in the realm we are discussing is the phrase, 'Erase our notes of indebtedness' in the *Abīnū Malkēnu* prayer recited on Jewish fast days,[12] which is undoubtedly influenced by the act of liberation entailed in the nullification of debts.

In Israel, the declaration of freedom (מישרים), which had served in the Ancient Near East to bring about equality and social rights of the citizens, became a model for the redemption of the soul and of forgiveness of sins on Yom Kippur.[13] Just as liberation (דרור) served as a model for the redemption of the individual, and particularly for the forgiveness of sins, so did it serve as a model for the redemption of the collectivity and the erasure of its sins at the End of Days. In the Qumran Scrolls, in the Melchizedek midrash (11Q Melch.) cited above, the

7. 'I wipe away (מחיתי) your transgressions (פשעיך) like a cloud, your sins (חטאתיך) like mist; come back to Me, for I redeem you'. Cf. Ps. 51.11: 'Hide your face from my sins, wipe out (מחה) all my iniquities;' cf. v. 3.

8. Indeed, this verse is incorporated into the *Amidah* for Yom Kippur.

9. See H. Tadmor, 'The Temple City and the Royal City in Babylon and Ashur', in: *Holy War and Martyrology: Town and Community, Lectures delivered at the 12th Convention of the Historical Society of Israel – December 1966* (1967), p. 192.

10. A.T. Clay, *Miscellaneous Inscriptions in the Yale Babylonian Collection* (YOS. 1.) (1915), no. 38, II.31–35: *aî ibbašši ešītsun, egītsunu limaṭṭēma, lipaššis hīṭetsun, sahmaštum lū ikkibšunuma.* Cf. C.J. Gadd, 'Inscribed Barrel Cylinder of Marduk-apla-iddina II', *Iraq* 15 (1953), p. 130; W. von Soden, *AHw*, p. 369, *ikkibu* 56.

11. Cf. M. Weinfeld. *Social Justice* (1995), pp. 171–72.

12. Cf. S. Singer, *The Standard Prayer Book* (1943), p. 68.

In the liturgical poem by Yannai (5–6 centuries CE) האוחז ביד מידת משפט, recited on Rosh Hashanah and Yom Kippur, immediately following the petition: 'find us righteous in judgement, O King of Judgement', we read: 'He who is equal (השווה), and makes equal great and small'. As noted by Y. Baer, this text expresses the Platonic ideal that God is 'equal' in the upper world, and therefore is a guarantor of the equality of human beings in the lower world; see: Y. Baer, 'The Ritual Sacrifice in Second Temple Times', *Zion* 40 (1974), pp. 95–153 (Hebrew). It is interesting that Yannai's point of departure for this view is the passage concerning the Jubilee year in Lev. 25:

You gave equality to all creatures
All are equal before You at the day of Creation
Let those who were sold for free be redeemed for free
And buyer and seller are equal as one.
Master of all, in all You have equalized all
Slave and his master, handmaiden and her mistress.

- *Qedusha* for the weekly portion [of the Palestinian cycle], 'and when you sell property' [Lev. 25.14], *Piyyutei Yannai* (ed. M. Zulai), pp. 168–69.

13. See above, n. 3.

verses from the Torah concerning the sabbatical year and the release (Lev. 25; Deut. 15) are interwoven with prophecies from Isa. 61.1–3, in which the prophet informs the people that he is sent 'as a herald of joy to the humble' and 'to proclaim release to the captives'. Isaiah 61.1, 'release' is interpreted there as a day of forgiveness of sins (see above) and as the day which concludes the year of grace of Melchizedek (cf. 1.9). The 'end', i.e., the time of redemption, will come during the first Sabbatical cycle of the Jubilee following nine Jubilee cycles, and will take place on the Day of Atonement. On this day, all the peoples of the earth will be judged: Melchizedek will execute vengeance for the divine judgements (cf. Isa. 61.2: 'and a day of vindication by our God' [יום נקם לאלהינו]). It is to this day that the Qumran midrash applies the words of the prophet: 'How welcome on the mountain are the footsteps of the herald announcing peace, heralding good fortune, announcing salvation' (Isa. 52.7). The author of the scroll goes on to say (line 18) that the harbinger is 'the anointed one of the spirit, of whom Daniel said, "until the [time of the] anointed leader is seventy weeks"' (Dan. 9.25).

The notion of release is here intertwined with the calculations of the end found in Daniel, connected with the 'seventy sevens' (Dan. 9.24), i.e., 7 × 70 = 490 years, which indeed corresponds to the end of the tenth Jubilee cycle (50 × 10), according to the calculations of the pešer of Qumran given here. Melchizedek thus fulfills here a function of the Messiah of the spirit, who foretells the redemption during the year of grace, which is [also] the year of release. Such an exegesis of Isa. 61.1–3 must have lain in the background of Lk. 4.16–19, in which Jesus sees himself as bearing to the reader news of freedom and a year of grace from the Lord.[14]

The prophecy in Isa. 61.1–3, whose source is connected with the Jubilee of years which passed between the destruction of the temple (586) and the declaration of Cyrus (536), acquires mystical-apocalyptic significance during the period of the second temple being motivated by calculations of the end of seventy sabbatical years (Daniel) and ten Jubilees (Midrash Melchizedek). It thus became a focus for the longings for redemption in both Judaism and Christianity.

The connection between the earthly, 'release of debts' and the divine one seems to be very old. It is not only found in Leviticus 25, where 'the day of atonement' (יום הכיפורים) is also the day of release of slaves and land (vv. 9–10), it is found to our surprise also in Ugarit.

In the Ugaritic text *KTU* 1.40 we find a Ugaritic ritual ceremony concerning the expiation of the sins of the children of Ugarit, men and women, king and queen and the foreigners (גר חמית אגרת) who live in Ugarit.[15] The citizens of

14. For a detailed discussion of the development of the prophecy in Isa. 61.1–3, from the Bible until Christianity, see J.A. Sanders, 'From Isaiah 61 to Luke 4', in J. Neusner (ed.), *Christianity, Judaism and other Greco-Roman Cults; Studies for Morton Smith at Sixty. Part One: New Testament* (1975), pp. 75–106. It seems to me that the function of Jesus as the harbinger of the kingdom of God (see Mk 1.14–15) is rooted in this ideology.

15. See recently: *Texts Ougaritiques, Tome II, Textes religieux rituels correspondance* (ed. A. Caquot and J.L. Cunchillos, 1989), pp. 140–49.

Ugarit have sinned with anger (אף) and impatience (קצר נפש) and they undergo an act of forgiveness while offering sacrifices. It was A. Caquot who identified the ceremony with the ceremonies of Yom Kippur.[16] Recently G. del Olmo lete suggested that the term משר which appears in this text so often is none other than Akkadian *mīšarum* which signifies a royal decree of freedom: release of debts etc.[17] Here it applies to sin and debts of religious nature, like the Israelite Jubilee.[18] As in the Ugaritic text the expiation of sins in Leviticus applies to the Israelites as well as to the alien residents (Lev. 16.29). Another text that is pertinent to the Ugaritic ceremony is Num. 15.22–26 where after an expiation offering brought on behalf of the people is (vs. 24–25) we read: 'The whole Israelite community and the foreigner residing among them shall be forgiven'. This formula is actually recited on the eve of יום כיפור in the synagogue until our day.

Here is a tentative partial translation of the Ugaritic text that we relate to.[19]

Lines 9–17: One offers the lamb of 'release' (משר) the 'release'
of the children of Ugarit…and the area (נפי)[20] of
Ugarit…they are…Hurrian, Hittite etc.
in your impatience (קצר נפשכם)[21] and in the loathful
deed
which you committed…we shall offer sacrifices…

Lines 18–25: One offers a sheep for the 'release' of… The foreigners of the walls of
Ugarit…You sinned with
your anger (באפכן) and in your impatience (קצר נפשכן)…
we shall offer sacrifices…
the father of the children of Il…
to the assembly of the gods.

Lines 26–34: one offers a donkey for the 'release',
the release of the children of Ugarit…
the 'release' of Niqmadu…
with your anger with your impatience.

16. A. Caquot, 'Un sacrifice expiatoire a Ras Shamra', *RHPhR* 42 (1962), p. 211.

17. G. Del Olmo lete, 'El Sacrificio de Expiacion Nacional en Ugarit (*KTU* 1.40 Y Par)', in *La Paraula al Servei dels Homes* (1989), pp. 43–56.

18. See M. Weinfeld, *Social Justice* (1995).

19. The text is divided into six sections marked by horizontal lines. Section one is hard to reconstruct. Section two refers to the people addressed in the masculine (נפשכם, באפכם), section three refers to the people in the feminine (באפכן,נפשכן); the third (26–34) addresses the people in the masculine and refers to the King *Niqmadu*; the fourth (35–41) addresses in the feminine and includes the Queen *Niṭitu*. For the most recent discussion of this text, see D. Pardee, 'The Structure of RS 1.002', in *Semitic Studies in honor of W. Leslau, II* (1991), pp. 1181–1196.

20. In my opinion נפי here is like Hebrew נפה, which designates district, especially that of דור (Josh. 11.2; 12.23; 17.11; 1 Kgs 4.11). According to M. Ben-Dov, 'נפה – A Geographical Term of Possible 'Sea People' Origin', *Tel Aviv* 3 (1976), pp. 70–73, the term *nph* is derived from Greek νάπη which designates forest in the plain, i.e., Sharon. The term was in use among the Sea People. See however N. Na'aman, *Borders and Districts in Biblical Historiography* (1986), pp. 184–85.

21. Cf. R.D. Haak, 'A Study and Interpretation of QṢR NPŠ', *JBL* 101 (1982), pp. 161–67.

Lines 35–41: He returns to recite…'release' of the children of Ugarit…
Of the foreigners of the walls of Ugarit
the expiation of *Niṯitu* (the queen)
We shall offer sacrifice…
the father of the children of Il.

The confession is recited here on behalf of the people, the foreigners, the king and the queen apparently by a priest, as we find it in the Yom Kippur ceremony according to Lev. 16.21 (compare *m. Yoma*).

Atonement on behalf of the people and its leaders, as we find in the Ugaritic text, actually appears in Leviticus 4 where purification offerings are prescribed for the high priest, the community, the chieftain and the commoner. Similarly in the Yom Kippur ceremony the high priest offers purification offerings on behalf of himself and his household (Lev. 16.11) and on behalf of the people (Lev. 16.24).

Chapter 16

THE CRYSTALLIZATION OF THE 'CONGREGATION OF THE EXILE' (קהל הגולה) AND THE SECTARIAN NATURE OF POST-EXILIC JUDAISM

As I have shown elsewhere,[1] apodictic law (thou shalt/shalt not do) was imposed on the people of Israel by its leaders, kings and rulers in the Early Israelite period. Moses and Joshua bind/command the people to observe the Lord's commandments (Exod. 15.25; 19.7–8; 24.3–8; Deut. 29.9–14; Josh. 24.25), as does Josiah (2 Kgs 23.1–3), and accordingly the laws are addressed in the second person, singular and plural. In the second temple period on the other hand, laws and commandments are worded in the first person plural – I refer to the pledge (אמנה) of Nehemiah in Neh. 10, in which the people assume, in first-person speech, the obligation of observing the commandments:

> We will not give our daughters in marriage to the peoples of the land (v. 31)
> ...we will not buy from them on the Sabbath (v. 32)
> We will forgo [the produce of] the seventh year... (v. 32)
> We have laid upon ourselves obligations...(v. 33)
> ...the first-born of our sons and our beasts...to bring to the House of our God (v. 37)

A similar form of expression has been found in the regulations of a religious-cultic group in Ptolemaic Egypt.[2]

> We shall assemble in the temple on holy days... we shall pay in coins of silver...we shall provide wine and beer...we shall offer burnt offerings (*kll.w*) and make libations.

Earlier before the appearance of the Persian Empire, the kings were responsible for establishing cultic practice: cf. Jeroboam setting up golden calves at Dan and Beth El (1 Kgs 12.28–30) and Hezekiah and Josaiah establishing the unification of the cult in Judah (2 Kgs 18.4; 22; 23.1–20). Priests who opposed these cultic reforms were slaughtered on their altars (2 Kgs 23.19). According to 2 Chronicles, King Hezekiah gave:

> ...the king's portion, from his property, for the burnt offerings
> – the morning and evening burnt offering, and the burnt offerings
> for sabbaths and new moons and festivals...(31.3)[3]

1. M. Weinfeld, 'The Origin of the Apodictic Law – An overlooked Source', *Vetus Testamentum* 23 (1973), pp. 63–75.
2. Cf. the demotic code from the days of Ptolemy III (223 BCE) cf. F. de Cemival, *Les associations religieuses en Egypte, d'après les documents démotiques*, 1972, Papyrus Lille 29, pp. 1–38.
3. Cf. also Ezek. 45.17.

During the Persian period religious observance became a voluntary matter. People assemble and accept obligations but are not subject to externally imposed laws. On the phrase in Exod. 19.17, '...and they took their places at the foot of the mountain', the Sages commented that God held a mountain over the people like a tub, i.e. forced a decision from them by overwhelming pressure, saying:

> If you accept my law – well and good; if not, this is where you shall be buried...
> (*b. Shab.* 88a)

Rabba adds that in the days of Ahasuerus the people nevertheless expressed their willingness to accept the commandments of the Torah:

> ...the Jews undertook and irrevocably committed themselves...(קימו וקבל)[4]
> (Esther 9.27)

And indeed the commitment that the returnees from Babylon undertook is worded as a voluntary consent and not as external dictation. They say:

> 'Now then, let us make a covenant with our God (נכרת ברית לאלהינו) to expel all these women and those who have been born to them...' (Ezra 10.3)

Cf. 2 Chron. 29.10 on Hezekiah:

> Now I wish to make a covenant with the Lord God of Israel...

'To make a covenant with' (כרת ברית ל) usually means the strong party dictating from on high, binding the weaker party on oath to observe the conditions the stronger lays down, cf., for example, Exod. 23.32; 34.15; Deut. 7.2; 1 Sam. 11.1; etc. In Ezra 10.3, by contrast, the returnees from exile commit themselves voluntarily to observe the commandments. Moreover, their undertakings do not apply to the whole of the people, as was usual in first temple times, but to the 'children of the exile' (בני הגולה) or the 'congregation of the exile'(קהל הגולה) (Ezra 4.1; 6.19,20; 8.35; 10.7, 16).

'The congregation of the exile' (קהל הגולה) was in dispute with the 'Remnant of Judah', as we can see from Ezek. 11.16 and 33.23ff. It was the exile or the exile of Judah that Jeremiah called 'the good figs' (Jer. 24.5; 29.17) that came to be accepted as the heirs of Judah and Israel and designated 'the men of Judah and Benjamin' (Ezra 10.9; cf. 4.1). The returnees demanded the status of Israel for themselves alone and were absolutely opposed to the claim of the 'Remnant of Judah' to the land, that the latter had put forward a hundred years earlier.[5]

The voluntary nature of the 'children of the exile's' obligations is most obvious in the commitment that we find in Nehemiah's Pledge to provide the annual wood offering (v. 35). Before the Exile there was no such duty as the royal administration or the national leadership provided all supplies for the sacrificial ritual. All changed after the destruction of the temple. In the Persian period, there being no

4. See S. Lieberman 'the Discipline in the so-called Dead Sea Manual of Discipline', *JBL* 71 (1952), pp. 199–206.

5. Cf. S. Japhet, 'The People and the Land in the period of the Restoration', *Studies in Jewish History of the Second Temple Period* (Collected by Daniel R. Schwartz [Hebrew], 1995), pp. 127–45.

royal administration to maintain the ritual, this duty was assumed by the religious community or a voluntary association. And in the Temple Scroll from Qumran (col. 23–24) we see that the supply of the wood offering has become an important matter. In the Hellenistic period it was one of the religious associations' central duties: I refer to the *xylonia*.[6]

A like case is the third-of-a-shekel annual temple contribution that the returnees committed themselves to, to finance its activities. In former times the king or another national leader would have taken care of this (see Num. 7; Ezek. 45.16–17). From the time of Nehemiah on, we are told of a pledge (אמנה) framing self-imposed commitments, in contrast to the externally imposed obligations typical of the first temple period. The formation and development of the various religious associations in the Persian period reflects this change. Politically, the subject kingdoms were subordinate to the Persian king, but, as though in compensation for this loss of independence, they were granted autonomy in their internal religious affairs.

Another reflection of this transition is the modification of the institution of the *ḥerem* (proscription). In pre-exilic times this entailed killing the individual (Exod. 22.19; Lev. 27.29) or the group (Deut. 13.13–19 – a condemned town; Judg. 20.48; 21.5,11) on whom the *ḥerem* had been laid. After the Exile, the institution took on the meaning of ostracism / excommunication, which also entailed the forfeiture of property; see Ezra 10.8:

> ...anyone who did not come in three days would...have his property confiscated (יחרם) and himself excluded from the congregation of the returning exiles (והוא יבדל מקהל הגולה).

We find a similar proscription in the regulations of the *Yaḥad* sect from Qumran:

> Every one of them who transgresses a commandment of the Law of Moses, with a lifted hand or a slack hand, shall be banished (ישלחהו) from the Council of the Community (1QS 8.22–23).

By failing to meet his self-imposed obligations, the transgressor had removed himself from the congregation that he had voluntarily joined and was thus expelled from the community of *Yaḥad*.[7]

The departure of prophecy from Israel in this period is also explained by the Persian ruling strategy not to permit political independence to small peoples, whereas the empires of Assyria and Babylon had allowed the existence of vassal kingdoms. In Israel's monarchical period the prophets had achieved the status of being both indispensable and unconstrainable. No significant political step could be taken without prophetical endorsement. Wars could not be undertaken without first consulting a prophet, and such was the case not only in Israel but in all the

6. See F. Poland, *Geschichte des griechischen Vereinswesen* (1909), pp. 258 nn. 2, 466; M.C. Youtie, 'The Kline of Sarapis', *Harvard Theological Review* 41 (1948), pp. 22–23; A.E. Raubitechek, 'A new Attic Club; (ERANOS)', *The S. Paul Getty Museum Journal* 9 (1981), line 42 (p. 94).

7. M. Weinfeld, *The Organizational Pattern and the Penal Code of the Qumran Sect* (1986), pp. 41–42.

states of the Ancient Near East. The loss of political independence made national prophecy redundant, and so the opening of the second temple period saw its disappearance. Haggai and Zechariah continued to prophesy since the hope still existed that Zerubbabel, of the line of King Yehoiachin of Judah, would re-establish the monarchy (cf. Hag. 2.21), but as soon as this hope had been extinguished prophecy as a national institution ended. Only individual prophecy survived, as E.A. Urbach has shown.[8]

The character of Judaism at the opening of the second temple period was determined by the deeds and decisions of Ezra and Nehemiah, who led the returnees. The returnee congregation saw themselves as the true Israel and dismissed other groups claiming the inheritance, e.g. 'the remnant of the people' (Hag. 1.12; Zech. 8.11,12) as unrepresentative of the true Israel. Whereas Haggai and Zechariah address themselves to the 'remnant of Israel' and entirely ignore the benefactions the returnees received from Cyrus and Darius, Ezra and Nehemiah accentuate the part the Persian kings played in the rebuilding of the temple and the restoration of Israel, released from its exile (Ezra 6.22; 7.27–28; 9.9).

The prophecy of Deutero-Isaiah also extols the rescue of Israel through the medium of Cyrus and his pronouncement in favour of rebuilding the Jerusalem Temple and returning the exiles to Judah and Jerusalem (Isa. 44.26, 28; 45.13).

As events have transpired, it was indeed the return of the Babylonian exiles that gave the Law of Moses dominion over Judah and thus liberated the Jews from false gods once and for all.

The traditional perception of the Sages who saw in the membership of *HaKnesset HaGedola* the embodiment of Ezra and Nehemiah's leadership is exactly right. The term *knesset* is equivalent to the Aramaic כנישתא which translates the Hebrew *kahal*. The Aramaic כנישתא passed into Akkadian (*Kiništu*) where it came to be applied to the founding assembly of the public around the new temple.

HaKnesset HaGedola refers, in the opinion of the Sages, to the assembly in the days of Ezra and Nehemiah and comprised elders, senior public officials, levites and priests (Ezra 10.8; Neh. 10.1). This is to be compared to 1 Macc. 14.28:

> ...*the great assembly* of priests and the people and the heads of the nation...[9]

The sectarian elements of second temple Judaism may be outlined as follows:

Pedigree

The sectarian character of the Community of the Exile is made very clear to us by a directive of Ptolemy IV Philopater (222–205 BCE). He ordered that all devotees of the Dionysos cult in Alexandria be assembled and be required to submit a signed declaration confirming from whom they had received the sacred rites, a declaration that was then to be verified to the third generation. The sacred list had to be signed and sealed by each devotee.

8. 'מתי פסקה הנבואה', *Tarbiz* 17 (1946), pp. 1–11.
9. Cf. M. Weinfeld, *The Organizational Pattern etc.* (see above n. 7), pp. 7f.

This incident reminds us that in the period of restoration the 'returnees were required to produce a written affirmation of ancestry before they could be accepted into the congregation and were rejected if no written proof could be submitted (Ezra 2.59; Neh. 7.61). The verification to the third generation ordered by Ptolemy IV recalls the order in Deut. 23.8–9 that only third-generation descendants of Edomites or Egyptians could be accepted into the congregation of the Lord' i.e. be accepted as a Jew.

The Manual of Discipline of the *Yaḥad* community also mentions candidates being registered by name:

> ...and they shall be registered in the order one before the other...
>
> (5.23;6.23;8.19)[10]
>
> And any new member of the community shall be measured by his deeds...and written down in his place in accordance with his share in the lot of the light.
>
> (Damascus Covenant 13.11–12)
>
> All shall be registered by name...and written down by name, each after his brother.
>
> (*Ibid.* 14.3–6)

Oath taking

Oath taking also assumed a prominent place in the internal organization of such communities. With respect to the returnees from the Babylonian exile we read that they will:

> ...take an oath with sanctions to follow the Teaching of God...
>
> (Neh. 10.30)

And with respect to the Qumran sect:

> Everyone who enters the community shall enter into God's covenant...He shall undertake a binding oath...He shall undertake by oath...
>
> (Manual of Discipline 5.8–10)

> And he who enters the covenant of all Israel...shall take on him the oath of the covenant...and shall be registered according to the oath of the covenant to which Moses swore the people of Israel...to return to the Law of Moses.
>
> (Damascus Covenant 15.5–9)

In a mystery sect of Isis in Egypt (Apuleius):

> Make yourself one of this order (militia) to which you have sworn an oath...
>
> (Metamorph 19.15, 30)

Baptism, Immersion

Joining one of these communities and entry into the covenant of Abraham, i.e. conversion to Judaism, entailed immersion/baptism. The same practice obtained in joining the Community of the *Yaḥad*, the Community of Christians, and the Isis Mystery sect in Egypt. With regard to the latter association, we find that Lucius immerses himself in water seven times before initiation.

10. *Ibid.*, pp. 22–23.

Another feature of the practice of these religious associations was the bestowal of prizes on temple builders: Zech. 6.9–16 relates how delegates of the exile bring silver and gold to make diadems for their leaders Joshua ben Yehozadak and, apparently, Zerubbabel, for their part in bringing about the rebuilding of the temple.

We find a similar happening in the Sidonian colony of Piraeus in Greece. The Sidonian settlers who had the status of an autonomous guild with their own temple, crown *Shema'*ba'al who had built a courtyard for the temple of Baᶜal-Sidon. The two events differ in that in Judah the delegates from exile crown the builder of a temple in their homeland, whereas in Sidon it is the builder of a temple in the Greek diaspora who is acknowledged:

> בים 4 למרזח בשת 14 לעם צדן תם בד צדנם בן אספת לעטר אית שמעבעל בן מגן אש
> אש נשאם לן על בת אלם עלת מעבת הרץ ויטנאי בערפת מת אלים על אש
> בדרכנם 20 ... לכתב האדמם אש נשאם לן על בת אלם עלת מצבת חרץ ויטנאי
> בערפת בת אלים ען אש.

On the 4th day of the feast, in the 14th year of the people of Sidon, it was decreed by the Sidonians in assembly to crown (*'ṭr*) Shamaᶜbaᶜal son of Mgn who had been the chief (*nś'*) of the community (*gw*) in charge of the temple and in charge of the buildings in the temple court, with a crown (*'ṭrt*) of gold worth 20 darics...the men who are in charge of the temple should write this decision on a stele and should set it up in the portico before the eyes of the men[11] (*Phoenician in Athens; KAI no. 60, 319* BCE)

This is to be compared with the episode in Zech. 6.10–14:

> לקוח מאת הגולה מחלדי מאת טוביה ... ובאת בית יאשיה בן צפניה אשר באו מבבל
> ולקחת כסף וזהב ועשית עטרות ושמת בראש יהוצדק הכהן הגדול ... הנה איש צמח שמו
> ומתחתיו יצמח ובנה את היכל ה׳... והעטרת תהיה לחלם ולטוביה ... לזכרון בהיכל ה׳.

Take silver and gold from the exiles, from Ḥeldai, Tobiah...and enter the house of Josiah...who have come back from Babylon. Take it and make a crown; put the crown on the head of Joshua son of Jehozadak, the high priest...these are the words... Here is a man named Zemah (=branch), he will show up from the ground where he is and build the temple of the Lord... The crown shall be in charge of Heldai...a memorial in the temple of the Lord.

The fact that a group minority develops a state is nicely depicted by Aristotle:

> For in early partnership we find mutual rights of some sort and also friendly feelings... All associations are part as it were of the association of the State. Travelers for instance associate together for some advantage, namely to procure some of their necessary supplies. But the political associations too, it is believed, was originally formed, and continues to be maintained, for the advantage of its members...Thus the other associations aim at some particular advantage; for example, sailors combine to seek the profits of seafaring in the way of trade or the like...some associations appear to be formed for the sake of pleasure, for example, religious guilds and dining clubs, which are unions for sacrifice and social intercourse. But all these associations seem to be subordinate to

11. H. Donner und W. Röllig, *Kanaanäische und Aramäische Inschriften*, No. 60; J. Teixidor, 'L'Assemblée Legislative en Phenicie d'après les Inscriptions', *Syria* 57 (1980), pp. 454–64.

> the association of the State, which aims not at a temporary advantage but at one covering the whole of life.
>
> The State as a Social Associate (Aristotle, *Nicomachean Ethics* [IX, 1–6])

As noted earlier, the books of Haggai and Zechariah show utter disregard of the returned exiles, in complete contradistinction to the books of Ezra and Nehemiah. The word 'exile' appears once only in the story (Zech. 6.10) of the delegation from Babylon that came in connection with the gold and silver for the diadems. The books of Ezra and Nehemiah, by contrast, are full of 'the children of the exile' and the 'congregation of the exile' that took shape after the Return to Zion. Haggai and Zechariah continued to function within a state-wide, all-Israel perspective, anticipating the re-establishment of the monarchy under Zerubbabel, of the line of King Yehoiachin of Judah. Ezra and Nehemiah, maintaining their loyalty to the kings of Persia, pursued a strategy based on voluntary associations.

We do not know at what point in the second temple period the diverse sects began to consolidate. The usual assumption is that the parties began to take shape in the Hasmonean period, but there is evidence for the existence of voluntary associations as early as the Persian era. For this reason Nehemiah's Pledge should be seen as signifying the transition from the dictation of state laws to the voluntary self-committal of a range of associations, of which the 'congregation of the exile' was one.

The existence of an autonomous institution called *kiništu* (Aramaic *kništa,* Hebrew *qahal*) from the late Babylonian period on also suggests that voluntary associations had begun to flourish under Persian sovereignty, replacing, for non-political purposes, the former organs of the state.

Chapter 17

'You will find Favour...in the Sight of God and Man' (Proverbs 3.4): The History of an Idea

A. *The Formula in the Bible*

In Proverbs 3.1ff., we read that a son who observes the teachings of his 'father', the sage, will be rewarded with length of days and years of life and well-being[1] and will find *ḥen* (favour) *wĕśekhel ṭôb* in the sight of God and man. *Śekhel ṭôb*, like the adjacent word *ḥen*, means '(the impression of) a good appearance'[2] = (cf. *Śkl – histakel* in late Hebrew),[3] as we find in connection with Abigail: 'The woman was *ṭōbat śekhel wiyĕfat tó'ar* (beautiful) (1 Sam 25.3), an expression synonymous with *yefat tó'ar weṭōbat mar'eh*[4] (see Esther 2.7, Gen. 29.17; 39.6). It should be added, however, that *śekhel*, as opposed to *mar'eh*, also connotes intelligence, and thus the double meaning of this root must be borne in mind (see below).

Śekhel in the sense of seeing and looking is also found in Gen. 3.6 in connection with the tree of knowledge, which is called: 'a delight to the eyes and...lovely *lĕhaśkil*'. *lĕhaśkil* should be interpreted here as 'to look (upon)', as it appears in the Aramaic Targums and as indicated by Ibn Janaḥ in his *Sefer Ha-Shorashim*. This meaning is confirmed by the description of the garden of the goddess Siduri in the epic of Gilgamesh. Of this garden, which contained trees bearing precious stones and diamonds (cf. Ezek. 28.13), it is said.[5] '(Clusters of grapes hang) lovely to gaze upon (*ana dagāla ṭābat*)...(bearing fruit,) beautiful to see (*ana amāri ṣâh*)'.

In this manner we can understand the phrase *śekhel ṭōb yitten ḥen* : 'good appearance wins favour' (Prov. 13.15), as well as other phrases cited by Ibn Janaḥ in *Sefer Ha-Shorashim*.[6] Of course, *śekhel* also means intelligence, like the

1. For a discussion of this verse (v. 2) and its division into parallel cola see: Y. Avishur, 'Phoenician Topoi in Proverbs 3', *Shnaton le-Miqra ule-Heqer ha-Mizrah ha-Qadum* 1 (1976), pp. 17ff. (Hebrew).

2. This was already noted by Jonah Ibn Janah in his *Sefer ha-Shorashim* and by David Kimhi in his *Sefer ha-Shorashim*. *Sakl* in Arabic means 'form', and on this point, it is interesting to note Tob. 1.13: χάριν καὶ μορφήν. According to P. Perles in 'A Misunderstood Hebrew Word', *JQR*, NS 17 (1926–27), p. 233, the Hebrew text, upon which the translator was dependent, read *ḥen weśekhel* (but see objection of J. Barr, *Comparative Philology of the Text of the Old Testament* (1968), pp. 244–45.

3. It is interesting to note that the hitpael form of *byn* also connotes seeing and looking.

4. See the translation of the Peshita. *'ntth špyr ḥzwh wšpyr qwbllh*

5. R.C. Thompson, *The Epic of Gilgamesh*, col. IX, vv. 49–51, Cf. *CAD* Ṣ, p. 66.

6. Such as 'Happy is he who looks to (= is thoughtful of) (*maśkil*) the wretched' (Ps. 41.2) and 'All this that the Lord has made me see (*hiśkil*) by his hand on me – the plan of all the works'

root *byn*, which includes the connotation of 'sight' (see n. 3). This being the case, it appears that in Gen. 3.6, as well as in 1 Sam. 25.3, the author intentionally used the verb *śekhel* to convey appearance so that he could also allude to the second meaning of the root, namely knowledge and intelligence.[7] Just as the tree of knowledge, which offers wisdom, is 'a delight to the eyes and *neḥmad… lĕhaśkil*, 'namely, both pleasant to look upon and desirable as a source of wisdom, so too is Abigail *ṭōbat śekhel* – both beautiful and intelligent. The story of Abigail, in fact, does attempt to stress her intelligence: 'And blessed be your prudence (*ṭa'amekh*)' (25.33), in other words, your intelligence (cf. *ṭēmu* in Akkadian).[8]

The verse under discussion (Prov. 3.4) cannot, therefore, be completely understood unless we interpret *śekhel ṭôb* to mean the good appearance of the son, through which he will find favour in the sight of God and man. The teachings and commandments that the son must learn in order to receive favour and *śekhel ṭôb* are likened to an item of jewellery bound about the throat (v. 3), which serves to adorn its wearer. Similar descriptions are also found in connection with instruction *(tôrāh)* and discipline (*mūsar*) in Prov. 1.8–9: 'My son, heed the discipline of your father, and do not forsake the instruction of your mother. For they are a graceful wreath (*liwyat ḥen*), upon your head, a necklace about your throat', and in conjunction with wisdom (*ḥokhmāh*) in Prov. 4.7ff: 'The beginning of wisdom is acquire wisdom…She will adorn your head with a graceful wreath (*liwyat ḥen*), crown you with a glorious diadem'. *Liwyat ḥen* in these passages is explained in detail by our verse: 'And you will find favour and *śekhel ṭôb* in the sight of God and man'.

Life, length of days and years, and favour in the sight of God and man, which appear in Prov. 3.1–4 as the rewards for observing the teachings and commandments, are also found in the Phoenician inscription of Yehawmilk, king of Byblos (fifth–fourth century BCE).[9] *tbrk bˁlt gbl ʾt yḥwmlk mlk gbl wtḥww wtʾrk ymw wšntw…wttn lw…ḥn lˁn ʾlnm wlˁn ˁm ʾrṣ z wḥn ˁm ʾrṣ…[lˁn] kl mmlkt*

[= May the mistress of Byblos bless Yehawmilk king of Byblos and grant him life and lengthen his days and years…and grant him…favour in the sight of the gods and the people of this land and favour with the land (in the sight of) every king.]

A shorter blessing, which from a linguistic standpoint is closer to Proverbs 3.4,

(1 Chron. 28.19). Compare Exod. 25.40: '*See* and do the design which you were shown on the mountain'.

7. See also the commentary of Benno Jacob. *Genesis, uebersetzt und erklaert* (1934), p. 107, regarding the double meaning of Gen. 3.6.

8. The double meaning of external appearance and intelligence is also found in Lk. 2.52: 'And Jesus increased in wisdom (σοφία) and in stature (ἡλικία) and in favour (χάρις) with God and man'. 'Stature' and 'wisdom' express both aspects of the word *śekhel*: external appearance and intelligence. The various interpretations of *śekhel ṭôb* have been noted and analysed by B. Couroyer, *Revue Biblique* 86 (1979), p. 961. Couroyer accepts the ecumenical translation: *tu passeras pour bien avise*. Indeed, *aviser* connotes seeing and understanding, as does *śekhel*. Couroyer, however, failed to notice that the root *śkl* also means 'seeing'.

9. Donner und Röllig, *Kanaanäische und Aramäische Inschriften* (=*KAI*) (1962), no. 10.8ff.

appears in a Phoenician inscription from Memphis in Egypt (second–first century BCE).[10]

> *[wy]tn lm ḥn wḥym lʿn ʾlnm wbn ʾdm*
>
> [= And (the gods) shall grant them favour and life in the sight of gods and men.]

The similarity between the Phoenician formulas and Prov. 3.1–4 gives rise to the assumption that these verses were influenced by Phoenician sources.[11]

However, the Ramesside letters, published by J. Černy[12] and later translated by E.F. Wente,[13] have revealed that blessing formulas such as these were more common in Egypt during the late Ramesside period (c. eleventh century BCE).[14] In one of the letters, for example, a man informs his friend that he is praying that the gods grant the friend life, health, and peace, length of days and old age, and give him favour (*ḥst*) before God and man.[15] This formula recurs in the letters in various forms.

Another interesting blessing that appears in the letters asks that the gods give the addressee life, health, and peace, and favour in the sight of the officer or general.[16]

Similar formulas are found in the Bible in connection with Egypt: Of Joseph it is said 'the Lord was with Joseph: He extended kindness to him and gave him favour in the sight of the chief jailer' (Gen. 39.21).

While here, as in the Phoenician inscriptions, the expression reads 'gave favour in the sight of *bĕʿēneŷ* whereas in the Egyptian letters it is 'gave favour before (*m b3ḥ*)', this difference is of no consequence,[17] since in Hebrew, too, 'in the sight of' can be interchanged with 'before (*liphnê*)'. Compare, for example, 'found favour in your sight' (Esther 7.3) and 'found favour before him' (Esth. 8.5). In Akkadian as well, the sign IGI stands for both eye (*īnu*) and face (*pānu*) (and also means before = *mahar*).

Three other verses that refer to God granting a person favour in the eyes of a superior also appear in connection with Egypt:

> And I will give this people favour in the sight of the Egyptians (Exod. 3.21).
> And the Lord gave the people favour in the sight of the Egyptians. Moreover, the man

10. *KAI* no. 48.
11. See Avishur (above, n. 1).
12. J. Černy, *Late Ramesside Letters* (*Bibliotheca Aegyptiaca* IX), 1939.
13. E.F. Wente, *Late Ramesside Letters* (*SAOC* 33, 1967). See recently E. Wente, *Letters from Ancient Egypt* (1990).
14. This has been recently discussed by Couroyer (above, n. 7), pp. 92–101.
15. Wente (above, n. 12), nos. 1,3,6, etc. The juxtaposition of life and favour in these letters and in the Phoenician inscriptions accounts for the parallelism of life (*ḥayyim*) and favour (*ḥen*) in Prov. 3.22. Avishur (n. 1, above), p. 14, saw a Phoenician influence here, as well, but as it is now apparent that the Egyptian formulas are earlier, it would be better to assume that the influence was Egyptian.
16. Wente (above, n. 12), nos. 8, 11, 14, 45.
17. I therefore do not believe that there is any particular significance in the fact that the Septuagint translates *bĕʿēneŷ* in Prov. 3.4 as ἐνώπιον (and not ἐν αφθαλοῖς), as Couroyer claims (above, n. 7), p. 96.

> Moses was very great in the land of Egypt, in the sight of Pharaoh's servants and in the sight of the people (Exod. 11.3).[18]
> And the Lord had given the people favour in the sight of the Egyptians (Exod. 12.36).

Clearly, it is no coincidence that the expression 'gave favour in the sight of (a superior)', a stereotypical phrase in the Egyptian letters, occurs in verses that make reference to Egypt.

Verses from a later period which contain this expression no longer speak of granting *ḥen* (favour) but rather of granting *raḥamim* (mercy, compassion) (compare Babylonian usage, below). However, it is not the use of the word *raḥamim* in place of the word *ḥen* that causes us to regard these verses as late, as *raḥamim* and *ḥesed* (kindness) are both synonyms of *ḥen*.[19] In the Joseph story, for example, we read: 'May El Shaddai grant you *raḥamim* (mercy) before the man' (Gen. 43.14).[20]

Rather, the lateness of these verses lies in their syntax: instead of 'grant *raḥamim* to so-and-so before someone', we read 'grant (or 'set') so-and-so *leraḥamim* before someone':

> Set them *leraḥamim* in the sight of their captors [=grant them mercy in the sight of their captors] (1 Kgs 8.50).
> He set them *leraḥamim* before all their captors [=made all their captors kindly disposed toward them] (Ps. 106.46).
> And God set Daniel *leḥesed uleraḥamim* before the chief officer [=disposed the chief officer to be kind and compassionate toward Daniel] (Dan. 1.9).
> And set him *leraḥamim* before this man [= dispose that man to be compassionate toward him (Neh. 1.1).

Compare also the phrase in the letters from Elephantine: '*wlrḥmn yśymk qdm drywhwš mlk*", 'may he set you before King Darius [= dispose Darius to be compassionate toward you]' (see below).

In fact, the Aramaic Targums (*Tg. Onq.*, *Tg. Ps.-J.*, and the Syriac) translate the phrase 'gave *ḥen* in the sight of', found in the earlier verses cited above, as *yhb lrḥmn qdm/b'yny* [= gave *lrḥmn* (*lě* + compassion) in the sight of]. Moreover, the phrase 'give *lěḥen lěḥesed ulěraḥamim* in the sight of' [= dispose favourably, kindly, and compassionately toward] is common in Jewish liturgy, as will be shown below.

18. Compare the Yeḥawmilk inscription quoted above: 'favour in the sight of the people of this land...and in the sight of every king and man', which recalls favour 'in the sight of Pharaoh's servants and in the sight of the people' in this verse.

19. Indeed, they are juxtaposed and parallel. See Y. Avishur, *The Construct State of Synonyms in Biblical Rhetoric*, 1977, pp. 110–11, 154 (Hebrew) (in Gen. 39.21, we find *ḥesed* beside *ḥen*). The triplet *ḥen*, *ḥesed*, and *raḥamim* recurs frequently in Jewish liturgy. See below, and my comments in the *Shnaton* 1 (1976), pp. 253–54.

20. It has already been noted that this verse shows evidence of the Priestly redactor (note the expression '*El Shadday*) and is thus later than the source of the story itself. Indeed, the use of the phrase 'gave compassion (*ntn rḥmym*) to so-and-so before someone', instead of the expression 'gave favour in the sight of someone' that appears in the other verses cited here, attests the lateness of the verse. Nevertheless, this formula is earlier than 'gave *leraḥamim* before so-and-so', which appears in the late verses to which we will shortly refer. Compare Deut. 13.18 'and gave you compassion' and Jer. 42.12 'and I shall give you compassion', with the verses soon to be cited in which the expression 'gave *leraḥamim*' appears.

Another verse relevant to the present discussion is Ps. 84.12: 'For the Lord God is sun (*šemeš*) and shield (*magen*): the Lord grants (*yitten*) favour and honour, and does not withhold good (*ṭôb*) from those who walk blamelessly'. God gives favour and honour to those who walk blamelessly, just as he grants blessing[21] to the innocent in Ps. 24.4–5. A. Ehrlich[22] has suggested that *šemeš* (sun) refers here to a neck ornament (cf. Arabic *šams*,[23] and he compares this verse to Prov. 1.9 and Prov. 1.3, the verse that engendered the present discussion (see above). Without mentioning Ehrlich, M. Dahood[24] compared the shield and the use of the verb *yitten* in Ps. 84.12 with Prov. 4.9: 'She will place (*titten*) upon your head a graceful wreath (*liwyat ḥen*): a crown of glory she will deliver to you (*tĕmagneka*)'. It is quite probable, therefore, that the 'sun and shield' are objects of the verb *yitten* and not divine epithets. They are the ornaments by virtue of which favour and honour are bestowed upon their wearer. As we shall see below, in the Bible (1 Sam. 2.26), and in Assyrian literature, 'good' (*ṭāb*) often replaces 'favour' (*ḥen*) in the phrase 'favour in the sight of', and it thus seems that the end of Ps. 84.12 also refers to 'finding favour'.

Two other verses that refer to 'granting favour' appear in Proverbs: 'and he shall grant favour to the lowly' (*lʿnyym* [*qere: lʿnwym*]) (3.34), and '*śekhel ṭôb* (good appearance/sense) wins (lit. grants) favour' (13.15). The book of Proverbs is replete with Egyptian influences, and thus it is not surprising that it contains both the stereotypical phrase 'find favour in the sight of God and men', found in Egyptian letters, and the concept of 'granting favour (*ntn ḥn*)'.

Other than in the verses cited above, the phrase 'grant favour' (*natan ḥen*) does not occur in the Bible.

B. *The Formula in Assyrian Literature*

The motif under discussion is also found in Mesopotamian literature of the first millennium BCE, especially in royal epistles from the neo-Assyrian empire. Here we find the formula 'good in the sight of gods and men'. Thus, for example, an official writes to his king, Ashurbanipal:[25]

> May Ishtar grant you length of days and years, physical health and joy of heart...the issue of my lord the king's mouth is good with gods and men (*ṣit pī ša šarri*...⌊*ṭāb itti*⌋ *ilī u amīlūti*)[26]

21. 'Blessing' (*berakhah*) appears together with 'shining of countenance' and 'granting favour' in the Priestly Benediction in Num. 6.25–26 'The Lord bless you... The Lord cause His face to shine upon you and grant favour to you (*wiyḥuneka*)', and in the final blessing of the eighteen Benedictions of daily prayer: 'Grant peace, goodness, and blessing, favour (*ḥn*), and kindness (*wḥsd*), and compassion (*wrḥmym*) to us...' See also below.

22. A.B. Ehrlich, *Die Psalmen* (1905), p. 203.

23. Compare the 'suns (*šĕvisim*) and the crescents' in Isa. 3.18. Since it has become apparent that špš in Ugaritic means sun, there is no longer any doubt that *šĕvis* is the Arabic *šams*, an adornment worn about the neck in the shape of a small sun. See also H. Wildberger, *Jesaja 1–12* (BK), 1972, p. 141.

24. M. Dahood, *Psalms II* (1968), p. 283.

25. L. Waterman, *Royal Correspondence of the Assyrian Empire* (1930), no. 1110.5f.

26. *CAD* A/II *amīlūtu*, p. 59, 2.

In another letter to the same king we find:[27]

> This act of kindness which is acceptable before gods and men (*ina* IGI DINGIR LÚ-*ti mahratuni*) which the king has done.[28]

A letter from Ashurbanipal to his courtier reads:[29]

> The things that you have done are good with gods and man (*ša ina muhhi ilī u amīli* [LÚ] *ṭābu šunu*).

Here we find the phrase 'gods and *man* (LÚ)', as in Prov. 3.4, rather than 'gods and *men* (LÚ-*tu*), as in the other references cited above.

The formula is found in the negative in the words of Esarhaddon:[30]

> Anything that is not good with gods and men (*ša eli ilāni u amīlūtu lā ṭâbu*)[31]

The formula 'good before (or: with) God and men' is reflected in 1 Sam. 2.26: 'and favour (*ṭôb*) both with (*ʿim*) the God and with (*ʿim*) men' (cf. Lk. 2.52). Here, *'im* is synonymous with *liphnê* (before). Indeed, these words are parallel in Ps. 72.5: 'Let them fear You as (*ʿim*) the sun [shines], as (*liphnê*) the moon [lasts], generations on end'.[32]

The words *ʿim* and *liphnê* (or *bĕʿēneŷ*) are also interchanged when they appear together with the word *hikkabed* (to be honoured). In 2 Sam. 6.22 we find: 'but among (*'im*) the slavegirls that you speak of, among them (*ʿimam*) I will be honoured (*ikkabedah*)', whereas in Lev. 10.3 we read: 'and I will be glorified (*ʾekkabed*) before (*ʿal pene*) all the people'. In Isa. 43.4 and 49.5 we find *hikkabed bĕʿēney*.

In Mesopotamia, as in Egypt, Phoenicia, and Israel, we also find prayers that God dispose god and men to treat the suppliant with compassion and goodness:

> May the good angel stand at my head, god and goddess and men provide me with well-being (*salīmu liršûni*).[33]

> May the god, the goddess, and men provide me with well-being, and show me compassion.[34]

27. Waterman (above, n. 25), no. 358.19.

28. Compare the identical formula in the treaty of Esarhaddon with the vassals: 'May that which is acceptable in the sight of God and men be acceptable in your sight and good for you' (11.296–97). See my translation in *Shnaton* 1 (1976), p. 102, and the note on this line on p. 84. See also K.H. Deller, 'Die Briefe des Adad-šumu-uṣur', *Festschrift von Soden*, *ADAT* 1 (1969), p. 50, which contains references to other places within the royal epistles in which this formula appears.

29. Waterman (above, n. 25), no. 1380.

30. R. Borger, *Die Inschriften Asarhaddons* (1956), p. 42, 1.42.

31. In Assyrian prayers we found 'the anger of God and men' (š*ibšat ilī u amilūti*). See E. Ebeling, *Akkadische Gebetserie 'Handerhebung*' (1953), p. 78.57.

32. In this verse, *liphnê* takes on the meaning of *ʿim* = as. See S. Paul 'Psalm 72.5, A Traditional Blessing of the Long Life of the King', *JNES* 31 (1972), pp. 351–55. In contrast, in 1 Sam. 2.26, *'im* means *liphnê* (before).

33. Ebeling (above, n. 31), p. 148: 24–25.

34. *Ibid.*, p. 78.61. According to the B text (see n. 10 in his book, in which we find *salīma rašû* as well as *rēma šakānu*), *rēma rašû* is identical to *salīma rašû/šakānu* and both express pardon and mercy.

> Provide me with a good angel...[may] the god, the goddess, and the men who are angry make peace with me, speak honestly to me.[35]

These Babylonian prayers make reference to 'well-being' and 'compassion' and not to 'favour'. Indeed, in biblical verses from the period of the Babylonian exile as well (see above), 'compassion' (*raḥamim*) appears in place of 'favour' (*ḥen*). Essentially, there is no difference between prayers for favour and requests for well-being and compassion. What they actually speak of is the development of a mutual relationship between the suppliant and God and men: According to one formula, the suppliant asks to find favour in the sight of God and men and according to the other, he asks that God and men make peace with him and show him compassion. The formulas we have quoted from the Assyrian royal inscriptions, however, differ from the west Semitic formulas in that they do not speak of finding favour in the sight of God and men, but rather request, as we have seen, that the individual be good with God and men; in terms of content, however, these prayers are identical.

In late biblical books we also encounter the phrase 'find peace' in the sight of someone, instead of 'find favour'. The verse 'So I became in his eyes as one who finds peace (*šalôm*)' (Song 8.10) is nothing but a variation of 'So I became in his eyes as one who finds favour (*ḥen*)'. Moreover, in late Jewish liturgy, the words *ḥen*, *ḥesed*, *raḥamim*, *ṭōbah*, *berakhah*, and *šalôm* (favour, kindness, compassion, goodness, blessing, and peace) frequently appear together, as in the final blessing of the Eighteen Benedictions of daily prayer:[36] 'Grant peace, goodness, and blessing, favour and kindness and compassion to us and all Israel Your people'. The origins of this blessing can be traced to the Priestly Benediction in Num. 6.25–26, in which we also find the combination of the words 'blessing' (*berakhah*), 'favour' (*ḥen*), and 'peace' (*šalôm*):

> The Lord bless you (*yebarekhekha*)...the Lord cause His face to shine upon you and be gracious to you (*wiyĕḥuneka*). The Lord lift up his countenance upon you[37] and grant you peace (š*alôm*).

And indeed, the rabbis interpreted *wiyĕḥuneka* to mean 'give you favour in the sight of mankind'[38] and 'grant you peace' as 'peace with every man'.[39] It seems that the Priestly Benediction and the final blessing of the Eighteen Benedictions are not prayers for pardon and mercy, in other words, requests that the suppliant be exempted from punishment; rather, they ask that God grant favour and peace to the people of Israel, so that others will love them and make peace with them, as in the formulas of 'granting favour' under discussion.[40]

35. *Ibid.*, p. 82.110ff.

36. See also my article in *Shnaton* 1 (1976) (above, n. 19), pp. 253–54.

37. *naśa' pānim* (lifting of countenance), like *pānu wabālu* in Akkadian (see *CAD* A I *abālu* A [*pānu* B, pp. 18–19], means to show kindness.

38. *Sifrê Naśo* 41 (Horowitz edition, p. 44).

39. *Ibid.*, 42 (p. 46).

40. I therefore prefer the translation appearing in the notes to the JPS translation (1962), 'make His face to shine upon thee and be gracious to thee', to the translation offered in the body of the text, 'deal kindly and graciously with you'. Also cf. the translation of the New English Bible. The 'shining

The 'good angel' mentioned in the Babylonian prayers asking for peace from god and men is a personal intermediary to whom the suppliant turns. In our opinion, he is identical to the Muses to whom Solon turns in his prayer (see below), as well as the angels who are asked to grant favour and kindness in late Jewish prayers (see below).

C. *The Formula in Letters from the Persian Period*

The Aramaic letters from the Persian period open with blessings for peace, longevity, happiness, and health (=strength), similar to those from Egypt and Assyria.[41] They also contain wishes for the attainment of peace and compassion from God, on the one hand, and from the king and ministers (=men), on the other. For example, in a letter to Bagohi regarding the construction of the temple at Elephantine we read:

> *šlm mrʾn ʾlh šmyʾ yšğl śgvʾ bkl ʿydn wlrḥmn*
> *yśymnk qdm dryhws mlkʾ wbny bytʾ ytyr mn ḥd ʾlp*
> *wḥyn ʾrykyn yntn lk wḥdh wšryr hwy bkl ʿydn*[42]
>
> [= May our Lord, God of the heavens, ask for much peace at all times, and dispose Darius the king and his household compassionately toward you a thousandfold more than now and grant you a long life, and may you be happy and healthy at all times.]

The 'thousandfold' blessing is found frequently in Neo-Assyrian letters. For example:

> May gods and men repay the kindness of the king, my lord, a thousandfold.[43]
> May the gods increase such blessings a thousandfold and grant them to the king, my lord.[44]

These blessings should be compared with Deuteronomy 1.11:

> May the Lord, the God of your fathers, increase your numbers a thousandfold, and bless you (see also 2 Sam. 24.3)

In another Persian letter (from 'Artahay to Nehtihur) we read:

of God's face' is explained in the final blessing of the Eighteen Benedictions of daily prayers: *barkhenu abinu be'or panekha* (bless us, our Father, with the light of your countenance), which recalls *Sefer Ha-Razim* (see below), in which the angels are asked to grant the brilliance of their countenance to the suppliant so that he will find *ḥen waḥesed* in the sight of all men.

41. Regarding the various blessing formulas in the Aramaic letters see J.A. Fitzmyer, 'Some Notes on Aramaic epistolography', *JBL* 93 (1974), pp. 214–15. See also B. Porten, 'The Archive of Jedeniah son of Gemariah of Elephantine – The Structure and Style of the Letters (I)', *Eretz Israel* 14 (1978). H.L. Ginzberg volume, pp. 165–66.

42. A. E. Cowley, *Aramaic Papyri of the Fifth Century* B.C. (1923), no. 30, 11, 1–3; cf. No. 31.11, 1–3; no. 38.11, 2–3.

43. Waterman (above, n. 25), no. 6, rev. 14.

44. *Ibid.*, no. 435, 1. 18, Deller (above, n. 28), p. 50j; *CAD* L s.v. *limu* B a.

šlm wšrrt śgy' hwšrt lk...kn 'bd kzy l'lhy' wl'ršm tḥd[y][45]

[= I am sending (blessings of) peace and much health,...act in order to appease God[46] and Arsam.]

The letter concludes with a prayer for peace:

[ṣlw kzy] ʾlhyʾ šlm yśmw lk

[= pray that the gods will grant you peace].[47]

D. *The Formula in Greek Literature*

In Solon's prayer to the Muses we read.[48]

ὄλβον μοι προς θεῶν μακάρων δότε καὶ προς ἁπάντων ἀνθρώπων αἰεὶ δόξαν ἔχειν ἀγαθήν

[= Grant that I inherit wealth from the immortal gods and good honour (favour)[49] always from all men.]

This call to the Muses resembles the call to the intermediary angels,[50] which was common in Babylonian and Jewish prayers (see below). The formula, however, differs from those we have discussed here: it is not favour and honour that is requested of gods and men, but rather wealth from God and honour from men. Nonetheless, these prayers are essentially the same, since the request to find favour in the sight of God and men is really a plea that the gods and men be good to the suppliant. In the case before us, the poet asks for wealth from the gods and honour from people.

E. *The Formulas in Late Hebrew Literature*

In the Book of Tobit 1.13, we learn that God gave Tobit favour and 'good appearance' (χὰριν καὶ μορφὴν)[51] before Shalmaneser the king, whereas in Eccl. 45.1ff. we read that Moses 'found favour in the sight of all mankind [and was beloved]

45. G.R. Driver, *Aramaic Documents of the Fifth Century B.C.* (1957), no. xlll.
46. Driver (above, n. 44) felt the need to translate *'lhy'* as 'his Majesty', but there is no basis for this.
47. Driver (above, n. 45), 1. 5.
48. For a recent discussion of this prayer see K. Alt, *Hermes* 107 (1979), pp. 389f.
49. Alt (above, n. 48), translates δόξε as *Ansehen*, which mean an appearance that inspires both respect and admiration. Cf. Ps. 84.12: 'God grants favour and honor (*ḥen wekhabod*)', cited above.
50. The Muses resemble the angels in many ways: they sing in a choir and offer praise to Zeus (Hesiod, *Theogony*, 11. 10ff) and to Apollo (Iliad I, 603–604), as do the angels in the Bible (Isa. 6.3; Ez. 3.12; Ps. 89.6ff.; Job 38.7); they are omniscient (*Iliad* 2.484ff.), as are the angels (2 Sam. 14.20); the Muses inspire the poet to prophesy (E.R. Dodds, *The Greeks and the Irrational*, 1959, p. 82), as does the angel who talks with the prophet (Zech. 1.9, 14, etc.); they appear out of a mist (Hesiod, *Theogony*, 9). Cf. Isa. 6.4; Ezek. 1.4–5; cf. My article 'The Heavenly Praise in Unison', *Meqor Hajjim, Festschrift für G. Molin* (1983), p. 434.
51. See n. 3, above. μορφή here is close in meaning to δόξα (= *Ansehen*) in the prayer of Solon, and See n. 49, above.

by God and men'.[52] Our interest, however, lies in the prayers to God that ask for favour in his sight and in the sight of man (literally, that God give the suppliant favour in the sight of others, see above). Such formulas are indeed found in Jewish liturgy. In the morning blessings[53] of the daily service we find:

> And give me today and everyday grace, favour and mercy (*leḥen ulĕḥesed ulĕraḥamim* in your sight and in the sight of all those who see me [= dispose them favourably, kindly, and compassionately toward me] (*b. Ber.* 60b).

Even more interesting are the formulas in *Sefer Ha-Razim*,[54] which appear in the context of the adjurations of the angels:

> I adjure you to grant favour, grace and mercy (*ḥen waḥesed weraḥamim*) to so-and-so from the brilliant grace, favour and mercy of your countenance...and cause me to find favour, grace, and mercy, and honour (*kabod*) in the sight of all mankind (p. 76).

From this we learn that the 'favour' (*ḥen*) on a person's countenance emanates from the countenances of the angels, and therefore one turns to the angels in this matter. As we have already mentioned, favour was necessary in order to charm the ministers and other superiors upon whom an individual was dependent. Indeed, the author of *Sefer ha-Razim* states explicitly regarding the angels who grant favour:

> These are the angels who change the minds of the king and the will of great ones, and chiefs, and rulers, and leaders and crown with favour and grace (*ḥen waḥesed*) all those who request *anything* of them in purity (p. 73).

The receipt of favour from the angels was dependent upon writing 'characters on a silver plate' and binding this plate to the tablet of the heart (p. 84), an act that recalls the verses in Prov. 3.3–4: 'Bind them about your throat, write them on the tablet of your heart, and you will find *ḥen weśekhel ṭôb* in the sight of God and man' (see above). The prayers in *Sefer ha-Razim* bear a striking resemblance to the Babylonian prayers, which are also adjurations accompanied by magical acts.

The act of turning to the angels in order to attain favour is preserved in the official liturgy, as well. Toward the end of the version of the Grace after Meals customary among Ashkenazi Jews we find the prayer:

> May those on high speak favourably on our behalf, so that we may have enduring peace. May we receive blessings from the Lord, justice from the God who saves us, and may we find *ḥen weśekhel ṭôb* in the sight of God and man.

In the Babylonian Talmud (*Ḥul.* 92a) we read that the princes of the nations (=angels)[55] intercede on Israel's behalf, and thus the above formula may indeed be regarded as a plea that the angels intercede on the suppliants' behalf, to ensure that they find favour in the sight of God and man.

52. Also cf. the Wisdom of Solomon 4.1: 'Perfection...will be recognized by God and men'.

53. Cf. my article 'The Morning Prayers (*Birkhot Haschachar*) in Qumran and in the Conventional Jewish Literature', *Revue de Qumran* 19 (1988), pp. 481–94.

54. M. Margalioth, *Sefer Ha-Razim* (1967). The editor dates the work to the third century CE.

55. See Rashi's commentary on this passage.

Even more instructive is a prayer that is said after the Priestly Benediction that is taken from a liturgical collection by Rabbi Nathan Hannover entitled *Shaʿarei Ziyyon*. The prayer is based on the names of angels. *'nqtm pstm pspsym dywnsym'* which are derived from the verses of the Priestly Benediction.[56] In it, we read:

> And set us *le'ahaba leḥen ulḥesed* in your sight and in the sight of all who see us' [= dispose them lovingly, favourable, and kindly to us].

This prayer is undoubtedly directed toward the angels, and indeed, in *Sefer ha-Razim*, Pesipiel (cf. *pstm pspsym*) appears as one of the angels to whom one turns if one wishes to find favour and kindness in the sight of superiors.[57]

F. *Summary*

Prayers for the favour of God and men, officials and rulers, first appear in Egyptian letters from the late Ramesside period (eleventh century BCE). They are later found in Phoenician inscriptions, one of which has been discovered at Memphis in Egypt. In the Pentateuch, such motifs appear in connection with Egypt: God gave Joseph favour in the sight of the keeper of the prison (Gen. 39.21); God gave favour to the Israelites in the sight of the Egyptians and Moses was esteemed among Pharaoh's courtiers (Exod. 3.21; 11.3; 12.36). The expression 'find *ḥen weśekhel ṭôb* in the sight of God and man' (Prov. 3.4) is even found in a collection of proverbs replete with Egyptian influences.[58] It seems, therefore, that the expression entered Israel through Egyptian influence.

In Mesopotamia as well, this expression was prevalent, but instead of the words 'find favour' (in the sight of God and men) we find 'to be good' (with God and men), a phrase which also occurs in 1 Sam. 2.26. Moreover, instead of 'favour', the Mesopotamian formulas ask for 'compassion and peace', requests that also occur in late biblical literature ('dispose him to be compassionate to') and in Jewish liturgy.

Furthermore, the Babylonian texts refer to a good angel who stands beside the one who asks for compassion and peace. This phenomenon was also recently discovered in *Sefer ha-Razim*, published by M. Margalioth.[59] Here, the angels are sworn to grant the suppliant favour and grace in the sight of all who see him, especially officials and rulers upon whom the suppliant is dependent. Prayers such as these filtered into the Jewish liturgy, despite the objections to praying to angels in the official liturgy.

56. A. Berliner, *Randbemerkungen zum taeglichen Gebetbuch* I (1909), pp. 32–34.

57. Margalioth (above, n. 54), pp. 83–84, 11. 38–56.

58. Regarding the Egyptian background of Prov. 1–9 see C. Kayatz, *Studien zu Prov. 1–9, eine form- und motivgeschichtliche Untersuchung unter Einbeziehung aegyptischen Vergleichsmaterial* (*WMANT*), 1966, 22. According to Couroyer (above, n. 7), pp. 98ff., the expression *śekhel ṭôb* in Prov. 3.4 is similar to the Egyptian *spd-hr* which appears there next to *hswt* = *ḥen*, as in Prov. 3.4, and it refers to one possessing sharpness and alertness.

59. See above, n. 53.

Addendum in the Light of Two New Epigraphic Discoveries

A. In the bilingual (Akkadian, Aramaic) inscription appearing upon the statue of the King of Gozan on the Habur, which was discovered at Tel Fekheriah in 1979,[60] we read, in the Aramaic section:

> *wlm'n 'mrt pmh 'l 'lhn w'l 'nšn tyṭb*
>
> [= (the statue) was erected in order that the words of his mouth (the king's request) will be good with God and men.]

This formula corresponds to the Assyrian formula quoted above: 'May the issue of the king's mouth be good with God and men'.[61] It should be noted that the statue and its inscription served as an intermediary, so to speak, for the transmission of the king's prayers to his God.[62] The statue is, therefore, a kind of 'good angel', an advocate of the king who ensured that god and men would grant the king's wishes, a matter which we have discussed above.

B. In a dedicatory engraving on Pithos B found at Kuntilat Ajrud, we read after an opening formula similar to the opening of the letter (said so-and-so...say to so-and-so).[63]

> May he bless you and keep you. Favour him (*ḥnnh*) with all that he may ask of man... And may YHWH give him as his heart [desires].[64]

Here too, we find a twofold request: (1) For favour in the sight of men so that everything asked[65] of people will be granted: (2) That God will grant the suppliant his wishes. The combination of 'all that he may ask of men' and 'favour' recalls verses from the story of the Exodus from Egypt, mentioned above: 'Tell the people to borrow, each man from his neighbour...and the Lord gave the people favour...' (Exod. 11.2–3) and 'and borrowed from the Egyptians...and the Lord gave the people favour...' (Exod. 12.35–36, and cf. Exod. 3.21–22).

It should also be added that the elements: 'The Lord bless you and keep you...and be gracious to you (*wiyeḥuneka*)' in the Priestly Benediction (see above) are reflected in the inscription from Ajrud: 'May he bless you and keep you (*ybrkk wyšmrk*)...and favour him (*ḥnn*)'.

60. Cf. *La Statue de Tell Fekherye et son inscription biblique assyro-aramenne* (ed. Ali Abou-Assaf, Pierre Bordreuil, Alan R. Millard, 1982).

61. The Akkadian in the Tell Fekhrye Inscription reads: *qibīt pišu eli ilāni u niše ṭubbi*, see *ibid.* (n. 60), p. 16.

62. Regarding this practice in Mesopotamia see W.W. Hallo, 'Individual Prayer in Sumerian: The Continuity of a Tradition', *JAOS* 88 (1968), p. 79 n. 74; *idem*, 'The royal Correspondence of Larsa', in *S.N. Kramer Anniversary Volume* (1976), p. 211.

63. See J. Naveh, 'Graffiti and Dedications', *BASOR* 235 (1979), p. 29.

64. I wish to thank Dr Z. Meshel for bringing this find to my attention.

65. Cf. the Panamuwa inscription: *wmz 'š'l mn 'lhy ytn ly* (Donner-Röllig, above, n. 9, 214.4) and see also the dedicatory inscription to Panamuwa II which concludes with a fragmentary blessing, of which the following words have survived: *qdm 'lh wqdm 'nš* (before God and before men) (*ibid.*, 215.23).

Chapter 18

Universalistic and Particularistic Trends During the Exile and Restoration[1]

It was the prophets, as is well known, who cultivated the religious universalistic ideal, articulating the visionary hope that all the nations of the world recognize YHWH, the God of Israel. Pentateuchal literature mentions no such idea. To the contrary, the Pentateuch actually contains the idea that YHWH himself apportioned 'the gods' among the nations of the world, and that these 'gods' constitute the natural focus of their faith. These second-order deities and the faith in them 'the Lord your God allotted to other peoples everywhere under heaven' (Deut. 4.19; cf. 29.25).[2] However, during First Temple times, the prophetic universalistic aspirations amounted to no more than a utopian wish, a vision to materialize only in the distant future. Israel during this period was not itself entirely clean of paganism, and the time had not yet ripened to speak of reforming other nations in this regard.

Only during the period of the Restoration did this prophetic universalistic ambition first find practical, concrete expression. This period saw the nation of Israel purified, purged of the sin of paganism, ready to have an impact on other nations as well. Deutero-Isaiah, who prophesied during this period, does not offer a vision of the eschaton or days yet to come, as had his prophetic forebearers, but rather envisions for the present, for the reality of his own times. This prophet, who watched the ancient geopolitical world disintegrate in the wake of Babylon's demise, turns to the bewildered Gentile refugees, saying in unequivocal terms: 'Turn to me and be saved...for I am God, and there is none else... To Me every knee shall bend, every tongue swear loyalty' (45.22–23). The prophet perceives his period as the right moment for fixing the world under the kingdom of God. The Babylonian kingdom, the land of idolatry, is falling apart, and on the horizon

1. Translated from the Hebrew by Simeon Chavel. *Addenda* placed at the end of the reprinted version of the article in 1979 have been integrated into the work.

2. This constitutes one of the verses which, according to Rabbinic tradition, the wise scribes revised in the copy of the Pentateuch they prepared for King Ptolemey. They wrote: 'the Lord your God allotted them *to illuminate for all the nations*' להאיר לכל העמים (*Mek.* to Exod. 12.40). Rashi brings this comment at Deut. 4.19, but it cannot be made to fit the parallel verse in Deut. 29.25, which says, 'gods whom they did not experience and whom He had not allotted to them'. On the character of the tradition about scribal revisions, see A. Geiger, *The Bible and Its Translations*, pp. 282ff. (Hebrew trans. of German original), and recently E. Tov, 'The Rabbinic Tradition Concerning the Alterations Inserted into the Greek Pentateuch and Their Relation to the Original Text of the LXX', *Journal for the Study of Judaism* 15 (1984), pp. 65–89.

arises Cyrus, the king seen by the prophet as YHWH's anointed (45.1), upon whom it falls to play an important role in realizing the universalistic objective.

Chapters 40–48 in the book of Isaiah, said against the background of Cyrus' rise and the conquest of Babylon,[3] contain prophecies in which the monotheistic message reaches the pinnacle of expression (41.4; 43.10; 45.5–7, 14, 18, 22). This message is directed mainly at the islands and peoples at the ends of the earth (41.1, 5; 42.4, 10, 12; 45.22; 49.1). Before this prophet's eyes stands the giant empire recently built by Cyrus; these distant islands and peoples, therefore, are apparently those of Greece, Asia Minor, and, in the East, those in the region of India, which Cyrus had recently conquered. According to this prophet, Cyrus fulfills a divine mission in that he spreads the monotheistic faith throughout the world. Plausibly, Cyrus suited this assignment more than any other king because he came from an aniconic religion, whose concepts resembled those of the Israelite faith more than the religions of other nations. Indeed, Cyrus is anointed by YHWH, called by him 'so that they may know, from east to west, that there is none but me; I am the Lord and there is none else' (45.6).

In the background of Deutero-Isaiah's prophecy stands the drama of a legal suit[4] against the Gentiles and their gods. Taking the gods of the Gentiles and their worshippers to court, the God of Israel asks them to lay out their arguments and proofs to substantiate the divine power of these supposed gods (41.1ff., 21ff., *et al.*). Since they cannot demonstrate the power to see the future, to envision the unfolding of history, they are false. By contrast, Israel testifies in this trial to the existence of prophecies from its God, proving the exclusive existence of its own God (43.10; 44.8). By the same token, additional pieces of evidence brought during the trial demonstrate Israel's God as the one and only. These proofs are both positive and negative. One line of reasoning argues that the gods of the Gentiles, mute idols, insignificant and empty, aspire vainly to represent the image of God, who transcends description through any sort of image or form (40.18, 25, *et al.*).[5] A second line of argument brings proof positive from the creation of heaven and earth: 'Lift high your eyes and see: who created these?' (40.26) – God created the luminaries and the forces of nature; these creations themselves are not divine. The case results in a clear verdict: 'I am He: before Me no god was formed and none shall exist' (43.10), 'I am God and there is none else' (45.22). Undoubtedly, this formulation has particular significance. The Pentateuch generally contains the expression, 'I am YHWH', whereas here the prophet says, 'I am God',

3. See M. Haran, *Between the First and the Last: A Literary and Historical Study of the Unit of Prophecies in the Book of Isaiah, Chapters 40–48* (1963).

4. For this motif in Deutero-Isaiah see L. Köhler, *Deuterojesaja stilkritisch untersucht*, *BZAW* 37 (1923). See also B. Gemser, 'The Rib-Pattern in Hebrew Mentality', *SVT* III (1955), pp. 120ff.

5. In this, he rebuts earlier conceptions, primarily the priestly one according to which God made mankind in his own image (Gen. 1.26–27; 5.1). Elsewhere I deal with Deutero-Isaiah's polemic against the anthropomorphic conception in Gen. 1 in connection with other images: God's work and rest (40.28), his consultation with the heavenly retinue (40.14; 44.24), and existence of primordial, formless matter (the deep, earth, and darkness) prior to Creation (45.7, 18–19). See my article in *Tarbiz* 37 (1968), pp. 105–132.

emphasizing the universal aspect of Israel's God.[6] Remarkably, the proofs for God's exclusive unity and existence come from the cosmic-universal sphere, not the national one. God appears here as the creator of the world, the 'maker and breaker' of kings (40.23), not as the one who, in particular, took Israel out of Egypt, as he appears elsewhere in the Bible, especially the Pentateuch.

The unique character of Deutero-Isaiah's universalistic prophecy also stands out in that it contains no mass movements of peoples and kingdoms to Mount Zion, as found in the prophecies of Isaiah son of Amoṣ and Micah in connection with the justice which will usher in world peace.[7] The prophet beckons the private individual, wherever he or she is, to bow to YHWH and swear by him (45.23). And indeed, different people from various places hearken his call, declaring their affiliation to the God of Israel: 'One shall say, "I am the Lord's", another shall use the name of "Jacob", another shall mark his arm,[8] "of the Lord" and adopt the name of "Israel" ' (44.5).[9] Even if this context deals with Israel, still Israel functions here as a tool in the universalistic mission. Israel bears the responsibility of bringing the monotheistic creed to the world and was 'elected' to this task. Indeed, election has a special significance in Deutero-Isaiah.

In two places the Bible demonstrates a fully formulated ideology regarding election, in Deuteronomy and in Deutero-Isaiah.[10] Deuteronomy sees election mainly as a privilege. From among all the nations on the face of the earth, YHWH chose Israel to be his holy people (Deut. 7.6; 14.2); He chose to favour only the forefathers of the Israelites (4.37; 10.15). In the chapters of the consoling prophet, by contrast, election constitutes an obligation and an assignment.[11] God chose Israel to serve as a covenantal people[12] and a light unto the nations (Isa. 42.6;

6. On the use of the formulation, 'I am YHWH', see J. Morgenstern, 'Deutero-Isaiah's Terminology for "Universal God" ', *JBL* 62 (1943), pp. 269–80; S.M. Blank, 'Studies in Deutero-Isaiah', *HUCA* 15 (1940), pp. 1–46; so, too, G.F. Moore, *Judaism* I, 1927, pp. 227ff.

7. The main idea in this prophecy does not consist of eschatological repentence, as B. Uffenheimer would have it ('History and Eschatology in the Book of Micah', *Bet Mikra* [1963], p. 53 [Hebrew]), but rather eternal peace, as Y. Kaufmann perceived (*History of the Israelite Faith*, III.204–205 [Hebrew]). The nations swarm to Zion not in order to know YHWH and accept his religion, but in order to fall under his legal sovereignty: 'Thus He will judge among the nations and arbitrate for the many peoples, and they shall beat their swords into ploughshares…they shall never again know war'. Indeed, the verses adjacent to this prophecy, in Isa. 2.5 and in Mic. 4.5 ('Though all the peoples walk, each in the names of its gods, we will walk in the name of the Lord our God forever and ever') demonstrate that the prophecy does not speak of eschatological repentance.

8. Hebrew יכתוב ידו means he will write on his hand to signal his affiliation, like the custom of marking slaves on their hands to establish their owners. See R. Yaron, *The Law of the Elephantine Documents* (1961), p. 49, and recently, M. Bar-Ilan, 'Magic Seals on the Body Among Jews in the First Centuries C.E.', *Tarbiz* 57 (1987), pp. 37–38 (Hebrew).

9. See *Avot de Rabbi Nathan* (Schecther edn) ch. 36: ' "and he shall be called by the name Israel" – these are the true proselytes גרי אמת'. S. Lieberman (*Greek and Hellenism in Israel*, p. 63) brings the following reading, which he prefers as more correct: 'these are the Gentile proselytes גרי אומות העולם'.

10. See G. Quell, *Theologisches Wörterbuch zum NT* IV, 1939, pp. 148ff.

11. See I. Heinemann, 'The Election of Israel in the Bible', *Sinai* 16 (1945), p. 22. He names this category of election, 'appointment'.

12. The word 'nation' (עם) in 42.6 means all humanity, as demonstrated by the previous verse

49.6).[13] In Deuteronomy, which sees paganism as the natural allotment of the Gentiles, election comes to distinguish Israel from the other nations, to distance Israel from them; in other words, election in Deuteronomy serves a nationalistic goal. In Deutero-Isaiah, election functions to draw the nations to Israel and its faith, namely, it serves a universalistic aim. The election of Israel here does not purport to bring great success to Israel itself, as in Deuteronomy, but rather to have Israel serve as a means for the spiritual advancement of the nations – for their own benefit. YHWH chose the 'servant of YHWH', that visionary image in Deutero-Isaiah[14] symbolizing the ideal and true Israel, even if not portraying Israel realistically, not only in order to firmly establish the Israelite tribes, but also to have them serve as a light unto the nations, bringing the salvation of YHWH to the furthest reaches of the earth (49.6). National redemption in Deutero-Isaiah, then, amounts to a means for a general universal redemption, which itself marks the true salvation.

The Beginnings of the Realization of the Universalistic Vision

If chs. 40–55 bring the universalistic message merely in the form of an entreaty, beseeching the nations of the earth, the later chapters in Deutero-Isaiah (56–66), said as far as one can tell in Israel and not in Babylon,[15] contain already the beginnings of the realization of the universalistic vision.

In ch. 56 the prophet turns to the Gentiles joining YHWH's ranks and to the eunuchs in the courts of the Gentile kings, promising them complete absorption into the congregation of Israelite faithful (vv. 1–8). This prophecy provides clear testimony to the existence of Gentile groups accepting the 'yoke of the kingdom of heaven'. It appears that the Jewish diaspora in Babylon and Persia in this period inspired excitement and activity among the Gentiles, particularly those in court circles. Judean exiles, including apparently the prophet himself, belonged to the Judean élite, so it should occasion no wonder that they played a role in the royal court. Some go so far as to say that Deutero-Isaiah was close to Cyrus and his courtiers.[16]

(42.5): 'Thus says God the Lord, who created the heavens and stretched them out, who spread out the earth and what it brings forth, who gave breath to the people upon it and life to those who walk thereon'.

13. At least from the point of view of the concept and theme of election, there is an identification between the 'servant of YHWH' spoken of here and Israel. Election and 'calling by name' are said of both Israel and the servant; see Haran, supra, pp. 33–37.

14. Zion and Israel undergo a process of personification in Deutero-Isaiah. Zion appears in the image of a widow-mother with a passive role (absorbing her sons), whereas he imagines Israel as YHWH's servant, fulfilling an active role in the service of its Lord.

15. This is the opinion of most scholars among both those who attribute these chapters to Deutero-Isaiah and those who attribute them to another prophet (Trito-Isaiah). I see no compelling reason to see in them the work of another prophet. One can explain the distinction between them as the result of different circumstances and not necessarily a different period. Haran (supra, pp. 83ff.) presumes that chs 49–55, too, display a Judean background; the presumption is a reasonable one.

16. M. Haller, 'Die Kyros Lieder Deuterojesajas, Eucharisterion Gunkel', *FRLANT* 36 (1923), I, pp. 261–77.

Daniel 1, too, speaks of Jewish children 'proficient in all wisdom, knowledgeable and intelligent', who serve in the king's court (v. 4). True, the stories of Daniel in their current form are not authentic; nevertheless, they reflect real historical circumstances, as exemplified by the descriptions of Nebuchadnezzar which fit the personality of Nabonidus and the events connected to him.[17] An historical background identical to that in the stories of Daniel stands behind the Prayer of Nabonides found in Qumran (4Q PrNab).[18] This text tells of a Jewish prophet who attempts to persuade Nabonides to abandon gods made of silver and gold and to admit to the existence and dominion of the Highest God. Recently R. Meyer[19] analysed this document, arguing that, composed in the Persian period, it preserves information about the Jewish settlements in the environs of Tema, the seat of Nabonides' rule.[20] The story's interests, in his opinion, reflect the universalistic spirit[21] which predominated in those times in the Diaspora in the East or among the Jewish communities in northern Arabia, a spirit which permeates the stories of Daniel as well.[22]

The Scroll of Esther may testify to the status of the Jews in the courts of the Persian kings as well. Behind the Wisdom veneer which currently colours the work,[23] stands an historical reality which accords with the Persian period, perhaps even the specific time of Xerxes I.[24] The case of Nehemiah, who served as the chief cupbearer in the court of Artaxerxes I, indicates the degree to which Jews penetrated the royal courts at that time.[25]

Presumably, the beliefs and ways of the Jews serving in the royal court set an example for the Gentiles, especially the cultured and enlightened among them, attracting many to Israel's religion. Indeed, this period sees the monotheistic creed spreading throughout the world for the first time. Malachi says:

> For from where the sun rises to where it sets, My name is honoured among the nations, and everywhere incense and pure oblations are offered to My name; for My name is honoured among the nations – said the Lord of Hosts' (1.11).[26]

17. See primarily W. von Soden, 'Eine babylonische Volksüberlieferung von Nabonaid in den Danielerzählungen', *ZAW* 53 (1935), pp. 81–89; *idem*, 'Kyros und Nabonid: Propaganda und Gegenpropaganda', *Archaeologische Mitteilungen aus Iran, Ergänzungen* 10 (1983).

18. J.T. Milik, 'Prière de Nabonide et autres écrits d'un cycle de Daniel', *RB* 63 (1956), pp. 407–415; D.N. Freedman, 'The Prayer of Nabonides', *BASOR* 145 (1957), pp. 31–32; Ch. Gevaryahu, 'The Prayer of Nabonaid from the Scrolls of the Judean Desert', in J. Liver (ed.), *Studies in the Scrolls of the Judean Desert*, 1957, pp. 12ff. (Hebrew); F.M. Cross, 'Fragments of the Prayer of Nabonidais', *IEJ* 34 (1984), pp. 260–64.

19. R. Meyer, *Das Gebet des Nabonaid* (*Sitzungsberichte der sächischen Akademie der Wissenschaften zu Leipzig, phil-hist. Kl.* 107/3, 1962).

20. *Ibid.*, pp. 67ff.

21. *Ibid.*, pp. 106ff.

22. A Bentzen, *Daniel*^{2} (*HAT*, 1952), pp. 27, 47.

23. S. Talmon, '"Wisdom" in the Book of Esther', *VT* 13 (1963), pp. 419–55.

24. *Ibid.*, p. 453.

25. See W. Rudolph, *Ezra und Nehemia* (*HAT*, 1949), p. 103.

26. There is no justification for striking this verse from Malachi, contra K. Elliger, *Das Buch der zwölf kleinen Propheten* (*ATD*), II.198.

Further on he says:

> For I am a Great King – said the Lord of Hosts – and My name is revered (נורא) among the nations (v. 14).

'Revered' (נוֹרָא) here means 'worshipped' and 'adored' (the *Nif'al* of ירא). Indeed, at that time a new circle of believers arose, going by the name 'the reverers of YHWH' (יִרְאֵי ה׳); no doubt they are the converts[27] to Judaism referred to in later times as φοβούμενοι, σεβόμενοι τόν θεόν.[28]

The Restoration psalms, especially the Psalms of Thanksgiving (Ps. 113–118), mention 'the reverers of YHWH' as a defined circle standing beside 'the house of Aaron' and 'the house of Israel' (115.9–11; 118.2–4; compare 135.19–20). Indeed, these psalms are saturated with universalistic ideas and thought processes found in the literature of the period. Similar to Malachi, the poet here says, 'From east to west the name of the Lord is praised' (113.3).[29] The continuation speaks of God's exaltation on one hand and his presence among the poor and lowly on the other (vv. 4–9), an idea found in Isa. 57.15. Psalm 114 recounts the *via triumphalis* of which Deutero-Isaiah speaks so often.[30] Psalm 115 polemicizes against pagan idolatry in quintessentially Deutero-Isaianic terms (compare primarily Isa. 44.9–20), and beside this polemic the poet solicits YHWH's blessing for both Israel and 'the reverers of YHWH'. Psalm 117 presents the praise offered by the Gentile nations,[31] while immediately following, in Psalm 118, appears the thanksgiving psalm of the house of Aaron, the house of Israel and the reverers of YHWH (vv. 1–4). The continuation describes the salvation from poverty and suffering, spoken of also in the songs of 'YHWH's servant', and the salvation and justice which, as we shall presently see, characterize Deutero-Isaiah.

A similar universalistic spirit defines the concluding section of Psalm 22 (vv. 23–32),[32] which too includes within it 'the reverers of YHWH'.[33] Gunkel[34] already

27. Cf. Esth. 9.27.

28. Acts 10.2, 22; 12.16; 16.14; 18.2. See further E. Schürer, *The History of the Jewish People in the Age of Jesus Christ*, rev. and ed. G. Vermes *et al.* (3 vols., 1973) III.166, and L. Rott-Gerson, '"Reverers of God" in Jewish Inscriptions from Sardis', *Eshel Beer Sheba* 1 (1976), pp. 88–93 (Hebrew), who argues correctly that the titles 'reverer of God' (θεοσεβής) found in two inscriptions with reference to persons who contributed to the floor-mosaic in the Sardis synagogue serve to signal the special standing of non-Jewish contributors. Second-order support for the phenomenon of eternalizing the names of Gentiles within the walls of holy places exists in a passage of the prophecy discussed in this article: 'I shall make for them in My house and within My walls a monument and a name' (Isa. 56.5).

29. The expression, 'May the name YHWH be blessed now and forever', in Ps. 113.2 has the character of Second Temple liturgy. See A. Hurvitz, *From Language to Language*, 1972, p. 100 (Hebrew).

30. Note the parallel between v. 8 in this psalm and Isa. 48.21. Isa. 48.20, which speaks of leaving Babylon, links up with v. 21, which mentions the exodus from Egypt (cf. Isa. 43.16–20; contra Haran, supra, pp. 70–71).

31. One should see this declaration against the background of Deutero-Isaiah's prophecy; so H.-J. Kraus, *Psalmen* I–II^2, 1961.

32. Many (Duhm [*KHC*], Schmidt [*HAT*] *et al.*) hold that these verses constitute a separate psalm. In any case, they do not fit organically with the verses preceding them.

33. See *Lev. Rabb.* 3.2: '*You who fear the Lord, praise Him! All you offspring of Jacob, honor*

recognized the sundry points of contact between the section and Deutero-Isaiah; indeed we read here of 'the reverers of YHWH' giving their praise alongside 'the offspring of Israel' (v. 24), of suffering and God's withdrawal (v. 25; cf. Isa. 53.3), of the base sinners returning to YHWH (v. 28; cf. Isa. 45.22), and of all earth-dwellers bowing before him (v. 30; cf. Isa. 45.23).

It appears that in this period the Jewish diaspora began exerting its influence over the nations among which it sat, in effect laying the groundwork for the Christian activity of a later period.[35] Against the background of the excitement generated by the Israelite religion among the nations in those times, an excitement by all appearances accompanied by Jewish propaganda, one can comprehend Zechariah's prophecy:

> In those days, ten men from nations of every tongue will take hold – they will take hold of every Jew by a corner of his cloak and say, 'Let us go with you, for we have heard that God is with you' (8.23).

The prophecies of that period even feature 'missionary' ideas: God gathers all nations and tongues to come see his glory, then marks them with a sign,[36] and sends emissaries (פליטים)[37] from them to relate his glory to the nations and distant islands who have not yet heard of him or seen his glory (Isa. 66.18–19).

The movement to accept Judaism received its impetus and encouragement mainly from the prophets of those times. With the Gentiles feeling their inferiority to the rooted Jews, the Restoration prophets felt it appropriate to encourage them to join the Jewish ranks. Indeed, as noted above, in chapter 56 Deutero-Isaiah (or, according to others, Trito-Isaiah) promises the Gentiles and the eunuchs complete integration into the Israelite congregation:

> Let not the foreigner say, who has attached himself to the Lord,
> 'The Lord will keep me apart from His people';
> And let not the eunuch say,
> 'I am a withered tree' (v. 3).

This verse comes to allay the fears of the Gentile converts concerning the particularistic tendencies among the Jewish 'men in the street'. Such anxiety certainly gained momentum from the antagonism beginning to dominate in that time between the Returnees and the 'peoples of the lands', so these words of the

Him!: *You who fear the Lord* R. Joshua b. Levi said, these are moral people; R. Ishmael b. Nahman said, these are the converts'.

34. H. Gunkel, *Die Psalmen* (*HKAT*[4]), 1926.

35. Wherever Paul goes in his travels he encounters the 'reverers of YHWH'. See above, n. 28.

36. The sign here serves as a banner raised to the nations; cf. 49.22; 62.10–11.

37. Hebrew פליט is not necessarily one who survives or escapes a battle, but rather one who leaves the front in order to report on events taking place on the battlefield; so 2 Kgs 9.15: 'allow no courier to leave the city to go and report (K: לגיד; Q: להגיד) this in Jezreel'. Compare Gen. 14.13; Ezek. 24.26–27; 33.21–22. Here, too, couriers are sent to recount YHWH's glory to the nations. YHWH does not gather the nations and tongues for the purpose of destroying them, as in Ezek. 38–39, but rather to draw them towards the God of Israel and so that they will bring with them the Israelites in faraway countries.

prophet constitute a polemic of sorts against those holding a narrow nationalistic view, who were unwilling to allow the Gentiles to participate in the (re)building of the temple and in the religious life of the people. This polemic finds expression also in the words of the prophet Zechariah, who was active during the height of the conflict that broke out between the Returnees and the 'peoples of the lands':

> Shout for joy, Fair Zion! For lo, I come; and I will dwell in your midst...
> Many nations will attach themselves to the Lord and become My people (2.14).[38]

The anonymous prophet from those times expresses similar ideas in Isa. 14.1:

> But the Lord will pardon Jacob,
> And will again choose Israel,
> And will settle them on their own soil.
> And strangers shall join them
> And shall cleave to the House of Jacob.[39]

Duhm argues that 56.1–8, which in his opinion begins a new prophecy,[40] has a particularistic character in contrast with the prophecies in chapters 40–55. However, a close examination of this prophecy will reveal a pervasive spirit unequivocally universalistic and moreover a dependence on the universalistic ideas of Deutero-Isaiah as articulated in chs 40–55.

The pericope begins (v. 1):

> Thus said the Lord:
> Observe what is right (משפט) and do what is just (צדקה);
> For soon My salvation (ישועתי) shall come, and My deliverance (צִדְקָתִי) be revealed.

Hebrew צדקה in this verse has two different senses,[41] a social set of actions[42] performed by human beings and a soteriological set of actions performed by God. Identical with salvation (ישועה), צדקה in the second stich of the verse comes as reward for human justice. This salvation soon to come and the deliverance about to appear mark the universalistic redemption whose significance means world-wide recognition of Israel's God, as Isa. 51.4–5 makes clear:

38. There is no reason to say that Haggai objects to this conception. The opinion of J.W. Rothstein (*Juden und Samaritener*, 1908, pp. 5ff.) that Haggai directed his prophecy in 2.10–14 against the Samaritans has no basis (see Kaufmann, *History of the Israelite Faith*, VIII.220–221 [Hebrew]). The pericope does not mention the phrases 'people of the land' or 'peoples of the lands', expressions so typical of the books of Ezra and Nehemiah regarding the Samaritans and their dependants (see E. Meyer, *Die Entstehung des Judentums*, 1896, p. 123). To the contrary, 'the people of the land' in Haggai refers to the entire people of Judah (2.4). This is also no justification for seeing Haggai as a nationalistic, particularistic prophet; see Kaufmann, *ibid.*, p. 220 n. 11.

39. For those who join up with the Jews in Second Temple times, see also Est. 9.27: 'The Jews...and all those who joined up with them'.

40. The distinction between two prophetic works in Isa. 40–66 and the line demarcating them were established first by Duhm in his commentary to Isaiah (B. Duhm, *Das Buch Jesaaja* [*HKAT*], 1892).

41. On the development of meanings within the prophecy of Deutero-Isaiah, see Kaufmann, *History of the Israelite Faith*, VIII.68.

42. On צדקה ומשפט as a *hendiadys* see E. Z. Melamed, '*Hendiadys* in the Bible', *Tarbiz* 16 (1945), pp. 173ff. (Hebrew); M. Weinfeld, *Social Justice in Ancient Israel and in the Nations* (1995).

Hearken to Me, My people,
And give ear to Me, O My nation,[43]
For teaching (תורה) shall go forth from Me,
My way (משפטי) for the light of peoples.
In a moment will I bring it:
The triumph (צדקי) I grant is near,
The success (ישעי) I give has gone forth;
My arms shall provide for (ישפטו) nations;
The coastlands shall trust in Me,
They shall look to My arm.

The collection of psalms from the period of the Return (Pss. 96–98), which have linguistic and ideational contact with Deutero-Isaiah,[44] contain hymns with this soteriological justice as their background. God judges the world justly (בצדק) and the nations faithfully (באמונתו) or fairly (במישרים) (96.10, 13; 98.9), and this in fact occurs after they sing to him 'a new song' and tell of his salvation among the nations and many islands (96.1–2; 97.1; 98.1; cf. Isa. 42.10, 12; 49.1). Deutero-Isaiah reports that salvation is nearly at hand and justice is about to be revealed; here, the poet announces that God has revealed his justice and made his salvation known to the Gentiles (98.2). As in Deutero-Isaiah, so, too, in these psalms all nations see YHWH's glory (Isa. 40.5; Ps. 96.3; 97.5) and the lowest of the earth witness God's salvation (Isa. 51.12; Ps. 98.3). National redemption here serves only as a precondition for universal redemption; its realization heralds the beginning of universal redemption.

43. The Peshitta reads 'O peoples...O nations'. It appears that this reading reflects a more original version; cf. 'Listen O coastlands to Me, and give heed, O nations afar' (49.1).

44. See Kraus' commentary to these psalms (H.J. Kraus, *Psalmen*, I–II^2, 1961). Mowinckel's opinion (S. Mowinckel, *Psalmenstudien* II, 1921, pp. 195f.) that these are First Temple coronation psalms upon which Deutero-Isaiah drew does not appear reasonable at all. Not only does the style they share determine that a direct link exists between these works, but so do the literary and conceptual motifs, which have their explanation in the conditions of the Return and appear expansively in the prophecy of Deutero-Isaiah. Note especially the Nature's songs (Ps. 96.11–12; 98.7–8; Isa. 44.23; 49.13), the message of the imminent salvation reaching the lowest people of the earth, the praise of the island peoples, and the 'new' song (see above), and the disparagement of paganism as well (Isa. 44.9–20; *et al.*; Ps. 96.5; 97.7). These psalms do contain deposits inserted from early psalms, but the insertions attain here new meaning. For example, the verses in 96.7–9 come from a more ancient psalm (Ps. 29) with roots in Ugaritic literature (see H. Ginsburg, *Ugaritic Writings*, 1936, pp. 129–31; F.M. Cross, 'Notes on a Canaanite Psalm in the O.T.', *BASOR* 117 [1950], pp. 19–21); however, whereas that psalm speaks of the 'sons of gods' giving honour and strength to YHWH (v. 1; cf. Ps. 89.7–8), here the 'families of nations' take this role (v. 7), which accords with Deutero-Isaiah's universalistic ambitions. Psalm 29 describes the 'sons of God' paying respect to the enthroned God establishing his kingship, whereas here the 'families of nations' bring him honour and strength by receiving his judgment, namely, by being saved by him. Ps. 96.10 actually quotes 93.1, but in 93.1 the context consists of the establishment of God's throne after his having subdued the 'Great Waters' and the 'Mighty Breakers' (vv. 3–4), whereas in 96.10 the citation refers to the judgment of the nations and its just decision. According to S. Loewenstamm (*Leshonenu* 27–28, p. 121 n. 20 [Hebrew]), the author of Ps. 96 replaces the 'sons of gods' by the 'families of nations' in order to preclude any formulation which may give the impression of legitimizing the 'gods of the nations' as real; this transformation, too, suits Deutero-Isaiah's world-view.

The universalistic motif continues in v. 2, in which the prophet says:

> Happy is the man who does this, the man who holds fast to it:
> Who keeps the Sabbath and does not profane it,
> And stays his hand from doing any evil.

The Hebrew words אנוש and בן אדם behind English 'man', denoting the human being as such, constitute terms found primarily in the Psalmodic-Wisdom literature in cosmic-universal contexts.[45] The observance of the Sabbath emphasized in this verse does not belong to the distinguishing particularistic features which coalesced in that time, as the Wellhausian scholars would have it. Strict Sabbath observance in Israel goes way back (Amos 8.5),[46] but conditions in the Exile turned it into the quintessential sign of belonging to the Jewish religion and, making a great impression upon the Gentiles, it attracted special attention from them.[47] The period of the Exile freed the Sabbath of its connection to the temple and the cult, linking it instead to the synagogue, where the people read from the Torah and pursued the knowledge of God. Indeed, this fact explains the juxtaposition of Sabbath and Gentile. The Gentiles learned about the Jewish religion during the Sabbath, when the Jews gathered to hear Torah-wisdom from the Sages;[48] perhaps, then, one may suppose that the prophet actually said his piece here on the Sabbath, in the same way that he delivered the message of ch. 58 on a fast day.

The following verse, more than any other, puts the universalistic imprint on the prophecy under discussion:

> I will bring them to My sacred mount
> And let them rejoice in My house of prayer...
> For My house shall be called a house of prayer for all peoples (v. 7).

This verse offers something of a challenge to those who would claim an exclusivity for the Israelite religion and espouse the rejection of those Gentiles wishing to participate in the rebuilding of the temple and the worship of God that goes on it. To this exclusivist group and its ideas we turn in the next section.

The Isolationist Ideology

Pentateuchal literature, especially in its two theological strands (P and D), contains many pronouncements whose main import intends to distance Israel from the nations, to separate Israel from them: 'You shall be holy to Me, for I the Lord

45. Cf. primarily Ps. 8.5; 144.3; Job 9.2; 15.14; 25.6 *et al.*
46. See my article in *Tarbiz* 37 (1968), pp. 127ff. (Hebrew)
47. With regard to a later period, see Josephus:

> The masses have long since shown a keen desire to adopt our religious observances; and there is not one city, Greek or barbarian, nor a single nation, to which our custom of abstaining from work on the seventh day has not spread (*Against Apion* 2.39; trans. H. St. J. Thackeray, *Josephus*, vol. I, Loeb edn, 1926, pp. 406–407).

48. Paul, for example, in his sermon in the synagogue on the Sabbath, turns to both the Jews and the 'reverers of God':" Ἄνδρες Ἰσραηλῖται καὶ οἱ φοβούμενοι τόν θεόν (Acts 13.16).

am holy, and I have set you apart from other peoples to be Mine' (Lev. 20.26); 'For you are a people consecrated (עם קדוש) to the Lord your God; of all the peoples on earth the Lord your God chose you to be His treasured people' (Deut. 7.6; 14.2).[49] Alongside these declarations sit concrete laws forbidding the maintenance of social contact and marriage connections with the nations in the land of Canaan (Deut. 7.3–4; cf. Exod 23.32–33; 34.12–16). Deuteronomy, laying particular stress on Israel's election and holiness, prepares a framework of laws meant not only to limit contact with the Canaanite nations, but also to prohibit members of the surrounding nations, even eunuchs, from joining the community of YHWH (Deut. 23.1–9). Although these laws intended to hurt the chances of eunuchs and Gentiles to assimilate into and be absorbed by Israel, in point of fact, these commandments could not by themselves stand in the way of such would-be members. Ultimately, the eunuchs who desired to join Israel, victims of monarchic despots, did not castrate themselves of their own accord; by the same token, the Gentiles who wished to participate in the Israelite congregation did not have Canaanite or even Ammonite or Moabite roots, whom the text prohibited from ever coming into YHWH's community (Deut. 23.4–7). The Gentiles' real worries did not come from these verses, written against the background of the cultural and political relationships of Israel and Judah with its neighbours in the First Temple period and earlier,[50] but rather from the movement which built upon these verses a new, radical ideology. This movement, from which Ezra and his group emerged, broadened and deepened the divide between the true Israelites and the Gentiles, developing an extremist religio-national brand of dogmatics based more on the hermeneutic interpretation of scripture then on the verses themselves. In Deuteronomy, and likewise in the priestly literature, separation from the Canaanite nations functions to preclude pagan abominations: 'lest they lead you into doing all the abhorrent things that they have done for their gods' (Deut. 20.18); 'for all those abhorrent things were done by the people who were in the land before you, and the land became defiled' (Lev. 18.27), while the reservations concerning the neighbouring, non-Canaanite nations have historico-national justifications, such as: 'No Ammonite or Moabite shall be admitted into the congregation of the Lord...because they did not meet you with food and water on your journey after you left Egypt' (Deut. 23.4–5). By contrast, the isolationist camp stripped the Pentateuch's separationist laws of their justifications, taking them instead in absolute terms. Moreover, they added to these laws their own explanation: 'mixing the holy seed among the peoples of the lands' (Ezra 9.2); Israel, the 'holy seed', must separate from every foreign nation regardless of its origins. They interpreted the rigoristic commandments in the Pentateuch with respect to the Ammonites and Moabites as covering the entire Gentile population:

49. For the nationalistic background of the concept of a 'holy nation' in Deuteronomy, see my article, 'The Awakening of Nationalistic Consciousness in Israel in the Seventh Century BCE', *Oz le-David: David Ben-Gurion Jubilee Volume* (1964), pp. 396–420.

50. See S. Mowinckel, 'Zu Dt. 23, 2–9', *Acta Orientalia* 2 (1923); K. Galling, 'Das Gemeindegesetz in Deuteronomium 23', *Bertholet-Festschrift* (1950), pp. 176–91.

> At that time they read to the people from the Book of Moses...that no Ammonite or Moabite might ever enter the congregation of God...When they heard the Teaching, they separated all the alien admixture (ערב)[51] from Israel' (Neh. 13.1–3).

Similarly, they explained the pentateuchal demand never to seek peace and joint prosperity with the Ammonites and Moabites (Deut. 23.7) as referring to all the peoples of the land (Ezra 9.12).

The 'holy nation' (עם קדוש) in Deuteronomy, which had had only a religio-*national* meaning, is transformed here into a 'holy seed' (זרע קדש), with a religio-*biological* meaning. The foreign women sent away by Ezra were not idolators, otherwise the text would have mentioned it explicitly, as elaborated by Y. Kaufmann.[52] The reason for their rejection consists solely of their foreign genealogical origins.

Instead of the generosity of religious spirit found in Isaiah 56, 'Let not the foreigner say... "The Lord will *keep me apart* (הבדל יבדילני) from His people"', Ezra denounces the fact that those of Israelite seed did not *keep themselves apart* (לא נבדלו) from all the Gentiles (Ezra 9.1; cf. Neh. 9.2). Ezra not only refused to accept converts and proselytes, but even insisted that those Gentile women who had married Jewish men and were considered Jewish converts[53] be ejected along with their children.

This isolationist program did not begin with Ezra. The rejection of the Samaritans during Zerubbabel's time also is anchored in this exclusivist world-view. The Samaritans did not engage in idolatry, but rather came from Gentile converts.[54] According to what they say, they look to the God of Israel and sacrifice to him since the days of Essarhaddon (Ezra 4.2), and there is no justification for doubting this testimony. They wish to participate in rebuilding the temple but the Returnees reject them on religious isolationist grounds: 'It is not for you and us together to build a House to our God, but rather we alone, the *yaḥad* (יחד), will build it to the Lord God of Israel' (Ezra 4.3). *Yaḥad* here functions as a noun similar to 1 Chr 12.18, with the meaning, as in the Dead Sea Scrolls, of a group of people tied by a single mutual covenant or council,[55] in other words, a closed community.

In contrast with this closed attitude, Deutero-Isaiah – as said above – sees in the temple 'a house of prayer for all nations' (56.7); presumably he would whole-heartedly support a joint effort together with the Gentiles in the rebuilding of the temple. The passage 'Aliens shall rebuild your walls' (60.10), even if in an eschatological context, rings with dissonance in a world where any partnership with Gentiles causes fuming and anger. One should take this verse, then, as representing a position opposed to the isolationist program. Likewise, the prophet's

51. Hebrew ערב here means 'alien admixture' not Arabian tribes (= Bedouin) as assumed by E. Meier, *Die Entstehung des Judentums*, S. 130 Anm. 2. See my essay in *EncMiq* VI, s.v. ערב רב, cols. 361–362.

52. *History of the Israelite Faith*, VIII.284ff.

53. *Ibid.*

54. *Ibid.*, pp. 189–90.

55. S. Talmon, 'The Sectarian יחד – A Biblical Noun', *VT* 3 (1953), pp. 133f.

promise to the eunuchs, 'I will give them, in My house and within My walls, a monument and a name' (56.5), may provide support for this assumption. Indeed, as against the confinement of the Jewish religious cult and the shutting of the gates before the Gentiles, the prophet strives for universalism in the cultic sphere as well.[56]

Universalism in the Cult

Deutero-Isaiah not only promises the Gentiles and the eunuchs inclusion in the Israelite congregation and its faith, but also declares for them complete participation in the Israelite religious worship. This acceptance of the Gentiles into Jewish worship does not find its expression solely in complete participation, but even in the temple service: 'And from them likewise I will take some to be priests and Levites, said the Lord' (66.21). One can certainly take this verse in two different ways: God will take priests and Levites either from among the Gentiles who bring the Israelite brothers, or from among the Israelite brothers brought by the Gentiles.[57] However, it appears that the emphasis in 'from them likewise', which contains something of an exaggeration, tilts the balance in favour of those who say that the verse refers back to the Gentiles.[58] Support for this view of the prophet, again, comes from ch. 56 in Isaiah. Here the prophet speaks about 'the foreigners who attach themselves to the Lord, to minister to Him' (v. 6). 'To minister (לשרת) to YHWH' – as opposed to the expression, 'to worship (לעבוד) YHWH' – means to participate in the holy chores in the temple set aside for the tribe of Levi: 'At that time the Lord set apart the tribe of Levi...to stand before the Lord, *to minister to Him* (לשרתו), and to bless in His name' (Deut. 10.8; cf. 17.12; 18.7; Jer. 33.21–22; Ezek 40.46; *et al.*). Indeed this language found in Isaiah 56 'to attach oneself to YHWH and to minister to Him', appears word-for-word in the priestly literature: 'they will be attached (וילוו) to you and minister (וישרתו) to you' (Num. 18.2). It appears reasonable, then, that the prophet intends to say that the Gentiles will serve as attendants of YHWH in the court of his holy dwelling.

This desire does constitute something new in the Israelite cult. Among the temple personnel the foreign element had always stood out (the Gibeonites, the Nethinim, and 'Solomon's slaves'); probably, the tribe of Levi originated in a group of unpropertied sojourners who offered their services to the temple[59] and

56. Admittedly, Malachi does come out against inter-marriage in 2.10–16, 'the only place in the entire prophetic corpus which mentions inter-marriage' (Kaufmann, *History of the Israelite Faith*, VIII.370), but he takes this critical stance against the background of the cruelty that emerged in a marriage from youth, so it differs from the criticism of Ezra which is based solely in the pentateuchal laws. Besides, Malachi's designation for the Gentile, 'daughter of a foreign God', reeks of paganism, an element entirely absent from the 'Gentile women' episode in Ezra's time.

57. See, for example, Skinner in his commentary.

58. See the thorough comments of Delitzsch on this verse (F. Delitzsch, *Jesaja* 1866, S. 648).

59. For a variety of opinions on the origins of the tribe of Levi, see recently J. Licht, *EncMiq* IV, s.v. Levi, cols. 460–478 (Hebrew).

later, with the establishment of the monarchy, to the king.[60] On the basis of the word 'לוא' in South Arabian inscriptions, many derive the name Levi from 'loan' (הלואה), namely, a person 'loaned' to the Temple. Indeed, like the Gentile temple slaves called *Nethinim*,[61] i.e., those given over, the Levites too are called 'given (נְתֻנִים)' to YHWH (Num. 8.16).

In this aspiration for universalism within the cult the prophet goes up against the circles of isolationist world-view, too. As is well-known, the congregation of Returnees debated the problem that they had only a small number of Levites and temple attendants. Ezra relates in his memoirs that among those who returned with him he found no Levites, and he seeks out Levites to serve as 'attendants for the house of our God' (Ezra 8.15ff.). The difficulties in locating Temple attendants resulted from the fact that the Returnees kept meticulous genealogical records with regard to cultic personnel (Ezra 2.62–63 = Neh. 7.63–64) and disallowed anyone not from the Levites, the *Nethinim*, or 'Solomon's slaves' from particpating in the maintenance of holy, temple matters (Ezra 8.20). Against this rigouristic exclusivism stands the radical liberalism of the prophet. Not only does he promise priesthood even for those not of Levite descent (61.5–6), but he also promises cultic jobs to the Gentiles now joining YHWH's ranks. These promises absolutely contradict Ezekiel's contention – grounded in priestly teachings – that only the Levitical priests of Zadokite descent may keep guard over the holy vessels, that the Levites will provide lesser services, and that the Gentiles are to be ejected from the temple entirely (Ezek 44.6–31).

The prophetic demand for universalism within the cult was so radical that later generations, unable to come to grips with it, attempted to soften and change it by manipulating the prophet's words. Instead of 'As for the foreigners who attach themselves to the Lord, to minister to Him (לְשָׁרְתוֹ), and to love the name of the Lord, to be His servants', 1QIsa[a] reads, 'As for the foreigners who attach themselves to the Lord to be His servants and to bless His name'. The author of the Scroll deleted the phrase 'to minister to Him', since the idea of a Gentile ministering in the temple did not suit him. A Gentile – according to this author – may worship YHWH ('עבוד' 'be his servants'), but not minister to him (שָׁרֵת). The concept of attendance (שָׁרֵת) indeed supercedes the concept of worship and service (עבודה). All subjects serve the king, but only a select few merit ministering to him (Gen. 39.4; 1 Kgs 1.4; Ps. 101.6; Prov. 29.12 *et al.*). For similar reasons the author of 1QIsa[a] revises the text from 'to love the name of the Lord' to 'to bless the name of the Lord'. Gentiles may – in this author's view – stand in the same grouping together with those who subject themselves to YHWH out of fear, but

60. Probably, the tithe, too, slated according to the priestly literature for the Levites, has its roots in the taxes the Levites collected from the populace and stored in their cities, 'the Levitical cities' (the blurring of sacral and royal tithes resulted from the fact that the temple was a royal one, benefitting from the king's patronage). In this case, we have uncovered another point of similarity to the Canaanite cities during the years of Egyptian rule, according to whose model the Levitical cities were built – in Mazar's opinion – because those cities included warehouses for storing the taxes collected from the people. B. Mazar, 'The Cities of the Priests and Levites', *SVT* VII (1960), pp. 193–205.

61. See E.A. Speiser, *IEJ* 13 (1963), pp. 69ff.

not with those who worship YHWH out of love. They may bless YHWH and praise him, but they do not love him.

Even if this reading does contain a measure of authenticity, still it appears that the original reading differed from the one offered by the author of the Scroll. In pentateuchal literature the Levites stand before YHWH *to minister to Him and to bless in His name* (Deut. 10.8; 21.5). It stands to reason, then, that the passage here also originally read, 'who attach themselves to the Lord *to minister to Him and to bless in His name*' in accordance with the formulation in Deuteronomy. 'To bless in His name' means to bless Israel in YHWH's name, as the priests must do according to the priestly literature: 'Thus shall you bless the people of Israel...Thus they shall link My name with the people of Israel' (Num. 6.22–27). This activity is quintessentially a cultic one given to the priests who administer in the holy precincts. By contrast, the author of the Scroll has, 'to bless His name', an expression found frequently in the liturgical literature[62] meaning to praise God.[63]

The Septuagint demonstrates the desire to soften this radical text as well. LXX translates 'minister' (שרת) here with δουλεύειν, a verb which normally conveys the concept of service and slavery. Indeed, beside this occurrence, this verb never renders 'minister' (שרת). LXX goes so far as to diverge from its normal practice with regard to 'attaching themselves' (הנלוים) as well, translating it by προσκέισθαι, a verb generally used in LXX to render 'sojourn' (גור).[64] Both the scrolls of the Judaean Desert and the Septuagint[65] in this verse reflect the difficulties later Judaism had with a prophetic universalistic world-view whose time had past.

Within the same period of time, then, there existed in Israel two opposing world-views, a universalistic one aspiring to draw Gentiles to Judaism and convert them and a particularistic one which desired to draw a sharp line of demarcation between Israel and the rest of the world's nations. Y. Kaufmann sees in this opposition the birthpangs of religious conversion.[66] Conversion by ethnic and geographical reaffiliation no longer existed then and religious conversion as it would develop in the *halakhah* had not yet taken its place. As he sees it, the

62. See Y. Kutscher, *The Language and Linguistic Background of the Great Isaiah Scroll from the Dead Sea Scrolls* (1959), p. 171 (Hebrew).

63. For the late character of the expression 'to bless YHWH's name', see Hurvitz, *From Language to Language*, p. 240.

64. I.L. Seeligmann (*The Septuagint Version of Isaiah*, 1948, pp. 45ff.) demonstrated how the Pentateuch influenced the translational methods of the Greek translators; in this case, the influence worked in a negative vein. The translator, who knew the pentateuchal formulation, προστεθήτωσάν σοι καὶ λειτουργείτωσάν, regarding the Levites, deliberately avoiding using it when speaking of the Gentiles; only the later translators (Aquilas, Symmacus and Theodotion), who translated more meticulously, re-introduced it into the text. Seeligmann (p. 117) found another example of Septuagint translators neutralizing a universalistic text (by giving it a nationalistic re-interpretation) in Isa. 19.24–25.

65. On an important tendentious change shared by the Septuagint and the Dead Sea Scrolls and bound up with pre-Gnostic influences, see I.L. Seeligmann, *Tarbiz* 27 (1958), 'δεῖξαι αὐτῷ φῶς', pp. 127ff.

66. Kaufmann, *History of the Israelite Faith*, VIII, 298–99.

people did not know how to behave towards those joining up with the Jews and taking Judaism upon themselves at that time, hence the confusion. It appears to me, though, that there was no confusion, but rather two different religious world-views, prophetic universalism and pentateuchal particularism. The prophetic universalistic line of thought neither contended with nor attempted to 'solve' the 'problem' of those taking on Judaism. Gentiles willing to join Israel clearly should be accepted with open arms; moreover, Jews had the grand task of drawing these Gentiles in, to be taken under God's wing. This world-view does not constitute long-term visionary thinking, some wish for future times. Deutero-Isaiah, after all, directs his words at concrete groups of eunuchs and Gentiles existing in his time and environs; he does not mean to pacify generations yet to come.

The pentateuchal particularistic line of thought did not offer an answer to the question of the Judaization of Gentiles either. The members of this movement inferred from the Pentateuch that Israel must not mingle with the nations, but separate from them. In opposition to each other stands the living, dynamic prophetic word of YHWH, which adjusts divine demands to the circumstances of the time and place, and the static, conservative word of YHWH enshrined in the Pentateuch, considered as an unchangeable one-time revelation. Ezra, scribe of the Mosaic Torah, anchoring himself in the Torah, especially in Deuteronomy whose nationalistic program stands out more, saw no possibility of attracting and attaching Gentiles to Judaism. By contrast, the later prophets, drawing upon the heritage of their prophetic forebearers, preached universalism and a liberal policy towards the Gentiles.

To the benefit of Second Temple Judaism, the gap between these two trains of thought progressively narrowed. The prophetic camp which had waved the banner of radical liberal policy had to agree to place practical, concrete demands on converts, while the pentateuchal camp had to forego its conservative isolationist policy. So evolved the institution of religious conversion, which at its root is universalistic, but enjoins the acceptance of the burden of observing the commandments. A Gentile may accept the Israelite faith in a moment's time,[67] but on the condition that he accept upon himself the national religious duties in Israel's Torah.

67. See *ibid.*, pp. 44–45.

Part IV

NEW TESTAMENT

Chapter 19

PENTECOST AS FESTIVAL OF THE GIVING OF THE LAW

It is still a prevalent view that Pentecost as a festival commemorating the revelation at Sinai and giving of the law (זמן מתן תורתנו)[1] cannot be earlier than the destruction in 70 CE. Thus, for example, E. Lohse in his article Πεντηκοστή[2] states that 'only in the Christian period do we find evidence that later Judaism linked this feast too with the events of the age of Moses, and particularly remembered the giving of the law at Sinai on this day. The immediate occasion for thus changing the meaning of Pentecost was the destruction of Jerusalem in 70 CE, which meant that the ancient pilgrimage could no longer be held nor the first fruits and sacrifices offered in the temple' (English Translation p. 48).[3] It is true, that in the last decade this view has been challenged, especially by French scholars. Thus J. Potin in his *La Fête Juive de la Pentécôte* (Lectio Divina 65, I–II, 1971)[4] argues that Pentecost as 'Festival of the Covenant' goes back to the second or even the third century BCE and in this he was actually anticipated by other French scholars.[5] In general, however, scholars still cling to the conventional view, i.e., that Pentecost as the festival of the giving of the law is late. It is admitted that some Jewish sects associated Pentecost with the Covenant but officially – so it is argued – the festival of the giving of the law was not celebrated before the second century CE. Thus, for example, J. Kremer in his recent monograph *Pfingstbericht und Pfingstgeschehen* (Stuttgarter Bibel Studien 63/64, 1973) states:

> die Erinnerung an die Gesetzgebung am Sinai, die im Rabbinischen Schriften mit Pfingsten verbunded wird, wurde allerdings erst nach der Zeit der Zerstörung des Tempels allgemein damit in Verbindung gebracht (p. 29).

1. Cf. *Amidah* liturgy of *Shavuot*. See I. Elbogen, *Der Jüdische Gottesdienst in seiner geschichtlichen Entwicklung*^{3}, 1931, p. 138.
2. *Theologisches Wörterbuch zum NT*, Band VI, 1959, s.v. (English translation in *Theological Dict. Of NT*, vol. VI, 1968).
3. Compare also 'Shavuot', *Encyc. Judaica*, vol. 14, col. 1320: 'In rabbinic times a remarkable transformation took place…the festival became the anniversary of the giving of the Torah'. Cf. Also J. Howard Marshall, 'The Significance of Pentecost', *Scottish Journal of Theology* 30 (1977), p. 349.
4. I am grateful to Professor R.J. Tournay O.P. for drawing my attention to this study.
5. Compare also R. Le Déaut, 'Pentécôte et tradition juive', *Assembleés du Seigneur* 51 (1963), pp. 22–38; M. Delchor, 'Pentécôte', in *Diction. de la Bible, Suppl.* VII 1966, 858–79, *idem.*, *RB* 79 (1972), pp. 610–14.

and this in spite of the fact that he himself associates the Pentecost story in Acts 2.1–13 with the Sinai tradition.

This skeptical attitude towards Pentecost as festival of the giving of the law has penetrated Jewish scholarship too, cf., e.g., G. Alon, מחקרים בתולדות ישראל, pp. 111 n. 91 and S. Safrai, העליה לרגל בימי בית שני, 1965, p. 189 and n. 143, although some leading Jewish scholars in the past argued for the antiquity of the festival.[6]

In this study we try to clarify the covenantal nature of the Pentecost by tracing its origins to the Old Testament literature (Psalms and Chronicles) and by showing its continuation in the Second Temple period.

Covenantal Festival

A. According to Exod. 19 the revelation at Sinai took place in the third month (Siwwan), the month in which Pentecost is due according to the Pharisaic as well as to the Essene and Qumran calendar. Though there is no evidence in the law that the Sinai theophany was commemorated as was Exodus (cf. Exod. 12) indications of such commemoration may be found in the Psalmodic literature. Psalm 50 opens with a theophany which is similar to that of Sinai; (compare especially מציון ...אלהים הופיע (v. 2) with Deut. 33.2 ה׳ מסיני בא...הופיע מהר פארן). However, there the scene takes place in Zion and not in Sinai.

> God, the Lord...spoke and summoned the world from east to west. From Zion, perfect in beauty God appeared – let our God come and not keep silence. Devouring fire runs before him, and rages around him fiercely. He summoned the heavens above, and the earth to the judgment of his people. Bring in my devotees who made a covenant with me over sacrifice...The heavens proclaimed his righteousness...

It seems that this passage reflects a dramatization of the Sinai theophany in Jerusalem. As at the covenant of Sinai so here God reveals himself in storm and fire, he calls from heaven to his people and asks to gather the ones who made a covenant with him over sacrifice (cf. Exod. 24.5). At last he proclaims.

Listen my people and I will speak	שמעה עמי ואדברה
O, Israel I will instruct you	ישראל ואעידה בך
I am God, your God.	אלהים אלהיך אנכי

The last sentence is none other than a chiastic quotation of אנכי ה׳ אלהיך of the decalogue, but because of its Elohistic setting (being embedded in the group of Elohistic psalms) the tetragrammaton was transformed into Elohim. In the continuation of the psalm we find admonition against stealing, adultery and false witness (vv. 18–19), crimes enumerated in the decalogue.

Another psalm in which the first two commandments of the decalogue are quoted is Ps. 81. Here a festival is explicitly mentioned:

6. Cf. H. Albeck, *Das Büch der Jubiläen und die Halacha*, pp. 15–16, J. Heinemann, *Philons Griechische und Jüdische Bildung*, p. 128.

Blow the horn of the New Moon
On the full moon for our feast day (ליום חגנו)
For it is a law for Israel
A ruling of the God of Jacob.
He imposed it as a decree upon Joseph
When he went forth from the land of Egypt
I heard a language that I know not.
I relieved his shoulder of the burden
His hands were freed from the basket…
I answered you from the secret place of thunder
I tested you at the waters of Meribah.
Hear my people and I will instruct you (ואעידה בך)
You shall have no foreign god
You shall not bow to an alien god
I the Lord am your God
Who brought you out of the land of Egypt…
(translation according to *Psalms*, JPS, 1972)

Here we find a festival involved in a theophany that occurs after the Exodus and is associated with the decalogue. The first two commandments are quoted chiastically לא יהיה בך אל זר ולא תשתחוה לאל נכר אנכי ה׳ אלהיך. Before the citation of the commandments the trial at the waters of Meribah is mentioned (v. 8) which reflects the sequence of the events as told in the Book of Exodus: waters of Meribah (ch. 17) and then the story of revelation (chs. 19–20).

In this revelation God is depicted as answering from the secret place of thunder אענך בסתר רעם which undoubtedly points to the Sinai tradition where God answered Moses in thunder (liter. voice and see below) from the cloud (Exod. 19.19, cf. Ps. 99.7 בעמוד ענן ידבר אליהם) while the horn was blowing. Similarly we read in Deut. 5.19 that God spoke to the congregation out of fire and cloud with a mighty 'voice', compare v. 20: 'You heard the voice out of the darkness'. The appearance of God in secret (סתר) out of the darkness while giving his voice (= thunder) is also mentioned in Ps. 18: 'He made darkness around him his secret place…the Lord thundered from heaven. The Most High gave forth his voice (וירעם בשמים ה׳ ועליון יתן קולו)' (vv. 12–14). It is clear that here 'thunder' equals 'voice' as we find elsewhere in the Bible and in the ancient Near East.[7] As in Ps. 50 where the verb העיד is used in connection with the commandments: שמעה עמי ואדברה ישראל ואעידה בך so in Ps. 81 the verb העיד precedes the quotation from the decalogue: שמע עמי ואעידה בך. The verse עדות ביהוסף שמו which occurs there likewise refers to these commandments. In fact העיד paired with עדות is found in 2 Kgs 17.15 and Neh. 9.34 and as Veijola has shown[8] it means 'to impose covenantal laws'. On the other hand העיד has the connotation of 'instruct' as pointed out by Couroyer.[9] It is interesting to note that in the Jewish Pentecost service a so-called liturgy of אזהרות (linked to the decalogue) was recited (I. Elbogen, *Gottesdienst*, p. 217) which seems to have very

7. Cf. My article in *Eretz Israel* vol. 14 (H.L. Ginsberg Festschrift).
8. T. Veijola, *Ugarit Forschungen* 8 (1976), pp. 343ff.
9. B. Couroyer, *Revue Biblique* 82 (1975), pp. 206ff.

ancient roots. Indeed הזהר like העיד means ‘to warn’[10] as well as ‘to instruct’ and it is possible that the liturgical tradition of אזהרות is traced back to liturgical situations like those reflected in Ps. 50 and 81. It is true that the festival implied here could also be the New Year as Mowinckel suggested[11] and as was interpreted by the Rabbis,[12] however this still remains a conjecture, whereas the sequence of events as depicted in Ps. 81 seem to point towards Pentecost and not the New Year. The blowing of the horn in Ps. 81 belongs to the ceremony of covenant renewal as may be learned from the Asa episode in 2 Chr. 15.10f., quoted below, where blowing the horn accompanies the covenantal oath. It is likely that just as the Jubilee which follows seven yearly weeks (שבע שבתות שנים) was inaugurated by blowing the horn (Lev. 25.9) so also the Pentecost which comes after seven weeks (Lev. 23.15: שבע שבתות) was celebrated by blowing the horn.

B. A covenant ritual performed in the third month and most likely on *Shavuoth* is described in 2 Chr. 15.10ff. Here we read that the people gathered in Jerusalem in the third month[13] and after sacrificing, entered the covenant to seek the Lord ‘with all their heart and soul’ and bound themselves by oath to the Lord through acclamation and sounds of trumpets and horns. The oath here is a covenantal oath[14] undoubtedly constituting a renewal of the first Sinaitic covenant ratified by a pledge accompanied by sacrifices (Exod. 24.3ff.).[15] The word שבועה, which occurs three times in the passage, points towards a connection with the name שבועות.[16] The double meaning of שבועות is explicitly referred to in the Book of Jubilees 6.21: ‘this feast is two fold and of double nature’.[17] The sounding of horns in the discussed passage finds its analogy in the sound of the horn at the

10. See I. L. Seeligmann, *Hebräische Wortforschung*, W. Baumgartner Festschrift (SVT 16), pp. 265ff.

11. S. Mowinckel, *Le décalogue*, 1927, p. 129f. Cf. also G. von Rad, *Gesam. Studien zum A.T.* (1961), pp. 28ff.

12. Cf. *b. Rosh Hash.* 8a, b.

13. The Targum adds in v. 11 here בחגא בשבועיא see A. Sperber, *The Bible in Aramaic* IVa, p. 45.

14. For ‘oath and covenant’ as hendiadys cf. my article ברית in *Theol. Wörterbuch zum AT*, I (1973).

15. 2 Chr. 15.15 recounts that the people ‘rejoiced at the oath because they had bound themselves with all their heart and had sought him with all their will’ (בכל רצונם). The ‘joy’ (שמחה) coupled with ‘willingness’ (רצון) found here, express the legal idea of free and uncovered will of the one who takes upon himself the obligation, cf. Y. Muffs, ‘Joy and Love as metaphorical expressions of willingness and spontaneity in cuneiform, ancient Hebrew and related literatures’, *Morton Smith Festschrift*, vol. III, 1975, pp. 1ff. Compare also the evening liturgy of the *Shema‘* Benediction. ומלכותו ברצון קבלו עליהם...בשמחה רבה ‘they took upon themselves his kingdom, willingly...with great joy’. For רצון and שמחה and its legal connotation cf. the discussion of Muffs, *op. cit.*, pp. 21ff.

16. On the tendency for ‘double meanings’ in the Book of Chronicles, cf. Y. Zakowitch, כפל מדרשי שם, MA thesis, Hebrew University of Jerusalem (1971), pp. 166ff.

17. Cf. R.H. Charles, *The Book of Jubilees* (1902) *ad loc.* Charles comments: ‘why this festival should be said to be ‘of a double nature’ I do not see’. (p. 53, n. 21). According to our view the double nature of the festival lies in the double meaning of the root שבע, which underlies חג שבועות. It should be added however, that Pentecost in the Book of Jubilees is of a double nature: it is associated with the pledge of the Lord to the Patriarchs on the one hand and with the pledge of the Israelites to the Lord on the other.

revelation at Sinai in Exod. 19.16, 19. As has been seen by Ehrlich[18], blowing the horn belongs to the oath ritual, a custom that persists in Judaism until this day.[19]

C. Pentecost as the covenantal festival par excellence is most clearly presented in the book of Jubilees. The covenants with Noah and Abraham were established on the fifteenth of the third month, which is the date of the Pentecost, in accordance with the calendar of this book[20] as well as with the calendar of the Qumran sect.[21]

We are told in the book of Jubilees that Noah was the first one to celebrate the feast of weeks and therefore was commanded that the future generations 'should celebrate the feast of weeks in this month once a year, to renew the covenant every year' (6.17). A similar injunction is proclaimed right after the covenant with Abram: 'On that day we made a covenant with Abram, according as we had covenanted with Noah in this month and Abram renewed the festival and ordinance for himself forever' (14.20).

Both covenants followed the offering of sacrifices (6.3; 14.19) as was the case with the covenant at Sinai (Exod. 24.3ff.) and the covenant of Asa mentioned above. The covenant with Abram, concerning circumcision, was also established in the middle of the third month (15.1) and the revelation to Jacob also takes place in the middle of the third month after celebrating the harvest festival (44.4ff.).

D. The people of Qumran used to renew the covenant annually (1QS 1.16ff.) and according to an unpublished text from Qumran cave 4 the annual covenant ceremony took place at Pentecost.[22]

Name of the Festival

The Hebrew and Aramaic names for Pentecost as reflected in the Mishnah (passim), the Targums[23] and Josephus are עצרתא/עצרת (ἀσαρθά, *Antiq.* III, 252). עצרת means 'assembly' or 'solemn gathering' which indicated that Pentecost was especially noted for its solemn convocation. It commemorated – in our opinion – the covenant assembly at Sinai. As has been shown by D.Z. Hoffman the designation עצרת for the Pentecost is to be explained against the background of biblical יום הקהל 'the day of assembly' which in Deuteronomy marks the day of revelation and giving of the law (9.10; 10.3; 18.16).[24] Indeed this is the only reasonable explanation for the name עצרת given to the Pentecost.

18. Cf. A. Ehrlich, מקרא כפשוטו, *ad loc.*

19. For blowing the horn in the oath ritual cf. *Aruch Completum* s.v. הסת (p. 229): ותוקעין בשופר עם האלה.

20. See Charles, *op. cit.* p. 52 to vv. 17–18.

21. Cf. S. Talmon, מחקרים במגילות הגנוזות,ספר זכרון לא. ל. סוקניק, 1957, 77ff.

22. Cf. J.T. Milik, *Ten Years of Discovery in the Wilderness of Judaea*, 1959, pp. 113ff.; for additional possible evidence cf. M. Delcor, 'Pentécôte', *Dict. Bibl. Supp*, 870–71.

23. *Tg. Onq.* and *Tg. Ps.-J.* Num. 28.26, *Targ. Neof.* I (facsimile 1970) Deut. 16.10 חגה דשבועיה היא עצרתה.

24. D.Z. Hoffman, *Das Buch Leviticus*, 1905–1906, II., p. 228f. Mark that *Tg. Ps-J.* and *Tg. Neof.* translate יום הקהל: ביום כנישת קהלא and in Deut. 18.16: ביומא דאתכנשו שבטיא למקבלא אורייתא.

That Pentecost was notorious for its solemn massive gatherings may be learned from Josephus and the New Testament. Josephus tells us twice about big gatherings in Jerusalem on Pentecost. One is at the time of the Parthian invasion in 40 BCE:

> when the feast called Pentecost came round the whole neighborhood of the temple and the entire city were crowded with country-folk (*War* 1.253, comp. *Antiq.* 14.337).

The second time is after the death of Herod in 4 BCE:

> on the arrival of the Pentecost...it was not the customary ritual so much as indignation which drew the people in crowds to the capital. A countless multitude flocked in from Galilee, from Idumaea, from Jericho, and from Peraea beyond the Jordan, but it was the native population of Judaea itself which, both in numbers and ardor, was preeminent (*War* 2.43, comp. *Antiq.* 17.254).[25]

In both cases the gathering is particularly noted. It is true, the gatherings were exploited for military activities, but these could not be upheld were it not for the particular solemn occasion.

Similarly we read in the Acts 2, that the crowd witnessing the miracles of the Pentecost included:

> Parthians, Medes, Elamites, inhabitants of Mesopotamia, of Judaea and Cappadocia, of Pontus and Asia, of Phyrgia and Pamphylia, of Egypt and the districts of Libya around Cyrene; visitors from Rome both Jews and proselytes, Cretans and Arabs... (vv. 9ff.).[26]

That Pentecost was outstanding for its pilgrimage may be also learned from Acts 20.16 according to which Paul wanted at all costs to spend Pentecost in Jerusalem. Philo marks Pentecost as a festival greater than another great feast (ἑτέρας ἑορτῆς μείζονος) (*Spec. Leg.* 2.176). In another place (*Spec. Leg.* 1.183) he calls Pentecost the most national celebration (δημοτελεοτάτη ἑορτή) and when describing the celebration of the Pentecost by the Therapeutae he refers to the festival as μεγίστη ἑορτή 'the biggest holiday'.

Pentecost in the New Testament

Most instructive for our purpose is the story about the founding of the Christian congregation on the day of Pentecost as told in the Acts of the Apostles:

> When the day of the Pentecost arrived (reached its course) they were all together, when suddenly there came from the sky a noise like that of a strong wind which filled the whole house...and there appeared to them tongues divided like flames of fire and rested on each one of them. And they were all filled with the Holy Spirit and began to talk in other tongues as the spirit caused them to utter... (2.1ff.).

The main components of this story may be found in the traditions of the law-giving at Sinai.

25. Translation according to Thackerey, Loeb Classical Library.
26. For a thorough analysis of this catalogue cf. J. Kremer, *Pfingstbericht* etc., pp. 145ff.

1. The heavenly noise and the fiery tongues have their roots in the description of the Sinai revelation as it was elaborated in the Midrashic literature of the Second Temple period. The Aramaic Targums as well as Philo explain the λόγοι coming out of the mouth of the deity at Sinai as blazing flames becoming words or voices, a concept based apparently on Exod. 20.18: וכל העם ראים את הקלות ואת הלפידים liter.: 'all the people saw the voices and the flashes/torches'. Philo recounts that the flames (φλόγες) became articulate speech in the language (διάλεκτος) familiar to the audience (Decal. 46). Targum Pseudo-Jonathan as well as Genizah Targum fragments and Neofiti similarly describe the word of God departing from his mouth as blazes and torches (Exod. 20.2).

> דבירא ... כד הוה נפיק מן פום קודשא יהי שמיה מברך הי כזיקין והי כברקין והי כשלהובין/ כלמפדין דינור, למפד מן ימינה ולמפד דאישא מן שמאליה, פרח וטייס באויר שמיא וחזר ומתחמי על משרייתהון דישראל וחזר ומתחקק על לוחי קוחי קיימא...[27]
>
> The word that went out from the mouth of the Holy one, may his Name be blessed, was like shooting stars and lightenings and like flames and torches of fire, a torch of fire to the right and a torch of flame to the left. It flew and winged swiftly in the air of the heavens and turned around and became visible in all the camps of Israel and by turning it became engraved on the two tablets of the covenant.

2. The idea of the division of flames into tongues is rooted in the Midrashic notion that each one of the Lord's words was divided into seventy tongues, that is, the languages of all the nations.[28] Thus we read in *b. Shab.* 88b: Rabbi Yohanan said: 'The Lord gives a command, those who bring the news are a great host' (Ps. 68.12), every *dibbur* that came from the Almighty was divided into seventy languages.[29] Another dictum by R. Yishmael: 'Behold my word is like fire declares the Lord – and like a hammer that shatters rock' (Jer. 23.29). It was taught by Rabbi Yishmael: Just as the sledgehammer (when shattered by harder rock) is divided into many slivers, so every word which was uttered by the Holy One was divided into seventy tongues.[30] Most significant is the overlap in phraseology between this tradition and the account in Acts: *the tongues of fire were divided.*

Rabbi Yishmael	Acts 2.3
דבור (כאש) נחלק לשבעים לשון	καὶ ὤφθησαν αὐτοις διαμεριζόμεναι γλῶσσαι ὡσει πυρός
The word (like fire) was divided into seventy tongues	There appeared to them tongues divided like flames of fire

27. For the variants in the Targums see J. Potin, *La Fête Juive* etc. Tome II, pp. 37ff.
28. Cf. the seventy nations in Gen. 10 and see my short commentary on Genesis (1975), *ad loc.*
29. Cf. Midrash Tehilim (ed. Buber) 92.3.
30. Amongst the various Rabbinic parallels that were adduced by Strack-Billerbeck to the episode in Acts 2, this dictum was also quoted but without noting its importance for understanding of the motif.

Cf. also: 'R. Yosi bar Haninah says: As a man who strikes with a hammer on stone and the fire sparks sprinkle around...so the Holy discharged the *dibbur* from his mouth and it was divided into luminaries' (*Midr. Ps*. to 92.3).

3. The fiery tongues that rested on each of them (Acts 2.3) remind us of the divine glory of the divine diadems[31] which were put on the head of the Israelites when they proclaimed 'we will do and obey' (נעשה ונשמע) at Sinai (*b. Shab*. 88a).[32]

The Speaking with Tongues

Following the revelation to the Christian congregation – we are told by Luke – the members of the congregation started to talk in different languages. Scholars do not know how to explain 'the talking in tongues' here. In their opinion it means 'ecstatic babbling', and according to E. Meyer, it reminds us of the activities of the bands of the popular prophets in ancient Israel.[33] Though one cannot deny the central place of the πνεύμα in this tradition (see below) there is no justification for understanding 'the speaking with foreign tongues' as ecstatic babbling. Luke in Acts 2 just wants to inform us that the revelation was destined not only for the Galileans who constituted the main bulk of the population present there (2.7) but for all the nations and 'tongues' of the world. Behind the story lies the Jewish tradition that the Torah was given in seventy languages, i.e., in the languages of all the nations in the world[34] and it is no mere coincidence that Rabbi Yishmael who expounded the verse about the fiery word of God dividing itself into seventy tongues, was also the author of the dictum that the Torah was written on the stone of Mount Ebal in seventy languages.[35]

Another Midrash speaks about God revealing himself at Sinai in four tongues (*Sifrei* to Deut. 33.2):

> When the Holy...revealed himself to give the Torah to Israel, he talked to them not in one language but in four:
>
> 1. 'God came from Sinai', that is, in Hebrew.
> 2. 'He shone forth from Se'ir', that is, in Roman.
> 3. 'He appeared from the Mount Paran', that is, in Arabic.
> 4. 'And came (ואתה) from רבבות קדש, that is, in Aramaic.[36]

31. The divine glory הדר/זיו/כבוד constitutes the fiery halo which surrounds the head and thus forms a crown. For the nature of the כבוד and its Akkadian and Egyptian equivalent *melammu* and *nsrt*, cf. my article in *Eretz Israel* vol. 13 (H. I. Ginsberg Festschrift).

32. According to the earlier tradition God himself tied the diadems upon their heads while the later tradition has it that the angels did it, see E. E. Urbach, *The Sages*, I, pp. 148–49.

33. Cf., e.g., E. Meyer, *Ursprung und Anfänge des Christentums* III (1923), pp. 142f., 221.

34. Cf. *t. Soṭ*. 8.7.

35. Cf. the *Mek*. on Deut. Discovered by Schechter, *J. Lewy Festschrift*, p. 189.

36. For other parallels cf. Potin, *La Fête Juive*, pp. 258ff.

Speaking Tongues as a Spiritual Gift

The 'fiery tongues' have their origin – as shown – in the Jewish Midrashic traditions about God's revealing the Torah in seventy languages. The 'speaking in tongues' by the members of the holy congregation[37] belongs however to another tradition and viz. the tradition about 'charismata' or the spiritual gifts bestowed upon the ones overtaken by the holy spirit (cf. 1 Cor. 12.10, 28; Acts 10.44–45).[38] This tradition has its roots according to our view, in the story of Num. 11 about the spirit of God descending upon the seventy elders (v. 25) who were to adjudicate the tribes of Israel. As is well known this story served as the prototype for the seventy members of the Sanhedrin in the second temple period and regarding them we are told that they should know and speak[39] seventy languages (*t. Sanh.* 8.1, *y. Šeqal.* 5.1,48d, *b. Sanh.* 17a, *Menaḥ.* 65a). The people of the elected body of the nation upon whom the spirit of God rested were thus endowed with the gift of tongues and this is exactly what we find in the miracle story of the Pentecost.[40] If it is true – as some argue – that it is only the Apostles who received the spirit in the upper room, then the analogy with Num. 11 is even stronger. Like the elders and the Sanhedrin, the Apostles too were in charge of judging Israel (Mt. 19.28, Luke 22.29) and therefore were in need of the divine spirit.[41] On the other hand it is possible that the whole community was considered as a council similar to that of the 'seventy' and therefore all its members received the holy spirit.

'Speaking in tongues' is a divine gift as is every propensity and talent but it is no more than a medium of communication. It was especially important for the Christian congregation which was comprised of people from different nations. 'Speaking in tongues' was needed not only for the translation of the message but also for understanding prayer, and this is what stands behind 1 Cor. 14. In this chapter we find the legitimation for praying in foreign languages.[42] 'Amen' can only be said when the prayer is understood:

37. It is not clear altogether whether Acts 2.4 refers to the 120 men mentioned in 1.15 or to the 12 Apostles. At any rate the writer has in mind here the holy body constituting the fountain of the Christian community.

38. Cf. Beare, *JBL* 83 (1964), cf. also Martin *JBL* 63 (1944).

39. Every member must understand the languages and should be able to speak at least two of them. The ability to speak the languages does not mean controlling them perfectly, cf. S. Lieberman, *Greek in Jewish Palestine* (1942), pp. 15–16.

40. It seems to us that the story in the Letter of Aristeas about the seventy-two elders who translated the Torah through divine inspiration, belongs to the same category. For the story in the letter of Aristeas and its connection with the account of the revelation at Sinai, cf. most recently H.M. Orlinsky, *HUCA* 46 (1975), pp. 94ff.

41. Cf. E. Stauffer, *ThLZ* 77 (1953), p. 202, who compares the 120 to the 120 members of the 'Knesset HaGedolah'.

42. Cf. *m. Soṭ.* 7.1

> I will pray with my spirit but I will also pray with my understanding. I will sing[43] with my spirit but I will sing also with my understanding. If you utter your praises in the spirit how is the person in a layman's position to say Amen to your prayer? For of course he does not know what you are saying (vv. 15ff.).

'Speaking in tongues' is – as Beare summarized in his study – 'one among many gifts, amid a great diversity and is less highly valued than the gift of prophecy or prayer and 'praise with the mind'.[44] It is a medium for disseminating the divine message and for understanding the prayer and is not an aim in itself.

Coming back to our main subject we may sum up in saying that the revelation as described in Acts 2 is patterned after the revelation at Sinai and the pouring of the spirit on the elders in the Sinai desert. Just as the revelation at Sinai occurred on the day of the Pentecost so the revelation to the first Christian community happened on this very day.[45] The date of the first revelation at Sinai, viz. the holiday of Pentecost served as a point of departure for other mystic experiences. Two episodes of later Jewish tradition are instructive in this respect. The first episode pertains to the mystic experience of Joseph Caro (1488–1575). During the vigil of the Pentecost night (*Order of the Night of Shavuot*), a voice came out suddenly of the mouth of Caro. The people around him heard the voice, fell on their faces and everybody fainted.[46]

The second episode relates to the proclamation of Shabbatai Tsevi (1626–1676) as Messiah. During the vigil of the night of *Shavuot*, the divine spirit rested upon Nathan of Gaza, and he fell into a trance and announced: 'Shabbetai Zevi is worthy to be King of Israel'.[47]

It is also possible that Josephus' story in *War* 6.299f. belongs to the same category. We are told there that at Pentecost night before the war, the priests heard a noise and then a divine voice: 'We are departing hence'.[48]

The Sinaitic Prototype of the Revelation to Jesus

Just as the revelation to the first Christian community was patterned after the revelation to the Israelites at Sinai so the revelation to Jesus was patterned after the revelation to Moses. In the Sinai stories we are told that Moses ascended the

43. 'Sing' here is associated with liturgy, cf. 1QS X9: אזמרה בדעת which comes before ועם מוצא ערב ובוקר אמר חוקיו עם מבוא יום ולילה אבואה בברית אל which points toward the recital of the *Shema'* in the morning and evening, cf. M. Weinfeld, *Shnaton, An Annual for Biblical and Ancient Near East Studies*, Vol. 1, 1976, p. 77 n. 245, *idem*. *Tarbiz* 45 (1976), p. 20. Cf. also H. Conzelman, *Der erste Brief an die Korinther*, 1969, *ad loc.*

44. *JBL* 83 (1964), p. 246.

45. E. Haenchen (The Acts of the Apostles, Commentary, 1971) who goes along with others in stating that evidence for the Jewish Pentecost tradition (associated with Sinai) has not been found earlier than the middle of the second century, nevertheless admits that Luke's story is influenced by the story of Sinai and that the tongues of fire which had become tongues of speech at Sinai (relying solely on Philo) influenced the story of Acts 2 (p. 174).

46. Cf. R.J.Z. Werblowsky, *Joseph Karo* (1962), pp. 19–21.

47. Cf. G. Scholem, *Shabbatai Tṣevi* (1975), pp. 217ff.

48. Cf. Tacitus, *Hist.* V, 13.

Mount together with Aaron, Nadab and Abihu (Exod. 24.9) and after six days of waiting God called from the cloud (Exod. 24.16) and Moses entered the cloud. Following the contact of Moses with the Lord his face changed (Exod. 34.28f.). Afterwards the tabernacle was built, when it was finished it was covered with a cloud (Exod. 40.34) out of which the Lord called unto Moses and commanded him (Lev. 1.1, cf. Deut. 31.14–15).

The story of the transfiguration has been similarly structured. Jesus ascended the Mount after six days (Mk 9.2; Mt. 17.1) together with his three followers: Peter, James and John. He was transfigured before them, following which booths were made for him and for Moses and Elijah who were with him there. After that a cloud overshadowed the booths and out of the cloud a voice was heard, proclaiming the election of Jesus.

The story of the transfiguration shows a perfect analogy with the stories about Moses at Sinai and there is no doubt therefore that the stories of the Gospels come to tell us that by ascending the Mount and speaking with Moses and Elijah Jesus became like them. As is well known, Moses and Elijah had revelations at Sinai and both of them together represent the supreme divine will as expressed in the Law and the Prophets, cf. Mal. 3.22–24, the concluding verses of the Torah and the Prophets.

It seems then that the revelation to Jesus as well as the revelation to the first Christian community were structured according to the Sinaitic narrative. The result achieved was that Jesus fulfills the role of Moses while the Christian congregation takes the place of the Israelite congregation at Sinai. The Jewish tradition about the Torah revealed by God through Moses from which Judaism drew its main inspiration was replaced in the Christian community by the revelation to Jesus on the Mount on the one hand and by the revelation to the first Christian community on Pentecost on the other.

Chapter 20

THE CHARGE OF HYPOCRISY IN MATTHEW 23 AND IN JEWISH SOURCES

Matthew 23 constitutes, as is known, a charge sheet against the Pharisees. The main charge is hypocrisy. The author compiled all sorts of traditions and structured them in a way that would enhance the image of insincerity and hypocrisy.[1] The chapter may be divided into three main parts: (1) the programmatic section (vv. 1–12); (2) seven passages that open with ‘woe to hypocrites’ (vv. 13–30); and (3) a concluding section about the doom of Jerusalem (vv. 31–39).

The programmatic section opens with a statement about the scribes and Pharisees who sit on Moses’ seat[2] and preach, but do not practise what they preach (vv. 2–4). Then comes a passage that exemplifies the false ostentatious behaviour of the scribes and Pharisees (vv. 5–7). This passage, which concludes with the accusation that the Pharisees love to be called ‘rabbi’, leads to the Christological passage (vv. 8–12) that elaborates the idea that the real ‘rabbi’ is Jesus.

The purpose of this study is to show that most of the accusations of hypocrisy contained in this chapter are rooted in Jewish tradition. In the programmatic section, moreover, this applies not only to the contents but also to the structure. Indeed, while the woes also have their roots in Jewish admonitions, the programmatic part already raises the fundamental issue (vv. 2–3):

> The scribes and the Pharisees sit on Moses’ seat, so practice and observe whatever they tell you, but not what they do, for they preach but do not practice. They bind heavy burdens hard to bear and lay them on men’s shoulders, but they themselves will not move them with their finger.

As has been seen by scholars,[3] the charge should properly refer to scribes (γραμματεῖς)[4] and *teachers of the Law* (νομικοί). For it was these two groups

1. Cf. D. Flusser, ‘Two Anti-Jewish Montages in Matthew’, *Immanuel* 5 (Summer 1975), pp. 37–45. For the nature of the composition of Mt. 23, cf. recently D.E. Garland, *Intention of Matthew 23* (Supplements to *Novum Testamentum*, 52, 1979).

2. ἐπὶ τῆς Μωυσέως καθέδρας, corresponding to the expression קתדרא דמשה in *Pesiq. Rav Kah.* 1.7 (Mandelbaum ed., p. 12). Such chairs were indeed discovered in various synagogues in the Land of Israel. See E.L, Sukenik, *Tarbiz* 1.1 (1929), pp. 150–51; J.N, Epstein, *ibid.*, p 152.

3. Cf. Garland, pp. 41ff.

4. The scribes (γραμματεῖς = סופרים) fulfilled administrative-judicial functions, as has been shown by D.R. Schwartz, ‘‘Scribes and Pharisees, Hypocrites’: Who Are the Scribes?’ (Hebrew), *Zion* 50 (1985), pp. 121–32. The scribes were identified with the Levites and the שוטרים; on the latter, see my ‘Judge and Officer in Ancient Israel and in the Ancient Near East’, *Israel Oriental Stuties*, I

who were in fact sitting on Moses' seat, rather than *all* the Pharisees as Matthew tries to present the matter. Indeed Luke 11, which contains a parallel to the woes passage, reflects some awareness of this distinction. There the first three 'woes' are addressed to the Pharisees (vv. 42, 43, 44), but the other three to the teachers of Law (vv. 46, 47, 52). Thus in Luke the charge of loading people with burdens hard to bear is directed at the latter group[5] and not at the Pharisees in general.

Condemnation of scribes and teachers who do not follow their own teaching goes back as far as Jer. 8.8:

> How can you say: 'We are wise and we possess the Torah of the Lord'?
> Surely, for naught has the pen labored, for naught the scribes.[6]

The prophet condemns the scribes and the wise men for not observing the teaching that they themselves had committed to writing. The pen of the scribes had made the Torah, as it were, into a lie.[7]

Condemnation of scribes and teachers of Torah who do not follow their own prescriptions is also well known from rabbinic literature. They are called there, as in Matthew, 'hypocrites in regard to Torah' (חנפי תורה). As we shall see presently, they are even accused of the same sins as in the Gospels. About such teachers there existed proverbial sayings in rabbinic literature, as for example:

> יש נאה דורש ואין נאה מקיים
> – 'there are those who preach well but do not practice well',[8]

and in positive form:

> נאין דברים כשהן יוצאין מפי עושיהן
> – 'good are the commands that come out of the mouth of those who perform them'.[9]

What is most instructive in these rabbinic sources, however, is that they link the contrast between preaching and practising to knowledge of the divine will or to the 'key of heaven', an idea that occurs also in the context of the woes passages in Matthew (23.13) and Luke (11.52). The sages admitted that it is hard to find a person whose teaching and practice are in complete harmony, since preaching implies the revealing of God's will, but knowledge of God's will is hard for a man of sinful nature. As *Avot de-Rabbi Nathan* 39 puts it:

> Because of his sin it is not granted to man to know what likeness is on high, and were it not for that, the keys would have been handed over to him and he might have known

(1977), pp. 83–86. But the νομικοί were of a scholarly character: teachers of the Torah (see next note).

5. νομικός = דורש תורה, 'the interpreter of the Law' (cf. Sir. 35.15 and the Qumran literature, passim), who was sometimes interchangeable with the scribe. Compare 4 Macc. 5.4 with 2 Macc. 6.18. Moses, on whose chair the teachers sit, is called נומיקה in the midrashic literature; cf. S. Lieberman, *Hellenism in Jewish Palestine* (1950), pp. 81–82.

6. Cf. the Jewish Publication Society's *The Prophets: A New Translation* (1978). לשקר here means 'in vain', as in 1 Sam. 25.21.

7. See my *DDS* (1972), p. 160.

8. *t. Ḥag.* 2.1; *t. Yebam.* 8.7 and the parallels in talmudic literature.

9. *t. Yebam.* 8.7; *Gen. Rab.* 3.4.6 (Albeck ed, p. 326).

> what heaven and earth were created with and would have obtained knowledge from the most High.... The one who follows the right path will be happy.[10]

Only the most outstanding of the sages, such as R. Eleazar b. Arakh, break their way through to heaven so as to get the divine knowledge. Thus *t. Ḥag.* 2.1 says that when Eleazar b. Arakh succeeded with his study Merkavah ('divine chariot', i.e., a knowledge not available to the many), Johanan b. Zakkai proclaimed:

> There are those who preach well but do not practice, there are others who practice well but do not preach well, but Eleazar b. Arakh preaches well and practices well. Happy are you Abraham, our father, that Eleazar b. Arakh descended from you who knows and understands to preach in honor of his Father in heaven.

As has been noted by S. Lieberman, what Johanan b. Zakkai meant was that receiving heavenly knowledge depends upon the performance of the Lord's will,[11] a view reflected in the statement of Rabbah bar Rav Huna in *b. Shab.* 31b:

> A man who possesses learning without the fear of heaven is like a treasurer who is entrusted with the inner keys but not with the outer; how is he to enter?

This passage provides a link between Mt. 23.13 and Lk. 11.52, showing that they reflect the same view: because of their non-compliance with divine norms, neither the teachers of the Law nor their students will enter the divine realm, whereby they are deprived of the key of knowledge. Each of these verses, however, contains half of the idea: Mt. 23.13 speaks about closing the way to heaven but says nothing about knowledge, whereas Lk. 11.52 talks of taking away the key of knowledge but says nothing about this knowledge being heavenly.

Also the position of the two verses is significant. The one opens the series of woes in Matthew where they are directed at 'hypocrites', while the other closes the series of woes in Luke where they are directed at 'teachers of the Law'. This woe is therefore a most important factor in both versions of the homily; it can be explained only against the background of the rabbinic sources according to which hypocritical teachers who do not observe what they preach cannot get the key to heavenly knowledge. Moreover, note the opening dictum in Mt. 23.13, which refers to those who shut the Kingdom of Heaven against themselves and their followers.

That Mt. 23.13 has close affinities with the preceding verses may be learned from the insertion of verse 14 after it. The interpolator of this verse, who missed in vv. 6–7 the clause about the devouring of the widows' houses (cf. Mk. 12.38–40, Lk. 20.46–47, and see below), found the proper place for it after the statement about shutting the way to heaven. He saw that v. 13 is an integral part of the introductory unit, although stylistically it belongs to the section of the seven woes of the next passage.

The programmatic section in vv. 1–12 opens with the charge of ostentatious behaviour. This charge is presented differently in the various Synoptic gospels.

10. Regarding the conclusion of the passage, we follow the manuscript in Schechter's edition, p. 75a. See S. Lieberman, *Tosefta Ki-Fshutah: Moed*, p. 1288.

11. Lieberman, *ibid.*

Mt. 23.5–7 reads:

> They make their phylacteries broad and their fringes long. They love to have the first couches at the table and the first seats in synagogues[12] and salutations in the market places and being called 'rabbi' by men.

Mark (12.38–40) and Luke (20.46–47; cf. 11.43) have:

> ...who like to walk around in long robes and to have salutations in the market places and to have the first seats in synagogues and the first couches at the table, who devour widow's houses and for a pretense make long prayers.

Before adducing evidence to show that the charges listed here are attested rabbinic literature, a general remark should be made: Pharisees are reproached as hypocrites in the rabbinic sources themselves. Thus *t. Soṭa* 22b contains a whole passage dedicated to this topic, opening with a *baraita* that lists seven types of Pharisees (פרושים).[13] The characterization of the types and the exact meaning of the definitions there elude us, because of the antiquated language of the tradition. It is clear, however, that some of those seven types of Pharisees are criticized for showing off their religious devotion in every possible way. Among them are one who 'carries his piety on his shoulder (פרוש שכמי), and one who looks for a task to perform in order to prove that he observes everything possible (פרוש דע חובתי ואעשנה).[14]

This *baraita* is followed by a dictum of R. Nahman b. Isaac, said in connection with the hypocritical types of Pharisee, which reminds us of the charge in Mk. 12.38 and Lk. 20.46 (see further below) about Pharisees who walk around in long robes: 'Let the great court call to account those who are wrapped up in a cloak [גונדאי]' (Rashi: 'those who wrap themselves in cloaks as though they were true Pharisees'). By way of association, the talmudic editor adduces a historical anecdote about Alexander Jannai (103–76 BCE):

> King Jannai said to his wife: 'Fear neither the Pharisees nor their opponents, but [fear] the hypocrites who pretend to be Pharisees but whose deeds are those of Zimri and who expect a reward like Phinehas'.

The true meaning of this episode may be understood against the background of Josephus' account (*Antiq.* 13.398f.) of how King Alexander Jannai advised his wife concerning her peacemaking with the Pharisees. The Pharisees knew how to influence Queen Alexandra and apparently not without flattery (cf., e.g., *Antiq.* 13.404–406).

The Qumran sect, too, accused the Pharisees of hypocrisy in this period. Its writings call them דורשי חלקות which means 'seekers of smooth things', paralleled by 'lying interpreters' (מליצי כזב) and 'seekers of deceit' (דורשי רמיה; cf.

12. πρωτοκλισία and πρωτοκαθεδρία correspond to Hebrew הסבה בראש and ישיבה בראש respectively.

13. For the *baraita* on the seven types of Pharisee, see also *y. Soṭa* 5.7 20c; *y. Ber.* 9.7, 14b. Cf. also *ARN* A.37 (Schechter ed., p, 109) and B.45 (*ibid.*, p124).

14. Cf. the explanations in the Talmud.

1QH 2.31–34). As has been shown by D. Flusser and others,[15] the 'seekers of smooth things' in Pesher Nahum (4QpNah 2.13–34, I.7; 3.6–7) and in other places in the Qumran literature are none other than the Pharisees. These are depicted there as hypocrites, 'who by their false teaching and their lying tongue and a deceitful lip lead many astray' (4QpNah 2.13–34, 2.8–9) אשר בתלמוד . שקרם ולשון כזביהם ושפת מרמה יתעו רבים.

The same source notes that they had invited Demetrius, the Greek king, to join them in their struggle against Alexander Jannai. It was for this reason the latter hanged them alive (4QpNah 169 3–4, 1.6–7). Apparently it was a period when the Pharisees exploited their status in order to assert power. This historical situation is what gave rise to the stigma of hypocrisy ascribed to the Pharisees. As we have seen, however, the Pharisaic literature itself preserves bad memories of that period, which find expression in the passage quoted from *t. Soṭa* 22b.

Let us now turn to some individual accusations made in Matt. 23.5–7 and their parallels in Mark and Luke. We shall inquire in what measure they, too, are reflected in Jewish-Pharisaic literature.

1. Ostentatious display of formal attire: parading in cloaks (ἐν στολαῖς Mk. 12.38 and Lk. 20.46). This accusation is quite common in rabbinic literature. In the passage from *t. Soṭa* 22b quoted above, R. Nahman b. Isaac denounces the sin of those who wrap themselves with cloaks in order to show off. Such demonstrations of one's formal position are often condemned by the rabbis. Thus ben Azzai said: 'It is easier to rule the world than to teach in the presence of two men wrapped in cloaks (העטופים בסדינים)'.[16] A somewhat different version is found in the Midrash on Psalm 18.44:

> 'You have rescued me from strife' – so that I will be saved from being judged before them. Ben Azzai said: 'It is easier to rule the world than to rule [influence] two men wrapped in robes.'[17]

This refers to the judges who used to wrap themselves in their robes before taking up a case (*b. Shab.* 10a).[18] As we shall see, this kind of admonition is directed toward judges and official leaders who care about their prestigious position but do not pay attention to the oppressed who need help.

It is not the formal attire itself that is condemned here, but the abuse of it. Sometimes, therefore, praise is given to those who, though wrapped in robes, do not flaunt their importance. Commenting on the meaning of Isa. 23.18, 'Rather shall her profits go to those who abide before the Lord', the sage says to Ishmael b. R. Jose: 'It refers to people like you and your friends and two –man wrapped in cloaks like you who do not feel yourselves important'.[19]

15. Cf. D. Flusser, 'Pharisees, Sadducees and Essenes in Pesher Nahum' (Hebrew), *Essays in Jewish History and Philology in Memory of Gedaliahu Alon* (1970), pp. 133ff. See also Y. Yadin, 'Pesher Nahum (4Qp Nahum) Reconsidered', *Israel Exploration Journal* 21 (1971), pp. 1–12.

16. *ARN* A.25 (end, Schechter ed.). On the attire of rabbinic school cf. S. Krauss, 'The Cloak of Rabbinic Scholars' (Hebrew), *Jubilee Volume for M.S. Bloch* (1905), pp. 83–93.

17. *Midr. Ps.*, Buber (ed.), p. 81.

18. Buber, *ibid.*, notes.

19. *Eccl. Rab.* 1.9.

2. Arrogant demonstrations of piety: exaggerated details of ritual attire (Mt. 23.5). Whereas Mark and Luke speak of 'cloaks', the parallel in Matthew speaks of the wearing of 'broad phylacteries' (φυλακτήρια, signifying תפלין)[20] and 'long fringes' (κράσπεδα, ציצית). These details, too, are mentioned in rabbinic criticism of Pharisaic peacockery, besides the already mentioned flaunting of cloaks to which those fringes were attached. Thus on the verse 'I further observed all the oppression...behold the tears of the oppressed, with none to comfort them' (Eccles. 4.1), *Ecclesiastes Rabbah* comments:

> R. Benjamin interpreted the verse as referring to hypocrites in regard to Torah (חנפי תורה). People suppose that they can read the Scriptures and the Mishnah, but they cannot. They wrap themselves in cloaks and put phylacteries on their heads. Of them it is written, 'Behold, the tears of the oppressed, with none to comfort them'. 'It is mine to punish', says God, as it is said: 'Cursed be they who do the work of the Lord deceitfully'. (Jer. 48.10)

The juxtaposition of the demonstration of ceremonial piety on the one act, and oppression of the underprivileged on the other, is thus clearly reflected in the rabbinic literature too. Similarly, in interpreting the commandment against taking God's name in vain, *Pesiqta Rabbati* 22.5 states.[21] 'You are to put on phylacteries and wrap yourself in your [fringed] cloak [טלית] and then go forth and commit transgression'.

To the ostentatious wearing of phylacteries and the fringed cloak, it adds the accusation of arrogating to oneself the first place at dinner, also mentioned in the Synoptic Gospels (Mt. 23.6, Mk. 12.39 and Lk. 20.46):

> 'Do not take God's name in vain' – R. Simon said: 'If this refers to a false oath, this is superfluous because it has already been said: "You shall not swear falsely by the name" [Lev. 19.12]. But what it means here is that you are not to wrap yourself in a cloak, cover yourself with the fringes, transgress the Torah in secrecy, presume to make the blessing first, open [the meal first or take the portion first.'[22]

Making the phylacteries broad as an ostentatious sign of status, exactly as found in Matt. 23.5, is mentioned in the testimony of R. Hai Gaon (l0th, century CE):

> It was the custom in the academy for the students to make their phylacteries small, no higher than a finger...whereas the great rabbis would make theirs some three fingers high, so that the students should not be equal to them.[23]

The term 'hypocrites in regard to Torah' (חנפי תורה), quoted above from *Eccl. Rab.*, is attested also in *Lev. Rab* interpreting Eccl. 5.5: [24]

> 'Do not let your mouth bring you into disfavor' – R. Benjamin interpreted this verse as referring to hypocrites in regard to Torah.

20. For the equation of φυλακτήρια in Matthew with תפלין, see J.H. Tigay, 'On the Tern Phylacteries (Mt. 23.5)', *Harvard Theological Review* 72 (1978), pp. 45–52.

21. Friedmann ed., 111b.

22. J. Mueller, *Teshuvot Ge'onei Mizrah u-Ma'arav* (1888), par. 132; cf. par. 171.

23. Cf. J.H. Tigay, *op. cit.*, p. 49 and reference there.

24. Margulies ed., p. 357.

3. Ostentatious behaviour in tithing all kinds of petty things: observing minutiae of the Law, such as tithing mint, dill and cumin, while sinning against the great principles of the Law (Mt. 23.23; Lk. 11.47). This, too, has its parallels in Jewish Pharisaic lore, which accuses Esau of exactly the same behaviour pattern. On Gen. 25.28, 'because [the meat from his] hunting was in his mouth' [כי ציד בפיו], the Midrash comments: 'He [Esau] used to ask his father, 'Does one give tithe from straw? Does one give tithe from salt or water?'[25] In 'mouthing' such questions, according to this interpretation, Esau 'hunted' his father's esteem by pretending to be a very pious man.

To sum up, accusations of Pharisaic hypocrisy in the Gospels contain motifs identical with the accusations in the rabbinic sources. These are: (1) not practising what one preaches; (2) ostentatiously wearing cloaks; (3) showing off phylacteries and fringes; (4) demanding the first place at dinner; (5) tithing trivial things. All these are denounced in rabbinic literature, a fact that shows that such a critique was prevalent in Judaism at the time when Christianity began to take shape.

It appears that the critique of Pharisaic hypocrisy was a common phenomenon in Judaism of the first centuries of the common era. When the authors of the Synoptic Gospels wrote about Pharisaic hypocrites, they were using material that was widespread in Pharisaic lore itself.

25. See *Gen. Rab.* 63.10, Albeck (ed.), p. 693, and note there.

Chapter 21

Hillel and the Misunderstanding of Judaism in Modern Scholarship

My point of departure for the discussed topic will be the view of J. Wellhausen on Judaism. Wellhausen was an outstanding scholar in Old Testament and New Testament whose life ambition was 'historical interpretation based on philological examination'.[1] Yet he readily admitted that he did not include rabbinic literature in his historical reconstruction of the second temple period. He read only Josephus. He admitted also that the theologians did not study even that.[2]

In his entry on 'Israel' in *Encyclopedia Britannica*, Wellhausen defined Judaism as follows:

> Judaism is historically comprehensible, and yet it is a mass of antinomies...The Creator of heaven and earth becomes the manager of a petty scheme of salvation; the living God descends from His throne to make way for the law [the very law which was the basis of Jesus' education! – M.W.]. The law thrusts itself in everywhere; it commands and blocks up the access to heaven; it regulates and sets limits to the understanding of the divine working on earth. As far as it can, it takes the soul out of religion and spoils morality. It demands a service of God, which, though revealed, may yet with truth be called a self-chosen and unnatural one, the sense and use of which are apparent neither to the understanding nor to the heart. The labour is done for the sake of the exercise. It does no one any good, and rejoices neither God nor man...The ideal is a negative one, to keep one's self from sin, not a positive one, to do good upon earth. The occupation of the hands and the desire of the heart fall asunder...There is no connection between the Good one and goodness.[3]

He goes on to claim that the gospel develops hidden impulses of the Old Testament, but it is a protest against the ruling tendency of Judaism. Jesus understands monotheism in a different way from his contemporaries... He feels the reality of God dominating the whole of life, he breathes in the fear of the Judge who requires an account for every idle word. This monotheism is not to be satisfied with stipulated services, how many and great soever; it demands the whole man, it renders doubleness of heart and hypocrisy impossible. Jesus casts ridicule on the works of the law, the washing of hands and vessels, the tithing of mint and cumin, the abstinence even from doing good on the Sabbath. Against unfruitful

1. See n. 12.
2. See n. 12.
3. *Encyclopedia Britannica*[9] (1881), Vol. XIII, pp. 269–431.

self-sanctification He sets up another principle of morality, that of the service of one's neighbour.[4]

What follows is much in the same vein. Wellhausen continues extolling the church and denigrating Judaism.

The same bias appears in Wellhausen's *Israelitsche und jüdische Geschichte*.[5] Here the New Testament is presented as the apex of the spiritual creativity of the 'true Israel', while the vast Hebrew literature which flourished in the Middle Ages did not, Wellhausen argues, emerge from the true roots of Israel's tradition.[6] Unlike Christianity, Judaism sees salvation as a miraculous event, unrelated to the religious and ethical behavior of the individual. The idea of individual responsibility before God, he concludes, is far-removed from Judaism.[7]

Wellhausen presents here a completely distorted view of the situation.[8] While it is true that Jewish halakha is, and has always been, a labour for its adherents,[9] its observance has never been a matter of 'labour done for the sake of the exercise'

4. Reprinted in J. Wellhausen, *Prolegomena to the History of Israel*, trans. J. Black and A. Menzies (Edinburgh, 1885), pp. 508–10. The German edition of this study appeared in J. Wellhausen, *Skizzen und Vorarbeiten: Erstes Heft* (1884).

5. Seventh edition (1914; originally published in 1894).

6. 'Die ausgedehnte jüdische Literatur des spätern Mittelalters kann man nicht eigentlich als ein Gewächs aus der alten Wurzel betrachten' (p. 358).

7. 'Israel', pp. 364ff.

8. His views correspond to those of his contemporaries in German, esp. E. Schürer and W. Bousset. Many of these never made an effort to study rabbinical sources or to read the literature of the Jewish school and synagogue. Nevertheless, they dared to define Judaism in a confident manner. Cf., e.g., the words of G.F. Moore: 'What Bousset lacked in knowledge, he made up, however, in the positiveness and confidence of his opinions...[by] unsupported assertion coming by force of sheer reiteration' ('Christian Writers on Judaism', *HTR* 14 [1921] p. 242).

On the prevailing anti-Jewish atmosphere of German theologians in the 19th century, cf. J. Blenkinsopp, *Prophecy and Canon* (1977), pp. 19–20. See also W. McKane and his reaction to Blenkinsopp in *JSOT* 17 (1979), pp. 66–67, and Blenkinsopp's response to McKane in *JSOT* 18 (1980), pp. 105–107. On the religious sentiments of Wellhausen's own time, see recently: L.H. Silberman, 'Wellhausen and Judaism: Julius Wellhausen and his *Prolegomena to the History of Israel*', *Semeia* 25 (1982), pp. 75–82.

R. Smend in his article, 'Wellhausen und das Judentum' (*ZTK* 79 [1982], pp. 249–82), has presented a thorough and valuable discussion of Wellhausen's attitude towards Jews and Judaism. Smend rightly concludes that in those days nobody would be blamed for thinking or talking like him. To be sure, this does not mean that he and his contemporaries were free of anti-Semititc feelings. Wellhausen was not happy at all about the survival of the Jews. On other occasions he did not hide his feeling of aversion to Jews. (See R. Smend, 'Wellhausen und das Judentum', p. 269 n. 95.)

According to W.R. Nicoll in the protocol of his meeting with Wellhausen in Eldena near Greifswald (March 8, 1881): 'Wellhausen hates Jews' (See T.H. Darlow, *William Robertson Nicoll: His Life and Letters* (1925), p. 42. See, however, the reservations of R. Smend in *ZTK* 78 (1981), p. 165. We should admit that Wellhausen's personal feeling do not count when it comes to scholarly matters. What we try to show is that whatever Wellhausen's personal feelings toward Jews may have been, his characterization of Judaism is false.

9. Hence the various complaints about its rigidity, stiffness, etc. See references, esp. the ones concerning Buber, in R. Smend, *ZTK* 79 (1982), p. 278 nn. 140–41. On Buber's attitude toward institutionalized religion, see Y. Amir, 'Buber and the Synagogue', *Here and Now: Studies in the Social and Religious Thoughts of M. Buber* (1982), pp. 115–18 (Hebrew).

but was rather an instructive discipline in the demanding multi-faceted service of God. A claim that halakha ignores the commandment of the heart and the 'reality of God dominating the whole of life' is simply misrepresentation. Wellhausen was apparently unaware that the biblical words 'I have set the Lord always before me' (Ps. 16.8)[10] are displayed prominently upon the lectern of every synagogue, and he apparently knew nothing of that Judaism which struggles against 'a commandment of men, learned by rote' (מצות אנשים מלומדה).[11]

Wellhausen himself testifies that besides some Mishnah and Mekhilta, he never studied any rabbinic literature,[12] which makes him ill-qualified to say what

10. In the translations of this and other biblical passages, I have made use of the recent translations of the Scriptures published by Jewish Publication Society of America. I have, where the context required, deviated from the Society's rendering.

11. See, e.g., Bahya ibn Paquda's *Duties of the Heart*, trans. M. Hyamson (1962), esp. Vol. II, pp. 144–51 ('Repentance', Chapter V) and pp. 198–201 ('Spiritual Accounting', Chapter III). The medieval philosopher's idea and its formulation derive from Isa. 29.13 (despite Wellhausen's idea of the inauthentic roots of medieval Jewish writings!).

12. See *Die Pharisäer*, p. 123 n. 1. In another note (p. 19 n. 1), he says that the Mishnah from beginning to end is characteristic of the Pharisees, and that there is no point in going to detail *as it is all the same*. Clearly no one who has studied Mishnah properly would make such a statement.

As pointed out by H. Liebeschütz in his survey of Wellhausen (*Das Judentum im deutschen Geschichtsbild von Hegel bis Max Weber* [1967], pp. 245–68), this conscious decision to forego the careful study of rabbinic literature is especially astonishing on the part of a scholar whose life's ambition was historical interpretation based on philological examination. Liebeschütz's study was brought to my attention by the late Professor I.L. Seeligman. As for Wellhausen's work on the Pharisees, his devoted friend Wilamowitz-Moelendorf testified that he wrote this work without any training in rabbinics. Wellhausen stated, 'I read only Josephus, the theologians do not even do that', *Erinnerungen* (1848–1914^2; [1928], p. 188).

This ignorance of Jewish sources crippled Wellhausen not only in his study of the Pharisaic period (i.e., the time of Jesus), but also in his evaluation of topics treated in the Priestly Code of the Pentateuch. For instance, in his dicussion of the 'shoulder, the two cheeks, and the maw' given to the priests, he makes reference to Josephus (*Prolegomena*^{6}, p. 14 n. 8 [ET, p. 154]), but not to the Mishnah (*Ḥul.* 10.1; cf. Sifra 17.6). Elsewhere, discussing P's outlawing of the high places since the time of the erection of the tabernacle, he cites (in Latin!) *m. Zebaḥ.* 14.4, but neglects to mention the Mishnayot which follow and speak of the subsequent legalization of the high places (*Prolegomena*^{6}, p. 37 n. 1 [not found in ET]). Y. Kaufmann accuses Wellhausen of willful distortion (*History of the Israelite Religion*, vol. 1 [1938], p. 132 n. 34 [Hebrew]), but it is just as likely that the case is one of citation from faulty, incomplete secondary sources. Wellhausen's superficiality in dealing with rabbinic material is far more serious a shortcoming than his hatred of Talmudists, a hatred he certainly did not lack (cf. *Die Pharisäer*, p. 123).

Regarding the lack of training in Judaic sources among the New Testament scholars of Wellhausen's age, cf. G.F. Moore in 'Christian Writers on Judaism' (note 4): 'It is not without significance that all these authors – Schürer, Baldensperger, Weiss, Bousset – were New Testament scholars, the oldest of them scarcely past thirty years old. Schürer was the only one who thought it was necessary to know anything about the rabbinical sources, and he found in Surenhusius' Mishnah just the right material for the demonstration of 'legalism'. Beyond this he never went; the others did not go so far'.

One of the biggest distortions of Judaism in Bousset's book about Jesus (*Jesus Predigt in ihrem Gegensatz zum Judentum*, 1892) is his statement that 'later Judaism had neither in name nor in fact the faith of the Father-God; it could not possibly rise to it' (cf. G.F. Moore, 'Christian Writers on Judaism', p. 242). Whoever opens a Jewish prayer book will hardly miss the phrases אבינו מלכנו ('our Father, our king') or אבינו שבשמים ('our Father in heaven').

Pharisaic Judaism is and is not. One Mishnaic passage which he certainly did not learn is the dictum that 'a man may offer much or little, *so long as he directs his mind toward heaven* (*m. Menaḥ.* 13.11). Had he learned it, he could not have claimed that Judaism separates the legal act from the proper thought and the 'understanding of the heart'.

It is also evident that Wellhausen failed to see that the Jewish religious experience is one of joy in fulfilling a commandment. The law is observed not for the sake of the exercise, but to perform the will of the Creator. Wellhausen entirely missed the fact that Judaism sanctifies life by eradicating the separation of *jus* from *fas* (of law from religion) by rendering all aspects of life – the synagogue, the home, and the market – a continuous act of divine service. Every step taken by the Jew is directed by awareness that he or she is fulfilling God's will.

The notion, which Wellhausen ascribed to Jesus as the antithesis of Judaism, that true monotheism is 'not to be satisfied with stipulated services...; it demands the whole man' is actually an authentically Jewish view. Rabbi Jose is quoted as saying 'and let all your deeds be done for the sake of Heaven' (*m. ʾAbot* 2.12). Elsewhere, this statement is attributed to Hillel the Elder, who is said to have performed such deeds as eating, drinking, and bathing for the sake of Heaven.[13] This same concept is expressed in the words of the amora Bar Kappara (*b. Ber.* 63a): 'Under which short passage are all the laws of the Torah subsumed? 'In all your ways know him' (Prov. 3.6)'.

Jesus was perpetuating a dispute current in the Judaism of his age: Hillel demanded, as we have seen, that one direct all his deeds to Heaven. Shammai held that such religious intent is necessary only for deeds that go into the performance of a divine command; it was not necessary for other actions.[14]

Although Wellhausen quoted Shammai and not Hillel, Judaism adopted Hillel's view.[15] Judaism understands the commandments as the concretization of a few ethico-religious principles:

> R. Simlai preached: Six hundred thirteen precepts were uttered to Moses: Three hundred sixty-five prohibitions, corresponding to the number of days in the solar year, and two hundred forty-eight injunctions corresponding to the number of organs of a man's body... David reduced the number to eleven as it is written: 'A Psalm of David: Lord, who may dwell in Your tent?' He who lives without blame, who does what is right...who has never done harm to his fellow' (Ps. 15.1–5).[16] ...Isaiah proceeded to

13. *ARN* B 30 (cf. Schechter edition, p. 66); see also E.E. Urbach, *The Sages: Their Concepts and Beliefs*, vol. 1 (1975), pp. 339–42. Urbach writes, 'One cannot overlook the danger to the observance of the precepts from the standpoint of Hillel, for if every act can be done in the name of Heaven, then something is abstracted from the absolute value of the precept and a way is opened for nullification of the worth of the ritual laws whose connection with knowledge of the Lord is not clear or simple. In truth, Jesus reached such extreme conclusions in his polemic agaisnt the Halakha, as is reported in the Gospels' (p. 341).

At any rate, it was not Jesus who invented this sort of montheism.

14. See Urbach, *Sages*, p. 450.

15. To characterize the Pharisaic attitude, Wellhausen quoted Shammai's and not Hillel's view about the Sabbath, and thus distorted the picture (*Die Pharisäer,* p. 19; ET p. 116). On the theological aspects of the controversy between Shammai and Hillel, see Urbach, *Sages*, p. 340.

16. Cf. my article in *Tarbiz* 62 (1993), pp. 5–15.

> reduce the number to six, as it is written, 'He who walks in righteousness, speaks uprightly' (Isa. 33.15). ...Micah further reduced the number to three, as it is written, 'He has told you, O man, what is good, and...the Lord requires of you to do justice... to love kindness...and to walk humbly' (Micah 6.8). ...Again came Isaiah and reduced the number to two, as it is said, 'Thus said the Lord: Observe what is right and do what is just' (Isa. 56.1). ...Amos finally reduced the number to one, as it is said, 'Thus said the Lord to the House of Israel: Seek me, and you will live' (Amos 5.4). (*b. Mak* 23b–24a)

The point of the homily is that the essence of the divine command and all the individual precepts it entails can be expressed in any number, however small, of the general religious-ethical demands, and that the classical prophets and psalmists had affirmed this fact. Another Talmudic view, that of R. Nahman bar Yishak, is that the reduction of the number of commandments to one, expressed according to R. Simlai in the passage from Amos, is better expressed in the words of Habakuk, 'The righteous shall live by his faith (באמונתו)' (Hab. 2.4). This notion that the 'faith of the righteous' is equal to the whole of the Law is found in Gal. 3.11–12. However, as opposed to the Talmudic passage, it appears there as part of the Pauline polemic against the observance of the precepts of the Torah.

Urbach realized that R. Simlai's homily was intended primarily to express the idea that humanity is to be wholly engaged in the fulfillment of God's will – both spacially and temporally.[17] The individual commandments are thus no more than a detailed elaboration and concretization of humanity's submission to and nearness to the Divine. Such a view is directly opposed to that voiced by Wellhausen in his book on the Pharisees:

> Die Summe des Abgeleiteten erstickte die Quelle, die 613 Gebote des geschriebenen und die tausend anderen des ungeschriebenen Gesetzes liessen für den Gewissen keinen Platz. Die Summe der Mittel wurde der Zweck, man vergass Gott über der Thora und der Zugang zu ihm über der Etikette, durch welche er ermöglicht werden sollte.[18]

The same R. Simlai preached that the Torah both begins and ends with acts of kindness. It opens with God's providing raiment for Adam and his wife, and ends with his attending to the burial of Moses (*Soṭa* 14a). The lesson is an obvious one: lovingkindness (חסד) as practised by God himself, is the alpha and omega of the Law.[19] Wellhausen's claim that Pharisaic Judaism was an outgrowth of the priestly religion and was therefore characterized by moral insensitivity is

17. Urbach, *Sages*, pp. 343–45.

18. *Die Pharisäer*, p. 19. Most Christian scholars failed to acquire a true understanding of the nature of Judaism and thus held views like this. The English biblical scholar G.A. Smith writes on Deut. 4.7, 'For what great nation is there that has a God so close?... Legal Judaism lost this sense of constant nearness of God [i.e., the one operative in Deut. 4.7] and did not compensate for the loss by its apocalypses' (*Deuteronomy*, Cambridge Bible [1918], p. 60). Only recently has the trend been reversed as Christian scholars have begun to get aquainted with Judaism; see C. Klein, *Theologie und Anti-Judaismus* (1975).

19. Cf. *Tg. Ps-J.* to Deut. 34.6 and cf. Mt. 25.31–39. Rabbi Simlai, a third century sage, was a kind of 'apostle' (or emissary-sage). In his preaching he polemicized with Christians (cf. B.Z. Rosenfeld, 'The Activity of Rabbi Simlai: A Chapter in the Relations Between Eretz-Israel and the Diaspora in the Third Century', *Zion* 48 [1983], pp. 229–39). It is against this background that we should understand the affinities of his sermons to the New Testament.

untenable.[20] Lev. 19 (cf. esp. vv. 14, 18, 32–34) and 25 (cf. esp. vv. 1, 17, 36, 43) are replete with moral demands, such as not putting a stumbling block before the blind (19.14), loving the neighbour (19.18), standing up before an old man (19.32), loving the foreigner (19.39), not cheating (25.17), not charging interest (25.36), and not ruling over a slave ruthlessly (25.43). The idea that the Priestly Code is morally apathetic is as distorted as the notion that Pharisaic Judaism is. Wellhausen did not feel the true pulse of Judaism. Proper intent (*kavvanah*) while performing the commandments was always a crucial issue to the Rabbis.[21] There would have been no place for the many Talmudic discussions of this topic if, as Wellhausen contended, the commandments were merely exercise.

Christian Morality

According to Wellhausen, religion reached its height in Christian morality. Yet this Christian morality itself is rooted in Pharisaic Judaism, as the Gospels themselves attest. Thus we read in Mt. 22.35f.,

> And one of them [the Pharisees], a legal expert [νομικός],[22] asked him, to test him: 'Master, which is the great commandment [ἐντολὴ μεγάλη] in the law?' And he said to him, '"You shall love the Lord your God with all your heart, and with all your soul, and with all your mind".[23] This is the first and great commandment, and the second is like it: 'You shall love your neighbour as yourself'. On these two commandments hang all the law and the prophets'.(Mt. 22.36–39)[24]

20. 'For what holiness required was not to do good, but to avoid sin', s.v. 'Israel', *Encyclopedia Britannica*, reprinted in ET of *Prolegomena*, p. 500.

21. Cf. Urbach, *Sages*, pp. 390–95.

22. Compare Lk. 10.25. In 4Macc. 5.4, Eleazar standing before Antiochus is called νομικός. In 2 Macc. 6.18 he is called 'one of the first scribes' (πρωτευόντων γραμματέων), i.e., one engaged in the interpretation of the Torah (δευτέρωσις, מדרש התורה); cf. תופש התורה (Sir. 15.1) and תורה דורש (35.15; see also Qumran passages). The latter are occasionally reckoned among the Pharisaic scribes, but are not identical to them; see, for example, Lk. 11.45, where the νομικός, does not see himself as one of the Pharisees. The Pharisees are the members of the sect; the *soferim* are the officials and assorted temple scribes, and the νομικόι are the learned preachers and interpreters of the Law. On Moses as a νομικός, see S. Lieberman, *Hellenism in Jewish Palestine* (1950), pp. 81–82.

23. ἀγαπήσς κυριον τὸν θεόν σου ἐν ὅλῃ τῃ καρδίᾳ σου…ψυχῇ σου…διανοίᾳ σου. The word διανοίᾳ (cf. Mk. 12.30; Lk. 10.27) never appears in the LXX for Heb. דעת, and represents, I believe Heb. יצר, as in the LXX of Gen. 6.5; 8.21; 1Chr. 29.18; in accord with the Midrashic comment in 'with all thy heart' (i.e., with both your inclinations יצריך; Sifre Debarim 32, ed. Finkelstein, p. 55 and refs.). In contrast σύνησις in Mk. 12.35 is the equivalent of Heb. *Mada'* of *da'at*, which replaces classical *leb* in rabbinic Hebrew (see A. Ben David, *Leshon Miqra Uleshon Hakamim*, vol. 1 [1967], p. 92); cf. also the commentary of Abraham Ibn Ezra to Deut. 6.5. לבבך נפשך ומאדך appear in Qumran as 'intelligence [דעת], strength [כח], and fortune [הון]' (1QS 1.12; cf. 3.2). The LXX rendered מאד in Deut. 6.5 with Greek ἰσχύς or δύναμις (see n. 25 below). The Aramaic translations render מאד *nks* (property) or *mmwn* (money; see below). Cf. also CD 13.11 and my article in *Iyunim bemiqra: Sefer zikkaron le-Y.M. Grintz* (1982), pp. 41–47.

24. See Sifra, Kedoshim 1.1: 'Why was [this chapter] said to the entire people? Because the essentials of the Law are subsumed in it'. See also D. Flusser, *Yahadut umeqorot hanatsrut* (1979), p. 36.

The Pharisee's questions about the 'great commandment' correspond in large measure to the dictum of Rabbi Akiba: '"Love your neighbor as yourself": that is the major principle [כלל גדול] in the Law' (Sifra Lev. 19.18).[25]

On the other hand, Jesus' statement that all the law and the prophets hang on these two commandments corresponds to Hillel's reaction to the heathen who wanted to be converted on the condition that Hillel teach him the entire Torah 'while standing on one foot'. Hillel replied, 'What is hateful to you do not do to your neighbour. This is the entire Torah; all the rest go and study [i.e., all the rest is a commentary]' (*b. Shab.* 31a).[26] This saying appears in the Palestinian Targum as a translation of Lev. 19.18: 'Love your neighbour as yourself'.[27] In the parallel of Mk. 12.28–33 we read:

> And one of the [Pharisaic] scribes came, and...asked him, 'Which is the first commandment of all?' And Jesus answered him, 'The first of the commandments is, "Hear, O Israel; the Lord our God is one Lord: And you shall love the Lord your God with all your heart, and with all your soul, and with all your mind, and with all your strength".[28] This is the first commandment. And the second is like it, namely, "You shall love your neighbour as yourself". There is none other commandment greater than these'. And the scribe said unto him, 'Well, Master, thou hast said the truth, for there is but one God; and there is none other but he: And to love him with all the heart, and with all the understanding [σύνεσις] and with all the soul, and with all the strength, and to love his neighbor as himself, is more than all burnt offerings and sacrifices'.

Both Luke 10.25–28 and Matthew 28 state clearly that the legal expert approached Jesus to test him, and Jesus stood the trial. Jesus thus revealed his awareness that the two commandments mentioned are the basis of Pharisaic Judaism.

By expressing the view of the Pharisees, Jesus reveals his own opinion as well. Christian interpreters have always realized this, though they have consistently felt compelled to stress the difference between the position of the Pharisees and that of Jesus. Bousset, for example, writes as follows:

25. See Flusser, *Yahadut*. It is best to avoid interpreting ἐντολή as 'principle' (כלל) as Flusser does, since כלל is not the same as מצוה at all (see M. Smith, *Parallels Between the Gospels and Tannaitic Literature* (1945).

The phrase ἐντολή μεγίστης appears in the letter of Aristeas in connection with the honouring of parents (§228). Second in importance is the love of neighbour, expressed in the language of LXX, 'your friend who is as yourself' (ὁ φίλος ὁ ἴσος τῆς ψυχῆς σου; Deut. 13.7). For the view that honouring one's parent is the most important commandment, see *y. Pe'ah* 1.1 (15d): 'R. Simeon ben Yohai says, the respect of father and mother is so great that the Holy One, Blessed be He, preferred it above His own honor... Said R. Abba bar Kahana: 'Scripture equates the easiest of the commandments with the most stringent. The easiest is to let [the mother-bird] leave the nest, *the most stringent is the honoring of father and mother*'. This same view may be present in Sifre-Deut. 13.7: 'Your friend who is as yourself; this is your father' (ed. Finkelstein, p. 151).

26. Cf. *ARN* B 26 (Schechter ed., p. 53).

27. For this saying and its sources, see Urbach, *Sages*, p. 589, and p. 955 n. 93.

28. The word used here is ἰσχύς. In Deut. 6.5, the word δύναμις appears (LXX). However, ἰσχύς is used in 2 Kgs 23.25. In Hebrew and Aramaic sources of the Second Commonwealth and thereafter, *me'od* is interpreted as 'money'. See CD 9.1; 12.10; *m. Ber.* 9.5; *Tg. Onq.* and *Tg. Yer.* to Deut. 6.5. The scribes at Qumran apparently understood *me'od* as fortunes.

> Die Heraushebung und Zusammenstellung der zwei Gebote tritt also nicht eigentlich also eigener Gedanke Jesu auf, sondern auch ein ehrlicher und nach dem Heil verlangender Schriftgelehrter konnte wissen, dass dies die wichtigsten Gebote des alten Bundes waren.…Aber die einzelnen ernsten Rabbiner haben nicht vermocht, diese Erkenntnis für die Welt fruchtbar zu machen; erst dadurch, dass Jesus für diese Anschauung eintrat, hat er gewissermassen die Seele der alten Religion entdeckt, aus der Umklammerung einer tausendgliederigen Gesetzesüberlieferung befreit und ihren edelsten Gehalt in die neue Religion überfuhrt. Der ganze Wust des Zeremonial-Gesetzes aber mit seinen zahllosen Einzelheiten ist damit zurückgedrangt und zum Absterben gezwungen.[29]

The tendentious inaccuracy of such interpretation speaks for itself. Neither the Pharisees nor Jesus considered the traditional meticulous observance of the commandments in any way a contradiction to the precepts of love of God and neighbour, nor did the authors of the Gospels themselves (cf. Mt. 5.17–20; Lk. 16.17). As a matter of fact, as we have stressed, the Pharisees considered observance to be the very realization of these ideals. It was Hillel, one of the greatest of the Pharisees, who saw – as indicated – in Leviticus 19.18 the basis of the whole Torah. And it was this same Pharisee Hillel who taught that man must 'love his fellow men and bring them near to Law' (*m. ᵓAbot* 1.12), a lesson which recalls Jesus' befriending of the sinners in order to bring them to faith. Hillel's school indeed ruled that Torah is to be taught to all men, even sinners, since 'many sinners in Israel, after having been brought to the study of the Torah, have become righteous, pious and proper men'. This view was opposed by the school of Shammai, who taught that 'one should teach only those who are wise, humble, of distinguished ancestry, and rich'.[30]

The difference between the attitudes of Hillel and Shammai in matters of formalities and etiquette comes to clear expression in the manner of recitation of the *Shema'* credo.[31] According to the school of Shammai, one should stand while reciting the *Shema'* in the morning, as written in Deut. 6.7: ובקומך ('at your rising'), whereas the recital of *Shema'* in the evening should be performed while reclining (ובשכבך). In contrast, the school of Hillel says, 'Everyone recites in his own way: one may stand, recline, walk, and even work during the recital'.

Shammai stresses the formal act: the ceremony during the recital. Hillel ignores altogether the ceremony and stresses instead the intention of the heart. R. Meir interprets Deut. 6.6, 'The words which I charge you will be on your heart' (והיו הדברים האלה על לבבך): 'the words will follow the intention of the heart'.

Concerning the objection to formal attire and etiquette, most interesting is the critique of hypocrisy in rabbinic literature. Here we find the same accusations as in Matthew 23. As in the Gospels, so in the rabbinic literature, we read about חנפי תורה, 'hypocrites in regard to the Torah', as shown in chapter 20.[32]

29. W. Bousset and W. Heitmüller, *Die Schriften des Nuen Testaments*^{4}, Band 1 (1929), p. 186.

30. *ARN* A 3 (ed. Schechter, pp. 14–15).

31. Cf. I. Knohl, 'A Parasha Concerned with Accepting the Kingdom of Heaven', *Tarbiz* (1983), pp. 11–32.

32. Cf. chapter 20, above.

Chapter 22

EXPECTATIONS OF THE DIVINE KINGDOM IN BIBLICAL AND POSTBIBLICAL LITERATURE

In this chapter I will try to show that the basic motifs of the divine kingship, such as longing for the coming of Yahweh, the revelation of God's kingdom, the speedy coming of the kingdom and the sanctification of the name of Yahweh in the universe, are reflected in the Old Testament but reached their apogee in Judaism and Christianity.

In the Old Testament these motifs were embedded in the prophecies while in Judaism and Christianity they were formulated as independent prayers and declarations. Thus the sanctification of God's name in the universe comes to expression in the Kaddish on the one hand and in the Christian Lord's prayer on the other. The longing for Yahweh's appearance appears as an attribute of holy persons both in Judaism and Christianity. By the same token the revelation of God's kingdom and the speedy coming of the kingdom are put in the form of a prayer. The following is a survey of the evidence.

The salvation of Israel was depicted from the beginning as *the coming of God*, the King, from his holy abode in order to save Israel from its enemies. This is already attested in the poetry of ancient Israel. According to the Song of Moses (Deut. 33), God appears from Sinai, Seir and Paran in order to help the tribes of Israel in the conquest of the promised land (Deut. 33.26–29). God acts there in the capacity of a king (v. 5) as he acted in Exodus (Exod. 15.18; Num. 23.21–22; 24.7–8). In Deut. 33.2,5 we read:

> Yahweh came (בא) from Sinai and shone forth (זרח)
> from Seir. he appeared (הופיע) from Mount Paran...
> There arose a King in Jeshurun
> when the heads of the people were assembled
> all the tribes of Israel together.

At the end of the poem one reads:

> There is none like the God of Jeshurun
> who rides the heaven to your help. . .
> who drove out the enemy before you (vv. 26–27).

Similarly in the Song of Deborah (Judg. 5), the God of Israel came to help the tribes of Israel in their encounter with the Canaanites by his appearance from Seir/Edom and Sinai (vv. 4–5). This is to compare with Ps. 68.8–9, 16–18 where

God figures as coming from Sinai with thousands of chariots (v. 17). Likewise, in the ancient poem of Habakkuk 3:

> God comes from Teman
> the holy one from Mount Paran
> his radiance overspreads the skies
> and his splendour fills the earth. . .
> he stands still and shakes the earth
> he looks and makes the nations tremble…
> the eternal mountains are riven
> the everlasting hills subside
> the tents of Cushan are shaking
> the tent-curtains of Midian flutter.

Here, next to the 'coming' is the revelation of his glory.

The theophany is also reflected in the inscriptions of Kuntilet-Ajrud of the beginning of the eighth century BCE that mention Yahweh Teman (cf. Hab. 3.3):

> and when El appears [shines forth, זרח]
> the mountains melt and the hills dissipate…
> to bless El on the day of war.[1]

The salvation of Israel appears mainly on the day of Yahweh, that is, when God appears to intervene on behalf of his people, as shown above.[2] There I have tried to demonstrate that the Day of the Lord is reflected in the Israelite prayers, as S. Mowinckel suggested,[3] however not in the New Year liturgy as he proposed, but in the liturgy in general.

I will try to show here in detail the components of the divine kingship as it developed in Judaism and Christianity.

1. *Longing for 'The Day of The Lord'*

Longing for 'the day of the Lord' is found for the first time in the prophecy of Amos (5.18) but the very longing appears as something known and traditional. It expresses the hope for divine salvation and is encountered in the other prophecies speaking about waiting for divine salvation (Mic. 7.4, 7: צפה, יחל; Isa. 8.17, 30.18: חכה; Hab. 2.3: 'If it delays, wait for it, for when it comes it will be no time to linger'; Zeph. 3.8: 'wait for me...for the day when I will stand up as witness'). Daniel continues this tradition into the second temple period with the exclamation: 'happy is the man who waits' (אשרי המחכה 12.12). The waiting for God's coming is reflected widely in the Jewish and Christian sources of the second temple period. Thus we read in the Qumran prayer devoted to Zion:

1. See M. Weinfeld, 'Kuntilet Ajrud Inscriptions and their Significance', *Studi Epigrafici e Linguistici* 1 (1984), pp. 121–30.
2. Chapter 4
3. S. Mowinckel, Zum israelitischen Neujahr und zur Deutung der *Thronbesteigungspsalmen*: Zwei *Aufsätze* (1952), pp. 26–38; *idem, The Psalms in Israel's Worship* (2 vols.1962), I, pp. 106–92.

> Great is your hope, O Zion...those who desire (המתאוים) the day of your salvation will rejoice in your plentiful glory...how they waited for your salvation... Your hope will never die, O Zion, and your aspiration will never be forgotten (11QPs[a] 22.2–11, *DJD*, IV, p. 43).

The sage Simeon Ben Shetah (first century BCE), is said to have opened his oath with the declaration: 'May I not live to see the Consolation (לא אראה בנחמה) if…' (*b. Mak.* 56).

Similarly, about Joseph from Arimathea it is said in the New Testament: 'that he lived in expectation of the kingdom of God' (Lk. 23.50), as with Simon the righteous and pious who was waiting for the consolation of Israel (Lk. 2.25); compare Lk. 2.38: Simon waiting for the redemption of Jerusalem (=גאולת ירושלים). The Aramaic Targum to 2 Sam. 23.4 refers to those who desired (מחמדין) the consolation (נחמתא) to come. Similarly, the Targum to Jer. 31.5 refers to those who desire (מחמדין) the years of consolation (נחמתא) to come, who say, 'when will we arise and go up to Zion?' The consolation is not necessarily the rebuilding of the temple but rather all eschatological hopes. The 'waiting' for the 'kingdom of God' or 'kingdom of heaven' was expressed clearly in the Jewish Liturgy. Thus is found in the *Kedusha* Liturgy of Sabbaths and festivals:

> from your abode, our King, appear and reign over us for we wait for you (כי מחכים אנחנו לך). When will you reign in Zion? Speedily, in our days, do you dwell there forever. May you be exalted and sanctified (תתגדל ותתקדש) in Jerusalem your city throughout all generations and to all eternity. May our eyes behold your kingdom, as it is said in your glorious Psalms by your truly anointed, David: 'The Lord shall reign forever, your God, O Zion, for all generations: Hallelujah *(Kedusha* liturgy).[4]

Surprisingly, this is confirmed by external evidence: Shenoute, Abbot of Athribis in Egypt, in the fourth century says.[5]

> They [the Jews] assemble, according to their customs…on the Sabbaths, New Moon days and festivals...to prostrate, calling in the Hebrew language: 'on which day will you come? at what time will you reveal yourself? because we are expecting your coming… Do not tarry, even if you tarry, we will wait'.

The anticipation of divine rule in Zion is found in every component of Jewish liturgy, starting with the ancient core of the daily service (the *Amidah*, = 'eighteen benedictions') and ending with the personal prayers of Talmudic sages now appended to the public service. Included in the official *Amidah* prayers are:

> Restore our judges as at first...reign you alone over us (some rites add: speedily), O Lord.[6]
> Make spring up speedily the branch of David for each and everyday we hope for your salvation.
> Blessed be the lord who makes spring up the horn of salvation (מצמיח קרן ישועה).

4. Cf. S. Singer, *The Authorized Daily Prayer Book* (1943), p. 99.
5. E. Amelineau, *Oeuvres de Schnoudi* (1914), 11, pp. 379–80.
6. *Authorized Daily Prayer Book,* p. 58.

Y. Liebes has suggested that the word ישועה here alludes to ישוע = Jesus, and that the Christian Jews formulated this prayer,[7] a very controversial thesis. It is probable however – in my opinion – that the Christian Jews interpreted this old Jewish Blessing as referring to Jesus, who was named Yeshua and considered to be a descendant of David.

2. The Revelation of The Glory of the Lord

The revelation of God's glory on the day of salvation is already attested in the ancient poems mentioned above in verbs like 'shine' (הופיע, זרח) and explicitly in Habbakkuk: 'his radiance overspreads the skies and his splendour fills the earth' (3.3). The Glory of God that fills the whole earth is mentioned in Num. 14.21 and also in the tris-hagion of Isa. 6.3. Compare Ps. 72.19.

The revelation of the glory of Yahweh is especially stressed in the prophecy of Deutero-Isaiah, see for example Isa. 40.5: 'the glory (כבוד) of Yahweh shall be revealed (ונגלה) and all flesh shall see it together'. The LXX renders the second part of this verse: 'and all flesh shall see the salvation of Yahweh', like the Masoretic Text of Isa. 52.10: 'Yahweh has revealed his holy arm in the sight of the nations and all the ends of the earth will see the salvation of our God'. According to H.L. Ginsberg, the term 'arm' in this context serves as a metaphor for salvation (cf. Isa. 51.5; 52.10; 53.1).[8] In fact, the revelation of the glory (כבוד) of Yahweh is synonymous with the revelation of his arm (זרוע) as well as of his righteousness (צדקה) see, for example, Isa. 62.2: 'the nations will see your righteousness and kings your glory (כבוד);' and Isa. 58.8: 'your righteousness will go before you and the glory of Yahweh will go after you'. The same is found in the ascension psalms, for example, like Ps. 98.1–3: 'his right hand and his holy arm helped him (הושיעה לו), Yahweh has proclaimed his salvation, in the sight of the nations he revealed his righteousness'.

In the prayer of Ben Sira (Sir. 36.19) is included the revelation: 'Fill Zion with your majesty (הוד), fill your tabernacle with your glory (כבוד)'.

Revelation of God's glory and splendour, so characteristic of the Day of the Lord prophecy, is likewise prominent in the second temple liturgy. In the *Aleinu* prayer is stated: 'We hope soon to behold your majestic glory'[9] and in the New Year *Amidah* we find: 'Reign over the whole universe with your glory and be exalted over all the earth in your grandeur, Shine forth (הופע) in your splendid

7. Y. Liebes, מצמיח קרן ישועה, in *Early Jewish Mysticism* (Jerusalem Studies in Jewish Thought, 3, 1984), pp. 313–48; cf. also, *idem*, 'The Angels of the Shofar and Yeshua Sar Ha-panim', in *Proceedings of the First International Conference on the History of Jewish Mysticism: Early Jewish Mysticism* (1987), pp. 1–2.

8. H.L. Ginsberg, '"The Arm of YHWH" in Isaiah 51–63', *JBL* 77 (1958), pp. 152–56.

9. *Authorized Daily Prayer Book,* p. 94. On this prayer, see J. Heinemann, *The Prayers in the Talmud: Forms and Patterns* (1977), pp. 173–75; and recently, Y. Ta-Shma: מקורה ומקומה של תפילת ״עלינו לשבח״ בסידור התפילה סדר המעמדות ושאלת סיום התפילה, *The Frank Talmage Memorial* (ed. B. Wallfish, 1993), I, pp. 85–98.

majesty (הדר גאון עזך) over all the inhabitants of your world'.[10] Similarly, in the Musaf for festivals: 'Reveal your glory of your kingship to us and appear and be exalted above us in the sight of all the living', and in the prayer *Al Hakkol* said before the reading of the Torah.[11] 'Let his kingship be revealed and seen over us speedily and very soon' (*Sop.* 14.1). Luke 19.11 says: 'the kingdom of God will be revealed soon' and the epistle to the Romans: 'the glory [of God] that will be revealed' (8.18).

The inclusion of eschatological motifs, and especially the notion of concluding a prayer with such motifs, is found in biblical hymns and prayers. The Song of the Sea concludes: 'The Lord shall reign forever and ever' (Exod. 15.18). Psalm 29 concludes with the establishment of God's kingdom on earth (v. 10). Psalm 68 concludes with a call to all the kingdoms of the earth to acknowledge God's majesty. The doxology following the second book of Psalms concludes with 'Let his glory fill the whole world. Amen and Amen' (Ps. 72.19, cf. Num.14.21). Psalm 22, a psalm of thanksgiving for salvation from distress, likewise ends with the hope that the whole world will acknowledge the divine salvation: 'Let all the ends of the earth pay heed and turn to the Lord, and the peoples of all nations prostrate themselves before you, for kingship is the Lord's and he rules the nations' (vv. 27–28 [Heb. 28–29]). Mesopotamian prayers also tend to end with an eschatological petition. The hymn to the god Shamash ends: 'may they bear your tribute... the wealth of the lands in sacrifice...may your throne-dais be renewed... whose utterance cannot be changed'.[12]

This tradition of eschatological prayer is continued in the book of Ecclesiasticus. In the prayers of Ben Sira (Sir. 36), many eschatological elements are later incorporated into the Jewish liturgy.

> Save us you God of all, put your awe upon all nations (שים פחדך על כל הגויים). Raise your hand against the heathen and let them see your power. As you became holy among us before their eyes, so be honored with us before our eyes. Let them learn, as we also have learned, that there is no God but you...Hasten the destined hour (קץ) and remember the appointed time (מועד). For who can tell you what to do? Gather all the tribes of Jacob (Sir. 36.1–11).

The beginning of the prayer is echoed in the opening of the New Year *Amidah* liturgy.[13] 'Put your awe upon all your creatures (תן פחדך על כל מעשיך)' (see above), while the continuation 'be honored with us' is echoed in the following section of this New Year prayer: 'Grant honor, O Lord, to your people (תן כבוד לעמך).'[14] The formula 'Raise your hand against the heathen' (v. 3) is reflected in the abridged form of the daily *Amidah*.[15] 'Raise your hand against evildoers' and

10. *Authorized Daily Prayer Book,* p. 353
11. *Authorized Daily Prayer Book*, p. 216
12. W.G. Lambert, *Babylonian Wisdom Literature* (1960), p. 138, 11. 196–99.
13. *Authorized Daily Prayer Book,* p. 350, 360.
14. *Authorized Daily Prayer Book,* p. 350, 360.
15. *Authorized Daily Prayer Book,* p. 67.

'let them learn that there is no God but you (v. 5). This parallels the second paragraph of *Aleinu*: 'May all the inhabitants of the world realize and know that before you every knee must bend'.[16]

'Hasten the destined hour (קץ), remember the appointed time (מועד)' refers to the era of salvation and these two words are used in Day of the Lord prophecies. The motif of the ingathering of the exiles, which follows, is also an integral part of the daily *Amidah*[17] and Jewish eschatology in general. The prayer of Ben Sira continues:

> Show mercy to the city of your sanctuary, Jerusalem, city of your dwelling place. Fill Zion with your majesty, fill your tabernacle with your glory. Give acknowledgement to your creation at the beginning; and fulifill the vision which has been spoken in your name (vv. 13–15).

Here is the motif of glorious revelation, which is attested in both the daily and New Year liturgy. The rebuilding of Zion and Jerusalem are described as the fulfilment of prophecy. This idea is echoed in the daily *Amidah*: 'Return in mercy to your city Jerusalem and dwell in it as you have promised (דברת)'.[18] The 'glory' which is to fill Zion is identical with the 'divine Presence' (שכינה) which according to the Abodah Benediction of the *Amidah*[19] is to be restored to Zion: 'Be appeased Lord, our God, and dwell in Zion (ושכון בציון)'. All these are to be traced back to the prophecy of Zechariah (2.14; 8.2).

Both the prayer of Ben Sira and the daily *Amidah* are rooted in the eschatological hopes of the prophets. As I have pointed out, these aspirations are likewise to be found in Mesopotamian prophecies,[20] but without the ideological-religious element of the elimination of idolatry. As in Israelite prophecy and Jewish liturgy, where expressions of aspiration are for the ingathering of the exiles, the restoration of ideal justice and the end of evil, and the establishment of a cultic centre, so Mesopotamian prayers ended with eschatological petitions.[21] As in Israel, both prayer and prophecy reflected eschatological hopes. It is likely that, as in many other cases, prophecy adapted liturgical material to its own purpose, and not vice versa. Although in later liturgy, verses from prophets were incorporated into prayer, the original desire for the revelation and God's kingdom predates classical prophecy. It lies behind the expectations of the people as described by Amos (5.18–20).

16. *Authorized Daily Prayer Book*, p. 94
17. *Authorized Daily Prayer Book*, p. 58.
18. *Authorized Daily Prayer Book*, p. 59.
19. *Authorized Daily Prayer Book*, pp. 61–62.
20. See above p. 301.
21. See 'The Šamaš Hymn', in Lambert, *Babylonian Wisdom Literature*, p. 138, 11. 196–99.

3. *The Sanctification of the Divine Name and The Establishment of the Divine Kingdom*

In the light of the above, it becomes clear that the belief in a future redeeming revelation is reflected in the prayers of the people. Although the people are aware, and the prophets constantly remind them, that this revelation is bound up with a last judgment in which even Israelite evildoers will not be spared, the central aspect of the revelation is the sanctification of God's name and the establishment of the God of Israel as King of the universe. This is expressed in Ezekiel's prophecy (38.18–23) regarding God: 'on that day…a terrible earthquake shall befall the land of Israel… I will punish him [the enemy] with pestilence and bloodshed...hailstones and sulphurous fire... I will be magnified (והתגדלתי) and sanctified and make myself known to many nations'. A similar expression is found in Zech. 14.9. 'The Lord will come forth and make war on those nations…there shall be a continuous day. .. only the Lord knows when – of neither day nor night...And the Lord shall be king over all the earth...the Lord will be one and his name one'. Compare also the passage in Isa. 5.15–16: 'humankind shall be brought low…humbled will be the haughty. And the Lord of Hosts is exalted in judgment: the Holy God sanctified by righteousness', a motif that belongs to Isaiah's Day of the Lord prophecy (2.9, 11, 17). These motifs of sanctification of God's name and the establishment of his kingdom became dominant in the liturgy. I have cited above references to God's kingdom in the liturgy; to these must be added references to the sanctification of his name.

The *Amidah* prayers of the New Year contain references to the sanctification of God's name along with reference to his kingship. After the petition 'Rule over us you alone speedily', follows: 'you are holy and your name is awesome (קדוש אתה ונורא שמך)'[22] in connection with which Isa. 5.16, 'And the Lord of Hosts is exalted by judgement; the Holy God sanctified with righteousness', is cited. A Benediction regarding the sanctification of God's name (קדושת השם) is contained in the daily *Amidah* as well,[23] and according to ancient sources (*Sifre* 343) and Geniza texts,[24] this Benediction also contained the above mentioned phrase 'you are holy and your name is awesome', now recited only on the New Year. The juxtaposition of God's holy name and his kingship is a dominant motif in all Jewish liturgy. The congregation must recite seven times daily the *Kaddish*,[25] which begins with the sanctification of God's name and establishment of his kingdom. Although its origins are unclear, the *Kaddish* has very ancient roots and it expresses the Israelite aspiration of the Day of the Lord. 'Magnified and Sanctified may be his name in the universe in the world that he created according to his will and let him make rule his kingship during your life and the life of all

22. *Authorized Daily Prayer Book,* p. 351, 361.

23. *Authorized Daily Prayer Book,* p. 55.

24. See recently, Y. Luger, 'The Weekday Amidah based on the Genizah' (PhD thesis, Bar-Ilan University, 1992), pp. 68–79.

25. See J.M. Epstein, *Aruch ha-Shulchan* (1903–1907), *Orah Hayyim* par. 55,4.

Israel speedily and fastly'. Compare the Hebrew Prayer before the recital of the Torah: 'Let his name be magnified and sanctified in the worlds that he created… according to his will'; in the Sabbath angelic liturgy: 'Let your name be sanctified and your mentioning, our king, be praised, on the heaven above and on the earth below (שמך אלהינו יתקדש וזכרך מלכנו יתפאר בשמים ממעל ועל הארץ מתחת)'.

These prayers parallel the Lord's prayer: 'Sanctified be your name. Your kingdom come; your will be done on earth as in heaven [throughout the world]' (Mt. 6.9; Lk. 11.2).

The *Complete Kaddish* is recited at the end of each service, and is the summit of all the prayers. Similarly, the *Aleinu* prayer is recited toward the end of each service. This poetic Hebrew prayer expresses the hope that idolatry will pass from the earth, that the world will be perfected in the kingdom of the Almighty and that all will accept the yoke of God's kingship. It is accepted in modern scholarship that this prayer is from second temple times (see above). It is in fact the credo recited by the worshipper at the end of the service. According to J. Ta-Shma this prayer stems from the Ma'amadot service when the people recited prayers during the worship of the priests of their turn (משמר).[26]

Other prayers that combine the sanctification of the divine name and the establishment of the divine kingdom include the prayer before the reading of the Torah, cited in tractate *Sop.* 14.1: 'Magnified and glorified…be the name of the supreme King of Kings…in the world which he has created…according to his desire… May his kingdom be revealed and seen by us',[27] which is in fact a Hebrew version of the Aramaic *Kaddish*. Compare also the prayer in the preliminary morning service, cited in the *Midrash Tanna debe Eliahu*: 'Reveal your holiness to those who sanctify your name. ..let all mankind realize and know that you alone are God over all the kingdoms on earth: gather them that hope for you from the four corners of the earth… who among all your creatures can say unto you: what are you doing?…'[28] This liturgy has much in common with the prayer in Sirach 36, quoted above; especially salient are the parallels in the motifs of sanctification of the Lord: the recognition of all the inhabitants of the world that there is no god besides Yahweh, the hope of the ingathering of the exiles, coupled with the idea of the absolute sovereignty of God ('who can say to God: what are you doing?').

4. *The Speedy Coming of the Divine Kingdom*

Public Prayers

The anticipation of the divine kingdom, and the wish that it be revealed 'speedily' and 'soon' (בעגלא ובזמן קריב, *Kaddish*, 'during your life') is also rooted in the prophecies of the Day of the Lord.

26. See Ta-Shma, n. 9 above.
27. *Authorized Daily Prayer Book*, p. 210.
28. *Authorized Daily Prayer Book*, p. 10.

'The great day of the Lord is approaching...most swiftly (קרוב ומהר מאוד) (Zeph. 1: 14).The time has come; the day is near (קרוב היום) (Ezek. 7.7).For the day is near. The day of the Lord is near (Ezek. 30.3).For the day of the Lord has come. It is close (קרוב) in the valley of decision (Joel 4.14).Yea, against all nations, the day of the Lord is close (קרוב) (Obad. 15). For the vision is a witness [read עֵד, for 'the appointed time'] a truthful יפח[29] for the destined hour... even if it tarries, wait for it still. It will surely come (בא יבוא) without delay' (Hab. 2.3).

Compare the following liturgical passages:

'Rebuild it [the Temple] soon, in our days... (בקרוב בימינו) (*Amidah*),[30] "Speedily cause the offspring of your servant David to flourish" (מהרה תצמיח) (*Amidah*).[31] "May his kingdom be revealed very soon" (prayer before the reading of the Torah).[32] "We hope (נקוה לראות)... soon to behold your majestic glory" (*Aleinu*).[33] "Speedily in our days (בימינו במהרה), in our lifetime do you dwell there forever"' (Sabbath morning *Kedushah*).[34]

All these should be compared with the following verses from the Gospel of Luke:

'...they thought that the reign of God would reveal itself at any moment (Lk. 19.11) ...you may know that the kingdom of God is near (ἐγγύς) (Lk. 21.31).The kingdom of God has come close (ἤγγικεν) to you (Lk. 10.9).The kingdom of God has come close (ἤγγικεν)' (Lk. 10.11).

The closeness of the Day of the Lord must encourage the people to repent. Thus Isa. 56.1: 'Observe what is right and do what is just (social justice), for soon my salvation shall come. .'. cf. 51.4–5: 'Hearken to me my people...The triumph I grant is near, the salvation has gone forth'; Mt. 3.2: 'repent for the kingdom of heaven is close to you (ἤγγικεν)', and Mk. 1.15: 'The time has come, the kingdom of God is close to you. Repent'.

29. For יפח = עד see S.E. Loewenstamm, *Comparative Studies in Biblical and Ancient Oriental Literatures* (AOAT, 204, 1980), pp. 137–45.

30. *Authorized Daily Prayer Book*, p. 59.

31. *Authorized Daily Prayer Book*, p. 60.

32. *Authorized Daily Prayer Book*, p. 83.

33. *Authorized Daily Prayer Book*, p. 94.

34. *Authorized Daily Prayer Book*, p. 199

APPENDICES

1. *Longing*

Jewish

May I not live to see the Consolation (לא אראה בנחמה) if I… (*b. Mak.* 56). Those who desire (מחמדין) the years of consolation (נחמתא) to come: who say: ‘when will we arise and go up to Zion’.

Great is your hope, O Zion… those who desire (המתאוים) the day of your salvation will rejoice in your plentiful glory… how they waited for your salvation… Your hope will never die, O Zion, and your aspiration will never be forgotten (11QPs[a] cols. 22.2–11 [*DJD*, IV, p. 43]).

Christian

he lived in expectation of the kingdom of God (Lk. 23.50).
Simon the righteous and pious who was waiting for the consolation of Israel (Lk. 2.25), compare Lk. 2.38: Simon waiting for the redemption of Jerusalem (= גאולת ירושלים)

2. *Revelation*

Reign over the whole universe with your glory and be exalted over all the earth in your grandeur. Shine forth (הופע) in your splendid majesty (הדר גאון עזך) over all the inhabitants of your world.
Save us you God of all, put your awe upon all nations (שים פחדך על כל הגויים). Raise your hand against the heathen and let them see your power. As you became holy among us before their eyes, so be honored with us before our eyes. Let them learn, as we also have learned,
that there is no God but you… Hasten the destined hour (קץ) and remember the appointed time (מועד). For who can tell You what to do? Gather all the tribes of Jacob (Sir. 36.1–11).

The kingdom of God will be revealed soon (Lk. 19.11).
The glory (of God) that will be revealed (Rom. 8.18).

3. *Sanctification*

Kaddish

‘Magnified and Sanctified may be his name in the universe in the world that he created according to his will and let him make rule his kingship during your life and the life of all Israel speedily and fastly’. Compare the Hebrew prayer before the recital of the Torah: ‘Let his name be magnified and sanctified in the worlds that he created. according to his will’.

The Lord’s Prayer

‘Sanctified be your name. Your kingdom come; your will shall be done on earth as in heaven [= ‘throughout the world’]’ (Mt. 6.9; Lk. 11.2).

4. *Speedy Coming*

The great day of the Lord is approaching… most swiftly (קרוב ומהר מאד) (Zeph. 1.14).
The time has come; the day is near (קרוב היום) (Ezek. 7.7).
For a day is near. A day of the Lord is near (Ezek. 30.3).
For the day of the Lord has come. It is close (קרוב) in the valley of decision (Joel 4.14).
Yea, against all nations, the day of the Lord is close (קרוב) (Obad. 15).
For the vision is a witness [read עד] for the appointed time… even if it tarries, wait for it still. It will surely come, without delay (Hab. 2.3).
Rebuild it (the Temple) soon, in our days...(בקרוב בימינו) (*Amidah*).[35]
Speedily cause the offspring of your servant David to flourish (*Amidah*).[36]
May his kingdom be revealed very soon (prayer before the reading of the Torah).[37]
We hope… soon to behold your majestic glory (*Aleinu*).[38] Speedily in our days, in our lifetime do dwell there forever (Sabbath morning *Kedushah*).[39]
May our eyes behold your return in mercy to Zion, blessed are you, O Lord who restores the divine presence to Zion.[40]

… they thought that the reign of God will reveal itself at any moment (Lk. 19.11).
… you may know that the kingdom of God is near (ἐγγύς) (Lk. 21.31).
The kingdom of God has come close (ἤγγικεν) to you (Lk. 10.9).
The kingdom of God has come close (ἤγγικεν) (Lk. 10.11).

35. *Authorized Daily Prayer Book*, p. 59.
36. *Authorized Daily Prayer Book*, p. 60.
37. *Authorized Daily Prayer Book*, p. 83.
38. *Authorized Daily Prayer Book*, p. 94.
39. *Authorized Daily Prayer Book*, p. 199.
40. *Authorized Daily Prayer Book*, pp. 58–62.

INDEXES

INDEX OF REFERENCES

BIBLE

Old Testament

Genesis

1.21	88
1.26–27	252
1.29	197
2.4	69
2.17	69
3.5	107
3.6	239, 240
3.22	107
5.1	252
6.5 LXX	291
8.21	122
8.21 LXX	291
9.1–17	205
9.13	197
10	274
12	196, 197
12.2	224
12.7	222
12.16	194
13.15	222
14.13	257
15	27, 218, 220, 222, 223
15.1	59
15.4–5	224
15.6	95
15.7	218
15.9	219, 220
15.10	29
15.13	207
15.17	220
15.18–21	223
15.18	197, 222, 223
15.19–21	224
16.2	213
16.6	207
17.1	205
17.6	224
17.7–8	222
17.7	223
17.8	222, 223
17.16	224
17.20	197
18.6	123
18.19	217
18.27	131
20	196, 197
20.4	196
20.5	196, 198
20.14–16	196
20.16	194, 195, 196
21.22	219
21.27	219
22.16	197, 201
22.18	201
23.11	197
24.7	222
24.40	205
25.28	285
25.31	211
25.33	211
26.3	222
26.4–5	204
26.5	201
26.24	202
26.26	219
27.27	124
28.4	222
28.13	222
29.17	239
29.33	215
30.3	213
30.33	209
31.45	30
31.49	23
31.51–52	30
31.53	23
32	47
32.2	61
32.21	197
32.25–33	61
35.1	224
35.12	222
39.4	264
39.6	239
39.21	204, 241, 242, 249
41.51–52	208
43.14	242
44.2	197
45.8	33
47.6	187
48.4	222
48.13–20	215
48.15	205
48.22	197
50.23	213

Exodus

1.11	207
3.6	84
3.21–22	250
3.21	241, 249
4.22	215
4.23–27	61
4.27	61
5.21	23
6.7	223
10.3	207

Exodus (cont.)
10.28 69
11.2–3 250
11.3 242, 249
12–13 113
12 161, 269
12.1–14 161
12.15–20 161
12.35–36 250
12.36 242, 249
12.40 251
13.1–10 113
13.3–4 162
13.7 162
13.11–16 113
13.14 209
15.11 41
15.18 50, 73, 294, 298
15.25 232
16.3–4 162
17 270
18.16 205
18.20 205
18.21 187
19–24 164, 191
19–20 164, 191, 270
19 82, 269
19.5–6 217
19.7–8 232
19.8 42
19.16 272
19.17 233
19.18 218
19.19 270, 272
20.2 274
20.6 202
20.18 274
20.22–23 164
20.33 164
21–23 164, 190–92
21 160
21.1–11 160, 190
21.2 160
22 159
22.1–3 161
22.15–16 159
22.19 234
22.28–29 190
23.4 161
23.8 197
23.10–19 191
23.10–11 190
23.14–19 190
23.15 161, 162
23.16 161
23.17 20
23.18 162
23.19 162
23.20 26
23.22 16
23.25–26 26
23.32–33 261
23.32 233
24 18, 29, 219
24.3–8 34, 232
24.3 164, 190, 191, 271, 272
24.5 29, 269
24.7 21, 42
24.8 29
24.9 278
24.16 278
25 164, 191
25.40 240
31.13 144
32.34 69
33.14–16 163, 191
33.16 163, 191
33.18 163, 191
33.22 84
33.33 217
34 163, 164, 191, 192
34.6 115
34.7 203
34.9 191
34.10 190, 191
34.11 162, 163, 168, 191
34.12–26 163, 191
34.12–16 261
34.12 217
34.15 233
34.18 161, 162
34.19–26 190
34.20 162
34.22 73
34.25 161, 162
34.28 278
40.34 278

Leviticus
1.1 278
2 122, 125
2.14 122
4 231
7.34 226
7.38 192
10.3 244
10.10–11 103
11–15 162
14.4 220
14.49 220
16.2 124
16.11 231
16.13 124
16.21 227, 231
16.24 231
16.29 230
17 160, 180
17.1–7 160
17.13–14 160
17.13 160
18.27 261
19 291
19.9 161
19.12 284
19.14 291
19.18 291, 293
19.27–28 162
19.32–34 291
19.32 291
19.39 291
20.26 260
21.5 162
21.8 64
22.28 159, 160
23 161
23.5 161
23.6 161
23.15 271
25 228, 229, 291
25.1 192
25.9–10 148, 229
25.9 271
25 291
25.1 291
25.10 227

25.14	228
25.17	291
25.30	222
25.36	291
25.43	291
26	217
26.12	223
26.31	122
26.34	190
26.39	60
26.44–45	217
26.46	190
27.29	234
27.34	192

Numbers

5.2	159
6.22–27	265
6.25–26	243, 245
7	234
8.16	264
11	276
13.21	224
13.22–23	224
14.18	115
14.21	297, 298
14.24	224
15.1–15	123
15.22–26	230
15.24–25	230
16.15	176
18.2	263
18.8	226
18.19	226
18.21	226
20.15 16	143
23.21–22	294
24.7–8	294
24.24	207
25.3 LXX	36
25.5 LXX	36
25.12–13	225
26.3–65	190
26.3	192
28	123
28.16–17	161
29	123
30	160
31	173, 174, 186
31.3	173
31.14	173, 186
31.28	173
31.43	173
31.49	173
31.53	186
32.11–12	224
33.3	186
33.50–34.29	190
33.50	192
35.1	192
36.1–13	190

Deuteronomy

1–30	162
1.1	158, 190
1.5	158, 159, 190
1.6	192, 193
1.11	246
1.36	224
3.24	138
4.7	290
4.9	17
4.10	32
4.19	251
4.26	22
4.29–31	218
4.37	253
5–6	113
5	113
5.1–6.1	112
5.10	202
5.19	270
5.20	270
5.28	164, 190–92
6.4–9	113
6.4	37, 166, 184
6.5	38, 291
6.5 LXX	291, 292
6.6	168, 293
6.7	17, 38, 293
6.20	209
7	26
7.2	233
7.3–4	261
7.4	162
7.6	253, 261
7.9–12	208
7.12	26, 217
8.5–10	112, 113
8.8	63, 114, 118, 120
8.9	63, 114
8.10	63, 114
9.10	272
10.3	272
10.4	164, 192
10.8	263, 265
10.14–17	138
10.15	253
11	113
11.13–21	113
11.13–15	162
11.13	38, 166, 168, 184, 217
11.14–17	38
11.19	17, 38
12	160
12.8	180
12.16	160
12.22	160
12.24	160
12.26	160
13	14, 15, 33
13.4	189
13.7 LXX	292
13.10	13, 14, 15
13.13–19	234
13.15	40
13.18	242
14	162, 168, 183
14.1–2	162
14.2	162, 253, 261
14.3–21	162
14.21	162
14.22–16.17	190
14.22–29	184
14.22	182
14.28	166
15	229
15.12	160
15.13	160
15.18	160
15.19	182
16.3	69
16.10	272
16.19	197

Deuteronomy (cont.)

17	165, 168, 169, 179
17.1	160
17.3	162
17.4	40
17.6–13	165
17.12	263
17.14–20	184
17.16–17	177
17.16	175
17.17	175, 179
17.18–19	184
17.18	179, 190
17.19	165, 172, 173
17.20	165, 175, 177
17.28	184
18.7	263
18.15–16	190
18.16	272
18.19	193
20.9	165
20.18	261
21.5	265
21.10–14	159
21.15–17	215
21.18–21	214
22.11	161
22.25	159
22.28–29	159
23.1–9	261
23.4–7	261
23.4–5	261
23.7	262
23.8–9	36, 236
23.18 LXX	36
23.22–24	160
23.22	189
24.5	165
26	163, 168, 191
26.3–4	163
26.5–11	137
26.5–9	143
26.7	208
26.10–19	163
26.12–15	184
26.12	166, 182
26.13–15	137
26.14	159
26.16–19	191
28	218
28.4	26
28.18	26
28.20	162
28.36	165
28.45	26
28.69	192
29.9–14	232
29.9	18, 164, 192
29.11–14	35
29.12	223
29.14	18
29.19	21
29.20	21
29.25	251
29.69	164
30.1–10	218
30.19	22
31.7–8	179
31.9	165, 179
31.10–13	184
31.11–12	165
31.12	167, 179, 180
31.13	17, 32, 184
31.14–15	278
31.25–26	165
31.28	22, 167
32	113
32.1	113
32.7	113
32.8	215
32.13	113
32.19	113
32.29	113
32.40	113
32.43 LXX	142
33	294
33.2	69, 81, 269, 294
33.5	294
33.8	203
33.12	116
33.26–29	294
33.26–27	294
33.28	81

Joshua

1.8	172, 179
4.6	209
4.21	209
8.31–35	179
8.31	190, 193
8.32	190
8.34–35	179
11.2	230
12.23	230
14.8	224
14.9	224
14.13–14	224
14.14	224
17.11	230
22.24	209
22.27	209
23.6	190, 193
24	18
24.2–13	143
24.24–26	34
24.24	42
24.25	232

Judges

1.20	224
5.4–35	81
5.4–5	294
5.4	69
5.11	206
6.19	123
13.19	123
13.23	123
16.26	41
20.26–27	78
20.48	234
21.5	29, 234
21.11	234

Ruth

4.6	213
4.7	40
4.9–10	211
4.14	211

1 Samuel

1.24	123, 220
2.26	243, 244, 249
8	168
8.9	168

8.20	181
9.8	132
10.25	7, 168, 170, 181
11.1	233
11.7	221
12	22
12.3	176
12.5	22
12.7–11	143
18.18	132
22.8	207
25.3	239, 240
25.21	280
25.33	240
26.19	122
27.6	225

2 Samuel

3.18	202
6.22	244
7	213
7.1	180
7.5	202
7.8–16	211
7.10	207
7.12	224
7.14	214, 223
7.15	203, 204
7.16	116
7.18	131
7.21	131
7.22–23	138
9.8	132
14.17	47, 107
14.20	107, 247
15.21	31
17.11	173
19.6	16
19.29	95
19.30	197
22	81
22.7–15	81
22.51	203
23.4	88
24.3	246

1 Kings

1.4	264
1.39	72
2.4	216
3.3	205
3.6	201, 203, 205, 208
4.11	230
5	173
5.17–18	180
5.18	129
6	173
8	183
8.10	124
8.12	102, 124
8.23–24	138
8.23	203, 208
8.25	216
8.32	145
8.34	145
8.36	145
8.39	145
8.43	145
8.50	242
8.53 LXX	102
8.54	182
8.66	182
9.4	201, 216
10.6	186
10.26	173, 186
11.4	201
11.6	201
11.39	207
12	171
12.7	202
12.28–30	232
14.8	201, 205
15.3	201, 205
18.36	124
18.38	124
19.13	84
19.19	35
22	106

2 Kings

8.13	132
9.13	72
9.15	257
11	168, 173–75, 186, 187
11.4	173, 186
11.6	175
11.8	174, 186
11.15	173, 186
11.19	173, 186
12.16	211
14.6	190, 193
17.15	270
18.4	232
20.3	205
22	232
22.7	211
23	165
23.1–20	232
23.1–3	232
23.2	18, 21
23.3	183
23.19	232
23.25	292

1 Chronicles

12.18	262
16.36	140
17.14	116
17.19	131
21	134
21.1	134
21.15	134
23.25	116
28.9	35
28.19	240
29.10–19	139
29.10–13	150
29.10	140
29.11	146
29.13	146
29.18 LXX	291

2 Chronicles

5.12–13	46
5.13	46
6–7	183
7.6	46
7.9	183
12.8	35
15.10	271
15.13	18
15.15	271
19.2	16
20.6	139
23	175
29.10	233
31.3	232

Ezra
2.59 36, 236
2.62–63 264
2.64 46
3.4–6 145
3.12 149
4.1 233
4.2 262
4.3 262
6.19 233
6.20 46, 233
6.22 235
7.27–28 235
8.15 264
8.20 264
8.35 233
9–10 36
9 60
9.1 262
9.2 261
9.5 124, 125
9.9 235
9.12 262
10.3 233
10.7 233
10.8 234, 235
10.9 233
10.16 233
10.44 215
13.9 36

Nehemiah
1.1 242
1.5 139, 141
7.5 36
7.61 36, 236
7.63–64 264
7.66 46
8–9 140, 149
8 140
8.3 105
8.4–5 140
8.4 183
8.6 140
8.8 140
8.18 140
9 60, 140, 141, 143, 145, 149, 150
9.2 36, 60, 262
9.5 139, 140
9.6–8 150
9.6–7 142
9.6 140, 142
9.7–9 142
9.8 140
9.9–12 142
9.13 141, 142
9.14 141, 142
9.25 118
9.27 145
9.28 145
9.32 140, 141
9.34 270
9.35 115, 118
9.36 115, 118
10 36, 232
10.1 40, 211, 235
10.30 236
10.31 232
10.32 232
10.33 40, 232
10.35 233
10.37 232
12.24 46
13.1–3 36, 262
13.5–9 122

Esther
1.19 42
2.7 239
2.21–23 13
6.1 13
7.3 189, 241
8.5 189, 241
8.15 195
9.23 170
9.27 40, 42, 170, 233, 256, 258
9.29 39
9.31 40

Job
4.18 106
9.2 260
9.24 197
15.8 107
15.14 260
15.15 106
24.14 105
25.5 106
25.6 260
38.7 46, 105, 247
40.10–13 84

Psalms
1 180
1.2 180
2 180
2.1 115
2.7–8 211
2.7 212
3 153
8.5 260
13.21–22 16
15.1–5 289
16.5–6 50
16.8 288
18 81
18.12–14 270
19.15 179
20.8 177
22 76, 298
22.23–32 256
22.24 257
22.25 257
22.27–28 76, 298
22.28–29 Heb. 76
22.28 257
22.30 257
24.4–5 243
29 83, 259
29.2 142
31.2 206
31.20 115
33.16 177
33.17 177
36.11 204
37.32–33 180, 184
37.35 69
40.6 109
40.18 133
41.2 239
44.3 115
44.15 115
45.7 116
47 80
47.5 80
50 270, 271

50.2 69, 269
50.5 29
50.18–19 269
51.3 228
51.11 228
51.17 142
68 81
68.12 274
68.18 51, 90, 94
69.14 124
70.60 133
71.2 206
72.5 244
72.19 155
73.26 50
74.16 103
75.3 70
75.4 70
80.18 211
81 269–71
81.8 270
84.12 243, 247
84.19–20 220
86.1 133
89 211
89.6 247
89.7–8 259
89.7 49, 259
89.8 96
89.9 96
89.15 96
89.20 203
89.22–26 212
89.27 212
89.28 215
89.34 203
89.35 213
89.38 22, 41
89.53 155
93.1 259
93.2 116
93.3–4 259
96–98 259
96 259
96.1–2 259
96.1 259
96.3 259
96.5 259
96.6 93
96.7–9 259
96.10 259
96.11–12 259
96.13 259
96.15 142
97.1 259
97.5 259
97.7 142, 259
98.1 259
98.2 206, 259
98.3 259
98.7–8 259
98.8 46
98.9 259
99 93
99.3 93
99.5 93
99.7 270
99.9 93
101 170
101.2 205
101.6 264
103.4 133
103.6 133
103.17–18 203
103.19–21 47
103.20 49
104.2–3 106
105.6 202
105.42 202
105.44 120
106.1–2 109
106.28 36
106.46 242
107 54
107.35 24
109.12 204
109.22 133
113–118 256
113.2 256
113.3 256
113.4–9 256
114 256
114.8 24, 256
115 256
115.9–11 256
115.10 179
117 256
118.1–4 256
118.2–4 256
119.113 135
119.12 127
119.29 134
119.63 203
132 208
132.1 207
132.12 213
135.19–20 256
135.21 155
136.7 99
141.2 122, 124
142.6 50
143.11 206
144.3 260
145.7 115
146.10 73
148 105, 141
148.1 141
148.3 105
148.6 141
148.9–10 109
149.7 115
150 55, 56
151 109
155 134

Proverbs
1–9 249
1.3 243
1.8–9 240
1.9 243
3.1–4 240, 241
3.1 239
3.2 239
3.3–4 248
3.3 240
3.4 240, 241, 244, 249
3.6 289
3.22 241
3.34 243
4.7 240
4.9 243
7.19–20 194
9.10 107
10.9 205
11.4 85
13.15 239, 243
13.24 213
16.14 197
23.14 213
29.12 264
29.14 116
30.3 107

Proverbs (cont.)
31 175
31.3 175
31.4–5 177
31.4 175
31.9 175

Ecclesiastes
4.1 284
5.5
11.2 183
11.6 46
36 69
45.1 247

Song of Songs (Cant.)
4.11–16 124
8.10 245

Isaiah
1.13 122
1.26 147
2 75, 79, 83–85
2.5 253
2.6 85
2.9 70, 300
2.11 72, 300
2.12–21 84
2.12–17 80
2.17 70, 80, 300
2.18 75, 82
2.19 72, 74, 83
2.20–21 72
2.21 72
3.18 243
5.15–16 85, 300
5.16–17 85
5.16 86, 300
6 124
6.3 45–47, 51, 149, 155, 247, 297
6.4 47, 95, 247
6.6 124
8.12 68
8.17 295
8.21 31
9 33
9.6 33
11.1 69
11.6 46
11.12 147
12.6 92
13 70
13.3 79
13.4–6 71
13.4 78
13.9–10 71
13.11 73
14.1 258
15.5 220
17.12–13 94
19.24–25 265
22.5 78
23.18 283
26.21 69
27.13 147
29.13 288
30.8 209
30.18 88, 295
33.15 290
34.4 115
34.5–6 78
34.6 79
35.2 72
38.14 179
38.18–19 153
40–66 258
40–55 254, 258
40–48 252
40.5 72, 259, 297
40.5 LXX 297
40.14 252
40.18 252
40.23 253
40.25–26 106
40.25 252
40.26 252
40.28 252
41.1 252
41.4 252
41.5 252
41.8 203, 212
41.9 212
41.10 211
41.21 252
42.4 252
42.5 254
42.6 253
42.10 252, 259
42.12 252, 259
42.21 95
43.4 244
43.9 115
43.10 252
43.15–20 256
43.23 122
43.25 228
44.5 253
44.8 252
44.9–20 256, 259
44.22 228
44.23 259
44.24 252
44.26 235
44.28 235
45.1 252
45.5–7 252
45.6 252
45.7 139, 252
45.13 235
45.14 252
45.18–19 252
45.18 252
45.22–23 251
45.22 252, 257
45.23 253, 257
48.20 256
48.21 256
49–55 254
49.1 252, 259
49.5 244
49.6 254
49.13 259
49.19–21 116
49.22 257
51.4–5 87, 258, 302
51.5 297
51.12 259
52.7 229
52.8 46
52.10 297
53.1 297
53.3 257
54.11 115
54.12 105
56–66 254
56 262, 263
56.1–8 254, 258
56.1 87, 206,

	258, 290, 302
56.2	260
56.3	257
56.5	256, 263
56.6	263
56.7	260, 262
57.15	256
58	260
58.8	297
58.13	194
59.11	179
60	99
60.1	95
60.10	262
60.21	50
61.1–3	229
61.1	229
61.2–3	116
61.2	229
61.5–6	264
61.6	217
61.8	147
61.10	116
62.2	297
62.4–5	116
62.5	116
62.10–11	257
63.7–64.11	60
63.7	115
65.17–18	115, 117
65.18	117
65.19–20	117
65.26	46
66.3	122
66.10–11	116
66.13	116, 120
66.18–19	257
66.21	263
66.22	117

Jeremiah

2.2	203
2.7	115, 203
3.4	211, 212
3.19	211, 212, 215
8.8	165, 280
10.1–16	75
10.13	94
17.26	122
18.20	205
22.5	197
22.13	207
23.5	147
23.16	193
23.29	274
24.5	233
25.15	70
29.17	233
31.1	203
31.3	204
31.5	88
31.8	57, 215
32.7–8	168
32.17–18	138
33.10–11	62
33.16	147
33.17	225
33.21–22	263
34	27, 222
34.8–22	221
34.9	160
34.18	27, 221
38.8 LXX	57
41.5	122, 123
42.12	242
46.3–10	78
46.10	78
48.10	284
48.34	220
51.13	94
51.14	31
51.16	94
51.63	8

Lamentations

1.12	78
2.22	78
3.23	97
5.19	116

Ezekiel

1	94
1.4–5	47, 247
1.20	46
1.24	93, 94
3.12	51, 247
3.13	45–47
7.6	70
7.7	87, 302, 304
7.19	85
7.24	73
10	94
10.5	94
10.19	46
11.16	233
11.22	46
13.4	78
13.5	78
13.6	40
20.1	144
20.12	144
20.34	147
20.41	147
21.30	70
21.31	70
22.26	103
24.26–27	257
28.12	107
28.13	239
30.3	87, 302
33.21–22	257
33.23	233
38–39	257
38.18–23	69, 85, 300
38.23	82
40–48	181
40.1–43.12	181
40.46	263
43.2	93, 95
43.2 LXX	94
43.7–19	182
43.9	116
43.11	182
43.13–27	181
44.1–13	182
44.6–31	264
45.8–12	182
45.13–16	182
45.16–19	182
45.16–17	234
45.17	232
45.18–25	182
45.24	123
46.1–3	182
46.4	123
46.16–17	182
46.18	182
46.19–24	182

Daniel
1.4 255
1.9 242
2.45 89
6.9 42, 195
6.13 39, 42
6.16 195
7.10 51, 90, 105
7.18 50
8.13 48
8.25 89
9 60
9.4 139, 141
9.7 60, 61
9.15–19 60
9.16 60
9.18–19 131
9.18 60, 130
9.19 60, 131
9.21 124
9.24 229
9.25 229
10.20 47
12.12 88, 295

Hosea
2.20 163
3.2 123
5.8 180
11.4 214
13.4 11

Joel
2.1 72, 87
2.17 60
4.14 69, 87, 302, 304

Amos
5 79
5.4 290
5.18–20 73, 77, 299
5.18 68, 69, 77, 295
5.20 69
5.21–25 73
5.21–24 80
5.21 122
6.6 207
6.8 31, 80
8.5 260

Obadiah
15 69, 87, 302, 304

Micah
1.3 69, 81
4.5 253
5.8 147
5.11–12 72
6.1–2 22
6.8 290
7.4 68, 295
7.7 68, 295
7.15 69

Nahum
1.3–5 81
1.5–6 81
1.12 207

Habakkuk
2.3 70, 87, 295, 302, 304
2.4 290
3 81, 295
3.3 69, 295, 297

Zephaniah
1.7 79
1.14–16 71
1.14 69, 87, 302, 304
1.16 78
1.17–18 85
3.8 68, 70, 295
3.9 72
3.20 132

Haggai
1.12 235
2.10–14 258
2.21 235

Zechariah
1.9 47, 247
1.14 247
1.16 147
2.14 77, 147, 258, 299
3.7 50
4.7 210
5.4 24
6.9–16 237
6.10–14 237
6.10 238
6.12 147
8.2 77, 302
8.4–5 62
8.11 235
8.12 235
8.23 257
9.11 29
13.2 134
14.3–9 85
14.9 37, 74, 82, 300

Malachi
1.11 122, 255
1.14 256
2.4 225
2.6 205, 225
2.7 50, 107
2.10–16 263
3.12 193
3.20 100
3.22–24 278
3.22 190

Apocrypha
Tobit
1.13 239, 247
3.4 227

Judith
9.1 124

Wisdom of Solomon
4.1 248
5.5 49

Ecclesiasticus (Sirach)
6.30 35
10 177
10.10 178
15.1 291
18.4–5 109
21.20 178
21.22–23 178
22.27 129

23.2	227
23.6	135
33.15	280
35.15	291
36	76, 86, 298, 301
36.1–11	76, 298, 303
36.1	129
36.3	298
36.5	299
36.13–15	77, 299
36.15	88
36.19	297
36.20–21	135
39.31	99
40.1	35
42.16–20	108, 109, 111
42.16	46
42.17	109
43.11	41, 53
50.2	105
50.8	105
51	146
51.17	35
51.23	35

Baruch

1.14	144
29.4	88

1 Maccabees

14	184
14.25	169
14.26	169
14.28	235
14.29–40	169
14.41–47	170
14.41	169
14.42	181
14.43	181
14.46	169
14.47	169
14.49	170
15.2	169

2 Maccabees

1.3–5	35
6.18	280, 291
11.19	8

New Testament

Matthew

3.2	87, 302
5.17–20	293
5.43	16
6.4–13	73
6.9–13	74, 150, 153, 303
6.9–10	86
6.9	301, 303
6.13	153
8.11	88
11.25	36
17.1	278
19.28	276
22.35	291
22.36–39	291
23	279, 293
23.1–12	279, 281
23.2–4	279
23.2–3	279
23.5–7	279, 282, 283
23.5	284
23.6–7	281
23.6	284
23.8–12	279
23.13–30	279
23.13	280, 281
23.14	281
23.16–22	24
23.23	285
23.31–39	279
25.31–39	290
26.29	88
27.6	197
28	292

Mark

1.14–15	229
1.15	87, 302
3.20–23	134
3.25	135
3.30	135
9.2	278
12.28–33	292
12.30	291
12.35	291
12.38–40	281, 282
12.38	282, 283
12.39	284
15.43	88

Luke

1.9	124
2.14	155
2.25	296, 303
2.38	296, 303
2.52	240, 244
4.16–19	229
10.9	87, 302
10.11	87, 302, 304
10.25–28	292
10.25	291
10.27	291
11.2–4	74, 150, 154
11.2	86, 301, 303
11.42	280
11.43	280, 282
11.44	280
11.45	291
11.46	280
11.47	280, 285
11.52	280, 281
13.29–30	88
14.15	88
16.17	293
16.29–31	65
19.11	87, 298, 302, 303
20.36	49
20.46–47	281, 282
20.46	282–84
21.31	87, 302, 304
22.18	88
22.29	276
23.50	296, 303
23.51	88
24.27	65
24.44	64

John

7.17–18	193
12.49	193
14.10	193

Acts
1.15 276
2 274, 275, 277
2.1–13 269
2.1 273
2.3 274, 275
2.4 276
2.7 275
2.9 273
3.1 125
10.2 256
10.3 125
10.22 256
10.30 125
10.44–45 276
12.16 256
13.16 260
16.14 256
18.2 256
20.16 273
20.18 49
20.26 49
20.32 49
24.14 65

Romans
8.18 298, 303

1 Corinthians
11.4 40
12.10 276
12.28 276
14 276
14.15 277
16.21 88

2 Corinthians
5.17 117

Galatians
3.11–12 290

Ephesians
1.11 49
1.18 35
5.8 35
6.6–7 35
6.11–13 35

Colossians
1.12 49

Hebrews
22.28–29 298
29.10 298
68 298
68.8–9 294
68.16–18 294
68.17 295
72.19 297, 298
98.1–3 297

Revelation
4.6 94
4.8 94
21 209
21.1 117
22.20 88

Other Ancient References

Pseudepigrapha
1 Enoch
2.1–3 99
18.13 106
21.3 106
39.4 49
41.7 106
45.4 49, 117
47.2 47
58 100
58.4 100
61.10–11 47
72.1 49
91.16 49, 100, 116

2 Enoch (Slavonic)
6.4 98

3 Enoch
7.1 48
18.6 48
27.2 48
35.1 48
42.2 48

2 Baruch (Syriac Apoc.)
48.9 107

3 Maccabees
7.11 8

4 Maccabees
3.12 187
5.4 280, 291

Apocalypse of Abraham
9–15 218

Epistle of Aristeas
176 178
189 177
190 177
191 177
193–196 177
209 177
245 177
263 177
264 177
270 177
279 177
280–281 177
283 173, 177
291–292 177

Jubilees
1.26 183
1.27 49
1.29 100, 117
2.2–3 110, 111
2.31–32 56, 144
6.3 272
6.17 272
6.21 271
14.9 218
14.19 272
14.20 272
15.1 272
31.14 105
32.10 183
44.4 272

Life of Adam & Eve
29 124

Ps. Philo
Biblical Antiquities
23.6–7 218

Psalms of Solomon
18.10–12 107

Testament of Levi
3.5 124
4.2–3 105

Qumran
CD (Damascus Covenant)
6.17–18 103
9.1 292
12.19–20 103
12.10 292
13.2–7 63, 64
13.2 67
13.11–12 236
13.11 291
14.3–6 236
15.5–9 236

1QH
1.1–4 108
1.3–14 98
1.6–7 49
1.11 102
1.14 116
1.18–19 102
1.20 116
1.21 102, 104
2.6 49
2.9 49
2.12 129
2.31–34 283
3.2 48
3.3–5 127
3.16 129
3.19 50, 133
3.20–23 108
3.20 49
3.22 49
4.6 100
5.3 49
6.13–14 49
6.13 105
7.11 48
10.4 49
11.3 127
11.6–7 49
11.11 48, 49
11.12 50
11.13–14 50, 142
11.13 48, 108
11.25–26 49
12.5–7 106
12.29–30 108
13.1–2 104
13.1 104
13.11–12 117
13.12 49
14.8–22 103
14.8 103
14.13–14 103
14.24 103
14.25 103
17.23 134
18.23 49, 105
18.27 49
18.29 100

1QM (War Scroll)
2.3 48
2.13 115
4.11 35
4.27 37
5.11 37
5.25 37
7.6 49
7.27 36
8.3 48
8.17 48
10.15–16 102
12.1–2 106
12.4 49
13.5 35
16.4 48
17.8 97, 100
17.11 48

1QS (Manual of Discipline)
1.1–5 180
1.2–3 67
1.4 16
1.5 180
1.7–8 180
1.9 102
1.10–11 16
1.12 291
1.16 272
2.3 35
2.15 16
2.19–20 64
2.19 20
2.22 48
2.26–3.2 19
3.2 291
3.15–19 102
3.15–16 116
3.15 98
4.2 35
4.6 36
5.8–10 236
5.8 19, 55
5.23 236
5.24 19
6.3–4 67
6.4–6 67
6.4–5 64
6.23 236
8.15–16 67
8.19 236
8.22–23 234
9.4 115
9.7 64
9.18 37
10.1–8 66
10.1–4 98
10.2–3 106
10.9–14 102
10.9 277
10.10 34, 65
10.11–12 97
10.14 63, 67
10.16 141
11.4 37
11.7–8 128
11.7 49
11.8 141
11.12 134
11.15–16 128
11.19 37

1QS[a]
2.17–22 67
2.17–21 67
2.22 63

1QS(b)
4.22–28 105
4.22–23 107

1QS(b) (cont.)
4.25 49
5.23 48

1Q27
5–6 57

1Q34
11.6 64

1Q34 (bis)
1.6 58
2 58
3ii 4–6 58, 66

4Q158
1–2 61

4Q400
2 104

4Q403
24.9 47

4Q405
20 108

4Q417
1.5–6 73

4Q434
2 112, 114, 121
2.1–12 115
2.1–4 114
2.2–3 116
2.2 116
2.3–4 117
2.3 116
2.4–5 117
2.4 117
2.5–13 115
2.7 118
2.8 118
2.9 119
2.10 119
2.11 119
2.12–13 116, 118

4Q501
1.2 61

4Q503
1.24–25 144
24–25 56
37–38 56
40–41 56

4Q504
1–2 60, 61
3.1–2 67

4Q508
2.4 58
3.1 58

4Q509
3 57

4QDeut.
8.8–9 114

4QPs
89 203

4 QpNah 3–4
1.6–7 283
1.7 283
2.8–9 283
3.6–7 283

4QS
24.9 48
40 48

6Q18
5 108

11QBer
1–2 116

11QMelch
9 229
18 229

11QPs[a]
19 66, 136
22 132, 135
22.2–11 296, 303
22.2–3 135
22.4 135
22.5–6 135
22.8 135
22.13–14 135
24 129
24.3–17 129
24.8 134
26.4–5 110
26.9–15 90, 111
26.9–12 55, 65
26.12 90
29 129, 132
29.1–4 133
29.7–8 130, 133
29.8–13 133
29.13–14 134
29.14–15 134
29.15–16 134
29.17–18 135
29.17 130

11QT (Temple Scroll)
1–29 185
1.9 173
2.11 164
11.5–6 173
11.9–11 186
12.15–16 181
17–30 182
18–22 183
23–24 234
29.8–10 117
29.9 49
30–43 183, 185
37 182
43 168
43–44 166
43.4 183
43.15–16 159
44 183
48.11–14 159
52.4–7 160
52.5 159
52.12 160
53.5–6 160
53.9–54.5 160
53.11 189
54.12 189
56.4–5 159
57–59 166
57.1 186
57.2 170
57.7–11 177
57.9–11 174

57.9	177
57.11–15	167
57.14	167
57.15–19	167
57.19	167
57.20–21	171
57.20	167
58.11–15	167
59.4–5	171
63.13–15	159
64.9	174
66.8–11	159

Targums

Aramaic

2 Sam. 23.4	296
Jer. 31.5	296

Neofiti I

Deut. 16.10	272

Onqelos

Deut. 6.5	292
Num. 28.26	272

Palestinian

Deut. 6.5	292
Lev. 19.18	292

Pseudo–Jonathan

Gen. 16.1	196
Deut. 34.6	290
Num. 28.26	272

Targ. Ezek.

1.24	94
3.12	94
43.2	94

Targ. Song.

4.11	124
4.16	124

Mishnah

Abot

1.12	293
2.12	289

Avoda Zarah

1.3	54

Berakhot

1.1	54
2.2	34, 55
4.4	150
5.2	103
6	53
6.1	53
6.8	63, 114
9.5	292

Giṭṭin

4.2	41
4.3	41

Hullin

10.1	288

Kelim

1.9	124

Ma`aserot

10	125

Makkot

3.15	95

Menahot

13.11	289

Parah

1.1	220

Pesah

1	125

Rosh Hashanah

4.5	71, 145

Sanhedrin

1.6	167
2.2	167
2.4	167, 178
4.3–4	179
10.1	50, 190

Soṭa

6.4	166
7.1	276
7.2	165
7.8	145, 165, 166, 180, 183, 184
11.13	166
14.22	166
26.12	166

Tamid

4.3	124
5.1	37, 38, 42

Yebamot

2.1	163
3.6	163

Yoma

7	145

Zebahim

14.4	288

Babylonian Talmud

B. Bathra

16a	134

Berakot

9b	180
16a–17a	154
16b	129
17a	74, 129, 130, 305
21a	37
28b	135
29a	76, 129
29b	61, 153
33a	150
33b	103, 138
35a	53
44a	114, 117, 118, 121
46b	114, 117, 121
48b	118, 120
49a	118, 120
58b	117
60b	59, 126–129, 248
63a	289

Giṭṭin

49v	64

Hagigah
12a 111
12b–13a 94
12b 97
13b 95

Horayot
12b 64

Hullin
84a 160
92a 248

Ketubot
8ab 114

Mo'ed Katan
28b 64

Makkot
5b 88
23b–24a 290
56 296, 303

Megillah
31a 182
41a 182

Menahot
65a 276

Nedarim
64 64

Pesahim
54b 88
104a 103, 104
118a 109

Rosh Hashanah
11b 57
31a 113

Šabbath
10a 283
110 62
115b 119
31a 292
31b 281
74b 123
88a 233
88b 274

Shebuoth
38b 29
39a 26

Sanhedrin
17a 276
42a 98, 107

Soṭa
22b
40a 146
41a 168

Ta'anit
12b 125

Yoma
36b 227
76b 135
87b 130

Jerusalem Talmud
Berakot
1.1, 2c 105
1.5, 3d 92, 146
1.9, 3d 118, 120
4.2, 7d 59, 127, 128, 131, 135, 155
4.3, 6a 76
4.3, 8a 115
4.4, 8b 153
4.5, 8c 118
5.1, 8d 129
5.2, 9b 103
9.7, 14b 283

Megillah
3.6, 74b 113

Pe'ah
1.1, 15d 292

Qidduhin
4.5, 66a 174, 186

Rosh Hashanah
4.659c 119

Sanhedrin
2.7, 20d 178

Šeqal
5.1, 48d 276

Soṭa
5.7, 20c 282
7.1, 44b 145
7.6, 22a 145

Ta'anit
2.3, 65c 92

Yoma
3.7, 40d 227
8.9, 45c 131

Tosefta
Avoda Zarah
1.4 54

Berakot
3.6 131
3.7 153, 155
6.5 53
7.6 117

Hagigah
2.1 280, 281

Rosh Hashanah
4.2.6 64

Sanhedrin
4.5 181
4.7 178
8.1 276

Soṭa
6.1 30
7.17 166
8.7 275

Yebamot
8.7 280

Kippurim
2.1 227
4.14 125

Midrashim
ARN
A25 283
A37 282
B26 292
B30 289
B45 282
39 280

Eccl. R
1.9 283, 284

Gen R.
3.4.6 280
6 172
16.1 196
21.5 107
63.10 285
65.21 95
78.1 97

Lev. R.
3.2 256
3.3 131
7.2 77

Midr. Pss.
18.44 283
92.3 275

Midr. Teh.
92.3 274

Pes K
1.7 279

Pes. R.
22.5 284

PRE
26.19 196
31 93

Sifra
17.6 288

Sifrē
Deut. 1.6 192
Deut. 13.7 292
Deut. 33.2 275

Sipre
160 167, 178
306 99
343 86, 93, 300

Philo
Abr.
98 196

Cong.
89 227
107–108 227

Decal.
46 274

Opif. Mund.
24.73 107

Plant.
3.12 107

Quod. Det. Pot. Ins.
63 227

Somn.
1.135 107

Spec. Leg. (Laws)
1.183 273
2.1.5 24
2.176 273
4.162 167
4.163 167
4.165–166 167
4.165 177
4.169 167
4.170 167

Virt.
33.178 36

Josephus
Antiquities of the Jews
1.161–165 196
1.183–185 218
10.63 28
12.89 178
13.282 124
13.398 282
13.404–406 282
14.337 273
14.45 173, 186
15.368 8, 19
17.254 273
17.42 8
18.124 8
3.252 272
4.223 167
8.184 173
8.185 186
9.143 175
9.153 169

Against Apion
2.39 260

The Jewish War
2.43 273
1.253 273
2.128 95, 99
2.131 64
2.139 16
2.8.5 113
6.299 277

Classical and Early Christian Literature
Aeschylus
Seven against Thebes
42–48 29

Aischines
2.115 15, 29
3.109 29
3.111 26

Andocides
On the Mysteries
96 14
97 32

Apostolic Constitutions
VII.35 48
VII. 35.3 94
VIII.12.27 51
VIII.12.27 90, 94

Apuleius
Metamorphoses
XI.1 37
XI.14 35

Metamorphoses (cont.)
XI.15 35
XI.21 37
XI.23 37
XI.25 37, 110
XI.30 35

Aristotle
Athenian Politeia
3.3 28

Ethica Nichomachea
IX.1–6 237

Politica
III.14.7 181

Cicero
(Epistula ad Atticum)
XIII.28 176

Clement of Alexandria
Stromateis
VII.12 51
VII.40.1 52

Clement of Rome
1 Clement
34.7 51

Didache
10 117, 118
10.6 88

Dio Cassius
59.9.2 10

Diodorus Siculus
I.70 172, 177, 187

Herodotus
1.74 29
3.8 29
3.71 12
6.86 25

Hesiod
Opera et Dies
II.283–285 26

Theogonia
9 47, 247
11.10 247
39 48

Homer
Iliad
1.603–4 247
2.484 247
2.485–494 110
2.594 47
3.103–7 219
3.268 219
8.442–443 82
Odyssey
4.746 29
10.381 29

Ignatius
Ephesians
4.1 51

Livy
III.28 34
IX.6 34

Maimonides
Guide for the Perplexed
22.5 107

Plato
Laws
753d 28, 220
Politicus
290d 188

Plutarch
Apophthegmata
198 176

Eumenes
12 16

Sulla
10.6 8

Polybius
3.61 19
7.9 24
7.9.7 10
7.9.8 9
15.25 169, 173, 187

Pliny
Ad Trajan
10.96 113
10.96.7 38

Suetonius
Divus Julius Caesar
2.84 33

Divus Augustus
17.2 19

Gaius Caligula
15.3 10

Tacitus
Annales
1.8 20
Histories
V.13 277

Thucydides
5.12.47 40
5.18.8 29
5.18.9 20
5.18.10 30
5.23.5 30

Virgil
Aeneid
VI.625–627 110

Xenophon
Anabasis
2.2.9 29

Respublica Lacedaemoniorum
15.7 169

Memorabilia
4.4.16 18

Papyri
Elephantine Papyri (AP)
30.21 122
30.25 122
31.21 122

32.9 122
33.10 122

Papyrus Lille
29.1–38 232

Other Ancient Texts
Hodayot
3.22–23 104
4.3–20 134
4.45 134
10.6 104
11.14 104
13.8 106
13.10 103

Middle Assyrian Laws (MAL)
1.22 194
14 196

Tractate Sefer Torah
1.7 178

Tractate Soferim
2.1.7 178
14.1 75, 86
18.11 80
19.5 75
19.10 98
13.6 127

INDEX OF AUTHORS

Abel, F.M. 170
Abramson, S. 37, 42, 129, 135
Albeck, C. 117
Albeck, H. 269
Allegro, J.M. 61
Alon, G. 88, 113, 118, 145
Alp, S. 4, 5, 7, 9, 14, 22
Alt, A. 212
Alt, K. 247
Altmann, A. 92
Amélineau, E. 68, 299
Amir, Y. 287
Asaf, S. 51, 90, 93, 127, 131
Assaf, S. 152
Avigad, N. 194, 195
Avishur, Y. 92, 239, 241, 242

Ba'ar, Y. 148
Baer, S. 130
Baer, Y. 60, 228
Baillet, M. 56, 57, 62, 151
Baltzer, K. 200
Bar-Ilan, M. 62, 92, 151, 253
Barr, J. 239
Bauer, Th. 40
Baumgarten, J.M. 62, 105
Beare, 276, 277
Begg, C.T. 218, 220
Ben Barak, Z. 168
Ben David, A. 291
Ben-Dov, M. 230
Bengtson, H. 9, 11, 12, 39
Bentzen, A. 255
Berliner, A. 97, 249
Bickerman, E. 9, 10, 24, 28, 29, 41, 148, 220
Biggs, R.D. 148
Blank, S.M. 253
Blenkinsopp, J. 287
Boer, P.A.H. de 208
Böhlig, A. 37
Boismard, M.E. 193
Borger, R. 18, 23, 41, 202, 221, 244
Bousset, W. 51, 90, 287, 288, 293
Bouyer, L. 96
Brettler, M.Z. 222
Brin, G. 65
Brown, R.E. 193
Büchler, A. 91, 117
Burkert, W. 219
Burrows, M. 210
Burton, A. 173, 187

Caquot, A. 229, 230
Cardascia, G. 194
Cary, E. 219
Cassin, E. 210, 213
Cassuto, U. 194–97
Cemival, F. de 232
Cerny, J. 241
Charles, R.H. 49, 271, 272
Childs, B.S. 208
Clay, A.T. 228
Clements, R.E. 200, 225
Coats, G.W. 132
Conzelman, H. 277
Cooper, J.S. 215, 220
Couroyer, B. 240, 241, 249, 270
Cowley, A.E. 209, 223, 246
Cross, F.M. 79, 109, 255, 259
Cumont, F. 30, 33, 35
Cunchillos, J.L. 229

Dahood, M. 105, 243
Dalman, G. 153
Darlow, T.H. 287
Davies, W.D. 101
Del Olmo, G. 230
Delatte, L. 176, 181

Delcor, M. 268, 272
Delitzsch, F. 263
Deller, K.H. 31, 244, 246
Dessau, H. 10, 15, 26
Diakonoff, I.M. 172
Dittenberger, W. 5, 8, 11
Dix, G. 96
Dodds, E.R. 31, 47, 247
Donner, H. 237, 240, 250
Draffkorn, A. 201, 219
Driver, G.R. 194–96, 214, 247
Driver, S.R. 163, 191
Duhm, B. 256
Duncan, J. 113

Ebeling, E. 22, 40, 83, 244
Ehrlich, A. 27, 215, 243, 272
Eissfeldt, O. 164, 192
Elbogen, I. 34, 37, 38, 45, 60, 74, 75, 92, 99, 100, 124, 126, 147, 268, 270
Elliger, K. 255
Epstein, J.M. 182, 183, 300
Eshel, E. 146
Eshel, H. 146
Everson, A.J. 78

Falk, Z.W. 13
Falkenstein, A. 212
Feigin, S. 215
Fensham, F.C. 200
Fiensy, D.A. 149
Finkel, J. 195
Fitzmyer, J.A. 3, 12, 17, 59, 153, 154, 194, 195, 221, 246
Fleischer, E. 45, 56, 68, 92, 95, 99, 143, 144, 150, 182
Flusser, D. 35, 48, 51, 58, 73, 90, 91, 126, 135, 142, 146, 155, 279, 283, 291, 292
Frankena, R. 31
Frazer, P.M. 173, 187
Freedman, D.N. 200, 255
Freydank, H. 9
Friedman, M. 50
Friedrich, J. 3, 9, 12, 20, 23, 201, 209, 214, 216, 222
Funk, F.X. 48, 51

Gadd, C.J. 220, 228
Galling, K. 261
Garland, D.E. 279
Gaster, Th. 28
Geiger, A. 251
Gemser, B. 252
Gevaryahu, Ch. 255
Gilat, Y.D. 153
Ginsberg, H.L. 41, 179, 205–207, 212, 297
Ginsberg, L. 76, 127, 128, 135
Ginsburg, H. 259
Ginzberg, L. 91, 100, 107
Glazov, G. 142
Glueck, N. 17, 203, 216
Goetze, A. 12, 13, 18, 31, 147, 204–206, 210, 212, 219
Goldschmidt, E.D. 74, 92, 117, 129, 131
Goldstein, J. 134, 181
Goodenough, R.E. 176
Gordon, A.L. 126
Green, J. 110
Greenberg, M. 70, 144, 217
Greenfield, J.C. 104, 109, 196, 211, 218
Greengus, S. 223
Greenstein, E.L. 207, 219
Grignachi, M. 176
Gruenwald, I. 48, 51, 104
Gruenwald, J. 45
Gulak, A. 39
Gunkel, H. 213, 257
Güterbock, H. 201
Gutmann, J. 36

Haak, R.D. 230
Haberman, A.M. 38
Hadot, P. 170
Haenchen, E. 277
Haller, M. 254
Hallo, W.W. 84, 250
Halperin, D.J. 94
Haran, M. 161, 162, 182, 252, 254, 256
Harrington, D.J. 195
Heinemann, I. 253
Heinemann, J. 45, 75, 90, 128, 153, 167, 297
Heitmüller, W. 293
Helck, W. 43
Held, M. 207, 217, 221
Heltzer, M. 4, 123, 226
Henninger, S. 220
Herrmann, P. 8, 10, 11, 17, 19, 20, 31
Higger, M. 98

Highby, L.I. 14
Hinz, W. 216
Hoffman, D.Z. 272
Hoffner, H.A. 212, 213
Holm-Nielsen, S. 49, 101, 105, 106
Hrozny, F. 31, 214
Huffmon, H.B. 217
Huffmon, M.P. 23
Hunger, H. 172, 179
Hurvitz, A. 119, 256, 265
Hurwitz, A. 109

Imparati, F. 210
Ivri, A.L. 108

Jacob, B. 214
Jacobsen, T. 213
Jacoby, F. 174, 188
Japhet, S. 233
Jawitz, Z. 101
Jellinek, A. 125
Jeremias, J. 81, 83

Kadari, M.Z. 40
Kasher, M. 164
Kaufmann, Y. 145, 182, 253, 258, 262, 263, 265, 288
Kayatz, C. 249
Kellermann, D. 124
Kempinski, A. 206
Kestemont, G. 170
Kimron, E. 49
King, L.W. 201, 224
Kister, M. 99
Kittel, B.P. 60
Klein, C. 290
Klengel, H. 214
Klima, J. 206
Klostermann, A. 162
Knohl, I. 55, 293
Koenen, L. 227
Kohler, J. 201, 205
Köhler, L. 252
Korošec, V. 169, 201, 209, 216
Košak, S. 206
Koschaker, P. 31, 210
Kraeling, E.G. 39, 203, 206
Kramer, S.N. 30, 34, 93, 142
Kraus, F.R. 216, 222
Kraus, H.-J. 259
Kraus, H.I. 256
Krauss, S. 283
Kremer, J. 268, 273
Kuhl, C. 90, 211
Kuhn, H.W. 48–50, 101, 105
Kuhn, K.G. 35, 105
Kühne, C. 9
Kutsch, E. 28, 29
Kutscher, E. 46
Kutscher, Y. 265

Lacheman, E.R. 213
Lake, K. 117
Lambert, W.G. 34, 47, 54, 76, 171, 298
Landsberger, B. 40, 206
Laroche, E. 11, 23
Le Déaut, R. 268
Lebrun, R. 147
Levi, I. 101
Lewis, D. 18
Lewy, J. 182
Liberman, S. 34, 36
Licht, J. 16, 19, 49, 98, 101, 102, 108, 141, 142, 263
Lichtheim, M. 170, 171
Lidzbarski, M. 38
Lieberman, S. 23, 30, 37, 40, 42, 53, 55, 95, 99, 116, 150, 166–68, 170, 178, 233, 253, 276, 280, 281, 291
Liebes, Y. 297
Liebeschütz, H. 288
Liebreich, L.J. 143, 144
Lipinski, E. 203
Liver, J. 224
Loewenstamm, S.E. 70, 83, 211, 216, 217, 218, 222, 259, 302
Lohfink, N. 200, 218
Lohse, E. 268
Lorton, D. 43
Luckenbill, D.D. 85
Luger, Y. 300
Luzatto, S.D. 45

Maier, J. 105
Malkhi, Y. 150
Malul, M. 210

Mann, J. 34, 59, 77, 92, 93, 95, 99, 101–104, 109, 127, 129, 131, 132, 135, 152, 153
Marcus, D. 207, 219
Margaliot, M. 75
Margalioth, M. 40, 45, 248, 249
Margulies, M. 62
Marshall, J.H. 268
Martin, 276
Masson, O. 27, 220
Mayer, W. 197
Mazar, B. 224, 226, 264
McCarter, K. 224
McCarthy, D.J. 200
McKane, W. 287
Meek, S. 195
Meier, A. 262
Meiggs, R. 18
Melamed, E.Z. 258
Mendels, D. 177, 187
Mendelsohn, I. 215
Mendenhall, G.E. 200
Mettinger, T. 180
Meyer, E. 174, 188, 258, 275
Meyer, R. 255
Miles, J.C. 194–96, 214
Milgrom, J. 123
Milik, J.T. 19, 113, 135, 203, 227, 255, 272
Millard, A.R. 34
Mirsky, A. 144
Mitford, T.B. 11, 32
Mitteis, L. 40
Moore, G.F. 253, 287, 288
Morag, S. 69
Moran, W.L. 7, 16, 211, 217
Morgenstern, J. 253
Mowinckel, S. 20, 71, 73, 77–80, 82, 259, 261, 271, 295
Mueller, J. 284
Muffs, Y. 203, 205, 208, 210, 223, 226, 271
Munn-Rankin, J. 216

Na'aman, N. 230
Naveh, J. 250
Negev, A. 38
Newsom, C. 56, 63, 95, 104, 108
Nicoll, W.R. 287
Nilsson, M.P. 28, 29, 31, 36, 37, 104, 219
Nock, A.D. 54
Noetscher, F. 205
Norden, E. 36
Nougayrol, J. 123

Odeberg, H. 48, 96
Oettinger, N. 222
Oppenheim, A.L. 4, 13, 36
Orlinsky, H.M. 276
Ostwald, M. 14
Otten, H. 9, 11, 209, 212

Pardee, D. 230
Parker, S.B. 217
Parpola, S. 221
Paul, S.M. 160, 212, 213, 215, 244
Perles, P. 239
Peterson, E. 38
Picard, C. 28
Pinches, T.G. 123
Ploeg, J. van der 46, 132, 133
Poebel, A. 38, 200
Poland, F. 234
Polotsky, H.J. 31
Polzin, R. 134
Pool, D. de Sola 73
Porten, B. 246
Postgate, J.N. 40, 201, 202, 208
Potin, J. 268, 274, 275
Preuss, H.O. 69
Priest, J. 28
Prümm, R. 37
Puech, E. 142

Quell, G. 253

Rabinowitz, J.J. 40, 208, 209, 222
Rad, G. von 50, 78–79, 82, 271
Raubitechek, A.E. 234
Rehm, M.D. 226
Reiner, E. 2, 9, 41, 172, 221, 222
Reitzenstein, R. 35–37
Richter, G. 176
Riemschneider, K. 201
Robertson Smith, W. 29
Rochbeg-Halton, F. 190
Rofé, A. 107
Röllig, W. 237, 240, 250
Rosenfeld, B.Z. 290

Rosenthal, E.S. 92
Rosenthal, F. 206
Rothstein, J.W. 258
Rott-Gerson, L. 256
Rudolph, W. 46, 175, 221, 255

Safrai, S. 150
Safran, J.D. 219
Sanders, J.A. 87, 90, 91, 94, 109, 152, 229
Sanders, J.P. 55, 59
Sarna, N.M. 211
Schäfer, P. 92, 109
Schalit, A. 186
Schechter, S. 44, 45, 51, 86, 90, 93, 98, 275
Scheiber, A. 110
Scholem, G. 48, 277
Schorr, M. 201, 214, 216, 225
Schottroff, W. 208
Schubart, W. 36
Schuler, E. von 4, 5, 7–12, 14, 17, 18, 23, 209
Schunk, K.D. 33
Schürer, E. 256, 287
Schwahn, W. 32
Schwann, J. 16
Schwartz, D.R. 279
Seeligmann, I.L. 21, 70, 80, 265, 271
Segal, M.Z. 64
Seidl, E. 31, 39
Seux, M.J. 34, 215
Shalit, A. 173
Shinan, A. 196
Siewert, P. 9, 24, 27
Simon, U. 159
Singer, S. 45, 46, 68, 90, 228, 296
Skehan, P.W. 93, 94, 109, 110, 142
Smend, R. 287
Smith, G.A. 290
Smith, M. 16, 292
Smith, S. 40, 219, 223, 225
Soden, W. von 34, 40, 69, 201, 228, 255
Sollberger, E. 123, 219
Sommer, F. 212
Speiser, E.A. 210, 212–15, 264
Sperber, A. 197, 271
Sperber, D. 140
Stadlhuber, J. 150
Stauffer, E. 276
Stefanini, R. 8
Stegemann, H. 113
Stegemann, M. 63
Steiner, G. 220
Steinmetzer, F.X. 201, 223
Stengel, P. 27–29, 219
Strassmaier, J.N. 220
Streck, M. 3, 18, 29, 172
Strugnell, J. 47, 108, 115
Sukenik, E.L. 279
Syme, R. 19
Szlechter, E. 219

Ta-Shma, Y. 297, 301
Tadmor, H. 171, 228
Talmon, S. 34, 102, 141, 255, 262, 272
Teixidor, J. 237
Thompson, R.C. 239
Thureau-Dangin, F. 208, 214, 215, 225
Tigay, J.H. 213, 225, 284
Tov, E. 57, 144, 251
Tsafrir, Y. 110
Tsevat, M. 21
Tucker, G.M. 211
Tur-Sinai, N.H. 107, 132, 163, 215

Uffenheimer, B. 253
Ulrich, E. 142
Ungnad, A. 201, 205
Urbach, E. 34, 75, 113, 235, 275, 289–92

Vaux, R. de 82, 209
Vavaignac, E. 214
Veijola, T. 270
Vellian, J. 96
Vermes, G. 146, 256
Von Dijk, J.J.A. 84
Von Premerstein, A. 10, 20
Vriezen, Th.C. 36

Wagner, M. 70
Walbank, F.W. 24
Watanabe, K. 221
Waterman, L. 4, 12, 32, 243, 244, 246
Weidner, E. 6, 8, 9, 13, 20, 21, 24, 27, 195, 201, 212, 221
Weinfeld, M. 2, 6–8, 11–15, 17, 18, 22–24, 26, 28, 32, 34, 36, 38, 40, 41, 46–48, 50, 54–56, 60, 64, 72, 73, 76–79, 81–83, 90, 93, 94, 103, 113, 118, 128, 134,

136–38, 141, 142, 146–52, 159, 160, 163–65, 169, 179, 182, 194, 195, 200, 202, 205–207, 216, 218, 221, 228, 230, 232, 234, 235, 245, 247, 248, 258, 260–62, 270, 271, 277, 295
Weingreen, J. 159
Weinrich, O. 15
Weinstock, S. 31
Weisberg, D.B. 13, 211
Weiss, M. 69, 71, 79, 82, 202
Wellhausen, J. 286–91
Wente, E.F. 241
Werblowsky, R.J.Z. 277
Wernberg-Moller, P. 54
Werner, E. 51, 88
Westermann, C. 218
White, S.A. 112
Widengren, G. 35
Wieder, N. 56, 57, 92, 93,103, 104, 140, 143
Wildberger, H. 243
Williamson, H.G.M. 140
Wilson, J. 31
Wiseman, D.J. 2, 41, 201, 202, 210, 212, 217, 218, 222
Wolff, H.W. 218
Wolfson, H. 36, 107, 167, 179
Woude, A.S. van der 46, 115
Wright, D.P. 220

Yadin, Y. 35, 37, 38, 46, 49, 65, 97, 108, 113, 158, 159, 163, 168, 173, 174, 176, 178–81, 183, 186, 187, 189, 191, 192, 194, 195, 283
Yahalom, J. 56, 144
Yailenko, V.P. 19
Yardeni, A. 146
Yaron, R. 40, 216, 223, 253
Youtie, M.C. 234

Zakovitch, Y. 196
Zakowitch, Y. 271